A·N·N·U·A·L E·D·I·T·I·O·N·S

Western Civilization Volume 1

11th Edition

The Earliest Civilizations through the Reformation

EDITOR

Robert L. Lembright
James Madison University

Robert L. Lembright teaches World Civilization, Ancient Near East, Byzantine, Islamic, and Greek/Roman history at James Madison University. He received his B.A. from Miami University and his M.A. and Ph.D from The Ohio State University. Dr. Lembright has been a participant in many National Endowment for the Humanities Summer Seminars and Institutes on Egyptology, the Ancient Near East, Byzantine History, and the Ottoman Empire. He has written several articles in the four editions of *The Global Experience*, as well as articles in the *James Madison Journal* and *Western Views of China and the Far East*. His research has concentrated on the French Renaissance of the sixteenth century, and he has published reports in the *Bulletins et memoires, Societe archaeologique et historique de la Charente*. In addition, Dr. Lembright has written many book reviews on the ancient world and Byzantine and Islamic history for *History: Reviews of New Books*.

McGraw-Hill/Dushkin
530 Old Whitfield Street, Guilford, Connecticut 06437

Visit us on the Internet
http://www.dushkin.com

Credits

1. The Earliest Civilizations
Unit photo—The Metropolitian Museum of Art. 8, 10, 11—The British Museum, 9 (top)—Photo by Michael Holford, 9 (bottom)— HT Archives

2. Greece and Rome: The Classical Tradition
Unit photo—Photo from the *Compendium of Illustrations in the Public Domain,* compiled by Harold H. Hart, Hart Publishing Company, 75—HT map by Ken Wass, 118—HT map by Tim Aspden

3. The Judeo-Christian Heritage
Unit photo—National Callery of Art.

4. Muslims and Byzantines
Unit photo—The Metropolitian Museum of Art, 121—Weidenfield Archives photo, 126—*The World and I* photo

5. The Medieval Period
Unit photo—WHO photo, 148—Philadelphia Museum of Art

6. Renaissance and Reformation
Unit photo—Library of Congress, 205—HT map by Ken Wass

Copyright

Cataloging in Publication Data
Main entry under title: Annual Editions: Western Civilization, vol. 1: The Earliest Civilizations through the Reformation. 11/E.
   1. Civilization—Periodicals. 2. World history—Periodicals. I. Lembright, Robert L. *comp.* II. Title: Western civilization.
901.9′05   82–645823   ISBN 0–07–242576–8   ISSN 0735-0392

© 2001 by McGraw-Hill/Dushkin, Guilford, CT 06437, A Division of The McGraw-Hill Companies.

Eleventh Edition

Cover image © 2001 PhotoDisc, Inc.

Printed in the United States of America   1234567890BAHBAH54321   Printed on Recycled Paper

Members of the Advisory Board are instrumental in the final selection of articles for each edition of ANNUAL EDITIONS. Their review of articles for content, level, currentness, and appropriateness provides critical direction to the editor and staff. We think that you will find their careful consideration well reflected in this volume.

In publishing ANNUAL EDITIONS we recognize the enormous role played by the magazines, newspapers, and journals of the public press in providing current, first-rate educational information in a broad spectrum of interest areas. Many of these articles are appropriate for students, researchers, and professionals seeking accurate, current material to help bridge the gap between principles and theories and the real world. These articles, however, become more useful for study when those of lasting value are carefully collected, organized, indexed, and reproduced in a low-cost format, which provides easy and permanent access when the material is needed. That is the role played by ANNUAL EDITIONS.

New to ANNUAL EDITIONS is the inclusion of related World Wide Web sites. These sites have been selected by our editorial staff to represent some of the best resources found on the World Wide Web today. Through our carefully developed topic guide, we have linked these Web resources to the articles covered in this ANNUAL EDITIONS reader. We think that you will find this volume useful, and we hope that you will take a moment to visit us on the Web at **http://www.dushkin.com** to tell us what you think.

What does it mean to say that we are attempting to study the history of Western civilizations?

A traditional course in Western civilization was often a chronological survey in the development of European institutions and ideas, with a slight reference to the Near East and the Americas and other places where Westernization has occurred. Typically it began with the Greeks, then the Romans, and on to the medieval period, and finally to the modern era, depicting the distinctive characteristics of each stage, as well as each period's relation to the preceding and succeeding events. Of course, in a survey so broad, from Adam to the atomic age in two semesters, a certain superficiality was inevitable. Main characters and events galloped by; often there was little opportunity to absorb and digest complex ideas that have shaped Western culture.

It is tempting to excuse these shortcomings as unavoidable. However, to present a course in Western civilization that leaves students with only a scrambled series of events, names, dates, and places, is to miss a great opportunity. For the promise of such a broad course of study is that it enables students to explore great turning points or shifts in the development of Western culture. Close analysis of these moments enables students to understand the dynamics of continuity and change over time. At best, the course can give a coherent view of the Western tradition and its interplay with non-Western cultures. It can offer opportunities for students to compare various historical forms of authority, religion, and economic organization, to assess the great struggles over the meaning of truth and reality that have sometimes divided Western culture, and even to reflect on the price of progress.

Yet, to focus exclusively on Western civilization can lead us to ignore non-Western peoples and cultures or else to perceive them in ways that some label as "Eurocentric." But contemporary courses in Western history are rarely, if ever, mere exercises in European tribalism. Indeed, they offer an opportunity to subject the Western tradition to critical scrutiny, to assess its accomplishments and its shortfalls. Few of us who teach these courses would argue that Western history is the only history that contemporary students should know. Yet it should be an essential part of what they learn, for it is impossible to understand the modern world without some specific knowledge in the basic tenets of the Western tradition.

When students learn the distinctive traits of the West, they can develop a sense of the dynamism of history. They can begin to understand how ideas relate to social structures and social forces. They will come to appreciate the nature and significance of innovation and recognize how values often influence events. More specifically, they can trace the evolution of Western ideas about such essential matters as nature, humans, authority, the gods, even history itself; that is, they learn how the West developed its distinctive character. And, as historian Reed Dasenbrock has observed, in an age that seeks multicultural understanding there is much to be learned from "the fundamental multiculturalism of Western culture, the fact that it has been constructed out of a fusion of disparate and often conflicting cultural tradition." Of course, the articles collected in his volume cannot deal with all these matters, but by providing an alternative to the summaries of most textbooks, they can help students better understand the diverse traditions and processes that we call Western civilization.

As with the last publication of *Annual Editions: Western Civilization, Volume I,* World Wide Web sites are included that can be used to further explore topics that are addressed in the essays. These sites are cross-referenced by number in the topic guide and can be hot-linked through the *Annual Editions* home page: *http://www.dushkin.com/annualeditions.*

This book is like our history—unfinished, always in process. It will be revised on a regular basis. Comments and criticisms are welcome from all who use this book. To that end a post-paid *article rating form* is included at the back of the book. Please feel free to recommend articles that might improve the next edition. With your assistance, this anthology will continue to improve.

Robert L. Lembright

Robert L. Lembright
Editor

Contents

UNIT 1

The Earliest Civilizations

Six articles discuss some of the dynamics of early civilizations. The topics include the development of social organization and communication, the early Mediterranean world, and an early civilization's military revolution.

The concepts in bold italics are developed in the article. For further expansion please refer to the Topic Guide and the Index.

v

UNIT 2

Greece and Rome: The Classical Tradition

Eight articles focus on Greek and Roman societies. Sports, military conquests, slavery, and the impact of philosophy and exploration on the development of Hellenic society are discussed.

The concepts in bold italics are developed in the article. For further expansion please refer to the Topic Guide and the Index.

Overview   **78**

UNIT 3

The Judeo-Christian Heritage

Five articles examine the impact that Jesus, women, politics, and clashing cultures had on the Judeo-Christian heritage.

The concepts in bold italics are developed in the article. For further expansion please refer to the Topic Guide and the Index.

vii

Muslims and Byzantines

Three selections discuss the effects of Greek Hellenic and Christian cultures on the development of the Muslim and Byzantine worlds.

UNIT 4

The Medieval Period

Twelve selections examine the medieval world. Topics include religion, health, military conquests, and culture.

UNIT 5

The concepts in bold italics are developed in the article. For further expansion please refer to the Topic Guide and the Index.

The concepts in bold italics are developed in the article. For further expansion please refer to the Topic Guide and the Index.

UNIT 6

Renaissance and Reformation

Eight articles discuss the importance of trade and commerce on the development of the modern state, the role of art in the Renaissance, culture, and the emergence of religion.

The concepts in bold italics are developed in the article. For further expansion please refer to the Topic Guide and the Index.

Topic Guide

This topic guide suggests how the selections and World Wide Web sites found in the next section of this book relate to topics of traditional concern to world civilizations students and professionals. It is useful for locating interrelated articles and Web sites for reading and research. The guide is arranged alphabetically according to topic.

The relevant Web sites, which are numbered and annotated on pages 4 and 5, are easily identified by the Web icon (◉) under the topic articles. By linking the articles and the Web sites by topic, this ANNUAL EDITIONS reader becomes a powerful learning and research tool.

TOPIC AREA	TREATED IN	TOPIC AREA	TREATED IN
Archaeology	2. Correspondence in Clay ◉ *9, 10, 11*		42. She-Devils, Harlots and Harridans in Northern Renaissance Prints ◉ *3, 7, 8, 9, 10, 11, 12, 13, 19, 20, 21, 22, 26, 27, 28, 29, 31*
Art	27. Monsters and Christian Enemies 42. She-Devils, Harlots and Harridans in Northern Renaissance Prints ◉ *3, 12, 29*	**Democracy**	8. Athenian Democracy and Its Slaves 24. Amazing Vikings ◉ *13, 23*
Christianity	15. Jews and Christians in a Roman World 16. Other Jesus 17. Women and the Bible 18. Ecstasy in Late Imperial Rome 19. Who the Devil Is the Devil? 27. Monsters and Christian Enemies 28. Women Pilgrims of the Middle Ages 30. Paris Bibles and the Making of a Medieval Information Revolution 34. Saints or Sinners? The Knights Templar in Medieval Europe ◉ *15, 16, 32*	**Empires, Ancient**	2. Correspondence in Clay 5. Coming of the Sea Peoples 6. Grisly Assyrian Record of Torture and Death 12. In the Year 1, Augustus Let the Good Times Roll 20. Survival of the Eastern Roman Empire ◉ *3, 7, 10, 11, 13, 14, 19*
Commerce	3. Cradle of Cash ◉ *26, 29, 30, 34*	**Exploration**	24. Amazing Vikings 38. Columbus—Hero or Villain? 39. Sir Francis Drake Is Still Capable of Kicking Up a Fuss ◉ *26, 30, 34*
Crime/Justice	10. Love and Death in Ancient Greece 34. Saints or Sinners? The Knights Templar in Medieval Europe ◉ *3, 12, 13, 14*	**Finance**	3. Cradle of Cash ◉ *7, 35*
Culture	4. Shards of Speech 12. In the Year 1, Augustus Let the Good Times Roll 13. Chariot Racing in the Ancient World 14. Friends, Romans, or Countrymen? Babarians in the Empire 20. Survival of the Eastern Roman Empire 21. Byzantium: The Emperor's New Clothes? 23. Scissors or Sword? The Symbolism of a Medieval Haircut 24. Amazing Vikings 25. Golden Age of Andalusia under the Muslim Sultans 27. Monsters and Christian Enemies 29. Britain 1100 30. Paris Bibles and the Making of a Medieval Information Revolution 35. Marsilio Ficino, Renaissance Man 36. Machiavelli	**Greek Society**	7. Winning at Olympia 8. Athenian Democracy and Its Slaves 9. Re-Running Marathon 10. Love and Death in Ancient Greece 11. Cleopatra: What Kind of a Woman Was She, Anyway? 13. Chariot Racing in the Ancient World ◉ *3, 5, 7, 12, 13, 14*
		Historiography	38. Columbus—Hero or Villian? ◉ *30*
		Islam	22. What Is Islam? 25. Golden Age of Andalusia under the Muslim Sultans 26. How the West Saw Medieval Islam 34. Saints or Sinners? The Knights Templar in Medieval Europe ◉ *11, 15, 20, 21*
		Jewish People and Judaism	15. Jews and Christians in a Roman World 17. Women and the Bible 19. Who the Devil Is the Devil? 25. Golden Age of Andalusia under the Muslim Sultans ◉ *15, 17*

2

● AE: Western Civilization I

The following World Wide Web sites have been carefully researched and selected to support the articles found in this reader. If you are interested in learning more about specific topics found in this book, these Web sites are a good place to start. The sites are cross-referenced by number and appear in the topic guide on the previous two pages. Also, you can link to these Web sites through our DUSHKIN ONLINE support site at http://www.dushkin.com/online/.

The following sites were available at the time of publication. Visit our Web site—we update DUSHKIN ONLINE regularly to reflect any changes.

General Sources

1. Archaeological Institute of America (AIA)
http://www.archaeological.org
Review this site of the AIA for information about various eras in human history.

2. The History of Costumes
http://www.siue.edu/COSTUMES/history.html
This distinctive site illustrates garments worn by people in various historical eras. The site is based on a history of costumes that was originally printed between 1861 and 1880.

3. Julia Hayden/Ancient World Web Meta Index
http://www.julen.net/ancient/
Julia Hayden's site will lead you to an astounding array of articles, museum displays, bibliographies, and Web links pertaining to the ancient world (and other eras), on topics such as religion, sexuality, and superstitions.

4. Library of Congress
http://www.loc.gov
Learn about the extensive resource tools, library services, exhibitions, and databases available through the Library of Congress in many subfields of historical studies.

5. Michigan Electronic Library
http://mel.lib.mi.us/humanities/history/
Browse through this enormous history site for an array of resources On the study of Western civilization, which are broken down by time period, geographic area, and more.

6. Smithsonian Institution
http://www.si.edu
Access to the enormous resources of the Smithsonian, which holds some 140 million artifacts and specimens in its trust for "the increase and diffusion of knowledge," is provided at this site.

The Earliest Civilizations

7. Ancient Economies I
http://sondmor.tripod.com/index-html
Ancient economies are previewed at this site. The importance of archaeology in discovering the cultures and practices of people who lived long ago is revealed.

8. Hypertext and Ethnography
http://www.umanitoba.ca/anthropology/tutor/aaa_presentation.html
This site will be of great value to people who are interested in culture and communication. Brian Schwimmer addresses such topics as multivocality and complex symbolization.

9. NOVA Online/Pyramids—The Inside Story
http://www.pbs.org/wgbh/nova/pyramid/
Take a virtual tour of the pyramids at Giza through this interesting site. It provides information on the pharaohs for whom the tombs were built.

10. The Oriental Institute/University of Chicago
http://www.oi.uchicago.edu/OI/default.html
Open this site to find information on ancient Persia, Mesopotamia, and Egypt, and other topics in ancient history.

11. WWW: Egypt and Near East
http://www.archaeology.org/wwwarky/egypt_and_near_east.html
Here is a guide to online resources for the archaeological study of the ancient Near (or Middle) East. An Egyptian fieldwork directory is included.

Greece and Rome: The Classical Tradition

12. Diotima/Women and Gender in the Ancient World
http://www.uky.edu/ArtsSciences/Classics/gender.html
This site features a wide range of resources on women and gender in the ancient and classical world.

13. Exploring Ancient World Cultures
http://eawc.evansville.edu
This electronic, college-level textbook has been designed by a worldwide team of scholars. Especially useful are the links to related Web sites. Learn about Greece and Rome, the pyramids of Egypt, and many more eras and topics.

14. WWW: Classical Archaeology
http://www.archaeology.org/wwwarky/classical.html
Useful information and links regarding ancient Greek and Roman archaeology are provided at this site.

The Judeo-Christian Heritage

15. Facets of Religion/Casper Voogt
http://www.bcca.org/~cvoogt/Religion/mainpage.html
Casper Voogt offers this virtual library of links to information on major world religions, including Islam, Judaism, Zoroastrianism, Baha'ism, and Christianity.

16. Institute for Christian Leadership/ICLnet
http://www.iclnet.org
This site of the Institute for Christian Leadership, a Christian organization, presents documents and other resources of use in the study of early Christianity. Internet links are provided.

17. Introduction to Judaism
http://philo.ucdavis.edu/Courses/RST23/rst23homepage.html
Use this site as a launching pad to Web resources on the history of Jews and Judaism, including a link to the comprehensive Shamash site. The page is provided by Religious Studies 23, a course at the University of California at Davis.

18. Selected Women's Studies Resources/Columbia University
http://www.columbia.edu/cu/libraries/subjects/womenstudies/
Click on extensive links to information about women in religion and philosophy and a wealth of other topics.

Muslims and Byzantines

19. Byzantium: The Byzantine Studies Page
http://www.bway.net/~halsall/byzantium.html
Paul Halsall provides this gateway to the Byzantine empire and many appealing and informative links to myriad related topics.

20. Islam: A Global Civilization
http://www.templemount.org/islamiad.html
This site presents information on Islamic history. It chronicles the basic tenets of the religion and charts its spread, including the period of the Umayyad Dynasty in Spain.

21. Middle East Network Information Center
http://menic.utexas.edu/menic/religion.html
This site provides links to a cornucopia of Web sites on Islam and the Islamic world. Information on Judaism and Christianity is also available.

The Medieval Period

22. Anglo-Saxon England
http://bay1.bjt.net/~melanie/anglo-sa.html
Explore life in Anglo-Saxon England after the Roman Empire began to crumble but before William of Normandy conquered England. Background text on the era is provided and links to related sites and bibliographies.

23. EuroDocs: Primary Historical Documents from Western Europe
http://www.lib.byu.edu/~rdh/eurodocs/
This collection is a high-quality set of historical documents. Facsimiles, translations, and transcriptions are included as well as links to information on Medieval & Renaissance Europe, Europe as a Supernational Region, and individual countries.

24. Feudalism
http://www.fidnet.com/~weid/feudalism.htm
Feudalism is covered in great detail at this site, which offers subjects such as feudal law, agriculture, development in Europe during the feudal period, and feudal terms of England, as well as primary source material.

25. The Labyrinth: Resources for Medieval Studies
http://www.georgetown.edu/labyrinth/
Labyrinth provides easy-to-search files in medieval studies. As a major site for topics in medieval history and lore, make it a primary stop for research.

26. The World of the Vikings
http://www.pastforward.co.uk/vikings/
For information on Viking ships and travel—and other aspects of Viking life—visit this site from Past Forward Ltd.

Renaissance and Reformation

27. Burckhardt: Civilization of the Renaissance in Italy
http://www.idbsu.edu/courses/hy309/docs/burckhardt/burckhardt.html
Jacob Burckhardt's famous book on the Renaissance is available chapter by chapter on the Net at this site.

28. Centre for Reformation and Renaissance Studies
http://citd.scar.utoronto.ca/crrs/databases/www/bookmarks.html
This list of bookmarks contains a selective yet extensive list of Web links that are useful to a study of the Renaissance and the Reformation.

29. Elizabethan England
http://www.springfield.k12.il.us/schools/springfield/eliz/elizabethanengland.html
Prepared by senior literature and composition students in Springfield High School (Illinois), this unusual site covers Elizabethan England resources in some detail: Historical Figures and Events, Everyday Life, Arts and Architecture, Shakespeare and His Theatre, and Links to Other Sources.

30. 1492: An Ongoing Voyage/Library of Congress
http://lcweb.loc.gov/exhibits/1492/
This site provides displays examining the causes and effects of Columbus's voyages to the Americas and explores the mixture of societies coexisting in five areas of the Western Hemisphere before European arrival. It then surveys the Mediterranean world at a turning point in its development.

31. History Net
http://www.thehistorynet.com/THNarchives/AmericanHistory/
The National Historical Society site provides articles on a wide range of topics, with emphasis on American history, book reviews, and special interviews.

32. The Mayflower Web Pages
http://members.aol.com/calebj/mayflower.html
These pages represent thousands of hours of research, organization, and typing. The site is a merger of two fields: genealogy and history.

33. Reformation Guide
http://www.educ.msu.edu/homepages/laurence/reformation/index.htm
This Reformation Guide is intended to provide easy access to the wealth of information on the Internet for this period. Topics include Martin Luther, John Calvin, the Reformation in England, Scotland, Ireland, and the United States, as well as the Counterreformation.

34. Sir Francis Drake
http://www.mcn.org/2/oseeler/drake.htm
Sir Francis Drake and in particular his "famous voyage"—the circumnavigation of the world during the reign of Queen Elizabeth 1 are the focus of this site. It is provided by Oliver Seeler's site, The History Ring.

35. Society for Economic Anthropology Homepage
http://sea.agnesscott.edu
This is the home page of the Society for Economic Anthropology, an association that strives to understand diversity and change in the economic systems of the world. The site presents data on the organization of society and culture, a topic of interest to students of the Renaissance and Reformation.

36. Women and Philosophy Web Site
http://www.nd.edu/~colldev/subjects/wss.html
This Web site provides online collections of resources, ethics updates, bibliographies, information on organizations, and access to newsletters and journals.

We highly recommend that you review our Web site for expanded information and our other product lines. We are continually updating and adding links to our Web site in order to offer you the most usable and useful information that will support and expand the value of your Annual Editions. You can reach us at: http://www.dushkin.com/annualeditions/.

www.dushkin.com/online/

5

Unit 1

Key Points to Consider

❖ How did Hatshepsut become the first female pharaoh in Egypt? How did her subjects react to this unusual situation?

❖ Why was the introduction of money important for the Mesopotamian civilizations?

❖ How did variations of the Indo-European language come to be the dominant languages in so much of Europe and Asia?

❖ Who were the "sea peoples," and how did their weapons and tactics launch a military revolution in the ancient world?

 **Links**   **www.dushkin.com/online/**

These sites are annotated on pages 4 and 5.

The Earliest Civilizations

Civilization is a relatively recent phenomenon in human experience. But what exactly is civilization? How do civilized people differ from those who are not civilized? How is civilization transmitted?

Civilization, in its contemporary meaning, describes a condition of human society marked by an advanced stage of artistic and technological development and by corresponding social and political complexity. Thus, civilized societies have developed formal institutions for commerce, government, education, and religion—activities that are carried out informally by precivilized societies. In addition, civilized people make much more extensive use of symbols. The greater complexity of civilized life requires a much wider range of specialized activities.

Symbolizations, specialization, and organization enable civilized societies to extend greater control over their environments. Because they are less dependent than precivilized societies upon a simple adaptation to a particular habitat, civilized societies are more dynamic. Indeed, civilization institutionalizes change. In sum, civilization provides us with a wider range of concepts, techniques, and options to shape (for good or ill) our collective destinies.

In the West, the necessary preconditions for civilization first emerged in the great river valleys of Mesopotamia and Egypt. There we find the development of irrigation techniques, new staple crops, the introduction of the plow, the invention of the wheel, more widespread use of beasts of burden, improved sailing vessels, and metallurgy. These developments revolutionized society. Population increased and became more concentrated and more complex. The emergence of cities ("the urban revolution") marked the beginning of civilization.

Civilization combines complex social, economic, and political structures with a corresponding network of ideas and values. The Sumerians organized themselves in city-states headed by kings who acted in the name of the local patron deity. The Egyptians developed a more centralized and authoritarian system based on loyalty to national divine kings. The Assyrians used force and intimidation to shape an international empire.

These early civilizations allowed for little individualism or freedom of expression. As historian Nels M. Bailkey notes in *Readings in Ancient History: Thought and Experience from Gilgamesh to St. Augustine* (1992), "Their thought remained closely tied to religion and found expression predominantly in religious forms." Elaborate myths recounted the deeds of heroes, defined relations between humans and the gods, and generally justified the prevailing order of things. Thus, myths reveal something of the relationship between values and the social order in ancient civilizations. The link between beliefs and authority, particularly in Egypt, is treated in the first article "Hatshepsut: The Female Pharaoh."

We are inclined today to make much of the limitations of ancient systems of thought and authority. Yet the record of the Mesopotamians and Egyptians demonstrates, from the very beginning, civilization's potential for innovation and collective accomplishment. They developed writing, as reported in "Correspondence in Clay"; mathematics, monumental architecture, law, astronomy, art, and monetary systems, as explored in "The Cradle of Cash"; and literatures rich with diversity and imagination. The record of ancient civilizations is full of cruelty and destruction, but it also includes an awakening concern for justice and moral righteousness. These early civilizations are notable, too, for their heroic efforts to bring nature under human control.

For a time the great river valleys remained islands of civilization in a sea of barbarism. The spread of civilization to rain-watered lands required that outlying areas find the means to produce a food surplus and to develop the social mechanisms for transferring the surplus from farmers to specialists. The first condition was met by the diffusion of plow agriculture, the second by cultural contacts that came about through conquest, trade, and migration. Along these lines, the article "Shards of Speech" explores the emergence and spread of Indo-European languages and dialects, a classic instance of diffusion of power and culture.

Several satellite civilizations evolved into great empires. Such enterprises grew out of conquest; their initial success and subsequent survival typically depend upon their relative capacity to wage war. "The Coming of the Sea Peoples" describes how an ancient military revolution affected the balance-of-power in the ancient Near East and furthered cultural exchange between diverse and dispersed societies. The problem of governing scattered and often hostile subjects required that conquerors create new patterns of authority. The growth of the Assyrian and Persian empires were not mere acts of conquest; they were innovations in government and administration. Still the earliest efforts to impose and maintain imperial hegemony could be both crude and cruel, as the report "Grisly Assyrian Record of Torture and Death" attests.

Hatshepsut

The Female Pharaoh

*Continuing our look at women in ancient Egypt, **John Ray** considers the triumphs and monuments of Queen Hatshepsut, the only female Pharaoh.*

John Ray

John Ray is Herbert Thompson Reader in Egyptology at Cambridge University.

The Pharaoh of ancient Egypt is normally described as the typical example of a divine ruler. The reality was more complex than this, since the Pharaoh seems to have been a combination of a human element and a divine counterpart. This duality is expressed not only in the ruler's titles, which often have a double aspect to them, but also in the king's names. Every Pharaoh had a human name, given to him at birth and used in intimate contexts throughout his life. These names are the ones by which we know them. Since such names tended to repeat themselves in families, we now need to distinguish kings with the same name by numbers. In addition, there was a throne-name, conferred at the accession and containing the immortal form of the ruler's divinity. The king was an embodiment of the sungod, an eternal prototype, and the human frailties of the individual ruler did not affect this embodiment: a convenient system, surely, for having the best of both worlds when it comes to government. The Pharaoh was essentially an icon, much as the imperial Tsar was an icon, and even the president of the United States sometimes appears to be.

How far can icons be stretched? Pharaoh was the manifestation of the sun in time and place: he could be old, young, athletic, gay, incompetent, boring, alcoholic or insane, but he would still be Pharaoh. Examples of all these types are known, or hinted at in the sources. But could he be female? The theoretical answer to this question may have been 'yes', since there are several ancient Egyptian texts describing creator-gods with both male and female attributes, but it was one thing to concede an abstract possibility and another to welcome its embodiment. Female rulers are attested in the long history of dynastic Egypt, and later tradition puts the names of queens at or near the end of both the Old Kingdom (*c.* 2200 BC) and the Middle Kingdom, some five centuries later. (The Old Kingdom one, Nitocris, later attracted considerable legends, and appears prominently in Herodotus). However, the important point was that tradition placed these queens at the end of their particular dynasties: female Pharaohs were unnatural, and meant decline and retribution. Egyptian society gave remarkable freedoms and legal rights to women—far more than in the rest of the Near East or in the classical world—but limits were limits, even by the Nile.

Egypt was, and is, a Mediterranean country, where the most powerful man can frequently be reduced to confusion and paralysis by a remark from his mother, but women were limited to their sphere: if they had no other title, they could always be honoured as 'lady of the house'. If they stayed within this domain, they could expect to retain status and protection. Agriculture beside the Nile was intensive, and this meant that women's contributions were essential, as opposed to the more nomadic societies of the Near East, where females were often seen as an encumbrance. Many Egyptian women may not have thought their position a bad bargain; pregnancy

A granite head of Tuthmosis III, the sidelined young Pharaoh who took revenge on his over-assertive aunt by erasing her inscriptions after her death.

Hatshepsut's standard bearer is followed by men carrying herbs and spices from the Punt expedition, underlining the ossibility that its motive was economic.

(Below) Loading up the Egyptian ships at Punt (from Howard Carter's drawings at the turn-of-the-entury of the Deir el-Bahri reliefs): among the 'booty' were the frankincense trees that stood in front of Hatshepsut's temple.

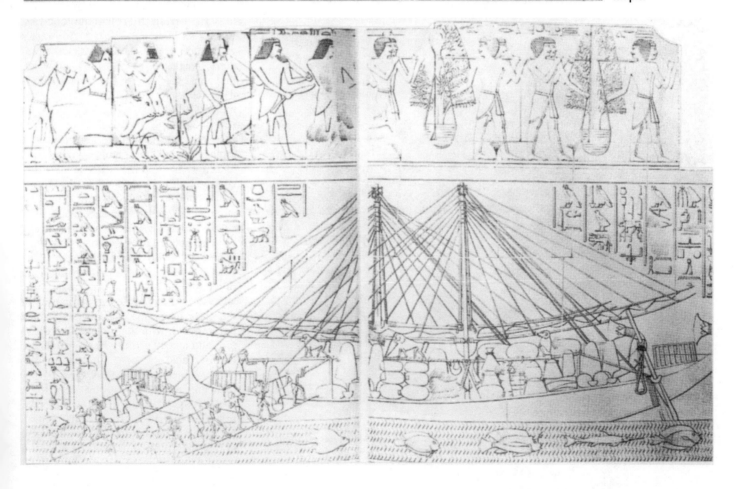

and childbirth were expected but dangerous, and support outside the family was unknown and perhaps impossible. Security, and the real possibility of influence over the holders of power, may not have seemed so poor a prospect, especially if a woman produced a son or two, while divorce and inheritance rules for females were relatively favourable. Why break the mould?

The early part of the Eighteenth Dynasty is often known as the Tuthmosid period, after the name of its principal rulers. Tuthmosis I (*c.* 1525–512 BC, although another reckoning would lower these dates by twenty-five years) was a warrior ruler, who took on the scattered principalities of Lebanon and Syria and carried his arms far beyond the Euphrates, setting up a victory stela on the banks of what the Egyptians described as the 'topsy-turvy' river, since it flowed the opposite way to the Nile. In retrospect, this is the beginning of something resembling an Egyptian empire in Asia, a subject which was to preoccupy foreign policy throughout the next two dynasties. However, retrospect is a one-way street, and contemporaries

may have thought that one show of force was enough. It may equally be that the modern concept of empire is an anachronism for the period: 'sphere of influence' might be a closer guide to Egyptian thinking. Tuthmosis I was followed by another Tuthmosis, a Pharaoh of whom little is known and arguably little worth knowing. However, he was married to Hatshepsut.

Hatshepsut was Tuthmosis II's half-sister (marriage to close relatives was not a problem in the Tuthmosid royal family, and this may explain the prominence given to queens in the early years of the dynasty; all were equally descended from the dynasty's heroic founder). However, it is likely that the king was worried about his wife's ambitions; her name, after all, meant 'Foremost of the noble ladies'. On his premature death (*c.* 1504 BC) he and Hatshepsut had produced only a daughter, Nefrure, and the official successor was Tuthmosis III, a young son by one of the king's minor wives. Clearly the boy was in need of a regent. His aunt thought herself qualified for the job; more importantly, she had convinced enough others of the same truth that she was able to

stage a coup. She and Tuthmosis III were declared joint Pharaohs. There were precedents for this in earlier dynasties, and this may have gone some way towards blurring the innovatory fact that one of the co-regents was not male. In a few early scenes she is shown dutifully following her partner, but this soon changes. This was to be a co-regency that was far from equal. For the next twenty-two years it would be 'goodnight from her, and goodnight from her'. The reign of Hatshepsut had begun, and her throne-name was Maatkare, 'Truth (a female principle which also embodies the ideas of justice and harmony) is the genius of the sungod'.

There is a sense in which all history is about the meanings of words, and it is certainly true that to change history involves colliding with the language in which it is expressed. Hatshepsut does this. Traditional Pharaohs were the embodiment of the god Horus; Hatshepsut is also Horus, but the epithets she adds in hieroglyphs are grammatically in the feminine forms. Furthermore, she describes herself as 'The she-Horus of fine gold', fine gold (electrum) being an amalgam of this metal with the rarer and more valuable silver. It is as if she were to style herself the platinum goddess. Like other Pharaohs, she regularly refers to herself as 'His Majesty' (a closer rendering might be 'His Person'). However, the word for majesty is turned into a new feminine equivalent. One is reminded of Elizabeth I of England, with her doctrine of the dual body of the monarch, one of which happens to be female. Rewriting language in the light of gender is not a twentieth-century discovery. It did not work in ancient Egypt (and it might not work now), but the attempt was none the less made. The changes either originated with the queen, or were approved by her, and they must correspond with her thinking. In conventional temple scenes, where the icon of a traditional Pharaoh is necessary, she appears as a male ruler. In sculpture, on the other hand, she is shown as female but imperial, with the typical Tuthmosid face and arched profile. Her portraits are unmistakable.

A characteristic of Hatshepsut is her preoccupation with historical context. It is as if she is trying to define her own role in events, to justify her intervention on to the stage and to issue a challenge at the same time. In a deserted valley in Middle Egypt, in the eastern cliffs about

A touch of the exotic—the 'fat lady' of Punt and her husband—one of the observations of Hatshepsut's artists from the walls of her temple on the expedition sponsored by the queen in years 8–9 of her reign.

175 miles south of modern Cairo, is an unusual rock-cut temple known by its classical name of Speos Artemidos, the grotto of Artemis. The goddess in question was known to the Egyptians as Pakhet, an obscure deity with the attributes of a lioness. On the facade of this temple is a long dedication, put there by Hatshepsut and her artists, designed, as she tells us, to 'record the annals of her supremacy for ever'. In this text she announced the theme of her reign, which is no less than a complete rebuilding of the land of Egypt. Solar imagery abounds in the text, and Hatshepsut is described without any attempt at modesty as the one predestined since the moment of creation to restore the ritual purity of the temples, to recapture the perfection of the world's origins:

> I raised up what was dismembered, even from the time when the Asiatics were in the midst of (the Delta), overthrowing what had been created. They ruled in ignorance of Re (the sungod), and acted not by divine command, until my august person.

This is a reference both to the resurrection of the god Osiris and to the occupation of Egypt by the alien Hyksos, which had preceded the Eighteenth Dynasty: an episode which was shameful, but by no means as barbaric as Hatshepsut makes out. Nor did it last as long as she pretended. This combination of historical perspective and return to religious purity is characteristic of Hatshepsut. Since her position as Pharaoh was unorthodox, an appeal to fundamentalism was necessary to correct the balance. This may well have corresponded to her own thinking, and need not be merely cynical.

Determination to rewrite history is also seen in the official version of the queens proclamation and accession, where the choice of her as ruler is made, not by inheritance or acclamation, but by the oracle of the god Amun, leader of the Egyptian pantheon and ruler of the royal city of Thebes. An oracle of this sort probably happened, since it is suspiciously convenient and could easily have been arranged by the queen's followers after her seizure of power. What is more important is that the queen is cutting out any human medium, and going straight for an identification with the divine. As Pharaoh, she had this identification automatically, and there would normally be no need to labour the point.

Hatshepsut is not normal, and she labours the point for all it contains, here and in her other inscriptions. The platinum goddess can be seen as the Egyptian equivalent of Gloriana, the mythical transformation of Elizabeth I. This is a comparison to which we will return.

One feature of Hatshepsut's reign is often noted: the apparent lack of military activity. There is evidence for minor campaigns in Nubia, and the period is not a complete blank, but the frantic action of the previous reign is lacking. This is sometimes explained as a delib-

Careful courtier: Senenmut, Hatshepsut's steward and one of the queen's closest advisers, shown here as a tutor cradling her daughter, the princess Nefrure.

erate attempt by Hatshepsut to adopt a pacifist and feminine approach to politics. This is so completely out of line with what can be deduced about her character that it cannot convince. Female rulers can be as warlike as any man, especially if they feel that they have something to prove. A more likely reason is that Hatshepsut could not trust the army. If she led a campaign herself, even if this were politically acceptable, what would happen if she lost? A female commander would be the natural thing to blame for defeat. If the army won, it might start agitating for more victories, and for a greater role for the queen's nephew, who would gain status as he grew in years. The whole subject was best avoided, especially if Tuthmosis I had already made the point that Egypt was the leading power in Asia. Some things could be left as they were.

If the army could not be used on a large scale, an outlet must be found elsewhere. This is one of the purposes behind the famous expedition to the land of Punt, which occupied the eighth and ninth years of her reign. The location of Punt is unknown, though it may have been Eritrea or part of Somalia, or somewhere further south, but it was the home of the frankincense-tree. The adventure is recorded on the walls of the queen's masterpiece, the great temple in the cliffs of Deir el-Bahri in western Thebes, the modern Luxor. Exquisite reliefs show the departure of the expedition, the arrival at the exotic land beyond the sea, the lading of Hatshepsut's ships with the produce of Punt, and the preparations for the voyage home.

The event was not simply a foraging mission, since it was accompanied by artists to record the flora and fauna of the Red Sea and of the African coast. It can almost be described as the beginning of comparative anthropology, even if the climax—the appearance of the grossly overweight queen of Punt accompanied by a donkey—has an element of the ridiculous about it. Part of the expedition found its way back to Egypt by way of the upper Nile, while five shiploads, including incense-trees, returned by sea. Walter Raleigh would probably have enjoyed Punt, although the reasons for the voyage are not entirely clear. It may have been imperial prospecting, although this is unlikely at this early stage in the dynasty. Perhaps it was economic, an attempt to corner part of the lucrative incense-trade for Egypt. It was certainly an exercise for an underemployed army, and it was propaganda for the queen as provider of the exotic. Perhaps it was also fun.

The roots of the incense-trees can still be seen before the Deir el-Bahri temple, where they were planted and where they perfumed the night air. The temple has been excavated slowly over the past century (its scenes were first copied by a young draughtsman named Howard Carter), and its plan is now clear. No one who walks the path over the mountain from the Valley of the Kings and looks down at the other side can ignore the series of terraces below, built into the western cliffs. It is one of the most dramatic sights in Egypt. The variety of its scenes, all showing the slightly austere elegance that is common to Tuthmosid art, the balance between light and shade which is necessary in such an exposed site, and the originality of its design make the building unique. Perhaps to contemporaries it was too unique; certainly the concept was never recreated. Manuals of classical architecture tell us that the Doric column was developed in Greece around the seventh century BC. The north colonnade of Deir el-Bahri was composed of them, eight centuries earlier.

Part of the temple was devoted to the divine birth of Hatshepsut, another piece of mythology which normal Pharaohs did not need to use. The god Amun himself desired to create his living image on earth, to reveal his greatness and to carry out his plans. He disguised himself as Tuthmosis I, went one day to see the queen, and the result, in due course, was Hatshepsut. Amun did not mind that his image was female, so why should anyone else?

Similar themes are explored in a rather strange medium, an inscribed pair of granite obelisks which the queen set up in her sixteenth year before the temple of Amun at Karnak opposite Deir el-Bahri. The entire work, she tells us, took seven months. Obelisks in Egyptian thinking were a representation of the first ray of light which inaugurated the creation, or what we would now call the Big Bang. In the text Hatshepsut knows the mind of God: she was present with the creator at the beginning, she is the luminous seed of the almighty one, and she is 'the fine gold of kings'—another reference to electrum. This metal was even used to coat the obelisks, to make her splendour visible. Her sense of posterity, and the force of her personality, are clear from the words she uses:

> Those who shall see my monument in future years, and shall speak of what I have done, beware of saying, 'I know not, I know not how this has been done, fashioning a mountain of gold throughout, like something of nature' . . . Nor shall he who hears this say it was a boast, but rather, 'How like her this is, how worthy of her father'.

She also tells us that her obelisks were situated by the gateway of Tuthmosis I, since it was he who began the obelisk habit. This preoccupation with the father is not accidental. Pharaoh was Pharaoh because his father had been Pharaoh; in Egyptian mythology, he was Horus to his predecessor's Osiris, one god ruling on earth while the other reigned over the netherworld. However, this was conventional, and orthodox Pharaohs did not need to make it explicit. Hatshepsut, the female Horus, was not orthodox. Her kingship depended on mythological props, and also on political ones; in fact, she would not have made a distinction between the two. But there may well be a third element at work, a personal one.

Tuthmosis I is prominent in many of her inscriptions, far more than is necessary. His sarcophagus was even discovered in his daughter's tomb, where it had been transferred from his own. Clearly she intended to spend eternity with the man who had been her father on earth. She left her husband, Tuthmosis II, where he was lying in the Valley of the Kings, and her inscriptions never mention him, even though he was presumably the parent of her child. This is a trait which prominent females sometimes show. Anna Freud turned herself into Sigmund's intellectual heir, Benazir Bhutto makes a political platform out of her father's memory, and one is reminded of a recent British prime minister whose entry in *Who's Who* included a father but no mother. Did Tuthmosis I ever call his daughter 'the best man in the dynasty', and is this why Hatshepsut shows no identification with other women? This is not entirely hypothetical: among Hatshepsut's inscriptions is an imaginative reworking of an episode when she was young, in which her father proclaims her his heir before the entire palace. Such a text could have been based on a coming-of-age ceremony, or even a chance remark to an impressionable child.

Hatshepsut was determined to hold on to power, and the way she achieved this is clear. After the gradual disappearance of her father's advisers, almost all her supporters are new men (women she could not have appointed, even if she had had a mind to). They owed nothing to the traditional aristocracy, little to conventional patronage: they were 'one of us'. They were hers, and if she fell, they would fall also. Their tombs are still visible in the cliffs above Deir el-Bahri. They are easily distinguished by the terraced effect of their facades, which resemble the royal temple; even in their architecture they showed whose men they were. This must have been a court where many lesser lights danced attendance on the sun-queen.

The most prominent courtier of Hatshepsut's reign is Senenmut. He dominates the temple of Deir el-Bahri, where he seems to be an overall but ill-defined master of works. His figure even appears in small niches in some of its chapels, worshipping the god Amun and his royal mistress. These niches are hidden behind the doors, but the gods would have known what was in them, and so probably did Hatshepsut. This must have been done with her approval. Senenmut's place in the royal household is confirmed by his position as tutor to the queen's daughter Nefrure, and statues survive showing Senenmut crouching in the guise of a patient client, while the head of the royal infant peeps out from between his knees. Senenmut was given permission to be buried within the precincts of the great temple, an unprecedented honour.

Around the seventh year of the reign Senenmut's mother died, and she too was interred in the temple. Senenmut exhumed the body of his father at the same time, and reburied him in splendour alongside her and other members of his family. The father had no title (otherwise the Egyptians, who were obsessed with titles, would have not failed to mention it), and his original burial was tantamount to a pauper's. Senenmut must have come from a small town along the Nile, and rose to prominence entirely through merit and the queen's patronage. This sheds unexpected light on what could happen in ancient Egypt. Senenmut seems never to have married. Perhaps he did not dare to; did not Walter Raleigh fall from grace as soon as he married one of Gloriana's maids?

Recently evidence has emerged that the reign of Hatshepsut could inspire distinctly tabloid reactions. Some years ago, in an unfinished tomb above the Deir el-Bahri temple, a series of graffiti were found. One of these is a feeble drawing of Senenmut, but on another wall there is a sketch showing a female Pharaoh undergoing the attentions of a male figure, in a way that implies her passive submission. This may be a contemporary comment on the relationship between Senenmut and the queen, or it may be a later satire on the notion of an impotent female Pharaoh, or it may simply be the fantasy of a little man for something he could never attain, rather on the lines of the stories which later circulated about Cleopatra or Catherine the Great. If the scene is genuine, it is extremely interesting, even if its meaning is less explicit than its drawing.

The queen died on the tenth day of the sixth month of the twenty-second year of her reign (early February 1482 BC). She was perhaps fifty. Tuthmosis III, so long cooped up, became sole Pharaoh and immediately led his army into Syria, where in seventeen campaigns he restored Egyptian overlordship of the Near East. At some point, though not for some years, he began a proscription of his aunt's memory. Probably he chose to wait until Senenmut and her other supporters had passed away. Perhaps he remained in awe of her. Her inscriptions were erased, her obelisks surrounded by a wall, and her monuments forgotten. Her name does not appear in later annals, which is why we refer to Tuthmosis by a Greek transcription, while hers is missing. The bodies of many of the New Kingdom Pharaohs survive, and are now in the Cairo Museum. As far as we know, hers is not among them. What we do know about her has been gained by excavation and careful epigraphy over the past hundred years. Perhaps this is as it should be, since the late twentieth century is a better time than most to think about the meaning of her reign. Will the feminist movement rediscover her, or will she be uncomfortable for us, as she was for some of her contemporaries?

FOR FURTHER READING:

Cambridge Ancient History (3 edn., vol. II, 1973, ch. 9); Peter F. Dorman, *The Monuments of Senenmut* (Kegan Paul International, 1988); Miriam Lichtheim, *Ancient Egyptian Literature II* (California, 1976); Donald B. Redford, *History and Chronology of the Eighteenth Dynasty of Egypt* (Toronto, 1967) and the same author's *Egypt, Canaan, and Israel in Ancient Times* (Princeton, 1992); John Romer, *Romer's Egypt* (Rainbird, 1982); Edward F. Wente, 'Some Graffiti from the Reign of Hatshepsut', *Journal of Near Eastern Studies 43* (1984).

Correspondence in Clay

Written by Barbara Ross

Photographs courtesy of the Museum of Fine Arts, Boston

I am going to have a house-warming," read the invitation. "Come yourself to eat and drink with me. Twenty-five women and 25 men shall be in attendance." The party favor promised was "10 wooden chariots and 10 teams of horses"—a lavish gift by ordinary standards, but this invitation was from royalty. It was sent some 3500 years ago by Kadasman-Enlil, king of Babylonia, to Akhenaten (Amenhotep IV), pharaoh of Egypt. The message was inscribed on a pillow-shaped clay tablet, small enough to be carried easily in one hand or slipped into a satchel.

The letter was one of hundreds uncovered in the late 1800's, when a peasant woman rummaging through the ruins of Akhetaten, an ancient city near modern-day Tell El-Amarna, came across a cache of small clay tablets covered with unfamiliar script. She took several to a merchant, who immediately purchased them. Word of the tablets spread quickly, and in a short time the site was buzzing with local residents, each hoping to find something of marketable value. The hoard was excavated, and most pieces were sold to the highest bidders. Today there are about 380 significant texts scattered among private collectors, antique dealers and museums, mostly in Egypt and Europe, and collectively these clay-table texts are known as the Amarna Letters.

The letters, which cover approximately three decades, hold a particular fascination because their place in Egyptian history is unique. They begin late in the reign of Amenhotep III and end during the first year of the reign of Tutankhamen; in between they cover the entire 17-year reign of Akhenaten, whose rule between 1353 and 1336 BC was perhaps the most dynamic and far-reaching in its effects of any reign in any of the 30 or so Egyptian dynasties that rules over the course of 3000 years. Often referred to as the "heretic king,"

BRITISH MUSEUM, LONDON

Among some 380 Amarna Letters known to exist is this one from a king of Mitanni—now northern Syria—a long-time ally of Egypt.

Akhenaten was the first Egyptian king to worship a single deity. (See *Aramco World*, September/October 1994). He forbade the worship of multiple gods, and he directed an entire society to worship one supreme being represented by the sun, which he referred to as "Aten." With his wife, Nefertiti, and their young daughters, the royal family moved from Thebes, the capital of Egypt, to a palatial city he had built along the east bank of the Nile some 300 kilometers (185 miles) to the north. He named his city Akhetaten ("Horizon of Aten"), and today it is known as Amarna.

Politically, Egypt was at its zenith, the most powerful kingdom the world had known, dominating the lesser empires of Babylonia, Assyria, Khatti, Mitanni and Alashiya (Cyprus), and the provinces of Syria, Palestine, Canaan and Kush. The Amarna Letters were diplomatic correspondence between the pharaoh and the rulers of these lands, or the vassals who governed towns and cities under Egyptian control.

Each letter observed a protocol, and in doing so it eloquently expressed the relationship of the sender with the Egyptian court—generally, in fact, with the pharaoh himself. John Huehnergard, professor of Near Eastern language and civilization at Harvard University, explains that the language of brotherhood and love so common in the letters "is meant sincerely, because it was also code for diplomatic relations. 'Brothers' were allies, and to 'love' one's brother was to be in a treaty relationship with the other king."

After a flurry of courteous salutations, most letters included a plea for money, gifts or military troops. This is a typical introduction: "Say to Nimmureya [Akhenaten], the king of Egypt, my brother, my son-in-law, whom I love and who loves me: Thus Tushratta, the king of Mitanni, your father-in-law, who loves you, your brother. For me all goes well. For you may all go well. For your household, for your wives, for your sons, for your magnates, for your chariots, for your horses, for your warriors,

ÄGYPTISCHES MUSEUM, BERLIN

In addition to its legacy of letters, the Amarna Period left an artistic legacy as well: a radical departure from 1500 years of iconographic idealism in favor of naturalism, exemplified in this relief of Nefertiti and Akhenaten holding three of their daughters under the life-giving rays of the sun-god Aten.

 Reprinted from *Aramco World*, November/December 1999, pp. 31–34. © 1999 by Aramco Services Company.

for your country and whatever else belongs to you, may all go very, very well."

The meat of the letter would quickly follow. In this case, Tushratta announced that he was sending one of his mistresses as a gift to the pharaoh. "She has become very mature, and she has been fashioned according to my brother's [Akhenaten's] desire. And, furthermore, my brother will note that the greeting gift that I shall present is greater than any before."

The letters were dispatched by messengers who were members of each monarch's council. When these emissaries were required to travel through unwelcoming territories, where they risked thieves, thugs and political enemies, their job was difficult—but so it might be once they arrived, too: Occasionally a messenger from abroad would be held by the pharaoh himself. In another letter, Tushratta complains of this problem:

"Previously, my father would send a messenger to you, and you would not detain him for long. You quickly sent him off, and you would also send here to my father a beautiful greeting-gift. But now when I sent a messenger to you, you have detained him for six years, and you have sent me as my greeting-gift, the only thing in six years, 30 minas of gold that looked like silver."

This testy passage is startling considering that Akhenaten was the richest and most powerful man in the world, for it implies that the Mitanni king was offended by a gift of what he suspected was counterfeit or debased gold. However, Tushratta and his father had maintained an unusually close relationship with Akhenaten's father and grandfather. The Mitanni, in western Mesopotamia, were among Egypt's most important allies, and several princesses had been sent as bridges to marry Akhenaten and his father, Amenhotep III. A kinship evolved between the rulers that elevated Tushratta above the role of a mere ally, and the terms of endearment in the letters to him were probably more than matters of protocol.

The written word of the time was cuneiform, a type of writing that had spread from Mesopotamia beginning in the third millennium BC, and was used to write several languages at different times and places. The Amarna Letters are mostly written in Old Babylonian, itself a dialect of Akkadian, a spoken and written language that developed in the city of Akkad, now in Iraq. At the time the letters were written, Old Babylonian had become infused with West Semitic and Egyptian words, and it had become the common regional language that unified international relations and trade, a *lingua franca*.

Because written tablets often carried political and commercial communications, their production was important business, and from the evidence in scenes etched on tomb walls, the scribes who wrote them enjoyed high status. Each country outside Assyria and Babylon, where Akkadian was the first language, had to maintain a staff of trusted, educated people who could interpret and write in Akkadian. For example, when the Egyptian king dictated a letter, his scribe probably wrote on papyrus. The scribe would then hand his text to a translator, who would inscribe it into clay in Akkadian. The tablet would then be dispatched by royal courier. If it was addressed, for example, to the Hittite king, the courier would have to gain admittance to that king's palace and hand the tablets to the Hittite king's interpreter, who would in turn translate the message into Hittite for presentation to his king.

This was an era in which diplomacy was often urgent, for throughout the Amarna period many of Egypt's vassals were at war with each other. Some let-

A profile of Akhenaten demonstrates the exaggerated realism of the early Amarna Period.

ters discredited the sender's enemy in these terms, as in this letter from Rib-Hadda, king of Byblos:

"Who is 'Abdi-Asirta, the servant and dog, that they mention his name in the presence of the king, my lord? Just let there be one man whose heart is one with my heart, and I would drive 'Abdi-Asirta from the land of Amurru."

In the same letter, Rib-Hadda eloquently pleaded for help: "Since he has attacked me three times this year, and for two years I have been repeatedly robbed of my grain, we have no grain to eat. What can I say to my peasantry? Their sons, their daughters, the furnishings of their houses are gone, since they have been sold in the land of Yarimuta for provisions to keep us alive. May the king, my lord, heed the words of his loyal servant and may he send grain in ships in order to keep his servant and his city alive."

In another letter, Rib-Hadda thanked the pharaoh for requesting help for him: "Moreover, it was a gracious deed of the king, my lord, that the king wrote to the king of Beirut, to the king of Sidon, and to the king of Tyre, saying, 'Rib-Hadda will be writing to you for an auxiliary force, and all of you are to go.' This pleased me, and so I sent my messenger, but they have not come, they have not sent the messengers to greet us."

Apparently, the troops never arrived. Although Rib-Hadda was a close ally and had dispatched numerous letters petitioning for help, Akhenaten did not go any further to assure his protection. As a result, Byblos was sacked, and the king was taken prisoner and put to death.

Scholars of the Amarna tablets wonder why Akhenaten did not respond more effectively to Rib-Hadda, but it was almost certainly a political calculation. "The Egyptian king had to balance his troop commitments," says Huehnergard. "He had troops deployed in the south [Nubia], west [Libya], and in garrisons in his Syro-Palestinian territories. To go to the aid of Rib-Hadda would have required a much larger force with the sole purpose of maintaining the status quo balance of minor powers in the region. The king opted instead to let the expansion of Amurru run its course, to poor Rib-Hadda's detriment."

In a tumultuous political sea, what remained fixed throughout Akhenaten's reign was his ardent adoration of Aten. Amarna was built with roofless court-

When finished, this serenely smiling bust of Nefertiti would have been polished, and the tenon would have anchored a separate headdress.

yards, temples, and shrines to facilitate worship directly toward the sun—although shade was provided for the royal family. An Assyrian king protested to the pharaoh on behalf of his emissaries:

"Why are my messengers kept standing in the open sun? They will die in the open sun. If it does the king good to stand in the open sun, then let the king stand there and die in the open sun. Then will there be profit for the king! But really, why should [my messengers] die in the open sun?"

Although many letters contain similarly heated protests of the pharaoh's ways, he appears to have remained largely unmoved, for his power dwarfed that of other empires. Tushratta, the king of Mitanni who was offended by a questionable gift from the pharaoh, plainly conceded, "In Egypt, gold is more plentiful than dirt." In the same letter, he elaborated on why he and his friends

Polychrome glass was a speciality among Amarna craftsmen, and this fish vessel vividly depicts a Tilapia species common in the Nile

were not impressed with the gift of gold recently sent to him:

"And with regard to the gold that my brother sent. I gathered together all my foreign guests. My brother, before all of them, the gold that he sent has been cut open. . . . And they wept very much saying, 'Are all of these gold? They do not look like gold.' "

Akhenaten may have incurred the ire of his vassals abroad, much as other great powers have throughout history, but there is evidence that he was a devoted husband and father. He and Nefertiti had at least six daughters, and reliefs found on shrines, temple walls, and burial sites show hints of intimacy and domestic contentment that are unique in pharaonic art. In one painting, the king and queen are seated under a sun-disc whose rays end in tiny hands, which symbolize the life-giving force of the sun. Their three eldest daughters, Meritaten, Meketaten, and Ankhesenpaaten, are often depicted in scenes that display an unusual degree of affection between them and their father.

Akhenaten died after 17 years of reign and was succeeded by Smenkhare, who had married Meritaten. Smenkhare ruled for four years, and was himself succeeded by Tutankhamen, who may have been either Akhenaten's younger brother, or Akhenaten's son by a minor queen. The nine-year-old pharaoh married Akhenaten's youngest daughter, Ankhesenpaaten, and ruled until his untimely death nine years later. This left his wife a widow while she was still, presumably, only in her teens.

During Tutankhamen's reign the capital was moved back to Thebes, and the old polytheism was reinstated. It is widely believed that the young king Tutankhamen was manipulated by older, craftier advisors who saw a return to past ways as a means of restoring their own power. One of the closest advisors to the king was a nobleman named Ay, who had been a faithful follower of Akhenaten. But after the political climate changed following Akahenaten's death, he had became sympathetic to the Theban priests who still prayed to the ancient Egyptian pantheon. In the absence of a male heir to Tutankhamen's throne, Ay became the designated candidate— but the prerequisite of his ascent was marriage to Tutankhamen's young widow, who was at least 30 years his junior.

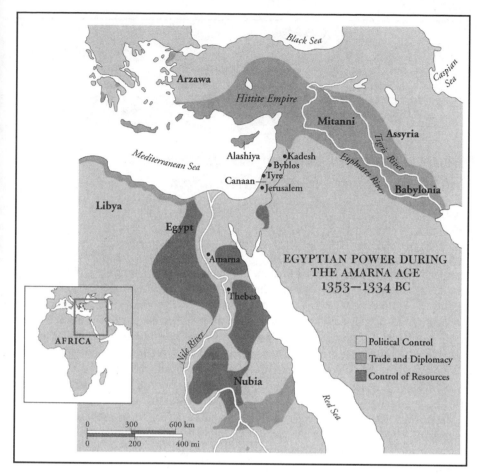

METROPOLITAN MUSEUM OF ART, NEW YORK

The yellow, semiprecious stone and high polish of this fragment suggest royalty, but it is not certain whom it represents.

To take Ay as her husband would have been ignominious for Ankhesenpaaten, and her desperate search for a suitor who might supplant him bespeaks a feisty and determined temperament. She scoured her own realm unsuccessfully and finally resorted to an unprecedented search beyond Egypt. That step produced one of the most famous and touching letters of the Amarna Period, authored by the distressed young woman. One of the only ones known to have been dispatched from Egypt rather than received there, it was discovered in the ancient city of Hattusas (modern-day Bogazköy in central Turkey), seat of the Hittite king Suppiluliumash.

"My husband has died," she wrote, "and I have no son. They say about you that you have many sons. You might give me one of your sons, and he might become my husband. I would not want to take one of my servants. I am loath to make him my husband."

It was earth-shattering for a woman of her stature, queen of a great empire, to request such a thing from one of Egypt's vassals, but the reference to her betrothed as a servant gave proof of her distaste for Ay. King Suppiluliumash

must have been stunned; yet he quickly took advantage of the opportunity and dispatched one of his princes. But the young man was murdered on his way to Egypt, and so Ankhesenpaaten did in fact marry Ay.

Ay reigned for four or five years, and he is believed to have continued the Theban building projects at Karnak and Medinet Habu. Ankhesenpaaten fades from the record, but a blue glass ring, inscribed with both her name and Ay's, was found in the ruins at Amarna. Ay was succeeded by Horemheb, who detested Akhenaten's monotheism and dispatched men to obliterate everything Akhenaten had created. What survives today of Akhenaten's legacy is but a small part of what once existed, and Horemheb's destruction is part of the reason that the reign of Akhenaten sank into obscurity until its rediscovery in the early 19th century. As for the Amarna Letters, although the form of communication doubtless continued, there have been no corresponding caches of correspondence found in Thebes, and thus the record ends approximately a year after the capital was moved back there from Amarna, during the reign of Tutankhamen.

The legacy of the Amarna Period is great. While some scholars credit Akhenaten with the inspiration for monotheism, more agree that his patronage of artistic realism left an even clearer legacy. In the vaulted halls of the Cairo Museum, silhouette statues of the "heretic king" are distinctly unlike those of prior pharaohs, who appear with broad shoulders, perfectly shaped features and robust physiques. Akhenaten chose a different iconography: he was depicted with narrow shoulders, a bulbous belly and swollen breasts. Whether or not this interpretation was Akhenaten's own choice, or merely the artists' realistic representation of the king's physique, has puzzled scholars ever since Amarna was uncovered.

Yet beyond scholarly questions, what makes the Amarna period riveting is the poignancy of the letters and the personal faces they present. Through them, we can clearly envision the indignant Assyrian king fuming over the treatment of his emissaries, the ill-fated Rib-Hadda pleading for relief, and the desperate royal widow embracing a lesser humiliation to avoid a greater one. The Amarna Letters are our only intimate glimpses into lives lived in a world so distant from our own in time, yet so similar in its humanity.

Free-lance writer Barbara Ross travels frequently to the Middle East and writes often on Egypt. She lives in Boston.

TRANSLATIONS ARE FROM: *The Amarna Letters,* trans. and ed. by William L. Moran (Johns Hopkins University Press, 1992, ISBN 0801842514).

The Cradle of Cash

*When money arose in the ancient cities of Mesopotamia, it
profoundly and permanently changed civilization.*

By Heather Pringle

THE SCENE IN THE SMALL, STIFLING room is not hard to imagine: the scribe frowning, shifting in his seat as he tries to concentrate on the words of the woman in front of him. A member of one of the wealthiest families in Sippar, the young priestess has summoned him to her room to record a business matter. When she entered the temple, she explains, her parents gave her a valuable inheritance, a huge piece of silver in the shape of a ring, worth the equivalent of 60 months' wages for an estate worker. She has decided to buy land with this silver. Now she needs someone to take down a few details. Obediently, the scribe smooths a wet clay tablet and gets out his stylus. Finally, his work done, he takes the tablet down to the archive.

For more than 3,700 years, the tablet languished in obscurity, until late-nineteenth-century collectors unearthed it from Sippar's ruins along the Euphrates River in what is now Iraq. Like similar tablets, it hinted at an ancient and mysterious Near Eastern currency, in the form of silver rings, that started circulating two millennia before the world's first coins were struck. By the time that tablet was inscribed, such rings may have been in use for a thousand years.

When did humans first arrive at the concept of money? What conditions spawned it? And how did it affect the ancient societies that created it? Until recently, researchers thought they had the answers. They believed money was born, as coins, along the coasts of the Mediterranean in the seventh or sixth century B.C., a product of the civilization

that later gave the world the Parthenon, Plato, and Aristotle. But few see the matter so simply now. With evidence gleaned from such disparate sources as ancient temple paintings, clay tablets, and buried hoards of uncoined metals, researchers have revealed far more ancient money: silver scraps and bits of gold, massive rings and gleaming ingots.

In the process, they have pushed the origins of cash far beyond the sunny coasts of the Mediterranean, back to the world's oldest cities in Mesopotamia, the fertile plain created by the Tigris and Euphrates rivers. There, they suggest, wealthy citizens were flaunting money at least as early as 2500 B.C. and perhaps a few hundred years before that. "There's just no way to get around it," says Marvin Powell, a historian at Northern Illinois University in De Kalb. "Silver in Mesopotamia functions like our money today. It's a means of exchange. People use it for a storage of wealth, and they use it for defining value."

Many scholars believe money began even earlier. "My sense is that as far back as the written records go in Mesopotamia and Egypt, some form of money is there," observes Jonathan Williams, curator of Roman and Iron Age coins at the British Museum in London. "That suggests it was probably there beforehand, but we can't tell because we don't have any written records."

Just why researchers have had such difficulties in uncovering these ancient moneys has much to do with the practice of archeology and the nature of money itself. Archeologists, after all, are

the ultimate Dumpster divers: they spend their careers sifting through the trash of the past, ingeniously reconstructing vanished lives from broken pots and dented knives. But like us, ancient Mesopotamians and Phoenicians seldom made the error of tossing out cash, and only rarely did they bury their most precious liquid assets in the ground. Even when archeologists have found buried cash, though, they've had trouble recognizing it for what it was. Money doesn't always come in the form of dimes and sawbucks, even today. As a means of payment and a way of storing wealth, it assumes many forms, from debit cards and checks to credit cards and mutual funds. The forms it took in the past have been, to say the least, elusive.

From the beginning, money has shaped human society. It greased the wheels of Mesopotamian commerce, spurred the development of mathematics, and helped officials and kings rake in taxes and impose fines. As it evolved in Bronze Age civilizations along the Mediterranean coast, it fostered sea trade, built lucrative cottage industries, and underlay an accumulation of wealth that might have impressed Donald Trump. "If there were never any money, there would never have been prosperity," says Thomas Wyrick, an economist at Southwest Missouri State University in Springfield, who is studying the origins of money and banking. "Money is making all this stuff happen."

Ancient texts show that almost from its first recorded appearance in the ancient Near East, money preoccupied es-

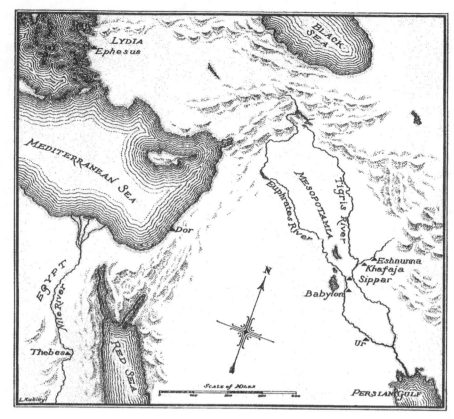

Illustrations by Laszlo Kubinyi

Cash first appeared in Mesopotamia then spread westward to the Mediterranean

stones across the plains and raising huge flat-topped platforms, known as ziggurats, on which to found their temples. Around their bases, they built street upon twisted street of small mud-brick houses.

To furnish these new temples and to serve temple officials, many farmers became artisans—stonemasons, silversmiths, tanners, weavers, boatbuilders, furniture makers. And within a few centuries, says Wyrick, the cities became much greater than the sum of their parts. Economic life flourished and grew increasingly complex. "Before, you always had people scattered out on the hillsides," says Wyrick, "and whatever they could produce for their families, that was it. Very little trade occurred because you never had a large concentration of people. But now, in these cities, for the first time ever in one spot, you had lots of different goods, hundreds of goods, and lots of different people trading them."

Just how complex life grew in these early metropolises can be glimpsed in the world's oldest accounting records: 8,162 tiny clay tokens excavated from the floors of village houses and city temples across the Near East and studied in detail by Denise Schmandt-Besserat, an archeologist at the University of Texas at Austin. The tokens served first as counters and perhaps later as prom-

tate owners and scribes, water carriers and slaves. In Mesopotamia, as early as 3000 B.C., scribes devised pictographs suitable for recording simple lists of concrete objects, such as grain consignments. Five hundred years later, the pictographs had evolved into a more supple system of writing, a partially syllabic script known as cuneiform that was capable of recording the vernacular: first Sumerian, a language unrelated to any living tongue, and later Akkadian, an ancient Semitic language. Scribes could write down everything from kingly edicts to proverbs, epics to hymns, private family letters to merchants' contracts. In these ancient texts, says Miguel Civil, a lexicographer at the Oriental Institute of the University of Chicago, "they talk about wealth and gold and silver all the time."

In all likelihood, says Wyrick, human beings first began contemplating cash just about the time that Mesopotamians were slathering mortar on mud bricks to build the world's first cities. Until then, people across the Near East had worked primarily on small farms, cultivating

barley, dates, and wheat, hunting gazelles and other wild game, and bartering among themselves for the things they could not produce. But around 3500 B.C., work parties started hauling

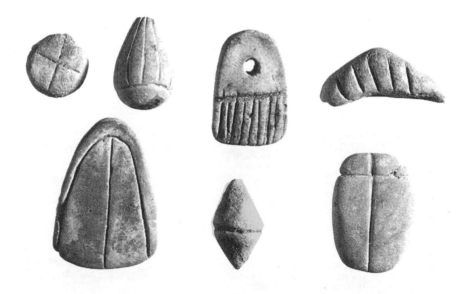

Courtesy Denise Schmandt-Besserat

These clay tokens from Susa, Iran, around 3300 B.C., represent (clockwise from top left): one sheep, one jar of oil, one garment, one measure of metal, a mystery item, one measure of honey, and one garment.

Ancient texts show that almost from its first recorded appearance in the ancient Near East, money preoccupied estate owners and scribes, water carriers and slaves.

issory notes given to temple tax collectors before the first writing appeared.

By classifying the disparate shapes and markings on the tokens into types and comparing these with the earliest known written symbols, Schmandt-Besserat discovered that each token represented a specified quantity of a particular commodity. And she noticed an intriguing difference between village tokens and city tokens. In the small communities dating from before the rise of cities, Mesopotamians regularly employed just five token types, repre-

senting different amounts of three main goods: human labor, grain, and livestock like goats and sheep. But in the cities, they began churning out a multitude of new types, regularly employing 16 in all, with dozens of subcategories representing everything from honey, sheep's milk, and trussed ducks to wool, cloth, rope, garments, mats, beds, perfume, and metals. "It's no longer just farm goods," says Schmandt-Besserat. "There are also finished products, manufactured goods, furniture, bread, and textiles."

Faced with this new profusion, says Wyrick, no one would have had an easy time bartering, even for something as simple as a pair of sandals. "If there were a thousand different goods being traded up and down the street, people could set the price in a thousand different ways, because in a barter economy each good is priced in terms of all other goods. So one pair of sandals equals ten dates, equals one quart of wheat, equals two quarts of bitumen, and so on. Which is the best price? It's so complex that people don't know if they are getting a good deal. For the first time in history, we've got a large number of goods. And

for the first time, we have so many prices that it overwhelms the human mind. People needed some standard way of stating value."

In Mesopotamia, silver—a prized ornamental material—became that standard. Supplies didn't vary much from year to year, so its value remained constant, which made it an ideal measuring rod for calculating the value of other things. Mesopotamians were quick to see the advantage, recording the prices of everything from timber to barley in silver by weight in shekels. (One shekel equaled one-third of an ounce, or just a little more than the weight of three pennies.) A slave, for example, cost between 10 and 20 shekels of silver. A month of a freeman's labor was worth 1 shekel. A quart of barley went for three-hundredths of a shekel. Best of all, silver was portable. "You can't carry a shekel of barley on your ass," comments Marvin Powell (referring to the animal). And with a silver standard, kings could attach a price to infractions of the law. In the codes of the city of Eshnunna, which date to around 2000 B.C., a man who bit another man's nose would be

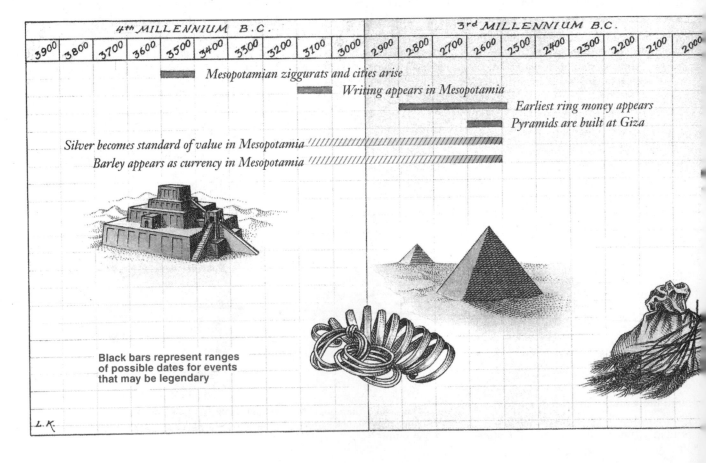

4th MILLENNIUM B.C.   3rd MILLENNIUM B.C.

| 3900 | 3800 | 3700 | 3600 | 3500 | 3400 | 3300 | 3200 | 3100 | 3000 | 2900 | 2800 | 2700 | 2600 | 2500 | 2400 | 2300 | 2200 | 2100 | 2000 |

Mesopotamian ziggurats and cities arise

Writing appears in Mesopotamia

Earliest ring money appears

Pyramids are built at Giza

Silver becomes standard of value in Mesopotamia

Barley appears as currency in Mesopotamia

Black bars represent ranges of possible dates for events that may be legendary

L. K.

MONEYFACT

The Bartering Ape

William Hopkins and Charles Hyatt at Yerkes Regional Primate Center report that chimpanzees were observed swapping items for food from humans.

First, a human experimenter knelt down and begged in front of a chimp cage (chimpanzees customarily beg from one another in the wild). At the same time, the experimenter also pointed at an item—an empty food case—in the chimp's cage and held out desirable food, like an apple or half a banana. Of 114 chimpanzees, nearly half caught the trading spirit and pushed the item out. Some even traded much faster for more desirable food—taking just 15 seconds to trade for a banana versus nearly 3 minutes to trade for typical fare. And some chimpanzees negotiated on their own terms, notes Hopkins. He has worked with four who refused to cooperate in experiments for their usual food reward when other, more preferable food was in sight.

until they balanced a small carved stone weight in the other pan. Other members of the upper crust favored a more convenient form of cash: pieces of silver cast in standard weights. These were called *har* in the tablets, translated as "ring" money.

At the Oriental Institute in the early 1970s, Powell studied nearly 100 silver coils—some resembling bedsprings, others slender wire coils—found primarily in the Mesopotamian city of Khafaje. They were not exactly rings, it was true, but they matched other fleeting descriptions of *har*. According to the scribes, ring money ranged from 1 to 60 shekels in weight. Some pieces were cast in special molds. At the Oriental Institute, the nine largest coils all bore a triangular ridge, as if they had been cast and then rolled into spirals while still pliable. The largest coils weighed almost exactly 60 shekels, the smallest from one-twelfth to two and a half shekels. "It's clear that the coils were intended to represent some easily recognizable form of Babylonian stored value," says Powell. "In other words, it's the forerunner of coinage."

fined 60 shekels of silver; one who slapped another in the face paid 10.

How the citizens of Babylon or Ur actually paid their bills, however, depended on who they were. The richest tenth of the population, says Powell, frequently paid in various forms of silver. Some lugged around bags or jars containing bits of the precious metal to be placed one at a time on the pan of a scale

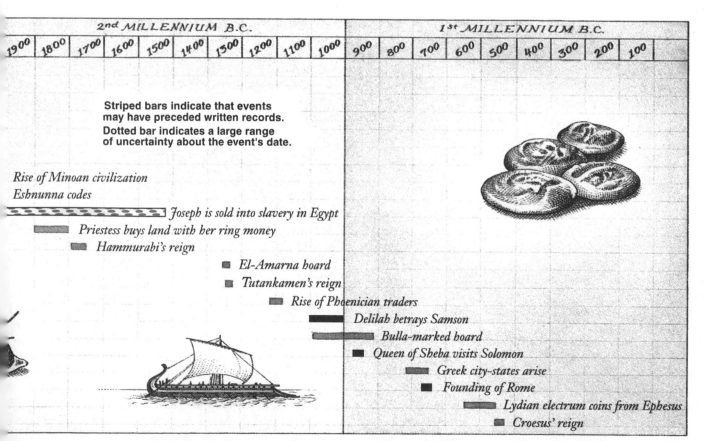

2nd MILLENNIUM B.C. | 1900 | 1800 | 1700 | 1600 | 1500 | 1400 | 1300 | 1200 | 1100 | 1000

1st MILLENNIUM B.C. | 900 | 800 | 700 | 600 | 500 | 400 | 300 | 200 | 100

Striped bars indicate that events may have preceded written records. Dotted bar indicates a large range of uncertainty about the event's date.

Rise of Minoan civilization
Eshnunna codes
Joseph is sold into slavery in Egypt
Priestess buys land with her ring money
Hammurabi's reign
El-Amarna hoard
Tutankamen's reign
Rise of Phoenician traders
Delilah betrays Samson
Bulla-marked hoard
Queen of Sheba visits Solomon
Greek city-states arise
Founding of Rome
Lydian electrum coins from Ephesus
Croesus' reign

The masses in Mesopotamia, however, seldom dealt in such money. It was simply too precious, much as a gold coin would have been for a Kansas dirt farmer in the middle of the Great Depression. To pay their bills, water carriers, estate workers, fishers, and farmers relied on more modest forms of money: copper, tin, lead, and above all, barley. "It's the cheap commodity money," says Powell. "I think barley functions in ancient Mesopotamia like small change in later systems, like the bronze currencies in the Hellenistic period. And essentially that avoids the problem of your being cheated. You measure barley out and it's not as dangerous a thing to try to exchange as silver, given weighing errors. If you lose a little bit, its not going to make that much difference."

Measurable commodity money such as silver and barley both simplified and complicated daily life. No longer did temple officials have to sweat over how to collect a one-sixth tax increase on a farmer who had paid one ox the previous year. Compound interest on loans was now a breeze to calculate. Shekels of silver, after all, lent themselves perfectly to intricate mathematical manipulation; one historian has suggested that Mesopotamian scribes first arrived at logarithms and exponential values from their calculations of compound interest.

"People were constantly falling into debt," says Powell. "We find reference to this in letters where people are writing to one another about someone in the household who has been seized for securing a debt." To remedy these disastrous financial affairs, King Hammurabi decreed in the eighteenth century B.C. that none of his subjects could be enslaved for more than three years for failing to repay a debt. Other Mesopotamian rulers, alarmed at the financial chaos in the cities, tried legislating moratoriums on all outstanding bills.

While the cities of Mesopotamia were the first to conceive of money, others in the ancient Near East soon took up the torch. As civilization after civilization rose to glory along the coasts of the eastern Mediterranean, from Egypt to Syria, their citizens began abandoning the old ways of pure barter. Adopting local standards of value, often silver by weight, they began buying and selling with their own local versions of commodity moneys: linen, perfume, wine, olive oil, wheat, barley, precious metals—things that could be easily divided into smaller portions and that resisted decay.

And as commerce became smoother in the ancient world, people became increasingly selective about what they accepted as money, says Wyrick. "Of all the different media of exchange, one commodity finally broke out of the pack. It began to get more popular than the others, and I think the merchants probably said to themselves, 'Hey, this is great. Half my customers have this form of money. I'm going to start demanding it.' And the customers were happy, too, because there's more than just one merchant coming around, and they didn't know what to hold on to, because each merchant was different. If everyone asked for barley or everyone asked for silver, that would be very convenient. So as one of these media of exchange becomes more popular, everyone just rushes toward that."

What most ancient Near Easterners rushed toward around 1500 B.C. was silver. In the Old Testament, for example, rulers of the Philistines, a seafaring people who settled on the Palestine coast in the twelfth century B.C., each offer Delilah 1,100 pieces of silver for her treachery in betraying the secret of Samson's immense strength. And in a well-known Egyptian tale from the eleventh century B.C., the wandering hero Wen-Amon journeys to Lebanon to buy lumber to build a barge. As payment, he carries jars and sacks of gold and silver, each weighed in the traditional Egyptian measure, the deben. (One deben equals 3 ounces.) Whether these stories are based on history or myth, they reflect the commercial transactions of their time.

To expedite commerce, Mediterranean metalsmiths also devised ways of conveniently packaging money. Coils and rings seem to have caught on in some parts of Egypt: a mural painted during the fourteenth century B.C. in the royal city of Thebes depicts a man weighing a stack of doughnut-size golden rings. Elsewhere, metalsmiths cast cash in other forms. In the Egyptian city of el-Amarna, built and briefly occupied during the fourteenth century B.C., archeologists stumbled upon what they fondly referred to as a crock of gold. Inside, among bits of gold and silver, were several slender rod-shaped ingots of gold and silver. When researchers weighed them, they discovered that some were in multiples or fractions of the Egyptian deben, suggesting different denominations of an ancient currency.

All these developments, says Wyrick, transformed Mediterranean life. Before, in the days of pure barter, people produced a little bit of everything themselves, eking out a subsistence. But with the emergence of money along the eastern Mediterranean, people in remote coastal communities found themselves in a new and enviable position. For the first time, they could trade easily with Phoenician or Syrian merchants stopping at their harbors. They no longer had to be self-sufficient. "They could specialize in producing one thing," says Wyrick. "Someone could just graze cattle. Or they could mine gold or silver. And when you specialize, you become more productive. And then more and more goods start coming your way."

The wealth spun by such specialization and trade became the stuff of legend. It armed the fierce Mycenaean warriors of Greece in bronze cuirasses and chariots and won them victories. It outfitted the tomb of Tutankhamen, sending his soul in grandeur to the next world. And it filled the palace of Solomon with such magnificence that even the Queen of Sheba was left breathless.

But the rings, ingots, and scraps of gold and silver that circulated as money in the eastern Mediterranean were still a far cry from today's money. They lacked a key ingredient of modern cash—a visible guarantee of authenticity. Without such a warranty, many people would never willingly accept them at their face value from a stranger. The lumps of precious metal might be a shade short of a shekel, for example. Or they might not be pure gold or silver at all, but some cheaper alloy. Confidence, suggests Miriam Balmuth, an archeologist at Tufts University in Medford, Massachusetts, could be won only if someone reputable certified that a coin was both the promised weight and composition.

Balmuth has been trying to trace the origins of this certification. In the ancient Near East, she notes, authority figures—perhaps kings or merchants—attempted to certify money by permitting their names or seals to be inscribed on the official carved stone weights used with scales. That way Mesopotamians would know that at least the weights themselves were the genuine article. But such measures were not enough to deter cheats. Indeed, so prevalent was fraud in the ancient world that no fewer than eight passages in the Old Testament forbid the faithful from tampering with scales or substituting heavier stone weights when measuring out money.

Such wealth did the newly invented coins bring one Lydian king, Croesus, that his name became a byword for prosperity.

Clearly, better antifraud devices were needed. Under the ruins of the old city of Dor along northern Israel's coast, a team of archeologists found one such early attempt. Ephraim Stern of Hebrew University and his colleagues found a clay jug filled with nearly 22 pounds of silver, mainly pieces of scrap, buried in a section of the city dating from roughly 3,000 years ago. But more fascinating than the contents, says Balmuth, who recently studied this hoard, was the way they had been packaged. The scraps were divided into separate piles. Someone had wrapped each pile in fabric and then attached a bulla, a clay tab imprinted with an official seal. "I have since read that these bullae lasted for centuries," says Balmuth, "and were used to mark jars—or in this case things wrapped in fabric—that were sealed. That was a way of signing something."

All that remained was to impress the design of a seal directly on small rounded pieces of metal—which is precisely what happened by around 600 B.C. in an obscure Turkish kingdom by the sea. There traders and perfume makers known as the Lydians struck the world's first coins. They used electrum, a natural alloy of gold and silver panned from local riverbeds. (Coincidentally, Chinese kings minted their first money at roughly the same time: tiny bronze pieces shaped like knives and spades, bearing inscriptions revealing places of origin or weight. Circular coins in China came later.)

First unearthed by archeologists early this century in the ruins of the Temple of Artemis in Ephesus, one of the Seven Wonders of the ancient world, the Lydian coins bore the essential hallmarks of modern coinage. Made of small, precisely measured pieces of precious metal, they were stamped with the figures of lions and other mighty beasts—the seal designs, it seems, of prominent Lydians. And such wealth did they bring one Lydian king, Croesus, that his name became a byword for prosperity.

Struck in denominations as small as .006 ounce of electrum—one-fifteenth the weight of a penny—Lydia's coinage could be used by people in various walks of life. The idea soon caught on in the neighboring Greek city-states. Within a few decades, rulers across Greece began churning out beautiful coins of varied denominations in unalloyed gold and silver, stamped with the faces of their gods and goddesses.

These new Greek coins became fundamental building blocks for European civilization. With such small change jingling in their purses, Greek merchants plied the western Mediterranean, buying all that was rare and beautiful from coastal dwellers, leaving behind Greek colonies from Sicily to Spain and spreading their ideas of art, government, politics, and philosophy. By the fourth century B.C., Alexander the Great was acquiring huge amounts of gold and silver through his conquests and issuing coins bearing his image far and wide, which Wyrick calls "ads for empire building."

Indeed, says Wyrick, the small change in our pockets literally made the Western world what it is today. "I tell my students that if money had never developed, we would all still be bartering. We would have been stuck with that. Money opened the door to trade, which opened the door for specialization. And that made possible a modern society."

Shards of Speech

The words you are reading are shrapnel from a five-thousand-year-old cultural explosion. Archaeologists and linguists now think they know where it erupted and who set it off.

David W. Anthony

David W. Anthony is an associate professor of anthropology at Hartwick College in Oneonta, New York, and director of the Institute for Ancient Equestrian Studies.

In June 1994, after centuries of trading words with England, France closed its linguistic borders. Long the lingua franca of diplomats, French had been usurped by English in this century and then, most gallingly, had been forced to collaborate with its conqueror. As American movies, fast-food chains and scientific journals inundated France. Hundreds of blunt Americanisms made their way into delicate French mouths, signaling a "process of collective self-destruction," in the words of a statement signed by 300 French intellectuals. Then came la Résistance. According to a law passed in 1994, terms such as *le microchip, le fast-food* and *le talk show* are never again to appear in French publications. Car manufacturers are to replace *les air bags* with *les sacs gonflables.* Businessmen, instead of discussing *le cash flow* while flying in *le jumbo jet,* are urged to discuss *la marge brute d'autofinancement* while in *le gros porteur.*

To many Americans, accustomed to the hybrid vigor of their own language, the French law seems futile, if not faintly comical. By maintaining that their language is under attack from "franglais," the government implies that

an older, purer French exists. Yet a brief review of linguistic history should only deepen their concerns. Modern French shares its source in Latin with more than ten other languages. Latin, in turn, is only one of myriad languages that sprang from a single, common linguistic stock: a language spoken more than 5,000 years ago, known as Proto-Indo-European (PIE).

In an age of multiculturalism and identity politics, Proto-Indo-European offers a welcome reminder of common origins. Ethnic roots, so often synonymous with ethnic differences, tend to converge in linguistic history: the deeper you dig, the closer they grow. The mother tongue itself has long remained beyond reach. But two centuries of scholarship is finally providing firm answers to some of history's most intriguing questions: Who were the speakers of PIE? Where did they live? What was their language? And how did its regional dialects become the dominant languages in so much of Europe and Asia?

Archaeological discoveries in Ukraine and Russia, together with new research methods in genetics and linguistics, now point independently to a region that has been a perennial candidate for the Indo-European homeland. If those findings are correct, the speakers of PIE lived east of the Dnieper River, in the grasslands of the Eurasian steppes. By introducing horseback riding and wheeled vehicles in the region, they revolution-

ized a pastoral economy. That revolution, I believe, set off a linguistic explosion that continues to expand with every century, echoing through voices from Scotland to China, shaping English and French (and Russian and Ukranian) and the words that pass from one to the other.

The Indo-European problem was first defined by William Jones, a justice in the high court of Calcutta. Jones's appointment, in 1783, signaled Calcutta's transition from a merchant colony to a seat of the British government. It did little, however, to dispel the city's reputation in England as a place of mythic exoticism. Fascinated with the complexities of Hindu law, Jones became a student of Sanskrit, an archaic language used throughout India in Hindu religious and legal texts. For three years he pored over Sanskrit texts, the oldest of which—the Rig-Veda—included hymns, accounts of rituals and stories of the heroic traditions of a people who called themselves Aryans. Then, in 1786, while presenting a paper at a meeting of the Asiatic Society of Bengal, Jones uttered the sentence now quoted in every introduction to historical comparative linguistics:

> The Sanskrit language, whatever be its antiquity, is of a wonderful structure; more perfect than the Greek, more copious than the Latin, and

more exquisitely refined than either, yet bearing to both of them a stronger affinity, both in the roots of verbs and in the forms of grammar, than could possibly have been produced by accident; so strong indeed, that no philologer could examine them all three, without believing them to have sprung from some common source, which, perhaps, no longer exists.

An accomplished linguist, familiar with Latin, Greek, Welsh and Gothic (an early Germanic language), Jones had put his finger on a truth wrapped in an enigma.

In the centuries since Jones's revelation, the search for his "common source" has proceeded in two disciplines: comparative linguistics and archaeology. Bit by bit, linguists have pieced together clues buried in ancient documents and in modern languages, defining the nature of the relations between the Indo-European languages with increasing precision. The Indo-European language family today comprises most of the languages of Europe, including Albanian, Bulgarian, Czech, Danish, Dutch, English, French, Gaelic, German, Greek, Italian, Latvian, Lithuanian, Norwegian, Polish, Portuguese, Romanian, Russian, Serbo-Croatian, Spanish, Swedish and Ukrainian (but not including Basque, Finnish, Hungarian or Turkish). In addition, Indo-European encompasses Armenian, Kashmiri, Kurdish, Persian and numerous tongues of India, including Bengali, Hindi and Urdu. Its extinct branches reach as far as Asia Minor and Syria, home of the Hittites, and into northwestern China, where Tocharian texts were discovered in the ruined caravan cities of Xinjiang. Those languages have been shown to share grammatical constructions and lexical roots that reveal their common ancestry.

Yet intriguing as it is, the linguistic evidence has long floated uncertainly in time and space, waiting for archaeologists to moor it to specific graves, settlements and material remains. Unfortunately, many archaeologists consider the Indo-European problem poisoned by propaganda. The Nazi myth of a Germanic "Aryan" superrace was based partly on the research of the German archaeologist Gustaf Kossinna, who argued in the 1920s that the Indo-European homeland was located in modern-day Germany. Today equally fanciful assertions are made in Russia and other Eurasian countries to justify racist beliefs and territorial demands.

Archaeologists not put off by the propaganda surrounding the Indo-European problem have split into three camps: those who distrust important parts of the evidence linguists have uncovered, particularly their ability to reconstruct the proto-language; those who root their theories in it; and those who dismiss the entire Indo-European problem as unsolvable.

The first camp is represented by the archaeologist A. Colin Renfrew of the University of Cambridge. In 1977 Renfrew proposed a scenario that remains popular among archaeologists: The speakers of PIE were pioneer farmers who lived in Anatolia (modern Turkey). Sometime before 6000 B.C. they moved northwest into Greece and the Balkans, and from there east into Romania, Ukraine and Russia, where they first established farms. Renfrew links the Indo-European linguistic expansion with a well-documented demographic and economic expansion from Anatolia into Greece and the Balkans. By placing the Indo-European homeland in Turkey, he also helps explain why certain words in Proto-Indo-European sound similar to words in both the Semitic languages of the Near East (Arabic, Hebrew and the like) and the non-Indo-European languages of the Caucasus (Chechen and Georgian, for example). His scenario is clean and simple—and therefore very appealing. It also suffers from a serious weakness.

To agree with Renfrew, archaeologists must dismiss most of what linguists have learned about the PIE lexicon in the past 200 years. That archaeologists have been willing to do so in great numbers demonstrates just how far apart archaeology and linguistics have drifted in recent years. Comparative linguistics is unreliable, archaeologists have charged. It relies too much on linear family trees, ignoring the ways languages can borrow, converge or create creolized versions of one another.

As an archaeologist of the second camp, I trust linguistic findings but not the way they are sometimes used. Some archaeologists have assumed that because PIE was a single language its speakers must have belonged to a single ethnic group. They have then associated telltale artifacts with that group—battle-axes, for instance—and have designated all sites that contain them as Indo-European. Such assumptions, though demonstrably false, cannot be blamed on the comparative method in linguistics, which is unconcerned with ethnicity. On its own terms, the comparative method has a proven record of success. It has predicted aspects of archaic languages (the sound of *w* and *k* pronounced simultaneously in Mycenaean Greek, for instance) well before their documentation in ancient inscriptions.

When comparative linguists try to explain changes in a language, they first look for unstable phonetic structures within the language. Only if that conservative approach does not work will they suggest that certain words, sounds or grammatical forms might have been borrowed from other languages. Although archaeologists, in their own work, are equally skeptical of external agents of change, they often take similarities between languages as evidence of borrowing. Nevertheless, no amount of linguistic borrowing or convergence has ever given rise to similarities as striking as the ones between Indo-European languages.

Languages are shaped by culture and by biology. Cultures invent and reinvent their own vocabularies, grammar and syntax, whereas the mechanics of speech set limits on cultural creativity. But words, once invented, tend to evolve in predictable ways. For example, *p*'s often turn into *f*'s (the Greek *pyr* became the English *fire*), but *f*'s less often become *p*'s.

When two words with a similar sound and meaning do appear in two or more languages, they may share a root, in which case they are known as cognates. The English word *horn* and the French word *corne,* for instance, each evolved from the PIE root word *krn-*. (An asterisk preceding a linguistic form indicates that the form is inferred but unattested in any manuscript materials.) Or two such similar words may simply be the same word, recently introduced into both languages (*café* and *coffee* both are versions of the Turkish *kahveh*). Separating cognates from borrowed words is a principal goal of the comparative method in linguistics. To do it, one must know how a particular sound in one language should sound in a particular foreign cognate. Fortunately, the rules of sound change are quite regular. If the word *coffee* had come from a PIE root, its French cognate might be *chef* or *cief*—but certainly not *café*. Given the rules of sound change in French and English, no PIE word of any phonetic shape could have evolved into both *coffee* and *café*.

Linguists have compared thousands of cognates, reconstructing important pieces of PIE vocabulary and grammar. The PIE root word **kmtom,* for example, was reconstructed from several cognates that mean "a hundred": *simtas* in Lithuanian, *centum* in Latin and *satem* in Avestan, an ancient Iranian language. Like pieces of a crossword puzzle in three dimensions, with words radiating from their every letter in every direction, PIE words have to satisfy several arcane criteria at once. For the *k* in **kmtom* to be accurate, it must, according the rules of evolutionary sound change, lead to the first letters of numerous cognates spoken in far-flung countries. The longer the proto-word, the more exacting the proof. Only random pieces of the proto-language emerge via that method, but the authenticity of the ones that do is thought to be highly reliable.

Reconstructed PIE is a priceless treasure, providing a window into the religion, kinship and descent systems, technology, social structure and economy of its speakers. To begin with, the very fact that many PIE words and grammatical rules can be unearthed suggests that PIE was a single language, perhaps with regional dialects, rather than a group of languages. Particular word clusters, in turn, reveal rituals and beliefs beyond the reach of archaeological evidence alone. They show that the speakers of PIE probably practiced patrilineal descent and patrilocal (husband's family) residence, recognized the authority of chiefs who were associated with a residential-kin group, had formally instituted warrior bands, practiced ritual sacrifices of cattle and horses, drove wagons, recognized a male or father sky deity, and avoided speaking the name of the bear for ritualistic reasons. They even demonstrate two senses of the sacred: "that which is imbued with holiness" and "that which is forbidden."

Some of the more mundane words have enabled linguists to circle in on the Indo-European homeland. For example, the speakers of PIE probably did not live in Greece or Turkey: The linguistic evidence makes it clear that they were familiar with horses, and wild horses were either rare or absent from that region, depending on how one reads the archaeozoological evidence. The speakers of PIE had words for *otter, beaver, birch* and *aspen,* and they shared euphemisms for *bear,* so they must have lived in a temperate environment. (On the basis of the cognates for names of trees alone, the American linguist and anthropologist Paul Friedrich suggested the PIE homeland was in what are now Ukraine and western Russia.) Finally, the Uralic language family (which gave rise to modern Finnish and Hungarian) borrowed words from early Indo-European languages, and the Caucasian language families borrowed words from PIE itself, so the speakers of those languages were probably neighbors.

Viewed in an archaeological context, some PIE words also hint at when their speakers lived. Terms for *domesticated sheep, pigs* and *cattle* suggest that the speakers of PIE lived after 6000 B.C., when the earliest Neolithic economies were established in the temperate zone. Terms for *wheel, axle* and *draft pole,* and a verb meaning "to go or convey in a vehicle" suggest that PIE existed as a single language after 3500 B.C., when wheeled vehicles were invented. Proto-Indo-European must have begun to disintegrate before 2000 B.C.: by 1500 B.C. three of its daughter languages—Greek, Hittite and Indic—had become quite dissimilar. Altogether, then, the linguistic evidence points to a homeland somewhere between the Ural and the Caucasus mountains, in what are now Russia and Ukraine, in the centuries between 3500 and 2000 B.C.

West of the Urals and northwest of the Caucasus the Dnieper River runs through the center of Ukraine and spills into the Black Sea. On the western bank of that river, near the modern village of Dereivka, people of the Sredni Stog culture built a Copper Age hamlet and cemetery between 4200 and 3800 B.C. They lived in buildings probably made of reed and timber; cooked stews in rough, plain clay pots; buried their dead in formal cemeteries near settlements; and decorated their bodies with pendants of boar's tusk and strings of beads made from shells and animal teeth. The few copper ornaments they had were imported from the west, probably by traders from the sophisticated Tripolye culture across the river.

People at the Dereivka site herded cattle, sheep and pigs, caught fish, and hunted deer and wild horses, relying on the latter for most of their meat. In the case of one horse, however, they made an exception: its hide, with its head and the bones of one foreleg attached, was ritually buried at the edge of the settlement along with the heads and pelts of two dogs. The horse's premolar teeth bear the unmistakable signs of bit wear (90 percent of modern horses that are frequently bitted show bit wear). Since 1987 I have studied bit wear in ancient and modern horses with Dorcas R. Brown, my wife and colleague at Hartwick College in Oneonta, New York. We have noted the relative effects of wear from metal, bone, rope and leather bits. The horse at the Dereivka site, a stallion between seven and eight years old, was bitted with a hard bit, probably bone, for at least 300 hours. Because it lived around 4000 B.C.— about 500 years before the wheel was invented—the horse was probably ridden. If so, it is the earliest direct evidence of the practice of horseback riding anywhere in the world.

Nowhere would learning to ride a horse have been more useful than in ancient Eurasia. At the center of that continent, the dry steppe extends 3,000 miles, from the mouth of the Danube to Mongolia. Steppe dwellers began to carve a secure, productive life from that desolate landscape sometime before 5000 B.C., when they learned to domesticate sheep and cattle. Horseback riding, practiced at Dereivka 1,000 years later, dramatically improved the pastoral life. It enabled scouts to search for good pasture at great distances, increased long-distance trade, expedited large-scale herding and conferred an important military advantage. When wagons arrived on the steppe between 3500 and 3300 B.C., the pastoral life completed its transformation. Herders could now pack up their tents and supplies, leaving their river-valley crops behind to follow their herds through the steppe for a season.

That package—herding, riding and wagon driving—was first put together by the Yamna culture. Descendants of the Sredni Stog people at Dereivka and similar groups on the Don and Volga rivers to the east, the Yamna people lived between 3500 and 2500 B.C. Their cemeteries, made up of between four and twenty-five kurgans, or low burial mounds, are scattered across the vast steppes north of the Caspian and Black seas, between the middle Ural River (around Orenburg) in the east and the lower Prut River in the west. In the west, Yamna kurgans were built on the ruins of Tripolye towns—once the largest human settlements in the world—that were abandoned around the time the Yamna culture appeared. The core of the Yamna area lay between the Dnieper and the middle and lower parts of the Volga.

The Yamna people introduced a new way of life to the steppe. They were the first to build some of their cemeteries in the deep steppe, far from permanent water sources—probably to mark off their distant pastures. They were the first to extensively exploit steppe copper ores and to hunt the saiga, an antelope of the deep steppe. Finally, they were the first to possess wagons and carts on the steppe, valuing them so highly that they sometimes buried them with their owners—perhaps to carry the soul toward distant pastures in the afterlife. Some 248 wagon or cart graves have been unearthed in the steppes between the Ural and Prut rivers, the earliest dating to around 3000 B.C.

Neither an empire nor a unified polity, the Yamna culture was still powerfully influential. The societies that adopted its way of life in the Dnieper-Volga steppes between 3500 and 3000 B.C. seem to have had common rituals—as their graves demonstrate—and they probably had a common language. That language, in all likelihood, was Proto-Indo-European.

According to a scenario first proposed by the American archaeologist Marija Gimbutas and later revised by the archaeologist James P. Mallory of Queen's University in Belfast, Ireland, and by me, the Yamna culture was the first to carry PIE into Europe. Cultures descended from it then carried related tongues across the steppes to Iran and India. Equipped with horses and wagons, the Yamna people and their descendants used ideology, alliances and trade to dominate their neighbors or exploit divisions among them, transforming Eurasian pastoralism as they went. The Yamna region may have included the entire language family to which PIE belonged. In that case, PIE

was a local language that gained high status and then gradually displaced its sister languages in the Dnieper-Ural steppes.

The Yamna people lived in the right place at the right time to plant the clues later discovered in the PIE lexicon. Unlike Renfrew's Anatolia, their homeland had a temperate climate, and it lay between the Ural and the Caucasus mountains. It was home to otter, beaver, bear, birch and aspen, and its location would explain the early ties between Indo-European languages, Uralic languages and the languages of the Caucasus. Our scenario, by setting Indo-European origins three millennia later than Renfrew does, would also explain how words for wheeled vehicles entered into PIE.

Renfrew argues that PIE never had terms for wheeled vehicles because it dispersed long before they were invented. Later Indo-European languages borrowed those terms from one another or from other languages, he maintains, when wheeled vehicles reached their cultures. For that to be true, Indo-European languages from India to Scotland would have had to pass along the same set of terms for wheeled vehicles that a single culture invented.

No archaeological evidence supports that idea, and much contradicts it. Wheeled vehicles appeared almost simultaneously in eastern Europe, the steppes and the Near East after 3500 B.C. No one knows where, when or by whom they were invented, but their spread, understandably, was quite rapid. The Indo-European words describing them fit seamlessly into their languages. The idea that terms describing them were borrowed between languages has never been supported by a linguistic study. On the other hand, numerous published studies have shown those terms to be true cognates derived from PIE. The speakers of PIE, the evidence shows, were clearly familiar with wheeled vehicles.

Linguists group Indo-European languages into at least nine subfamilies—Albanian, Anatolian, Balto-Slavic, Celtic, Germanic (which includes English), Greek-Armenian, Italic, Indo-Iranian, Tocharian and perhaps Thracian—but they have long disagreed on when each subfamily split from the mother tongue. Recently, however, the linguists Ann D. Taylor and Don Ringe, and the information science

specialist Tandy J. Warnow, all of the University of Pennsylvania in Philadelphia, have created a robust evolutionary tree for Indo-European. Using a modified form of cladistics (a mathematical method used to define relations between biological species), they have shown that pre-Celtic and pre-Italic separated from the Indo-European core quite early. Pre-Tocharian, pre-Greek-Armenian and pre-Indo-Iranian followed next. Pre-Germanic probably began to separate from Balto-Slavic around the time the speakers of pre-Greek-Armenian became isolated. After the speakers of pre-Germanic became fully separated from Balto-Slavic, they established contact with and began to borrow numerous words from the speakers of pre-Italic and pre-Celtic. Finally, pre-Baltic and pre-Slavic developed into two distinct languages.

The Yamna region gave rise to two migrations that help explain the shape of that evolutionary tree. The first migration, inferred on the basis of well-dated archaeological sites and vestigial genetic patterns in European populations, flowed from the western steppes into the lower Danube Valley, the Balkans and eastern Hungary between 2900 and 2700 B.C. Pockets of Yamna migrants seem to have coexisted, at least at first, with indigenous societies. Seventeen Yamna cemeteries have been mapped in Bulgaria, each including between five and twenty kurgans.

They continue up the Danube Valley and into the eastern part of Hungary, where one specialist has counted 3,000 kurgans. Kurgans in Bulgaria and eastern Hungary match those in the steppe in every detail: the occupants are laid on their backs with knees raised, their heads to the northeast; daggers and silver temple rings serve as grave gifts; mats painted with red and white stripes or other geometric forms lie on the grave floor or grave cover; red ocher or hematite lumps are placed at the body's hip or shoulder; and the grave pits are covered in timber and topped with carved stone stelae (broken and undecorated in Hungary, decorated in Bulgaria like the ones in the steppes). In Bulgaria one kurgan contains a wagon. In eastern Hungary the immigrants had to import hematite for their graves. When hematite was not available, they laid a lump of dirt next to the occupant's shoulder and painted it red. They went to great lengths, in other words, to cling to Yamna traditions.

The Carpathian Basin went on to become a crossroads for interregional trade, powerfully influencing the cultures of central and western Europe during the Bronze Age. The proto-Celtic languages, in particular, are widely thought to have been associated with the Hallstatt culture, which evolved in the mountains west of Hungary. The first Yamna migration took place at the right time and place to spawn Italic as well.

The second migration out of the Yamna region took place between 2200 and 2000 B.C., and it flowed east from the Volga-Ural region into the steppes east of the Ural Mountains. The Poltavka culture, which gave rise to it, grew directly from late Yamna at the northeastern boundary of the Yamna world. (I am now investigating Yamna and Poltavka sites in the lower Samara River Valley with support from the National Geographic Society.) East of the Urals, the migrants interacted with people of a different tradition, establishing the remarkable Sintashta culture. The Sintashta people built compact, fortified settlements, forged weapons and ornaments in bronze and buried chariots in kurgans with their dead warriors or chiefs. Aside from those burials, traces of Yamna and Poltavka ancestry can be seen in Sintashta weapons, pottery and head-and-hoof horse sacrifices.

Like the small figurine nesting within a wooden babushka, Sintashta gave shape to ever expanding cultures. First it joined with the related Petrovka complex to engender the Andronovo cultural horizon, which spread across the eastern steppes to the Tien Shan and the borders of Iran and Afghanistan. Andronovo helped shape the Indo-Iranian culture which, in turn, led to a Persian culture that retained some traces of Sintashta, including chariotry, horse sacrifices and the myth of the horse-headed human.

With Indo-Iranian, the path to PIE comes full circle. Sanskrit is also a daughter tongue of Indo-Iranian, so similar to Old Persian that it could have sprung only from the same source. Like the Persians, the Aryans kept some Sintashta customs alive—elaborate mortuary rituals and horse and cattle sacrifices, for example. But they considered Sanskrit too sacred to set it down in writing. The hymns and rituals of the Rig-Veda, with their gambling heroes, chariot races and paeans to plump cattle, were passed on orally for centuries, even after Sanskrit passed out of daily use. Transcribed, at last, and dispersed throughout India, they made their way to Calcutta and the curious mind of William Jones. Five thousand years after disappearing on the steppe, the mother tongue had begun to be found.

The Coming of the Sea Peoples

*A low-tech revolution in Bronze Age battlefield tactics
changed the history of the Western world.*

by Neil Asher Silberman

In the long annals of Western military history, one important group of battlefield innovators—whose archaeological traces have been uncovered from mainland Greece to the coasts of Lebanon and Israel—has often been overlooked. Around 1200 B.C., a wave of sword-wielding warriors streamed southward across the Aegean and eastward toward Asia Minor, Cyprus, and Canaan. By around 1175, some of them had reached the borders of Egypt, where they were finally repulsed by the land and sea forces of Pharaoh Ramesses III. Yet in their stunning military successes throughout the region, these warriors exerted an enormous impact on the development of ancient warfare and proved instrumental in the transformation of Mediterranean society. In subsequent centuries, the rising kingdoms of Israel and Phoenicia and the city-states of Classical Greece all adopted their tactics, arms, and strategic mentality.

Who were these invading forces and where did they come from? What was it about their weapons and tactics that proved to be so deadly to the great Late Bronze Age empires—and so influential in shaping the societies that succeeded them? For the past 150 years, historians

have recognized that the twelfth century B.C. was a time of great upheaval, in which ancient empires were toppled and new societies were born. They have ascribed this dramatic transformation not to innovations in warfare but to vast population movements, spearheaded by a coalition of northern tribes and ethnic groups who are mentioned repeatedly in ancient Egyptian inscriptions—and whom nineteenth-century scholars dubbed the "Sea Peoples" or the "Peoples of the Sea." These Sea Peoples were not simply Bronze Age Vikings but were a haphazard collection of farmers, warriors, and craftspeople, as well as sailors who originated in the highlands of the Balkans and the coastlands of Asia Minor. Their only common trait seems to have been their movement across the Mediterranean toward the centers of trade and agriculture of the Near East.

Their impact on the Near Eastern empires was dramatic, though scholars are deeply divided on the reasons. Some maintain that the Sea Peoples were displaced from their homelands by famine, natural disasters, or political breakdown and were able to overcome the sophisticated, cosmopolitan empires of the Mediterranean by their sheer barbarian

savagery. Others suggest that a closer analysis of the historical records and archaeological remains from this period can pinpoint a more specific agent of change connected to the era's vast population movements. There is reason to believe that only a small, specialized class of professional warriors, in the midst of the much more massive migratory waves, was responsible for the military attacks of the Sea Peoples. As a skilled caste of mercenary foot soldiers who drifted southward to find employment in kingdoms throughout the region, this group of Sea Peoples had both the tactical know-how and the weaponry to recognize—and demonstrate—just how pitifully vulnerable the great Late Bronze Age powers had become. The civilization of the Late Bronze Age (c. 1550 to c. 1200 B.C.), to which these northern mercenary contingents gravitated, was typified by grand monuments, opulent palace cultures, and some of the most complex administrative and accounting systems the Mediterranean world had ever seen. In Egypt, the powerful pharaohs of the New Kingdom resided amid the splendor of Thebes in Upper Egypt. There they prospered from the rich agricultural produce of the Nile

This article is reprinted from the Winter 1998 issue of *Military History Quarterly* magazine, pp. 6-13, with permission of Cowles Enthusiast Media, Inc. (History Group), A PRIMEDIA Publication. © 1998, Military History Quarterly magazine.

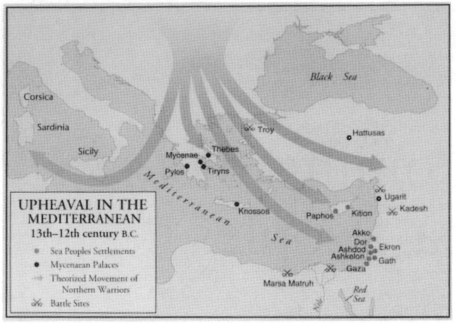

UPHEAVAL IN THE
MEDITERRANEAN
13th–12th century B.C.

* Sea Peoples Settlements
● Mycenaean Palaces
→ Theorized Movement of
    Northern Warriors
⚔ Battle Sites

GEOSYSTEMS, COLUMBIA, MD

Not long after appearing in Egypt, Sea People warriors fought for the Egyptians at Kadesh (c. 1275 B.C.). They would become agents of radical change, likely bringing down Mycenaean civilization and enfeebling the great empires of the ancient world.

valley and enjoyed the luxury goods acquired from a far-flung trade network reaching from Africa and the southern coast of Arabia to the islands of the Aegean Sea. To the north of Egypt, in the city-states of Canaan, on the island of Cyprus, and at the cosmopolitan port of Ugarit, local dynasties ruled over docile peasant populations and vied with one another for diplomatic or commercial advantage. In the vast continental expanse of Asia Minor, the Hittite empire maintained its feudal rule from the stronghold of Hattusas. And across the Aegean Sea, on mainland Greece, Crete, and the islands, a unique palace-based civilization of regional rulers, with their coteries of servants, craftsmen, priests, and mercenary forces, comprised the chivalric society that was at least partially reflected in the physical details of Homer's *Iliad*.

Despite these differences in styles and traditions, all the empires of the Late Bronze Age were united in their dependence on a single military technology. No self-respecting kingdom could exist for long without attack forces based on the light battle chariot, which was then the most sophisticated and reliable vehicle of war. The chariots of this period were constructed with considerable skill—and at considerable cost—from sturdy yet highly flexible laminates of

wood and bone that enabled them to travel at high speed and with great maneuverability. Propelled by a specially bred and trained two-horse team, the chariot was manned by a professional driver and a combat archer, whose composite bow, also constructed of laminated materials, could launch arrows with extraordinary accuracy and force. These factors all added up to make the light chariot a high-powered, highly mobile weapons delivery system that could swoop down on static infantry forces with frightening speed and velocity.

The figure of the charioteer—as an embodiment of individual skill and courage—became, in many respects, a symbol for the age. The firepower of the new-style chariots was so overwhelming on the battlefield that no ruler who hoped to maintain his throne against his local or regional rivals could afford to be without them—any more than any truly modern nation can afford to be without an effective air force. As a result, Bronze Age kings, pharaohs, and princes scrambled to assemble chariot forces. And just as the kings and potentates of other eras strutted in the guise of knights-errant, cavalry officers, or naval commanders, Late Bronze Age Egyptian pharaohs and Mycenaean, Hittite, and Canaanite kings were all grandly depicted on their monuments in

the pose of triumphant charioteers. Yet as the chariot buildup continued through the fourteenth and thirteenth centuries B.C., and as chariot formations gradually rendered infantry battles obsolete in conflicts between rival city-states or empires, a costly arms race began to get out of control.

By the time of the Hittite-Egyptian confrontation at the battle of Kadesh in Syria in 1275 B.C., relatively modest chariot corps of a few dozen vehicles had expanded to enormous contingents. At Kadesh, the Hittite chariot corps alone numbered at least 3,500 vehicles. This placed a strain on even the wealthiest kingdoms. The cost of chariots and horses was substantial. And the skilled craftsmen, chariot drivers, archers, and horse trainers required to maintain the battle-readiness of a kingdom's chariot force could—and did—demand lavish personal support, generous land grants, and conspicuously privileged status at each court they served. Thus, at times of shortage brought about by drought, flood, disease, or poor crop yields, the demands of the charioteers and their staffs could force individual kingdoms toward the breaking point. And yet the Late Bronze Age powers had all become dangerously dependent on this method of warfare. Little wonder, then, that when its tactical vulnerability was discovered, the whole edifice came tumbling down. The result was one of the great turning points in history dubbed by some the Great Catastrophe. Within the span of just a few decades before and after 1200 B.C., the Bronze Age civilizations of Greece and Asia Minor were shattered, and Egypt gradually lost its role as a regional superpower. At the same time, the sudden arrival and settlement of new peoples on Cyprus and along the coast of Canaan ushered in a new era of small kingdoms and city-states.

Just beyond the confines of the civilized regions of the Mediterranean world, in the mountainous areas of the Balkan peninsula and in the rugged hinterlands of western and southern Asia Minor, the chariot had no power. It was suited only to action on the relatively level battlefields of the lowlands and the plains. On the occasions when the great empires felt the need to mount punitive expeditions against the inhabitants of the highlands, they dispatched infantry forces for brief, brutal demonstrations of force. For the most part, however, the highlanders were left alone as long as they handed over the demanded tribute and did nothing to interfere with the main routes of trade. Among the tribal societies of these regions, internal disputes were settled in contests of single combat between experienced professional warriors. Archaeological finds from warriors' tombs across western and central Europe, from Scandinavia to the Black Sea, have provided evidence of this mobile, deadly kind of hand-to-hand warfare, waged with long, two-edged swords that could be swung with enough momentum to decapitate an opponent or cut off a limb. Small round shields seem also to have been used to deflect rapid parries. Helmets of various designs and light body armor of many shapes and materials were also common in this individualistic style of war. In terms of weaponry and personal aggressiveness, the warriors of the frontier areas were much more formidable than the typical infantries of the Mediterranean empires, whose members were usually conscripted from the local peasantry, poorly trained, and armed only with short daggers, spears, or clubs.

The reason for the neglect of the infantry by the Mediterranean empires was the overwhelming importance accorded to chariot forces, which comprised the main tactical elements. Lines of chariots would charge against each other like modern tank forces, and, having penetrated or outflanked the opposing formation, would wheel around quickly and charge against the opposing chariots again. Foot soldiers were used in the decidedly secondary capacities of guard duty, road escort, frontier patrols, and routine police work. The only battlefield function reserved for foot soldiers was as "runners" who raced behind and among the chariots, snatching up fallen enemy booty and finishing off wounded enemy chariot crews. This mopping-up function was of little tactical significance. But by the time of the battle of Kadesh, the appearance of a new kind of runner proved to be an omen of the way that subsequent wars in the Mediterranean region would be waged—and won.

In a provocative new book entitled *The End of the Bronze Age: Changes in Warfare and the Catastrophe, ca. 1200 B.C.*, Robert Drews, a professor of ancient history at Vanderbilt University, ar-

gues that the arrival of northern-style warriors in the Mediterranean upset the unquestioned domination of the chariot. By so doing, it undermined the foundations of the regimes the chariots were meant to defend. Drews notes that barely ten years before the battle of Kadesh, Egyptian hieroglyphic reliefs recorded the ominous movements of a people named the "Sherden," who had arrived "in their warships from the midst of the sea." Wearing trademark horned helmets and armed with long swords and small round shields, they obviously made a profound impression on the Egyptians. By the time the Egyptian chariot forces moved north to confront the Hittites, contingents of Sherden had been recruited by the Egyptians to serve as bodyguards and particularly deadly "runners" among the chariots.

In contrast to the usual runners, who merely mopped up after the chariot charges, the Sherden apparently became an independent offensive force. They are shown in the reliefs of the battle of Kadesh using their weapons to slash, hack, and dismember enemy charioteers. Their weapons, which were originally designed for individual combat, made Sherden warriors far more mobile and adaptable to changing battlefield conditions than the traditional formations of infantry. And with significant numbers of aggressive, northern-style warriors swarming among the chariots, deflecting arrows with their shields and pouncing on disabled vehicles with long swords swinging, they would have posed a sudden, unexpected threat to the firepower and mobility of even the most impressive concentrations of chariotry. While the traditional Bronze Age foot soldiers marched together in relatively slow-moving formations and used weapons such as clubs and spears, which had only a limited radius of effectiveness, the Sherden seem to have ranged widely, pouncing on vulnerable chariot crews.

No less important, they possessed weapons far more effective in combat than those of standard Bronze Age foot soldiers. Ancient pictorial representations of Sherden runners suggest that they were also skilled in the use of the hunting javelin, commonly used in this period for felling wild game. In combination with the long sword, the hunting javelin would have been especially deadly. Drews makes a persuasive—if admittedly speculative—case for suggesting that these new weapons could

transform units of runners into an effective battlefield strike force. "For the 'hunting' of chariot horses the javelin must have been ideal," Drews writes, "although it seldom would have killed the horse that it hit, the javelin would have surely brought it to a stop, thus immobilizing the other horse, the vehicle and the crew."

The battle of Kadesh ended in a stalemate between the Egyptians and the Hittites, ushering in a brief period of military balance between the two powers. But by the middle of the thirteenth century B.C., new groups of northern warriors armed with long swords and javelins were drawn in increasing numbers toward the centers of the Late Bronze Age empires, where they were destined to upset the delicate geopolitical balance. Initially, they found employment as mercenaries just as the Sherden had done. Among the names mentioned in Egyptian records and in the archives of Ugarit and the Hittite empire were—in addition to the Sherden—groups known as the Shekelesh, Tursha, Lukka, Shardana, and Ekwesh. Linguistic analysis of these names has enabled scholars to identify them with peoples mentioned in classical and biblical literature: Sicilians, Tyrrhenians, Lycians, and Achaean Greeks. The Sherden have been identified as a group originating on the island of Sardinia, or, according to some scholars, as its eventual conquerors.

It is important to recognize, however, that these Sea Peoples mentioned in the ancient records were not entire nations displaced from their homelands, but a particular military caste represented by warriors from many ethnic groups. Like the pirates and freebooters of the seventeenth-century Caribbean, their many separate nationalities were as conspicuous as the threatening uniformity of their weapons and hand-to-hand fighting techniques.

Archaeologists are generally agreed that the relative tranquility of the Late Bronze Age world following the battle of Kadesh was rocked sometime after 1250 B.C. by a great wave of destructions and upheavals that seems to have begun in the Aegean basin. The Mycenaean palace of Thebes in Boeotia was destroyed and abandoned. The flourishing city of Troy, guarding the trade routes to the Black Sea, was likewise destroyed in a great conflagration, to be succeeded by a much more modest settlement. There is suggestive evidence that these destructions may not have resulted from normal clashes between chariot forces. The hasty construction of a great fortification wall across the Isthmus of Corinth and the strengthening of the defenses around other Mycenaean palace complexes may reflect apprehensions about a far more pervasive danger, perhaps a threat by potential attackers that Bronze Age chariotry would have been unable to withstand. And those apparent fears of attack and conquest seem to have been justified, for by the middle of the next century, the destruction of all the Mycenaean palace complexes was virtually complete.

There may, of course, have been many specific, local reasons for this wave of upheaval. In some places, rivalries between regional centers could have led to the violence. In others, widespread social unrest caused by growing inequalities in late Bronze Age society may have led to local uprisings and the overthrow of the palace elite. Yet in a thought-provoking hypothesis that has already aroused considerable scholarly discussion, Drews pulls together tactical analysis, archaeological evidence, and the colorful testimony of heroic Greek myth to offer a novel reconstruction of the events. He suggests that the legendary accounts of the attacks against Thebes by a coalition of champions (immortalized by Aeschylus in his play *Seven Against Thebes*) and Homer's epic poem about the sack of Troy by Agamemnon's forces preserve memories of the first dramatic triumphs of free-lance northern infantry concentrations, fighting in the new style.

The gradually increasing scope of such encounters may suggest that news of the vulnerability of chariot forces spread among northern mercenary contingents. And in this very period, a wave of northern warriors now made their way southward in search of plunder, not employment. In looking anew at Homer's poetic metaphors about the epic battle between Achaeans and Trojans, it may well be—as Drews suggested—that the repeated description of the Achaean hero Achilles as "fleet-footed," and the characteristic description of the Trojans as "horse-taming," preserve memories of an epic clash between foot soldiers and horse-powered troops. Even though the *Iliad* was set down in writing several centuries later, at a time when chariot warfare had long

been abandoned, the vivid image of Achaean soldiers streaming from the Trojan Horse may eloquently express, at least in mythic language, the sudden emergence of a new style of infantrymen—whose hidden power was revealed in an age of horse-based warfare. In their conquest of Troy, the Achaean foot soldiers departed from the empty wooden horse, thereby symbolically leaving behind the horse (and chariot) as the preferred weapons platforms of the age.

The violent events in the Aegean do not seem to have affected the great capitals and emporia of the Near East—at least not immediately. International commerce continued throughout the thirteenth century B.C., and a certain measure of prosperity was enjoyed in the royal courts of the Near East. New Kingdom Egypt (where at least some Sea People had gone to find work as mercenary runners) therefore beckoned as a tempting target for plundering attacks. The aging pharaoh Ramesses II (c. 1279–c. 1212 B.C.), after having emerged from the battle of Kadesh in a military stalemate with the Hittites, still presided over a vast territory and trade network extending from Canaan, south to Nubia, and as far west as Libya. Excavations at Late Bronze Age port cities and recovered cargoes from sunken merchant ships of this period throughout the eastern Mediterranean have emphasized the volume of international trade—and the extent of interaction between nations, cultures, and ethnic groups during this cosmopolitan age. Only recently have excavations uncovered the ruins of a once busy Late Bronze Age trade depot—littered with sherds of pottery from Mycenaean Greece, Egypt, Cyprus, and Canaan—on a sandy island known as Bates's Island off the coast of Egypt's western desert, about 120 miles east of the modern border with Libya.

It was surely no coincidence or accident that the first major attack by northern warriors on Egypt was launched from this direction. Far from being an isolated wilderness, Libya was connected to Egypt by land and sea trade routes. At a time of reported famine, it was a Libyan leader named "Meryre, Son of Did," who instigated the first major operation in which a coalition of northern warriors played a promi-

nent role. Scholars have always puzzled over how and why Libyans forged a coalition with the various Sea Peoples. Yet the archaeological evidence of an offshore trade depot so close to Libya indicates that it was not a cultural backwater but on one of the main routes in the movement of people and goods. It is entirely conceivable that Meryre was aware of events going on elsewhere in the eastern Mediterranean, possibly through the contact his subjects had with the polyglot gangs of sailors, stevedores, and workers who were drawn into the networks of long-distance trade. More important, he seems to have been keenly aware of the recent—one might even say revolutionary—developments in the art of warfare. Indeed if Meryre had heard about recent successes achieved by northern warriors in direct assaults on chariot forces in Greece and Asia Minor, his subsequent actions in recruiting Sea People warriors for his own campaign would suddenly be understandable.

Why else would he contemplate an invasion of Egypt with only foot soldiers? If he were planning a less organized infiltration of the border lands, he would not have needed to form the grand coalition he did. Yet soon after the death of Ramesses II around 1212 B.C., Meryre began to organize a campaign against the western Nile Delta, for which he gained the cooperation of a number of warrior bands. Later Egyptian records note that they came from "the northern lands"—which could indicate an origin in any of the territories along the northern shores of the Mediterranean. The specific mention of Ekwesh, Lukka, Sherden, Shekelesh, and Tursha (identified as Achaeans, Lycians, Sardinians, Sicilians, and Tyrrhenians) suggests that Meryre's appeal attracted recruits from many lands. He promised them a share of the fertile territory and booty to be gained in attacking the forces of the new pharaoh, Merneptah, the long-lived Ramesses' already elderly son. Seen in the context of the times, Meryre thus made an audacious tactical gamble: in recruiting tens of thousands of northern-style foot soldiers along with his own sizable infantry contingents, he was confident that he could overcome the Egyptian chariotry.

As things turned out, Meryre lost his gamble but proved to be a strategist ahead of his time. Merneptah's chariots met the advancing Libyan-Sea People coalition in midsummer 1208 B.C. in the western desert, at a site probably not far from the later and also fateful battlefield of El Alamein. The Egyptian forces reportedly slew 6,000 Libyans and more than 2,200 of the invading Ekwesh, with significant casualties suffered by the other Sea Peoples as well. Yet the list of spoils taken in the battle by the Egyptians gives a clear indication of the novel nature of the encounter: more than 9,000 long swords were captured from the invaders—with only an utterly insignificant twelve Libyan chariots being seized. For the time being, the pharaoh's chariots had prevailed over massed formations of swordsmen and javelineers. But new troubles were not long in coming for the pharaoh. Frontier populations in other regions were growing restless, and Merneptah soon had to undertake a punitive campaign into Canaan, where he was forced to reassert his control over some important cities and pacify the highlands. In typically bombastic prose he reported one of the most gratifying outcomes of the encounter: "Israel is laid waste; his seed is not!" The clear, if mistaken, implication was that this people had been so thoroughly defeated that they or their descendants would never appear on the stage of history again.

The quotation, which comes from Merneptah's so-called Victory Stele at the Temple of Karnak, contains this earliest mention of the people of Israel outside the Bible, and it may also indicate the extent of the tactical revolution spreading throughout the Mediterranean world. For in the hill country of Canaan at precisely this period, c. 1250–c. 1200 B.C., archaeologists have discovered the sudden establishment of scores of hilltop villages throughout the modern area of the West Bank. Being far from the lowland Canaanite urban centers and outposts of Egyptian presence in fortresses along the coast and major trade routes, they represent the earliest settlements of the Israelites. Their defense against outside powers was not based on chariot warfare but most likely on coordinated militia campaigns. Certainly the biblical books of Joshua and Judges are filled with references to the defeat of the Canaanite kings and the destruction of their chariot forces. Although many historians have come to question the historical reliability of the story of the Israelite Exodus from Egypt, the vivid scriptural account of the drowning in the

Red Sea of the pharaoh's pursuing army—and its great chariot corps—might preserve in dreamlike narrative an indelible historical memory of an era of great victories over chariotry.

The threats by northern-style raiders against Egypt and the other great centers of the Bronze Age civilization continued to intensify in this period, with port cities, fortresses, temples, and trade depots throughout the region put to the torch, and in some cases never fully reoccupied again. It is likely that in the spreading chaos, movements of people grew more frequent. Warriors and mercenaries were on the move, of course, but so were other groups formerly serving as craftsmen, servants, or functionaries in the palace centers that had been destroyed by hostile attacks. All of these groups were the "Sea Peoples," both the victims and the perpetrators of the spreading wave of violence. In certain places on Cyprus and along the coast of Canaan, settlers from the Aegean world arrived to establish new communities in the ruins of destroyed Late Bronze Age cities. And the characteristic Mycenaean-style pottery they produced at sites such as Ashkelon, Ekron, and Ashdod in Canaan clearly indicates that whether they themselves were marauders or refugee craftsmen and officials from the destroyed palace centers of the Aegean, the course of their lives and communities had been disrupted by upheavals throughout the Mediterranean world.

Although it is impossible to follow precisely the sequence of raids, conquests, and refugee colonizations in Greece, Cyprus Egypt, and Canaan, there is suggestive evidence that the use of new weapons and tactics by the invaders continued to play a crucial role. In the rubble of the great trading emporium of Ugarit on the coast of modern Syria, for example, excavators have found a number of hunting javelins scattered in the destruction ruins. And the discovery of several newly cast long swords (one even bearing the royal cartouche of Merneptah!) hidden away in hoards at the time of the city's destruction may reflect a desperate, last-ditch effort by some local commanders to equip their forces with the same deadly weapons borne by the marauding Peoples of the Sea.

The last and greatest of attacks by contingents of northern warriors against the centers of Bronze Age civilization is memorialized in ex-

acting detail on the outer walls of the Egyptian temple of Medinet Habu in Upper Egypt, built by Pharaoh Ramesses III, who ruled from c. 1186 to c. 1155 B.C. The Medinet reliefs depict what was one of the most notable events of Ramesses' reign: thousands of Egyptian foot soldiers, sailors, and archers are shown engaged in battles on land and sea against a bizarrely costumed coalition of invaders, who include—in addition to the Sherden and the Shekelesh of the earlier invasions—people known as the Tjekker, Denyen, Weshesh, and Peleset (whom scholars have identified as the biblical Philistines).

This invasion was apparently different and far more threatening than earlier actions. The tone of Ramesses III's official inscription accompanying the pictorial representations conveys an atmosphere of deep crisis that gripped Egypt when word arrived that seaborne and overland coalitions of northern warriors "who had made a conspiracy in their islands" were approaching. Although the precise origin of these warrior bands has never been pinpointed, the mention of "islands" suggests that the threat came from the direction of the Aegean Sea. Ramesses' chronicle goes on to trace the progress of the invaders across the region, in which many separate actions seem to have been combined for rhetorical purposes to heighten the drama of the events.

"All at once the lands were removed and scattered in the fray," reported the inscription in tracing the path of the invaders southward from the Hittite empire, through the cities of Cilicia, Cyprus, and Syria, toward Canaan, which was also known as Amor. "No land could stand before their arms from Hatti, Kode, Carchemish, Arzawa, Alayshia on, being cut off at one time. A camp was set up in one place in Amor. They desolated its people, and its land was like that which has never come into being. They were coming forward to Egypt, while the flame was being prepared before them," the inscription continued. "They laid their hands upon lands as far as the circuit of the earth, their hearts confident and trusting, 'Our plans will succeed!' "

In retrospect, we can see that Pharaoh Ramesses III was placed in an impossible situation in the Great Land and Sea Battles of 1175 B.C. When this last and greatest wave of Sea Peoples' invasions burst upon Egypt, Ramesses was forced to confront forces that had proved they could successfully overcome chariots—which remained the backbone of the Egyptian defense. In response, he apparently tried to change radically the fighting capabilities of his forces—as many desperate, doomed warlords have attempted to do throughout history. Indeed, as analysis of the Medinet Habu reliefs suggests, the vaunted Egyptian chariotry played almost no role in the fighting. Ramesses III's inscriptions can be seen as a commemoration of the heroism of his own infantry. He boasted that the Egyptian foot soldiers—once scorned as insignificant tactical factors—had fought "like bulls ready on the field of battle" and that the militiamen who engaged the enemy in hand-to-hand fighting aboard their ships "were like lions roaring on the mountaintops." No less significant is the fact that in one scene Ramesses himself is depicted as an unmounted archer—not a charioteer—with his two royal feet firmly planted on the bodies of fallen Sea People enemies.

Yet in discarding the ethos and discipline of chariot warfare on which his empire had become so dependent—and in mobilizing his foot soldiers to fight on the same terms and with the same weapons as the invaders—Ramesses sealed the fate of New Kingdom Egypt as surely as a defeat at the hands of the Sea Peoples would have done. For even though the Sea Peoples' invasion was repulsed, and some of the Sea Peoples, like the Philistines, were permitted to settle peacefully in colonies along the nearby coast of Canaan, Egypt would never regain its former strength. The Egyptian Empire—like all other Late Bronze Age kingdoms—had been built and maintained over hundreds of years as a towering social pyramid in which the king, his court, officers, and chariot forces reserved the pinnacle for themselves. The new method of marshaling units of highly mobile, highly motivated infantry against chariot forces required unprecedentedly large numbers of trained fighters. Egypt was never a society that viewed its general population as much more than beasts of burden; to accord peasant recruits respect and intensive training within the armed forces was something that the highly stratified society of New Kingdom Egypt found extremely difficult to do. The strict hierarchy began to crumble, and the growing power of mercenary units and local infantry bands caused widespread social unrest. By the end of the twelfth century, the power of New Kingdom Egypt was ended, and the country entered a new dark age. In contrast, the new world that unfolded in the centuries after the appearance of the Sea Peoples in Greece, Cyprus, Asia Minor, and Canaan drew its strength from the new cultural pattern, which was based on the solidarity and military might of local levies of foot soldiers, not elite units of courtly charioteers.

Chariot forces would again be used on the field of battle—as in the later campaigns of the Assyrian empire in the ninth and eighth centuries B.C.—but only in a supporting role to the infantry. And with the development of effective tack and stirrups during the subsequent centuries, the chariot could be dispensed with altogether, except perhaps as a battlefield conveyance for generals and kings. The Sea People warriors themselves were eventually assimilated into the general populations of the refugees from the great upheavals. Along the coast of Canaan and on Cyprus, new societies derived from Mycenaean models and led by descendants of refugees were born. Even in the rising kingdoms of Israel, Phoenicia, Aramea, Cilicia, Phrygia, and the city-states of Greece, where new forms of military and social organization emerged after the end of the Bronze Age, the legacy of the Sea Peoples—though dramatically transformed—could still be perceived. Just as the fleet-footed Achaean warrior Achilles became the role model for the citizen soldier of the archaic Greek polis, the image of the young David, surrounded by his band of mighty men of war, remained a cherished biblical symbol of national solidarity. And there were to be even more far-reaching developments in the use of large infantry formations as the kingdoms of Assyria and Babylonia swelled into great empires with enormous populations. Eventually, the massive formations of infantry units evolved into the Macedonian phalanx and the Roman legion.

The sweeping scenario of scattered contingents of Sea People warriors streaming together from their distant islands and hill country homes to overcome the elite chariot forces of the Bronze Age Mediterranean has not been without its critics. Scholars who still favor explanations such as natural disasters, generalized social breakdown, or the gradual cultural shift from Bronze Age chariot empires to Iron Age infantry kingdoms are skeptical of a single military cause. But without minimizing the possibility that natural or economic crises may indeed have undermined the political order and intensified social tensions, there is much to be said for the contention that only something as dramatic as the introduction of new weapons and tactics could have triggered violent upheavals on such a massive scale.

And there is, even beyond the specific questions of this remote period, a far more basic historical point. We must not merely see the episode of the "Sea Peoples" as a bizarre and bloody episode that took place in a far-off region more than 3,000 years ago. The long swords, javelins, and body armor of the invading Sea Peoples may seem quaintly rustic to us in a day of Stealth fighter-bombers and Tomahawk missiles. Yet they offer an important object lesson in the way that complacent dependency by great powers on expensive and complex military technology can suddenly be undermined. The grand catastrophe of the end of the Bronze Age and the role of the Sea Peoples in it should show us how unexpectedly simple weapons in the hands of committed warriors can topple great empires. Societies in any age can become dangerously presumptuous about the invulnerability of their advanced military technologies. Over centuries or even decades the society molds itself, in its religion, political order, and social hierarchy, to conform to the dominant technology. If that technology is undermined by groups with little stake in preserving the existing system, the results can be catastrophic. Today we speak of terrorists with homemade bombs and shoulder-fired missiles, but at the end of the Late Bronze Age in the eastern Mediterranean, it was northern warriors with long swords and hunting javelins who laid the groundwork for a dramatic transformation of society.

Neil Asher Silberman is an author and historian specializing in the ancient history of the Near East. He is a contributing editor to Archaeology *magazine.*

Grisly Assyrian Record of Torture and Death

Erika Bleibtreu

Assyrian national history, as it has been preserved for us in inscriptions and pictures, consists almost solely of military campaigns and battles. It is as gory and bloodcurdling a history as we know.

Assyria emerged as a territorial state in the 14th century B.C. Its territory covered approximately the northern part of modern Iraq. The first capital of Assyria was Assur, located about 150 miles north of modern Baghdad on the west bank of the Tigris River. The city was named for its national god, Assur, from which the name Assyria is also derived.

From the outset, Assyria projected itself as a strong military power bent on conquest. Countries and peoples that opposed Assyrian rule were punished by the destruction of their cites and the devastation of their fields and orchards.

By the ninth century B.C., Assyria had consolidated its hegemony over northern Mesopotamia. It was then that Assyrian armies marched beyond their own borders to expand their empire, seeking booty to finance their plans for still more conquest and power. By the mid-ninth century B.C., the Assyrian menace posed a direct threat to the small Syro-Palestine states to the west, including Israel and Judah.

The period from the ninth century to the end of the seventh century B.C. is known as the Neo-Assyrian period, during which the empire reached its zenith. The Babylonian destruction of their capital city Nineveh in 612 B.C. marks the end of the Neo-Assyrian empire, although a last Assyrian king, Ashur-uballit II, attempted to rescue the rest of the Assyrian state, by then only a small territory around Harran. However, the

Babylonian king Nabopolassar (625–605 B.C.) invaded Harran in 610 B.C. and conquered it. In the following year, a final attempt was made by Ashur-uballit II to regain Harran with the help of troops from Egypt, but he did not succeed. Thereafter, Assyria disappears from history.

We will focus here principally on the records of seven Neo-Assyrian kings, most of whom ruled successively. Because the kings left behind pictorial, as well as written, records, our knowledge of their military activities is unusually well documented:

1. Ashurnasirpal II—883–859 B.C.
2. Shalmaneser III—858–824 B.C.
3. Tiglath-pileser III—744–727 B.C.
4. Sargon II—721–705 B.C.
5. Sennacherib—704–681 B.C.
6. Esarhaddon—680–669 B.C.
7. Ashurbanipal—668–627 B.C.

Incidentally, Assyrian records, as well as the Bible, mention the military contracts between the Neo-Assyrian empire and the small states of Israel and Judah.

An inscription of Shalmaneser III records a clash between his army and a coalition of enemies that included Ahab, king of Israel (c. 859–853 B.C.). Indeed, Ahab, according to Shalmaneser, mustered more chariots (2,000) than any of the other allies arrayed against the Assyrian ruler at the battle of Qarqar on the Orontes (853 B.C.). For a time, at least, the Assyrian advance was checked.

An inscription on a stela from Tell al Rimah in northern Iraq, erected in 806 B.C. by Assyrian king Adad-nirari III, informs us that Jehoahaz, king of Israel (814–793 B.C.), paid tribute to the

Assyrian king: "He [Adad-nirari III of Assyria] received the tribute of Ia'asu the Samarian [Jehcahaz, king of Israel], of the Tyrian (ruler) and the Sidonian (ruler)."[1]

From the inscriptions of Tiglath-pileser III and from some representations on the reliefs that decorated the walls of his palace at Nimrud, we learn that he too conducted a military campaign to the west and invaded Israel. Tiglath-pileser III received tribute from Menahem of Samaria (744–738 B.C.), as the Bible tells us; the Assyrian king is there called Pulu (2 Kings 15:19–20).

In another episode recorded in the Bible, Pekah, king of Israel (737–732 B.C.), joined forces with Rezin of Damascus against King Ahaz of Judah (2 Kings 16:5–10). The Assyrian king Tiglath-pileser III successfully intervened against Pekah, who was then deposed. The Assyrian king then placed Hoshea on the Israelite throne. By then Israel's northern provinces were devastated and part of her population was deported to Assyria (2 Kings 15:29).

At one point, Israel, already but a shadow of its former self and crushed by the burden of the annual tribute to Assyria, decided to revolt. Shalmaneser V (726–722 B.C.), who reigned after Tiglath-pileser III, marched into Israel, besieged its capital at Samaria and, after three years of fighting, destroyed it (2 Kings 18:10). This probably occurred in the last year of Shalmaneser V's reign (722 B.C.). However, his successor, Sargon II, later claimed credit for the victory. In any event, this defeat ended the national identity of the northern kingdom of Israel. Sargon II deported, according to his own records, 27,290

Courtesy of the *Biblical Archaeology Review,* January/February 1991, pp. 52–61. © 1991 by the Biblical Archaeology Society, 3000 Connecticut Avenue, NW, Suite 300, Washington, DC 20008.

Israelites, settling them, according to the Bible, near Harran on the Habur River and in the mountains of eastern Assyria (2 Kings 17:6, 18:11).

Later, in 701 B.C., when King Hezekiah of Judah withheld Assyrian tribute, Sargon II's successor, Sennacherib, marched into Judah, destroying, according to his claim, 46 cities and besieging Jerusalem. Although Sennacherib failed to capture Jerusalem (2 Kings 19:32–36), Hezekiah no doubt continued to pay tribute to Assyria.

The two principal tasks of an Assyrian king were to engage in military exploits and to erect public buildings. Both of these tasks were regarded as religious duties. They were, in effect, acts of obedience toward the principal gods of Assyria.

The historical records of ancient Assyria consist of tablets, prisms and cylinders of clay and alabaster. They bear inscriptions in cuneiform—wedge-shaped impressions representing, for the most part, syllables. In addition, we have inscribed obelisks and stelae as well as inscriptions on stone slabs that lined the walls and covered the floors of Assyrian palaces and temples.

In all of these inscriptions, the king stands at the top of the hierarchy—the most powerful person; he himself represents the state. All public acts are recorded as his achievements. All acts worthy of being recorded are attributed only to the Assyrian king, the focus of the ancient world.

The annals of the kings describe not only their military exploits, but also their building activities. This suggests that the spoil and booty taken during the military campaigns formed the financial foundation for the building activities of palaces, temples, canals and other public structures. The booty—property and people—probably provided not only precious building materials, but also artists and workmen deported from conquered territories.

The inscriptional records are vividly supplemented by pictorial representations. These include reliefs on bronze bands that decorated important gates, reliefs carved on obelisks and some engravings on cylinder seals. But the largest and most informative group of monuments are the reliefs sculpted into the stone slabs that lined the palaces' walls in the empire's capital cities—Nimrud (ancient Kalah), Khorsabad (ancient Dur Sharrukin) and Kuyunjik (ancient Nineveh).

According to the narrative representations on these reliefs, the Assyrians never lost a battle. Indeed, no Assyrian soldier is ever shown wounded or killed. The benevolence of the gods is always bestowed on the Assyrian king and his troops.

Like the official written records, the scenes and figures are selected and arranged to record the kings' heroic deeds and to describe him as "beloved of the gods":

> "The king, who acts with the support of the great gods his lords and has conquered all lands, gained dominion over all highlands and received their tribute, captures of hostages, he who is victorious over all countries."[2]

The inscriptions and the pictorial evidence both provide detailed information regarding the Assyrian treatment of conquered peoples, their armies and their rulers. In his official royal inscriptions, Ashurnasirpal II calls himself the "trampler of all enemies . . . who defeated all his enemies [and] hung the corpses of his enemies on posts."[3] The treatment of captured enemies often depended on their readiness to submit themselves to the will of the Assyrian king:

> "The nobles [and] elders of the city came out to me to save their lives. They seized my feet and said: 'If it pleases you, kill! If it pleases you, spare! If it pleases you, do what you will!' "[4]

In one case when a city resisted as long as possible instead of immediately submitting, Ashurnasirpal proudly records his punishment:

> "I flayed as many nobles as had rebelled against me [and] draped their skins over the pile [of corpses]; some I spread out within the pile, some I erected on stakes upon the pile . . . I flayed many right through my land [and] draped their skins over the walls."[5]

The account was probably intended not only to describe what had happened, but also to frighten anyone who might dare to resist. To suppress his enemies was the king's divine task. Supported by the gods, he always had to be victorious in battle and to punish disobedient people:

> "I felled 50 of their fighting men with the sword, burnt 200 captives from them, [and] defeated in a battle on the plain 332 troops. . . . With their blood I dyed the mountain red like red wool, [and] the rest of them the ravines [and] torrents of the mountain swallowed. I carried off captives [and] possessions from them. I cut off the heads of their fighters [and] built [therewith] a tower before their city. I burnt their adolescent boys [and] girls."[6]

A description of another conquest is even worse:

> "In strife and conflict I besieged [and] conquered the city. I felled 3,000 of their fighting men with the sword . . . I captured many troops alive: I cut off of some their arms [and] hands; I cut off of others their noses, ears, [and] extremities. I gouged out the eyes of many troops. I made one pile of the living [and] one of heads. I hung their heads on trees around the city."[7]

The palace of Ashurnasirpal II at Nimrud is the first, so far as we know, in which carved stone slabs were used in addition to the usual wall paintings. These carvings portray many of the scenes described in words in the annals.

From the reign of Shalmaneser III, Ashurnasirpal II's son, we also have some bronze bands that decorated a massive pair of wooden gates of a temple (and possibly a palace) at Balawat, near modern Mosul. These bronze bands display unusually fine examples of bronze repoussé (a relief created by hammering on the opposite side). In a detail, we see an Assyrian soldier grasping the hand and arm of a captured enemy whose other hand and both feet have already been cut off. Dismembered hands and feet fly through the scene. Severed enemy heads hang from the conquered city's walls. Another captive is impaled on a stake, his hands and feet already having been cut off. In another detail, we see three stakes, each driven through eight severed heads, set up outside the conquered city. A third detail shows a row of impaled captives lined up on stakes set up on a hill outside the captured city. In an inscription from Shalmaneser III's father, Ashurnasirpal II, the latter tells us, "I captured soldiers alive [and] erected [them] on stakes before their cities."[8]

Shalmaneser III's written records supplement his pictorial archive: "I filled the wide plain with the corpses of his warriors. . . . These [rebels] I impaled on stakes.[9] . . . A pyramid (pillar) of heads I erected in front of the city."[10]

In the eighth century B.C., Tiglath-pileser III held center stage. Of one city he conquered, he says:

"Nabû-ushabshi, their king, I hung up in front of the gate of his city on a stake. His land, his wife, his sons, his daughters, his property, the treasure of his palace, I carried off. Bit-Amukâni, I trampled down like a threshing (sledge). All of its people, (and) its goods, I took to Assyria."[11]

Such actions are illustrated several times in the reliefs at Tiglath-pileser's palace at Nimrud. These reliefs display an individual style in the execution of details that is of special importance in tracing the development of military techniques.

Perhaps realizing what defeat meant, a king of Urartu, threatened by Sargon II, committed suicide: "The splendor of Assur, my lord, overwhelmed him [the king of Urartu] and with his own iron dagger he stabbed himself through the heart, like a pig, and ended his life."[12]

Sargon II started a new Assyrian dynasty that lasted to the end of the empire. Sargon built a new capital named after himself—Dur Sharrukin, meaning "Stronghold of the righteous king." His palace walls were decorated with especially large stone slabs, carved with extraordinarily large figures.

Sargon's son and successor, Sennacherib, again moved the Assyrian capital, this time to Nineveh, where he built his own palace. According to the excavator of Ninneveh, Austen Henry Layard, the reliefs in Sennacherib's palace, if lined up in a row, would stretch almost two miles. If anything, Sennacherib surpassed his predecessors in the grisly detail of his descriptions:

"I cut their throats like lambs. I cut off their precious lives (as one cuts) a string. Like the many waters of a storm, I made (the contents of) their gullets and entrails run down upon the wide earth. My prancing steeds harnessed for my riding, plunged into the streams of their blood as (into) a river. The wheels of my war chariot, which brings low the wicked and the evil, were bespattered with blood and filth. With the bodies of their warriors I filled the plain, like grass. (Their) testicles I cut off, and tore out the privates like the seeds of cucumbers."[13]

In several rooms of Sennacherib's Southwest Palace at Nineveh, severed heads are represented; deportation scenes are frequently depicted. Among the deportees depicted, there are long lines of prisoners from the Judahite city of Lachish; they are shown pulling a rope fastened to a colossal entrance figure for Sennacherib's palace at Nineveh; above this line of deportees is an overseer whose hand holds a truncheon.

Sennacherib was murdered by his own sons. Another son, Esarhaddon, became his successor. As the following examples show, Esarhaddon treated his enemies just as his father and grandfather had treated theirs: "Like a fish I caught him up out of the sea and cut off his head,"[14] he said of the king of Sidon; "Their blood, like a broken dam, I caused to flow down the mountain gullies";[15] and "I hung the heads of Sanduarri [king of the cities of Kundi and Sizu] and Abdimilkutti [king of Sidon] on the shoulders of their nobles and with singing and music I paraded through the public square of Nineveh."[16]

Ashurbanipal, Esarhaddon's son, boasted:

"Their dismembered bodies I fed to the dogs, swine, wolves, and eagles, to the birds of heaven and the fish in the deep. . . . What was left of the feast of the dogs and swine, of their members which blocked the streets and filled the squares, I ordered them to remove from Babylon, Kutha and Sippar, and to cast them upon heaps."[17]

When Ashurbanipal didn't kill his captives he "pierced the lips (and) took them to Assyria as a spectacle for the people of my land."[18]

The enemy to the southeast of Assyria, the people of Elam, underwent a special punishment that did not spare even their dead:

"The sepulchers of their earlier and later kings, who did not fear Assur and Ishtar, my lords, (and who) had plagued the kings, my fathers, I destroyed, I devastated, I exposed to the sun. Their bones (members) I carried off to Assyria. I laid restlessness upon their shades. I deprived them of food-offerings and libations of water."[19]

Among the reliefs carved by Ashurbanipal were pictures of the mass deportation of the Elamites, together with severed heads assembled in heaps. Two Elamites are seen fastened to the ground while their skin is flayed, while others are having their tongues pulled out.

There is no reason to doubt the historical accuracy of these portrayals and descriptions. Such punishments no doubt helped to secure the payment of tribute—silver, gold, tin, copper, bronze, and iron, as well as building materials including wood, all of which was necessary for the economic survival of the Assyrian empire.

In our day, these depictions, verbal and visual, give a new reality to the Assyrian conquest of the northern kingdom of Israel in 721 B.C. and to Sennacherib's subsequent campaign into Judah in 701 B.C.

NOTES

1. Stephanie Page, "A Stela of Adad-nirari III and Nergal-eres from Tell al Rimah," *Iraq* 30 (1968), p. 143.
2. Albert Kirk Grayson, *Assyrian Royal Inscriptions,* Part 2: *From Tiglath-pileser I to Ashurnasir-apli II* (Wiesbaden, Germ.: Otto Harrassowitz, 1976), p. 165.
3. Ibid., p. 120.
4. Ibid., p. 124.
5. Ibid.
6. Ibid., pp. 126–127.
7. Ibid., p. 126.
8. Ibid., p. 143.
9. Daniel David Luckenbill, *Ancient Records of Assyria and Babylonia,* 2 vols. (Chicago: Univ. of Chicago Press, 1926–1927), vol. 1, secs. 584–585.
10. Ibid., vol. 1, sec. 599.
11. Ibid., vol. 1, sec. 783.
12. Ibid., vol. 2, sec. 22.
13. Ibid., vol. 2, sec. 254.
14. Ibid., vol. 2, sec. 511.
15. Ibid., vol. 2, sec. 521.
16. Ibid., vol. 2, sec. 528.
17. Ibid., vol. 2, secs. 795–796.
18. Ibid., vol. 2, sec. 800.
19. Ibid., vol. 2, sec. 810.

Unit 2

Unit Selections

Key Points to Consider

❖ Describe the functions of sporting events in ancient Greece and Rome.

❖ Did Athenian democracy depend upon the existence of slavery? Defend your answer.

❖ How did the Athenians win the battle of Marathon over the Persians?

❖ What was life like for Athenian women?

❖ How did Cleopatra influence Roman history?

❖ Why might Augustus Caesar deserve the title "Man of the Year" for 1 A.D.?

❖ Were the barbarians, on the whole, good or bad for the Roman Empire?

 **Links**   **www.dushkin.com/online/**

These sites are annotated on pages 4 and 5.

It has been conventional to say that, for the West, civilization began in Mesopotamia and Egypt, but that civilization became distinctly Western in Greece. These matters no longer go undisputed: witness recent academic debates over Martin Bernal's thesis that Greek civilization derived from the older cultures of Egypt and the eastern Mediterranean.

Those disputes aside, the Greek ideals of order, proportion, harmony, balance, and structure—so pervasive in classical thought and art—inspired Western culture for centuries, even into the modern era. Their humanism, which made humans "the measure of all things," not only liberated Greek citizens from the despotic collectivism of the Near East, but also encouraged them, and us, to attain higher levels of creativity and excellence. In "Winning at Olympia," Donald Kyle recounts how the Greeks motivated and honored athletic excellence.

Though the Greeks did not entirely escape from the ancient traditions of miracle, mystery, and authority, they nevertheless elevated reason and science to new levels of importance in human affairs, and they invented history as we know it. It was their unique social-political system, the polis, that provided scope and incentives for Greek culture. Each polis was an experiment in local self-government. But to many moderns the Greek order was tainted because it rested on slavery and excluded women from the political process. In the essay "The Athenian Democracy and Its Slaves," Dimitris Kyrtatas offers perspectives on the Greek social and political order. Kenneth Cavander discusses the place of Greek women in "Love and Death in Ancient Greece."

Yet for all its greatness and originality, classical Greek civilization flowered only briefly. From the great Athenian victory, as Barry Baldwin details in "Re-Running Marathon," the weaknesses of the polis system surfaced during the Peloponnesian Wars. After the long conflict between Athens and Sparta, the polis ceased to fulfill the lives of its citizens as it had in the past, and the Greeks' confidence was shaken by the war and subsequent events.

But it was not the war alone that undermined the civic order. The Greek way of life depended upon unique and transitory circumstances—trust, smallness, simplicity, and a willingness to subordinate private interests to public concerns. The postwar period saw the spread of disruptive forms of individualism and the privatization of life.

Eventually, Alexander the Great's conquests and the geographical unity of the Mediterranean enabled the non-Greek world to share Greek civilization. Indeed, a distinctive stage of Western civilization, the Hellenistic age, emerged from the fusion of Greek and Oriental elements. At best the Hellenistic period was a time when new cities were built on the Greek model, a time of intellectual ferment and cultural exchange, travel and exploration,

scholarship and research. At worst it was an era of amoral opportunism in politics and derivative styles in the arts. It may be argued that Cleopatra (see "Cleopatra: What Kind of a Woman Was She, Anyway?") came to represent the best and worst of these ideals.

Later, the Greek idea survived Rome's domination of the Mediterranean. The Romans themselves acknowledged their debt to "conquered Greece." Modern scholars continue that theme, often depicting Roman culture as nothing more than the practical application of Greek ideals to Roman life. The popularity of chariot racing would seem a direct link between Greece and Rome, yet Greeks and Romans differed in their view of the sport, as Dirk Bennett notes in "Chariot Racing in the Ancient World." The Romans were not merely soulless imitators of the Greeks. They were creative borrowers (from the Etruscans, as well as from the Greeks). In addition, the Roman Republic invented an effective system of imperial government and a unique conception of law. Their accomplishments can be found in Lionel Casson's essay "In the Year 1, Augustus Let the Good Times Roll." Finally, the decline of the Roman Empire is addressed in "Friends, Romans, or Countrymen? Barbarians in the Empire."

The Romans bequeathed their language and law to Europe and preserved and disseminated Greek thought and values. The Greeks had provided the basis for the cultural unity of the Mediterranean; the Romans provided the political unity. Between them they forged and preserved many of the standards and assumptions upon which our tradition of civilization is built—the classical ideal.

Winning At Olympia

New studies challenge traditional notions about Greek athletes and why they competed.

Donald G. Kyle

Donald G. Kyle, associate professor of history at the University of Texas at Arlington, has published extensively on the history of Greek athletics. His research, reviews, and teaching have contributed to the emerging field of ancient sport studies.

You say, "I want to win at Olympia." ... *If you do, you will have to obey instructions, eat according to regulations, keep away from desserts, exercise on a fixed schedule at definite hours, in both heat and cold; you must not drink cold water nor can you have a drink of wine whenever you want. You must hand yourself over to your coach exactly as you would to a doctor. Then in the contest itself you must gouge and be gouged, there will be times when you will sprain a wrist, turn your ankle, swallow mouthfuls of sand, and be flogged. And after all that there are times when you lose.*

Epictetus, *Discourses* 15.2–5,
trans. W.E. Sweet

This summer in Atlanta athletes, officials, spectators, promoters, and reporters will once again witness the spectacle of the modern Olympics. Many will assume that the modern games are a true reflection of the ancient ones, that the events and ceremonies and the ideology of universal brotherhood and amateurism recall the Olympics of Greece's golden age. They would be surprised to learn that the ancient contests were quite different from our own, and that Greek athletes were not amateurs.

A generation ago the study of ancient sport focused on antiquarian concerns—how Greeks threw the discus or how far they could jump. Glossing over the violent, erotic, and materialistic aspects of Greek sport, and downplaying abuses and opportunism, scholars simply accepted idealistic notions about who these athletes were and why they competed. Now, using a variety of evidence, we are demythologizing the ancient Olympics. Excavations at Olympia and at the sites of other games have led to a new understanding of athletic participation and the role of spectators in ancient sport. Archaeology and art history, especially epigraphy and the reexamination of vase paintings, have allowed us to test and revise ancient literary accounts of how athletes trained, worshiped, competed, won, and celebrated, and how they were motivated, rewarded, and honored.

Every four years heralds traveled throughout the ancient Greek world proclaiming a sacred truce, affording safe passage through any state for all travelers to and from the games. All Greeks were invited to attend or compete in the great festival and games at the sanctuary of Zeus at Olympia. And come they did, from 776 B.C. (the traditional date of the first Olympiad) to at least the late fourth century A.D., making the games the most enduring of Greek institutions. These panhellenic gatherings were vital to Greek ethnicity. They were multinational, but only free, male Greeks could compete. At Olympia visitors and participants from Greek city-states throughout the Mediterranean shared a common culture in which religious piety and enthusiasm for sport were of pivotal importance. By the mid-sixth century Olympia had emerged as the pinnacle of a circuit of four great panhellenic sacred "crown" games with wreaths awarded to the victors. The others, at the sanctuaries of Delphi, Isthmia, and Nemea, were held sequentially, with at least one festival each year culminating in the finale at Olympia. Named after the winner in the men's sprint race, the Olympiads provided a common chronology at a time when each city-state had its own calendar.

Athletics were only part of a religious festival at Olympia that honored Zeus with processions and sacrifices. One end of the original racecourse may have extended close to the Altar of Zeus, where athletes swore oaths on slices of boar's flesh that they would abide by the rules of the games. Athletes competed for the glory of Zeus, and the ancient Greeks felt that victors were divinely favored. The sole prize was a crown of olive leaves cut from Zeus' sacred grove. Over time the competitions became a larger part of the festival, with more events and expanded facilities, but the games never became fully secular.

Excavations have taken place at Olympia for more than a century, but interpretations of the early history of the site have recently been revised. Archaeologists now suggest that major athletic events were not part of the earliest festivals at Olympia. Scholars have claimed variously that the original contests served as sacred rituals, funeral games, offerings to gods, initiations, or reenactments of myths. The second-century A.D. traveler Pausanias and others recount myths that Herakles founded the games to honor Zeus or that they were established by King Pelops after winning a chariot race against King Oinomaos of Pisa. Traditions also speak of a refounding or reorganization of the games during the Greek Dark Age (ca. the ninth century B.C.). The earliest literary account of athletic competition, Patroklos' funeral games in Homer's *Iliad*, reflects the athletic world of the eighth century or earlier. Homer mentions valuable prizes (bronze cauldrons and tripods; horses, cattle, and women;

Myths about the Ancient Games

David C. Young

Many aspects of our Olympic Games have been justified by specious ancient antecedents. Until recently we believed competitors had to be amateurs because we believed ancient Greek Olympians were amateurs. Nonsense. The ancient Olympics had no such rule, and the Greeks did not even have a word for amateur. Ancient Olympic athletes were professionals. The Olympic Truce, while guaranteeing safe passage to athletes and spectators on their way to the Games, did not, contrary to popular belief, stop all wars in Greece: Sparta was fined for attacking Elean territory in 420 B.C., and Arcadians invaded the sanctuary at Olympia in 364. Modern Olympic officials, citing an ancient inscription from Delphi that had been translated "Wine cannot be taken into the stadium," have assumed that ancient athletes abstained from strong drink, setting an example for today's competitors. It now seems the correct translation is "Wine cannot be taken *out* of the stadium."

As especially beguiling myth is that the five interlocked Olympic rings—among the world's best-known logos—were an ancient Greek symbol for the games. Several recent books include a photograph of a stone block from Delphi with the five rings inscribed on it. The books identify it as ancient and say that the five rings "later adopted as the symbol of the modern Olympics" create "a link between the ancient and modern Olympics" and are "considered by experts to be 3,000 years old." More nonsense. The five rings were invented in 1913 by Pierre de Coubertin, president of the International Olympic Committee. There had been five modern Olympiads by that time, and Coubertin's writings suggest each ring was intended to represent a completed Olympiad, the first five host countries united in "Olympism" and peace. Apparently he expected to add a sixth ring after Olympiad VI, to be held in Berlin in 1916, and so on, until there was a flagful of rings and "universal peace." But Olympiad VI was preempted by World War I, so Coubertin gave the symbol a different official meaning: each ring represented one of the five continents of the world, united in Olympism (to Europeans, the "continents" number only five).

Thus the logo froze at five and stays there today, a fossil of pre-World War I Europe, when hopes of world peace briefly flowered. How did the inscription of the five-ring logo come to be a Delphi? The infamous 1936 Nazi Olympics of Berlin provide the answer. Leni Riefenstahl filmed the 1936 Olympic torch relay as the flame moved from ancient Olympia toward Berlin for her acclaimed movie *Olympia*. For a scene where a torch runner circles the photogenic stadium at Delphi, a crude stone block was inscribed with the symbol of the five rings, and placed in the stadium. Years later American authors Lynn and Gray Poole observed the old movie prop in the stadium, mistook it for an ancient inscription, and published their error, which soon spread to other books, where it continues to mislead the unwary.

The custom of lighting the flame at ancient Olympia and relaying the torch to the modern Olympic stadium is also a legacy of the Berlin games, although many wrongly think it derives from the ancient Olympics. Carl Diem, organizer of the 1936 Olympics, seeking to glamorize them with an ancient aura, staged the first lighting of the Olympic Flame, now a hallowed ritual in which thousands delight. The first Olympic torches were made by the Krupp Company, better known for providing weapons for two world wars. The association of the Olympic torch with peace came later, as the flame arrived at more peaceful venues.

Despite the myths linking modern and ancient games, a similarity of spirit is authentic. Those who revived the Olympics succeeded in making the games live again. Our Olympics are, like those of the ancients, a magnificent sporting and cultural event, a source of national pride, and a showcase for outstanding individual achievement.

David C. Young *is a professor of classics at the University of Florida. His new book,* The Modern Olympics: A Struggle for Revival, *is forthcoming from Johns Hopkins University Press.*

armor and iron) and contests (chariot racing, boxing, wrestling, running, armed combat, discus, archery, and javelin), but his poems contain no specific reference to games at Olympia. Although archaeologists have found evidence of funeral games in the Late Bronze Age (thirteenth and twelfth centuries B.C.) elsewhere in Greece (a funerary coffer from Boeotia with scenes of mourning and various contests; vases with scenes of boxers and chariot races), there is no evidence for them at Olympia.

German archaeologists Alfred Mallwitz and Klaus Herrmann reject the idea of Mycenaean games associated with Pelops and argue that cult activities preceded athletics at Olympia. They note that there are earlier remains in the area but those suggesting a sanctuary (e.g.,

votives) are not older than the Geometric period (from about the tenth century to 750 B.C.), and that the Pelopeion, the shrine of Pelops at Olympia, is later than a stratum of black ash, animal bones, and votive figurines dated to about 700. Recent studies by Catherine Morgan, a Cambridge University archaeologist, and others suggest that the numerous metal figurines and tripods found at Olympia are dedications rather than prizes for athletic competitions. Morgan's study characterizes early Olympia (from the late tenth until the eighth century) as a rural shrine for a rustic cult of Zeus. According to Mallwitz, the oldest wells near the stadium date to the early seventh century. It would appear from the archaeological evidence that the first games, traditionally dated from

776, were humble and local, and that major athletic competitions did not emerge until ca. 700 or even 680, when the addition of equestrian contests allowed more conspicuous displays of the status and resources of competitors. Owning horses in poor and rocky Greece was a sign of great wealth, and Isocrates and Aristotle both wrote that "the breeding of racehorses is possible only for the very rich." Rivalries among emerging city-states contributed to increased participation and intensification of competition.

For centuries the events and facilities at Olympia were spartan for both athletes and spectators. Sources such as Epictetus' *Discourses* mention the heat, the crowds, the makeshift accommodations, and the poor sanitation. In striking contrast to the grandeur of the temples of Zeus and Hera, the classical stadium was a simple running track outside the sacred precinct. Only judges and diplomatic representatives had permanent stone seats in a small area on the southern embankment. Spectators camped out nearby or came early, standing or sitting on the grassy embankments to watch the competitions.

Held in late summer, the ancient Olympics had no winter events, no water or ball sports, and no oval tracks. There were no women's events, and adult women were barred from attending the games on pain of death (see box, "Games for Girls"). Age classes for men and boys (perhaps from 12 to 17 years old) developed, but there were no team sports and no second prizes. The games included various footraces (of about 200, 400, and at most 4,800 meters) and even a race in armor, but there was no ancient marathon (see box, "Stadia and Starting Gates"). Olympia also had equestrian events, horse and chariot races for which the owners, not the drivers, were declared the victors. Owners did not even need to be present, and often hired drivers or jockeys, a circumstance allowing monarchs, tyrants, and even women to become Olympic victors. Alcibiades, the Athenian politician and general, entered seven chariots in the games of 416 B.C. We do not know if he personally drove any of them but he "won" first, second, and third or fourth place. Kyniska, daughter of a Spartan king, won the four-horse chariot race in 396 and 392 B.C. According to Suetonius, in A.D. 67 the Roman emperor Nero made a travesty of the games by competing personally in a ten-horse chariot race held for his benefit. Even though he fell from his chariot and did not finish the race, Nero was declared the victor. The Greeks later rejected those games and his victory as unofficial.

There was a pentathlon—discus throw, javelin throw (using a throwing thong), long jump (using hand-held weights), footrace (probably 200 meters), and wrestling—but no decathlon. A debate on the system of choosing the winner in the ancient pentathlon has now gone on longer than the modern Olympics. There are theories about elaborate point systems, lots, byes, rematches, and comparative victories or relative placements, but most scholars favor some system of progressive elimination of competitors down to two opponents who wrestled each other in the final event.

Wrestling, boxing, and the *pankration,* a combination of the two, were known as "heavy" events because, without weight classes or time limits, bigger athletes dominated. In these events byes were allotted if there was an odd number of entrants, and a competitor might have to face an opponent who had just sat out a round. In the *pankration* punching, kicking, choking, finger breaking, and blows to the genitals were allowed; only biting and eye gouging were prohibited. A recent study by Michael Poliakoff, a leading authority on ancient combat sports, has shown that pankratiasts could wear light boxing "gloves" made of strips of leather and designed, like all Greek boxing gloves, to protect the hands of the puncher, not the face of the opponent. The bronze boxer at the Terme Museum in Rome and a fragment of a relief on a tombstone at the Kerameikos Museum in Athens show scarred faces, broken noses, and cauliflower ears. Vase paintings of boxing matches show bloody noses. Satirical epigrams claim that boxers became so disfigured their dogs did not recognize them and they could not claim inheritances:

When Odysseus returned safely to his home after 20 years, only his dog Argos recognized him when he saw him. But you, Stratophon, after you have boxed for four hours, neither dogs nor your fellow citizens can recognize. If you will be so kind as to view your face in a mirror, you will affirm with an oath, "I am not Stratophon." (Lucillius, *Greek Anthology* 11.77, trans. W.E. Sweet)

O Augustus, this man Olympikos, as he now appears, used to have nose, chin, forehead, ears, and eyelids. But then he enrolled in the guild of boxers, with the result that he did not receive his share of his inheritance in a will. For in the lawsuit about the will his brother shows the judge a portrait of Olympikos, who was judged to be an imposter, bearing no resemblance to his own picture. (Lucillius, *Greek Anthology* 11.75, trans. W.E. Sweet)

Wrestling matches were decided by falls, but boxing and *pankration* bouts continued until one athlete gave up or was incapacitated. Stories tell of deaths and even a posthumous victory: before he died in a stranglehold, the pankratiast Arrhichion is said to have dislocated his opponent's ankle, forcing him to give up.

Athletes had legal immunity in cases of unintentional homicide, but the Olympic judges denied victory to one Kleomedes of Astypalaia, apparently for intentionally killing his opponent in boxing.

Although the number of events of Olympia remained limited, local athletic festivals offered a vast array of competitions in male beauty, dancing in armor, chariot dismounting, torch racing, team events, and more. Epigraphic studies, such as the publication of new victor lists from the Panathenaic Games at Athens and numerous inscriptions recording contests in Hellenistic and Roman times from Alexandria to Aphrodisias, continue to reveal more about games beyond Olympia. The inscriptions reflect the proliferation of prizes, honors, and festivals throughout the Mediterranean. Some new games were modeled on Olympia, but Olympia and the other panhellenic games remained the most revered. Finally historians and inscriptions record gifts of money and buildings and the patronage of Olympia and athletes by such famous figures as Herod, king of Judaea, and Roman emperors including Hadrian.

Historians debate whether "sport" as we know it is a modern phenomenon—the word has no classical equivalent—or a continuation of ancient traditions. Some see modern sport as distinctive in its secularism and its concern with quantification and records, but others see ancient and modern sport as part of a continuum, an enduring heritage. Whether sport is modern or timeless, great athletes have always understood effort and agony. On occasion the media undermine our sense of athletic awe by bringing us too close, showing anorexic beauties and anabolic beasts. Who were the athletes of Greece, and how different were they? How were they prepared and rewarded? What motivated them to risk shame and injury? How did they react to victory and sudden fame? How did they see themselves, and what was their place in society?

Ancient competitors went to Olympia on their own initiative and at their own expense; they were not screened at home by athletic trials or officially supported by local committees. Access to state gymnasiums was usually open and free, but training required time, money, and instruction. Although there were a few state entries in chariot races, for centuries after the games began there is no certain evidence of state subsidies for

Games for Girls

Thomas F. Scanlon

Pericles' statement, "Fame will be great ... for the woman whose reputation for excellence or blame is least known among males," reflects a typical attitude toward women's activities in ancient Greek literature. Yet tantalizing fragments of evidence suggest that some Greek girls did engage in athletic competitions, mostly at religious festivals marking their progress toward womanhood.

According to mythology the Olympics were founded by King Pelops after he defeated Oinomaos, king of Pisa, in a chariot race. For his victory Pelops won the princess Hippodameia as his wife. In thanksgiving he founded the games to honor Zeus, while Hippodameia established the Heraia, a festival honoring Hera, Zeus' wife. Most of what we know about the Heraia is from a description by the second-century A.D. author Pausanias, who noted that the Heraia had only one event, a footrace for maidens. This was run in the same stadium as the men's races, but with a course shorter by one-sixth, corresponding to the average shorter stride of women. Their festival, like the men's, took place every four years and may well have been open to girls from all Greek states. The Heraia was probably held during the Olympic year, just prior to the men's games, since the participants probably would have traveled to the sanctuary with the males in their families.

There were three footraces, one for each of three age divisions unspecified in the ancient sources, but perhaps ranging from six to 18. Winners, like victors in the men's games, received an olive wreath crown and a share of the one ox slaughtered for the patron deity on behalf of all the participants. Heraia victors attached painted portraits of themselves to Hera's temple in the Olympic sanctuary. The paintings are now gone, but the niches into which the votives were attached on the temple columns remain.

Unlike men, who competed nude, girls wore a short dress called an "off-the-shoulder chiton," which left the right shoulder and breast bare. This style, not in imitation of Amazon warrior women as some have speculated, was an adaptation of a typical light garment worn by men in hot weather or while performing hard labor. Thus the girls dressed like men, a ritual custom often followed in ceremonies of initiation to adulthood, an inversion of gender roles, perhaps to experience the status of the "other" before assuming one's own role.

Adult women were prohibited from attending the men's Olympics on penalty of death. The laws of Elis, the city that hosted the games, dictated that any woman caught entering the Olympic assembly on the forbidden days or even crossing the river that borders the site was to be hurled to her death from the high cliffs of Mount Typaion opposite the stadium. There is no evidence that such executions were ever carried out. Kallipateira, who attended disguised as a trainer and leapt into the stadium to congratulate her victorious son, went unpunished out of respect for her illustrious family. But to prevent such a violation from happening in the future, trainers thereafter had to enter the stadium naked. Yet maidens could attend the men's games, probably to familiarize them with the world of men. The only married woman permitted to watch the Olympics was the priestess of Demeter, whose privilege probably derived from the location of an ancient altar and sanctuary of that goddess in the middle of the stadium seating area.

In Sparta girls were favored with an exceptional educational system that included training in most of the same athletic events as boys. The aim was eugenic: healthy women produced healthy citizen-warriors. The contests were restricted to unmarried girls, who competed either nude or wearing only skimpy dresses. Boys were admitted as spectators, a practice intended to encourage marriage and procreation. Some Spartan maidens ran a special race for Dionysos, god of adult females, and this athletic ritual may also have celebrated their communal rite of passage.

At the sanctuaries of Brauron and Mounychion in Attica, girls celebrated the Arkteia or "Bear Festival," a quadrennial mystery ritual in honor of Artemis, goddess of wild animals and maidens. Legend says that this was a prenuptial festival required of all girls of Attica. A series of vases found at the Arkteia sanctuaries depicts girls, both nude and in short chitons, apparently performing various ritual activities, including dancing and running. The scenes of running appear to show girls chasing one another in a contest symbolic of their change of status from "wild" to "tame."

Only after the classical period did Greek girls come to compete in men's athletic festivals. References to this are few and late, suggesting exceptional social circumstances and perhaps the pressure of the Roman political system, which allowed the daughters of the wealthy to participate in men's festivals. Several noble girls are recorded as victors in the chariot race at Olympia and elsewhere, but they were owners, not drivers. A first-century A.D. inscription found at Delphi records young women who personally competed in chariot races or footraces at Delphi, Isthmia, and Menea, but not the Olympics. Yet these girls probably competed only against other girls, as in a race for daughters of magistrates at the Sebasta festival in Naples during the imperial period and the races for women instituted by Domitian at the Capitoline Games in Rome in A.D. 86.

Thomas F. Scanlon *is a professor of classics at the University of California, Riverside. He is director of the program in comparative ancient civilizations and has written books and articles on ancient athletics and on Greek and Roman historical writing.*

athletes, so family resources were an important advantage. The first evidence for government subsidies is an inscription from Ephesos, dated to about 300 B.C., that records a trainer's request for funds for an athlete. Other inscriptions show both the continuing involvement of the urban elite, who sometimes referred to themselves as the "gymnasium class" and who received physical training as youths (*epheboi*) in young men's organizations, as well as the rise, from the first century B.C. on, of guilds of full-time vocational athletes (with membership certificates, officers, and pensions). Olympians had to swear that they had been in training for ten months, and for one month prior to the games they had to

Stadia and Starting Gates

Hugh M. Lee

In 776 B.C., according to legend, a runner named Koroibos sprinted toward the alter of Zeus and crossed the finish line, becoming the first Olympic victory in history. Both distance and contest were called the *stadion,* or stade. The shortest race in Greek athletics, a stade was 600 *plethra,* but the length of the *plethron* used to lay out the track varied from site to site. While the Olympic stade was 192.28 meters, the stade in the Pythian Games at Delphi was 177.5 meters. the stadium in which Koroibos won has not been found, though we are reasonably sure it was somewhat west of the stadium visible today, which was built in the fifth century B.C.

Other Olympic footraces included a double stade (the *diaulos*) in which runners raced up the field, turned around a post, and returned; the *dolichos,* literally the "long race," of seven to 24 stades (1,400 to 4,800 meters); and the armed race (the *hoplitodromos*) in which runners, wearing a helmet and shin guards and carrying a shield, ran a *diaulos.* The marathon is a modern invention, first held during the 1896 Olympics in Athens. The Greeks were, however, known to run ultramarathon distances. Before the battle of Marathon in 490 B.C., the Athenian courier Philippides ran to Sparta seeking help, a distance of 135 miles, in less than 48 hours.

Unlike the modern oval track surrounding an infield, the ancient running course was a rectangular field marked off at each end by stone blocks set into the found in a line or sill called a *balbis.* The *balbis* usually had parallel grooves carved along its length, as well as sockets at regular intervals for posts. The posts in the *balbis* served a dual purpose, as part of the starting gate and as turning posts (*kampteres*). The grooves marked the positions for the runners' feet. As sculpture and vase painting reveal, the runners employed a standing start, the left foot slightly ahead of the right. The back end of the grooves was vertical to allow the runners to grip with their toes and shove off, whereas the forward end was beveled toward the track to keep the runners from stubbing their toes.

Corinth experimented with the form of the starting line in its stadium, built ca. 500 B.C. The *balbis* was curved so that in races with turns the runners on the outside did not have to run farther than those on the inside. Furthermore the runners placed their toes into individual toe grooves, not a continuous groove along the sill. The front and rear grooves were two or three feet apart, indicating the runners employed a wide starting stance.

In the *diaulos* the runners had individual turning posts and two lanes for the run up the track and back. Colored dust was probably used to mark off the lanes. For the *dolichos* the runners turned around single posts at each end. Where were these posts located? The fourth-century B.C. stadium at Nemea sheds some light. A stone block with a socket hole is 5.3 meters on the track side of the *balbis* and 3.4 meters to the west of the central longitudinal north-south axis. The socket hole held a turning post, and a similar one must have existed at the other, unexcavated, end of the stadium. The runners therefore clustered to their right as they approached the posts at each end.

How did the Greeks start their races? Originally, they probably used an auditory signal, either an official saying "Go" or perhaps a trumpet blast. Runners could anticipate the signal and start too soon, hence the invention of a starting gate, or *hysplex.* Inspired by the representation of a gate on a fourth-century Athenian vase, Stephen G. Miller of the University of California, Berkeley, and his Greek colleague Panos Valavanis reconstructed a form of the *hysplex* on the *balbis* of the stadium at Nemea in 1993. This *hysplex* functions like the simple mousetrap. Between poles at each end of the *balbis,* ropes are stretched to form a barrier. Utilizing torsion from twisted ropes, the gate is lowered onto the ground, then raised against the tension and kept in a vertical position by a ring and cord fastened to larger stationary posts at each end. The rings are also attached to ropes held by an official standing behind the runners. When he jerks the ropes, the rings slip off the poles, the gate slams forward, and the runners spring onto the track.

Hugh M. Lee *is an associate professor of classics at the University of Maryland, College Park.*

---

train at Elis, the city that hosted the festival and games at nearby Olympia. At Elis they were scrutinized, sometimes punished for fouls or disobedience, and possibly removed from competition if determined to be unworthy athletically by priestly judges equipped with unchallenged authority and whipping sticks.

By roughly the sixth century athletes were specializing in particular events and hiring expert coaches to hone their skills. Training was intensive and there were experiments and fads concerning diet, exercise, and sex. Fads led some athletes to favor cheese, figs, or grain, others to distrust fish or pork. Possibly influenced by the sixth-century philosopher Pythagoras or the medical school at Kroton, athletes from Kroton in southern Italy believed in the value of a meat diet and saw the consumption of beans as taboo. Milo of Kroton, the greatest Olympic wrestler, reputedly ate 40 pounds of meat and bread at one sitting, washing it down with eight quarts of wine. In the *Laws* Plato notes that Ikkos of Tarentum, a victor in the Olympic pentathlon (perhaps in 444 B.C.), was said never to have touched a woman, or a boy, while in training. Weight lifting was not an event nor was it a major part of training, for which shadow boxing, punching bags, and even dancing were recommended. Flute music often accompanied training, and many festivals included contests for musicians, dancers, and heralds.

The basic equipment of an athlete consisted only of an unguent jar (*aryballos*) of oil and a scraping instrument (*strigil*) for anointing and cleaning himself, though for various events a competitor might need other gear: a pick to soften the ground, boxing thongs, jumping weights, discus, or javelin. He had no shoes, no jockstrap, no uniform, and no endorsements. As Plato said in the *Republic,* classical Greeks, unlike barbarians, were not ashamed to appear in the nude. This custom may have been introduced in the eighth century, and by the sixth it was the norm. Ancient explanations for the nudity of competitors at Olympia (only chariot drivers were clothed) included safety or improved performance: speculative anecdotes recorded by Pausanias and Isidore suggest that one early runner dropped his loincloth intentionally and ran better without it, and that another was killed when his loincloth slipped down and tripped him. In contrast, modern theories of athletic nudity and even of the practice of infibulation (tying up the foreskin) favor cultic explanations: nudity was a costume, a state of ritual purity as in rites of passage; nudity and wreaths were remnants of hunters' rituals; or athletes were proclaiming their sexual abstinence. Only recently have we begun to admit that ancient athletics had an erotic dimension. *Kalos* inscriptions or love-names appear on many drinking vessels with athletic scenes, and the entrance tunnel to the stadium at Nemea bears a graffito in which one athlete applauds the beauty of Akrotatos, probably the Spartan prince and king from 265 to 252 B.C. Vase paintings show handsome young athletes pursued by mature men with gifts of hares and gaming cocks, and in literature wrestling was a metaphor for sex. Gymnasium hours were regulated and boys were carefully supervised, because, as Mark Golden, a scholar of Greek childhood, put it, gymnasiums were "prime pick-up points."

The historian Herodotus tells how the Persian king Xerxes, on hearing that Olympia awarded only wreath prizes, marveled that Greeks competed not for material reward but "only for honor." Then as now, however, Olympic victory brought more than its own rewards. Until the 1970s it was said that early Olympic athletes were idealistic, noble amateurs but that over time specialization, material rewards, and lower-class professionals corrupted athletics. Rejecting this scenario, revisionist scholars led by classicist David C. Young have concluded that the notion of amateurism in Greek sport is anachronistic, that the Greeks had neither the concept of nor a word for amateur athletics, and that ancient victors, whatever their background, accepted valuable prizes and benefits eagerly and with impunity. The prize wreath at Olympia was symbolic, but home cities rewarded Olympic victors substantially with cash bonuses, free meals, and more. In the sixth century Solon legislated rewards of 500

Reviving Nemea's Games

More than 650 people from some 30 countries were set to doff their shoes, don tunics, and run in the stadium at Nemea in southern Greece this past June, bringing the games held there in antiquity back to life after a 2,300-year hiatus. The ancient games at Nemea were one of the four panhellenic competitions that also included contests at Olympia, Delphi, and Isthmia. Inspiration for the revival came from races run in 1994 to mark the opening of the stadium as an archaeological park. A Society for the Revival of the Nemean Games—composed of archaeologists, classicists, citizens of modern Nemea, politicians, and business people—planned the event. The Olympic torch, on route to Atlanta from Olympia, stopped at Nemea on April 1 to rekindle symbolically the spirit of the ancient games. Excavated since 1974 by Stephen G. Miller of the University of California, Berkeley, the side includes ruins of a locker room, a tunnel (marked with the graffiti of ancient athletes) leading into the stadium, and the stadium itself.

The track's clay surface and re-created starting gate (see preceding page) are authentic, but not all aspects of the ancient games were followed in this year's competitions. The events included only 100-meter and 7.5-kilometer (4.5-mile) footraces. Boxing, wresting, and *pankration* were not on the schedule. "We wanted to avoid legal problems if someone was injured wrestling or boxing," says Miller. Unlike their ancient counterparts, contestants were to be clothed, wearing a light tunic modeled on classical Greek dress. "The ancient games were always conducted in the nude," says Miller, "but that is one step we were not prepared to take." Organizers did, however, promise that false starters would be flogged by the judges, according to ancient practice.

The new Nemean games were open to people of all ages and occupations; no training or physical aptitude was required. Among those scheduled to run were U.S. ambassador to Greece Thomas Niles; University of California, Berkeley, chancellor Chang-Lin Tien; former U.S. Olympic track coach Payton Jordan; gold medalist Rafer Johnson; Angelos Delivorrias, director of Athens' Benaki Museum; Yiannis Tzedakis, director of antiquities in the Greek Ministry of Culture; and Doreen Spitzer, president of the American School of Classical Studies.

The competition was to be friendly, with no records kept. Winners were to receive only the traditional wild celery wreath that was given to victors in the ancient games. "By running barefoot at Nemea we wanted to recognize our common humanity with those who came before us, and with all those who participated," said Miller.

—MARK ROSE

drachmas (more than $300,000) for Athenian Olympic victors. Athletes usually represented their native cites, but they could compete for another state. Astylos of Kroton, the first known free agent, won races at Olympia in 488 and 484 for Kroton, but then won races in 480 for Syracuse. States such as Athens, Kos, Macedon, and Syracuse realized that games were good publicity and good business, and they promoted their games and athletes through prizes, coins, and monuments. Beyond the "crown" games, there were many local games offering valuable material prizes and sometimes even appearance money for stars. Victory in the men's sprint at the Panathenaic Games brought a prize of 100 amphoras of olive oil (the equivalent of $67,000).

Debate continues on the class origins and social status and mobility of athletes. Competitors from lower classes were not excluded but, even with the proliferation of material rewards, they

were at a disadvantage concerning leisure time and finances for training and travel. Aristocrats certainly did compete, and later tales of rustics becoming early victors may be romantic fabrications. One epigram, attributed to the poet Simonides, speaks of a victor who used to be a fish porter, but Aristotle comments that the man's accomplishment was exceptional. Some famous athletes, such as Milo and the renowned penthathlete Phayllos, went on to be leaders in war and politics. Often, however, it is impossible to tell if an ancient athlete had status and resources before or because of his victory.

We have no autobiographies or diaries that describe what went through the minds of ancient athletes. At best, commissioned victory odes, epigrams, and statues tell us how athletes wanted to be regarded. From whatever class and however mixed their motives, athletes embraced and espoused a traditional, aristocratic athletic value system with themes of piety, endurance (*ponos*), and humility (*aidos*). Although they accepted material prizes and rewards, ancient athletes referred to them as gifts (*dora*) not wages (*misthos*), matters of glory (*kleos*) not greedful gain (*kerdos*). Aristic scenes of victorious athletes being crowned usually depict them with downcast eyes and a modest posture. Ancient athletes, however, cheated earlier and more often than purists would like to believe. Even Homer mentions foul play and the dangers of excessive competitiveness in the games honoring Patroklos: While spectators wagered and bickered at the finish line, Antilochos nearly caused an accident in the chariot race by driving dangerously and refusing to yield; afterward he and Menelaos nearly came to blows in a dispute over placements and prizes.

Although they swore a sacred oath to abide by the rules, ancient Olympians sought unfair advantages. False starting in a race brought whipping, as did infractions in combat sports. Inscriptions show that as early as the sixth century the judges at Olympia had established rules against cheating in wrestling. An inscription of the last quarter of the sixth century from Olympia declares: "The wrestler shall not break any finger . . . the judge shall punish by striking except on the head . . ." (trans. J. Ebert).

By the fourth century, bronze statues of Zeus, known as Zanes and paid for from fines for lying, bribery, and cheating, lined the route to the Olympic stadium. Pausanias says the first six statues were established in the 98th Olympiad (388 B.C.) when the boxer Eupolos of Thessaly bribed his opponents. An inscription on the base of one of the first statues declares that "an Olympic victory is to be won not by money but by swiftness of foot or strength of body" (trans. S.G. Miller). Inscriptions on other bases similarly urge piety and warn against violations. In A.D. 93 an Alexandrian athlete who arrived late was expelled and fined for lying. He had claimed being delayed by weather when in fact he had been delayed by competing in prize games in Ionia. A fellow Alexandrian exposed his lie and was declared the victor without a fight. Lead curse tablets show that athletes even tried to hex rivals at Isthmia and elsewhere with pleas to underworld deities such as "let them not prevail in running."

Greek athletes also knew stress and pressure. Competing individually, they nonetheless represented their families, communities, and city-states. Carrying the heavy burden of a great investment of effort and emotion onto the track, Olympians gave their all for god and country. Participation was not enough; winning was the only thing. Pindar (518–438 B.C.), the greatest poet of victory odes, says that athletic victory was the greatest height to which mortals can aspire; he also writes of defeated athletes slinking home by back streets.

Victors were feasted and feted at Olympia by relatives and countrymen. Sometimes things got out of hand: Alcibiades, to his discredit, used sacred vessels for a party celebrating his chariot victory. Most ancient Olympians, however, probably would have said that their feelings could not be expressed in words, that their victories were neither won by themselves alone, nor for themselves alone, and that it was all worth it. As ancient Greeks they would have felt an obligation to thank the gods, and as victors they would have felt the urge to celebrate the moment and commemorate the achievement. Most athletes apparently followed traditional customs: a party followed by a dedication of the wreath or a votive to an appropriate deity. Among the many exciting finds at Nemea was a votive pit containing a pentathlete's equipment—an iron discus and javelin points, a lead jumping weight, and a *strigil*—and drinking cups from 550–525 B.C.

More celebrations, songs, and commemorations awaited victors returning home. Sometimes a city would put up a statue of a local victor, and local veneration over time could reach the level of a hero cult. Theagenes of Thasos, who won the boxing (480 B.C.) and *pankration* (476 B.C.) at Olympia, claimed some 1,400 wins in his long career. After his death his city commissioned a statue of him that became the focus of a hero cult. Supposedly an enemy of Theagenes flogged the statue, whereupon it fell on him and killed him. When thrown into the sea, the statue brought famine to Thasos until it was restored. Major victories brought privileges, including free meals and seats of honor at civic gatherings for life. Years later one might still be known as "the athlete" or "the *stadion*-runner." Athletic fame sometimes even brought wartime clemency. During the Peloponnesian War Athens freed without ransom Doreius of Rhodes, a thrice victorious Olympic pankratiast. Alexander the Great, who supposedly disliked athletics, spared the home of Pindar while destroying Thebes in 335, and later freed the Theban Olympic victor Dionysiodoros captured after the Battle of Issus in 333 B.C.

The Greek athlete's world was not without its critics. Protests against the inappropriateness of honors for athletes rather than intellectuals reverberated, with no effect. Aristophanes' *Clouds* laments the passage of the "good old days" of proper and proficient gymnastic education, and the writings of Euripides and Plato contain criticisms and caricatures of athletes as unnatural, overdeveloped, socially burdensome, and unsophisticated louts: "the worst of the thousand ills of Greece." However, the archaeological record—stadiums and gymnasiums, dedications, prizes, and artworks—shows that society at large, then as now, heralded games and athletes as cultural treasures. Even Plato admitted that the majority of Greeks deemed the life of Olympic victors "most happy," and, in his *Myth of Er,* Atalanta chooses the life of an athlete because of its great honors. Ancient Greeks would have agreed with the sentiment expressed in Homer's *Odyssey* that, "There is no greater fame for a man than that which he wins with his footwork or the skills of his hands" (trans. S.G. Miller).

The Athenian Democracy and Its Slaves

'All men are equal...' but some, though excluded from citizenship in classical Athens, were still taken into account through various mechanisms designed to promote stability in the body politic. Dimitris Kyrtatas examines how slaves were not necessarily just menials in the Athenian state.

Dimitris Kyrtatas

Dimitris Kyrtatas is Assistant Professor of Ancient History at the University of Crete and author of Slaves, Slavery and the Slave Mode of Production *(in Greek, Polites, 1987).*

Ancient Greek city-states had too many external enemies to be happy with anything weakening their defensive or offensive capacity. To cope with their internal problems, the Greeks were quite inventive. Colonisation was a successful remedy for land-hunger, which was probably among the principal causes of social discontent. Arbitrators and lawgivers, often called from abroad, were able, on several occasions, to mediate between conflicting factions and secure workable solutions. By exiling political leaders, alone or along with their supporters, Greek cities gave other leaders a good chance of proceeding with their programmes unchallenged. Wars with neighbours may not always have been victorious, but even when they did not lead to the annexation of productive land, they normally strengthened the internal front. Furthermore, ritual purifications, religious festivities and athletic contests served, among other purposes, the cause of civic cohesion.

The most inventive and lasting protection against threatened internal strife, however, was the establishment of majority rule. The originality of this device, which was the essence, though not the exclusive privilege, of Athenian democracy, lay in its ability to keep a community united, without evading the issues that divided it. Far from suppressing existing differences, a political system working on the principle of majority rule could accommodate diametrically opposed views. All sides would be allowed to advance their arguments and, at the peak of the debate, when everything would suggest that the community was on the verge of an open conflict, everybody was prepared to accept the verdict of the majority. Those in favour of peace were ready to lead an expedition; those who had argued for the capital punishment of an accused person were ready to accept him as a full member of the community.

The ability of a community to reunite so speedily after a formal declaration of a split within it is impressive. Behind this consensus there must have functioned very powerful factors. Whatever the origins of these factors, by the fifth century they were in full operative force. At the height of its development, when Athenian democracy was self-assured and optimistic, it welcomed this 'good division' as a sign of a healthy constitution.

Decision-making by majority rule, however, was strictly located within the limits of a citizen body. In Athens, as elsewhere, it was only full citizens who were entitled to participate 'in Judgement and Authority', as Aristotle formulated it in his *Politics* (1275a). Slaves and foreigners, including those with permanent residence, were excluded—and so were, of course, women and children. This simple fact, acknowledged theoretically by most scholars, though often forgotten thereafter in their investigations, is deeply problematic. A city was interested in securing the unity of its total population, not just of its privileged élite. *Pace* Aristophanes, the citizens of Athens had no reason to question the loyalty of their women and children, and the same held true for resident foreigners, called metics. Such foreigners had chosen to live in Athens of their own free will, and some of them had prospered in the great city for generations. But a reasonable question to ask is whether the Athenians expected some kind of loyalty from their slaves as well. Did they feel that living in a democratic city had positive effects upon their slaves or did they rely exclusively upon their coercive institutions to secure their domination?

Political oratory suggests that slaves were regarded as natural enemies of the political order. They were kept in bondage in accordance with the laws and customs of the city and they were, therefore, expected to hate the system that maintained their servile status. This view must have been shared by most Athenians, though not without significant qualifications. Political oratory was concerned with the behaviour of citizens, not slaves. The point made by the orators was that citizens of servile origin should never be trusted. In particular, those among them aspiring to leading positions were a potential threat to the community's interests. By proving that a politician had servile or even servile-like origins, his opponents thought that they were disqualifying him from serving his city.

Given the purpose of the argument, it is understandable that only the negative side of a slave's feelings was considered. There was at all times plenty of evidence reminding every master how dangerous slaves could be. Xenophon and Plato, among others, gave vivid accounts of the terror a master was expected to experience if ever he was left to confront his slaves alone (*Hieron* 4.3; *Republic* 9.578d-9a). Given the opportunity, as Thucydides records in his account of the Peloponnesian War, slaves would run away to join the enemy camp (7.27). Significantly, even though there were no large-scale slave rebellions in classical Athens, masters were being constantly reminded that they should take precautions. One piece of advice, the neglect of which proved disastrous in Roman times, was that a master should never keep together large numbers of slaves of the same nationality.

Under normal circumstances, however, the Athenians had no major problems with their slaves. Slaves were to be found in most households occupied with almost any kind of service. Some were trusted to live on their own or even to take charge of their masters' affairs. Numbers of slaves were constantly being manumitted. Occasionally, an emancipated slave would be granted citizenship status. Admittedly, this was very rare, but the fear of the orators about politicians with servile origins would have been ungrounded had such politicians never existed. In fact, a comprehensive investigation of the ancient sources reveals that the Athenians had, to some extent, ambivalent feelings towards their slaves. Besides regarding them as the natural enemies of their democratic order, there are also signs that, sometimes, they regarded them as potential allies.

Faithful slaves often made their appearance on stage. Expressions much as, 'master's luck is mine' (*Agamemnon* 32) or 'to a slave his master's affairs mean

a great deal' (*Helen* 728) are quite common in classical tragedy. An Athenian in Plato's *Laws* (776d) was aware of stories according to which slaves had saved their masters along with their family and property. Naturally, such accounts are not representative of the feelings of real slaves—although we should not rush to the conclusion that no such slaves ever existed. But it is interesting to observe that the Athenians were happy to believe that they were often surrounded by trusty or even friendly slaves.

More significantly, some positive remarks are also made about slaves in a political context. The fact is that slaves seem to have been present in almost all the most important developments in the history of the democracy. Already in the early sixth century, Solon's political reforms prohibited loans on the security of the person, and all Athenian debt-bondsmen were liberated. Debt-bondsmen (whom we may loosely think of as serfs) were not slaves in the strict sense, but under certain circumstances some Athenian citizens were liable to seizure and could be sold along with their children. Solon is also credited with bringing back to the city such Athenians as had been sold abroad. These reforms would not have made Athenians more attractive to slaves at large. The liberation of Athenian bondsmen was followed by mass importation of foreign slaves who had no reason to expect similar treatment in the future. The collective memory preserved, however, that at the very foundation of the first real constitution (which Athenians were later to identify with the origins of their democracy) former bondsmen and slaves were incorporated into the citizen body. Far from suppressing the tradition, the Athenians recorded it with pride.

The establishment of the democracy at the end of the sixth century was also associated with a benevolent attitude towards slaves. Dealing with the problems of citizenship rights, Aristotle in the *Politics* gives as an example the case of Athens 'after the expulsion of the tyrants, when Kleisthenes made many foreigners and slaves citizens by enrolling them in the tribes' (1275b). The idea was, of course, that such enrolment strengthened the democratic side against the aristocrats. Modern scholars have doubts about this passage, but it must have seemed reasonable enough to Athenian readers. According to Thucydides (3.73), in 427 the slaves of Kerkyra had

also sided with the democrats against the oligarchs, when, in their conflict, both parties were appealing to them for support.

In conditions of extreme danger, slaves were called upon to aid the Athenians against external threats. One such occasion was the battle of Marathon. The normal procedure would be to free the slaves in advance. After the battle those of them who had died were buried with honour, but separately from the citizens. The effects of emancipation would not have been negligible, but they were hardly adequate under the circumstances. In return for their freedom, slaves were expected to risk their lives. Although the evidence is meagre, there are reasons to believe that by allowing them to fight at their side (mostly as rowers), masters were hoping to see some kind of enthusiasm on the part of their former slaves.

The way metics were encouraged at wartime may be, to a degree, relevant. Thucydides gives the details of a battle that was to prove decisive in the Peloponnesian War (7.63). Addressing himself to the metics participating in the Sicilian expedition, the Athenian general, Nicias, made a number of remarks. He reminded them of the honours they had been receiving throughout Greece and of the advantages of the empire they were enjoying, as if they were Athenians, although, in fact, they simply spoke their language and imitated their manners. The general was, therefore, expecting them not to betray the Athenians in a time of need. That metics fighting along with full citizens had to be addressed in such a fashion is understandable. But it is also reasonable to expect that ex-slave combatants would have been encouraged in some similar way. What sort of help could the Athenians expect from their former slaves if they did not have something persuasive to tell them? For the present argument, it makes little difference that the numbers of such slaves were small. The important fact is that they existed and that their generals would have found the appropriate rhetoric to address them.

In *406* BC metics and slaves were fighting on Athenian ships in the naval battle of Arginusae. As usual under such circumstances, slaves were manumitted, but this time they were also promised, along with the metics, Athenian and Plataean citizenship. The Athenians won an important victory against the Spartans and did not neglect to reward those who had helped them row the ships. The incident seems to have made a great impression, since Aristophanes pays an unusual tribute to the slaves who had 'fought in the naval battle'. In his *Frogs* (190-1), he makes Charon refuse to ferry over the river Styx to the underworld any slave other than them. The whole affair was a very rare occurrence, but not altogether exceptional.

Slaves became important once more in a later act of the democratic drama. In 404 the Peloponnesian War ended with the humiliation of the Athenians by the Spartans. Their long walls and their league were dissolved and their democracy dismantled. For a brief period a tyranny was imposed. Soon after, however, through a full-scale social and political uprising, democratic rule was restored. Important details are given in Aristotle's *Athenian Constitution* (40.2). In their struggle, the democrats were aided by metics and slaves. Just before the election of the new archons, a motion was passed in the Assembly 'which was to give a share in the citizenship to all who had joined in the return from the Piraeus, some of whom were palpably slaves'. The decree was eventually annulled and non-citizens were less generously rewarded. In this case slaves may not have been incorporated into the citizen body. The conscription of metics and slaves to the democratic front, however, remains a fact, and so does the intention that existed among many Athenians to grant them citizenship status.

The evidence presented above should not be over-estimated The incidents recorded were few and untypical. Overall, the slaves in Athens did not exhibit true respect towards their masters and their masters' democracy. For the most part they were never really given the opportunity to express their true feelings. It is characteristic of the mentality of the Athenians that the testimony of slaves in court was only accepted when they were under torture. Even if they were ever allowed to express themselves freely, it is hardly likely that they would have spoken highly of the democracy. Athenians were obviously aware of this reality. They knew that the general attitude of their slaves was hostile and that not much could be expected from them and their descendants. This plain and clear reality, however, does not make the cases of co-operation between citizens and slaves difficult to explain. Among

the thousands of slaves in democratic Athens at any given time, it would not have been hard to find some with respect for their masters. Others would have calculated that their chances of success were greater than their risks.

Manumission alone would have been a great incentive. Aristotle was quite explicit in the *Politics* (1330a). He argued that 'it is a good thing that all slaves should have before them the prospect of receiving their freedom as a reward'. His expectation was, obviously, that with the reward in their minds, slaves would work harder and exhibit some kind of respect towards their masters as well as towards the city, its customs and its laws. The Athenians did not follow the suggestion, but they constantly manumitted small numbers of slaves nevertheless. Most among them were domestics and artisans, some of whom would have been living on their own. Upward social mobility, from slave to metic and from metic to citizen, minimal though it must have been, was an acknowledged fact.

What is somewhat perplexing is the willingness of the Athenians to record the incidents in which they had been aided by their slaves. As is clearly shown from the funeral oration attributed to Perikles, in standardised appraisals of the city and its constitution there was normally only a place for citizens and hardly any for their women. Slaves were not so much as mentioned. Why was it that the Athenians made some exceptions to this rule? And why was it that these exceptions were related to the most important developments in the history of the democracy?

As the Athenians saw things, their democratic state was preferable for slaves to the Spartan state, or any other state with a less democratic constitution than their own. According to one witness known as Old Oligarch, 'slaves and metics in Athens lead a singularly undisciplined life; one may not strike them there, nor will a slave step aside for you'. The anonymous author of this pamphlet had an anti-democratic mentality and was clearly grossly exaggerating. He claimed that in Athens slaves 'live in luxury, and some of them in considerable magnificence' and went as far as to argue that 'in the matter of free speech we have put slaves and free men on equal terms' (1.10-2). The account cannot be taken literally, but it may reflect a widespread myth.

The Athenians had no problem in acknowledging the exploitation of their slaves. They had no desire to convince slaves that they were their equals and they would have had no chance of succeeding had they made such an attempt. The myth was not so much concerned with class relations as it was with the democracy. The anonymous author was not attacking slaves; he was attacking the constitution that granted them what seemed to him unacceptable privileges. Other Athenians were happier with the 'general benevolence' of their democracy.

In his *Poroi*, Xenophon advanced a scheme that would improve, in his opinion, the Athenian economy. If it were followed, he argued, all citizens would profit. To begin with, metics and foreign traders should be treated with more respect. Some should be honoured by the city. All should be encouraged to carry on their enterprises in ways benefiting to them as well as to the Athenians. Furthermore, the Athenian economy, which was suffering after the end of the Peloponnesian War, would improve if the city invested in more than a thousand slaves. All of them would be hired out to individual entrepreneurs to be employed in the silver mines of Laurion. Regarding slaves, the last thing which Xenophon had in mind was to conceal the bare fact of exploitation.

Nothing of what he writes gives the impression that those slaves could ever be integrated into Athenian society and life. The work they performed was probably the worst a slave ever did in Athens. As he admits, a slave would work in the mines for as long as he lasted. In due course he would have to be replaced by a younger one—no thought of family relations, manumission, good clothing or treatment, let alone 'freedom of speech'. In fact, to protect the city from fraud, the slaves would be branded as state property.

Xenophon's pamphlet has no clear political aims. It is exclusively concerned with the physical subsistence of the city and it addresses problems of production and trade. Consequently it deals with metics, traders, artisans and slaves. Yet, at the very end of the long arguments it does not avoid a reference to war, a political act *par excellence*. What it says is revealing. The value of slaves, it argues, is twofold. On the one hand they are productive; on the other they can fight. If circumstances demand, even the most oppressed slaves can be armed:

> For what instrument is more serviceable for war than men. We should have enough of them to supply crews to many ships of the state; and many men available for service in the ranks as infantry could press the enemy hard, if they were treated with consideration (42).

It is unlikely that Xenophon or any other Athenian statesman believed that branded slaves working in the silver mines under exceedingly harsh conditions would fight in earnest for the citizens' cause. The idea, however, was not altogether absurd. The Athenians recorded and publicised the cases in which they had been aided with profit by their slaves. The accounts were clearly of greater importance to them than they were to the slaves. They strengthened their sense of security and they reassured them that at a deep level the city was united. It could face its external enemies without real dangers from within. The contrast with Sparta could

hardly be more obvious, as the helots would never miss an opportunity to revolt and were a greater threat than help whenever they were armed. It was otherwise in Athens. Given the proper incentives, numbers of slaves would not only fight but, having fought, would not pose any problem to the city. In Athens, emancipated slaves could be easily incorporated into the free population and even into the citizen body. Potentially, the democratic system was open to anyone the citizens cared to invite.

Athenians were always reluctant to give slaves their freedom, and even more reluctant to grant citizenship rights. They knew, however, that they could do both easily whenever they wished. This, they thought, was one of the advantages of their constitution. They therefore kept reminding themselves of the occasions on which they had done so with profit. Perhaps they also wanted their slaves to know about these occasions. What the slaves thought is difficult to say. Under conditions of slavery it is unlikely that they bothered to meditate on the advantages of democ-

racy. As free men, however, they would have certainly preferred to live in democratic Athens. Whatever the politicians may have argued in their debates, the democratic constitution gave all citizens the same rights. Even better, as Perikles is reported to have claimed, the system was called a democracy because it served the interests not of the few but of the majority (2.37).

FOR FURTHER READING:

The best introductions to democracy and slavery are Aristotle's *Politics* (Penguin, 1962) and *The Athenian Constitution* (Penguin, 1984). For modern discussions see G. E. M. de Ste. Croix, *The Class Struggle in the Ancient Greek World* (Duckworth, 1981) and M. I. Finley, *Ancient Slavery and Modern Ideology* (Chatto and Windus, 1980); important points are also made by Nicole Loraux, *The Invention of Athens* (Harvard University Press, 1986) and Josiah Ober, *Mass and Elite in Democratic Athens* (Princeton University Press, 1989). For comparison with the helots of Sparta it is useful to consult Paul Cartledge, *Agesilaos and the Crisis of Sparta* (Duckworth, 1987).

Re-running Marathon

The Battle of Marathon has long been presented as the decisive moment at which Greeks—led by the newly democratic Athenians—gained the upper hand over the despotic Persians. **Barry Baldwin** *reappraises the battle, and explains why it is still a byword for endurance.*

The mountains look on Marathon,
And Marathon looks on the sea.
And musing there an hour alone,
I dreamed that Greece might still be free,
For standing on the Persian's grave,
I could not deem myself a slave.

(Lord Byron, *The Isles of Greece*)

To Greeks and Romans, the battle of Marathon in 490 BC tended to be the ultimate proof of courage, patriotism, and that the gods (despite Napoleon) are not always on the side of the big battalions. Traditionally it has been seen as a turning-point, not just in ancient history. Had Marathon gone the other way, classical Greek civilisation would have been stifled, and we would not have the pleasures and profits of Greek art, literature and thought.

In his *Histories,* written a generation or so after the Persian Wars, Herodotus produced the classic account of the campaign, but, in the words of the classicist and novelist Frederic Raphael, 'Herodotus contributed hugely to the swelling of Greek heads. He enjoyed a breakthrough success when he recited his work at Athens. Paid ten talents and made an honorary citizen for his PR work on behalf of the Athenians, he was the first man to prove that history had a market, if you told the right stories.'

Herodotus traced the origin of the Graeco-Persian conflicts back to the Trojan War. We shall not here follow him all that distance, but to the reign of Cyrus, founder and first ruler (559–530 BC) of the Achaemenid Persian Empire. After his conquests of Lydia (in western Asia Minor) and Babylonia and the cap-

ture of their respective capitals Sardis (546 BC) and Babylon (539 BC), Cyrus had within twenty years acquired an empire the largest the world had yet seen. He spent his last eight years organising these new possessions into an efficient working order. He carved the empire into twenty provinces, each governed by a local plenipotentiary known as a satrap. Two of these districts contained Greek subjects: Lydia subsumed the Ionian coastline, whilst Phrygia embraced the Dardanelles, the Propontis and the Black Sea's southern littoral—all areas colonised by Greek cities. For many Greeks, rule by Persia rather than Lydia made no difference to their lives. Herodotus reports Cyrus' death with brisk neutrality and never assails him as a despot. By the fourth century, he was idealised by the pro-Spartan military adventurer Xenophon, who had sold his own mercenary sword to a later Cyrus in a dynastic civil war.

Nevertheless, when Cyrus attempted to drive a wedge between the powerful Miletus and the other Ionian islands, the latter Greeks appealed to Sparta for help. Not for the last time, the Spartans refused assistance to their overseas compatriots. But they did send a single ship to see what was going on; also an ambassador was dispatched to Sardis to warn the king to keep his hands off the Greek cities or risk Spartan displeasure. An astonished Cyrus asked who these impudent Spartans were and how many men did they have to back up such a demand. Upon being informed, he made a crisp response: 'I have never yet been afraid of men who have a special meeting-place in the centre of their city

where they swear this and that and cheat each other'. Herodotus took this to be scorn of the free market and barter systems of the Greek agora; but it may also reflect a king's suspicion of incipient democracy.

The short reign (530–522 BC) of Cambyses was mainly concentrated on the Persian conquest of Egypt, but when Cyprus and Phoenician states submitted to him the Persians inherited a much-needed navy. It was the ambition and drive of his successor Darius I (522–486 BC) that generated the conflicts that would lead to Marathon. He had in mind the conquest of the Pontic-Caspian steppes from the Danube to the river Jaxartes. The execution of Polycrates, tyrant of the Ionian city of Samos, was followed by a large Persian army crossing the Danube in 513 BC, invading the northern steppes of Scythia. It also swept through Thrace and took control of the vital ports of Byzantium and Chalcedon at the Black Sea entrance to the Propontis. Darius was now a threat both to the military security and grain supplies of mainland Greece.

By 499 BC Miletus and the other Ionians who had helped Darius cross the Danube now broke out into armed revolt against him, with Miletus' exiled ruler Aristagoras appealing both to Sparta and Athens for help. The reactions of these two cities were complicated by the recent military and political involvements of Sparta in Athenian domestic politics, the outcomes of which had been the expulsion of the tyrant Hippias and the implementation of Cleisthenes' democratic reforms in Athens. The Spartan King Cleomenes (who had ousted Hippias)

This article first appeared in *History Today*, May 1998, pp. 44-49. © 1998 by History Today, Ltd. Reprinted by permission.

laughed the suppliant Aristagoras out of the room when he unwisely confessed that armed assistance would take the Spartans a good three months march inland. Aristagoras had learned his lesson. He moved on to Athens and by a combination of wild promises and economy with the truth (claiming the Persians would be easily beaten since they fought without shields and spears) persuaded the Assembly to send help. Herodotus commented wryly: 'apparently it is easier to dupe a crowd than an individual', adding 'the sailing of the Athenian fleet was the beginning of trouble, not only for Greece, but for the rest of the world'.

The twenty ships sent by Athens were joined by five from the small city of Eretria which felt it owed a debt of honour to Miletus for having taken their side in a previous local war. By 494 BC Darius had crushed the uprising. A good measure of Athenian alarm is what happened to the playwright Phrynichus when in the following year he presented what was probably the first-ever historical drama on the Athenian stage, *The Capture Of Miletus*. The audience was reduced to tears of grief and shame, the play was banned, and its author heavily fined 'for reminding the Athenians of their misfortunes'—a far cry from the reception accorded some twenty years later to Aeschylus' triumphalist *The Persians*. However, their capture and burning of Sardis in 498 BC had been a great coup for the Greeks and a major embarrassment for the Persians.

Early in the summer of 490 BC, Darius launched his invasion of Greece. Under the command of his nephew Artaphernes and the Median admiral Datis, this armada allegedly consisted of 600 ships (troop and transport, provided and manned by subject allies) and an unspecified number of Persian infantry and cavalry, described by Herodotus as 'powerful and well-equipped'. Despite the fibs of Aristagoras, the Persian infantry did have proper weapons. As to cavalry, the Persians had developed the then novelty of special horse-transport vessels to get them across the sea.

The ostensible targets were Athens and Eretria—a reprisal for their role in the Ionian Revolt—but few doubted that all of Greece was the ultimate ambition. Darius had indeed already sent to individual cities his demands for earth and water, the traditional tokens of surrender. Many complied, but when the Persian ambassadors came to Athens they

were gaoled; at Sparta they were flung down a well, the inhabitants remarking that if they wanted earth and water that was the place to find them.

Having captured a number of other Greek cities and islands en route, the Persians besieged Eretria which succumbed after six days, weakened from within by party political strife and a pro-Persian faction which betrayed the city. A few days later, the Persians sailed for Attica, 'in high spirits and confident' (Herodotus). Marathon was selected as the best spot to invade, being closest to Eretria and also the most suitable for cavalry manoeuvres. At least, such was the advice of Hippias who was with this Persian force which he hoped would restore him to power. It was here that his father Pisistratus had landed in 546 for his successful bid for the tyranny in Athens.

Hippias was also buoyed up by a dream in which he was in bed with his mother. He took this to mean he would return to Athens, regain power, and die peacefully at home in his old age. Alas, poor Hippias! As he was superintending the Persian disembarkation at Marathon, he was seized with a violent fit of coughing and sneezing which dislodged one of his many loose teeth. Having failed to find it in the sand, Hippias sadly remarked that this was the only part of him fated to lie in native soil.

Athenian resistance was led by ten generals. The outstanding personality among them was Miltiades. He was connected to Athens through family, though he had been a tyrant elsewhere, in the Chersonese area of Greece. Miltiades' own father had been banished from Athens by Hippias' father, Pisistratus. Further cachet accrued to him from his father's triple Olympic chariot-racing victories, a feat otherwise accomplished only by the Spartan Evagoras.

Despite this, an ex-tyrant was out of place in the new democratic atmosphere of Athens after Cleisthenes. Indeed, Miltiades' personal enemies managed to launch a prosecution against him for 'past crimes' in the Chersonese, but under the looming threat of invasion, proceedings were quashed and he was elected to the board of generals. No doubt Miltiades drew heavily on the fact that back in 513 BC he had tried to thwart Darius by destroying his bridge across the Danube while the king was cut off in Scythia. The plan had failed, thanks to opposition from the top Ionian

leaders. Still, according to his admiring Roman biographer Nepos, the scheme had won him the reputation of being 'a friend of liberty'.

As a democratic reformer, Cleisthenes himself has been seen by some to be more of an opportunist than an ideologue. He had been restored from exile to Athens by Spartan arms and he rushed some spokesmen off to Sardis to gain Persian recognition and a formal alliance to keep himself in power. Still, up to a point, this can be excused: he knew the exiled Hippias was already bidding for the same support.

In 490 BC, Athenian democracy introduced by Cleisthenes in 509–7 still looked like a frail bloom. Though both fought at Marathon with distinction, Aristides and Themistocles, the men most associated with Athenian democracy, would not have their brightest days in the sun until the next war, against Xerxes. Herodotus' says nothing about civilian politicians or the Assembly during the Marathon crisis: everything is decided by the generals.

A message for help was sent from Athens to Sparta with the runner Pheidippides. According to Herodotus, Pheidippides covered the 156 miles in one day, being a professional long-distance runner. This probably means that he carried messages for a living. In a recent re-creation, an amateur Greek runner, a nightwatchman, won by completing the distance in twenty-one hours, fifty-three minutes, suitably crossing a finishing-line marked by the statue of an ancient Spartan king. A version by the satirist Lucian (second century AD) had Pheidippides run straight back to Marathon to join the battle, then immediately to Athens (twenty-six miles and a bit, hence the modern marathon distance) to announce the victory before—suitably —dropping dead.

The Spartans were impressed by Pheidippides' running, his bad news, and his stirring appeal, reported verbatim by Herodotus:

> Men of Sparta, the Athenians ask you to help them, and not to stand by while the most ancient city of Greece is crushed and subdued by a foreign invader; for even now Eretria has been enslaved, and Greece is the weaker by the loss of one noble city.

But they refused to help, at least immediately, on religious grounds: they had to wait until the next full moon to complete an important local ceremony (the Carneia) in honour of Apollo. A question rarely asked, but surely obvious in the light of the 1973 Yom Kippur War, is: did the Persians know of this, via Hippias, and time their invasion accordingly? Plato, in *The Laws,* attributes the Spartan delay either to their being distracted by a war with Messene 'or some other reason—I'm not aware of any information being given on the point'. Is this just dramatic persiflage, or veiled ridicule of the lunar explanation? It is inconceivable that Plato would not know Herodotus' version. But lunar superstitions were not restricted to the Spartans—an Athenian army in Sicily fatally delayed because of one—and there was the awkward truth that virtually all of the Greeks stayed out of the campaign. This national disgrace would be largely repeated in the second and much bigger war a decade later. Of the 700 or so independent city states that made up Greece at the time, only thirty-one have their names inscribed on the war memorial set up to honour the victory over Xerxes in 480 BC.

Athens, however, did not stand by herself. In gratitude for previous services rendered, the little central Greek town of Plataea came to her help—Plataea was to be ruthlessly destroyed sixty years later in the Peloponnesian civil war.

The generals were divided over strategy. Five opposed any offensive urging a waiting game. They knew the enemy had chosen the site; to attack might play into Persian hands. There was also the chance of eventual help from Sparta. But the others were swayed by a fiery Death or Glory speech from Miltiades, including the War Archon (Minister) Callimachus who gave his support. In the battle Callimachus, commanded (by tradition) the right wing, the Plataeans held the left, leaving—as often in ancient engagement—a deliberately weak centre.

According to Herodotus, the Greeks charged 'at a run' (*dromo* is his operative word) from just over a mile away from the Persians, a first in their military history. And a stupid move, to judge from a recent American re-enactment: the cardiovascular strain and energy requirements make such a run impossible. No wonder Herodotus reports the Persians were delighted to see the Greek charge, calling it 'lunacy'. Still, in terms

of metabolic energy cost, a jog-trot could have been feasible: the heroic story would grow in the telling and *dromo* may be more a technical term than a literal one.

The struggle was protracted in this 'never to be forgotten' fight (Herodotus). The weak Athenian-Plataean centre fell back, but both wings prevailed. The Persians were driven back towards their ships, seven of which were captured, at the cost of Callimachus' life. Herodotus says he died in the last phase of the battle, fighting bravely. The memory of Callimachus, dimmed over the centuries, has been refurbished by the recent discovery of the victory statue with an inscription commemorating his role.

Another distinguished casualty was Cynegeirus, brother of the playwright Aeschylus. Cynegeirus clung to a Persian ship until one hand was severed by an axe blow.

A famous puzzle attends the battle. Why are Persian cavalry not mentioned in Herodotus' account? Some think the horses were kept on, or returned to, the ships, ready for a dash on Athens. Others have them grazing up on the northern part of the plain, thus missing the conflict. A Byzantine encyclopaedia, compiled around AD 1000, explains the proverb 'The Cavalry Aren't Here' by saying that just before dawn some Ionian Greeks from the Persian side slipped across to the Athenian camp, and told their compatriots that the Persian horses were away, so this was the moment to attack. Nepos mentions that the Greeks were camped where the terrain was broken by bushes and trees, hence the Persians may simply have decided against using them. This rather invalidates Hippias' reason for choosing Marathon. Another possibility is that the horses, never good travellers on water, were ill from the voyage and so unusable. A final theory is simplest of all: the horses were there, and took part, but Herodotus did not consider it worth mentioning.

The Persians then sailed fast around Cape Sunion, hoping to capture Athens itself. Some said they were drawn by a flashing shield signal from within the city by a group of pro-tyrant sympathisers, namely the Alcmaeonidae family of political aristocrats. Herodotus accepts the incident, but not the explanation, going out of his way to acquit the Alcmaeonidae of treason. Assuming such a signal could even be seen

and deciphered, we are better employed asking what it meant: Invade Now? or The Plot Has Failed? Whatever the truth, after lingering a few days, the Persian fleet withdrew. Artaphernes and Datis returned to the Persian capital of Susa with little to show for their expedition but some prisoners-of-war from Eretria whom Darius treated with mercy, settling them in new homes within his empire. The king, in Herodotus' words, was dismayed but not deterred by his setback and spent the next three years preparing a second, bigger armada. Death, however, cut him off, and it was left to his son and successor Xerxes to mount the second invasion. But that is another story.

6,400 Persians fell. For them, there is no monument. Pausanias looked in vain for a grave, concluding that the Athenians must have dumped their corpses into a pit. On the Greek side, 192 Athenians and an unspecified number of Plataeans gave their lives. In 1970, the archaeologist Spyridon Marinatos discovered the Plataean burial mound a mile west of the Athenian one. He claimed its position supports Herodotus' statement that the Plataeans comprised the left wing of the infantry line. Its most poignant content was a clay jar in which was the skeleton, with weapons, of a ten-year-old boy. Marinatos unearthed 'eleven scores of bodies', then stopped and declared that the tomb should be left as a monument to the war dead of all ages.

Some Greek artistic depictions and later legends ascribed a role and personal appearances upon the battlefield to the Olympian gods, a theophanous tradition that extends from Homer's *Iliad* to the Angel of Mons in the First World War. Pausanias claimed that the plain of Marathon echoes every night with the sound of horses whinnying and men fighting. There is none of this in Herodotus, but he does relate one fine tale:

> During the action, a very strange thing happened. Epizelus, the son of Cuphagoras, an Athenian soldier, was fighting gallantly when he suddenly lost the sight of both eyes, though nothing had touched him at all—neither sword nor spear nor missile. From that time he remained blind for the rest of his life. I am told that he used to say, when talking about what had happened to him, that he thought he was opposed by a huge

man in heavy armour whose beard overshadowed his shield; but this phantom passed by him and struck down the soldier at his side.

The full moon came, and with it the Spartans, marching 140 miles in three days in full armour. They observed the Persian dead, remarked 'the Athenians have done well', and marched back home again. Shortly afterwards, the Athenians rewarded Miltiades by fining him fifty talents (an enormous sum of money) for 'defrauding the people'—he had failed in a subsequent military operation. The hero of Marathon was prosecuted as he lay in court on a stretcher, thanks to a leg smashed in action and turned gangrenous. His prosecutor was Xanthippus, father of Pericles. This shameful (not a word found in Herodotus' cool account—I prefer the indignation of Nepos) episode is well glossed by the cynical remark of the father of Themistocles who was himself destined to be distinguished in, then disgraced after, the war against Xerxes. Pointing out to his son some old ships rotting on the beach, he observed that the Athenians treated their leaders in the same way, dumping them when they had served their purpose.

Herodotus viewed the battle more as the end of the Ionian Revolt than the beginning of the Persian Wars proper. Although unstinting with his praise, he does not pile up superlatives on the scale of his accounts of Salamis (a sea victory for which Athens provided half the fleet, but Sparta the commander), or Thermopylae and Plataea —victories on land against Xerxes redounding most to the glory of Sparta. Similarly, Themistocles refused to celebrate the result, says Plutarch, warning his fellow-Athenians that Marathon was not the end but only a prelude to a far greater struggle. Such a linkage is implicit in the mini-epic poem written between 478 and 468 BC by Simonides, fragments of which were found and published as re-

cently as 1992, incorporating both invasions. It is explicit in *The Persians* of Aeschylus, in an exchange between Darius' widow, Atossa, and a Persian councillor who attributes the Athenian victory to their democratic system— free men versus vassals. Aeschylus reduces the Spartan contribution to Xerxes' defeat to a single mention of Dorian spears.

Aristophanes has a couple of set-pieces (*Acharnians* and *Clouds*) on the men of Marathon. In his *Laws,* Plato makes an Athenian interlocutor claim that although the sea battles of Artemisium and Salamis saved the Greeks, it was the land battles of Marathon and Plataea that improved them. He, too, sees Marathon as a link in a chain of events: it got the Greeks out of danger, Plataea finally saved them. For his part, Aristotle (*Politics*) maintains that their sea victories over the Persians gave the Athenian people an inflated view of themselves, and this came to impair their judgement when choosing leaders.

During the Roman period, Marathon became more rather than less exalted. Pausanias asserts that the local people of Attica worshipped its battle heroes as divine. He is one of several later writers to claim that Aeschylus at the end of his life preferred to commemorate his presence at Marathon rather than that at Salamis or his poetic fame, leaving an epigram which boasts that the witnesses of his manhood were the trees of Marathon and the Persians who landed there. Nepos, the Roman biographer of Miltiades, commented that: 'the battle of Marathon is a great monument to valour; never have so few performed so well in the face of so many'.

Samuel Johnson later observed, 'that man is little to be envied, whose patriotism would not gain force upon the plain of Marathon'. To John Stuart Mill, 'the battle of Marathon, even as an event in English history, is more important than the battle of Hastings'. In *Childe Harold's Pilgrimage,* Byron wrote of the day 'when Marathon became a magic

word'. Sir Edward Creasey in 1851 (*Fifteen Decisive Battles Of The World, Extending From Marathon to Waterloo*) thought that Marathon 'secured for mankind the intellectual treasures of Athens, the liberal enlightenment, the great principles of European civilisation'.

Some of this is overheated. Assuming the Greeks went on to win the final conflict it is probably fair to say that the men of Marathon would have been almost as celebrated had they lost the battle. The best synthesis of the various verdicts, ancient and modern, is this one by Peter Green:

> Marathon, practically speaking, was no kind of final solution: it merely postponed the day of reckoning. On the other hand, this unprecedented victory gave an enormous boost to Athenian morale. It showed that a well-trained Greek army could beat the Persians on land—something the Ionians had never contrived to do. Psychologically speaking, the legend became almost more important than the actual battle.

FOR FURTHER READING:

A.R. Burn, *Persia and the Greeks: the Defence of the West 546–478 BC* (Edward Arnold, 1962); J.A.S. Evans, 'Herodotus and Marathon', *Florilegium 6* (1984), 1–26; P. Green, *The Greco-Persian Wars* (University of California Press, 1997); C. Hignett, *Xerxes' Invasion of Greece* (Clarendon Press, 1963); J.F. Lazenby, *The Defence of Greece: 490–478 BC* (Arts & Phillips, 1993); W.K. Pritchett, *Marathon* (University of California Press, 1960).

Barry Baldwin *is Emeritus Professor of Classics and Fellow of the Royal Society of Canada. He is editor of* The Latin and Greek Poems of Samuel Johnson *(Duckworth, 1995).*

Love and Death in Ancient Greece

Catching him in the act, an obscure citizen of Athens slew his wife's lover. But was it a crime of passion—or premeditated murder?

Kenneth Cavander

Euphiletos was tired. He had been out in the country all day attending to business, and now he was home trying to get some sleep, and the baby was crying. His house was on two floors; the baby slept with a maid on the first floor; above, there was a combined living-dining-sleeping area for him and his wife. Euphiletos told his wife to go downstairs and nurse the baby. She protested that she wanted to be with him; she'd missed him while he was in the country—or did he just want to get rid of her so that he could make a pass at the maid, as he had the time he got drunk? Euphiletos laughed at that and at last his wife agreed to go downstairs and hush the child, but she insisted on locking the door to their room. Euphiletos turned over and went back to sleep. It never occurred to him to ask why his wife had gone through the charade of keeping him away from the maid, or why she had spent the rest of the night downstairs. But a few days later something happened that made him ask these questions, and by the end of the month a man was dead, killed in full view of a crowd of neighbors and friends.

This drama took place nearly two thousand five hundred years ago in ancient Athens. The characters were none of the brilliant and celebrated figures of the times—Socrates, Plato, Euripides, Aristophanes, Alcibiades—but members of the Athenian lower-middle class, obscure people who receded into the shadows of history. Their story is a soap opera compared to the grander tragedies being played out at the festivals of

Dionysos in the theater cut into the slopes of the Acropolis.

By a quirk of fate and an accident of politics the speech written for the murder trial that climaxes this story was the work of a man named Lysias. As a boy, Lysias sat in the company of Plato and Socrates, who often visited his father's house. As an adult, he was active in politics, and when a coup by the opposition party sent his family into exile, his property was confiscated and he narrowly escaped with his life. But a countercoup soon allowed him to return to Athens, and Lysias, now without a livelihood, had to find a profession.

He found one in the Athenian legal system. Athenian law was complex and attorneys were unknown; every citizen had to prosecute or defend himself in person. As a result, a class of professional legal advisers emerged that made a living supplying litigants with cogent, legally sound briefs. In time, Lysias became one of the most sought-after of these speech writers and several examples of his elegant and literate Greek style have been preserved, including the speech written for the defendant in this case.

Euphiletos, like many Athenians of modest means, lived in a small house in the city and commuted to the country to attend to his farm or market garden. He cannot have been well-off, for his house had the minimum number of slaves— one. Even a sausage seller or baker had at least one slave. Euphiletos had recently married and he was a trusting husband, so he said, giving his wife any-

thing she asked for, never questioning her movements, trying to please her in every possible way. The most exciting event in the marriage was the birth of their child, whom his wife nursed herself. But the most significant event was the death of his mother: the whole family attended the funeral and, although Euphiletos did not know it at the time, his marriage was laid to rest that day along with his mother.

After the birth of their child Euphiletos and his wife had rearranged their living quarters. It was too dangerous to carry the baby up and down the steep ladder to the upper floor every time the child needed to be washed or changed, so the family was split up. Euphiletos and his wife moved into the upper part of the house, while the baby, with the slave girl to look after it, stayed downstairs.

The arrangement worked well, and Euphiletos's wife often went down in the middle of the night to be with the baby when it was cranky. But on the evening of the day Euphiletos came back tired from the country, two things in addition to the little drama of the locked door struck him as unusual. One was his wife's makeup: it was only a month since her brother had died—yet he noticed that she had put powder on her face. And there were noises in the night that sounded like a hinge creaking. When his wife awakened him by unlocking the bedroom door the next morning, Euphiletos asked her about these sounds. She said she had gone next door to a neighbor's house to borrow some oil for the baby's night light, which had gone out. As for the makeup, when Euphiletos thought about it he remembered his wife saying how much she had missed him and how reluctantly she had left him to go down and take care of the baby. Reassured, he dismissed the whole episode from his mind and thought no more about it—until something happened to shatter this comforting domestic picture and rearrange all the pieces of the puzzle in quite a different way.

One morning, a few days later, Euphiletos was leaving his house when he was stopped in the street by an old woman. She apologized for taking his time. "I'm not trying to make trouble," she said, "but we have an enemy in common." The old woman was a slave. Her mistress, she said, had been having an affair, but her lover had grown tired of her and left her for another woman. The other woman was Euphiletos's wife.

"The man is called Eratosthenes," said the old slave. "Ask your maid about him. He's seduced several women. He's got it down to a fine art."

In the midst of his shock and anger Euphiletos revealed a streak of something methodical, almost detached, in his character. Instead of going straight to his wife or her lover, he proceeded like an accountant investigating an error in the books.

He retraced his steps to his house and ordered the maidservant to come with him to the market. His wife would see nothing unusual in this, for respectable married women did not go out shopping in fifth-century Athens. That was left to the men and the slaves. Halfway to the market Euphiletos turned aside and marched the girl to the house of a friend, where he confronted her with the old woman's story. The girl denied it. Euphiletos threatened to beat her. She told him to go ahead and do what he liked. He talked of prison. She still denied it. Then Euphiletos mentioned Eratosthenes' name, and she broke down. In return for a promise that she would not be harmed, she told Euphiletos everything.

Her story was bizarre as well as comic and macabre. It began at the funeral of Euphiletos's mother. Eratosthenes had seen Euphiletos's wife among the mourners and had taken a fancy to her. He got in touch with the maid and persuaded her to act as go-between. Whether it was a difficult or an easy seduction we don't know; but, as

the old woman had said, Eratosthenes was a practiced hand.

This love affair, first planned at a funeral and then set in motion by proxy, was carried on mostly at Euphileto's house when he was away in the country. On one occasion his wife may have contrived to meet her lover away from the house, for she had gone with Eratosthenes' mother to the festival of the Thesmophoria, one of several festivals celebrated in honor of feminine deities. During these festivals a woman could leave the seclusion of her own house without arousing suspicious comment.

The slave girl also told Euphiletos that on the night he came back tired from the country, her mistress had told her to pinch the baby to make it cry, which gave her an excuse to go downstairs. His wife's parade of jealousy, Euphiletos now realized, was an act, designed to provide her with a reason to lock the door on him. So while he was a temporary prisoner in his own bedroom, his wife was downstairs in the nursery with her lover, and the maid was keeping the baby quiet somewhere else.

In a crisis, a person will often revert to archetypal behavior. For the Greeks of the fifth century B.C. the Homeric poems provided a mythological blueprint for almost any life situation, and it is interesting to see how Euphileto's next move re-created a scene out of the legends. In *The Odyssey* Homer tells the story of what happened when Hephaistos, the god of fire, found out that his wife, Aphrodite, had been sleeping with the war god, Ares. Hephaistos decided not to face Aphrodite with her infidelity; instead, he wove a magical net that was sprung by the two lovers when they climbed into bed together. Then, as they lay there trapped, Hephaistos invited the other Olympians to come and view the guilty pair, "and the unquenchable laughter of the gods rose into the sky." In his own mundane way, but without the magic net, Euphiletos would follow the example of Hephaistos. He made his slave promise to keep everything she had told him a secret; then, pretending to his wife that he suspected nothing, he went about his business as usual and waited for a chance to spring his trap.

The part of cuckold is a mortifying one to play, and it was particularly so in ancient Athens where the relative status of men and women was so unequal. A freeborn Athenian woman was free in little more than name. She could

not vote, make contracts, or conduct any business involving more than a certain sum of money; legally she was little more than a medium for the transmission of property from grandfather to grandchildren through the dowry she brought with her to her husband. Her husband, of course, was invariably chosen for her by her father or by the nearest male relative if her father was dead. Almost the only thing she could call her own was her reputation, which depended on good behavior, an unassertive demeanor, a life spent dutifully spinning, weaving, dyeing clothes, cooking, bearing and raising children, and, above all, on not interfering in the serious business of life as conducted by the men. In a famous speech in praise of the Athenian men who died during the Peloponnesian War, Pericles makes only one reference to women: according to Thucydides, who reports the speech in his history of the war, Pericles said that women should never give rise to any comment by a man, favorable or unfavorable. In the tragic dramas, moreover, women who offer their opinions unasked or who go about alone in public usually feel they have to apologize for behaving in such a brazen and immodest way.

Such was the official status of women. Unofficially, the women of ancient Athens found ways, as their sisters have done in every age and culture, to undermine the barriers of male prejudice. In Euripides' play *Iphigeneia at Aulis* (written within a year or two of Euphiletos's marriage), Agamemnon tries to assert his authority over his wife, Clytemnestra, in order to get her out of the way while he sacrifices his own daughter, Iphigeneia, to Artemis. Clytemnestra, with a show of wifely stubbornness that surely came out of the playwright's contemporary observation, refuses to be dismissed and finally cuts the conversation short by sending her husband about his business. In another play by Euripides, *Hippolytos,* there are some lines that might have been written specifically for Euphiletos himself to speak. Hippolytos, told that his stepmother, Phaidra, is in love with him, remarks scathingly: "I would have no servants near a woman, just beasts with teeth and no voice, [for] servants are the agents in the world outside for the wickedness women do."

Drink and sex are the traditional outlets for the oppressed. The comedies of

Aristophanes are studded with snide references to the excessive drinking habits of women. According to Aristophanes, festivals such as the Thesmophoria were excuses for massive alcoholic sprees. More likely, these mystery cults were the safety valve for pent-up emotions, a chance to transcend the cruelly narrow boundaries imposed on women by their roles in a rigidly male society.

As for sex, women were the weaker vessel when it came to this human urge. In *Lysistrata* Aristophanes has the women wondering whether they can hold out long enough to bring the men to their knees. And in the legends that canonized popular wisdom on the subject there is a story about Zeus and Hera squabbling over who gets the greater pleasure out of sex—the man or the woman. When they finally appeal to Teiresias, the blind seer and prophet, who, as part man and part woman, ought to be able to settle the question for them, he duly reports that in the sexual act the woman, in fact, gets nine-tenths of the pleasure, and the man only one-tenth.

These scraps of myth and folklore, however, filtered through male fantasy as they are, reveal a sense of unease about women. In the Orestes myth, for instance, it is Clytemnestra who takes over the reins of government in the absence of Agamemnon, then murders him when he returns; and it is her daughter Electra who pushes a faltering Orestes into taking revenge for the slain king. A whole army of formidable heroines—Electra, Clytemnestra, Antigone, Hecuba, Andromache, Medea—marches through the pages of Greek drama. The Fates, the Muses, and the Furies are all women. None of these female figures is anything like the meek and passive drudge that the Greek woman of the fifth century was expected to be.

But were they real types, these mythological heroines, or were they phantom projections of male fears and desires, mother imagoes, castration anxieties dressed up as gods, embodiments of the part of a man he most wants to repress—his own irrational and emotional side, his moon-bound, lunatic aspects—thrust onto women because he dare not admit them in himself?

It is possible. Every mythologized figure embodies inner and outer worlds. We see what we wish to see, and the picture we perceive turns into a mirror. Were there actual women in Athens capable of organizing a fully functioning

communistic state and pushing it through the assembly, like the Praxagora of Aristophanes' play *Ekklesiazousai?* Were there Electras and Clytemnestras and Medeas? If there were, they never reached the pages of the history books. We hear of Aspasia, Pericles' "companion" (the Greek word is *hetaira,* meaning "woman friend"), for whom he divorced his legal wife. But Aspasia was a member of the demimonde of "liberated" women who lived outside the social order, not necessarily slaves, but not full citizens either. They were often prostitutes, but some of them were cultured and educated, better traveled and more interesting to Athenian men than their own wives. Custom permitted one or more relationships with *hetairai* outside the marriage, but a *hetaira* had no legal claim on a man, and he could sell her or dispose of her any time he liked. Meanwhile, for the trueborn Athenian woman who wanted a more varied life than the one prescribed by convention, what was there? Gossip with the neighbors. The bottle. A festival now and then. A clandestine love affair.

Four or five days passed while Euphiletos brooded over the wrong done to him. Suppose a child was born from this liaison: who could tell whether it was his or Eratosthenes'? All kinds of complications might follow. But whatever he was feeling, Euphiletos managed to hide it from his wife. She never suspected that he knew anything at all.

Euphiletos had a good friend named Sostratos. Less than a week after his interview with the maid Euphiletos met Sostratos coming home from the country, and since it was late Euphiletos invited his friend to his house for supper. This casual meeting was to become important later at the trial. The two men went upstairs, ate and drank well, and had a pleasant evening together. By custom Euphiletos's wife was not present. After Sostratos had gone home Euphiletos went to sleep.

Some time in the middle of the night there was a knock on his door. It was the maid. Eratosthenes had arrived.

Leaving the maid to keep watch, Euphiletos slipped out a back way and went around the neighborhood waking up his friends. Some of them were out of town, but he managed to collect a small group who went to a nearby store and bought torches. Then they all trooped off to Euphiletos's house where they stood outside in the street holding

the lighted torches while Euphiletos tapped on the door. Quietly the maid let him into the courtyard. He pushed past her into the room where his wife was supposed to be asleep with the baby. A few of Euphiletos's friends managed to crowd in behind him.

For a split second the scene must have been like a tableau out of Homer: Eratosthenes naked in bed, Euphiletos's wife in his arms, the two lovers trapped in the light of torches held by the neighbors.

Then Eratosthenes, still naked, sprang up. Euphiletos shouted at him, "What are you doing in my house?" and knocked him off the bed, pulled his wrists behind his back, and tied them.

Eratosthenes offered to pay Euphiletos any sum he named. Euphiletos had a choice: he could accept the bribe, or he could take a form of revenge allowed by law—brutalizing and humiliating Eratosthenes by such methods as the insertion of tough thistles up his rectum. There was also a third option open to him under the circumstances: since he had caught Eratosthenes in the act, and there were witnesses present, Euphiletos could kill him.

Euphiletos interrupted the other man's pleas. "I won't kill you," he said, and then, in the kind of logical twist the Greeks loved, he added, "but the law will."

And in the name of the law he killed Eratosthenes.

Athenian homicide law required the dead man's family, not the state, to bring charges of murder. Eratosthenes' family undertook the task, and approximately three months later Euphiletos found himself facing a jury of fifty-one Athenians in the court known as the Delphinion, located in the southeast corner of Athens, where cases of justifiable homicide were tried. Eratosthenes' family charged Euphiletos with premeditated murder on the grounds that he had sent his maid to lure Eratosthenes to the house; they may also have tried to prove that Eratosthenes was dragged into the building by force, or took refuge at the hearth before he was killed. In the speech he writes for Euphiletos, Lysias sets out to rebut all these charges.

Lysias puts into Euphiletos's mouth some ingenious legal arguments. The law (of which a copy is read to the court) says that a seducer caught in the act may be killed. "If you make it a crime to kill a seducer in this way," he argues, "you will have a situation in which a thief, caught burglarizing your house, will pretend that he is an adulterer in order to get away with a lesser crime." Lysias also refers the jury to the law on rape. Rape carries a lower penalty than seduction. Why? Because, theorizes Lysias, the rapist simply takes the woman's body, while the seducer steals her soul.

Nevertheless, in spite of Lysias's able and sophisticated defense, there is a flaw in Euphiletos's argument. His defense rests on the assumption that his action was unpremeditated, committed in the heat of the moment, under the shock and stress of finding his wife in bed with another man. That is surely the intent of the law, and Euphiletos goes to great lengths to prove he had not planned the encounter. He cites the dinner invitation to Sostratos, which, he says, is not the behavior of a man planning murder. But the rest of his story contradicts this. The signals by which the maid warned him that Eratosthenes had arrived and by which he let her know that he was waiting at the front door; the rounding up of friends to act as witnesses; the presence of the murder weapon on his person—all point to prior preparation. Euphiletos may prove to the jury's satisfaction that he did not lure Eratosthenes deliberately to his house that night, but he fails to prove that he was taken totally by surprise or that he

tried to do anything to stop the affair before it reached that point. His action looks suspiciously like cold-blooded revenge executed under color of a law that forgives even violent crimes if they are committed in the heat of passion.

Neither the speech for the prosecution nor the testimony of witnesses has survived, so we do not know if the wife or the maid gave evidence. Though women were not allowed to appear as witnesses in court cases, the rules for murder trials may have been different. A slave could not testify at all, but a deposition could have been taken from her under torture and read to the court. On the other hand, Euphiletos may have wanted to avoid bringing the women into it: after all, they had been in league against him throughout the whole unhappy affair.

There is something touching in the alliance between the slave, an object without rights or status, and the wife, legally a free citizen but in reality a kind of slave too. The maidservant probably accepted a bribe from Eratosthenes, but all the same she had a moment of heroism when, threatened with a beating and prison, she refused to incriminate her mistress. Afterward, when she became Euphiletos's accomplice, there is an eerie reversal of the situation: the slave admits her master to the house in the same stealthy way that she had opened

the door for her mistress's lover a few minutes earlier. But still, there was a moment when Euphiletos was the outsider, barred from his own house and his wife's arms, with only his rage and his group of male friends for company.

Finally there is the wife herself, the center of the drama and its most shadowy character. Apart from his grudging admission that she was thrifty and capable and a good housekeeper, Euphiletos tells us little about her. From what we know of Athenian marriage customs, we can guess that she was probably married at fourteen or fifteen to a virtual stranger and expected to keep house for this man who spent much of his time away from home on business. Was she satisfied with the trinkets that Euphiletos says he let her buy, and with all of the household duties and her young baby?

A small fragment survives from a lost play by Aristophanes in which a character says, "A woman needs a lover the way a dinner needs dessert." Euphiletos's wife was no Lysistrata, able to express her frustration and rebellion in some dramatic act of revolutionary will, but she did find a way to rebel all the same. It cost her dear. By Athenian law, if a man discovered that his wife had been raped or seduced, he was expected to divorce her. And from what we know of Euphiletos's character, we can be sure that he obeyed the law.

Cleopatra: What Kind of a Woman Was She, Anyway?

Serpent of the Nile? Learned ruler? Sex kitten? Ambitious mom? African queen? History is still toying with the poor lady's reputation

Barbara Holland

Barbara Holland, who often writes wryly about history and politics for the magazine, is the author of several books, including Endangered Pleasures *(Little, Brown).*

Until now, everyone has had pretty much the same fix on Cleopatra: passion's plaything, sultry queen, a woman so beautiful she turned the very air around her sick with desire, a tragic figure whose bared bosom made an asp gasp when she died for love. Inevitably, the best-known incarnation of her is Hollywood's: Theda Bara, Claudette Colbert, Elizabeth Taylor, telling us what fun it was to be filthy rich in the first century B.C., spending days in enormous bathtubs and nights in scented sheets. Drinking pearls dissolved in vinegar. (Do not try this at home; it doesn't work.) Lounging around on a barge, being waited on hand and foot.

Sometimes the asp looks like a small price to pay.

Hollywood's queen rests less on George Bernard Shaw's Cleopatra, who is a clever sex kitten, than on William Shakespeare's; in the Bard's *Antony and Cleopatra* she's a fiercer soul, downright unhinged by love for Mark Antony. Of course, they both had to leave out her children. Everyone does. It's tough being the world's top tragic lover with four kids underfoot. Even if you can get a sitter, it doesn't look right.

The latest version, part of the current debate about the possible influences of Africa on Greek and Roman culture, suggests that she was black. The last time we looked she was a Macedonian Greek, but the black-Cleopatra advocates like to point out that since nobody knows anything about her paternal grandmother except that she wasn't legally married to Ptolemy IX, it is possible that she was black.

Most classical scholars disagree. Some note that though Ptolemy II, more than a century earlier, had an Egyptian mistress, the Ptolemies were wicked snobs, so proud of their bloodline, not to mention the line of succession to their throne, that they tended to marry their brothers and sisters to keep it untainted. When they picked mistresses, they customarily chose upper-class Greeks. They felt so superior to the Egyptians, in fact, that after 300 years in Alexandria, they couldn't say much more than "good morning" to the locals in their native tongue; Cleopatra was the first in her family to learn the language.

Nobody should be surprised at such claims, however. For the fact is that for purposes political and otherwise, people have been fooling around with Cleopatra's image to suit themselves for centuries. In *All for Love* John Dryden gives us a traditional Cleo less a queen and a ruler than an addictive substance. Shaw made her stand for everything unBritish and thus deplorable. In the course of his *Caesar and Cleopatra* she evolves from a superstitious, cowardly little girl into a vengeful, bloodthirsty little girl. To underline his point he lops five years off her actual age and leaves her under the thumb of a sturdy Roman governor, forerunner of the wise and kindly British administrators of later colonies full of childish foreigners.

Of course, nearly everyone's story goes back to Plutarch, the first-century Greek biographer, who included two versions of Cleo. He knew the writings and stories of people in her part of the world who remembered her as a scholar in their own refined tradition, so unlike the ignorant, loutish Romans; a mothering goddess; a messiah sent to liberate the East from under the jackboots of Rome. On the other hand, he had the Roman story, largely attributed to her enemy in war, and conqueror, Octavian (who later became the emperor Augustus—portrayed as the clueless husband of the evil Livia in the television series *I, Claudius*). Octavian worked hard to set her up as everything scheming, treacherous, female, foreign and, most of all, sexually rapacious. His Queen Cleopatra was a drunken harlot, the wickedest woman in the world.

Actually, where we can reasonably deduce them, the facts are more interesting than these exotic scenarios.

Cleopatra VII was born in 69 B.C, the third child of Ptolemy XII, called Auletes, known as the Flute Player. Egypt was still rich, then, but its ancient empire had been nibbled away, and the natives, unfond of their Macedonian masters, were restless. The Flute Player kept going to Rome to get help in holding onto his throne. He may have taken Cleopatra along when she was 12; she may have watched the Roman loan sharks charge him 10,000 talents, or nearly twice Egypt's annual revenue, for services to be rendered.

Not only couldn't he control his subjects, he couldn't do a thing with his children. While he was away his eldest daughter, Tryphaena, grabbed the throne. After she got assassinated, second daughter Berenice grabbed it next—until Ptolemy came back with Roman

help and executed her. Cleopatra, now the eldest, had cause to ponder. She knew Egypt needed Roman help, but paying cash for help was beggaring the state. She knew she had to watch her back around her family. I suppose you could call it dysfunctional.

She seems to have found herself an education. Cicero, like most Romans, couldn't stand her, but he grudgingly admits she was literary and involved like him in "things that had to do with learning." The Arab historian Al-Masudi tells us she was the author of learned works, "a princess well versed in the sciences, disposed to the study of philosophy." According to Plutarch she spoke at least seven languages.

In 51 B.C., when Cleopatra was 18, the Flute Player died and left the kingdom to her and her 10-year-old brother (and fiancé) Ptolemy XIII. The reign got off on the wrong foot because the Nile refused to flood its banks to irrigate the yearly harvest. A court eunuch named Pothinus reared his ugly head; he'd got himself appointed regent for little Ptolemy, squeezed Cleopatra clear out of town and began giving orders himself.

Cleopatra's looks are one of the burning issues of the ages.

Rome, meanwhile, was in the process of shedding its republican privileges to become an empire. An early phase involved the uneasy power-sharing device called the First Triumvirate, with Caesar, Pompey and Crassus (a money man) jointly in charge. It wasn't Rome's brightest idea. Caesar and Pompey quarreled, Caesar defeated Pompey in Greece, Pompey took refuge in Egypt.

Not wanting to harbor a loser, the Egyptians had him murdered and cut off his head and presented it to victorious Caesar when he sailed into Alexandria to collect the defunct Flute Player's debts. Pothinus had reason to hate and fear Rome. He was very likely plotting to do in Caesar, too, who took over the palace and stayed on with a guard of 3,000 Roman soldiers. He couldn't take his ships and go home; the winds were unfavorable.

Cleopatra needed a secret word with him, so as we've all heard, she got herself rolled up in some bedding and had herself delivered to Caesar as merchandise. According to Plutarch, Caesar was first captivated by this proof of Cleopatra's bold wit, and afterward so overcome by the charm of her society that he made a reconciliation between her and her brother. Then he killed Pothinus. So there was Cleopatra, at the price of being briefly half-smothered in bedding, with her throne back. And of course, sleeping with Caesar, who was in his 50s and losing his hair.

How did she do it? Cleopatra's looks are one of the burning issues of the ages. European painters tend to see her as a languishing blue-eyed blonde with nothing to wear but that asp. However, there's a coin in the British Museum with her profile on it, and she looks more like Abraham Lincoln than a voluptuous queen. Most people who have written about her agree that she commissioned the coins herself and, being a woman, was vain of her looks, so even this profile could have been downright flattering. In any case, it launched a lot of cracks about her proboscis. Had Cleopatra's nose been shorter, according to 17th-century French writer Blaise Pascal, the whole face of the world would have been changed. However, there's no evidence that Antony was unhappy with her nose the way it was.

Or maybe it wasn't so long. Maybe she thought more of her kingdom than her vanity and wanted to scare off possible enemies by looking fierce. Considering the speed with which she corrupted Rome's top commanders—both of them widely traveled, experienced married men—it's possible she looked more like a woman and less like Mount Rushmore than she does on the coins. Besides, the second-century Greek historian Dio Cassius says Cleopatra seduced Caesar because she was "brilliant to look upon . . . with the power to subjugate everyone." (She knew a few things about fixing herself up, too, and wrote a book on cosmetics full of ingredients unknown to Estee Lauder, like burnt mice.) And Plutarch reports that "It was a pleasure merely to hear the sound of her voice, with which, like an instrument of many strings, she could pass from one language to another. . . ."

She bowled Caesar over, anyway, and when reinforcements came he squelched the rebellious Egyptian army for her. In the process he had to burn his own ships, and the fire spread and took out part of Alexandria's famous library, which housed most of what had been learned up to the time—Shaw called it "the memory of mankind." When the smoke cleared they found Ptolemy XIII drowned in the Nile in a full suit of golden armor, but as far as we know, his sister hadn't pushed him. Caesar then married her to her youngest brother, Ptolemy XIV, age 12, whom she ignored. When Caesar left, she was pregnant. Anti-Cleopatrans scoff at the notion that Caesar was the father, claiming he never admitted it himself, but there was plenty he never admitted, including his whole Egyptian fling, and somehow it seems likely. Giving the childless Caesar a son was a much shrewder move than getting pregnant by your 12-year-old brother; as policy it might have done wonders for Egypt. She named her son Ptolemy Caesar, always referred to him as Caesarion, and took him with her to Rome in 46 B.C. Mindful of her father's mistake, she took Ptolemy XIV, too, so she could keep an eye on him.

In Rome she was Caesar's guest. They gave fabulous parties together. He put up a golden statue of her in the temple of Venus Genetrix, causing a scandal that made him more vulnerable to the people who were plotting to kill him, as they did in March of 44. After he got stabbed, it turned out that he hadn't named Caesarion as his heir, but his great-nephew Octavian, so Cleopatra had to pack up and go home. When brother Ptolemy XIV conveniently died,

she appointed the toddler Caesarion as coruler.

Here the record loses interest in her for several years, between lovers, but she must have been busy. She'd inherited a country plagued by civil wars, Egypt was broke, and twice more the Nile floods misfired. Somehow, though, by the time the West began to notice her again, peace reigned even in fractious Alexandria. She'd played her cards deftly with Rome and her subjects loved her. According to the first-century A.D. Jewish historian Josephus, she'd negotiated a sweetheart real estate deal with the Arabs and in general managed the economy so well that Egypt was the richest state in the eastern Mediterranean. So rich that Mark Antony came calling in 41 B.C. in search of funds to finance an attack on the Parthians.

. . . like any Washington lobbyist with a pocketful of Redskins tickets, she was putting her time and money where they mattered most.

By then the Romans were pigheadedly pursuing the triumvirate notion again, this time with Octavian, Lepidus and Antony. If you believe Plutarch, Antony was simple, generous and easygoing, though a bit of a slob. Cicero says his orgies made him "odious," and there's a story that, after an all-night party, he rose to give a speech and threw up into the skirt of his toga while a kindly friend held it for him. Still, he was doing all right until Cleopatra came along, when he was, as Dryden laments, "unbent, unsinewed, made a woman's toy."

Plutarch's description of their meeting on her barge makes poets and movie producers salivate. Who could resist those silver oars and purple sails, those

flutes and harps, the wafting perfumes, the costumed maidens, and the queen herself dressed as Venus under a canopy spangled with gold? Not Antony, certainly. She knew what he'd come for and planned to drive a hard bargain. Naturally, they became lovers; they also sat down to deal; she would pay for his Parthian campaign, he would help fight her enemies and, for good measure, kill her sister Arsinoe, her last ambitious sibling.

Antony came for money and stayed to play. A sound relationship with Rome was tops on the whole world's agenda at the time. So, like a perfect hostess, Cleopatra lowered her standards of decorum and encouraged her guest in rowdy revels that have shocked the ages. The ages feel that all that frivoling means she was a frivolous woman, and not that, like any Washington lobbyist with a pocketful of Redskins tickets, she was putting her time and money where they mattered most.

She drank and gambled and hunted and fished with him. Sometimes they dressed as servants and roamed the town teasing the natives. Plutarch's grandfather knew a man who knew one of her cooks and reported that each night a series of banquets was prepared. If Antony wanted another round of drinks before dinner, the first banquet was thrown out and a second was served up, and so on. Anyone standing outside the kitchen door must have been half-buried in delicacies.

Back in Rome, Antony's third wife, Fulvia, and his brother raised an army against Octavian. (Lepidus, like Crassus, fizzled out early.) She got whipped, and Antony had to bid the fleshpots farewell and go patch things up. Then Fulvia died, and Antony sealed a temporary peace by marrying Octavian's sister, Octavia. Within weeks of that ceremony in Rome, Cleopatra had twins, Alexander Helios and Cleopatra Selene.

At the news of Antony's marriage, Shakespeare's queen has hysterics and tries to stab the messenger, but the Bard is guessing. The real queen probably took it in stride. She could recognize a political move when she saw it; she had Antony's alliance and a son to prove it, and a country to run besides.

SHE HAD NO TIME TO LOLL IN ASS'S MILK

No one suggests that she had a prime minister, and after Ponthinus, who would? No one denies, either, that Egypt was in apple-pie order. So there sits our drunken harlot, with Caesarion and the twins in bed, working late by oil light, signing papyri, meeting with advisers, approving plans for aqueducts, adjusting taxes. Distributing free grain during hard times. Receiving ambassadors and haggling over trade agreements. She may hardly have had time to put eyeliner on, let alone loll in ass's milk, and apparently she slept alone.

Antony finally got it together enough to invade Parthia. He needed help again, so he sent for Cleopatra to meet him at Antioch and she brought the children. Some see this as strictly business, but Plutarch insists his passion had "gathered strength again, and broke out into a flame." Anyway, they were rapturously reunited, and she agreed to build him a Mediterranean fleet and feed his army in exchange for a good deal of what is now Lebanon, Syria, Jordan and southern Turkey.

Did she really love him, or was it pure ambition? Ambition certainly didn't hurt, but it seems she was fond of him, though he probably snored after parties. Sources say she tried to introduce him to the finer things in life and dragged him to learned discussions, which at least sounds affectionate.

After a happy winter in Antioch, he went off to attack Parthia and she was pregnant again. The Parthian campaign was a disaster, ending with the loss or surrender of nearly half his army.

But for Cleopatra it was another boy, Ptolemy Philadelphus. When she'd recovered, she went to Antony's rescue with pay and warm clothes for the survivors. Presently Octavia announced that she, too, was coming to bring supplies. Antony told her to forget it and stay home. Octavian felt his sister had been dissed and suggested to the Romans that Antony was a deserter who planned to move the capital of the empire to Alexandria and rule jointly with his queen from there.

You could see it that way. In a public ceremony in Alexandria, Antony assembled the children, dressed to the teeth and sitting on thrones, and proclaimed Cleopatra "Queen of Kings" and Caesarion "King of Kings." He made his own three kids royalty, too, and gave them considerable realms that weren't, strictly speaking, his to give. Worst of all, he announced that Caesarion, not Octavian, was Julius Caesar's real son and the real heir to Rome.

Then he divorced Octavia.

All hands prepared for war. If the lovers had been quick off the mark, they might have invaded Italy at once and won, but instead they retired to Greece to assemble their forces, including Cleopatra's fleet. She insisted on sailing with it, too; her national treasury was stowed in the flagship. The upshot was that in 31 B.C. they found themselves bottled up at Actium, facing Octavian across the Ambracian Gulf. The standard version of the Battle of Actium is that while the fight hung in the balance, Cleopatra took her ships and left, because, being a woman, she was a coward and deserted in battle. The besotted Antony, we're told, followed her like a dog, and the fight turned into a rout.

With battles, the winner gets to tell the tale. Octavian was the winner, and he saw Cleopatra as a threat to Rome, a lascivious creature, and himself as a noble Roman able to resist her Eastern blandishments. All we really know is that it was a bloody mess, from which she managed to retreat with the treasury intact, enough to build another fleet with change left over. Octavian wanted that money to pay his troops. She wanted Egypt for her children. Perhaps deals could be made. Antony even suggested killing himself in trade for Cleopatra's life, but Octavian was bound for Egypt and he wouldn't deal.

Thus threatened, the queen swiftly stuffed a big mausoleum with treasure, along with fuel enough to burn it down if all else failed, and locked herself in with her serving maids. It's unclear whether Antony was told she was dead or he just felt depressed, but anyway he disemboweled himself. He botched the job—it's harder than you'd think—and lingered long enough to be hauled to the mausoleum and hoisted through the upstairs window, where presumably he expired in Cleopatra's arms. Victorious Octavian marched into town. He sent his henchmen to the queen, and they tricked their way in, snatched away her dagger, taking her—and her treasure—prisoner.

. . . she and her ladies dressed up in their best finery and killed themselves. Octavian did the handsome thing and had her buried with Antony.

According to Plutarch, at 39 "her old charm, and the boldness of her youthful beauty had not wholly left her and, in spite of her present condition, still sparkled from within." It didn't help, so she and her ladies dressed up in their best finery and killed themselves. Octavian did the handsome thing and had her buried with Antony. Then he tracked down and killed Caesarion and annexed Egypt as his own personal colony.

The best-remembered Cleo story is the asp smuggled in with the basket of figs. Plutarch, who saw the medical record, mentions it as a rumor, wrestles with the evidence and concludes that "what really took place is known to no one, since it was also said that she carried poison in a hollow comb . . . yet there was not so much as a spot found, or any symptom of poison upon her body, nor was the asp seen within the monument. . . ."

Later it was suggested—probably by Octavian—that she'd tried various substances on her slaves and, so the story usually goes, opted for the asp, but in truth its bite is even less fun than disemboweling. Maybe she used a cobra, whose effects are less visible. But where did it go? Some people claimed there were two faint marks on her arm, but they sound like mosquito bites to me. Others insist they saw a snake's trail on the sand outside; fat chance, with all those guards and soldiers and distressed citizens milling around shouting and trampling the evidence.

It looks likelier that she'd brewed up a little something to keep handy. She was clever that way; remember the second brother. Octavian's men had patted her down—"shook out her dress," Plutarch says—but she was smarter than they were. And why gamble on the availability of snakes and smugglers when you could bring your own stuff in your suitcase? When Octavian led his triumph through Rome, lacking the actual queen, he paraded an effigy of her with her arm wreathed in snakes, and the asp theory slithered into history. Maybe he'd heard the rumor and believed it, or maybe he started it himself. It would have played well in Rome. In Egypt the snake was a symbol of royalty and a pet of the goddess Isis, but in Rome it was strictly a sinuous, sinister reptile, typical of those Easterners, compared with a forthright Roman whacking out his innards.

History has always mixed itself with politics and advertising, and in all three the best story always carries the day. But why did the man who was now undisputed ruler of the known world work so hard to ruin a dead lady's reputation? Maybe she'd been more formidable than any of our surviving stories tell. We do know she was the last great power of the Hellenistic world, "sovereign queen of many nations" and the last major threat to Rome for a long time. She might have ruled half the known world or even, through her children, the whole thing, and ushered in the golden age of peace that she believed the gods had sent her to bring to the Mediterranean.

At least she would have left us her own version of who she was, and maybe it would be closer to the truth than the others. And then again, given the human urge to tell good stories, maybe not.

In the Year 1, Augustus Let the Good Times Roll

The Year 2000 Is Almost Upon Us, But What in the (Western) World Was Happening When The Counting Began?

BY LIONEL CASSON

AS THE SECOND MILLEN-nium of the Christian Era draws to an end, the editors of *Time* will be pondering their choice for the outstanding figure of its last year, Man of the Year A.D. 1999, to put on the cover of the appropriate issue. What if they had to add a choice for the first year of the era, Man of the Year A.D. 1? More specifically, Man of the Year A.D. 1, in the Western world, this being where the reckoning of time from the birth of Christ was invented and took hold. Our system of dating was thought up by a learned Christian monk, Dionysius Exiguus (Little Dennis), who lived in Rome around the close of the fifth century A.D. and the beginning of the sixth. The system in his day had been insti-tuted by Diocletian, a Roman emperor infamous for his merciless persecution of the Christians. Dionysius, deeming it no fit system for Christians, devised a new one that was, and, as we all know today, chose the birth of Jesus Christ, as he calculated it, as his starting point (SMITHSONIAN, February 1999).

In the year Dionysius would choose to start with, one man bestrode the West-ern world like a colossus. He was not Shakespeare's Julius Caesar, whose be-striding had ended abruptly on the Ides of March, 44 years earlier, but his

The Romans diluted their wine liberally with water—despite this, they managed to get tight.

grandnephew Augustus, whom Julius Caesar had named as his heir. Augustus was a youth of 18 when Caesar's murder propelled him into the Roman political arena; he was only 32 when Mark An-tony's suicide in 31 B.C. left him over-lord of territory that reached from Spain to Syria. He transformed that territory into the Roman Empire, with the reins of power securely gathered into his own hands. He put in place the machinery of government that ran it; he created the army and navy that protected its bor-ders. He did such a good job that the Roman Empire endured for centuries af-

ter, the first two of which were the cen-turies of the celebrated Pax Romana, the longest period of peace the Western world would ever enjoy.

The year 1 was the 30th in the reign of Augustus, who ruled over the empire with absolute power. By this time the government he had put in place was op-erating smoothly. The curtain had also gone up on the prosperity that peace can bring. The whole Mediterranean was now open to commerce, and its sea-lanes were safe, since the Roman navy, with no enemies to fight, concentrated on getting rid of pirates.

Massive amounts of commodities moved over the waters in vessels that could be as large as the East Indiamen of the 18th century. Grain was the prime commodity, for making the bread and porridge that were the basis of the an-cient diet. Olive oil and wine were run-ners-up. Olive oil was shipped in quantity because, for Greeks and Ro-mans, it was considerably more than a food item. It did what electricity and soap do for us—people burned it for light in lamps and anointed themselves with it as a cleanser. And wine was shipped in quantity because it was more than something to drink with meals. They took a cup of it when we would have one of coffee or tea, both unknown in antiquity. Since whiskey, brandy and other alcoholic beverages were equally unknown, the sole drink at all festive occasions was wine. The Romans diluted it liberally with water—the view was that only barbarians and sots took it straight—but despite this, they managed to get tight; some famous figures, such as Alexander the Great and Mark Antony, were notorious drunks, and so was one of the gods—Hercules, who imbibed as mightily as he fought.

For rowers in the navy, an inducement to join up was the discharge benefit—Roman citizenship.

A shipper could prosper handling cheap and bulky commodities like oil and wine. If he hankered for a richer return, he went in for importing silks and spices and similar expensive luxuries from far-off India—goods whose value made a vessel a veritable treasure ship. Whether dealing in olive oil or exotic silks, the trader got the sizable sums he needed to finance his venture through maritime loans, in which he pledged as security the cargo he would buy with the borrowed funds. He would have to pay interest of 30 percent or better; no matter, the profit he could turn when he sold his goods easily covered it. Besides, under the laws governing maritime loans, he repaid only after the cargo arrived safely home. If the ship went down, the lenders stood the loss. Investors were ready to take the risk. In ancient Greece and Rome, where real estate rarely went on the market, where there were no corporations, and such things as stocks and bonds did not exist, maritime loans were among the few ways available to make a financial killing. There was no shortage of men willing to stake a shipper to the equivalent of hundreds of thousands of dollars, even though a bit of bad luck with wind and weather might wipe out

the total investment. For, if the ship came in, and most of the time it did, they reaped over three times what they would have netted on an ordinary loan.

Though the big money was to be made on the sea, in those peaceful times the land also offered good opportunities. Tradesmen and craftsmen could do very well—and manufacturers especially well. One of the major areas of manufacture was the molding and firing in quantity of clay utensils. These included not only small items, such as oil lamps, dishware and cookware for household use, but also the huge clay jars, or amphorae, commonly standing about five feet high, that served as containers for shipping oil, wine and other foodstuffs, since wood was too expensive to use for barrels. Huge numbers of these jars were needed: the ordinary oil or wine freighter held 3,000 or so of them, and a large freighter, as many as 10,000. If several vessels arrived at a port to load, it could well take tens of thousands of amphorae to fill the holds. The manufacturing of such numbers of large jars was done, like all other manufacturing in ancient times, by hand, in small factories. The organization and direction that made it possible must have been ruthlessly efficient.

In A.D. 1, the poor in Roman cities washed more often than many Americans will in A.D. 2000.

Not only the many who prospered but also their less fortunate neighbors enjoyed the public amenities supplied by the towns or cities they lived in. A town was not a proper town, the Romans felt, unless it offered its denizens paved streets, a water supply, which often had to be brought in over aqueducts from miles away, and public baths with hot, warm and cold pools—baths that were open to everyone, rich or poor. In A.D. 1, the poor in Roman cities and towns drank better water and washed

more often than many of their counterparts in American cities and towns will in A.D. 2000.

Another amenity the towns and cities supplied free to the denizens was entertainment, including the Roman spectator sports par excellence, chariot racing and gladiatorial combats. Chariot races were part of the program at official religious festivals; gladiatorial combats were also put on, not as a regular feature but as added attractions paid for by ambitious politicians or, in Augustus' time and after, by the emperor. Augustus, in the course of his reign, gave the public eight gladiatorial shows in which no fewer than 10,000 men fought—an average of 1,250 per show. One of the eight took place in 2 B.C., and it must have been a big one, for it was part of the ceremonies at the dedication of the temple of Mars Ultor, "Mars the Avenger," which the emperor erected in thanks for his victory in the decisive battle against Caesar's assassins, a vital step in his path to the throne. In his day, gladiatorial contests were no longer necessarily associated with religious festivals, although chariot racing continued to be. In either case the spectators were unaffected: admission was gratis.

Health care was, if not free, at least within the reach of the poor. The source of the benefaction in this case was not the government but religion. The payment required was a donation to the god, and he compassionately accepted whatever he was given. The god was Asclepius, whose sanctuaries, equipped with the appropriate buildings and staffed by priests with the appropriate training, provided the services of a medical center. Patients from all over flocked to them because there, they knew, their case would be handled by an infallible doctor—the god himself. After receiving a solemn ritual preparation, they passed the night in a sacred dormitory, and he appeared in their dreams and prescribed the treatment to be carried out. If the dream was unclear, the temple priests were there to offer an interpretation. From the patients' accounts the priests could usually prescribe standard remedies such as a change in diet, exercise, medicines, purging, bleeding. None of these cures would have helped much with the two most prevalent maladies in antiquity, malaria and tuberculosis, and probably did little for many of the other maladies that confronted the priests, but what unquestionably helped in all cases was the psychological effect of the impressive procedure.

A major contributor to the bright days of A.D. 1 as well as the years before and after it—the thriving economy, the flourishing towns and cities with their public services and entertainment—was the security the empire enjoyed, thanks to the armed forces. Before Augustus' time, troops were recruited and warships launched only when the need arose; one of Augustus' greatest accomplishments was his establishment of a standing, professional army and navy. Both were of top quality. The members were all volunteers, who eagerly signed on for hitches of at least 20 years because the services gave a man status, lodging, good pay and benefits on discharge to boot. The biggest item in the army's budget was the payroll, since the men bought their own weapons and food. The biggest item in the navy's budget was the ships. The standard man-of-war was the trireme, a combat galley large enough to accommodate almost 200 oarsmen, arranged in three superimposed lines, and marines, who boarded other vessels or repelled boarders. Some combat galleys were larger, with even more oarsmen.

The fleets had a total of several hundred such vessels, and each represented a sizable outlay. The timber that went into each combat galley was the finest, and to ensure proper strength in the hull, the construction was more like cabinetwork than carpentry; the planks were fastened to each other with thousands of closely set mortise-and-tenon joints, each, of course, painstakingly hand cut.

The navy had a sizable payroll to meet, too, for the rowers, contrary to a common misconception, were not slaves; they were freemen who, though they received less than the soldiers of the army, still got a fair wage. (The galley slave does not enter history until long after the end of the ancient period.) The navy had no trouble recruiting the thousands of men it needed to pull the oars of its galleys; they came from Rome's subject provinces, and for them a strong inducement to join up was the discharge benefit—Roman citizenship.

An aspect of life that benefited enormously from the security the army provided on land and the navy on the sea was tourism. Before Augustus' day, chronic warfare and generally unsettled conditions discouraged sight-seeing. Be-

sides, few were wealthy enough to go in for it. In the years of the Pax Romana, the conditions were propitious, and the general prosperity made the number who could afford to travel far greater than ever before or for centuries thereafter. And travel they did, even though it was not easy. Getting anywhere overseas meant booking deck passage on a freighter (there were no passenger ships as such), while getting anywhere overland meant jolting along in a springless carriage. Moreover, once on the road, travelers were more or less out of communication with home. The only organized postal service in existence was strictly of and for the government. A private person who wanted to send a letter had to find someone heading for the desired destination who was both willing to carry it and to take the trouble to locate the addressee—no easy task in an age when there were few streets with names, none with street signs, and no such thing as house numbers.

Tourists willingly undertook the hardships. The attraction was, as it often is today, the magnetism of relics of the past. We trek to where Washington spent a night, where Monet lived, where Napoleon is buried. They trekked to where Alexander the Great spent a night, where Socrates lived, where Achilles was buried. We flock to England for a visit to Shakespeare country; they flocked to Troy in Asia Minor for a visit to Homer country (where they were shown the beach along which the Greek ships were pulled up, the plain where Hector and Achilles rampaged, the cave where Paris gave his fateful judgment, and so on). They went to Egypt to see the very things we do—the Pyramids, the great Sphinx, the Valley of the Kings. We know many of the specific spots they visited because they had the same habit people have today, of scribbling their names on the sites they visited. One graffito, left by a Roman traveler on the wall of the Temple of Isis on the island of Philae, far up the Nile at the First Cataract, runs: *L. Trebonius Oricula hic fui*, or "I, L[ucius] Trebonius Oricula, was here." The ubiquitous Kilroy of World War II fame, had his native tongue been Latin, would have used these words. Trebonius adds the date: the eighth day before the Kalends of April in the 13th consulship of Augustus—which works out to be just two years before the beginning of our era, March 25, 2 B.C.

And, like his modern counterpart, the ancient tourist came home with souvenirs of his travels. One of the major sights of Antioch, for example, was a famous statue of Tyche, the goddess of fortune. A multitude of miniature copies of it have been found, from two inches to a foot high and in all sorts of materials—glass, clay, bronze, silver, stone; they were tourist gimcracks, the ancient equivalent of the miniatures of Michelangelo's *David* that are peddled in Florence today, or of the Eiffel Tower that are sold in Paris. It was the trade in such souvenirs that caused so much trouble for Saint Paul when he was in Ephesus: one of the city's great sights was the Temple of Artemis, and the silversmiths who made little Artemis shrines for sale to visitors were upset at the potential effect on their business of his preaching against the gods.

In foreign affairs, over which Augustus did not have the control he had over domestic matters, he experienced some failures. Although he had the finest army in the Western world at his command, in maintaining the peace he preferred diplomatic maneuvering and negotiation to force. In 4 B.C., for example, he faced potential trouble in Palestine, a place where maintaining the peace was always a delicate business. Herod the Great, king of the region, had managed to do it for more than three decades by combining ruthless handling of enemies with deft handling of religious and political divisions. But his death in 4 B.C. removed him from the scene, and problems soon arose. He had married ten times and sired numerous sons, and though he killed off a number of them, enough were left to start a wrangle about the succession. Augustus settled the argument Solomonically by dividing the kingdom among the three eldest. His solution proved to have momentous consequences: the son who acquired the southern part, which included Judea and Jerusalem, got himself so disliked that in A.D. 6 Augustus removed him, sent him into exile, and annexed his territory to the empire as a province governed by a Roman official. The sixth such official was Pontius Pilate. As we know, Pontius Pilate would make his own contribution to the year 1. In A.D. 30, he would preside over Jesus Christ's condemnation to death by crucifixion, thus starting the process that would lead the little Christian monk, Dennis, 500 years later, to choose Christ's birth as the starting point for his new, Christian era.

One area where Augustus couldn't resort to diplomacy or negotiation was along the northern frontier between Gaul, which was part of the empire, and certain lands adjoining it that were held by German tribes, who consequently had easy access for raiding Gallic villages and took advantage of it. Here he had to use the army, and in the opening years of the century, operations went well. Then he chose to put in charge the

In A.D. 9, Varus led a force some 20,000 strong straight into a German trap in the Teutoberg Forest, and it was wiped out; he committed suicide.

wrong man, Quinctilius Varus. In A.D. 9, Varus led a force of some 20,000 strong straight into a German trap in the Teutoberg Forest, and it was wiped out; he committed suicide. The Germans captured the standards of three legions, the greatest of all humiliations for the Roman army. After Augustus got the news, for months he let his hair grow wild, didn't shave, and every so often would bang his head on a door screaming, "Varus! Give me back my legions!" The defeat had its long-term consequences: it contributed to keeping much of Germany out of the embrace of the Roman Empire, and as a result, Germans today speak their own language and not some version of Latin.

The border to the east was also a source of worry, and here Augustus managed to achieve what he was after with diplomacy. Across the border was Rome's only rival power, the Parthian kingdom, occupying the ancient land of Persia beyond the Euphrates River. The Parthians were formidable because of their army. The Romans relied on a highly trained, well-disciplined mass of infantry whose prime weapons were spear and sword; the Parthians relied on lightly armored cavalrymen whose prime weapon was the bow. One of their specialties was the "Parthian shot": they would feign retreat and, as they galloped away, suddenly fire backward at unwary pursuers. In 53 B.C., a Roman general ventured across the Euphrates with a big army and senselessly chose a flat plain on which to meet the Parthian force that came to stop him. Its cavalry, shooting at his infantry masses like ducks on a pond, administered one of the worst defeats Rome had ever suffered; the Parthians went home with the Roman legionary standards and thousands of prisoners. For decades the Romans agonized about the situation, much the way we did about Americans taken captive during the Vietnam War. Finally, in 20 B.C., Augustus, mingling diplomacy with a show of force, succeeded in getting everything and everybody back.

The Parthian kings, checked by Rome in the west, expanded eastward, into India. Today India, with all its linguistic and religious and cultural divisions, is at least a political unit; at the beginning of the Christian Era it was not even that. The Parthians held the northwest, invaders from Central Asia the rest of the north, a powerful native dynasty the center, and a number of local rulers shared the south. Under this political diversity, life was recognizably Indian: the population was split, as it had been for centuries, into castes; women committed suttee; rice was the staple diet (resident traders from the west, longing for bread, used to include a bit of grain in their shipments from home); there was the

welter of familiar religions—Buddhism, Jainism, Hinduism.

Beyond India lay the Chinese empire, bracketing the known world on the east as the Roman Empire did on the west. These two great states knew of each other, but only barely, and what contacts they had were indirect. Western traders were aware that the silk they bought in India to ship to the Mediterranean came from China: as one of them wrote, "There is a very great inland city called Thina from which silk floss, yarn, and cloth are shipped. . . . It is not easy to get to this Thina, for rarely do people come from it and only a few." He probably got his information from Malayan or Indian seamen, who plied the waters between China and India, or from Central Asian caravaners, who plied the routes on land. It was too bad for the Western world that relations weren't closer, for it might have gotten some useful things much earlier than it eventually did. Chinese smiths, for example, knew how to make cast iron, Chinese laborers had that humble but supremely efficient instrument, the wheelbarrow, for carting loads, and Chinese children were having fun flying kites; the West knew none of these until the Middle Ages and even later.

In A.D. 1, the Roman Empire, having been brought into being by Augustus less than 30 years earlier, was young and vigorous. There was peace; commerce and industry prospered; people, including the rank and file, enjoyed urban amenities and free entertainment. Rome's neighbors were quiet, except for the Germans, and the trouble they were causing would not become serious until later. The credit goes chiefly to Augustus—Man of the Year, even as he had been for more than a decade before and would be for more than a decade after.

Lionel Casson, a professor of classics at New York University, has often written about the ancient world for SMITHSONIAN.

Chariot Racing in the Ancient World

Dirk Bennett *sheds new light on the origin and history of chariot racing as a sport, and explores its popular and political role from pre-classical Greece to the fall of the Roman Empire.*

Antilochos the fourth driver, the glorious son of Nestor, that king of lofty heart, the son of Neleus, got ready his horses with gleaming coats. Swift horses born in the land of Pylos drew his chariot. And his father, standing by his side, giving good advice to one who was himself naturally prudent, spoke wisely thus: 'Antilochos, although you are very young, Zeus and Poseidon have both loved you and taught you all kinds of skills at driving a chariot; therefore we need not teach you, for you know how skilfully to turn around the post. But your horses are the slowest. I therefore think that the race will be sorrowful to you. True, their horses are swifter, but the drivers do not know more than you. And so, my son, contrive a plan in your heart, so that the prize will not elude you ... Drive chariot and horses so close to this (the post) as to graze it, and lean the wellwrought car slightly to the left horse, and calling upon the right horse by name, prick him with your goad and let out its reins from your hand. Let your horses graze the post so that the hub of the well fashioned wheel will seem to touch it. But avoid making contact with the stone, so that you will not injure your horses and wreck your chariot, which would be a joy for your opponents and a distress to you.'

(Homer, *Iliad* 23, 334–348)

Horse racing, the ancient equivalent to Formula One, does not, however, begin here. The history of equestrian sports could change our perception of the ancient world in general, and our idea of Greece as the cradle of European civilisation in particular. In fact, when the first horses appeared from Central Asia in Mesopotamian and near Eastern societies in the 2nd millennium BC, Greece and Italy, as well as the rest of Europe, lay very much on the outskirts of the civilised world.

In the beginning there was no question about using the animals in sport. However, a technological revolution in warfare comparable maybe to the introduction of battle tanks in the twentieth century took place that was to have a far reaching and lasting impact. The old chariots pulled by mules or oxen did not stand a chance against the swift new horse-vehicles. The armies of the empires of Sumer, Egypt, Ur, the Hittites and others increasingly relied on contingents of charioteers. In the battle of Kadesh (*c.* 1275 BC), the Hittite army consisted of 20,000 soldiers, 3,500 of whom were charioteers. It is roughly at this time that we get the first hint that chariots must have been known to the predecessors of the classical Greeks. In a letter to the 'Wanax Agamemnon' the great Hittite king mentions that the brother of the Greek king, Eteokles, had been riding on the same chariot with his driver. Even if this is not Homer's Agamemnon, this letter is a strong indication that Homer, in the *Iliad*, does not simply write from the point of view of his times (ie *c.* seventh century BC), as some might have it, but actually describes a much older society.

All of this, however, is little proof of the use of horses in a sporting environment. There are leisurely activities like hunting or shooting at targets from chariots by the great kings of Persia, the Egyptian pharaohs or the Hittite kings, but they have little to do with what we would regard as real competitive sport. These pastimes served more as imperial propaganda, displaying the skills and strength of the rulers.

To find the origins of actual chariot racing we have to turn to Greece and the islands of the Aegean. In the fourteenth to twelfth centuries BC, first the Minoan, and later the Mycenean, culture inhabited what was subsequently seen as the cradle of European civilisation. The ongoing excavations and exciting discoveries of the last hundred years are still changing our view of the world before the classic age. They have also shed some light on the development of horse racing as a sport. Finds in the archives of the cities of Knossos, Mycene, Tiryns and Pylos illustrate the richness of their rulers, the administration of their realms and the structure of their societies. The inventories of the place of Pylos for example contain not only livestock and precious goods, but—and this is of particular importance for us—hundreds of spoked wheels. The same applies to the tables found in Tiryns, Mycene and

Knossos. We read about wheels and chariots, and of their number and condition. Additionally, discoveries of clay models give an idea of their shape and even the different types in use. Still, we could not be sure about their use other than in warfare without further proof: a number of fragments of pottery from Tiryns show two or more chariots, obviously in the middle of a race. The vehicles, a turning post and the flowing hair of the charioteers can all be seen.

This is a clear indication that chariot racing existed as a sport from as early as the thirteenth century BC. The other 'evidence' is well known—the *Iliad* and numerous other Greek legends that describe it. For example, the tale about the notorious King Oinomaos of Olympia is said to describe the origins of the Olympic Games: In order to win the hand of his daughter, the suitor had to beat him in a chariot race, otherwise the unlucky contestant had to suffer death at the hands of Oinomaos. The hero Pelops managed to win the attractive prize, but only by replacing the nails which held the wheels of the king's chariot with some made of wax. The result of this sabotage was the destruction of the chariot and the death of the king. Thus the most famous games in the world began with a fraud.

Illustrations and legends also make clear that many of the early races took place in funerary surroundings. In the *Iliad*, for example, games are held to honour the fallen Patroklos, friend of Achilles. It also gives an idea of the enormous prizes which could be won:

First he (Achilles) ordered the noble prizes to be set aside for the swift charioteers. The first prize was a woman skilled in graceful handicraft and a tripod with two handles holding twenty-two measures. And for second, he designated an unbroken mare, six years old, carrying in her womb a mule foal. And for third prize he set aside a handsome kettle that had never been put over the fire, holding four measures, still as bright as it was on the day it was made; and for fourth he set aside two talents of gold; and for fifth he put a double cup which had never been put over the fire . . .

Thus it seems certain that horse racing took place at least in the thirteenth to twelfth centuries BC. After that the attacks of the 'Sea People' and the 'Doric Migration' put an end to Mycenean civilisation. Both terms and both

phenomena have come under scrutiny recently and are nowadays only used with caution to describe events which led to the so-called 'Dark Ages'. This period, characterised by a lack of sources, stretches roughly to the eighth century BC. From then on begins the Archaic Age which lays the foundations for the classical culture as we know it. From this time the archaeological sources begin to flow again: chariot races are depicted on late Geometric vases, and in 680 BC we see the official birth of chariot racing as a sport when it was included in the programme of the Olympic Games. This development is also remarkable as a turning point in social history: formerly the leisurely occupation of a few aristocrats (and before that of kings), the chariots were now increasingly driven by professionals. Nevertheless, although the chariot owners mostly did not actually drive themselves, victory always belonged to them, not to the drivers—a parallel to racing programmes today which list owners first, then horses and lastly jockeys.

As a result of the rise of the Greek cities of the classic period, other great festivals emerged. There were literally hundreds of competitions in Asia Minor, Magna Graecia and the mainland providing the opportunity for athletes to gain fame and riches. Apart from the Olympics, the best respected were the 'Crown Games', the Isthmians in Corinth, the Zeus Games at Nemea, the Pythians in Delphi and the Panatheneans. This last name derives from the attributes for the winners—wreaths of laurel, olive, pine and wild fennel. But these were only the official signs of victory. More substantially, for example, in Athens the victorious charioteers received up to 140 amphorae of olive oil (much sought after and precious in ancient times). Prizes at other competitions included corn in Eleusis, bronze shields in Argos and silver vessels in Marathon.

In addition, the returning athletes gained various benefits in their native towns, like tax exemptions, free clothing and meals and even prize money. A winner from Athens obtained 500 drachmas, the equivalent of a year's wages for a craftsman. Statues in precious metals were erected in their honour and they were often granted political posts, priesthoods and honorary offices.

An even more professional approach to sport came when the hippodromes were taken over by the new political

power, Rome, a change which was also to have deep social and cultural impact. Here horse racing had allegedly been introduced by the former Etruscan kings—Romulus or, other sources say, Tarquinius Priscus, who after Livius laid the foundations for the Circus Maximus. For the first few centuries of the city, however, racing as sport was slow to take off, perhaps understandable in a '*res publica*' mostly inhabited by peasants and in constant conflict with its surrounding neighbours. After the defeat of the Carthaginians, the expansion towards the Greek south of Italy and the arrival on the Greek mainland, from the third to the second centuries BC, unimaginable riches began to flow to Rome. The privileged citizenry of the capital had to be amused and kept at bay. Thus began the rise of a 'leisure industry' which was to coincide with the decline of the Greek festivals.

The history of the first century AD is of decades of civil war, during which the changing political leaders used games as a political means to draw the support of the masses. It was also at this time that the *factiones* first appear; parties supporting different racing stables distinct by colour: green, blue, red and white—and later for a short time, purple and gold. Finally, under the emperors, the phenomenon of '*bread and circuses*' came into play and the circus became the favourite public form of entertainment. The growing attraction of the circus is evident in the increasing use of racing motifs on items of everyday use, on mosaics, wall paintings, and in funeral art, where putti, goddesses, fauns, in short every living form, were put into the context of racing.

The masses who gathered divided into their favourite colours. The seating order reflected the different strata of Roman society with the first rows reserved for senators, high ranking officials and the Vestal Virgins. Then came the knights, the guilds and colleges and finally the common people. Even the different orders of priests had their own place.

The more the citizens of Rome lost their former political role and influence to the emperors the more they were drawn to the races. It is no accident that circuses all over the Roman world were built close to the local palaces of the emperors or officials. The *pulvinar*, or *kathisma*, the royal box, which in the new circus of Constantinople replaced the tribunal, was the place where the emperor was expected to appear on certain occasions, and, even if he did not watch the races, at least to open them by throwing the *mappa*—a piece of cloth. A number of vivid descriptions exist telling how the audience—in the Circus Maximus between 100,000–250,000—noisily greeted the emperor, addressed him with thoroughly orchestrated chants, gained benefits, had officials suspended or simply expressed their dedication to their rulers. It was here where political events and personalities were discussed and approval or discontent expressed. Often enough riots broke out in the heated atmosphere of the races with horrific results.

A number of yearly calendars listing public holidays, festivals and celebrations give us an idea of the programmes and extent of the races. One of them, the so-called calendar of Philocalus, quotes no less than 180 public holidays in Rome for the year 354 AD, all of which included races. The number increased from only a few to twelve and later up to twenty-four races a day in the fifth and sixth centuries AD. Horse racing proved no less popular in the Christian era than in the pagan centuries before. However, with the decline of the Roman empire, it eventually disappeared in the east. A print of the Hippodrome in Constantinople from the fifteenth century shows a derelict site, a few walls still standing, the *spina* (central reservation) robbed of its splendour. Today only obelisks and the Serpent Column stand where for centuries the spectators gathered.

One might ask why the concentration was so heavily on chariot racing? The answer is simple: horse racing was not as widespread and attractive to the ancient public. At the local Greek games some races of this kind took place—the best known are probably the Apobatoi competitions of the Panathenians—but compared with the masses who went to the chariot races they had comparably little attraction.

The design of hippodromes and chariots throws significant light on both the inventiveness and technical capabilities of contemporary engineers and builders. However, it was not before the Romans took up chariot racing that massive changes and improvements took place. Hardly anything is left of the Classical Greek sites, even in Olympia where the most important races took place. The ancient traveller Pausanias

describes the site, which he saw in the second century AD:

> As one passes out of the stadium . . . one comes to the hippodrome and the starting gate for the horses. This starting gate looks like the forepart of a ship, with the projecting bows pointing towards the track. The prow is the widest where it is nearest the Stoa of Agnaptos; at the very tip of the projection is a bronze dolphin on a pole. Each wing of the gate, with the stalls built into it, is more than 400 feet long. The entrants for the equestrian events draw lots for the stalls; the barrier in front of the chariots and ridden horses consists of a cord passing through the stalls. For each Olympiad a plinth of unbaked brick is built at about the middle of the prow, and on this plinth is a bronze eagle with its wings fully extended. The starter works the mechanism on the plinth: when it is set in motion, it causes the eagle to jump up so it becomes visible to the spectator, while the dolphin falls to the ground. The traps at each end . . . open first . . .
>
> (Pausanias VI, XX. p10)

One after the other the chariots were released with the ones in the middle starting last. After 320m in straight lanes, a trumpet was blown, on which signal they were allowed to leave the lanes and the race began in earnest. Now they entered the U-shaped course itself, marked by two turning posts, in Greek *'nyssa'*, with a distance of three stadiums between them, i.e. 576m. It seems most likely that there were short, middle and long distance races. Apart from these, there were different disciplines, like two- and four-handed races, or different animals were raced; foals, mares, stallions, mules and asses. It has been suggested that races with female drivers took place but this seems unlikely.

Many of the Greek local games survived throughout antiquity, attracting participants and spectators from far and wide. The last Olympic chariot races took place around a thousand years after they began.

The racing in the Roman era was altogether different. Its main aim was to attract and distract the masses. Although the Circus Maximus—the most famous race course of the Roman Empire for centuries—has disappeared under later buildings, we have a very good idea of the scale and design of these buildings. This is partly because Roman-style chariot racing spread throughout the

Mediterranean. Almost every town had its own racecourse. The best preserved circuses today are probably the one in Leptis Magna in modern Libya and the Circus of Maxentius besides the Via Appia. Vivid descriptions of races by Ovid, Cassiodor, Sidonius and many others, inscriptions, the *Forma Urbis* (a third century marble map of Rome) and the obelisk of Theodosius help complete the picture.

Like the hippodrome, the course resembled a stretched 'U', with a long starting straight and the actual racecourse. Other than in Greece, however, the chariots started from a curved line leaving the stalls, the *carceres,* twelve in the Circus Maximus, in marked lanes. On contemporary sarcophagi we can see the *carceres,* closed by barred doors, and above them, in the middle of the stalls, the *tribunal editoris,* the box of the official in whose name the games were held. A white line marked the point from where the lanes could be left. Everybody then headed for the best position to enter the track at the near turning post, the *meta.* This was connected to its corresponding post by a highly decorative structure, called the spina, which separated the two halves of the track. A historian who witnessed the fall of Constantinople in 1204 describes the decorative objects that graced the hippodrome, such as the famous horses above the carceres, which can be seen today in Venice, the Serpent Column, statues of the 'star-driver' Porphyrius, the obelisks of the Theodosian dynasties and so forth. Some places included a waterchannel, used to water the sand of the arena, a highly dangerous duty carried out by little boys, the *sparsores.* On the spina of the Circus Maximus there also was a counting device, a combination of rising and falling figures (silver eggs and dolphins) which indicated the laps. Around the spina the chariots made their laps, accompanied by *hortatores* and *moratores,* who had to spur on or slow down the horses of the chariots as the situation required.

It is amazing how many of the participants' horses and drivers alike, are still known to us by name—a fact that illustrates their importance during their lifetimes. For them poems were written, statues erected, names preserved in winner's lists, or handed down by historians. In early Greek times we find the names of many local rulers on the lists, the tyrants of Sicily, kings of Sparta, of

Pergamon etc, and later wealthy tradesmen and politicians. In Rome the race courses and the fame clearly belonged to the jockeys. One of the earlier celebrities of the track was Scorpus, active at the end of the first century AD, who was honoured with an epitaph by the poet Martial:

> I am Scorpus, the glory of the roaring circus, the object of Rome's cheers, and her short-lived darling. The Fates, counting not my years but the number of my victories, judged me to be an old man.

And impressive his record was at the time of his premature death—almost certainly on the race course—for he had won 2,048 races. Racing was a dangerous sport, and a number of epitaphs tell the stories of drivers who died in their mid-twenties. The clothing of the drivers clearly did not provide enough protection: a helmet, leather cuirass over the tunic in the colours of their team, and trousers which were sometimes strengthened with leather and greaves. But then, what could have protected them when their chariots, as often happened, collided or crashed against the barriers? The drivers were lucky if they managed to cut themselves free from the reins which they usually had looped around their waists.

Probably the most famous charioteer of the Roman world was Porphyrios Calliopas. Born in Libya, he was brought up and taught his dangerous business in Constantinople shortly before 500 AD. He started racing at an early age, probably younger than eighteen (though this was not exceptionally young for a charioteer) in the great hippodrome of Constantinople which had by then taken over from the Circus Maximus in Rome as the centre of chariot racing. In the more than forty years of his career Porphyrios became so successful that at least six statues were erected for him on the spina of the hippodrome in Constantinople, three by the Greens and three by the Blues. It was not uncommon for drivers to change between the Blues and Greens and also the minor stables of the Reds and Whites during their career. A specialty of Porphyrios' was the *diversium*. In order to prove his outstanding supremacy over the other jockeys he used to swap chariots with them during the race—and still win.

The drivers were well travelled. Porphyrios is reported to have raced in Alexandria, Constantinople and Antioch, where he was the catalyst to an infamous incident that took place in 507 AD. Here he had been engaged by the local Green party to help them back to a winning streak after a long row of defeats—a turnabout he promptly achieved. Incensed by the success of their opponents the Blues rampaged through the city to the noble suburbs of Daphne where a synagogue was set alight. After a series of battles against the Greens imperial troops were brought in and the situation finally defused. We do not know of the consequences of this fraças, but for Porphyrios it did not seem to hinder his career in the long run. Years later we find him defending the Emperor Anastasius against the attempt of the usurper, Vitalian, on the walls of Constantinople. He was probably still involved in racing when the Nika incident took place in 532 AD, one of the worse riots ever to break out at the circus, which left some 30,000 dead.

The horses became almost as famous as the drivers, like one appropriately named Victor, belonging to the second-century champion, Publius Aelius Gutta Calpurnianus. The poet Martial complains about the fame of 'Andraemon' (horse of the aforementioned Scorpus) being bigger than his own. On mosaics horses are often depicted with their names—Romulus, Jubilator, Lupus (Wolf) etc. The names of his horses accompany Porphyrios on the bases of his statues, such as Nikopolemos, Radiatos, Halieus, Anthypathos, Aristides, Palaestiniarches and his two favourites, Pyrros and Euthynikos.

> Now let me describe the mass of people, unemployed and with too much time on their hands . . . For them the Circus Maximus is a temple, home, community centre and the fulfilment of all their hopes. All over the city you can see them quarrelling fiercely about the races . . . They declare that the country will be ruined if at the next meeting their own particular champion does not come first out of the starting-gate and keep his horses in line as he brings them round the post. Before dawn on a race day they all rush headlong for a place on the terraces at such a speed that they could almost beat the chariots themselves.
>
> (Ammianus Marcellinus, XXVIII, iv28)

However, as we have seen these were not simply disorganised masses. The factions were much more than mere 'fan clubs'—their involvement was two-fold.

On the one hand, they employed the teams of charioteers, horses, coaches and provided stables, technical and medical support—in short everything that was needed for the running of a successful winning team. On the other hand, they also rallied the fans. Originally in private hands, from the first century AD onwards, the clubs in Rome were in fact run by the emperors and their officials. They appointed the directors, known as the *'domini factionum'*. The factions were at their most sophisticated in the Byzantine era. The bureaucracy consisted not only of the *demarchoi*, the heads and their deputies, but also of *notarii, factionarii, archontes,* etc, all of whose functions are not entirely clear, but also, significantly, of poets, musicians and conductors, whose duty was to direct the audience in acclamations, applause, chanting and singing against the opposition.

The effect must have been breathtaking and not unlike the spectacle at football stadiums in Naples, Rome, or Milan today. Long before the races started the crowds streamed into the circus. Sun roofs protected them from the heat. While the course was prepared, the ground levelled and sprinkled with water, racing programmes were sold on the terraces, refreshments offered and cushions distributed. Maybe shortly before the event commenced the Emperor would appear in the pulvinar, to the sound of an organ accompanied by elaborate acclamations from the masses: 'God is one. Victory to the Romans. Our Lord have pity on us, our Lord is victorious for ever! May the victory of Theodosius grow strong! May the victory of Valentinia Augustus increase! May the victory of our Lords increase . . .'

A procession, the *'pompa'*, opened the games. The poet Ovid describes the scene:

> But now the parade is coming! Now is the time to cheer and clap; the golden procession is here. First is Victory with her wings spread . . . Here's Neptune. Let the sailors applaud him, terra firma is enough for me. And leave it to the soldiers to cheer for Mars; I loathe the violence, I'm all for love and leisure . . . Next comes Venus; she's the one for my money, she and her cupid with the bow . . .
>
> (Ovid, Amores III, 2)

The procession also included the officials for the race, the umpires, their assistants and the stars of the games—the chariots manned by the jockeys. Then the chariots of the first, the most important, race would draw lots and take up their places in the traps. All eyes would be on the tribunal or kathisma now. Here stood the steward of the games, mappa in hand—and as he dropped it, the gates would open and hell break loose—the chariots racing forward in the straights, towards the nearest meta, where the first collisions would occur. The noise of the crowd must have been overwhelming as the vehicles headed along the spina towards the turning point—hortatores and moratores galloping alongside, doing their best to support their team. The spectators on the opposite side of the spina, unable to see what was happening, would greet the chariots as they turned the bend, guided by the *sinstri funales,* the lead horses on the left, with a tremendous roar:

> When you had covered the open stretch of the track, the part where it narrows and is enclosed by the long spina with its channel and lap counter caught you from our gaze. But when the turn round the far post restored you to our view, your second string was in the lead; your two opponents had passed you, and you were lying fourth. The two drivers in the middle hoped that the leader would swing out to the right on one of the turns and allow them to slip inside him and secure the inner berth. You kept your horses reined back, reserving your effort for the seventh lap. Sweat flew from horses and drivers, and the roar of the crowd grew louder . . .
>
> (Sidonius, Carmina XXIII, p360)

Once the horses had passed, officials hastened onto the course to clear it from debris before the chariots reappeared for the next lap and water was sprinkled onto the sand to settle it.

After the race the victorious charioteer was honoured by the *actuarius.* A lap of honour concluded the first part of the day. Outstanding jockeys, and we can assume that Porphyrius counted among them, additionally won the right to wear the *kassidion,* a silver helmet. Intervals between the races were filled with performances of jugglers, pantomimes and the dance of the factions. Sometimes a gladiatorial fight might take place, or at least a deer hunt. In the later days even death sentences were carried out in the circus. After an exhausting day watching twenty-four races spectators would leave the stadium in the afternoon. Discussions, heated arguments with members of the other colours, maybe a little fight would take place on the way home, but already expectations for the next day's racing were building up.

Ancient horse racing was much more than just a sport, as we have seen. It performed a key role—political, social and cultural. It also serves to illustrate how civilisation spread from the old centres in the east to Greece, Rome and finally the European world. But racing in the ancient fashion perished with the decline of the ancient empires only surviving for a short time in the east with the heiress of Ancient Rome, Byzantium.

FOR FURTHER READING:

O. Olivova, *Chariot Racing in the Ancient World* (Nikephoros 2, 1989); H. A. Harris, *Sport in Ancient Greece and Rome* (Thames & Hudson, 1972); A. Cameron, *Circus Factions, Blues and Greens at Rome and Byzantium* (Oxford University Press, 1976).

Dirk Bennett *studied ancient history and archaeology at Regensburg University.*

Friends, Romans or Countrymen?

Barbarians in the Empire

Lead in the water, over-indulgent lifestyles, rampant inflation—the list of explanations for the fall of the Roman Empire in the west has been endless. But in a new study, Stephen Williams and Gerard Friell turn the spotlight on the 'barbarians' who shored up Rome's armies and frontiers, and discuss if they were Rome's salvation or doom.

Stephen Williams and Gerard Friell are the authors of Theodosius: the Empire at Bay, *Published by Batsford, priced £30.*

The importing of tribal 'barbarian' peoples (mainly Germanic) to the Roman Empire was a permanent imperial policy which expanded in scale over the centuries, and was continued by Byzantium after the Western empire had crumbled in the fifth century—supposedly destroyed by those same Germanic peoples. Like any strategy it had its risks and its critics. 'The introduction of barbarians into the Roman armies,' intones Gibbon, 'became every day more universal, more necessary, and more fatal.'

It is a sombre observation that so many modern historians have split into anti- and pro-barbarian camps, like Roman writers themselves. To Gibbon, Bury, Piganiol, the Germans were a dangerous fifth column which undermined and eventually wrecked the empire. To German historians such as Otto Seeck (1923), W. Ensslin (1941, 1959) and Joseph Vogt (1964), they were an injection of new and vigorous blood which defended and then inherited an exhausted empire. This is not much of an advance on the rival polemics of the Greek rhetorician, Themistius, and the philosopher Synesius in the fourth century. It is surely time to free ourselves from this Punch and Judy approach.

In the early first century, following the disastrous defeat of Varus' three legions in the German forests by Arminius the chief of the Cherusci, Augustus abandoned the earlier ambition of conquering Germany to the Elbe, and set limits to the empire. The Rhine and Danube were to be permanent frontiers. Henceforth, frontier policy involved not just roads, garrisons and fortified points, but an active diplomacy among the external tribes. Trade, protectorship, assistance, subsidies and influence in tribal politics played just as important a role as war or the threat of war.

The Roman aim was to encourage small, friendly client chieftainships who would both respect the Roman frontiers and protect them against other tribal threats, often in return for Roman help against their tribal enemies. Only in this indirect way, carefully conserving the strength of the legions, could the thousands of miles of frontier be policed and maintained. The clients would be formally recognised as 'allies and friends' of Rome (*socii et amici*), although the true relationship was not, of course, between equals. Chieftains would be honoured with Roman citizenship or, more palpably, money subsidies with which to impress and reward their followers. By the mid-first century there was a chain of clients from the lower Rhine to the middle Danube: Frisii, Batavii, Hermunduri, Marcomanni, Quadi and Sarmatians.

The system did not always work smoothly, if only because the tribes were first and foremost warrior peoples to whom seasonal warfare was the normal mode of life. Nor could their nobles always control them, having no coercive apparatus in the manner of sophisticated kingdoms. But, like Highlanders, Pathans, Gurkhas, Zulus, the Germans were recognised not only as a potential threat, but also an enormous reservoir of warlike recruits. It was axiomatic that they would invariably fight each other in any case—let them do it in Roman interests. From the earliest, Germans had been recruited into the specialist auxiliaries in the Roman army, troops of lower pay and status than the legions, though not necessarily inferior in fighting skills. Arminius, who had massacred the three legions in Germany, had himself served as an auxiliary.

To the Germans, Rome represented boundless riches, magnificence and almost unlimited power, which might be plundered but was just as attractive as a high-paying employer of warriors. The German noble who was invited to cross the Rhine to meet Tiberius, said:

> I have today seen those gods, whom until now I had only hear tell of. . . . Our young warriors are foolish to try and defeat you, instead of gaining your trust.

A further move in the diplomatic repertoire was settling barbarians in Roman territory with their families and moveable wealth. As early as 38 BC. Agrippa allowed a German tribe, the Ubii, to settle west of the Rhine, and similar settlements continued intermittently throughout the first century. By the time of Marcus Aurelius in the second century, such transfers had become common practice: Marcus settled barbarians in Dacia (Romania), Pannonia (Western Hungary), Moesia (Romania-Bulgaria), the Rhineland and Italy itself, although the last-named settlement was not a success. Moves of this kind were presented to the Germans as concessions: in fact, they worked to Roman advantage. They dispersed and weakened the aggressive potential of the tribes, transferring part of this potential into Roman control instead. The barbarian youth were ever eager to fight—but now, within the framework and command structure of the Roman army, not their tribal warrior band.

The condition of immigration varied, as did the motive and the initiator. Sometimes it was a compulsory transfer by the Romans to defuse a situation, sometimes it was requested by the tribes who wanted land and security, and sometimes it was refused. Usually it was part of a peace treaty which reflected the degree of Roman ascendancy. After a crushing defeat, of course, prisoners of war who were considered to have no rights might be sold as slaves. Alternatively, captives and family groups would be assigned land as tenant farmers (*coloni*) tied to large landowners or imperial estates, where they would be liable to rent, tax and, later, military service. Increasingly, the defeated enemy was required to supply a specified quota of warriors who would be judiciously distributed among the Roman army.

Where the peace treaty was on more equal terms, different conditions operated. The tribes might supply whole units of troops on a contract basis, such as the 5,500 élite Sarmatian cavalry based at Ribchester (*Bremetennacum*) in the Ribble Valley: at the end of their service they naturally settled in Britain, where many of them had married and raised families, rather than return to their distant Hungarian homeland. Equally common was to allow specified numbers of a population land on which to settle, not as coloni but as the *Laeti:* a community of freehold farmers with all their livestock and moveable wealth, their families and their tribal leaders. They would be disarmed, and subject to the overall authority of a Roman governor, the *Praefectus,* and encouraged to farm the land by subsidies, technical help, temporary tax exemption and whatever else was needed to promote a loyal, thriving community. In time, it was reasonably hoped, they would become Romanised as so many other provincials had done.

By the mid-third century the balance of power on the frontiers had shifted dramatically away from the empire. Great migration pressures were at work southward and eastward, down the Russian rivers, into the Donetz basin and the Hungarian plain, and the Vistula and Oder regions. Continuous tribal warfare, displacements and amalgamations had replaced the old familiar groupings with far larger tribal agglomerations—Visigoths, Ostrogoths, Vandals, Sarmatians, Burgundians, Alemanni, Franks, Saxons—who were a much more formidable threat to Rome. At the same time the Praetorian Guard and then the regional army groups themselves were setting up and murdering emperors in rapid succession. Between 235 and 284 there were fifteen 'legitimate' emperors and many more usurpers, almost every one of which died a violent death.

The military anarchy was both cause and effect of the heightened external threat. Continuous war on all frontiers simultaneously stretched the economic and military resources of the empire beyond their limits. Frontiers were breached, cities sacked and plundered, provinces temporarily overrun, communications disrupted. Continuous war demands and the shrinkage of productive land in the emergencies, drove up taxation and led to uncontrolled money inflation. Regional armies, continually fighting the invaders and demanding ever-higher pay and status, would support their own commanders' ambitions against a distant, in-

effective emperor in Rome whose orders were increasingly irrelevant. This meant treason, and treason meant civil war, which denuded the frontiers yet further. Several main regions of the empire, including Gaul, Spain, Britain, Egypt and Syria, temporarily split off to form separate regional empires.

The empire was eventually bolted together again, most efficiently, by a series of tough soldier-emperors such as Aurelian, Diocletian and Constantine, between about 270 and 330: but it was now a different empire: autocratic, centralised and regimented, a fortress designed for indefinite siege. The armies were expanded, the various enemies defeated, the frontiers restored and greatly strengthened. Painfully but effectively, Roman superiority was everywhere reasserted.

In these circumstances, the need for military manpower was acute. General conscription was introduced, but it proved disappointing. As later empires were to discover, the very spread of civilisation and urbanisation made the populations less willing to become soldiers than their fathers had been. The idle Roman city plebs even cut off their thumbs to avoid the colours. As the fourth-century historian Ammianus observed, as the emperor negotiated a new immigration of Sarmatians from beyond the Danube:

> . . . now that foreign troubles were over and peace was made everywhere, he would gain more childbearing subjects and be able to raise a strong force of recruits: for the provincials would always rather pay tax in gold, to avoid offering their bodies.

It was always the more rustic peoples still with a strong warrior tradition, like today's rural Turks, who made the best and most willing soldiers. Roman recruitment had steadily run through the Gauls, the Spaniards, the Illyrians, and now had to look more and more to the Germanic peoples beyond the frontiers. Diocletian's army contained distinct units of almost every major tribe: Saxons, Franks, Alemanni, Vandals, Goths, Quadi, Sugambri and others.

So long as they were under clearly perceived Roman overlordship, laeti settlements made excellent sense, achieving three imperial policy aims simultaneously. They removed barbarian aggressive pressure by providing settlement land; they got vacant or deserted lands under cultivation again and yield-

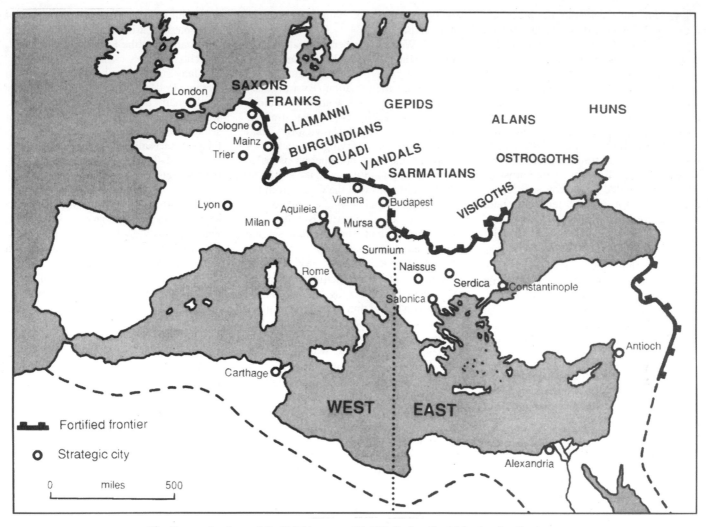

The Roman Empire and its Neighbours *c.* AD 375 (before the Visigoth migration.)

ing a tax: and they provided a steady flow of hardy recruits, which in time was converted into a system of conscription. Instead of money tax, the laeti were asked for men; and once a man had taken the military path, the obligation to serve was automatically passed on to his sons, in a way suggestive of later feudalism.

Laeti settlements were, of course, quite different from modern immigration into European nation-states that were originally ethnically and culturally homogeneous. The Roman Empire was always a multi-national conglomeration in which Greeks, Gauls, Copts, Britons, Dacians, Arabs co-existed but retained much of their national and cultural identity, including language and religion. It was reasonable to see the barbarian settlements as just one more component in this mosaic. After a generation, the difference between Roman and Barbarian would blur. The great melting-pot was the army.

A veteran returning from his service would have been accepted by a military culture which honoured his prowess, but which was very different from the tribal war band and the mead-hall: he would be accepted in the powerful regimental traditions of those who served the great Caesar Augustus, and he would see remote parts of the world of which his people knew nothing. He might gain honours and promotion as so many did, and he would automatically enjoy the respected social rank of *Honestior,* the right to wear the gold rings which was denied to a mere peasant or artisan. His attitudes would have changed by the time he returned to his community a prosperous and respected man, if indeed he returned at all. Like the Sarmatian cavalry, many Germanic soldiers would marry and settle far away from their original community.

The Illyrian soldier-emperors greatly expanded the laeti settlements: Vandals

and Burgundians in Britain, Franks and Memanni in Gaul and Italy, Carpi in Pannonia, Visigoths in Moesia. Constantine settled some 300,000 Sarmatians in Italy, Macedonia, Thrace and Syria. By about 350, perhaps 10 or 15 per cent of the empire's people, and certainly a majority of its army, were of barbarian origin. Constantine's reorganisation of the officer structure for the first time allowed officers of barbarian origin, who were very numerous, to reach the topmost commands. Generals such as Bauto, Arbogast and Richomer (Franks), Nevitta, Fravitta and Modares (Goths), Dagalaif (Alemanni), Victor (Sarmatian) proved superb commanders. They saw themselves not at all as mercenary tribal warriors but loyal Roman commanders and respected members of the ruling classes—which is just what they were.

Everyone recognised the basic distinction between these men, and the Germanic tribes beyond the frontiers.

They, and the Germanic troops in the ranks and lower officer corps, would fight whoever the emperor commanded them to fight, including their own former kinsmen, without hesitation. There was no possibility for them to return to their former tribe—they would be killed on the spot if they did, as the Frank Silvanus discovered when, caught up in a treason plot, he thought of returning to his tribe, but was forcibly warned what would happen. Equally, their barbarian origins precluded them for aspiring to the imperial throne, and tended to hold them in check politically.

Diocletian and Constantine had stabilised the frontiers and the imperial throne with the establishment of a strong dynastic system (Constantine's house ruled, with colleagues, for seventy years) and the standard practice of collegial emperors of East and West, whose regional presence was necessary to control the thousands of miles of threatened frontiers.

But by the late fourth century new and unforseen external threats emerged, which altered the whole strategic situation. The seemingly irresistible pressure of the Huns into the Ukraine region subjugated or evicted the great nations of Goths and Alans, and completely disrupted the carefully balanced diplomatic-defensive system along much of the Danube frontier. The defeated Visigoths and Ostrogoths both desperately petitioned the Eastern emperor Valens to be admitted as laeti, in order to survive as independent people. Valens agreed to the first but refused the second. The immigrant numbers proved huge and unmanageable. They were neither properly disarmed, nor fed, nor dispersed, and their plight was shamefully exploited by the local Roman officials. A major revolt broke out, which was so dangerous that Valens had no alternative but to march against the Visigoths with the main Eastern field army. Their tribal kinsmen the Ostrogoths took advantage of the confused state of the Danube defences to cross also.

On the faithful day of August 9th, 378, the combined forces of the Goths met the Roman army outside Adrianople (modern Edirne), and owing to Valens' incompetent mistakes, the result was the most catastrophic Roman defeat for centuries. Over two-thirds of the army—perhaps 20,000 men—were slain, including Valens himself. The East was virtually defenceless as the Goths roamed unopposed, plundering Greece and the Balkans.

The Western emperor, Gratian, appointed the general, Theodosius, Emperor of the East, with the daunting task of restoring the situation. By ruthlessly scraping together a new army of dubious quality, by skilful use of the strategic fortified cities, by local victories, manoeuvre and by starving the Goths of supplies, the two coemperors were at last able to regain the military initiative. They could not expel the Goths from the empire (they had nowhere else to go), nor destroy them in battle. But they split their forces and their loyalties, and weakened them sufficiently to bring them to a peace treaty in 382.

This granted them settlement land in Moesia and Thrace as 'allies' (Foederati) with obligation to provide military forces for the emperor on demand. Despite contemporary—and modern—criticisms of this treaty, it was probably the very best that could be had in the desperate circumstances. Superficially, it was represented in imperial propaganda as 'business as usual', a continuation of earlier settlements. In reality, both the emperors and the Goths knew it was a distinct new departure. The clear pre-condition of all the earlier settlements—perceived, unambiguous Roman supremacy—was no longer there. The Visigoths were settled not as a disarmed community of laeti, subject to a Praefectus and supplying individual recruits or small units to be integrated into the Roman command structure. They were a semi-independent nation in arms, subject to their own tribal chieftains who had concluded an equal treaty with the emperor: they would fight *en masse* as a national allied army under their own leaders. It was open to them to see the treaty of 382 as a concession they had finally prized out of the Romans as a result of their victory at Adrianople. All the manoeuvres, shifts and bargainings of frontier diplomacy were now having to be enacted *within* Roman territory.

This step could not be reversed, but Theodosius tried hard to stop it becoming a precedent. He badly needed the Gothic manpower to rebuild his armies, and he probably hoped that given time, the Gothic state-within-a-state could be brought under firmer overlordship, like the conventional laeti. He followed a deliberate public policy of conciliation between Romans and barbarians, wooing their nobles with benefits of 'Roman-ness' and co-operation, to the disgust of the senatorial aristocracy. His own niece was married to the loyal Vandal general, Stilicho.

Many responded. Some powerful Gothic leaders became enthusiastically pro-Roman, but now they knew there were far more favourable conditions of settlement than the old laeti: they saw themselves as allies, not subjects, and they husbanded their forces as the only ultimate safeguard against imperial bad faith. Still, the settlement worked acceptably during Theodosius' reign. The Visigoths kept their part of the bargain, helped him win two costly civil wars, and also made it possible for a fresh Ostrogoth invasion to be repulsed on the Danube in 386.

The situation might have stabilised at this point. But in 395 its architect, Theodosius, suddenly died, leaving the twin thrones of East and West to his two immature and inexperienced sons, Arcadius and Honorius. This was a gravely dangerous new situation. Inevitably, real power was wielded by ministers, generals, empresses, who could be no substitute for strong, militarily respected emperors. The traditional loyalty between the thrones of East and West was not only suspended, but turned into its opposite, as the two courts intrigued against each other like separate states. The Visigoths were not slow to occupy the power vacuum.

Their leader Alaric had wanted a full Roman generalship, which Theodosius had wisely refused. Alaric now had himself proclaimed king, and led his warriors on another grand plundering expedition, until the Eastern government, in desperation, granted him the top military command in Illyricum (Yugoslavia and the Balkans) which legitimised his plundering and gave him access to the Roman arms factories.

For the next fifteen years the volatile Alaric was a very destructive third force in the empire, who could be held in check and occasionally defeated, but not destroyed or tamed. To assemble the forces desperately needed against him, to crush a revolt in Africa and repel an Ostrogothic invasion of the Italian heartland, the Western generalissimo Stilicho was forced to buy barbarian troops on almost any terms: *ad-hoc* treaties ceding yet more territory to new Foederati. To defend Italy itself, he was forced to strip Britain and the Rhine defences below the danger level, and in 407 hordes of Vandals, Suevi, Alans and others poured across the frozen Rhine into Gaul, never to be dislodged again. This ultimately cost him his position and his life. In 408 his enemies procured his execution on a trumped-up treason charge. Half his soldiers deserted in disgust to Alaric.

Freed of the one military leader who could defeat him, Alaric went on to sack Rome in 410. Henceforth, the Roman military rulers in the West—Constantius, Aetius and others—not only had to rule through incompetent puppet emperors, but had to accept the military reality of new 'Foederati' in Pannonia, Gaul, Spain and then Africa, hoping to play off one against another. By now they dropped even the nominal pretence that these were Roman subjects, and officially recognised them as kings and allies. Alaric had set the dangerous precedent of uniting the two offices of Roman field-marshal (*Magister Militum*) and Gothic King. Henceforth other supreme warlords such as the Goth Ricimer could rule in reality, setting up and discarding imperial puppets at will,

until eventually even these empty symbols were unnecessary, and in 476 were simply dropped. Insofar that a veneer of Roman legitimacy was needed, the kings looked to Constantinople, where there was still a real emperor. In the West, many Roman officers and civil servants made the best of things by serving the new kingdoms and hoping to civilise them.

There was no casual continuity between the earlier policies of controlled barbarian immigration, and the later carving out of large sections of the former Western empire into German proto-kingdoms. The nationalist picture of Germanic infiltration and subversion, and the opposing idealistic picture of heroic German saviours and newcomers, are both shallow and unhistorical. The Roman empire, perhaps more than any other on earth, disregarded ethnic origins and rewarded loyalty, skill and energies within its imperial system. Many of its greatest emperors were themselves Spaniards, Africans and above all, Illyrians. What happened in the Roman West

in the fifth century had very little to do with ethnic origins or even culture. It was a breakdown of crucial political parameters, beginning with the treaty of 382, which time and events did not allow to be re-established.

The Germanic allies did not initially seek to destroy or replace the Roman framework, provided they could find a strong, respected, federal place within it—which, in more favourable conditions, might well have been achieved. By 800 Charlemagne wanted nothing so much as the fictional crown of Holy Roman Emperor, equal to the emperor at Constantinople.

FOR FURTHER READING:

J.B. Bury, *The Later Roman Empire* (1923: Dover paperbacks, 1958); A.H.M. Jones, *The Later Roman Empire*, (Vol 1, Blackwell, 1964); J.M. O'Flynn, *Generalissimos of the Later Roman Empire* (Edmonton, 1983); P.J. Heather, *Goths and Romans*, (Clarendon, 1991).

Unit 3

Unit Selections

15. **Jews and Christians in a Roman World,** Eric M. Meyers and L. Michael White
16. **The Other Jesus,** Kenneth L. Woodward
17. **Women and the Bible,** Cullen Murphy
18. **Ecstasy in Late Imperial Rome,** Dirk Bennett
19. **Who the Devil Is the Devil?** Robert Wernick

Key Points to Consider

❖ Describe the relationship that existed among Jews, Christians, and pagans during the Roman era.

❖ How do Jews, Buddhists, Hindus, and Muslims view Jesus as opposed to the Christian interpretation?

❖ Why do you think ancient Jewish and early Christian writings ignored or downplayed the importance of women?

❖ How did the various religions of the Near East view the Devil?

 **Links**   **www.dushkin.com/online/**

15. **Facets of Religion/Casper Voogt**
    http://www.bcca.org/~cvoogt/Religion/mainpage.html
16. **Institute for Christian Leadership/ICLnet**
    http://www.iclnet.org
17. **Introduction to Judaism**
    http://philo.ucdavis.edu/Courses/RST23/ rst23homepage.html
18. **Selected Women's Studies Resources/Columbia University**
    http://www.columbia.edu/cu/libraries/subjects/womenstudies/

These sites are annotated on pages 4 and 5.

Western civilization developed out of the Greco-Roman world, but it is also indebted to the Judeo-Christian tradition. If Western civilization derives humanism and materialism, philosophy, politics, art, literature, and science, from the former, it derives its God and forms of worship from the latter. It is perhaps difficult or misguided to separate these traditions, for the Judeo-Christian heritage comes to us through a Hellenistic filter. This angle is explored in the first unit article, "Jews and Christians in a Roman World."

On the political surface the history of the Jews seems similar to that of other small kingdoms of the Near East, closely situated as they were to such powerful neighbors as the Babylonians, Assyrians, and Persians. Yet of all the peoples of that time and place, only the Jews have had a lasting influence. What appears to differentiate the Jews from all the rest, writes historian Crane Brinton, is "the will to persist, to be themselves, to be a people." The appearance of Israel on the map of the modern world 2,000 years after the Romans destroyed the Jewish client-state is a testimonial to the spirit described by Brinton.

The legacy of the Jews is a great one. It includes the rich literary traditions found in their sacred texts. And they have bequeathed to Western civilization their unique view of history, which is linear and miraculous—God intervenes in history to guide, reward, or punish his Chosen People. They also gave birth to the morality within the Ten Commandments, the moral wisdom of the prophets, and a messianic impulse that inspired Christianity and other cults. Their monotheism and their god, Yahweh, formed the model for Christian and Muslim ideas of God.

A brief comparison of Yahweh and the Greek god Zeus illustrates the originality of the Jewish conception. Both gods began as warrior deities of tribal cultures. But, as Zeus evolved, he was chiefly concerned with Olympian rather than human affairs. Yahweh, on the other hand, was more purposeful and had few interests except for his people. And unlike Zeus, who was in and out of the universe, Yahweh was the creator of the universe.

Certainly Christianity bears the stamp of Judaism. After all, Christ himself was a Jew. To his early followers, all of them Jews, he satisfied the powerful messianic messages inherent in Judaism. The New Testament recounts the growth and spread of Christianity from an obscure Jewish sect in Palestine to a new religion with great appeal in the Roman world. Yet Jesus, the central figure in this great drama, remains shrouded in mystery, for there is a dearth of firsthand evidence. The Gospels, the greatest and most familiar source, contain wide gaps in their account of the life of Jesus. Nonetheless, they remain a profound record of early Christian faith. In the essay "The Other Jesus," Kenneth Woodward describes the ways in which Jesus is viewed by Jews, Christians, Hindus, and Buddhists. Next, Cullen Murphy, in "Women and the Bible," assesses scholarly efforts to understand why

ancient Jewish and early Christian writings ignored or downplayed the role of women.

As it separated from Judaism, Christianity took on new dimensions, including the promise of private salvation through participation in the sacraments. From the beginning, its theology reflected the teachings of St. Paul, who changed the focus from converting the Jews into spreading the faith among the Gentiles. Then, as it took hold in the Near East, Christianity absorbed some Hellenistic elements—Stoicism, Platonism, and the Roman pantheon. The latter is the subject of Dirk Bennet's essay, "Ecstasy in Late Imperial Rome." The way was prepared for a fusion of classical philosophy and Christianity. The personal God of the Jews and Christians became the abstract god of the Greek philosophers. Biblical texts were given symbolic meanings that might have confounded an earlier, simpler generation of Christians. The Christian view of sexuality, for instance, became fraught with multiple meanings and complexities. In effect, Christianity was no longer a Jewish sect; it had become Westernized. Eventually it would become a principal agent for Westernization of much of the world.

The last essay in this section deals with evil in a personal form. "Who the Devil Is the Devil?" by Robert Wernick recounts the origins and influence of the Devil from the ancient religions until the modern day.

Jews and Christians in a Roman World

New evidence strongly suggests that both in Roman Palestine and throughout the Diaspora, Judaism, Christianity, and paganism thrived side by side.

Eric M. Meyers and L. Michael White

More than a century ago, archaeologists began to rediscover the ancient world of the Mediterranean: the world of Homer and the Bible. Much of the early fieldwork in the classical world arose from a romantic quest to bring ancient literature to life. One thinks instinctively of Schleimann at Troy, a shovel in one hand and a copy of Homer in the other. In the Holy Land, the first biblical archaeologists were theologians and ministers who sought to identify and explore cities of the biblical world and to authenticate biblical stories and traditions; thus they arrived with preconceived ideas drawn from biblical texts and other literary sources. Because many were Old Testament scholars, New Testament archaeology in the Holy Land took a back seat. Outside the Holy Land, it remained for years in the shadow of classical archaeology.

Since World War II, and especially since the discovery of the Dead Sea scrolls in 1947, archaeology has been more attentive to the world of the New Testament. But the new archaeological knowledge has only slowly begun to have an impact because New Testament scholars have been slow to take archaeology seriously. Some scholars think archaeology is of peripheral concern to early Christian studies, concluding debatably that the "earthly" dimension of early Christianity is irrelevant. New Testament archaeology is also given low priority in Jewish studies, which traditionally have placed far greater emphasis on sacred texts. Many believe New

Testament archaeology to be of limited value in the study of ancient Palestine, erroneously assuming that the archaeological time frame is restricted to only two generations, from the time of Jesus to the destruction of Jerusalem in the year 70. In fact, one cannot understand the development of either Judaism or Christianity without looking at the historical context over centuries, beginning with the introduction of Greek culture into the ancient Near East.

THE HOMELAND

Scholarly understanding of Judaism and Christianity in the Roman province of Palestine during the early Common Era (abbreviated C.E. and chronologically the same as A.D.) has long been burdened by some dubious suppositions. One is the belief that after the First Jewish Revolt against Rome in 66–70 C.E., the new Jewish-Christian community fled the Holy Land. Certainly there was significant emigration to the Mediterranean lands, but in light of archaeological evidence from the first two or three centuries C.E., a growing number of scholars have found the idea of wholesale Jewish-Christian migration untenable.

Actually, the first followers of Jesus were basically indistinguishable from their fellow Jews. Although they believed Jesus was the Messiah and professed a radical love ethic that had few parallels in Judaism—for example, love for one's enemies—the first Jewish-

Christians observed most of the Jewish laws and revered the Temple in Jerusalem. They apparently got along well with their fellow Jews, contrary to the impression created in the Gospels and other New Testament writings, where the Pharisees, the "mainstream" religious party of ancient Judaism, are presented in a negative light. The new Christians, in fact, were at odds mostly with the Sadducees, who were much more rigid in their religious outlook than the Pharisees, and far fewer in number. When the Apostles were persecuted by the Sadducean high priest, it was the Pharisee Rabbi Gamaliel who intervened to save them (Acts 5:17–42); when Paul was called before the Sanhedrin (the High Council) in Jerusalem, he obtained his release by appealing to the Pharisees (Acts 22:30–23:10); and according to the Jewish historian Josephus, when Jesus' brother James was put to death by order of the Sadducean high priest in 62 C.E., the Pharisees appealed to the king to depose the high priest. Jesus' natural constituency was the Pharisees, whose doctrine of love for one's fellow humans must surely have been the foundation for Jesus' ethical teaching.

The belief that all or most of the Jewish-Christians left Palestine after the First Revolt stems partly from the lack of clear material traces of the Christian community in the Holy Land from about 70 to 270 C.E. Early Christianity, however, vigorously sought to win converts both among gentiles and in the many Jewish communities throughout the

Surprise Findings From Early Synagogues

The synagogue provides a rare opportunity to study the Jewish people—and Jewish-Christians—as they forged a new religious way in Roman Palestine after the fall of Jerusalem. Even within a given region, we find a great variety of architectural forms and artistic motifs adorning the walls and halls of ancient synagogues. This great divergence of synagogue types suggests great variety within Talmudic Judaism, even though the members of different congregations belonged to a common culture.

Such diversity resulted in part from the catastrophe of 70 C.E., after which many sectarian groups were forced to fend for themselves in a new and often alien environment. Some groups settled in town, others in urban centers; their choices reflected their understanding of how hospitable a setting their beliefs would find in either the sophisticated cities or the agrarian towns.

Synagogue excavations also attest to the primacy of Scripture in Jewish worship and provide a clearer view of the place held by the *bema,* or raised prayer platform, and the Ark of the Law. The Ark is the fixed repository for the biblical scrolls, which were stored in a central place in the synagogue by the third century C.E. Until recently, the dominant view was that the Ark remained portable throughout most of antiquity.

Some synagogue mosaics even suggest that Jewish art played an integral part in the composition of new poetry recited in the synagogue. In late Roman synagogue mosaics, themes based on the zodiac begin to appear. These mosaics are followed in the textual record by poems that name the actual constellations of the zodiac. The setting for reciting such poems, or *pzyyutim,* was undoubtedly the synagogue, where the intelligentsia would have gathered and included the poems in their worship.

Finally, survey and excavation of numerous synagogue sites in the Golan Heights have revealed an astonishingly lively and vigorous Jewish community in Palestine in late Roman, Byzantine, and early Islamic times. The supposed eclipse of Jewish life at the hands of early Christendom—especially after the conversion of Constantine and, later, the establishment of Christianity as the state religion in 383 C.E.—needs to be reexamined. In fact, one of the surprises of recent synagogue studies is the generally high level of Jewish culture in Palestine at the end of the Roman period (third and fourth centuries C.E.) and the continued though sporadic flourishing of synagogue sites in the Byzantine period (from the middle of the third century to 614 C.E., the year of the Persian conquest of Palestine). All the evidence points to a picture of a Judaism in Palestine that was very much alive until the dawn of the medieval period.

Mediterranean. It is exceedingly hard to imagine these efforts bypassing the large Jewish community in Palestine.

Moreover, Jews from Jerusalem and the surrounding area fled in large numbers to Galilee after the revolt was crushed. Would the first Jewish-Christians have ignored Galilee, where Jesus spent his childhood and where he conducted his ministry? Later generations of Christians certainly did not, as evidenced by the numerous churches they built in Galilee. The presence of important Christian centers of worship makes it difficult to imagine a great Christian "repopulation" of Palestine between the third and fifth centuries. Rather, it seems there was a large community of Jewish-Christians in Palestine from the first century onward, a community later augmented by pilgrims in the age of Constantine.

Jerusalem is central in the study of early Christianity. It is there that the new religion received its most compelling moments of inspiration in the death and burial of Jesus; and it is from there that its followers took their message to the other cities and towns of the land. As long as the Temple stood, the first Christians continued to worship there and in private household meetings. With the destruction of the Temple, however, both Jews and Christians had to establish new patterns of worship. Thus the local synagogue, which was both a meeting place and a center of worship, became the focus of spiritual life for Jew and Jewish-Christian after 70 C.E.

Recent synagogue excavations have revealed that Jewish life enjoyed remarkable vitality in Palestine during the Roman period, and in some localities into the Byzantine period and beyond. In the pre-Constantinian era, the synagogue was quite possibly where Jewish-Christians worshiped as well. Although the archaeological record shows very little definitive evidence of Christianity until the end of the third century, the textual record is quite clear. In a reference that may go back to 100 or 120 C.E., the Jerusalem Talmud implies that Christians are a sect of *minim,* or heretics. Irenaeus, the first Christian theologian to systematize doctrine, speaks of Ebionites, who read only the Gospel of Matthew, reject Paul, and follow the Torah and the Jewish way of life. Epiphanius, another early Christian writer, speaks of Nazarenes, or Elkasaites, as Christians who insist on the validity of the Torah and laws of purity.

Whether one looks at early Christianity or rabbinic Judaism in Roman Palestine, it is clear that this was a period of great cultural and religious pluralism. One finds this pluralism in the Lower Galilee, at Sepphoris, and at the great site of Capernaum on the northwestern shore of the Sea of Galilee. The octagonal Church of St. Peter in Capernaum is built over what some excavators believe is a Jewish-Christian "house-church" dating back to about the third century. The excavators have also found evidence of a first-century house below this church edifice that may have been Peter's residence. It is clear that by the fourth century, Christians venerated the site by erecting churches there. Next to these Christian structures are Jewish buildings, including a reconstructed synagogue. Archaeologists once thought the synagogue was from the first century C.E., the very building in which Jesus would have walked. Today there is universal agreement that it is a later structure, dating to the fourth or fifth century, that survived for hundreds of years into the early medieval period. Excavators have recently claimed finding another synagogue, from the first century, beneath this fourth- or fifth-century synagogue. If they are right, then in Capernaum a Jewish synagogue and a Jewish-Christian church existed side by side from the end of the first century on. The grander structures above both the early synagogue and the house of Peter in Capernaum suggest that Jewish and Christian communities lived in harmony until the seventh century. The continuous Christian presence for six centuries also casts serious doubts on the idea that the early Christians fled Palestine after 70 C.E. Evidence like that found in Capernaum is plentiful in the Beth Shean Valley and in the Golan Heights, although the evidence there begins later, toward the end of the Roman period and into the Byzantine period.

In the middle of the fourth century, pluralism began to suffer as the Roman period in Palestine came to an end and the Byzantine period began. The transition from Roman to Byzantine culture as revealed by the archaeological and textual records was dramatic and coincides with either the so-called Gallus Revolt against Roman occupation in 352 or the great earthquake of 363. In the case of the revolt, the Byzantine emperor might have taken the opportunity to place the unruly province under his direct rule. In the case of the earthquake, the damage to Roman buildings would have presented the opportunity for a Byzantine architectural and cultural style to emerge as cities were rebuilt.

In either case, the revolt and the aftermath of the earthquake mark the beginning of a difficult period for Jews, in which they had little choice but to adjust to Christian rule. The Palestine of the Roman period, when Jewish sages spoke in Greek and when Rabbi Judah the Prince reputedly numbered the Roman emperor among his friends, became a land undergoing thorough and vigorous Christianization after the conversion of Constantine. Money poured into Palestine, and much of it went into building churches.

Nevertheless, archaeological evidence prompts us to exercise caution. Pockets of Judaism and Christianity remained in close contact during the Byzantine period. They may well have continued the harmonious relations established during the period of pluralism, even as Christianity became the dominant religion.

THE DIASPORA

Archaeology has also enriched our understanding of the New Testament world outside Palestine. It is significant to both Jewish and Christian history that the bulk of the New Testament is set outside the Jewish homeland. Jews and Christians alike called their communities outside Palestine the Diaspora, or "dispersion."

While the religious heritage of the New Testament may be Hebrew, its language is Greek. Its cultural heritage is not that of the ancient Near East but that of Greece and Rome. The world of the New Testament was fluid and pluralistic, with an extensive transportation network crisscrossing the Mediterranean. Christians and Jews traveled the highways and seaways, carrying their religion with them. This mobility is vividly reflected in the extensive journeys of Paul.

The work of archaeologists should not be used to prove New Testament stories about Paul. The remains of his day are simply too hard to find.

The New Testament record of Paul's travels provided early investigators with both an itinerary for their archaeological work as well as a "case" to be proved. From the 1880s to the 1920s, for example, the eminent Sir William Ramsay sought to corroborate the account given in the Acts of the Apostles of Paul's activities on his way to Rome, in Ephesus, Athens, Corinth, and Philippi. Shaping Ramsay's approach were attractive images of Paul, such as the one in chapter 17 of Acts, where he is depicted preaching to the philosophers on the Areopagus, or Mars Hill, below the entrance to the Acropolis. The story in Acts, and later Christian legends attributed to Paul's followers, are the only evidence we have for this. Paul left no footprints on the Areopagus for archaeologists to follow. It is also interesting that Paul, in his own letters, never once mentioned his activities or this episode in Athens. Still, this remains a popular tourist spot, and the legacy of early archaeologists like Ramsay lives on.

All over the eastern Mediterranean, tourists play out variations on this theme with local guides. (Though Paul was a tireless traveler, if he had visited every one of these places, he might have died of old age before he got to Rome.) Often

the difficulties arise when local legends, which seem to grow like stratigraphic layers, become attached to a site. A prime example of this occurs at Paul's *bema* at Corinth.

Excavations at Corinth have revealed a fifth-century Christian church erected over what appears to be a bema, or speaking platform. The obvious assumption was that this was the site of Paul's defense before the Roman governor Gallio in Acts 18:12 ("But when Gallio was proconsul of Achaia, the Jews made a united attack upon Paul and brought him before their tribunal"). Indeed, the story is given further credence by the discovery of an inscription from Delphi that bears the name of Gallio as well as his title. This inscription has been very important in dating Paul's stay in Corinth to around the years 51 and 52 C.E. But it is most difficult to place Paul's trial on this particular bema, since the South Stoa of Corinth, where the bema is found, was expanded and rebuilt during the next two centuries. Other evidence found at Corinth does little to clear matters up. A pavement bearing the name of Erastus, the city treasurer named in Romans 16:23, identifies him as an *aedile,* a minor administrative official, not as treasurer ("Erastus, the city treasurer, and our brother Quartus greet you"). Is this a tangible record of a follower of Paul at Corinth? One cannot be sure. As at the Areopagus, the best advice may be *caveat* pilgrim.

Similar problems arise in trying to place Paul or John in Ephesus, since Byzantine and medieval accounts have been overlayed on the biblical stories. Current excavations at Ephesus have revealed an elaborate Roman city of the second to sixth centuries C.E., but evidence of the first-century city remains sparse. Extensive excavations at Philippi, in Macedonia, have uncovered a second-century forum and main roadway, but most of the remains come from churches and basilicas dating from the fourth to the seventh centuries. Once again, the remains of Paul's day are difficult to identify.

In some cases, the connection of a site with Paul is demonstrably wrong. For example, Christian pilgrimage and devotion in Philippi helped to equate a Hellenistic pagan crypt with Paul's "prison," as described in chapter 16 of Acts. In the late fifth century, a basilica was built around this site. In short, the work of archaeologists should not be

Palestine's Sophisticated Cities

In recent decades, a number of important cities besides Jerusalem have undergone major excavation, yielding evidence of a sophisticated life-style in Palestine. These were Roman cities, built for the administrative infrastructure of imperial rule, but they also became conduits through which Greco-Roman culture was introduced into Palestine.

These cities dominated Palestine, except for the upper Galilee and Golan regions in the North, but the level of sophistication dropped steeply when one moved away from these urban cores. In the surrounding areas, the older agrarian life-style was still very much dominant, and it was town more than city that ultimately encompassed most of Jewish, and Jewish-Christian, life in Palestine.

Nonetheless, there were some Hellenized centers of Jewish life, mostly along the major roadways, the Lower Galilee, the Rift Valley, and the coastal plain. The primary language here was Greek, and the surrounding Jewish population used Greek for trade and day-to-day discourse. In time, Greek eclipsed Hebrew as the common language, and many of Israel's most important sages buried their loved ones, or were themselves buried, in containers or sarcophagi that bore Greek epigraphs or Greco-Roman decorations. In striking contrast, virtually no Greek is found in the Upper Galilee or the Golan.

Such tombs are exceptionally instructive. For example, the Jewish catacombs of the sages in Beth Shearim, excavated in the late 1920s, attest to the high level of Greek spoken by the sages. They attest as well to the fact that the sages were comfortable with a style of decoration in their tombs that was thought by contemporary scholars to be incompatible with Jewish sensibilities and law, and with the proscription against representational and figural art contained in the Second Commandment. With the discovery in 1987 of the extraordinary Dionysos mosaic at Sepphoris, the heartland of the Jewish sages, an exciting new perspective was provided on the Hellenization of Roman Palestine.

It is not yet clear who commissioned the colorful mosaic stone carpet, found near both the Roman theater and Jewish buildings and homes, but the ramifications of the discovery are most significant. The mosaic dates to about 200 C.E., the time of Rabbi Judah the Prince, who was both a leader in the compilation of the Mishnah (Jewish traditional doctrine) and reputedly a close friend of the Roman emperor Caracalla. The central panel of the carpet shows Herakles/Dionysos in a drinking contest. The 15 panels that surround this scene depict the life and times of Dionysos, god of wine, the afterlife, revelry, fertility, and theater. What is so amazing is that they are all labeled in Greek, either to clarify the contents for those who didn't know Greek mythology—a gap in knowledge probably not uncommon in these eastern provinces—or to jog the memory of those who ate in the hall in which the stone carpet was located.

The implications of this discovery are many, but the three most important may be summarized as follows: the extent of Hellenization in Palestine by the third century C.E. is greater than was previously believed; Jews were more accepting of great pagan centers than was previously believed, and had more access to them; Jewish familiarity with Hellenistic culture in urban centers such as Sepphoris was a positive force affecting Jewish creativity. It hardly seems coincidental that the Mishnah was codified and published at Sepphoris during the very same period when a highly visible Hellenistic culture and presence flourished in Palestine.

---

used to prove such New Testament stories. Instead, archaeological work should be used more as a "backdrop" for the discussion of Paul's letters to Christian congregations living in these cities of the Roman world. The focus of archaeology should be placing the Christians and Jews in a cultural context.

More recent archaeological perspectives shed light on the development of Jewish and Christian institutions of the New Testament world. Originally, "church" (the Greek *ekklesia*) and "synagogue" (the Greek *synagoge*) were synonymous terms for assembly or congregation. Especially in the earliest days of the Diaspora, Christian groups including gentile converts, were considered to be following a form of Jewish practice. Only in the second century would the terms "church" and "synagogue" begin to become specific to Christians and Jews. In fact, distinct architectural differences between them did not begin until the fourth century. In other words, if we were following Paul through Ephesus or Corinth, we would not be able to distinguish Christian or Jewish meeting places from the exteriors of the buildings.

Most of the congregations founded by Paul met in the houses of individual members. Significantly, Diaspora Jewish groups would have met in houses, too; but over time, more formal synagogue buildings appeared. If anything, house-synagogues were in use earlier in the Diaspora than in Palestine (as early as the first century B.C.E.). Of the six early Diaspora synagogues known from excavations—at Delos, Priene, Ostia, Dura-Europos, Stobi, and Sardis—five were originally houses that were renovated and adapted to special religious use. The earliest of these, from Delos, dates to the very beginning of the Common Era, or even slightly earlier.

There is evidence that Jews and Christians worshiped as neighbors in the Diaspora, as in Roman Palestine. One of the most impressive discoveries in this regard comes from Dura-Europos, a Roman garrison on the Euphrates River in what is now Iraq, dating to before 256 C.E. On one street was a house that had been renovated, in three stages, into a sanctuary of Mithras, a Persian god whose cult spread throughout the Roman empire from the second half of the first century C.E. onward. Farther down the same street, another house had been converted, in two stages, into a synagogue. Its assembly hall contained one of the earliest datable Torah niches, and on its walls were elaborate frescoes depicting stories from the Hebrew Scriptures. Farther down the same street was a house that was renovated to become a Christian church, with a small assembly hall and a room set aside for baptism. The baptistry room in particular has attracted considerable attention, since it contains some of the earliest clearly datable Christian art, including representations of Jesus in scenes from the Gospels.

More evidence of religious pluralism in the Diaspora can be seen in Rome. Excavations beneath several basilicas, such as those of St. Clement and SS. John and Paul, reveal earlier buildings—houses or apartment complexes—that were being renovated for religious use as early as the first century. The house-church of St. Clement, for example, is generally identified with the first-century levels below St. Clement's Basilica. Interestingly, the second-century house adjacent to the house-church of St. Clement was used as a Mithraic cult sanctuary. Seven such Mithraic halls are known from Rome, and another 14 from the nearby port of Ostia. In addition, inscriptions from Jewish catacombs suggest at least 11 synagogues existed in Rome during imperial times.

The complex society that sustained such pluralism is now the focus of much research. A new group of biblical archaeologists, using what they refer to as a "social history" approach, are attempting to bring biblical texts and archaeological evidence into a more cohesive historical framework. The basis of their work is the use of archaeological evidence not merely as proof or illustration but as a key to the historical and social context of religion. In the Hellenized Roman cities of Palestine, such as Sepphoris, and in major urban centers of the Diaspora, such as Corinth, the activities of Jews and Christians must be seen as part of a complex culture and viewed over several centuries of development.

For example, textual evidence shows the existence of a Jewish community at Sardis in Roman Lydia (western Turkey) since the time of Julius Caesar; however, the first significant archaeological evidence of its activities comes hundreds of years later with the renovation of a public hall, part of the bath-gymnasium complex, to serve as a synagogue. Thus we know that Jews and Christians were both in Sardis for a long time, but apparently with no distinctions by which we can recognize their daily activities. The synagogue was in use from the third century to the sixth century, and its size and opulence attest to the vitality of Jewish life in Sardis. The synagogue was renovated by Jews at least twice after its initial adaptation, and these renovations were extensive and costly. Moreover, its inscriptions give evidence of the social standing and connections of the Jewish community: a total of 12 known donors to the renovations are titled "citizen" or "city councillor," and in some cases both. Other notables, including several Roman bureaucrats, are also named in the roster of donors. Here the archaeological record yields a picture of a Jewish community, over several centuries, that was politically favored and socially "at home" in the civic life of Sardis. To understand the life of the Jews of Sardis, however, one must place them not only in the context of their city but also ask how their local conditions compare to other Jewish groups from the Diaspora.

The evidence suggests that Jews and Christians were able to live in much closer harmony with one another than has often been assumed.

This same social history approach may be applied to Christian groups as well. At stake are a number of traditional assumptions about Judaism and Christianity in relation to their social and religious environment. It would seem that Jews and Christians were able to live in much closer harmony both with one another and with their pagan neighbors than has often been assumed. To an outsider, both church and synagogue might have resembled foreign social clubs or household cults.

The mobility within the Diaspora produced cultural as well as theological diversity, even within the Jewish and Christian traditions. We should not assume that the Diaspora synagogue communities conformed to Talmudic Judaism. A good case in point is seen in recent archaeological evidence, especially from inscriptions, for active participation and even leadership by women in Diaspora synagogues—something also seen in the homeland. This could eventually shed light on the significant role of women in Paul's churches. To date, however, the main information comes from the New Testament writings, which give evidence of women as house-church patrons, as in Romans 16:2–5.

There are numerous ways in which Jews and Christians of the Diaspora were influenced by their cultural environment. Especially noteworthy are conventions of letter writing drawn from the analysis of papyri, which can enhance our understanding of the letters of Paul. Likewise, conventions of building or donation inscriptions offer a means of understanding many synagogue inscriptions, such as those at Sardis. Still more common are Jewish and Christian burial inscriptions. Both in burial inscriptions and in funerary art one finds that the earliest Jews and Christians, when one can distinguish them at all, regularly used motifs and language common in the larger pagan environment.

Thus there is a wide array of new and old archaeological data available for students of Judaeo-Christian antiquity. Whether it comes from East or West, whether it is inscribed with letters or decorated with figural art, it constitutes the most significant body of evidence for reconstructing the cultural context in which Jews and early Christians lived.

Of all the human sciences, archaeology is best equipped to deal with such complex matters. When strongly tied to the literary and historical disciplines, it becomes the most reliable tool for reconstructing the ancient societies in which Judaism and Christianity, orphaned from Jerusalem, found new homes.

The Other Jesus

*To Christians, he is the Son of God. But the world's other great
religions have their own visions of a legendary figure.*

By Kenneth L. Woodward

*Christ is absolutely original and ab-
solutely unique. If He were only a
wise man like Socrates, if He were a
prophet like Muhammad, if He were
enlightened like the Buddha, without
doubt He would not be what He is.*
                            —John Paul II

EVER SINCE HIS ELECTION, JOHN
Paul II has wanted one thing:
to walk where Jesus walked,
preach where Jesus taught and pray
where Jesus was crucified, died and was
buried. This week the pope finally gets
his chance. Weary in body but ecstatic
in spirit, John Paul makes his long-
anticipated pilgrimage to the Holy
Land. For him it is a personal "journey
with God"; there will be no intruding
television cameras when, lost in prayer,
he communes alone at Christianity's
holiest shrines. But the land of his
heart's desire is holy to Jews and Muslims as well. And so the pope will visit
the Western Wall, Judaism's most sacred
site, and the Mosque of El Aqsa atop
the Temple Mount. He will also meet
with Muslim and Jewish religious leaders and—in one particularly resonant
moment—pause to pray at Yad Vashem,
Israel's memorial to victims of the
Holocaust.

Like his powerful plea for forgive-
ness a fortnight ago, the pope's trip is
also an exercise in religious reconciliation. More than 90 times since he took
office, John Paul has acknowledged past
faults of the church and begged pardon
from others—Muslims and Jews, as well
as Protestant and Orthodox Christians—
for sins committed in the name of Ca-

tholicism. Like the sound of one hand
clapping, however, his efforts have
brought few echoing responses. Now, at
the high point of this jubilee year for
the church, he comes to Jerusalem, the
city of peace, hoping to erect bridges
among the three monotheistic faiths.

There are, of course, important com-
monalities among these three religious
traditions. All three believe in one God
who has revealed his will through sacred
Scriptures. They all look to an endtimes
when God's justice and power will triumph. And they all recognize the figure
of Abraham as a father in faith. What is
often overlooked, however, is another
figure common to the three traditions:
Jesus of Nazareth.

The Christ of the Gospels is certainly
the best-known Jesus in the world. For
Christians, he is utterly unique—the
only Son of God and, as the pope puts
it, the one "mediator between God and
humanity." But alongside this Jesus is
another, the Jesus whom Muslims since
Muhammad have regarded as a prophet
and messenger of Allah. And after centuries of silence about Jesus, many Jews
now find him a Jewish teacher and reformer they can accept on their own
terms as "one of us."

Jesus has become a familiar, even
beloved, figure to adherents of Asian
religions as well. Among many contemporary Hindus, Jesus has come to be revered as a self-realized saint who
reached the highest level of "God-consciousness." In recent years, Buddhists
like the Dalai Lama have recognized in
Jesus a figure of great compassion much
like the Buddha. "I think as the world

grows smaller, Jesus as a figure will
grow larger," says Protestant theologian
John Cobb, a veteran of interfaith dialogues.

Perhaps. Each of these traditions—
Judaism, Islam, Buddhism and Hinduism—is rich in its own right, and each
has its own integrity. As the pope calls
for better understanding among the
world's great religions, it is important to
recognize that non-Christian faiths have
their own visions of the sacred and their
own views of Jesus.

JUDAISM

THAT JESUS WAS A JEW WOULD SEEM
to be self-evident from Gospels.
But before the first Christian
century was out, faith in Jesus as universal Lord and Savior eclipsed his early
identity as a Jewish prophet and wonder
worker. For long stretches of Western
history, Jesus was pictured as a Greek,
a Roman, a Dutchman—even, in the
Germany of the 1930s, as a blond and
burly Aryan made in the image of Nazi
anti-Semitism. But for most of Jewish
history as well, Jesus was also a deraci-
nated figure: he was *the* apostate, whose
name a pious Jew should never utter.

Indeed, the lack of extra-Biblical evidence for the existence of Jesus has led
more than one critic to conclude that he
is a Christian fiction created by the early
church. There were in fact a half dozen
brief passages, later excised from Talmudic texts, that some scholars consider
indirect references to Jesus. One alludes

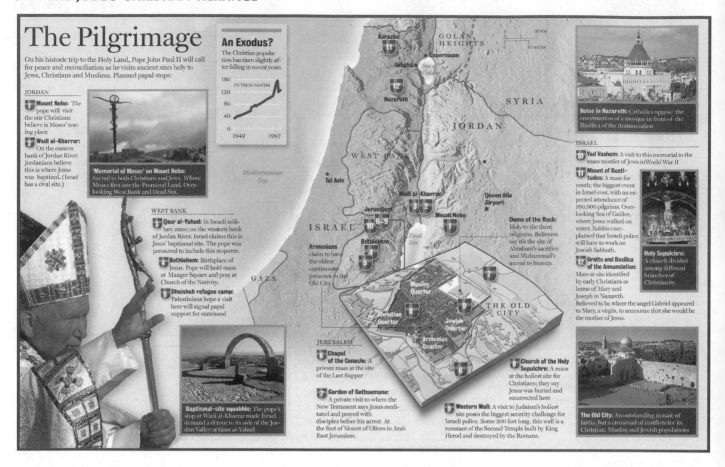

The Pilgrimage

On his historic trip to the Holy Land, Pope John Paul II will call for peace and reconciliation as he visits ancient sites holy to Jews, Christians and Muslims. Planned papal stops:

An Exodus?
The Christian population has risen slightly after falling in recent years.

IN THOUSANDS
160
120
80
40
0
1949   1997

JORDAN

1 Mount Nebo: The pope will visit the site Christians believe is Moses' resting place

2 Wadi al-Kharrar: On the eastern bank of Jordan River. Jordanians believe this is where Jesus was baptized. (Israel has a rival site.)

'Memorial of Moses' on Mount Nebo: Sacred to both Christians and Jews. Where Moses first saw the Promised Land. Overlooking West Bank and Dead Sea.

WEST BANK

3 Qasr al-Yahud: In Israeli military zone; on the western bank of Jordan River. Israel claims this is Jesus' baptismal site. The pope was pressured to include this stopover.

4 Bethlehem: Birthplace of Jesus. Pope will hold mass at Manger Square and pray at Church of the Nativity.

5 Dheisheh refugee camp: Palestinians hope a visit here will signal papal support for statehood

Baptismal-site squabble: The pope's stop at Wadi al-Kharrar made Israel demand a detour to its side of the Jordan Valley at Qasr al-Yahud.

JERUSALEM

6 Chapel of the Cenacle: A private mass at the site of the Last Supper

7 Garden of Gethsemane: A private visit to where the New Testament says Jesus meditated and prayed with disciples before his arrest. At the foot of Mount of Olives in Arab East Jerusalem.

Armenians claim to have the oldest continuous presence in the Old City

Dome of the Rock: Holy to the three religions. Believers say it's the site of Abraham's sacrifice and Muhammad's ascent to heaven.

8 Church of the Holy Sepulchre: A mass at the holiest site for Christians; they say Jesus was buried and resurrected here

9 Western Wall: A visit to Judaism's holiest site poses the biggest security challenge for Israeli police. Some 200 feet long, this wall is a remnant of the Second Temple built by King Herod and destroyed by the Romans.

ISRAEL

10 Yad Vashem: A visit to this memorial to the mass murder of Jews in World War II

11 Mount of Beatitudes: A mass for youth; the biggest event in Israel ever, with an expected attendance of 100,000 pilgrims. Overlooking Sea of Galilee, where Jesus walked on water. Rabbis complained that Israeli police will have to work on Jewish Sabbath.

12 Grotto and Basilica of the Annunciation: Mass at site identified by early Christians as home of Mary and Joseph in Nazareth. Believed to be where the angel Gabriel appeared to Mary, a virgin, to announce that she would be the mother of Jesus.

Noise in Nazareth: Catholics oppose the construction of a mosque in front of the Basilica of the Annunciation

Holy Sepulchre: A church divided among different branches of Christianity

The Old City: An outstanding mosaic of faiths, but a crossroad of conflicts for its Christian, Muslim and Jewish populations.

---

to a heresy trial of someone named Yeshu (Jesus) but none of them has any independent value for historians of Jesus. The only significant early text of real historical value is a short passage from Falvius Josephus, the first-century Jewish historian. Josephus describes Jesus as a "wise man," a "doer of startling deeds" and a "teacher" who was crucified and attracted a posthumous following called Christians. In short, argues Biblical scholar John P. Meier of Notre Dame, the historical Jesus was "a marginal Jew in a marginal province of the Roman Empire"—and thus unworthy of serious notice by contemporary Roman chroniclers.

Christian persecution of the Jews made dialogue about Jesus impossible in the Middle Ages. Jews were not inclined to contemplate the cross on the Crusaders' shields, nor did they enjoy the forced theological disputations Christians staged for Jewish conversions. To them, the Christian statues and pictures of Jesus represented the idol worship forbidden by the Torah. Some Jews did compile their own versions of a "History of Jesus" ("Toledoth Yeshu") as a parody of the Gospel story. In it, Jesus is depicted as a seduced Mary's bastard child who later gains magical powers and works sorcery. Eventually, he is hanged, his body hidden for three days and then discovered. It was subversive literature culled from the excised Talmudic texts. "Jews were impotent in force of arms," observes Rabbi Michael Meyer, a professor at Hebrew Union Seminary in Cincinnati, "so they reacted with words."

When skeptical scholars began to search for the "historical Jesus" behind the Gospel accounts in the 18th century, few Jewish intellectuals felt secure enough to join the quest. One who did was Abraham Geiger, a German rabbi and early exponent of the Reform Jewish movement. He saw that liberal Protestant intellectuals were anxious to get beyond the supernatural Christ of Christian dogma and find the enlightened teacher of morality hidden behind the Gospel texts. From his own research, Geiger concluded that what Jesus believed and taught was actually the Judaism of liberal Pharisees, an important first-century Jewish sect. "Geiger argued that Jesus was a reformist Pharisee whose teachings had been corrupted by his followers and mixed with pagan elements to produce the dogmas of Christianity," says Susannah Heschel, professor of Jewish studies at Dartmouth. Thus, far from being a unique religious genius—as the liberal Protestants claimed—Geiger's Jesus was a democratizer of his own inherited tradition. It was, he argued, the Pharisees' opponents, the Saducees, who became the first Christians and produced the negative picture of the Pharisees as legalistic hypocrites found in the later Gospel texts. In sum, Geiger—and after him, other Jewish scholars—distinguished between the faith *of* Jesus, which they saw as liberal Judaism, and the faith *in* Jesus, which became Christianity.

The implications of this "Jewish Jesus" were obvious, and quickly put to polemical use. Jews who might be attracted by the figure of Jesus needn't convert to Christianity. Rather, they could find his real teachings faithfully recovered in the burgeoning Reform Jewish movement. Christians, on the other hand, could no longer claim that Jesus was a unique religious figure who inspired a new and universal religion.

HIS ROOTS: Christian and Jewish scholars accept that much of what Jesus taught can be found in Jewish Scriptures, but Jews still see Christ as an 'admirable Jew,' not the Son of God

Indeed, if any religion could claim universality, it was monotheistic Judaism as the progenitor of both Christianity and Islam.

The Holocaust occasioned yet another way of imagining Jesus. If some Jews blamed Christians—or God himself—for allowing the ovens of Auschwitz, a few Jewish artists found a different way to deal with the horror of genocide: they applied the theme of the crucified Christ to the Nazis' Jewish victims. This is particularly evident in harrowing paintings of Marc Chagall, where the dying Jesus is marked by Jewish symbols. And in "Night," his haunting stories of the death camps, Elie Wiesel adopted the Crucifixion motif for his wrenching scene of three Jews hanged from a tree, like Jesus and the two thieves on Golgotha. The central figure is an innocent boy dangling in protracted agony because his body is too light to allow the noose its swift reprieve. When Wiesel hears a fellow inmate cry, "Where is God?" the author says to himself; "Here He is. He has been hanged here, on these gallows." "There's no lack of suffering in Judaism," says Alan Segal, professor of Jewish Studies at Barnard College and Columbia University, "and no reason why Jews shouldn't pick up an image central to Christianity."

Today, the Jewishness of Jesus is no longer a question among scholars. That much of what he taught can be found in the Jewish Scriptures is widely accepted by Christian as well as Jewish students of the Bible. At some seminaries, like Hebrew Union, a course in the New Testament is now required of rabbinical candidates. Outside scholarly circles, there is less focus on Jesus, and most Jews will never read the Christian Bible. And, of course, Jews do not accept the Christ of faith. "They see Jesus as an

A Rabbi Argues with Jesus

A noted Talmudic scholar insists that Jews must remain faithful to the words of the Torah.
BY JACOB NEUSNER

IMAGINE WALKING ON A dusty road in Galilee nearly 2,000 years ago and meeting up with a small band of youngsters, led by a young man. The leader's presence catches your attention: he talks, the others listen, respond, argue, obey—care what he says, follow him. You don't know who the man is, but you know he makes a difference to the people with him and to nearly everyone he meets. People respond, some with anger, some with admiration, a few with genuine faith. But no one walks away uninterested in the man and the things he says and does.

I can see myself meeting this man, and, with courtesy, arguing with him. It is my form of respect, the only compliment I crave from others, the only serious tribute I pay to the people I take seriously. I can see myself not only meeting and arguing with Jesus, challenging him on the basis of our shared Torah, the Scriptures Christians would later adopt as the "Old Testament." I can also imagine myself saying, "Friend, you go your way, I'll go mine, I wish you well—without me. Yours is not the Torah of Moses, and all I have from God, and all I ever need from God, is that one Torah of Moses."

We would meet, we would argue, we would part friends—but we would part, He would have gone his way, to Jerusalem and the place he believed God had prepared for him; I would have gone my way, home to my wife and my children, my dog and my garden. He would have gone his way to glory, I my way to my duties and my responsibilities.

Why? Because the Torah teaches that the kingdom that matters is not in heaven, but the one we find ourselves in now: sustaining life, sanctifying life, in the here and the now of home and family, community and society. God's kingdom is in the humble details of what I eat for breakfast and how I love my neighbor.

Can the Kingdom of God come soon, in our day, to where we are? The Torah not only says yes, it shows how. Do I have then to wait for God's Kingdom? Of course I have to wait. But while waiting, there are things I have to do. Jesus demanded that to enter this Kingdom of Heaven I repudiate family and turn my back on home: "Sell all you have and follow me." That is not what the Torah says.

On Sinai Moses told how to organize a kingdom of priests and a holy people, conduct workday affairs, love God—how to build God's kingdom, accepting the yoke of God's commandments. As a faithful Jew, what I do is simply reaffirm the Torah of Sinai over and against the teachings of Jesus. Moses would expect no less of us. So when I say, if I heard those words, I would have offered an argument, my dispute would have been with a mortal man walking among us and talking with us. Only the Torah is the word of God.

I think Christianity, beginning with Jesus, took a wrong turn in abandoning the Torah. By the truth of the Torah, much that Jesus said is wrong. By the criterion of the Torah, Israel's religion in the time of Jesus was authentic and faithful, not requiring reform or renewal, demanding only faith and loyalty to God and the sanctification of life through carrying out God's will. Jesus and his disciples took one path, and we another. I do not believe God would want it any other way.

NEUSNER *has just been named research professor of religion and theology at Bard College. He is the author of "A Rabbi Talks With Jesus."*

A MAN OF LOVE: Buddhists depersonalize the Jesus who walked this earth and transform him into a figure more like the Buddha. Some regard him as a bodhisattva, a perfectly enlightened being who vows to help others.

admirable Jew," says theologian John Cobb, "but they don't believe that any Jew could be God."

ISLAM

A T THE ONSET OF RAMADAN LAST year, Vatican officials sent greetings to the world's Muslims, inviting them to reflect on Jesus as "a model and permanent message for humanity." But for Muslims, the Prophet Muhammad is the perfect model for humankind and in the Qur'an (in Arabic only), they believe, the very Word of God dwells among us. Even so, Muslims recognize Jesus as a great prophet and revere him as Isa ibn Maryam—Jesus, the son of Mary, the only woman mentioned by name in the Qur'an. At a time when many Christians deny Jesus' birth to a virgin, Muslims find the story in the Qur'an and affirm that it is true. "It's a very strange situation, where Muslims are defending the miraculous birth of Jesus against western deniers," says Seyyed Hossein Nasr, professor of Islamic studies at George Washington University. "Many Westerners also do not believe that Jesus ascended into heaven. Muslims do." Indeed, many Muslims see themselves as Christ's true followers.

What Muslims believe about Jesus comes from the Qur'an—not the New Testament, which they consider tainted by human error. They also draw upon their own oral traditions, called *hadith,* and on experts' commentaries. In these sources, Jesus is born of Mary under a palm tree by a direct act of God. From the cradle, the infant Jesus announces that he is God's prophet, though not

God's son, since Allah is "above having a son" according to the Qur'an.

Nonetheless, the Muslim Jesus enjoys unique spiritual prerogatives that other prophets, including Muhammad, lack. Only Jesus and his mother were born untouched by Satan. Even Muhammad had to be purified by angels before receiving prophethood. Again, in the Qur'an Muhammad is not presented as a miracle worker, but Jesus miraculously heals the blind, cures lepers and "brings forth the dead by [Allah's] leave." In this way Jesus manifests himself as the Messiah, or "the anointed one." Muslims are not supposed to pray to anyone but Allah. But in popular devotions many ask Jesus or Mary or John the Baptist for favors. (According to one recent estimate, visions of Jesus or Mary have occurred some 70 times in Muslim countries since 1985.)

Although Muhammad supersedes Jesus as the last and greatest of the prophets, he still must die. But in the Qur'an, Jesus does not die, nor is he resurrected. Muslims believe that Jesus asked God to save him from crucifixion, as the Gospels record, and that God answered his prayer by taking him directly up to heaven. "God would not allow one of his prophets to be killed," says Martin Palmer, director of the International Consultancy on Religion, Education and Culture in Manchester, England. "If Jesus had been crucified, it would have meant that God had failed his prophet."

When the end of the world approaches, Muslims believe that Jesus will descend to defeat the antichrist—and, incidentally, to set the record straight. His presence will prove the Crucifixion was a myth and eventually he will die a natural death. "Jesus will return as a Muslim," says Nasr, "in the sense that he will unite all believers in total submission to the one God."

HINDUISM

T HE GOSPELS ARE SILENT ABOUT the life of Jesus between his boyhood visit to the Jerusalem Temple with his parents, and the beginning of his public ministry at the age of 30. But in India there is a strong tradition that the teenage Jesus slipped away from his parents, journeyed across Southeast Asia learning yogic meditation and returned home to become a guru to the Jews. This legend reveals just how easily Hinduism absorbs any figure whom others worship as divine. To Hindus, India is the Holy Land, its sacred mountains and rivers enlivened by more than 300,000 local deities. It is only natural, then, that Jesus would come to India to learn the secrets of unlocking his own inherent divinity.

A VIRTUOUS MAN: Many Hindus are drawn to Jesus because of his compassion and his devotion to nonviolence, but they find the notion of a single god unnecessarily restrictive.

As Gandhi was, many Hindus are drawn to the figure of Jesus by his compassion and nonviolence—virtues taught in their own sacred Scriptures. But also like Gandhi, Hindus find the notion of a single god unnecessarily restrictive. In their perspective, all human beings are sons of God with the innate ability to become divine themselves. Those Hindus who read the Gospels are drawn to the passage in John in which Jesus proclaims that "the Father and I are one." This confirms the basic Hindu belief that everyone is capable through rigorous spiritual practice of realizing his or her own universal "god-consciousness." The great modern Hindu saint Ramakrishna recorded that he meditated on a picture of the Madonna with child and was transported into a state of *samadhi,* a consciousness in which the divine is all that really exists. For that kind of spiritual experience, appeal to any god will do. "Christ-consciousness, God-consciousness, Krishna-consciousness,

Buddha-consciousness—it's all the same thing," says Deepak Chopra, an Indian popularizer of Hindu philosophy for New Age Westerners. "Rather than 'love thy neighbor,' this consciousness says, 'You and I are the same beings.'"

BUDDHISM

THE LIFE STORIES OF JESUS AND THE Buddha are strikingly similar. Both are conceived without sexual intercourse and born to chaste women. Both leave home for the wilderness where each is tempted by a Satan figure. Both return enlightened, work miracles and challenge the religious establishment by their teachings. Both attract disciples and both are betrayed by one of them. Both preach compassion, unselfishness and altruism and each creates a movement that bears the founder's name. Thich Nhat Hanh,

a Vietnamese Zen Buddhist monk with a large Western following, sees Jesus and Buddha as "brothers" who taught that the highest form of human understanding is "universal love." But there is at least one unbridgeable difference: a Christian can never become Christ, while the aim of every serious Buddhist is to achieve Buddhahood himself.

Thus when Buddhists encounter Christianity they depersonalize the Jesus who walked this earth and transform him into a figure more like Buddha. "Buddhists can think of Jesus Christ as an emanation or 'truth body' [*dharmakaya*] of the Buddha," says Buddhist scholar Robert Thurman of Columbia University. For Tibetan Buddhists, Jesus strongly resembles a bodhisattva—a perfectly enlightened being who vows to help others attain enlightenment. But to reconfigure Jesus as a Buddhist is to turn him into something he was not. Jesus, after all, believed in God, the creator and sustainer of the universe, which

The Karma of the Gospel

A spiritual leader finds connections between Christian teachings and his own traditions.
BY THE DALAI LAMA

AS A BUDDHIST, MY attitude toward Jesus Christ is that he was either a fully enlightened being, or a bodhisattva of a very high spiritual realization. I see common notes between Buddhism and Christianity. Here are a few:

Transfiguration. In Buddhism, when an individual practitioner reaches a high degree of realization in his or her spiritual evolution, the transformation can manifest itself at the physical level, as well. We find such stories about the Buddha in the sutras. They begin when Buddha's disciples notice a physical change in his appearance. A radiance shines from his body. Then one of the disciples asks the Buddha, "I see these changes in you. Why are these changes taking place?" These parables are similar to the Gospel passages on the Transfiguration when Jesus' face is suddenly glowing.

Karma. In another Gospel passage, Jesus says: "I have not come to judge the world but to save it.... The word I have spoken will be his judge on the last day." I feel this closely reflects the Buddhist idea of karma. There is not an autonomous being (God) "out there" who arbitrates what you should experience and what you should know; instead, there is the truth contained in the casual principle itself. If you act in an ethical way, desirable consequences will result; if you act in a negative way, then you must face the consequences of that action as well.

Faith. In the Buddhist tradition, we speak of three different types of faith. The first is faith in the form of admiration that you have toward a particular person or a particular state of being. The second is aspiring faith. There is a sense of emulation: you aspire to attain that state of being. The third type is the faith of conviction.

All three types of faith can be explained in the Christian context as well. A practicing Christian can have a very strong devotion to and admiration for Jesus by reading the Gospel. That is the first level of faith, the faith of admiration and devotion. After that, as you strengthen your admiration and faith, it is possible to progress to the second level, which is the faith of aspiration. In the Buddhist tradition, you would aspire to Buddhahood. In the Christian context you may not use the same language, but you can say that you aspire to attain the full perfection of the divine nature, or union with God. Then, once you have developed that sense of aspiration, you can develop the third level of faith, a deep conviction that it is possible to perfect such a state of being.

Empathy. One of the grounds on which the presence of Buddha-nature in all people is argued is the human capacity for empathy. Some people may have a stronger force, others less; but all of us share this natural capacity to empathize. This Buddha-nature, this seed of enlightenment, of perfection, is inherent in all of us. To attain perfection, however, it is not enough that a spiritual practitioner merely possess such a nature; this nature must be developed to its fullest potential. In Buddhist practice, you require the assistance of an enlightened guide, a guru or teacher. Christians believe that all of us share this divine nature but it is only through Jesus that one perfects it. Through Jesus it comes into full bloom and becomes unified, one, with the Father.

THE DALAI LAMA *is the author of "The Good Heart"* (Wisdom Publications, Boston), *from which this is excerpted.*

A TRUE SAVIOR: The Christ of the Gospel is the best-known Jesus in the world. For Christians, he is unique—the only Son of God.

Buddhists do not. He believed in sin, which is not a Buddhist concept. Jesus did not teach compassion as a way of removing bad karma, nor did he see life as a cycle of death and rebirth. In short, says the Dalai Lama, trying to meld Jesus into Buddha "is like putting a yak's head on a sheep's body." It doesn't work. Indeed, nothing shows the difference between the Jesus and the Buddha better than the way that each died. The Buddha's death was serene and controlled—a calm passing out of his final re-birth, like the extinction of a flame. Jesus, on the other hand, suffers an agonizing death on the cross, abandoned by God but obedient to his will.

Clearly, the cross is what separates the Christ of Christianity from every other Jesus. In Judaism there is no precedent for a Messiah who dies, much less as a criminal as Jesus did. In Islam, the story of Jesus' death is rejected as an affront to Allah himself. Hindus can accept only a Jesus who passes into peaceful samadhi, a yogi who escapes the degradation of death. The figure of the crucified Christ, says Buddhist Thich Nhat Hanh, "is a very painful image to me. It does not contain joy or peace, and this does not do justice to Jesus." There is, in short, no room in other religions for a Christ who experiences the full burden of mortal existence—and hence there is no reason to believe in him as the divine Son whom the Father resurrects from the dead.

Even so, there are lessons all believers can savor by observing Jesus in the mirrors of Jews and Muslims, Hindus and Buddhists. That the image of a benign Jesus has universal appeal should come as no surprise. That most of the world cannot accept the Jesus of the cross should not surprise, either. Thus the idea that Jesus can serve as a bridge uniting the world's religions is inviting but may be ultimately impossible. A mystery to Christians themselves, Jesus remains what he has always been, a sign of contradiction.

With ANNE UNDERWOOD *and* HEATHER WON TESORIERO

Women and the Bible

*Motivated variously by historical, theological, and personal concerns,
a rapidly growing cadre of scholars, most of them women, is exploring
one of the great overlooked subjects in scholarship: the domain of Jewish
and Christian women in ancient times*

Cullen Murphy

Cullen Murphy is the managing editor of The Atlantic Monthly. *He writes the comic strip* Prince Valiant *and is the author, with William Rathje, of* Rubbish!: The Archaeology of Garbage *(1992). Murphy's article "Who Do Men Say That I Am?", about research on Jesus, was* The Atlantic's *cover story in December of 1986.*

Perhaps a rumor of impending persecution lay behind it, as several scholars have speculated. Perhaps the reason for concealment was something else entirely. We can never know why twelve ancient codices and a fragment of a thirteenth came to rest where they were found. The place was a rugged curtain of cliffs rising above the valley of the Nile River, near where today there is a village called Nag Hammadi. The time was the late fourth century or early fifth century A.D. For whatever reason, someone, perhaps a monk from the local monastery of St. Pachomius, took steps to preserve some holy books—Coptic translations of works that had originally been written in Greek, works of the kind that had been denounced as heretical by Athanasius, the archbishop of Alexandria. The words of the prophet Jeremiah may have played through the mind of the person hiding the codices: "Put them in an earthenware jar, that they may last for a long time." For it was in an earthen jar, hidden in a cavity under a rock at the base of the cliffs, that

the papyrus manuscripts were eventually discovered.

The Nag Hammadi library, as these texts have come to be called, was brought to light in 1945. By the early 1950s, after feuds and transactions of Levantine complexity, almost all of the Nag Hammadi collection was in the safe but jealous hands of the Coptic Museum, in Cairo, which for many years proved exceedingly particular about whom it would allow to study the documents. It was clear very early, however, that the codices, which contained forty previously unknown works, would offer unprecedented access to the world of the Gnostics, a variegated group of Christian communities, active as early as a century after the time of Jesus, that diverged sharply from the emerging Christian orthodoxy in many ways—one of them frequently being the prominence, both in theology and in community life, of women.

Elaine Pagels was a doctoral student in religion at Harvard University during the late 1960s, when mimeographed transcriptions of the Nag Hammadi library were circulating among American and European scholars. Her area of interest was the history of early Christianity. There were no women then on the faculty of Harvard's program in religion, and the dean who accepted Pagels as a doctoral candidate had turned her down

the first time she applied. In this field, he explained in a letter, women didn't last. But now, after applying again, here she was, with the working knowledge of Latin and Greek that anyone dealing with early Christian texts requires, and the Nag Hammadi mimeographs caught her attention. Because the transcriptions were in Coptic, which is Egyptian written with the Greek alphabet and a few other characters, Pagels added Coptic to her repertoire (and also Hebrew) and got to work.

Sitting one afternoon recently in her office at the Institute for Advanced Study, in Princeton, I spoke with Pagels about her Harvard years and other matters. Pagels, who is a professor in the religion department at Princeton University, works at certain times at the institute, which offers scholars a chance to pursue research without the distraction of teaching. It is a modern and spacious place, set impersonally among vast lawns. In Pagels's office a photograph of her late husband sat upon the sill. A girl's bicycle was propped against a wall. Pagels has two young children, and a demeanor that somehow manages to be calmer than her circumstances are.

"I discovered," Pagels said, thinking back to her initial encounter with the Nag Hammadi materials, "as did the other graduate students, that our professors had file folders full of Gnostic texts

From *The Atlantic Monthly*, August 1993, pp. 39–45, 48, 50–55, 58, 60, 62–64. © 1993 by Cullen Murphy. Reprinted by permission of the author.

of secret Gospels that many of them told us were absurd and blasphemous and heretical—but interesting. And I *did* find these texts interesting. And exciting. I think that perhaps my empathy for them had something to do with being a woman in an environment that was almost exclusively male. I found things among the heretics that were startlingly congenial." Pagels became part of the team that would translate the Nag Hammadi texts into English and provide a critical apparatus for them.

The Creation stories form the basis for a view of humanity as existing in a fallen state, of woman as having led humanity astray, of man as being ordained to be the master of woman.

Not until 1975, five years after completing a doctoral dissertation on certain aspects of the Nag Hammadi library, did Pagels have an opportunity to inspect the documents themselves. At various times during a stay in Egypt, Pagels would visit the small, unprepossessing room in the Coptic Museum where the Nag Hammadi library is kept, one day perhaps to examine The Interpretation of Knowledge, another to examine A Valentinian Exposition or The Gospel of Mary. The documents looked, she remembers thinking, like tobacco leaves. Each fragile page, each fragment, lies flat between sheets of hard plastic, the black lettering stark against a mottled golden background, the underlying weave of the crushed papyrus fronds plainly visible. The Coptic Museum was a place of columns and courtyards and quiet. The only interruption was caused by the cleaning woman, and Pagels and any other scholars present would continue working at their desks when she came in, lifting their legs as soapy water

was spilled and spread beneath them over the stone floors.

In a book called *The Gnostic Gospels* (1979), which received wide attention when it was published and occasioned a sometimes bitter scholarly debate, Pagels took some of those fragments that lie flat between plastic and sought to give them dimension, set them in history, bring ancient sensibilities back to life. She described Gnostic groups who saw God as a "dyad" embodying both masculine and feminine aspects, and who explicitly invoked the feminine aspect in their prayers: "May She who is before all things, the incomprehensible and indescribable Grace, fill you within, and increase in you her own knowledge." Some groups conceived of the third person in Christianity's trinitarian God—a God consisting of Father, Son, and Holy Spirit—to be female, and so rendered the Trinity, logically enough, as Father, Son, and Mother. Powerful feminine imagery and ideology suffuse many Gnostic texts, and this found parallels in the practice of a number of Gnostic groups, which permitted women to hold priestly office. Gnostic thought was disorderly and fantastical, and for a variety of reasons was spurned by Christian polemicists (although some elements seem to find echoes in the Gospel of John). But it preserves some early Christian traditions, and is valuable for its reflection of currents in popular religion that are only dimly reflected in the canon of sanctioned Christian works—currents important to an understanding of Christianity's unruly beginnings.

Some of the Gnostics were much intrigued by the Creation stories in the Book of Genesis. Pagels, too, became intrigued, and in 1988 she produced *Adam, Eve, and the Serpent* a book more ambitious than *The Gnostic Gospels*. The Bible's Creation stories—or, perhaps more precisely, the interpretation of the Creation stories that came to be accepted—form the basis for a view of humanity as existing in a fallen state, of woman as having led humanity astray, of man as being ordained to be the master of woman, and of sexuality as a corrupting aspect of human nature. And yet, as Pagels shows, this is not how the Creation stories were interpreted by many Jews and early Christians, and it is sometimes difficult to see how such conclusions came to be drawn. Pagels points to other traditions in Jewish and Christian thought: of the Crea-

tion stories as parables of human equality, men and women both being formed in the image and likeness of God, of the stories as evocations of God's gift of moral freedom. *Adam, Eve, and the Serpent* traces the clashes of interpretation in the early Church, which culminated in the triumph of Augustine, whose harsh views on the subject would become those of much of the Western world—would help define Western consciousness—for a millennium and a half.

The point is, Pagels told me, early Christianity was a remarkably diverse and fractious religious movement. There were traditions within it that the evolution of a stronger, more institutionalized tradition would largely destroy. Acknowledging this fact has implications for our own time and for people who have often felt excluded or even oppressed by the dominant tradition. It has implications in particular for women. "The history of Christianity has been told from a single point of view," Pagels said. "If that point of view is no longer tenable historically then it enables people to develop other perceptions."

The work of Elaine Pagels is but one manifestation of a larger phenomenon: the rapidly expanding influence of feminist scholars in the study of Jewish and Christian history, and the reassessment of certain issues that has ensued as a result. The body of work that these scholars have produced is by now substantial. Virtually all of it has been published within the past fifteen years. Most has been published within the past ten. While the writing can at times be difficult—some scholars don methodology like chain mail—a strikingly large proportion, whether in specialized journals or in books, is written so as to be broadly accessible to readers outside academe.

The motivations, besides simple intellectual curiosity, that lie behind this work are not difficult to discern. There is the perception that the Hebrew Bible and the New Testament deal with women unfairly in many spheres; the need to understand why they do; the suspicion that an alternative past awaits recovery. Among some scholars there is a conviction, too, that recovering the past could help change the present—for example, could help make the case for giving women access to positions in religious ministry and religious leadership from which they are now barred. Although half of all Christian denominations permit the ordination of women, as do Reform and Conservative Judaism, the issue remains a matter of strongly felt conflict. The work of feminist scholars, both individually and collectively, has been greeted in some quarters with impatience, irritation, dismissiveness, even contempt. But it has also established women's issues as a permanent focus of biblical studies. That it has done so is one important element of the broader engagement of feminism with every aspect of organized religion.

A few years ago I set out to explore this branch of scholarship—to meet some of its practitioners and become familiar with some of their work. My focus was not on politics but on research. The people whose work is touched on here are drawn not from the sometimes airy or angry outskirts of the feminist biblical enterprise but from its solid scholarly core. They come from several religious backgrounds, represent several scholarly disciplines, and, as feminists, display a range of stances toward religion in general and the Bible in particular. Their work thus defies easy summary. My intention is to let it speak for itself.

THE PATRIARCHY PROBLEM

The women's movement has as yet had meager impact on some academic realms, but the realm of religion is not among the scarcely affected. Even if the convergence of feminism and religion has prompted developments on the fringes of popular culture which would strike some as bizarre (the proliferation of neo-pagan "goddess" movements comes to mind), the truly significant consequences have occurred closer to the mainstream of ministry and scholarship. Walk into the department of religion or the divinity school at any major university today and the bulletin board will paint the same picture: seminar after workshop after lecture on almost any conceivable matter involving women and religion. The influx of women into divinity-school programs has by now received considerable attention. So has the movement to adopt "inclusive" language, when appropriate, in translations

of Scripture, and to correct mistranslations of Scripture that have served to obscure feminine references and imagery. This movement saw its most important victory in 1990, with the publication by the National Council of Churches of the New Revised Standard version of the Bible. But much of the work being done by women in biblical scholarship and related fields—work that demands immense erudition—remains far less well known.

The Bible has always been a compelling object of study, both because questions of religious faith are inextricably involved and because it is a window—albeit one whose refractions may distort and occlude—onto much of human history. With respect to issues of gender the Bible is also, of course, highly problematic, to use a word that no feminist scholar I've spoken with can help uttering in a tone of ironic politeness. It is a central tenet of contemporary feminism that a patriarchal template governs the way people have come to think and behave as individuals and as societies. The Bible is no stranger to patriarchy. It is an androcentric document in the extreme. It was written mostly if not entirely by men. It was edited by men. It describes a succession of societies over a period of roughly 1,200 years whose public life was dominated by men. And because the Bible's focus is predominantly on public rather than private life, it talks almost only about men. In the Hebrew Bible as a whole, only 111 of the 1,426 people who are given names are women. The proportion of women in the New Testament is about twice as great, which still leaves them a small minority.

As a prescriptive text, moreover, the Bible has been interpreted as justifying the subordination of women to men: "In pain you shall bring forth children, yet your desire shall be for your husband, and he shall rule over you." "Wives, be subject to your husbands as you are to the Lord." "Indeed, man was not made from woman, but woman from man. Neither was man created for the sake of woman, but woman for the sake of man." As a text that has been presumed by hundreds of millions of people to speak with authority, moreover, the Bible has helped enforce what it prescribes. There is no getting around the disturbing character, for women, of much of the Bible, short of an interpretive reading (a "hermeneutic," to use the term of art) that may represent some-

thing of a stretch—short of what one biblical scholar has called an act of "hermeneutical ventriloquism."

The subjection of the Bible to historical and critical scrutiny, a revolution in scholarship that began during the latter half of the nineteenth century, was undertaken almost entirely by men. It did not occur to these men that the way the Bible treats women—or, just as important, fails to treat women—might be a fit matter for study. The Society of Biblical Literature, which remains to this day the leading professional group in the field, was founded in 1880, and inducted its first woman member in 1894. But the relative handful of women who embarked on careers in biblical studies in the nineteenth century and the first half of the twentieth showed virtually no interest in women's issues. As the historian Dorothy Bass, of the Chicago Theological Seminary, has shown, it was women outside academe who first pursued the matter: women like the abolitionist Sarah Grimké, in the 1830s, and, later, Frances Willard, of the Women's Christian Temperance Union.

Their aims, initially, were two. The first was to identify and critically confront passages and stories about women which they deemed objectionable—the stories, for example, of Delilah, in the Book of Judges, and of Jezebel, in I Kings. The second aim was to seek out and elevate to greater prominence passages and stories about women which are positive and ennobling—for example, the remarkable image of Wisdom personified as a woman, in Proverbs, and the stories of Deborah, in Judges, and of the prophetess Huldah, in II Kings. Both these strands of the early feminist response to the Bible have survived, in increasingly sophisticated forms, down to the present.

The suffragist leader Elizabeth Cady Stanton made a contribution by means of that remarkable fin-de-siècle document *The Woman's Bible*, the first volume of which was published in 1895. Though well into her eighties, Stanton oversaw a committee of female editors who scrutinized and critically glossed every passage in the Bible having to do with women. She came to the conclusion that little could be salvaged from Scripture which was fully compatible with the belief system of a rational modern feminist. None of the women who worked on *The Woman's Bible* was a biblical scholar. Female biblical scholars refused to participate in the project, afraid, Stanton believed, "that their high reputation and scholarly attainments might be compromised by taking part in an enterprise that for a time may prove very unpopular."

Female biblical scholars did not face up to issues of gender—did not, as Frances Willard had urged, "make a specialty of Hebrew and New Testament Greek in the interest of their sex"—in any significant way until the 1960s. One call to action came from a professor of biblical literature at Smith College, Margaret Brackenbury Crook, who in a book called *Women and Religion* (1964) took aim at the "masculine monopoly" on all important matters in all the world's great faiths. She repeated the plaintive question of the biblical figure Miriam: "Has the Lord spoken only through Moses?" By the 1970s, of course, a generalized version of that question could be sensed almost everywhere in the culture. Departments of religion and divinity schools were merely two among the crowd of institutions that saw more and more women seeking access, bringing with them unfamiliar questions and ways of thinking.

Biblical scholarship is still a predominantly male endeavor, but inroads by women have been substantial. The female membership of the Society of Biblical Literature amounted to three percent of the total in 1970. It now exceeds 16 percent. The share of the student membership that is female—a harbinger, surely—is 30 percent. In 1987 the society elected its first woman president, Elisabeth Schüssler Fiorenza, a theologian who at the time was a professor at Episcopal Divinity School, and who now teaches at Harvard. The joint annual meeting of the SBL and the American Academy of Religion today features a large number of sessions on women's issues, chiefly by women but sometimes by men. "Prostitutes and Penitents in the Early Christian Church." "Redeeming the Unredeemable: Genesis 22—A Jewish Feminist Perspective." "Rape as a Military Metaphor in the Hebrew Bible." The opening address at the AAR portion of last year's joint meeting was given by Mary Daly, whose first two books, *The Church and the Second Sex* (1968) and *Beyond God the Father* (1973), were a source of inspiration to many women with an interest in religion. (Daly herself has ventured not only beyond God the Father but also beyond

Christianity, and is by now well off the beaten track; she maintains an uneasy professorship in the department of theology at Boston College, a school run by Jesuit priests.) At the next joint meeting, this coming November, the SBL will install its second woman president: Phyllis Trible, of Union Theological Seminary.

It was Schüssler Fiorenza's work—most notably her book *In Memory of Her* (1983), to which I was introduced almost a decade ago in the course of research on a related subject—that drew me into the world of women whose academic lives revolve, one way or another, around the central texts of the Jewish and Christian traditions. Schüssler Fiorenza, a soft-spoken native of Germany, is the Krister Stendahl Professor of Divinity at the Harvard Divinity School. She is also a founder and a coeditor of the *Journal of Feminist Studies in Religion*, one of several academic journals in the field with a focus on women. Schüssler Fiorenza is quick to acknowledge that coming to the United States, as she did in 1970, with a fresh doctorate in New Testament studies from the University of Münster, marked a turning point in her interests. The United States offered what Germany at

---

After the crucifixion it was women who helped hold together the Jesus movement. Women were the first to discover the empty tomb, the first to experience a vision of a resurrected Jesus.

---

the time did not: a strong and active feminist movement and a university system whose faculties—crucially, whose theology-department faculties—were open to women. Schüssler Fiorenza, in her own words, "began doing theology as a woman and for women." Her writing

has focused primarily on the role played by women during the conception, birth, and infancy of Christianity.

Historical reconstruction of the Jesus movement is risky . . . . Among other things, as Schüssler Fiorenza reminded me during a conversation one afternoon, "within both Judaism and Christianity the patriarchal side won"—thus determining the lens through which interpretation would look. One must approach the texts with a "hermeneutic of suspicion," to use a phrase that is by now a cliché in feminist biblical circles. The references to women that do exist in Christian works, Schüssler Fiorenza said, surely represent the tip of the iceberg, though unfortunately much of the part that is submerged now is likely to remain submerged forever.

And yet, she went on, there is some significant material about women to work with, if only we are not blind to it. The Gospels, she noted, are unequivocal in placing women prominently among the marginalized people who made up so much of Jesus' circle. Women are shown as having been instrumental in opening up the Jesus community to non-Jews. After the Crucifixion it was the women of Galilee who helped hold together the Jesus movement in Jerusalem as other disciples fled. Women were the first to discover the empty tomb and the first to experience a vision of a resurrected Jesus. Jesus' message was in part a radical attack on the traditional social structures of the Greco-Roman world—structures that limited the participation of women in the public sphere, and that the Jesus movement sought to replace with what Schüssler Fiorenza calls "a discipleship of equals."

And after Jesus was gone? Christianity's penumbral first centuries can be difficult to apprehend. The texts that would make up the New Testament—not to mention the many other texts that survive from Christian communities—were at this time being written, edited, and re-edited, each text created in the context of certain communities and to fulfill certain purposes. What emerges from Schüssler Fiorenza's reading is a Christian missionary movement that in its initial stages "allowed for the full participation and leadership of women." She notes in *In Memory of Her* that in the authentic letters of Paul, women are singled out by name and given titles the same as or comparable to those held by male leaders. Prisca, a traveling missionary, is described by Paul as a peer, a "co-worker." Phoebe, in Cenchreae, is called a *diakonos*, a title Paul also gives himself.

Some scholars have in the past tried to explain away evidence like this, Schüssler Fiorenza writes, by arguing that when held by women such titles must have been mere honorifics. Or they have translated the titles differently. *Diakonos*, for example, which is usually translated as "minister," "missionary," or "deacon" when associated with men, has usually been downplayed as "deaconess" or even "helper" when associated with women. Scholars have also argued that people whose names are apparently female must actually have been men. Schüssler Fiorenza observes that the social mores of the time left ample room for women to wield authority in early Christianity. For one thing, the rituals of Christianity evolved in a network of churches based in homes, and within the home, women could claim important rights and responsibilities. Schüssler Fiorenza argues, finally, that early Christianity was built around a theology of equality; that Paul's famous reiteration in Galatians 3:28 of the ancient baptismal formula—"There is no longer Jew or Greek, there is no longer slave or free, there is no longer male and female; for all of you are one in Christ Jesus"—represents not a radical and temporary breakthrough in Paul's thinking but an expression of broad and ordinary Christian belief. In Schüssler Fiorenza's view, Galatians 3:28 is "the magna carta of Christian feminism."

Schüssler Fiorenza is a theologian, and she has an explicitly theological agenda. In her approach to Scripture she aims to highlight themes of unfolding liberation and emancipation. But large portions of her work exemplify a strategy pursued by non-theologians as well: the attempt to pierce the veil of the sources, to discern what was social and religious reality in a distant time. This may involve textual scholarship—training attention on vocabulary, on rhetorical style, on whatever can be inferred about the editing process. It may involve the disciplines of archaeology and anthropology—coming at early Jewish and Christian life from the outside, and looking at what the physical record has to say. All this work presupposes a broad grounding in some very obscure aspects of history. The work can be frustrating in the extreme. The materials

available are often meager, and the conclusions drawn sometimes precarious and insubstantial.

Elaine Pagels spoke about some of the endeavor's hazards and intricacies and opportunities in one of our conversations. We had been talking about the issue of an author's point of view. Pagels observed that in some instances the documentary record of certain suppressed opinions consists only of the surviving criticisms of those opinions. Before the discovery of the Nag Hammadi library, Gnostic thinking was a prime example: many Gnostic beliefs had been scathingly summarized in the writings of Irenaeus of Lyons, a second-century theologian and foe of heretics. Images of women can sometimes be made out in the same way. "We have to read the texts aware that the point of view may not reflect the whole social reality," Pagels told me. "It will reflect the point of view of the people writing the texts, and the groups they represent. And generally women were not doing the writing. So we have to make a lot out of the few clues that are found."

She reached for a comparison to bring home the nature of this situation. "Imagine," she said after a moment's reflection, "having to re-create the thinking of Karl Marx on the basis of a handful of anti-communist tracts from the 1950s."

SALVAGE OPERATIONS

Union Theological Seminary, in New York, occupies two city blocks along Broadway, in a neighborhood that might be thought of as upper Manhattan's religion district. The Jewish Theological Seminary of America lies across the street to the northeast, taking up much of a third city block. Across the street to the southwest, taking up a fourth city block, lies The Interchurch Center, which houses scores of religious organizations: groups devoted to social work, missionary work, publishing, broadcasting. (The square, clunky structure is known as "the God box.") And across the street directly to the west, occupying a fifth city block, is Riverside Church, long a bulwark of social activism with a mildly hallowed cast. Union is an example of the kind of liberal, nondenominational seminary whose student body in recent years has become increasingly female: almost 55 percent of its more

than 300 students are women. It is a comfortable, reassuring place. The architecture is monastic, preserving outwardly in cool stone a way of life that no longer prevails inside. In the library's reading room, whose shelves hold the leather-bound classics required for exegetic work, and from around whose perimeter gleam the marbled pates of learned men, it is perhaps possible to believe that this is still the Union Seminary of Paul Tillich and Reinhold Niebuhr.

Trible believes that the Bible can be "reclaimed" as a spiritual resource for women. The Bible, she said, is sometimes not as patriarchal as translations would make it seem.

But in the hallways of the living quarters the tricycles and toys betray a changed demography. The omnipresent flyers announcing meetings also tell a story. "Hunger Strike Demanding Action for Peace and Reunification in Korea." "Feminists for Animal Rights." "Lesbian-Gay Caucus Sez Howdy." These people, one senses, are busy, committed. They do not lack up-to-date agendas.

Phyllis Trible is the Baldwin Professor of Sacred Literature. Her office at Union sits high above the quadrangle, under the eaves, and in it one can occupy a certain chair at a certain angle and almost be persuaded that the world outside the window is the world of Oxford or Cambridge. On a wall of Trible's office hangs a photograph of a white-haired man in a dark suit and tie—James Muilenburg, who was a professor at Union when Trible was a student here, in the late 1950s and early 1960s, and who taught the first class she attended at the seminary. "I'll never forget that class," Trible recalled one day. She speaks with precision in an accent shaped by her native Virginia. "He walked in with a stack of syllabi under his arm and he put them down on the table and started quoting Hebrew poetry: the 'Sword of Lamech,' in Genesis. And he dramatized the whole thing—took the sword and plunged it in. He asked us where that sword reappeared, and jumped to Peter in the New Testament. I was utterly captivated, and have never gotten over it to this day." Trible is but one of several female biblical scholars I've met who, whatever problems being a woman may have caused them in academe, warmly acknowledge a close intellectual relationship with a male mentor.

Trible is the author of two books, *God and the Rhetoric of Sexuality* (1978) and *Texts of Terror: Literary–Feminist Readings of Biblical Narratives* (1984), that would appear in anyone's canon of feminist biblical studies. Even colleagues who have no affinity with Trible's work—who differ radically in outlook—may acknowledge a debt. Ask graduate students in their twenties or established scholars in their thirties or forties how an interest was awakened in women's issues and biblical studies, and the answer will often turn out to involve an article or a book by Trible.

It is important to recognize where Trible stands in a spectrum that ranges, as she explained to me, "from some fundamentalists who claim that they are feminists but say they have no problem with the Bible to those at the other extreme who are unwilling to concede the Bible any authority at all." Trible is in the middle. She doesn't forget for a minute, she said, that the Bible is a thoroughly patriarchal text. But she is hardly a member of the rejectionist camp. She believes that the Bible can be "reclaimed" as a spiritual resource for women. And in all fairness, she said, it must be pointed out that the Bible is sometimes not as patriarchal as translations would make it seem. This is not just a matter of exclusive language. Trible pulled down a copy of the Revised Standard Version of the Bible, opened it to Deuteronomy 32:18, and read this passage: "You were unmindful of the Rock that begot you, and you forgot the God who gave you birth." She said, "Those words 'gave you birth' are from a Hebrew term for 'writhing in labor,' so the translation, if accurate, is tame. But here is how the Jerusalem Bible translates it: 'fathered you.' "

The work that initially brought Trible to prominence was a pair of journal articles in the 1970s on the two Creation stories in the Book of Genesis. These articles—the first ones written on the subject from a feminist perspective—were an attempt at reclamation. Trible argued that properly understood, the Creation stories, including the story of Adam and Eve, did not actually say what centuries of interpretation have made them say. For example, is woman to be considered subordinate to man, as some traditional interpretations would have it, simply because she was created after he was? If that is the case, Trible argued, then why are human beings not regarded as subordinate to animals, since Genesis 1:27 plainly declares that human beings were created after the animals were?

But that is almost beside the point, because it is a mistake, in Trible's view, to think of the first human being, Adam, as male. She points out that the Hebrew word '*adham*, from which "Adam" derives, is a generic term for humankind—it denotes a being created from the earth—and is used to describe a creature of undifferentiated sex. Only when the Lord takes a rib from '*adham* to make a companion are the sexes differentiated, and the change is signaled by the terminology. The creature from whom the rib was taken is now referred to not as '*adham* but as '*ish* ("man"), and the creature fashioned from the rib is called '*ishshah* ("woman"). In Trible's reading, the sexes begin in equality. It is only after the act of disobedience occasioned by the serpent's temptation, and the departure of '*ish* and '*ishshah* from their initial and intended condition, that the sexes fall out of equality. It is only then, in this disobedient state, that the man establishes his dominance. Oppression of women by men, then, is not what was meant for humanity, even if it is what we have come to. "Rather than legitimating the patriarchal culture from which it comes," Trible concluded, "the myth places that culture under judgment."

Much as one hears the polite word "problematic" applied to material in the Bible which some feminist scholars deem to be negative, so also one hears the polite word "optimistic" applied to interpretations that some feminist scholars deem to be too positive. Trible is not unfamiliar with the latter charge. Her response would be that "optimistic" is a term that makes sense only if one assumes that the relationship people have with the Bible is as with something dead. She thinks of the Bible differently—as if it were a pilgrim forging new relationships over time. There are ways, she believes, of articulating a conversation between feminism and the Bible in which each critiques the other.

I was familiar, of course, with how feminism might critique the Bible. I asked Trible what critique the Bible offers of feminism. She replied that there was sometimes a tendency to make too 'much of feminism, to put it on a pedestal,' and that the Bible calls attention to that kind of propensity. "It warns," she said, "against idolatry."

Trible's specialty is a form of criticism known as rhetorical criticism, which pays particular attention to a document's literary architecture. During one conversation Trible walked me through some passages that, together, may offer an instance of a biblical woman's falling victim to editorial manhandling. The passages tell the story of Miriam—the sister of Moses and Aaron, a woman who was perhaps considered by the Israelites to be the equal of her brothers, but of whom few traces survive in the Bible as it has finally come down to us.

We meet Miriam in the Book of Exodus. It is she who persuades Pharaoh's daughter to raise the infant Moses—left in a basket among the rushes on the banks of the Nile—as her own, and to bring along Moses' mother as nurse. Miriam is not at this point given a name; the woman who saves the infant's life is identified only as his sister. And as the story of Moses proceeds, Miriam disappears—until the crossing of the Red Sea. Then, when the Israelites reach the far shore, Pharaoh's armies having been destroyed, there is a song of rejoicing: the poetic Song at the Sea, sung by Moses and the people of Israel. It begins, "I will sing to the Lord, for he has triumphed gloriously; / horse and rider he has thrown into the sea." No sooner has Moses finished than there comes a small fragment of text that appears out of place. The fate of Pharaoh's armies is for some reason quickly retold, and then, with the Israelites once again safely on shore, we learn that "the prophet Miriam, Aaron's sister," begins to sing the very same Song at the Sea. She sings the first two lines. The text then moves on to other business.

Trible paused. There are several interesting things here, she said. One is that we learn for the first time that the sister of Aaron, who must also be the sister of Moses, has a name, and that it is Miriam. We also see that she is called a prophet and that this occurs at a place in the text well before the place where Moses is first called a prophet, though the precise meaning of "prophet" in the context of Exodus remains unclear. What this piece of text about Miriam represents, Trible said, is the dogged survival of an earlier version of the Exodus story. Indeed, she pointed out, scholars have argued that in the most ancient Israelite traditions the singing of the Song at the Sea was ascribed not to Moses but to Miriam. The role was only later shifted away from Miriam. (As an aside, Trible observed that the first work on the attribution of the Song at the Sea to Miriam dates back to the mid-1950s—and was done by men. She added pointedly, "I'm not one to say that you can't use the previous generation of scholarship—not at all.")

Miriam moves with the people of Israel into the desert, whereupon she disappears from the Book of Exodus. But she reappears later in the Bible, in connection with what seems to be a severe clash within the leadership, one from which Miriam emerges the loser—accounting, perhaps, for her diminished prominence. The reappearance occurs amid the jumble of the Book of Numbers, wherein Miriam and Aaron are heard to question the authority of their brother, asking the question that Trible and others ask more broadly: "Has the Lord spoken only through Moses?" The Lord does not punish Aaron, but Miriam is struck down with a skin affliction, possibly leprosy, for her rebelliousness, and later dies in the wilderness of Zin.

And yet there are signs that the memory of Miriam in the Israelite consciousness remains an active and uplifting one. Miriam has always been associated with water, Trible noted—remember the basket among the rushes? remember the Song at the Sea?—and the text immediately following the notice of Miriam's death again brings up the subject of water. It reads, "Now there was no water for the congregation." In standard editions of the Bible that sentence starts a new paragraph, as if the subject is suddenly being changed. Trible said, "Written Hebrew doesn't have such breaks. The paragraph marking after the end of

the Miriam story is artificial. It makes you miss the idea that what is happening is connected to Miriam's death. Nature is mourning the loss of Miriam." Henceforward in the Bible, Miriam reappears only in hints and fragments, as in this passage from Deuteronomy: "Remember what the Lord your God did to Miriam on your journey out of Egypt." But she survives in real life—in the form of the continuing popularity of the name Miriam. The New Testament, compiled more than a millennium after Miriam's death, is populated with a multitude of women named Mary—the Hellenized version of the Hebrew Miriam. It is no coincidence, Trible has argued, that the Magnificat, the great canticle of Mary the mother of Jesus, borrows imagery directly from the Song at the Sea.

Miriam, Trible said, is only one of a number of apparently powerful women in the Bible who are alluded to almost in passing, the modesty of the references at odds with the importance of the roles these women seem to play. The references hint, perhaps, at the existence of a class of women in Israel whose history

Miriam is only one of a number of apparently powerful women in the Bible who are alluded to almost in passing, the modesty of the references at odds with the roles these women seem to play.

has in essence been lost, or can today be recovered only by means of the most delicate salvage, even then yielding mere wisps of insight. But that the references survive at all—that the editors believed some mention of these women had to be made—is itself suggestive.

"It shows," Trible said, "that the stories just couldn't be squelched."

THE EARLIEST ISRAELITES

During part of almost every year for thirty years Carol Meyers, a professor of religion at Duke University, has left behind the comforts of university life for the rigors of archaeological excavations in the Middle East. For the past five summers she and her husband, Eric, have led excavations at a place called Sepphoris, in Israel, a site with remains as recent as the Crusades and as ancient as the Iron Age. Sepphoris, near Nazareth, in Galilee, is said in Christian tradition to be the birthplace of Mary. [In 1993] Carol and Eric Meyers excavated an Iron Age site at Sepphoris, one that dates to the earliest years of the Israelite people.

I visited Carol Meyers not long before her latest tour of duty in the Middle East, and she began describing the conditions under which she and her colleagues worked there. We were in her Gothic office at Duke, and the crowded shelves around us held books like *L'architecture domestique du Levant* and *Catalogue of Ancient Near-Eastern Seals in the Ashmolean Museum*—the sort of books that elicit in me a vague yearning for baked earth and native porters. When you step off the plane in Israel, Meyers said, it is always a visual shock. Even with the achievements of modern irrigation—even in the rainy season—much of the landscape is forbidding: barren, rocky, thorny. And in the summer it is *hot*. And in the winter, as people abroad often do not realize, it is *cold*. There is wind and hail and sleet.

These conditions are at their most extreme in the hill country of Judea and Samaria and Galilee, where the Israelites first emerged, inhabiting the unforgiving uplands because the Canaanite city-states controlled the fertile bottomlands. In this marginal ecological niche, where water was scarce and soils were bad, the tribes of Israel clung to a tenuous subsistence. They terraced the hills to make fields. They built cisterns lined with slaked-lime plaster to hold water.

Precisely who the Israelites were and where they came from remain matters of debate, but their appearance in the Land of Canaan can be dated to roughly 1250 B.C. The period of the Israelite monarchy, the kingdom of Saul and David and Solomon and their successors, was two centuries away, and the demands of social organization fell almost entirely upon the family—or, more precisely, upon clusters of related families. There was no central government, no structured politics, no sense of a public domain.

In this inhospitable and tribalized world, Carol Meyers believes, men and women functioned in social parity. The books of the Bible that describe this period of Israel's history—Judges and Joshua, primarily—do not necessarily show this to be the case, of course. Having achieved final form centuries later, they depict a society in which most of the important roles were played by men. But, as Meyers observed, there is frequently a big disjunction between a society's public stance and the everyday social reality; and everyday social reality in ancient Israel has only recently become an object of scrutiny. In biblical studies as in many other kinds of scholarship, social history has been a latecomer, and it is in social rather than political history that women tend at last to emerge from the background.

That Carol Meyers developed an interest in biblical studies at all is an accident of history. When she was an undergraduate at Wellesley, in the mid-1960s, a course in the Old Testament and the New Testament was required for graduation. Wellesley's insistence on biblical education, now long since dropped, had deep historical roots: Wellesley was a college where female biblical scholars had since the late nineteenth century found a congenial home. The first woman to present a paper at a meeting of the Society of Biblical Literature (1913) was a Wellesley professor, as was the first woman to publish a paper in the society's *Journal of Biblical Literature* (1917). Meyers found herself drawn to the world of the Bible and after a summer spent on an archaeological excavation in Wyoming, run by Harvard University, she knew that she wanted to combine biblical studies and archaeology. She began studying biblical Hebrew and then took up Akkadian, a Semitic language with many Hebrew cognates. In graduate school at Brandeis she was the only woman in most of her classes, and she had no female professors.

Needless to say, there was no such thing as feminist biblical studies. Nor did Meyers feel an inner tug in that direction. "It really was only once I began teaching at Duke," she recalled when we spoke, "that I became aware of the need

and of the potential for gender studies with respect to Scripture. It really wasn't even at my own initiative—and I'm not embarrassed to say that. When I started teaching here, my colleagues said, 'Listen, you have to put a couple of courses on our curriculum that are of your own design. Why don't you think about doing some course on women and the Bible, or something like that?' This was in the mid-seventies, and I was the only woman in the department. Of course I said yes. When I started trying to put such a course together, I found out that there was no material. No one had done any research on it; no one had written about it. And that's when I started doing work myself."

Much of that work is embodied in *Discovering Eve: Ancient Israelite Women in Context* (1988), a book that draws on biblical sources and, more important, the insights offered by archaeology and social anthropology to reconstruct aspects of life in Israel before the dawn of monarchy and complex political institutions.

Meyers is cautious about applying the label "patriarchal" too broadly. Who knows what this nineteenth-century construct even means when applied to ancient Israel?

The economic functions of men and women at that time would have been separate and distinct, Meyers writes, with the men disproportionately responsible for tasks involving brute strength and the women responsible for tasks requiring technology or specialized skills or social sophistication: shearing wool and weaving cloth, processing and preserving food, teaching children, and managing a complex

household whose membership excavated floor plans suggest, usually went far beyond the nuclear family. In pre-monarchic Israel, as in primitive societies today where the household is the basic political and economic unit, women would have been central and authoritative figures.

Meyers observes further that the God of Israel, in sharp contrast to the gods of all other contemporaneous religions, was perceived at this time as asexual. Moreover, when God had to be described metaphorically, both male and female imagery was used. The prominence of God as father is a very late development in Israelite religion, Meyers argues, and makes only rare appearances in the Hebrew Bible itself (the term "father" is used in association with God just ten times).

The editors of the Bible have preserved traces of what Meyers believes was a relatively egalitarian regime. The Book of Judges, which reached its final form around the time of the Babylonian Captivity (586–538 B.C.), depicts life in Israel half a millennium earlier, and contains material that is very old. It brings to our attention an unusually large number of self-assured and powerful women. One of these, Deborah, is referred to as both a prophet and a judge. The "judges" in these earliest times were not magistrates but rather those few individuals among the Israelites whose authority extended beyond household and tribe and might be thought of as somehow national. Some scholars have even speculated that one portion of the Book of Judges, the so-called Song of Deborah, may have been composed by a woman. (Resolving such matters of authorship is at this point impossible. It should be noted that the recent and widely publicized *Book of J*, in which the literary critic Harold Bloom entertains the conceit that one of the authors of the Pentateuch, the so-called J source, was a woman, is not held in high regard by biblical scholars, whatever the truth about J's identity may be. An earlier and more reliable book that speculates briefly on the same question is *Who Wrote the Bible?* by Richard Elliott Friedman.)

To Israelite women's economic productivity—at least equal in importance to that of men—must be added the essential element of reproductivity. Meyers reads the Bible mindful of the precarious demographic circumstances confronting the early Israelites. "It's wrong," she said, "to impose our idea of the individual on a society in which that may not have been a driving force in human development. The 'me-ness' or the 'I-ness' of our own contemporary life cannot be superimposed upon another era. The demands of community survival meant cooperation and a sense that what people were doing was in order for the group to survive. I get annoyed at some feminist critics who don't consider the social-history perspective. They see things like 'Be fruitful and multiply, and fill the earth' as meaning that the sole purpose of a woman is to conceive children. And all her interactions with God or with her husband seem to be to bring that fact about. They say, 'Well, a woman is just giving up her body for her husband.' I would counter by saying that in an agrarian society large families are essential. And that the Israelites were settling into marginal lands that had never been developed before. And whether they would make it or not depended on a certain population base. So the injunctions for fertility—and remember, they are addressed to both men and women—can be seen as a way of encouraging something that was beneficial if not essential for community survival."

It was a hard life. Infant mortality approached 50 percent. Excavations of burials show that female life expectancy, owing in part to the risks involved in repeated pregnancies, was perhaps thirty years, ten years less than life expectancy for men. Meyers told me that whenever she is on an archaeological dig in the Middle East, she inevitably begins to imagine herself as one of those women of ancient Israel. During an excavation Meyers is working the same remorseless terrain as did the Israelites 3,000 years ago, the two sexes side by side. The toil is unremitting and tedious, the environment dry and dusty. The days when scores of local laborers were supervised by aristocrats in pith helmets are long over. Archaeology is a complex enterprise, group-oriented in the extreme. Being a mother, Meyers for years had other responsibilities as well: young children for whom she had to care, on the site, even as the excavations proceeded.

Meyers's research has now moved beyond the formative centuries of Israel to the Israelite monarchy, which was instituted under Saul around 1020 B.C. This is the Israel of the two books of

Samuel and the two books of Kings, a unified monarchy until, after the death of Solomon, around 920 B.C., the country was partitioned into northern and southern kingdoms. Under its kings, political structures in Israel became increasingly centralized and urban centers became increasingly important. A market economy grew up alongside the subsistence one. During this period, too, at least in urban settings, the position of women relative to men became more unequal—came more to resemble the kind of society we see in the Bible. It is hard to know how closely the situation in, say, Jerusalem, reflected life elsewhere. Jerusalem, Meyers explained to me, was always an anomaly. After the Assyrians overran the Northern Kingdom, in 721 B.C., the population of Jerusalem, the capital of the Southern Kingdom, was swollen by refugees. The city grew to be ten times as large as the next largest city in Israel. Its inhabitants no longer had ties to the land, and women no longer had a central role in economic life. There was poverty and chaos and great social stratification. There were large numbers of foreigners. There was something called public life, and it was in the hands of men. This is the time and the place in which much of the Hebrew Bible was fashioned. No wonder, Meyers said, that it is androcentric.

Kraemer noted that, commonplace assumptions notwithstanding, nowhere do the New Testament writings identify Mary Magdalene, who was prominent in Jesus' circle, as a prostitute.

And yet, Meyers went on, some 90 percent of the people of Israel continued to live in agricultural villages in the countryside. She is cautious about applying the label "patriarchal" either too broadly or too loosely. Often the social

patterns that prevail in the city are quite different from those that survive in the country. The term "patriarchy" may be legitimate in some places and times and not in others. Who knows what this nineteenth-century construct even means when applied to a pre-modern society like that of ancient Israel? "It does a disservice," Meyers said, "to a complex piece of literature, the Bible, and to a society that existed for a thousand years, and changed and grew."

Our gaze is deflected, too, Meyers said, by the very focus of the Bible on public life. On the relatively rare occasions when it affords a glimpse of private life, a patriarchal society is not always what we see. The Song of Songs offers such a glimpse. It contains much archaic material, and is especially noteworthy for the amount of text written in a woman's voice, and in the first person. Some of the terminology is suggestively feminine, and even hints at female authority. For example, whereas in most of the Bible the standard term for a household is *bet'ab*, or "father's house," the term used in the Song of Songs is *bet'em*, or "mother's house." Indeed, there has been speculation that the Song of Songs was written by a woman.

> My beloved is mine and I am his;
> he pastures his flock among the lilies.
> Until the day breathes and the shadows flee,
> turn, my beloved, be like a gazelle
> or a young stag on the cleft mountains.

Regardless of the author's sex, the love poetry in the Song of Songs expresses an emotional bond not between a master and a subordinate but between equals.

PATRONS AND PRESBYTERS

"Do you know what a 'squeeze' is?" Under other circumstances I might have confidently given a reply, but after several hours of conversation with Ross S. Kraemer, a fellow at the University of Pennsylvania's Center for Judaic Studies, I had a feeling that the answer would be unexpected. We had met in Philadelphia, where Kraemer lives, and we talked over lunch and during a drive through town (interrupted by calls to a housekeeper on the car phone). Kraemer spoke about the Greek cult of Dionysus, which, though little attention has been paid to the fact, was in its ecstatic rites the province of women. (A study of the cult of Dionysus had been the nucleus of her doctoral dissertation at Princeton.) She spoke about Mary Magdalene, one of the women who figured most prominently in the circle around Jesus, and noted that, commonplace public assumptions notwithstanding, nowhere do the New Testament writings identify her as a prostitute. (The tradition may have been developed deliberately as part of an attempt to diminish Mary's stature, particularly in comparison with that of the Apostle Peter.) She spoke about the ancient "purple trade"—the trade in expensive purple-dyed fabric, the participants in which could be presumed to enjoy a certain affluence. This information bears on a woman named Lydia, a "dealer in purple cloth" from the city of Thyatira, who appears in the Acts of the Apostles and is an example of the kind of independent woman of means who seems to have played an especially active role in early Christianity.

A squeeze is a mold of an ancient inscription carved in marble or other stone, obtained by coating the hard surface with a pliable substance—latex has supplanted papier-mâché as the medium most commonly used—and then peeling it off. Epigraphers, as those who study inscriptions are called, typically have a selection of them in their possession, along with files of photographs and transcriptions. The subject of squeezes had come up when Kraemer began describing the types of sources auxiliary to the Bible on which scholars can rely in the study of women and ancient religion. As time moves forward from primitive epochs, the sources become more plentiful. They include works of art and works of history and literature. They include a diverse array of documents involving women: for example, letters, tax receipts, wet-nurse contracts. And they include large numbers of inscriptions and fragments of inscriptions from buildings and monuments. Kraemer pointed to the work of one colleague whose analysis of Greek and Latin epigraphical evidence led her to conclude, contrary to the prevailing scholarly consensus, that at least sometimes Jewish women occupied prominent leadership roles in the ancient synagogue.

That the sources become more plentiful suggests a Mediterranean world that was becoming more complex. By the end of the sixth century B.C. the monarchic period in Israel had drawn to a close. The Israelites had endured a half century of exile in Babylon and then been allowed to return to their homeland. During the several hundred years that elapsed before the birth of Jesus, this homeland would be ruled by Persians, by Greeks, by Romans. The entire region would feel the influence of new economic and cultural systems. This is also the period when, in the Temple precincts of Jerusalem, the Hebrew Bible gradually cohered into the form in which we have it now, a collection of thirty-nine canonical texts, some of them incorporating material of great antiquity passed down through the ages more or less verbatim. (I remember Carol Meyers's once pointing out that the enormous stylistic variety of the Bible's Hebrew is one characteristic that eludes translation.) The canon of the Hebrew Bible was closed—no books would subsequently be added—toward the end of the first century A.D. By then the Romans had razed the Temple in Jerusalem, and the sacred texts of a new religious force, Christianity, were in the process of being compiled.

How egalitarian was that new religious force? More important (and borrowing the title of an influential and controversial 1971 article by Leonard Swidler, a professor at Temple), was Jesus a feminist? Such questions unfailingly stir up a range of scholarly responses. I asked Ross Kraemer to talk about those questions, and the conversation gravitated naturally to the work of Elisabeth Schüssler Fiorenza. Kraemer acknowledged the enormous debt that everyone owed Schüssler Fiorenza, acknowledged that her work had been groundbreaking in providing a new but also comprehensive and coherent way of viewing the Jesus movement and its context. But she added that she was less, well, optimistic than Schüssler Fiorenza. "I'm not as optimistic not so much in terms of her recovery of what she thinks women in early Christianity did, what roles they played—I think she's likely to be right about a lot of that. Where I would part company is with her argument that the earliest theology of Christianity is *intentionally* egalitarian and feminist. I'm really not persuaded of that, though I

think that Christianity in many communities may have had egalitarian consequences. Elisabeth wants to locate the intent in Jesus himself. It's not so much that I think she's wrong as that I'm simply not convinced we can know that she's right. It's very hard to argue that we know *anything* about what Jesus really thought, and the few things that any scholar would be willing to attribute to Jesus himself with any confidence don't address this particular issue."

The difficulty is that the Gospels and other early texts are encrusted documents, layered accretions formed out of a mixture of sources and motivations. On women's issues as on other matters, they may be surer guides to the communities in which they were formed than to the community around Jesus that they ostensibly describe. Kraemer used the various Resurrection stories and the part played by women in those stories to illustrate the pitfalls. All four Gospels depict women as having been the first to discover the empty tomb of Jesus, and in two of the Gospels, Jesus first appears after the Resurrection to Mary Magdalene. This would certainly seem to make a point about the position of women in the Jesus movement, some scholars say, and would also bolster a claim to female authority in Christian affairs—at the time of Jesus or later. Others note, however, that the account of the Resurrection in Paul's first letter to the Corinthians, which was written at least twenty years before the Gospels existed in written form, makes no mention of Mary Magdalene or indeed of any women, and it makes no mention of the empty-tomb tradition.

What is going on? One possibility, of course, is that in his account Paul is deliberately ignoring a tradition he is fully aware of—perhaps so as not to deflect emphasis from the authority of men (and himself). This could suggest that the process of diminishing the authority of women in Christianity began at a very early date. If that is the case, the survival of the women-at-the-empty-tomb tradition in the Gospels—decades after Paul—suggests its sheer durability. Thus we should perhaps take at face value, after all, what the Gospels have to say about the prominent position of women in the Jesus movement.

But wait: What if Paul was unaware of the empty-tomb tradition? What if, indeed, it arose *after* Paul—arose, as some have ventured, in conjunction with a growing belief among Christians in the prospect of a physical resurrection of an uncorrupted body after death, a belief that Paul himself would have regarded as crudely simplistic, whether applied to Jesus' Resurrection or to a more general resurrection of the dead? If the tradition did arise after Paul, Kraemer argues, then casting women as the first to see the empty tomb might have subtly helped to explain why it took so long for the good news about the physical Resurrection of Jesus to spread: because they were women, the original witnesses had been afraid to divulge what they knew, or had been widely disbelieved. In either case, of course, the result is an implicit denigration of women.

The situation is something of a mess. As Kraemer points out in her book *Her Share of the Blessings*, the basic problem is that "early Christian communities, especially after the death of Jesus, experienced considerable conflict over the appropriate roles of women, and tended to retroject their positions about this conflict back onto the stories they told about the women who encountered the earthly Jesus."

Her Share of the Blessings is a wide-ranging exploration of the role of women in Greco-Roman religions—pagan, Jewish, Christian—from about the fourth century B.C. to the fifth century A.D. The comparative approach Kraemer takes has great advantages, allowing her to see how structures in one realm may have influenced those in another. If she believes that, for whatever reason, early Christianity was more egalitarian in terms of gender than it later became— and she does—it is not only because of the interpretation she accepts of early Christian writings. She knows also from looking at the larger context that it was not unusual for women to hold cultic office in pagan religion, not unusual for them to play the role of patron. In light of the social mores of the time, the emphasis in much of early Christianity on sexual asceticism would also have served to enhance female independence: it offered free women a radical new option, a door to open other than the traditional one of marriage and child bearing and domesticity. Another force conducive to egalitarianism was the expectation among many early Christians that the present early order would soon pass—that the Lord was about to return in glory. In such a climate attachment

to social structures that were plainly "of the world" was considerably lessened. Did women serve as priests? The formal establishment of a priesthood in Christianity came very late, Kraemer writes, but a diverse body of evidence shows that women in early Christianity held the title *presbytera*, and that people who held this title performed all priestly functions: they taught, they baptized, they blessed the Eucharist.

There are, of course, tensions. One cannot read very far into the writings of Paul without becoming aware of his inner conflict when it came to questions of gender and sexuality. George Bernard Shaw once characterized Paul as the "eternal enemy of woman." In the epistle to the Galatians, Paul embraced an egalitarian formula, but in I Corinthians he showed himself to be clearly disturbed by the powerful and independent women in the Christian community at Corinth. He did not forbid the Corinthian women from prophesying, but he demanded that they cover their heads when they prayed in public, and he added a statement that defines women as subordinate to men. Is this last statement (along with some other problematic passages) a later interpolation, as some scholars believe? Perhaps. But tensions exist nonetheless, Kraemer writes, and they become deeper and more intolerable as Christianity moves further away in time from its origins, and moves closer to the contemporaneous social establishment.

Conflicting perspectives on women are apparent in later writings. One perspective is embodied in the apocryphal Acts of Thecla, probably written in the second century A.D., which celebrates the life of an ascetic female missionary supposedly sent out by Paul himself to teach and spread the word of the Lord. The Acts of Thecla, it must be said, has many decidedly odd elements (for example, Thecla is described as baptizing herself by jumping into a pool of hungry seals), but this text and many others like it enjoyed wide popularity. The other perspective is embodied, for example, in the epistles to Timothy, written in the second century, which contain some of the most stringent passages about women in the New Testament, passages that were then ascribed to Paul:

Let a woman learn in silence with full submission. I permit no woman to

teach or to have authority over a man; she is to keep silent. For Adam was formed first, then Eve; and Adam was not deceived, but the woman was deceived and became a transgressor.

This is the perspective that hardened when Christianity became the religion of the Roman state.

WOMEN WHO LEAD

Was Junia, whom Paul, in his epistle to the Romans, called "prominent among the apostles," a man or a woman? What about the person named Jael, who is referred to in an inscription from Aphrodisias, in Asia Minor, as being the presiding officer or patron of a Jewish community there? These questions are not academic. They speak to issues of gender, status, and leadership.

Some would argue that Junia and Jael had to have been men. How, after all, could a woman be a Christian apostle or the presiding officer of a Jewish community, when we know that women were barred from such honors? This is the kind of reasoning that brings a note of both excitement and exasperation to Bernadette Brooten's voice. Brooten is a professor of Scripture and interpretation at the Harvard Divinity School and the woman who made the study of Greek and Latin inscriptions which Ross Kraemer referred to. [In 1993] she. . . joined the faculty at Brandeis University. It is bad enough, Brooten said during a conversation one day, for women to be invisible in ancient Judaism and Christianity because men didn't think to mention them or because they weren't in a position to be mentioned. Must we also argue away the few women in plain sight?

Junia was a common female name in the ancient world, Brooten said. Several ancient religious commentators, such as Origen of Alexandria and John Chrysostom, assumed as a matter of course that the Junia mentioned in Romans was a woman. This assumption prevailed until the Middle Ages. Then a reaction set in. Paul reserved the title "apostle" for persons of great authority—people who had served as missionaries and founded churches. To a medieval mind, such people had to have been men. Junia underwent a change of sex. Later Martin Luther popularized a reinterpretation of Junia as *Junias*, an apparently masculine name—the diminutive, perhaps, as scholars would later speculate, of Junianius or Junilius. There is only one problem, Brooten said. The name Junias cannot be found in antiquity: not on documents, not in inscriptions. It does not exist as a name, diminutive or otherwise. All that we have is Junia, a common name for a woman—in this case, the name of a woman "prominent among the apostles."

As for the name Jael, Brooten said, the only reason the question of gender has come up at all is that there is an important title attached to the name, and the name sits at the top of a list of other names, all of which are male. In less politically charged circumstances, this Jael would simply have been assumed to be a woman. Jael was—is—a well-known woman's name. A woman named Jael is prominent in Judges. But scholars have hunted through Scripture and other ancient sources to see if they can find precedent for a Jael who is a man, because it seems to them so unlikely that this Jael could have been a woman. In some manuscripts of the Book of Ezra, as it appears in the Septuagint, they have found such a Jael. The name is in a list of male exiles who had married foreign women and were now repudiating them upon their return to Israel. The identification is highly tentative, however. The Septuagint is the Hebrew Bible as translated into Greek, and the transliteration of Semitic names from Hebrew into Greek is haphazard and inconsistent. What this means, Brooten went on, is that to take Jael as a man's name one has to accept an instance that may be nothing more than an artifact of transliteration. One has to prefer this to the attestation of Jael as female in a major book of the Bible, the name being that of a well-known figure whose story was probably a staple of synagogue readings.

"All of which," Brooten said, "raises several questions for me. How many women do there have to have been for there to have been any? And if it's part of the marginalization of women that women are very rarely leaders to begin with, then even in those circumstances in which women do occur as leaders, they may be either perceived as not being women or perceived as not being leaders." The note of frustration in Brooten's voice gave way to something slyer as she summoned up an image of scholars one day confronting a document that referred to Prime Minister Margaret Thatcher and the members of one of her all-male Cabinets. It would be only a matter of time, Brooten said, before some scholar came along and pronounced Thatcher a man.

Harvard Divinity School is one of the many divinity schools to whose revival an influx of women has contributed greatly. Applicants are plentiful, with women accounting for well over half the enrollment in the school's various programs. Whatever this portends for the future, women as yet remain distinctly underrepresented among the school's senior faculty.

Brooten joined the Harvard faculty in 1985. She had received her doctorate from Harvard a few years earlier, and in the intervening period had taught at Claremont. Part of her academic training took place in Tübingen, the cobbled and timbered university town in Germany whose name has long been associated with new departures in theology. She describes the German academic environment for women in much the same way Schüssler Fiorenza does. "German theologians," Brooten told me, "will just say outright that they don't want women." Oddly, though, Tübingen is where Brooten took her first women's-studies course: Leonard Swidler, on leave from Temple, happened to be a visiting professor there for a year, and offered a seminar on women and the Church. Brooten was one of two students who signed up for it. "In the university as a whole," she recalled, "there was no interest in such things at all."

Brooten's office at Harvard has the dusky flavor of a Dickensian garret. Narrow pathways thread among tumuli of tables and books. Some of the books are old, spines worn to a dull sheen by centuries of palms. There is not even a computer to suggest the late twentieth century, though Brooten does use one at home. It is now standard in the field to have computer software that can print in Greek, Hebrew, and Coptic fonts. Computers have also made some kinds of research much easier for biblical scholars. For example, the great bulk of the writing that survives from antiquity in Greek, Latin, and Hebrew—not just works of literature but also snippets from tens of thousands of papyrus fragments and stone inscriptions—is now available on CD-ROM.

A capsule summary of the implications of Brooten's earliest research might read like this: with respect to roles played by women, there was more differentiation within Judaism in the Greco-Roman world than many scholars acknowledge. This touches on a highly sensitive issue. Some scholars, particularly among those who want a liberalization of Christian church policies concerning women, have argued that if early Christianity fell short of an egalitarian ideal, the cause lay in part in the nature of the Jewish world out of which Christianity emerged. Thus, one argument runs, there might have been more women leaders in Christianity if only there had been more in Judaism. Looking at the matter another way, to the degree that egalitarianism did exist in early Christianity, it is sometimes presented as a sharp break from Jewish tradition. Often implicit, this kind of thinking amounts, in the view of some, to locating the origins of patriarchal misogyny in the Hebrew Bible and those who inhabited its shadow. That is perhaps stating the problem too unsubtly, but it exposes a place where the nerve is raw. Brooten's view is that the spectrum of tolerable practice among Jews in ancient times was broad—just as it is in modern Judaism, just as it was and is in Christianity.

In her doctoral dissertation, later published in book form as *Women Leaders in the Ancient Synagogue*, Brooten considered nineteen carved inscriptions dating from as early as 27 B.C. to as late as the sixth century A.D., in which Jewish women are accorded official titles relating to the communal life of a synagogue—titles such as "head of the synagogue," "leader," "elder." Titles like these, when applied to women, had long been interpreted as honorific rather than functional. "Rufina, a Jewess, head of the synagogue, built this tomb for her freed slaves and the slaves raised in her house"—these words come from a marble plaque, inscribed in the second century A.D., that was found in Smyrna. The traditional view has been that Rufina, the "head of the synagogue," the *archisynagogos*, had no real functional authority and was in all likelihood merely the wife of the true *archisynagogos*. Rufina is seen to have the title, as Brooten wryly notes, "*honoris causa.*" In dense, meticulous arguments that cannot be reviewed here, Brooten mounts an assault on that view. She takes up the cases of Rufina and the eighteen other women, and exposes what she deems to be the flawed presuppositions and tortured reasoning necessary to conclude that their titles were not functional. Women leaders of the synagogue were, of course, never the norm and were perhaps always the great exception. But, Brooten states, it is wrong to see the emergence of women leaders in Christianity as unprecedented.

Brooten's more recent work involves the writings of Paul, in particular his views on the proper place of women in society and where those views came from. One clue lies in Paul's condemnations of same-sex love. As Brooten explains, in a discussion that draws not only on religious texts but also on ancient materials as diverse as medical and astrological writings, Paul was in this regard no more than a man of his time. Whatever the exceptions in practice, on the normative gender map of the Roman world some behavior is appropriately masculine and some appropriately feminine, and the line is not supposed to be crossed. In sexual relations between members of the same sex this distinction is violated. One man becomes "like a woman"; one woman becomes "like a man." Underlying all this was a world view that, Brooten argues, saw the distinction between "active" and "passive" as more fundamental even than distinctions of sex. It was the basis of social order and social hierarchy. It was the origin of the tension in Paul. Forward-looking in many ways, Paul could not let it go.

"Paul was happy to work with women as colleagues, and encouraged them," Brooten said. "So, for example, he mentions Junia, and he acknowledges Prisca and Tryphaena and Tryphosa and Persis and other women. He teaches with them, and he recognizes their prophecy, and he works with them as missionaries in the Roman world. On the other hand, while he was very willing to make a religious and societal break with Jewish tradition on points that were considered very central to Judaism, such as the issue of dietary laws and the circumcision of men, in order to permit Jew and Gentile to come together alike to accept Jesus as the Christ, with some customs concerning women he's not willing to make that kind of break. For example, the issue of the hairstyling and veiling of women. And, indeed, at that very point in the text he describes Christ as the head of man, and man as the head of woman, which goes beyond tolerating a custom and gives a theological underpinning to gender differentiation. I see his position as essentially ambivalent. On certain issues—gender, slavery, Roman power—he is very much interested in maintaining social order. But what's fascinating about Paul is that he experiments."

Toward the end of a long conversation we lingered for a moment on the nature of that first-century world of which Paul was a part: a world that those who know it well describe as more alien from our own in its psychology and belief systems and outlook than we imagine. How confident do you feel, I asked Brooten, that we can span the gulf between these two cultures, ours and theirs—can reconstruct something trustworthy about the dynamics of *then*?

The work of feminist scholars has been greeted by some with impatience, irritation, even contempt. It has also established women's issues as a permanent focus of biblical studies.

"That's something I ask myself about all the time," Brooten said. And then she laughed. "I've often had this thought: that I'll die, and go to heaven, and Rufina will meet me, and I'll greet her as archisynagogos. And she'll say, '*Archisynagogos*? Nah. That was just my husband's title.'"

THE WRITING ON THE WALL

To focus on the work of a handful of scholars is necessarily to leave aside the work of scores of others. And there are, literally, scores. Their research by now covers just about every conceivable aspect of the Hebrew Bible and the New Testament. It has spread deeply into the fields of history and theology and literary criticism. I once asked David Tracy, the prominent Catholic theologian, what he thought would be the result of feminism's encounter with religion, and he said simply, "The next intellectual revolution." That assessment may sound overblown, but it isn't. Phyllis Trible used the metaphor of a conversation between feminism and the Bible. Feminism's larger conversation with religion touches every aspect of it, leaves no subject off the table. It engages doctrine, liturgy, ministry, and leadership, and it engages them all at once.

Scholarly work on women and the Bible faces certain inherent problems, certain inherent risks. In my talks with people in the field, the same worries were voiced by one scholar after another. A fundamental one has to do with the distinction between deriving an interpretation *from* a text and reading an interpretation *into* a text. It is one thing for a contemporary personal agenda—a desire, say, to see women enjoy a position of full equality in religious institutions—to direct one's research focus. Agendas of one sort or another frequently drive scholarship. But can't they also get out of hand? Another concern is an issue raised by Bernadette Brooten: the sometimes facile comparisons made between Christianity and Judaism. This has already begun to stir animosity outside the field of biblical studies, as evidenced by an eloquent recent essay in the Jewish bimonthly *Tikkun*.

The range of scholarly output on matters involving women and the Bible has been enormously diverse. As in any academic endeavor, the work has been of uneven quality. Much of the research remains tentative and preliminary, and there are severe limits, given the sparseness of what is likely to be the available evidence, to what can ever be known with certainty. The most we can hope for, Bernadette Brooten has written, is "a quick glimpse through a crack in the door." What has been accomplished thus far? One achievement is simply the staking out of ground. Several decades ago no one was particularly concerned—indeed, the thought rarely occurred to anyone—that the entire academic biblical enterprise was based on what was known about men's lives, was one that generalized from men to all humanity. Those days are gone. Another achievement has been a new emphasis on the sheer variety of thought and practice which sometimes existed within ancient religious groups. Scholars who perhaps went searching after some lost Golden Age—driven by the "earlier-is-better" bias that seems to be a characteristic of human thought—have stumbled into worlds that are more confused and complex than they may have anticipated, worlds that are in that sense not unlike our own. Yet another achievement is simply this: leaving aside the specific details, scholars have gone a long way toward bringing women in biblical and early Christian times into sharper relief. They have also shown how meaning has been shaded by the lacquer of interpretation. A good distillation of much of the research on women can be found in *The Women's Bible Commentary*, edited by Carol A. Newsom and Sharon H. Ringe.

Perhaps the most important lesson offered by the work of feminist biblical scholars comes in the form of a reminder: that in religion, as in other spheres, circumstances have not always been as we see them now. Evolution occurs. Some things, it turns out, are *not* sacred. This point may be obvious, but with respect to religion, especially, it is frequently overlooked—and, in fact, sometimes hotly denied. Whatever one believes about the nature of their origin, the handful of immutable precepts at any religion's core are embedded in a vast pulp of tradition, interpretation, and practice. And that pulp bears an all-too-human character. It is variously diminished, augmented, scarred, sculpted, and otherwise shaped by powerful human forces in every society and every time period through which it passes. Sometimes the change occurs slowly and almost invisibly. Sometimes it happens quickly and right before one's eyes, as I believe it is happening now—the proliferation of feminist scholarship on the Bible being both consequence and cause.

I write these last words on the day of my daughter's first communion in a denomination that still restricts the role of women, and I write them in the expectation that with respect to the position of women, matters will not remain—will simply not be able to remain—as in some places we see them now; in the expectation, to employ a biblical turn, that the present way's days are numbered.

Ecstasy in Late Imperial Rome

Dirk Bennett describes the crowded religious calendar of pagan Rome, and the spiritual market place in which Christianity had to fight for domination.

The sacred cry strikes to heaven with the praises of the eternal Lord and the pinnacle of the Capitol totters with the shock. The neglected images in the empty temples tremble when struck by the pious voices, and are overthrown by the name of Christ. Terrified demons abandon their deserted shrines. The envious serpent pale with rage struggles in vain, his lips blood-stained, bemoaning with his hungry throat the redemption of man, and at the same time now, with unavailing groans, the predator writhes around his dry altars cheated of the blood of sacrificial cattle. . . .

(Paulinus of Nola)

This is Rome in the fourth century after Christ. The Church Fathers unanimously drew a picture of an overwhelming triumph of their creed. According to them, with the conversion of Constantine in AD 312 the old and tired heathen religions gave way to a youthful new belief. Victories of Roman emperors were now interpreted as victories of God; the history of mankind equalled the history of His church. They argued that the old gods could not prevent the defeats, plagues and misfortunes of the past and present, and only since the arrival of Jesus Christ had the Empire achieved its vocation: to spread the true faith all over the world.

Contemporaries, though, saw the situation differently. A closer look at these statements reveals them to be wishful thinking and propaganda: pagan culture still had a huge following. Mid-fourth-century Rome had a colourful mix of religions. Christians, Jews, Manichaeans, Neoplatonists, followers of the old gods, of the Great Mother, of Bacchus and of hundreds of domestic gods taken from the conquered nations all populated the city.

Their brotherhoods, chapels, temples, shrines and sanctuaries spread all over the city and their festivals and celebrations added to the Roman year. Of these, the so-called calendar of Filocalus for the year 354 has survived and lists no less than 177 official holy days for a seemingly endless variety of gods and goddesses. Not one Christian celebration is to be found among them.

The highest festival of ancient origin was the Great Roman Games. The pinnacle of the celebrations, which stretched over several days, was September 13th, according to tradition the day the foundations had first been laid for the great temple of Jupiter on the Capitoline Hill. No expense was spared when the highest god of the community was celebrated, together with his wife and daughter, Juno and Minerva. Statues of all three of them were to be found inside the temple. Around the main event there were days of *epulones* (festive meals for the gods), huge processions along the Via Sacra, markets and, of course, the games in the Circus Maximus.

A special priesthood, appointed for the occasion, prepared the *epulones*. They purified and adorned the statues, prepared rooms and the sacred meal itself. This was shared between a select group of deserving members of society and the gods, who were symbolised by the statues lying on beds. Similar meals were held all over town on a smaller scale by Roman families.

The Plebeian Games also took place, in honour of the gods Ceres, Flora and Apollo. These festivities, as the celebrated deities show, were closely connected to the peasant origins of the town. The most ancient brotherhoods— the Pontifices, the Sacerdotes, the Flamines, Auguri, Vestal Virgins, Epulones, the Salii, the Arval and Luperci—wearing their traditional robes, processed through town to their temples. Each of these offices followed their own specific and often strict codes. The high priest of Jupiter, for example, the *Flamen Dialis* or 'Divine Flame', was forbidden to touch horses, goats, dogs or meat, dead or alive. Ivy, beans, wheat and bread were prohibited. He was not allowed to have any knot tied on him or cut his nails and hair with an iron knife. By the fourth century, these ancient rituals and instructions had lost their meaning to the people and even to the priests themselves.

The 'Divine Flame' was present at another ancient ritual, again connected to the town's rural origins: the Lupercal. Its celebration is documented up to the late fifth century when Pope Gelasius protested against it. On February 15th, at the Lupercal—the cave where according to legend the she-wolf had fed Romulus and Remus—a number of male goats were sacrificed. A priest then touched the foreheads of two young noblemen with the bloody knife. The blood was then wiped away with a lump of wool soaked in milk, the two young men would laugh out loud and, wrapped in the fur of the killed animals, would start a boisterous race around the borders of the ancient town. On their way they lashed bystanders, especially young women, with whips made from the skin of the goats.

Many other ancient holidays survived, including April 21st, official birthday of the city of Rome, 'Eternal City' of the pagan world, as well as countless birthdays of the domestic and state gods. On February 2nd, there was Hercules; on March 1st, Mars; April 3rd, Quirinus; April 8th, the divine twins and protectors of the town, Castor and Pollux; in August, Salus, Sol and Luna (the goddesses of public wealth, the sun and the moon). Other days were reserved for Fortuna, Persephone, Hermes, the Penates, Diana and others.

Former emperors and empresses were considered gods, and membership of their priesthoods was highly sought after. The duties of the Augustales priesthood included the observance of the birth- and death-dates of the former heads of state. In the fourth century these alone amounted to no fewer than ninety-eight days a year.

The celebration of all these cults reflected the ancient polytheistic attitude towards religion, in which sacrificing on one altar did not exclude the believer from prayer at another. Tomb inscriptions of Roman magistrates show how many sacred offices and priesthoods could be taken on:

> To the Divine Shades, Vettius Agorius Praetextatus, Augur, Priest of Vesta, Priest of the Sun, Member of the Fifteen, Curial of Hercules, Consecrated to Liber and the deities of Eleusis, Hierophant, Superintendent Minister, initiated by the bull's blood Father of Fathers. . . .

Some historians have called late antiquity the age of spiritually, a time when many believers tried to get to the core of things and gain deeper understanding of the meaning of life. In contemporary opinion, there was more than one way of achieving this. Symmachus, probably the most famous exponent of paganism of his time, expressed it thus:

> It is reasonable that all the different gods we worship should be thought

of as one. We see the same stars, share the same sky, the same earth surrounds us: what does it matter what scheme of thought a man uses in his search for the truth? Man cannot come to so profound a mystery by one road alone. . . .

The idea is typical for the fourth century, but it also corresponded with a practical and very Roman view of religion. The relations between gods and humans resembled a contract in which both sides had to fulfil certain 'mutually agreed' conditions. The gods' entitled rites and instructions had to be thoroughly observed, and they, in return, were expected to provide health and wealth to the people. It therefore followed logically that the more gods you attended, the more goods you would have. As head of state and the human most responsible for mankind playing its part, the emperor had the important role of supervising all cults and religions as a supreme priest, or Pontifex Maximus.

In a frenzy the most faithful castrated themselves, an act which entitled them to enter the priesthood

---

The mystery religions have over the centuries aroused the interest of academics and the public alike. Arguably, the cult which has attracted the most attention is that of Demeter—the Great Mother of Earth, also known as Magna Mater and Kybele—and her lover Attis. Soldiers on campaign in the east in the second century BC had first been initiated into the cult's rites and brought it back to Rome. It soon raised the eyebrows of the senatorial elite, for whom its novel ceremonies presented a serious threat to the Roman way of life, undermining the state. It was declared illegal but was re-established under the emperors, and proved to be one of the firmest

and most successful religious communities in and beyond the capital.

The highest ceremonies, in March of each year, described the story of the love between Demeter and Attis, his death and resurrection. The main celebrations began on March 22nd. A freshly cut pine tree was solemnly taken into the temple of Demeter on the Capitoline Hill, where it was adorned with ribbons and pennants under prayers and cantations. Violets symbolised the blood shed by the young god, when he committed suicide under the tree. Then a portrait of Attis himself was attached to the trunk. The following day was dedicated to the preparation of the faithful. We read about festive music, trumpets and prayers. The third day was the 'Day of Blood'. The high priest, or Archigallus, cut his arm with a knife and shed his own blood over the tree, followed by the other priests. They then led the whole community in an ecstatic procession of wild dances and flagellation through the streets. In a frenzy the most faithful few, the so-called *fanatici*, even castrated themselves, an act which entitled them to enter the priesthood. The procession ended in tears and sorrow, the community mourning the death of the god and burying his effigy as a symbol of their grief.

Firmicus Maternus, a Christian author, described what happened next:

> One night an image is laid face upwards on a couch and lamented with tears and rhythmic chants, Then, when they have glutted themselves with fake mourning, the light is brought in. The throats of all who have lamented are then anointed by the priest and, after the anointing, the priest whispers these words in a soft murmur: 'Take courage, initiates of the mystery of a god now saved. For you will come salvation from suffering.'

The joy and elation about salvation expressed itself in the celebrations extended over the 'Day of Jubilation'. After that, a day of recuperation, fasting and contemplation was necessary. On the 27th, the statue of the goddess was taken out of the temple and put on an ox-drawn cart. Down the steep streets of Capitol Hill it went, through the town to a little river, the Almo, nearby, where the effigy, together with the cart and instruments of worship, were solemnly dropped into the stream and purified.

Now, finally, everything was taken back to the temple under heaps of flowers in preparation for the reappearance of the young god.

But these lavish public rituals were but one aspect of the cult, displayed only once a year. There were numerous smaller events like fasts, sacred meals and a peculiar baptising ceremony, the details of which particularly incensed Christian onlookers:

A trench is dug, and the high priest plunges deep underground to be sanctified. He wears a curious headband, fastens fillets for the occasion around his temples, fixes his hair with a crown of gold, holds up his robes of silk with a belt from Gabii. Over his head they lay a plank-platform crisscross, fixed so that the wood is open not solid; then they cut or bore through the floor and make holes in the wood with an awl at several points till it is plentifully perforated with small openings. A large bull, with grim, shaggy features and garlands of flowers round his neck or entangling his horns, is escorted to the spot. The victim's head is shimmering with gold and the sheen of the goldleafs lends colour to his hair. The animal destined for sacrifice is at the appointed place. They consecrate a spear and with it pierce his breast. . . . (Prudentius)

The Egyptian cult of Isis was another highly influential community in Rome. The sources quote two main events in the 'Church of Isis': The *Navigium Isidis* (or 'Vessel of Isis') and 'Isia'. The first, on March 5th, officially opened the shipping season and consisted of a colourful procession to the harbour. The main ceremonies, however, took place between October 28th and November 3rd, and also described a love story, on this occasion between Isis and her brother Osiris. The latter is killed by his envious brother, Seth, and, after a long and adventurous search, resurrected by his sister.

The symbol of Isis, a golden calf in a black veil, was paraded through the streets of Rome. The procession recreated Isis's search for her vanished husband and brother Osiris, with key figures represented: the soldier, the fisherman, the hunter, the gladiator, the civil servant, the philosopher and the woman. Female worshippers sprinkled perfume, incense and flowers, others carried the toiletries of the goddess, combs and polished mirrors. Singers and torchbearers

followed. Only linen and cotton clothes were permitted. The women were veiled, while the heads of the men were shaved. Then came the priests:

First of all is the singer . . . and after him follows the watcher of the hours; he holds in his hands a clock and palm branch as the symbols of astrology. . . . Then the divine writer appears; he wears a feather on his head and in his hands a book and a basket, in which there is an inkwell and a magic wand. . . . After that comes the steward; he carries the hand of justice and a pitcher for libation. . . . And at last appears the speaker of the words of god and he holds, visible for all, the water pitcher in his lap; he is followed by the men, who carry the bread to be distributed. . . . (Clemens of Alexandria)

Many early Christian churches were built over caves dedicated to a highly secretive and, quite literally, underground cult: that of Mithras. However, they succeeded only partially in suppressing the evidence of this thriving community. Numerous inscriptions, altar stones and statues to the cult survive. The cult differed from other mystery religions from the East in one aspect above all. Only men were allowed into the community. Not surprisingly, its biggest following was with the army. In military outposts all over the empire its symbols and caves can be found.

There were seven grades of initiation to the cult of Mithras: raven, bridegroom, soldier, lion, Persian, heliodrome and the father, each standing under the protection of a particular planet and god. Most of the strange symbols that adorn the caves are now meaningless to us and we know little about the mythology. The caves seem to symbolise both the world and the birthplace of the saviour god Mithras.

Underground chapels have been found under the Piazza Navicella, the San Stefano Rotondo and elsewhere. These rooms were small, and only rarely offered space for more than thirty or forty of the faithful. They were furnished with statues of the planet gods, among them Chronos, the lionheaded, half-human half-animal, guardian of time, a snake winding around his body. The ancient scriptures mention atmospheric illuminations, which seems appropriate for a god connected with sun and fire, and is supported by archae-

ological findings. The grottoes are full of light shafts, openings and hidden niches for lamps or candles. There were benches along the walls for the worshippers and mosaics on the floor depicting the 'Mithras ladder', the climb from one grade to another. Everything was concentrated towards one end of the room where the statue of Mithras stood flanked by his helpers Cautes and Cautophates, sunrise and sunset, slaying the bull and bringing salvation to the world. Reliefs surround the central scene, telling the legend of the god. One Christian author describes a baptism:

Some flap their wings and imitate the cry of a raven, while others roar like lions. Some have their hands bound with fowls' entrails and water is spilled over them, while someone appears with a sword, cuts the ties and calls himself 'the saviour' . . . (Ps. Augustinus)

How did Christianity overthrow these ancient cults? Some historians have pointed to the organisation of the church, and others to Christian intolerance, which proved an effective weapon against the pagan cults. Its consistent ideology might also have played a part. Opportunism on the part of the emperors is another well-known explanation. The Roman emperors recognised and made use of the unifying potential of Christianity throughout the Empire. A decisive point was reached in AD 392 when Theodosius officially banned the practising of pagan ceremonies.

However, without question, the success of Christianity could not have occurred to such an extent if it had not held huge appeal to the masses in its own right. Perhaps the 'age of spiritualism' had tired of the old beliefs, which contained no notion of an afterlife. Mystery religions were one step closer, but it is doubtful whether their promises and visions were truly focused on the afterlife. They were also aimed at elite societies with no interest in converting the masses or bringing wider salvation.

The genuine appeal of Christianity to people in the fourth century cannot be underestimated. However, it faced a real threat from two very different quarters: from Manichaeism (or Gnosticism) and from the heretic sects. The first resembled Christianity at first glance and offered a seemingly more consistent and logical ideology. The second introduced life-threatening division into the Christian community.

The Manichaean church had an elaborate organisation, and a message which pointed to salvation in the afterlife. Many who later became Christian dignitaries began their religious life as Manichaeans, including St Augustine. Their ascetic priests spread the word of their founder Mani far and wide.

According to Mani, the world was divided between the principles of good and evil linked in a cosmic, predestined battle. For mankind there was no escape and no free will, like angels, demons, gods and prophets—Jesus being one of them—they were participants, messengers or helpers in a war which ultimately would lead to salvation.

In the end, however, this dark and unworldly vision could not match the positive message proclaimed by the great Christian scholars, who from the fourth century sought and gained the initiative. Manichaeism ultimately turned back to its roots in the East. In the years following the Council of Nicaea in 325, the Christian church faced heated arguments between different factions about the nature of Jesus. Splinter groups had their own variations in teaching and ritual—the Judaeo-Christians, Novatians, Paulianists and many more. But so strong was its message, the Christian creed still triumphed.

What happened to the rich world of ancient paganism, to its rituals, symbols, instruments, holy days and holy places? Certainly, paganism survived until long after the fall of the Western Empire to the barbarian king Odoacer in 476. The frequent repetition of laws and numerous complaints from bishops and popes against pagan practices show that it was still very much alive until late into the sixth century.

The Christian church took over many pagan elements, transformed and made them into their own. Even statues like that of Demeter with the small Dionysus were reinterpreted as Mary and Jesus. Pagan ceremonies were transformed into Christian holy days, best known of which is Christmas which replaced the birthday celebrations for the sun god. Incense found its way into Christian liturgy. Symbols like the crescent moon of Isis became a symbol for the Virgin Mary, while Christian churches were erected on the sites of, or sometimes even built into, pagan temples. Priestly robes still resemble their pagan predecessors—especially the papal costume with its extensive use of the imperial purple which directly emphasised the role of its hearer as the new Pontifex Maximus.

FOR FURTHER READING

J. Ferguson, *Greek and Roman Religion. A Sourcebook* (Noyes Classical Studies, 1982); M. R. Salzmann, *On Roman Time, The Codex Calendar of 354 and the Rythms of Urban Life in Late Antiquity* (University of California Press, 1990); B. Cook & J. Harris, *Religious Conflict in 4th Century Rome* (Sydney University Press, 1982); R. Turcan, *The Cults of the Roman Empire* (Oxford University Press, 1996). W. Burkert, *Ancient Mystery Cults* (Cambridge/Mass., London 1987).

Dick Bennett studied ancient history and archaeology at Regensburg University

Who the Devil Is the Devil?

BY ROBERT WERNICK

WITH THE RAPID APPROACH of the third millennium, many people can't help wondering what role the Devil will be playing in it. But a cursory examination of the mainstream press of America reveals almost no mention of him, and even using the Internet services that promise to keep track of everything, it's much easier to find information on Monica Lewinsky than on the Devil.

What a humiliating comedown for one the mere mention of whose name was once enough to make the hair of kings stand up in terror; of whom Saint Augustine said, "The human race is the Devil's fruit tree, his own property, from which he may pick his fruit."

To appreciate the full extent of that downfall, try to put yourself someplace in Western Europe in the year 999, as the second millennium was about to bow in.

In the tenth century and for at least half a millennium thereafter, the Devil was everywhere. He leered out of every church door, he capered through castle and church and cottage, and his plots and pranks and temptings of humans were spelled out in sermons, on the stage, in paintings, in pious books, and in stories told in taverns or in homes at bedtime.

No corner or cranny of daily life escaped him. He lurked outside every orifice of the human body, waiting for the chance to get at the human soul inside— one reason why to this day we say "God bless you" when we hear someone sneeze.

The Devil fathered children on sleeping women, he stirred up conspiracies and treasons, he led travelers astray. He caused boils, plagues, tempests, shipwrecks, heresies, barbarian invasions. Whatever he did, his name was on everyone's tongue, and he went by many names: Satan, Lucifer, Beelzebub, Belial, Mastema, the Prince of Darkness, the Lord of Lies. In the Bible he was the Accuser, the Evil One, the Prince of this World.

This suave, sardonic Devil is actually a new kid on the block.

Today, a few scant hundred years later, he has dropped so far out of sight that some believe he is gone for good. It may be true that 48 percent of Americans tell the pollsters they believe in the existence of the Devil and another 20 percent find his existence probable. But though they use him often enough in common lighthearted expressions (give the devil his due, the devil is in the details) and in the privacy of their hearts may put the blame on him when they covet their neighbor's wife or cheat on their income tax, they do very little talking about him out loud. Reported physical appearances of the Devil are far rarer

than sightings of UFOs. In practical terms, people have banished him from public life.

Yet most everyone who discusses moral standards in pulpits or on television talk shows or in the *New York Times* is agreed that morals are lower than ever before. The Devil should be out in the streets and on the airwaves, roaring like a lion about his triumphs. Where has he gone? It all depends on precisely what you mean by "the Devil."

Theologians have been arguing for centuries (and sometimes have gone to the stake for expressing the wrong opinion) to achieve a satisfactory definition. But today the average person with no theological axe to grind is apt to envisage the Devil as a sleek, dark-complexioned male figure, with black chin-whiskers, little horns and cloven hooves, perhaps with a foxy glint in his eye and a trace of a foreign accent, but on the whole handsome, worldly-wise, a persuasive talker, a friendly sort of customer. He may tell you anything, try to talk you into something too good to be true. Only later, when you've taken that risky bet or signed the shady contract, and he comes to collect his due, do you realize you have signed away your immortal soul. He is unquestionably the Lord of Lies.

This suave, sardonic Devil is actually a new kid on the block; he has been around for barely a few hundred years, a mere stutter in the long swell of human misery and woe. And the Devil in general, the Devil with a capital *D*, as opposed to the legions of lowercase devils, demons, imps, satyrs, fiends and so on, first entered human history less than 3,000 years ago.

But humans indistinguishable from us have been around for many thousands of years, and it seems fair to assume that from the very beginning they were all aware of unseen powerful presences affecting their lives and everything around them. Every ancient religion that we know of, as well as many modern religions with hundreds of millions of followers, perceives a bewildering array of such spirits: gods, demigods, angels, devils, demons, sprites, imps, goblins, ghosts, fairies, fauns, nymphs, jinns, poltergeists. Some of them are benevolent, some are malignant, though most of them alternate between the two extremes. The gods of ancient Greece are typical: Zeus was a wise ruler up on Mount Olympus, but he became a serial rapist when he came down to the lowlands; Persephone was goddess of life in spring and goddess of death in autumn. None of these ancient religions ever developed a single Devil concentrating all the essence of evil, any more than they ever concentrated the essence of good in a single God.

The Old Testament, which was composed between the tenth and third centuries B.C., has little trace of the Devil with a capital *D*, and in its earlier books, none at all. God, speaking through the mouth of the prophet Isaiah, says, "I form the light and create darkness, I make peace and create evil, I the LORD do all these things." The serpent who tempted Adam and Eve in the Garden of Eden was later identified by Jewish rabbis and Christian church fathers with the Devil, the principle of Evil; but in the third chapter of Genesis as written, he is only a snake. It took another few hundred years before both snake and Devil were identified with Lucifer ("light-bearer," the Latin translation of the Hebrew and Greek words for the morning star, the planet Venus) who in Isaiah is thrown down from Heaven for having presumed to set his throne high above the stars of God.

Ancient Hebrew had a noun, *satan*, meaning "obstructor" or "accuser," and several satans appear in the Old Testament being sent by God on different errands, such as blocking the path of Balaam's ass or giving King Saul a fit of depression. When the Old Testament was translated into Greek beginning in the third century B.C., *satan* was rendered *diabolos*, "adversary," from which

come the Latin *diabolus*, French *diable*, German *Teufel*, English "devil." The first time the word appears with a capital *S*, defining a particular person, is in the Book of Job, where Satan is a sort of celestial J. Edgar Hoover, sent by the Lord to check up on the loyalty of the folks down on earth.

The first Devil, the first concentration of all evil in a single personal form, appears in history some time before the sixth century B.C., in Persia. His name is Ahriman, described by the prophet Zoroaster (Zarathustra) as the Principle of Darkness (evil) engaged in ceaseless conflict for control of the world with Ormazd or Mazda, the Principle of Light (good).

Satan was once an angel who had led a rebellion in Heaven.

The Jews were under Persian domination for almost two centuries, and it is likely that Ahriman had some influence on the formation of the figure of their Satan. He appears for the first time acting independently in the third-century Book of Chronicles, where the text of the much older Book of Samuel is changed from "The LORD incited David," to read "Satan incited David." In the next few centuries of the so-called Intertestamentary Period between the compilation of the Old and New Testaments, when a major subject of theological speculation and literature was the apocalypse—the final struggle between good and evil at the imminent end of the world—this Satan grew in stature as the leader and embodiment of the forces of evil. The Jewish rabbis soon lost interest in him, and though he runs wild through folklore, he is a very minor figure in modern Judaism. He would be a major figure, however, as the Satan or Lucifer of the Christians or the Iblis or Shaytan of the Muslims. Whatever he does, and however powerful he may be at times, none of these religions have ever followed Zoroaster in allowing the Devil an independent existence apart

from God. He is always separate but far from equal, though exactly to what extent separate and unequal has been the subject of perpetual debate on the questions that the postulation of a Devil naturally calls up: Why did a good God create an evil Devil in the first place? And if he had to, why did he give him so much power and let him reign so long? Or, as Friday asked Robinson Crusoe, "If God much strong, much might as the Devil, why God no kill the devil, no make him no more do wicked?" Such questions were being debated in Latin by 12th-century scholars in Paris in almost the same terms as by 12th-century scholars in Baghdad, and they are still being debated by scholars all over the world today.

The Christian Devil, who is the one most familiar in today's literature and art, appears often, but with only sketchy details, in the New Testament. It took three or four centuries of debate and speculation for the church to settle on a unified but not quite consistent picture of his history and functions. He was once an angel—some said the firstborn and chief of all the angels—who had led a rebellion in Heaven (some said out of pride; some said out of envy either of God himself or of the man, Adam, created in God's image; some said out of sexual lust for pretty women) and had been cast down to Hell (some said on the very first day or hour of the creation of the world, others after the creation of Adam, others after the Fall of Man, others during the time of Noah), had tempted humankind into sin, which allowed him to rule the world until the coming of Christ (or until the Second Coming), and would on the Day of Judgment be condemned to perpetual torment along with all the sinners of the race of Adam.

At the beginning there was curiously little interest in the particular features of this Devil, who does not appear at all in the first six or seven centuries of Christian art. Perhaps the early Christians, members of a small persecuted sect faced with the daily possibility of meeting the representatives of the Roman state in the form of gladiators, lions and howling mobs in arenas, did not need to dream up faces for the Devil. After Christianity became the state religion of Rome in the early fourth century, the fight against the enemy changed in character. The heroes were not martyrs in an arena: they were monks who went out into the deserts to meet Satan face-to-face. Satan appeared to all of them to tempt them, and it was then that Satan first acquired a recognizable physical form, appearing variously as lion, bear, leopard, bull, serpent, hyena, scorpion and wolf.

Around the tenth century, the Devil began to assume monstrous forms.

Still, for hundreds of years no one thought of putting an image of the Devil on paper or a church wall. There is a sixth-century manuscript of the Gospels in Syriac that shows a couple of little black-winged creatures fleeing from the mouth of a man being exorcized. Not till the ninth century, in an illustrated manuscript known as the *Utrecht Psalter*, does a recognizable Devil appear, as a half-naked man holding a three-pronged pitchfork. The Devil would appear often like this in the next couple of centuries, human or at least humanoid in form, sometimes wearing the halo of his old angelic days in Heaven.

Then, some time around the pre-millennial tenth century, the Devil began, all over the Western world, to assume monstrous forms. He appeared on the illustrated pages of books now written for the first time in the vernacular languages, and on the painted walls and ceilings and the carved doors and columns and watersprouts of churches and cathedrals. Everywhere there were scenes from sacred history intended to teach the illiterate masses the way to salvation, and the Devil played a prominent, sometimes predominant, role in these scenes.

He appeared in a thousand grotesque and horrible guises. His features might be derived from those of old gods of Greece and Rome whose broken images still cluttered the soil of Europe, or the newer gods of the barbarian Germans and Scandinavians, or more ancient supernatural beings from Mesopotamia, Egypt, Persia, even China, who spread their wings on imported silks and tapestries. He borrowed horns and hairy legs with cloven hooves from the Greek god Pan, a hooked nose and grimacing lips from the Etruscan death god Charun, a pitchfork from the Roman sea god Neptune, an animal head from the Egyptian god Anubis. Sometimes he was a furry black monkey with great black bat's wings. Sometimes he was a snake, a wolf, a frog, a bear, a mouse, an owl, a raven, a tortoise, a worm. Often he appeared as a combination of human and animal forms, with a tail, spiky flamelike hair, an apish body, a goat's hairy thighs, an ass's feet, a boar's tusks, a wolfish mouth, an eagle's claws, a monkey's paws, a lizard's skin, a snake's tongue. When he led the revolt of the angels in Heaven, fighting Saint Michael, he was a scaly dragon. Enthroned in Hell, he was a potbellied imbecilic old man, with snakes growing out of his head and limbs, mindlessly chewing on the sterile souls of naked sinners as they dropped down to him on Judgment Day.

He was meant to be both frightening and disgusting, to demonstrate both the horror and the folly of sin. The fright was all the greater because the devices like bone-vices, spine-rollers and red-hot prongs being used to torture sinners down in Hell were copied from those being used to torture heretics in public up on earth.

The static visions on the church walls were regularly brought to life in plays staged in front of churches or in public squares. Surrounded by elaborate scenery and firecrackers, the Devil was always a popular performer when, clothed in snakeskin and with a woman's face, he dangled an apple before our First Parents in Eden, or with fanged mask and hairy goat's body, he grimaced and grunted and growled as he prodded wailing sinners into a Mouth of Hell that could open and shut and spit flames.

One of the most popular stories throughout the Middle Ages, retold hundreds of times in many European languages, was that of Theophilus of Cilicia, a sixth-century ecclesiastic who signed a pact with the Devil, exchanging his soul for a powerful and profitable position in the church. He was then able to lead a life of unbridled pride and corruption till one day the Devil reappeared and demanded his payment. In terror, Theophilus repented and threw himself on the mercy of the Virgin Mary, who took pity on him, descended into Hell, grabbed the pact from Satan, then interceded for the sinner at the throne of God. He was pardoned, and the Devil was cheated of his due.

This tale played a major role in establishing the cult of the Virgin in Catholic Europe. It had the subsidiary effect of familiarizing everyone with the idea of diabolical pacts. The authorities of church and state took advantage of this when sometime in the 15th century they claimed to discover a vast conspiracy by a confederation of witches dedicated to the subversion of all order. There were, of course, plenty of supposed witches around, mostly old countrywomen who knew the traditional herbs and chants and charms that would attract a handsome lover or stop an unwanted pregnancy or blast the crops in an unfriendly neighbor's field. But for the space of two or three centuries, tens of thousands of accused witches, most of them women, most of them poor illiterates, were hanged or burned after being forced to confess to taking part in secret midnight meetings at which they ate babies, copulated with the Devil and signed blood compacts with him.

Ben Jonson summed it up in one of his plays, The Devil is an Ass.

The Salem witch trials of 1692 are the most familiar to Americans, having left an indelible stain on the name of our Puritan forebears. Perhaps the most interesting thing about them is that, compared with what had been going on in Europe for the previous three centuries, they were on such a very small scale: 18 women, one man and two dogs put to death in obedience to the biblical command "Thou shalt not suffer a witch to live." And there were no more witch trials in the Colonies after Salem.

For by the year 1700 few educated people really believed in witches anymore, and increasingly they were coming not to believe in the Devil himself. The reason was that Western Europe, followed in more or less short order by the rest of the world, was entering the modern era, the world of exploration, discovery, science, technology, individualism, capitalism, rationalism, materialism, democracy, progress. In such a world the old Devil was getting to seem both embarrassing and superfluous. When he appeared on the stage with his monkey suits and his conjuring tricks, he was only an unsightly clown—Ben Jonson summed it up in the title of one of his plays, *The Devil is an Ass*. And when you got down to the business of explaining what was going on around you, the Devil only got in the way. When Shakespeare's Othello learns too late how he has been tricked into murdering his wife and losing his soul, his first, medieval instinct is to look down at Iago's feet; then he pulls himself together and says, "But that's a fable." Iago doesn't need supernatural cloven hooves; he has all the wickedness he needs stored up in his own human heart. Bit by bit, the Devil's possessions and prerogatives were stripped from him.

When Benjamin Franklin called down a great spark from Heaven with a mere key hanging on a kite, all the army of infernal spirits that had been swarming through the air vanished, and the atmosphere became nothing but a mass of nitrogen and oxygen and other atoms, whirling around according to laws that Satan had never heard of.

Where the 13th-century Cistercian abbot Richalm blamed the Devil for the "wondrous sound that would seem to proceed from some distemper" of his stomach or bowels, a modern monk sends for a gastroenterologist. Great storms are no longer conjured up by the Devil, but by El Niño currents, and no one blames the wreck of the *Titanic* on anything but errors of judgment and faults of design. People are still possessed by devils, and the Roman Catholic church among others provides means of exorcizing them. But their numbers are infinitesimal compared with the number of people who are daily put under the care of psychiatrists.

The old-fashioned horror-show Devil virtually disappeared from the fine arts with the coming of the Renaissance. In 1505 Raphael painted a traditional picture of Saint Michael beating the Devil out of Heaven; the Devil is a kind of outsize science-fiction insect with horns and wings and a madman's gasping face. Thirteen years later he did another

painting on the identical theme, but the Devil this time, though a pair of bat wings grows out of his shoulders, is otherwise wholly human, a young man writhing in the despair of defeat, a much more arresting and moving figure than the bland self-satisfied saint who is poking him with a spear.

To adjust to this modern world, the Devil has had to change his ways.

The real gravedigger of the old brutal, terrifying, physically threatening Devil was John Milton, whose *Paradise Lost* was to influence the world's conception of Satan in a way no other work of art has ever done, though not at all in the way the author intended. It was designed to be an epic poem like those of Homer or Virgil, but told to "justify God's ways to Man," and dealing with creation, sin and salvation. In outline, it is a very orthodox story of pride and sin eventually humbled and destroyed by the infinite wisdom and goodness of God. Milton's Satan follows the theologically correct process of transformation from the most radiant of angels to the loathsome crawling serpent of Book Ten. Few readers, however, get to Book Ten of *Paradise Lost*. They are more apt to let themselves be lost in fascination with the Satan of the first books, a heroic figure of the first order, young, proud, self-confident, self-reliant, inventive, ingenious, yielding to no obstacle, defiant, who will not accept defeat even if defeat is inevitable, who values his own freedom more than happiness, who would rather "reign in Hell than serve in Heaven." These might be considered features of the tireless visionary entrepreneurs from Columbus to Bill Gates whose dreams and exploits have shaped so much of modern history, and provided the heroes for so many modern movies and novels.

But to the modern Devil, even more galling than his loss of physical power, his control of earthquakes and unholy wars, must be his loss of respect. The

Prince of Darkness has become, in the view of Prof. Andrew Delbanco of Columbia University, in a book called *The Death of Satan*, a superannuated athlete who has gone on the lecture circuit.

He can always get a supporting role in a horror movie like *Rosemary's Baby* or a science-fiction thriller about a professor of comparative literature who carves up and cooks his more attractive students. But no one takes him really seriously. He is toned down, domesticated. Bowdlerized, he has become politically correct. As one of the title characters in John Updike's *Witches of Eastwick* remarks, "Evil is not a word that we like to use. We prefer to say 'unfortunate' or 'lacking' or 'misguided' or 'disadvantaged.'" Even hellfire preachers who make a speciality of describing in detail the horrors of the afterlife no longer say, as the church fathers of a more robust age used to do, that one of the joys of being in Heaven will be to watch sinners writhing in the hands of the Devil.

To adjust to this pallid modern world, the Devil has had to change his ways. Always an expert shape-changer, he now comes on most often in the form of Mephistopheles. The name was made up in a 15th-century German updating of the old Theophilus legend, which has Mephistopheles signing a pact with Dr. Johann Faustus, a professor-turned-magician who is more than willing to trade his soul for 24 years of unbounded knowledge, power and sex. Christopher Marlowe's play of *Doctor Faustus* would launch both the Faust story and the character of Mephistopheles on a fabulously successful career. He was followed two centuries later by Goethe with his epic drama *Faust*. Between them they created the modern Devil, witty, ironic, disillusioned, a much more complex and interesting character than Doctor Faustus himself. Unlike Faust, however, Mephistopheles never *does* anything; he just talks.

He talks very well, of course. He talks very wittily and convincingly in Dostoyevsky's *Brothers Karamazov* and in George Bernard Shaw's *Man and Superman*. He is funny in a sinister kind of way when in C. S. Lewis' *Screwtape Letters* he becomes a conscientious bureaucrat filling reams of paper with instructions to an Englishman on how to get on his mother's nerves. He looks very handsome and winning when he is played by Al Pacino in the movies. But out in the world of commerce, politics, wars and gross national product, he is little more than a joke.

For some observers like Professor Delbanco and Prof. Jeffrey Burton Russell, of the University of California, Santa Barbara, whose five-volume biography of the Devil is the most authoritative, this is a tragic situation; it means that America, like the modern world generally, has lost its sense of evil, and without a sense of evil a civilization must go straight to Hell.

Perhaps, however, he is not dead after all; he may only be in hiding. A 17th-century Englishman, Richard Greenham, was apparently the first to coin the phrase, later borrowed or reinvented by Baudelaire, Dostoyevsky, G. K. Chesterton and Whittaker Chambers, "it is the policy of the Devil to persuade us that there is no Devil." The Devil, after all, if he is anything, is the personification of evil, and no one can deny that there is plenty of evil around even in today's comparative peace and prosperity.

The psychiatrist Viktor Frankl was a young doctor in Vienna in 1940 when he and his wife were picked up by Nazi thugs and sent off to concentration camps. She was soon murdered, but he managed to survive through all five years of the war. One night, as he climbed up to his wooden bunk, he found the man next to him moaning and roaring and thrashing, in prey to the worst nightmare Frankl had ever seen in his years of medical practice. His every humane instinct as a doctor told him to wake the man up before he hurt himself, but as he reached out to shake him he suddenly remembered that the reality he would be waking the man up to was Auschwitz, with all its stenches and screams and heavy thudding blows, and that was a hundred times worse than anything the mere human imagination could make up in the confines of a narrow human skull. So he let the nightmare gallop on.

Common sense tells us that we will go on performing wicked deeds.

There were no devils running Auschwitz, only human beings doing an ill-paid job that they must have found unpleasant at times but which was clearly preferable to being sent to die in the hell of the Russian front. That does not mean the Devil was not there.

Most everyone these days has taken the pledge that there will be no more Auschwitzes. But such pledges have been taken before. Common sense tells us that we will go on performing wicked deeds of one sort or another till an automated virtue machine is patented or (more likely) till the end of the world.

Madame Carmelita, a psychic on the Upper East Side of Manhattan, has assured me that the world will end on or about my 100th birthday, February 18, 2018. And a science-fiction scenario might have the world (meaning human life) come to an end when a giant comet hits the earth, clearing the ground for little polyps that will evolve into creatures much nicer and more spiritual than us mere mammals. A scientist has assured me that the world (meaning life on earth) will come to an end when our sun becomes a red giant in the year 4,000,001,999. If in the meanwhile a sleek gentleman dressed as a prosperous options-and-derivatives salesman offers you fantastic odds on a bet that he will not be around right up to the last second on any or all of those occasions, and you take him up on it, you will probably be making a bad bet.

Robert Wernick reports that he has received many offers from the Devil but thus far has resisted his blandishments.

Unit 4

Key Points to Consider

❖ Why was the Eastern Roman Empire able to survive after the West had fallen?

❖ Was the Byzantine civilization merely an extension of late Roman culture, or was it a new departure?

❖ What are the basic beliefs and duties of Islam?

 **Links**

www.dushkin.com/online/

These sites are annotated on pages 4 and 5.

After the collapse of the Roman Empire, three ethnic/religious entities emerged to fill the vacuum. Germanic kingdoms arose in central and western Europe. In the Balkans and Asia Minor, the eastern remnants of Rome evolved into the Byzantine Empire. The Near East, North Africa, and much of the Iberian Peninsula fell under the control of the Arabs. Each area developed a unique civilization, based in each instance upon a distinctive form of religion—Roman Catholicism in most of Europe, Orthodox Christianity in the Byzantine sphere, and Islam in the Arab world. Each placed its unique stamp upon the classical tradition to which all three fell heir. The articles in this unit concentrate on the Byzantine and Muslim civilizations. The medieval culture of Europe is treated in the next unit.

Western perceptions of Islam and Arabic civilization have been clouded by ignorance and bias. To European observers during the medieval period, Islam seemed a misguided or heretical version of Christianity. In the wake of Arab conquests, Islam increasingly came to represent terror and devastation, a dangerous force loosed upon Christendom. Reacting out of fear and hostility, Christian authors were reluctant to acknowledge the learning and high culture of the Arabs.

Muslim commentators could be equally intolerant. Describing Europeans, one of them wrote: "They are most like beasts than like men . . . . Their temperaments are frigid, their humors raw, their bellies gross . . . they lack keenness of understanding . . . and are overcome by ignorance and apathy."

The stereotypes formed in the early encounters between Christians and Muslims survived for generations. Centuries of hostility have tended to obscure the extent of cultural exchange between the Arab world and the West. Indeed, as historian William H. McNeil has observed, "Muslims have been written out of European history."

However, the domain of Islam encroached upon Europe at too many points for the two cultures to remain mutually exclusive. In western Europe, Islam swept over Spain, crossed the Pyrenees, and penetrated France; in the central Mediterranean, it leaped from Tunis to Sicily and then into southern Italy; in eastern Europe, Islam broke into Asia Minor, the Balkans, and the Caucasus. In its expansion, early Islam was exposed to Jewish, Christian, and classical influences. History and geography determined that there would be much cross-fertilization between Islam and the West.

Yet there is no denying the originality and brilliance of Islamic civilization. There is the religion of Muhammad, unquestionably one of the world's most influential faiths. The essay "What Is Islam?" highlights essentials of that faith. Additional evidence of Arab creativity can be found in the visual arts, particularly in the design and decoration of the great mosques. The Arabs also made significant contributions in philosophy, history, geography, science, and medicine.

The medieval West borrowed extensively from the Arabs. The magnificent centers of Islamic culture—Baghdad, Cairo, Cordoba, and Damascus—outshone the cities of Christendom. The Arab administration of Andalusia was a model of successful governance. Islamic scholars surpassed their Christian counterparts in astronomy, mathematics, and medicine—perhaps because the Arab world was more familiar than medieval Europe with the achievements of classical Greece. (European scholars eventually regained access to the Greek heritage, at least partially, through translations from the Arabic!)

As for the Byzantine Empire, it was for nearly 1,000 years a Christian bulwark against Persians, Arabs, and Turks. In "The Survival of the Eastern Roman Empire," Stephen Williams and Gerard Friell describe the reasons for the East's survival while Western Europe fell into destruction. It also made important cultural contributions. The beautiful mosaics and icons of Byzantine artists set the pattern for later visualizations of Christ in the West. Byzantine missionaries and statesmen spread Orthodox Christianity, with its unique tradition of Caesaro-Papism, to Russia. Byzantine scholars and lawmakers preserved much of the classical heritage. Even hostile Islam was subject to a constant flow of ideas and traditions from the Byzantines. Alexander Kazhdan discusses the strengths and weaknesses of Byzantine civilization in "Byzantium: The Emperor's New Clothes?"

The Survival of the Eastern Roman Empire

Stephen Williams *and* **Gerard Friell** *analyse why Constantinople survived the barbarian onslaughts in the fifth century, whereas Rome fell*

THE OLD ATTITUDE still prevails in some quarters that what we know of as the Roman Empire was dismembered in the fifth century, and that what survived in the East was something different—Byzantium, Greek and Christian; fascinating, no doubt, but no longer the real Rome. This quite misleading picture is often accompanied by another: that the survival of the Eastern half in the terrible fifth century, when the West went under, was a more or less natural development—even unconsciously anticipated by Constantine's wise foundation of his new capital in the wealthier, more urbanised East.

The reality of course was very different. Despite the administrative division into East and West, which predated Constantine, the empire was everywhere seen as one and indivisible. At the beginnings of the fifth century both halves faced similar chronic problems: immature or inept emperors, rebellious armies, external barbarian invaders and the large and dangerous settlements of barbarian 'allies' within imperial territories. By difficult expedients and innovations the East was eventually able to overcome these problems, while the West was not. After several attempts, Constantinople accepted that it had not the strength to save the West, but it still treated it as a group of temporarily lost provinces to be recovered when the situation permitted—a view that the emperor Justinian in the sixth century took entirely literally.

After the disastrous defeat by the immigrant Visigoths at Adrianople (Edirne) in 378, the new Eastern emperor, Theodosius, was eventually able to fight and manoeuvre them into signing a treaty in 382, settling them in the Balkans as 'allies' (*foederati*), since they could not possibly be expelled. They were obliged to support the emperor, militarily, on request, but this was nonetheless a radically new departure in foreign policy, the result of Roman weakness. Instead of mere farmer-settlers under Roman administration, this was an entire armed Germanic nation established deep within Roman territory under its own tribal leaders. It could not help but be a precedent for other land-hungry barbarians. Theodosius, however, had no option but to hope that in time the Goths could be assimilated as others had been.

After Theodosius's death in 395, his two young sons, Arcadius (377–408) and Honorius (384–423), inherited the thrones of East and West respectively. Both boy-emperors were immature and incapable (Honorius was practically retarded), and although strong loyalty to the dynasty kept them on their thrones, they were entirely managed by individuals or factions within the two courts. Instead of the cooperation that was badly needed, the two governments of East and West intrigued and manoeuvred against each other like hostile states for over ten years, with damaging consequences.

On Theodosius's death the Visigoths immediately broke out of their assigned territories and ravaged the Eastern provinces, under their leader Alaric, who now declared himself king. Temporarily without their main army, the Eastern government, dominated by the eunuch chamberlain Eutropius, was able to deflect Alaric westwards by granting him a top military command in Illyricum (Yugoslavia). The combined status of Roman general and tribal warlord created yet another dangerous precedent. Alaric was able to exploit the deep hostility between the two governments, becoming a destabilising force over the next fifteen years.

In the West, real power was legitimately in the hands of the commander-in-chief Stilicho, of Vandal origin, who had been appointed guardian of the boy-emperor Honorius. He was resented and feared by the ruling circles at Constantinople, who had him declared a public enemy. Stilicho, hoping in vain to force Alaric back into his former alliance, was able to defeat him several times but not destroy him. He had to crush a revolt in Africa (encouraged by Constantinople) and then defeat an Ostrogothic invasion of Italy itself. He was by now forced to buy barbarian fighting men from any source and on any terms, often with personal promises, and even grants of land.

To defend Italy, Stilicho had to strip Britain and the Rhine frontier of troops, and at New Year 407 multiple barbarian invaders crossed the frozen Rhine into Gaul virtually unopposed, never to be expelled again. For this, Stilicho's political enemies in the Senate contrived to have him condemned and executed on the weak emperor's orders, whereupon thousands of his loyal barbarian troops, fearing for themselves and their families, fled over to join Alaric. With Stilicho removed, nothing could prevent Alaric from besieging and finally sacking Rome in 410.

The East had rid itself of the menace of Alaric by propelling him westwards, but this did not free it from other barbarian dangers. What Alaric's Visigoths could do, others could imitate. A new revolt broke out in 399 among the recently-settled Ostrogothic federates. Gainas, the general sent to suppress it, mistrusted the government and was himself of Gothic origin and the commander of other Gothic federate troops. The two Gothic groups joined forces, marched on Constantinople and occupied it, with Gainas dictating his terms to the emperor. However, he was met by a violent anti-Gothic, popular backlash and total hostility from the civil government. Having achieved nothing, he attempted a clumsy withdrawal from the capital in which many Goths and their families were massacred by the mob. Those that escaped were later defeated by loyal units (also commanded by a Goth).

These events had a profound effect on the civilian ruling circles in Constantinople. Henceforth they were determined to keep a firm grip on imperial power and curb ambitious generals, especially those of Gothic origin, even though many were entirely loyal. For several years Goths were excluded from top commands, armies were thinned in numbers, and care was taken to avoid any new settlements of barbarian federates. The Praetorian Prefect, Anthemius, the acknowledged leader of the state, invested instead in strengthening the defences on the Danube frontier, building a new and massive belt of land walls to protect Constantinople, its emperor and government, from both barbarian invasions and its own potentially dangerous armies.

The exclusion of Gothic generals did not last long. With the federate crises past, and a growing external threat from the Huns, able professional commanders such as Plinta, Aspar and Areobindus once again rose to the top *Magister* posts. The fact that they were divorced from any federate or tribal power base (unlike Alaric and Gainas) made them acceptable. They remained what they had been in the previous century—loyal members of the Roman ruling class.

The really farsighted achievement of the Eastern empire during this period was not so much the weakening of the power of the army, as the institutionalising of it within a central ruling establishment at Constantinople, which included the palace and civil bureaucracy. The Eastern field army, about 100,000 strong, was already divided into five regional mobile groups, and the commands carefully balanced between men of Gothic and Roman origin. Two

of these groups—the Praesental armies—were stationed in the vicinity of Constantinople and their commanders, of whatever background, were senior members of the senate and members of the emperor's inner council of state, the Consistory.

Any successful, ambitious general was faced with a choice and a temptation. He could use external military violence to try to dominate the emperor at Constantinople, perhaps even making himself emperor, or at least military dictator. Or he could use the army's indispensability and natural leverage within the legitimate, established power structure where there was a place for him at the top table.

Gainas had attempted the first option and had been ruined. Other military leaders overwhelmingly chose the second. Though politically powerful, the army was only one of several competing, but also interlocking, forces around the throne. To break out of this careful web of power risked losing everything. Certainly, there were bitter conflicts within the Constantinople establishment. For many years the deficiencies of the pious and bookish emperor Theodosius II (408–450) were heavily compensated by his dominating sister Pulcheria, who did everything possible to keep power within the palace and the imperial family rather than the civil ministers and generals. But even she had to negotiate with these other power centres.

The solidarity of the inner establishment was strikingly demonstrated when confronted by the end of an imperial dynasty, when all the old threats of factional coup, military violence and even civil war reared their heads in the struggle to place a new emperor on the throne. Aware of what each stood to lose, palace, bureaucracy, army and, later, church found ways to fight their conflicts behind closed doors and then present an agreed imperial choice to be acclaimed by the senate, the troops, the people and the wider world.

This orderly transmission of imperial power was achieved in the elevation of Marcian in 450, Leo in 457 and Anastasius in 491, all of them dynastic breaks. Through these precedents, buttressed by an increasingly elaborate ceremony of emperor-making, violent coups and civil wars became the exception. Even if a declared rebel succeeded in gaining wide support outside, he still had to cash in his imperial claims in the

capital itself, in the face of the central establishment and the city's virtually impregnable defences: if he did not already enjoy powerful allies within the city this was a daunting task.

Thus, an important factor in the durability of the establishment was simply the acknowledged geographical concentration of power and authority in a single capital, Constantinople, which was in every sense what Rome had once been. The emergence of a viable, rival power base was made very difficult, and this, as much as the city's strategic position and fortifications, contributed heavily to the stability and survival of the Eastern state.

Of all the elements in the establishment, stability was most steadfastly provided by the civil bureaucracy, which provided experience, statecraft and continuity. They kept the impersonal, administrative machine functioning even during violent conflicts within the palace, or purges of this or that faction. These senatorial mandarins, in fact, represented a new service aristocracy created by Constantine. Frequently of modest origins, they owed their power and status not to birth or landed wealth, but entirely to government service. Consequently, regardless of whether a particular emperor was strong or weak, they took great care to uphold and strengthen the imperial authority itself, since their careers, and hence their prosperity, completely depended on it.

In contrast, the great Western senatorial clans such as the Anicii and Scipiones were only concerned to husband their already huge accumulated family wealth, and treated high state positions as no more than honorific perquisites. Part of the East's undoubtedly greater financial muscle, therefore, was due not just to its inherently greater wealth but also to these mandarins' more honest management of the tax machine, even when it bore on their own aspiring social order.

In the West, the response to the problem of a weak unmilitary emperor was quite different. Real power was concentrated in a military strongman such as Stilicho who ruled on his behalf and enjoyed extraordinary authority, making appointments and issuing laws in the emperor's name. The long reign of the feeble Honorius, the multiple military emergencies and the need to raise and move armies rapidly made this new ruling figure indispensable. After a few

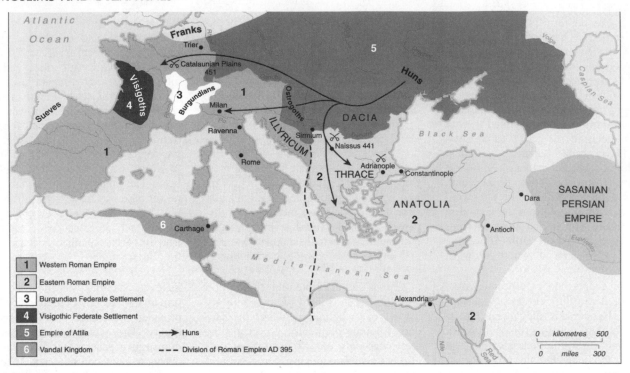

By 450, the Western empire was already a patchwork of barbarian settlements whereas the East retained its integrity.

years of turmoil the general Constantius stepped into this new position, now vaguely designated 'Patrician' and perhaps better described as military dictator or *generalissimo*. After him came Aetius. Both were patriotic and energetic rulers but had no legally acknowledged position beyond their monopoly of military force, and no regular way of transferring their power to a successor. Each had to intrigue or fight his way to dominant power, which was destructive and destabilising.

Inevitably they came to depend more on their personal popularity and prestige among the troops, whom they recruited and paid. A gulf steadily grew up between the real power of the warlord with his army, and the symbolic, legal authority with the emperor in his palace. During the invasion of Italy, Stilicho had persuaded Honorius to shift the imperial capital from Milan to the safe refuge of Ravenna, creating a geographical split in addition to the political one.

Constantius achieved a degree of stability in the West, but at enormous cost. Visigoths, Burgundians, Franks, Suevi and Vandals were all settled as federates on large tracts of Gaul and Spain, and were evolving into Germanic kingdoms under only the most nominal Roman overlordship. Constantius and Aetius

skillfully exploited their rivalries to maintain some ascendancy. But having relinquished control of so much taxable land and its populations, the regular Roman armies were only one force among many, and no responsible leader could do more than hold the balance, and avoid risking this force if possible.

The Hun menace took on an entirely new dimension with Attila, who had unified them under a single king and subjected all the remaining tribes to Hun rule. His object was not land to settle, but plunder, tribute and glory, and once again the blow fell initially on the East. His hordes ravaged the Balkans three times in the 440s, sacking and ruining many major cities and enslaving their populations. The Roman armies that met him in the field were repeatedly beaten by his cavalry, but he was always deterred by Constantinople whose defences he could not storm. After each invasion he had to be bought off by an increasingly ignominious 'treaty' and larger annual payments, involving heavier taxation of the senatorial classes. In all, the East paid him about nine tons of gold, until the new emperor Marcian finally tore up the treaties and defied him.

Yet here, the two great resources of the East came to the rescue: the impassable fortifications of Constantinople and

the enormous taxable wealth of the Asiatic provinces—Anatolia, Syria, Palestine, Egypt. So long as this great land gate was kept shut and so long as these provinces remained secure—meaning peaceful relations with Persia—Attila could always be bought off and much of the Balkan territories temporarily lost without mortal damage to the empire.

Relations with Persia were always a crucial consideration if the empire was to avoid the perils of fighting on two frontiers simultaneously. Unlike other potential enemies, Persia was a centralised, sophisticated state, and both empires were continually involved in a chess game of military and diplomatic manoeuvres which at intervals broke down into open war. In set battle the Romans could usually win, but at quite huge logistical costs. The 1,400-mile frontier zone along the Euphrates was already the most expensive in terms of providing troops and resources. The danger was not so much that Persia would conquer the Roman provinces, as that they would disrupt the whole delicate defensive system of Arab alliances and force the empire to a great commitment of forces, imperilling other frontiers.

But, although Persia tried to take advantage of the empire's difficulties elsewhere, its war aims were limited and it was usually amenable to negotiation. After nearly twenty years of peace, a brief Persian attack in 441 was halted and led to a new treaty involving Roman payments. At the same time, Persia's ambitions were severely checked by pressure from their own northern enemies, the Ephthalite horse peoples, akin to the Huns, who were tacitly encouraged by Constantinople. Whatever martial propaganda they still broadcast to their peoples, the two empires gradually came to accept the advantages of avoiding costly and unrewarding wars, and sought if possible to resolve conflicts by other means. As a result, a mature and structured diplomacy became as important as the military strategy.

Finally, after suffering heavier casualties in battle for diminishing returns of plunder, Attila decided to cut his losses and invade westward. Here Aetius, with all his carefully cultivated barbarian friendships, performed a diplomatic miracle in uniting and commanding the mutually hostile Germanic kingdoms in a great coalition to stop Attila in 451. After a huge and bloody battle on the Catalaunian plains of northern Gaul, Attila was forced for the first time to retreat. The next year he mounted an abortive invasion of Italy. Soon afterwards, he died suddenly in a drunken stupor. Within a short time his always personal and charismatic 'empire' collapsed.

In the West, Aetius was immediately concerned to disperse the more numerous and powerful Germanic armies as quickly as possible. But now that the main barbarian threat seemed removed, he was treacherously murdered by the emperor Valentinian III (425–455) who had long hated him. In revenge, Aetius's partisans assassinated Valentinian shortly afterwards, ending the Theodosian dynasty.

The next *generalissimo* figure, Ricimer, was himself a barbarian and naturally well-qualified to deal with the overwhelmingly barbarian army and allies. He was related both to the Visigoth and Sueve royal houses, and very willing to allow more federate settlements. Ricimer was a leader spanning two worlds. He saw the Roman empire more as a prestigious, unifying symbol than a political reality, and he set up and deposed puppet emperors at will. In the end it was only logical that a barbarian king should step into the ruling role of patrician and *generalissimo*. When that

happened there was no need to retain even a figurehead emperor in the West. In 476 the barbarian king Odovacer forced the emperor Romulus Augustulus to abdicate, and sent an embassy to Constantinople declaring that he would henceforth rule as the viceroy of the Eastern emperor. The fiction of a single united Roman empire was still retained.

The East had tried, and partially succeeded, in arranging the fragments of Attila's old empire to its advantage, but it had been forced to accept two large blocs of Ostrogoths, formerly subjects of Attila, as federates in Illyricum (Yugoslavia) and Thrace (Bulgaria-Romania). These were a destabilising element, each too strong to be defeated by a single Roman field army. In the confused reign of Zeno (474–491) all the dangerous elements erupted again: open conflict in the imperial family, civil wars for the throne, rebellion by the Gothic federates. At one point there was fighting within the capital itself. There seemed a real danger that the Ostrogoths would carve out permanent kingdoms for themselves in the way this had happened in the West.

For a time, the central establishment lost control, but they had several strong advantages. There was always a strong core of regular Roman troops to balance the federates, and they continued to be steadily recruited. All the soldiers, Roman or federate, could only be paid from the central treasuries, which were a potent lever in negotiations, as were timely bribes of gold. The Goths also suffered periodic food shortages which the imperial government, with its network of cities and supply depots, naturally exploited. The two Gothic blocs were often in competition and could easily be played off against each other. Their aims were opportunistic and their long-term goals uncertain. One king, Theoderic (471–526), wanted larger, more secure territories for his people, while the other, Strabo, aimed at a top Roman command and a seat at the centre of government.

By the time Zeno had managed to crush or conciliate his other domestic enemies, by adroit and unscrupulous manoeuvring, Strabo was dead and all the Goths followed Theoderic. In 488, with only one king to deal with, Zeno played the masterstroke. Instead of poor and precarious lands in the Balkans, he invited Theoderic to take Italy from

Odovacer. Theoderic did so, finally freeing the East of the federate problem.

It was left to the next emperor Anastasius (491–518) to consolidate these gains. Himself a civil bureaucrat who knew the government machinery intimately, he overhauled and improved the entire fiscal system to produce considerably greater sums for the treasury without injuring the mass of taxpayers. With these funds he expanded the armies by raising pay, built new defences, revived and re-populated much of the Balkans, and fought a successful war against Persia, still leaving a healthy surplus. It was with these great resources that Justinian was soon to embark on his ambitious schemes of reconquest.

The East had certain long-term advantages: a strategically placed capital, shorter vulnerable frontiers, a wealthier agricultural base. But it demanded a high order of statecraft to overcome all the external and internal threats of the fifth century. Individually, its leaders were no more skilful than their Western counterparts, but they managed to evolve institutions and practices which applied these skills and perpetuated them. The Constantinople establishment; the constitutional rituals of imperial succession; the integration of the top army commands; the opposition to federate settlements; the centralised pool of administrative, fiscal and diplomatic experience—all these enabled the East to avoid the unravelling process of diminishing control which occurred in the West.

FOR FURTHER READING

A.H.M. Jones, *The Later Roman Empire* (2 vols, Oxford University Press, 1990); J.B. Bury, *History of The Later Roman Empire,* (Dover paperbacks, 1958); R.C. Blockley, *East Roman Foreign Policy* (ARCA, 1992); J.H.W.G. Liebeschuetz, *From Diocletian to the Arab Conquest,* (Oxford University Press, 1990); J.H. W.G. Liebeschuetz, *Barbarians and Bishops: Army, Church and State in the Age of Arcadius and Chrysostom* (Oxford University Press, 1991); C. Mango, *Byzantium. The Empire of New Rome* (London, 1980).

Stephen Williams and Gerard Friell are also the authors of Theodosius: the Empire at Bay *(Batsford, 1994).*

Byzantium: The Emperor's New Clothes?

Eastern Europe and Russian are the subject of intense scrutiny at present as questions of power, identity, and political structures are pursued at breath-taking speed. 'History Today' contributes a commentary on these events. . . . Alexander Kazhdan, senior research associate at Dumbarton Oaks, Washington, D.C., considers the influence of totalitarianism and meritocracy in the Byzantine empire—and its relationship to the growth of the Russian and other successor states in the East.

The state of Byzantium, the so-called Byzantine empire, has never existed; the term was invented in the sixteenth century to designate the empire the capital of which was Constantinople, the city on the Bosphorus, which was supposedly founded in 330 and destroyed by the Ottoman Turks in 1453. Byzantion (in the Latinised form Byzantium) was the name it held before being renamed by and in honour of the Emperor Constantine the Great (324–37), and throughout the Middle Ages the Byzantines were the citizens of Constantinople only, not the subjects of the emperor who reigned in Constantinople. These subjects did not even notice that they stopped being Romans and began being Byzantines—they continued to consider themselves Romans until they woke up under the rule of the sultans.

Thus the nomenclature itself is confused, and some purist scholars prefer to call the population of the Constantinopolitan empire Romans or Greeks, and terms such as 'the Eastern Roman empire' or 'Greco-Roman law' are still in use. But this is only the beginning of the problem, and we are in trouble when trying to define the date of birth of Byzantium. Was it 330, when Constantine celebrated the inauguration of his new residence on the Bosphorus? Was it 395, when the Emperor Theodosius I died and bequeathed the empire to two different rulers, his sons Arkadios in Constantinople (395–408) and Honorius (395–423) in Milan and later Ravenna? Was it in 476, when the Herulian (or Hun) Odoacer deposed the last western emperor, Romulus Augustulus, and sent his regalia to Constantinople. Or was it in 554, when Justinian I (527–65), after having reconquered Italy, issued the Pragmatic Sanction and determined the status of this old-new province? None of these events had a lasting effect on the empire. All we can say is that Byzantium was not born in a day, and the changes were various and gradual.

The idea that radical ethnic changes gave birth to Byzantium was popular in the nineteenth century and still remains popular among some East European scholars; the Slavs are said to have invaded the Roman empire, settled in Greece and Asia Minor, rejuvenated the decrepit empire, become the backbone of the new victorious army and, even more, that of the Orthodox monarchy. Unquestionably, the Slavs invaded the Balkans in the first half of the seventh century. They left behind some traces in Balkan place-names. The Slavic influence on the administration, legal and fiscal systems, and military organisation is another matter—there is no data for such an assertion.

Territorial changes are more evident. In rough outline they coincided with the Slavic invasion, and took place during the seventh century. The Mediterranean Roman empire disappeared, and was replaced by a new formation, concentrated around Greece and Asia Minor, the areas dominated by the Greek language and culture. But could not the empire retain its old character within a more restricted framework?

Religious changes seem to be attached to the activity of a single man, the Emperor Constantine. Tradition has it that he saw a vision of the cross and promulgated the Milan edict liberating the Christian church from discrimination. For medieval chroniclers this was a radical turning point, the creation of the Christian empire. We know now that the edict of tolerance was issued before Constantine, in 311, by the Emperor Galerius, whom Constantine's staunch flatterers depicted as a scoundrel. We also know that Constantine did not com-

 This article first appeared in *History Today*, September 1989, pp. 26–34. © 1989 by History Today, Ltd. Reprinted by permission.

Power over God and Man; the Empress Irene, 752–803, whose achievements during a tumultuous career included the re-establishment of icon worship and the deposition of her own son Constantine as emperor in her bid for sole imperial power.

pletely abandon pagan cults, particularly the worship of the solar deity (or deities), and that when Constantine, on his deathbed, formally accepted Christianity, he accepted the new religion in its heretical denomination, Arianism. Moreover, paganism regained momentum soon after Constantine, during the reign of Julian the Apostate (361–63). At the court of the Very Christian Emperor, Theodosius I, pagan politicians were influential, and the fifth century saw a revival of pagan culture represented by such men as the philosopher Proklos and the historian Zosimos. Even in the sixth century, paganism was alive in the countryside, and the aristocratic intelligentsia, while paying lipservice to the official creed, stuck to the ancient philosophical and cultural traditions. Thus, the question arises: which phenomenon is more momentous: Constantine's cautious baptism or the seventh-century triumph of Christianity that had behind it the gigantic work of the church fathers who had elaborated the system of the new belief? The Trinitarian and Christological disputes, out of which this system emerged, came to halt only in the middle of the seventh century.

The changes in the administrative system are the most evasive, and some scholars place the roots of these changes in the reign of Justinian I, or even earlier. The search for these roots is a futile one—any important phenomenon has its roots in the past. What matters is not embryonic development but the critical mass. It is, however, very difficult to measure the critical masses of historical process, especially for the seventh century, notorious for its scarcity of available sources. Of course, Byzantium remained a monarchy in and after the seventh century, and was, at least in theory, administered from Constantinople, but it now seems sure that the new administrative system of districts, the so-called 'themes', appeared in the seventh century. The exarchates of Ravenna and of Carthage, organised by the end of the sixth century, were the direct predecessors of the themes; the themes were powerful organisations until the mid-ninth century and decided the destiny of the throne of Constantinople. Indeed, all major uprisings until the ninth century were based on themes.

In central government during the same seventh century, late Roman departments were replaced by new offices. The main functionaries such as praetorian prefect and *magister officiorum* disappeared, and the central bureaux worked under the supervision of the so-called *logothetai*. Some late Roman designations survived, although often in a changed sense. For example, the Byzantine hypatos-consul was worlds away from the magnificent consuls of the sixth century, and the Byzantine *magistros* was a title, rather than an office, like the late Roman *magister*. Some change of function must have occurred beneath the veneer of this terminological stability.

And did society remain late Roman? We can divide the question into two sections: the urban and the rural. It seems that in the seventh century the Roman provincial city was in decline and that when it reappeared by around the tenth century, it had a new, medieval, character. Archaeological excavations are usually witness to the decline of cities, and the findings of coins from the second half of the seventh century become rare. In addition the setting of hagiographical literature shifts from the provincial city to either the capital or the countryside. The available data about the countryside between the seventh and late ninth centuries are scanty, and we are forced to build our conclusions more on the silence of our sources than on direct evidence. Silence, however, is fairly evocative. We hear little about large estates, slaves and *coloni* of this period; the most discussed case is that of St Philaretos who is said in his *Vita* to have possessed approximately fifty allotments (*proasteia*). Such figures are usually exaggerated, and we cannot take them for granted, the more so since Philaretos was the son of a peasant and could perfectly well manage his team of ploughing oxen. On the other hand, the so-called Farmers' Law, the Byzantine counterpart of the western *leges*, deals with free peasants. Certainly, the text is enigmatic, imprecisely dated and probably reflects some local conditions, but this is what we have—direct evidence about the free peasantry and very questionable data concerning large estates.

If we assume that the leading class of the ancient *polis*, the urban landowners, disappeared, or at least lost its former significance, a strange phenomenon coinciding with those changes becomes clearer: the disappearance of family names. Rare after the fourth century but still known in the sixth century, they are practically unknown between the seventh century and the end of the

ninth century. Does this mean that the aristocracy or at least the concept of aristocracy ceased to exist? Certainly, we do not know of any powerful family from this period, and at the end of the tenth century Basil II (976–1025) wrote with astonishment and indignation about those families which had been pre-eminent for some seventy to one hundred years; so the phenomenon must have been a new one in his reign.

Thus all information converges on the seventh century; and although it is far from extensive or dependable, it allows us to hypothesise that in the seventh century some slow changes occurred and that establishing the seventh century as a watershed at least does not conflict with the available evidence.

But why should we bother our heads about Byzantium? Today we take for granted the impact of ancient cultural traditions—they are considered to be the foundation of western civilisation. In our perception of the past, Byzantium plays the role of a stepdaughter, a Cinderella; we allow it to store and transmit the *oeuvre* of great Greek minds. Byzantine culture is seen not as an achievement in its own right, but as an imitation and copy of the great classical paragon. The art has been looked at and the literature has been read with this presupposition in mind; as non-creative, repetitive, slavishly following ancient originals, disconnected from contemporary problems, concentrating on ridiculous theological niceties, and so forth. And since the purpose of their art, literature, philosophy, law and science was to imitate the great predecessors, Byzantine culture allegedly knew no development.

But was this really true? Bearing in mind the social and political changes of the seventh century already alluded to, can we see a cultural transformation taking place at the same time? Certainly building activity almost stopped, literary work contracted and even the most medieval genre, hagiography, was almost nonexistent in the eighth century. Manuscripts copied at that time are extremely few, and philosophical thought came to a halt. Thus, as in the West, the Byzantine Middle Ages began with a cultural gap that was followed by a revival around 800.

What is interesting in this revival is its social background: the vast majority of the known authors of this time belonged to the monastic world. But from the mid-ninth century onwards a different type of *literatus* came to the fore—

the imperial or ecclesiastical functionary. In the twelfth century, again, a new type of writer emerges: the professional author, frequently called the 'beggar poet' since his existence depended upon the gifts and stipends from the emperor and others, and soliciting these gifts occupied a substantial part of his concerns and of his poetry.

The genres of literature were also in flux; in the twelfth century the saintly biography went through a crisis, very few contemporary biographies were produced, the writers preferring to revise old hagiographical texts, and Eustathios of Thessalonike, a rhetorician and commentator on Homer, issued a *vita* that was, in its core, a denial of traditional hagiographical virtues. This *vita* of a (fake?) saint, Philotheos of Opsikion, was a eulogy to a rich married man living in the world. However, while hagiography was fading a new genre appeared, or rather was revived, after a long absence: the romance. Poetic and prose panegyrics of secular leaders were of no significance before the eleventh century; the ethical ideal had remained either monastic or imperial. And the memoir did not come into being before Michael Psellos in the eleventh century.

The well-entrenched concept of Byzantine cultural uniformity does not stand up to examination, not only because Byzantium's cultural development was in a state of flux. A distinction can be drawn not only between difference generations but also between members of the same generation of different class and with different taste.

A classic example of such a distinction is a group of addresses to the emperor Alexios III Angelos (1195–1203) celebrating his victory over rebellious John Komnenos the Fat. Four orations survive; three of them are traditional, that is lacking in concrete detail, symbolic and full of propaganda. The fourth, by Nicholas Mesarites, is rich in details, dynamic and ironic. Mesarites does not strive to exclude reality in the interests of a higher moral truth; his aim is to make actual events vivid.

But if Byzantine culture was not a plain imitation of antiquity, then what was the difference between the two, and what was the former's contribution? Antiquity is a broad notion whatever characterisation we formulate, and what we now accept as essential may be perceived by other scholars in other times as incidental. There was clearly a considerable transitional period between the Roman and the Byzantine worlds. On the other hand, Byzantium is not 'linear', one-dimensional and simplistic; moreover, it was consciously orientated toward ancient culture. The Byzantines called themselves Romans, believed in this definition, and did not see a demarcation line between themselves and antiquity. Homer was their poet. Aristotle their philosopher, and Augustus their emperor. In their writings they followed ancient Greek (although they spoke vernacular), and they filled their works with ancient quotations, proverbs and dead words. The cultural line between Rome and Constantinople is as indistinct as the chronological line between them.

There are, however, some points of difference which seem obvious. Byzantium was Christian, antiquity pagan; Byzantium was uniform, antiquity variegated; Byzantium was autocratic, antiquity republican. Unfortunately none of these statements is completely correct: Christianity was born in antiquity and inherited many ancient ideas; Byzantium's uniformity was relative; and both Hellenistic and Roman monarchies existed within the framework of ancient civilisation. But relative as they are, these oppositions reflect partial truth and highlight the direction of search.

Another set of obvious or half-obvious dichotomies refers to a different aspect of reality. Marxist theoreticians contrast ancient slave ownership with Byzantine feudalism. The word 'feudalism' is too questionable to be a useful tool of analysis, but it is plausible that the forms of exploitation differed between antiquity and Byzantium, even though slaves (and not only the household slaves but slaves in the fields, at the herds and in the workshops) were numerous in Byzantium. We can also say that the urban life so typical of antiquity lost its role in Byzantium and that the family not the *municipum* formed the main social unit and determined the structure of many other units.

Before we take the final step and attempt to define along very rough lines, the 'Byzantine particularity', let us shift from chronological to territorial distinctions, let us juxtapose not Byzantium and antiquity but Byzantium and the western medieval world. Of course, the western medieval world was diverse, nevertheless, some feeling of unity prevailed: the Byzantines, at least from the eleventh century onward, spoke of the

'Latins' as a specific group, differing from the Byzantines insofar as their beliefs, costumes and habits were concerned. For the westerners as well, the 'schismatic Greeks' formed a separate set of people; one could marry a Greek woman, trade in Greek ports, serve at the court of Constantinople, but the gap remained and even widened as time went on.

From the viewpoint of the westerners the Byzantines entertained a wrong theology, believing that the Holy Spirit proceeded from God the Father only; they were too bookish and bad soldiers; they adorned their churches with icons and not the sculptured crucifix, and their priests were married. But there was one point that usually dominated in the mutual contrasting of two societies.

In 1147 crusading armies arrived in Constantinople. The Greek historian, John Kinnamos, who was almost contemporaneous with the event, described them in great detail. Among other things, he noticed with a subdued surprise that:

> Their offices (or dignities) are peculiar and resemble distinctions descending from the height of the empire, since it is something most noble and surpasses all others. A duke outranks a count; a king a duke; and the emperor, a king. The inferior naturally yields to the superior, supports him in war, and obeys in such matters.

What struck Kinnamos was the hierarchical structure of western aristocracy, the system of vertical links.

In 1189 Isaac II (1185–95) sent an embassy to Frederick Barbarossa. The Byzantine historian, Niketas Choniates, relates that Frederick ordered the Greek ambassadors to be seated in his presence and had chairs placed in the hall even for their servants. By so doing, comments Choniates, the German ruler made fun of the Byzantines, who failed to take into consideration the virtue of nobility of different members of society and who appraised the whole population by the same measure, like a herdsman who drove all the hogs into the same pigsty.

Western society was perceived by both the Greeks and the Latins as one organised on the aristocratic and hierarchical foundation, Byzantine society as 'democratic', although in Byzantium the word '*demokratia*' had a pejorative tinge and was usually applied to the domination of the *demoi*, the unbridled mobs.

To sum up, Byzantium was an atomistic society with the family as its cornerstone. The man was primarily the member of the family and not of the *municipium* (as he was in Greco-Roman antiquity) or community or guild (as he was to be in the medieval West). Formal wedding ceremonies, prohibition of divorce, abolition of concubinage; all these contrasted with the 'free' late Roman family. Lineage played an insignificant role, and vertical (hierarchical) links remained practically unknown. Small family-like monasteries were common, and family-orientated terminology permeated both political and ecclesiastical relations.

The aristocratic principle was underdeveloped. This does not mean that all the emperor's subjects were equal in rights and wealth, even though western observers kept repeating disparagingly that they were; in the tenth century, for instance, the German ambassador Liutprand asserted that all the participants in the imperial procession in Constantinople wore shabby and frayed costumes. The principle of inequality in Byzantium differed from that of the West; the Byzantines created a meritocracy based not on individual's 'blood' or origin but on his place in the bureaucratic machine. A system which, while less stable than nobility in the West, enabled more vertical mobility. This does not mean that they were less arrogant, but it does mean that, while less restricted by tradition, they were less defiant of the emperor's omnipotence.

The imperial power was both feeble and strong. It was strong since the emperor, in theory, was not restricted by law; he was the law itself. He combined in his hands legislative, administrative and judicial power, was the supreme army commander and claimed control of ideology. But he was poorly protected against schemes and plots, and half of all the Byzantine emperors ended their rule as victims of violence. Feeble as individuals (certainly some emperors had a strong personality) they were omnipotent as symbols of government; the emperors themselves might be criticised, but the principle of unlimited monarchical power was never questioned.

In practice, of course, everything was more complex, and many an emperor met social and religious resistance, even blunt bureaucratic intransigence. However, we can call the Byzantine empire a totalitarian state. And it was the only totalitarian state of the European Middle Ages. As such, Byzantium gives us material to observe a totalitarian state over a long period and to analyse its liabilities and assets, its roots and mechanism.

Several points are of importance. Was the totalitarian organisation of power interconnected with the atomistic structure of society? It seems quite plausible that western system of vertical and horizontal bonds created a better protection for the man, certainly for a nobleman, against the supreme power that condescended to respect the noble as the king's peer. I do not think that the western *villanus* was better protected than Byzantine *paroikos*, but probably western guilds gave more protection to their members than did Byzantine *somateia*, their counterpart. At any rate, atomistic feelings and fears, rejection of friendship and emphasis on individual way of salvation (rather than the role of sacraments) could contribute to the concept of the lonely man, a helpless slave in front of the powerful emperor, a toy of relentless doom. The political misfortunes of ever-shrinking Byzantium reinforced this concept; late Byzantine philosophers were unable to grasp why the most Christian, the 'chosen people' should be exposed to the crashing attacks of the Ottoman Turks.

How did the totalitarian state function? So much ink has been spilled to describe the unwieldy and rotten Byzantine governmental mechanism, and undoubtedly there is much truth in these two adjectives—based on the bitter words of contemporary critics. But there are some stubborn facts that cry out for explanation. How could the Eastern Roman empire, where centralised authority was more strongly developed than in the West, repel the same barbarian attacks that subdued Italy and Gaul? Why was it that, until the twelfth century, totalitarian Byzantium was economically and culturally ahead of the West? A century ago Russian Byzantinists developed a theory according to which the Byzantine emperors, especially in the tenth century, protected the peasantry and the village community against the so-called *dynatoi* ('powerful', i.e. the wealthy and influential members of the ruling class) and thus secured the existence of a strong army and of plentiful taxes. When, in the eleventh century, the emperors yielded to western feudalism, abandoned 'the minor brethren', and turned away from the principles of the Orthodox (and Slavic) monarchy, the decline of Byzantium began. This theory is political more than scholarly. The

tenth-century state did not protect the peasantry either (it protected state taxes that were burdensome enough and the centralised power over the countryside), nor was the period of the eleventh and twelfth centuries that of decline. On the contrary, it was a period of economic growth and cultural upsurge. But in spite of all its weakness, totalitarian Byzantium managed to flourish during several centuries while the split-up ('federal') West suffered from shortages of food, dress and housing.

The problem is intensified by Byzantine ideological duplicity. A striking example is the fate of Roman law in Byzantium, the Roman law summarised and codified by Justinian I during the last stage of the late Roman empire. It was never abolished, although some attempts to make it simpler were made. Byzantine legal text-books adhered to Roman law, repeating, time and again, formulations that were in disaccord with reality. For instance, the official law-book of the ninth century, the *Basilika*, described administrative institutions that existed during the sixth century and had ceased to exist by the ninth. Furthermore, the agrarian terminology of the *Basilika*, translated from Latin into Greek, applied to no Byzantine reality, and often made no sense whatever. Whereas Roman law reflected the principles of the legal state, protecting individual rights and private ownership, the Byzantine empire did not give any legal protection to its subjects. Emperors could execute any citizen without trial and could confiscate any land without argument. Texts of the tenth century state that any land on which the emperor had put his foot could be taken from its owner. As more private documents have been published in recent decades, we can see more clearly that the Byzantine law of things and law of obligations deviated from Roman norms and that Byzantine tribunals acted on principles distinct from the Roman; but the words often remained the same, and private ownership of land was repeatedly affirmed in legal text-books.

This contrast between theory and practice had a strong impact on Byzantine mentality. I am not referring to the notorious Byzantine diplomacy or the lack of fealty, of which the Latin neighbours accused them; indeed I doubt that such accusations could be taken at face value. In fact they can be applied equally to many medieval leaders. Much

more substantial was the Byzantine skill of allusion. Of course, their literature is in no way short of direct and open invectives against political and ideological enemies, but they loved, and knew how to say without saying, to evoke by an apparently occasional hint a broad gamut of emotions. They were much more attentive towards those details and nuances which usually escape modern understanding. One of the most drastic examples is the Byzantine insistence on the resemblance of their icons to sitter or subject, whereas modern art historians are unable to perceive individual elements in Byzantine icons and are inclined to deny such resemblance. Equally, we are unable to catch allusions, political and personal, in their writings, particularly in their favourite game, the use of ancient and Biblical imagery.

Two conclusions can be drawn from this observation. In the first place, the Byzantines frequently cared more about nuances than general statements. Any totalitarian or uniform ideology possesses an established set of concepts which are above discussion; Byzantine ideology was no exception, with a set of political or religious formulae, perceived by everyone as final truth and rarely, if ever, discussed. But they certainly had discussions, and very vehement ones. These usually began over slight terminological differences, and it gradually becomes clear that behind such niceties loomed crucial dissentions. We are facing a paradox: an allegedly uniform ideology did not prevent the Byzantines from bitter disputes, only these disputes seemed to be limited to innocuous and insignificant problems: should the churches be adorned with images? Was the Holy Spirit proceeding from God the Father only or from the Son as well? How could Christ be at the same time the sacrifice offered to God, the priest offering the sacrifice, and God receiving it? Can one see the divine light, the divine energy with sensual eyes? And so on.

In the second place, we must reconsider the role of Byzantine intellectuals. Their indiscriminate eulogies addressed to those in power sound abominably grovelling to our ears. But as soon as we become acquainted with the nuances and methods of the rhetoric it is possible to strip them of the shroud of uniformity and flattery and understand the profound content concealed beneath the surface. Of course, most of their allusions have been lost in the passage of time and still remain incomprehensible to the modern reader, but even that little part of them that can be deciphered compels us to discard the traditional image of literary barrenness.

The Byzantine world was totalitarian; many will agree with such a statement. But it is hard to accept this heritage; we are more willing to reject it, to restrict the survival of the Byzantine 'axe and icon' to Eastern Europe, Slavic and/or Communist countries. The recent celebration of the millenium of the Russian Church sharpened this point yet more. Totalitarian Russia seems to be as natural a successor of totalitarian Byzantium as the Russian icon is the heir of Byzantine images or Russian obscuring eloquence is the heir of Byzantine rhetorics.

The problem is once again, however, not that simple. Kievan Rus certainly had contacts with Byzantium. But did it experience Byzantium's direct impact beyond the ecclesiastical sphere? In fact Kievan temporal society absorbed very little of Byzantium: their weaponry came from the West, their glass producers followed western, not Byzantine recipes, their political structure was as distanced from the Byzantine one as possible. Political marriages of high rank between the two countries were almost unknown. Kievan Rus as a state did not travel the path the Byzantines had worn.

Only in the fifteenth century when Russian grand princes began to build up their centralised monarchy did they discover their Byzantine ancestry; Russia did not inherit Byzantine totalitarianism but used the model for their political ends. The process was not genetic or automatic—it was a part of the ideological programme, whether consciously or unconsciously applied.

It would be very tempting to assume that only those countries (Bulgaria, Serbia, Rumania, Russia) that were in direct contact with Byzantium developed a tendency to totalitarianism—but I am afraid that this is not true. Not only did Russia become totalitarian only after it had severed direct relations with Byzantium, (when it was separated from Byzantium by Mongolian seminomads and Italian trade republics which dominated the Black Sea coast), but there were also countries that for centuries had such contact and did not become totalitarian: Armenia, Georgia, Hungary, Italy. On the other hand, totalitarian governments could be traced in various European countries whose contacts with Byzantium were very slight, such as Spain and France, from the fifteenth century onwards. The French model of the Sun King followed the Byzantine paragon, and it is not sheer chance that sixteenth-century France contributed so much to the development of Byzantine studies.

Byzantium was an interesting historical experiment. It teaches us how totalitarian systems work, what a meritocracy (*'nomenklatura'*) is, what the place of intellectuals in a totalitarian state is, and who owns the land and the means of production. It shows the advantages and disadvantages of the totalitarian system, and reveals under the surface of stagnation the suppressed class of political and ideological contrasts.

FOR FURTHER READING:

Romilly Jenkins, *Byzantium: the Imperial Centuries*. A.D. 610–1071 (Weidenfeld & Nicolson, 1966); Cyril Mango, *Byzantium. The Empire of New Rome* (Weidenfeld & Nicolson, 1980); Arnold Toynbee, *Constantine Porphyrogenitus and his World* (Oxford University Press, 1973); Alexander Kazhdan and Ann Wharton Epstein, *Change in Byzantine Culture in the Eleventh and Twelfth Centuries* (University of Berkeley Press, Los Angeles, 1985); R. Browning, *The Byzantine Empire* (Charles Scribner's Sons, New York, 1980); N. G. Wilson, *Scholars of Byzantium* (The Johns Hopkins University Press, Baltimore, 1983).

TAKING THE MYSTERY OUT OF ISLAM

WHAT IS ISLAM?

*Islam, a great monotheistic religion, provides spiritual and moral life,
and cultural and sometimes national identity, to more than a billion people.*

ABDULAZIZ SACHEDINA

In the mass media, Islam and Muslims are frequently depicted as the "other" in global politics and cultural warfare. The Iranian revolution under Ayatollah Khomeini in 1978–79, the tragic death of 241 marines near Beirut airport in 1983, and the bombing of the World Trade Center in New York in 1993 are among the violent images associated with Muslims. But those images resonate poorly with the majority of Muslims. Most Muslims, like other human beings, are engaged in their day-

to-day life in this world, struggling to provide for their usually large extended families, working for peaceful resolution to the conflicts that face them, and committed to honor universal human values of freedom and peace with justice.

Muslims in general take their religion seriously. For many it is the central focus of their spiritual and moral life. For others, less religiously inclined, it remains a source of their cultural and sometimes national identity. So the word *Islam* carries broader ramifications than is usually recognized in the media. As the name of the religion, *Islam* means "submission to God's will." It is also applied to cultures and civilizations that developed under its religious impulse.

Historically as well as psychologically, Islam shares the monotheistic religious genome with Judaism and Christianity. Islamic civilization has acted as the repository of the Hebrew, Persian, Indian, and Hellenistic intellectual traditions and cultures.

HISTORICAL DEVELOPMENT

Islam was proclaimed by Muhammad (570–632), the Prophet of Islam and the founder of Islamic polity, in Arabia. Seventh-century Arabia was socially and politically ripe for the emergence of new leadership. When Muhammad was growing up in Mecca, by then an important center of flourishing trade between Byzantium and the Indian Ocean, he was aware of the social inequities and injustices that existed in the tribal society dominated by a political oligarchy.

Before Islam, religious practices and attitudes were determined by the tribal

aristocracy, who also upheld tribal values—bravery in battle, patience in misfortune, persistence in revenge, protection of the weak, defiance of the strong, generosity, and hospitality—as part of their moral code. The growth of Mecca as a commercial center had weakened this tribal moral code and concern for the less fortunate in society, leaving them without any security. It

Islam: One of the World's Great Religions

Islam was proclaimed by Muhammad (570–632), the Prophet of Islam and the founder of Islamic polity.

After Muhammad's death, the Islamic community divided into the Sunni ("people of tradition") and the Shiites ("partisans").

The Sunni have mostly a quietist and authoritarian stance, while the Shiites tend to be more activist and radical.

The Muslim faith is built on Five Pillars.

Islam today continues to inspire more than a billion people to go beyond a self-centered existence to establish a just society.

was in the midst of a serious socioeconomic imbalance between the rich and the poor, between extreme forms of individualism and tyrannical tribal solidarity, that Islam came to proclaim an ethical order based on interpersonal justice.

THE FOUNDER AND HIS COMMUNITY

Muhammad's father died before he was born, and his mother died when he was only six years old. In accordance with Arab tribal norms, he was brought up first by his grandfather and then, following his grandfather's death, by his uncle. As a young man he was employed by a wealthy Meccan woman, Khadija, as her trade agent. He was twenty-five when he accepted a marriage offer from Khadija, who was fifteen years his senior. When Muhammad received his prophetic call at the age of forty, Khadija was the first person to become "Muslim" ("believer in Islam").

Meccan leadership resisted Muhammad and persecuted him and his followers, who were drawn mainly from among the poor and disenfranchised. Muhammad decided to emigrate to Medina, an oasis town in the north. This emigration in 622 marks the beginning of the Muslim calendar, as well as the genesis of the first Islamic polity. (Muslims marked their new year, 1418, on May 8, 1997.)

Muhammad as a statesman instituted a series of reforms to create his community, the Umma, on the basis of religious affiliation. This also established a distinctive feature of Islamic faith, which does not admit any separation between the religious and temporal spheres of human activity and has insisted on the ideal unity of civil and moral authority under the divinely ordained legal system, the Shari'ah.

At Muhammad's death, he had brought the whole of Arabia under the Medina government, but he apparently left no explicit instruction regarding succession to his religious-political authority. The early Muslim leaders who succeeded him as caliph (meaning political and spiritual "successor") exercised Muhammad's political authority, making political and military decisions that led to the expansion of their domain beyond Arabia. Within a century Muslim armies had conquered the region

from the Nile in North Africa to the Amu Darya in Central Asia east to India.

This phenomenal growth into a vast empire required an Islamic legal system for the administration of the highly developed political systems of the conquered Persian and Byzantine regions. Muslim jurists therefore formulated a comprehensive legal code, using the ethical and legal principles set forth in the Qur'an.

Differences of opinion on certain critical issues emerged as soon as Muhammad died. The question of succession was one of the major issues that divided the community into the Sunni and the Shiites. Those supporting the candidacy of Abu Bakr (ca. 573–634), an elderly associate of the Prophet, as caliph formed the majority of the community and gradually came to be known as the Sunni ("people of tradition"); those who acclaimed 'Ali (ca. 600–661), Muhammad's cousin and son-in-law, as the "imam" (religious and political leader) designated by the Prophet formed the minority group, known as the Shiites ("partisans").

The civil strife in Muslim polity gave rise to two distinct, and in some ways contradictory, attitudes among Muslims that can be observed even today: quietist and activist. Those upholding a quietist posture supported an authoritarian stance, to the point of feigning unquestioning and immediate obedience to almost any nominally Muslim political authority. Exponents of an activist posture supported radical politics and taught that under certain circumstances people had the right to revolt against evil Muslim rulers.

Gradually the quietist and authoritarian stance became associated with the majority Sunni Muslims, although every now and then they had their share of radicalism, as seen in the assassination of Egyptian President Anwar Sadat in 1981. The activist-radical stance came to be associated with Shiite Islam, represented by Iran today.

The Muslim community has continued to live in the shadow of the idealized history of early Islam, when religious and secular authority was united under pious caliphs. Efforts to actualize this ideal today give rise to radical politics among a number of religious-minded Muslim groups, usually designated pejoratively as "fundamentalists," who regard jihad (war)

against their corrupt rulers as a legitimate tool for change.

WHAT DO MUSLIMS BELIEVE?

Muslims derive their religious beliefs and practices from two sources: the Qur'an, which they regard as the "Book of God," and the Sunna, or the exemplary conduct of the Prophet. The Qur'an consists of the revelations Muhammad received intermittently over the twenty-two years from the time of his calling in 610 until his death. Muslims believe that the Qur'an was directly communicated by God through the archangel Gabriel, and accordingly, it is regarded as inerrant and immutably preserved. It has served as the normative source for deriving principal theological, ethical, and legal doctrines. The Sunna (meaning "trodden path") has functioned as the elaboration of the Qur'anic revelation. It provides details about each and every precept and deed attributed to Muhammad. The narratives that carried such information are known as *hadith*. In the ninth century, Muslim scholars developed an elaborate system for the theological and legal classification of these hadith to derive certain beliefs and practices.

In this connection it is relevant to remember the Rushdie affair of the 1980s. Salman Rushdie's novel *The Satanic Verses* was directed toward discrediting both the Qur'an and the Prophet as the normative sources for Muslim religiosity, which, understandably, enraged more than a billion Muslims around the world. And while many Muslims may not have endorsed the death sentence passed on Rushdie by the Ayatollah Khomeini, they unanimously condemned the novel for its profanity in connection with the founder of Islam and Muslim scriptures.

THE FIVE PILLARS OF ISLAM

The Muslim faith is built upon Five Pillars, as follow:

The First Pillar is the *shahada*, the profession of faith: "There is no deity but God, and Muhammad is the messenger of God." This is the formula through which a person converts to Islam. Belief in God constitutes the integrity of human existence, individually and as a member of society. The Qur'an speaks about God as the being whose presence is felt in everything that exists; everything that happens is an indicator of the divine. God is the "knower of the Unseen and the Visible; . . . the All-merciful, the All-compassionate, . . . the Sovereign Lord, the All-holy, the Giver of peace, the Keeper of faith, the All-preserver, the All-mighty, the All-powerful, the Most High" (Qur'an, 59:23). Faith in God results in being safe, well integrated, sound, and at peace.

Human beings are not born in sin, but they are forgetful. To help them realize their potential God sends prophets to "remind" humanity of their covenant with God (7:172). Noah, Abraham, Moses, Jesus, and Muhammad are regarded as "messengers" sent to organize their people on the basis of the guidance revealed by God.

The Second Pillar is daily worship (*salat*), required five times a day: at dawn, midday, afternoon, evening, and night. These prayers are short and require bowing and prostrations. Muslims may worship anywhere, preferably in congregation, facing Mecca. They are required to worship as a community on Fridays at midday and on two major religious holidays.

The Third Pillar is the mandatory "alms-levy" (*zakat*). The obligation to share what one possesses with those less fortunate is stressed throughout the Qur'an. The Muslim definition of the virtuous life includes charitable support of widows, wayfarers, orphans, and the needy. Although zakat has for the most part been left to the conscience of Muslims, the obligation to be charitable and contribute to the general welfare of the community continues to be emphasized. In a number of poor Muslim countries this benevolence provided by wealthy individuals has underwritten badly needed social services for those who cannot afford them.

The Fourth Pillar is the fast during the month of Ramadan, observed according to the Muslim lunar calendar, which has been in use since the seventh century. Since the lunar year is some ten days shorter than the solar year, the fasting and all Muslim festivals occur in different seasons. During the fast, which lasts from dawn to dusk, Muslims are required not only to refrain from eating, smoking, and drinking; they are also to refrain from sexual intercourse and acts leading to sensual behavior. The end of the month is marked by a festival, Eid al-Fitr, after which life returns to normal.

The Fifth Pillar is the *hajj*, or pilgrimage to Mecca, which all Muslims are required to undertake once in their lives, provided they have the financial means. The pilgrimage brings together Muslims of diverse cultures and nationalities to achieve a purity of existence and a communion with God that will exalt the pilgrims for the rest of their lives.

The Islamic ethical-legal system, known as the Shari'ah, was developed to determine normative Islamic conduct.

MUSLIM MORAL AND LEGAL GUIDANCE

The Islamic ethical-legal system, known as the Shari'ah, was developed to determine normative Islamic conduct. The Shari'ah is the divinely ordained blueprint for human conduct, which is inherently and essentially religious. The juridical inquiry in discovering the Shari'ah code was comprehensive because it necessarily dealt with every case of conscience covering God-human relations, as well as the ethical content of interpersonal relations in every possible sphere of human activity. Most of the legal activity, however, went into settling more formal interpersonal activities that affected the morals of the community. These activities dealt with the obligation to do good to Muslims and guard the interests of the community.

Islamic legal theory recognized four sources on the basis of which judicial decisions could be deduced: the Qur'an, the Sunna, consensus of the early community of Muslims, and analogical reasoning, which attempts to discover the unknown from the known precedent. Ash-Shafi'i (767–820), a rigorous legal thinker, systematically and comprehensively linked the four sources to derive the entire legal system covering all possible contingencies. The legal precedents and principles provided by the Qur'an and Sunna were used to develop an elaborate system of rules of jurisprudence. Human conduct was to be determined in terms of how much legal weight was borne by a particular rule that ren-

dered a given practice obligatory or merely recommended.

As Islamic law became a highly technical process, disputes about method and judicial opinions crystallized into legal schools designated by the names of prominent jurists. The legal school that followed the Iraqi tradition was called "Hanafi," after Abu Hanafi (669–767), the great imam in Iraq. Those who adhered to the rulings of Malik ibn Anas (ca. 715–795), in Arabia and elsewhere, were known as "Malikis." Ash-Shafi'i founded a legal school in Egypt whose influence spread widely to other regions of the Muslim world. His followers were known as Shafi'is. Another school was associated with Ahmad ibn Hanbal (780–855), who compiled a work on traditions that became the source for juridical decisions for Hanbalis.

The Shiites developed their own legal school, whose leading authority was Imam Ja'far ibn Muhammad (ca. 702–765). Normally, Muslims accept one of the legal schools prevalent in their region. Most of the Sunni follow Hanifah or Shafi'i, whereas the Shiites follow the Ja'fari school. In the absence of an organized "church" and ordained "clergy" in Islam, determination of valid religious practice is left to the qualified scholar of religious law known as a *mufti* (the one who issues a *fatwa,* or decree).

MUSLIM FAMILY LAW

In Islamic family law, the rights of women, children, and other dependents are protected against the male head of the family, who, on the average, is stronger than a woman and more independent, since he is free of pregnancy and immediate care of children. Islamic marital rules encourage individual responsibility by strengthening the nuclear family. The Shari'ah protects male prerogative as the one who is required to support the household, whereas a woman is protected primarily by her family. All schools give a husband one-sided divorce privileges, because for a woman to divorce a man would mean to unsettle her husband's economic investment. Under these rules a husband could divorce a wife almost at will, but a wife who wished to leave her husband had to show good reason. The main legal check upon the man in divorce is essentially financial and a matter of contract between equal parties that includes

Islam and the Arabic Language

By Tamara Sonn

Those are the verses of the glorious book. We have revealed it as an Arabic recitation, so that you will understand. (Qur'an, 12:2)

These words from Islamic scripture, and others like them, reveal the integral relationship between the Arabic language and Islam. Muslims believe that all revelation comes from the same divine source, so there is no need to be concerned that the Jews have their Torah and the Christians have their Gospels, for example. The Qur'an is simply divine revelation sent to speakers of Arabic, according to this sacred book. "Yet before it was the Book of Moses for a model and a mercy; and this is a book confirming in Arabic, to warn the evil-doers and bring good tidings to the good-doers" (46:11–12). The Qur'an, therefore, is essentially Arabic. But that does not mean Islam is only for Arabs.

According to the Qur'an, no one can be forced to convert. "In matters of religion there is no compulsion" (2:256). But those who choose to become Muslim must pray five times a day, reciting from the Qur'an in Arabic. The role of the Arabic language in Islam, therefore, remains central, despite the fact that the vast majority of Muslims are neither Arab nor Arabic speaking.

The majority of Muslims worldwide today "read" Arabic for prayer the way Roman Catholics used to "read" Latin at mass. They can make out the words but know the general ideas represented primarily through vernacular interpretations. Yet there is no movement to substitute the vernacular for the original language, as there was in Catholicism before the Second Vatican Council. On the contrary, emphasis on the importance of studying Arabic is increasing.

Only one country has ever authorized a translation of the Qur'an. Turkey, created after the breakup of the Ottoman Empire in World War I, stressed the Turkish language in an effort to distinguish itself from the rest of the Muslim world. Even in Turkey, however, prayer continued to be in Arabic, and today there is a strong movement to return to Arabic as the universal language of Islam.

Part of the contemporary stress on Arabic results from the worldwide movement of rebirth (*al-nahda*) in Islam. After centuries of eclipse and Euro-Christian domination, the Muslim world entered the twentieth century with a renewed commitment to its roots as a means of reviving both cultural strength and political independence. Formal independence from colonial control, however, left most of the Muslim world afflicted with severe economic and political underdevelopment. Experiments with European-style social and political models have been judged failures, benefiting only a few. The result has been a populist call for "the Islamic solution," religiously based cultural and political identity. Renewed emphasis on the Qur'an—and with it, Arabic—is an integral part of this "Islamist" movement. As a result, the Arabic language is being studied more widely than ever.

The Islamist stress on Islamic and therefore Arabic studies, however, should not be confused with another modern movement known as Arabism (*'urubah*). Arabism stresses not only the centrality of the Arabic language to Islamic identity but the dominance of Arab culture. Early proponents described Islam as "the highest moment of consciousness" of Arab culture. Therefore, as people become Muslim, they actually become Arab as well, at least to a certain degree. Some see Arabism as simply a religiously oriented version of the Arab nationalist movement.

A controversial movement from the outset, Arabism has declined in popularity with the rise of Islamism, although its echoes can still be heard. In a recent speech, Sadek Jawad Sulaiman, former ambassador of Oman to the United States, stressed the centrality of Arabism to Islam: "Outside its repository of Arabic culture, Islam is left with little form or substance."

The majority of those who stress the importance of Arabic believe they are simply following the Qur'an's own teaching. The Qur'an repeatedly refers to the power and beauty of its language. It tells of Prophet Muhammad being an illiterate (or unlettered) orphan and yet producing a work of such splendor that it challenges his detractors to match it (10:38–9, 11:13–16, 28:49). Even today, non-Muslim Arabic speakers are awed by its beauty. Undoubtedly, the book's inherent beauty and power would suffer in translation. Beyond aesthetic concerns, however, is recognition of the insidious effect of translation on understanding.

Even so, Muslims agree that fluency in Arabic is no guarantee that one will be moved by the Qur'an or be a good Muslim. As the Qur'an teaches, "God summons to the abode of peace and guides whomsoever he will to a straight path" (3:27). Islam enters "through the heart," according to Qur'anic metaphor. It is primarily a turning of the will toward God, an inner transformation. This transformation may or may not be prompted by the power of the Qur'an. The Qur'an counts among the believers anyone—including Jews and Christians—who believes in God and does good deeds. For at its core, Islam is a matter of behavior rather than words: "Woe betide those who pray, yet are neglectful of their prayers—those who pray for show and yet refuse charity" (107:1–7).

Tamara Sonn is a professor in the Department of Religious Studies at the University of South Florida, Tampa.

---

a provision about the bridal gift. The man pays part of the gift, which might be substantial, at the time of marriage; if he divorces her without special reason, he has to pay her the rest.

The Muslim woman can own property, and it cannot be touched by any male relative, including her husband, who is required to support her from his own funds. Moreover, she has a personal status that might allow her to go into business on her own. However, this potential feminine independence was curbed primarily by cultural means, keeping marriages within the extended family, so that family property would not leave the family through women marrying out.

All schools of Islam, although tending to give men an extensive prerogative, presupposed a considerable social role for women. The Qur'anic injunction to propriety was stretched by means of the Sunna to impose seclusion. The veil for women was presented simply in terms of personal modesty, the female apartments in terms of family privacy.

In the patriarchal family structures, and not necessarily in the Shari'ah, women were assigned a subordinate role in the household and community. Here, the term *Islam* is being used in the sense of culture or local tradition. And it is precisely in the confusion between normative Islam and cultural practices that we find tension in ethical and legal formulations among Muslims.

In some parts of the Muslim world women are victims of traditional practices that are often harmful to them and to their children's well-being. One controversial and persistent practice is female circumcision (*khafd or khifad*), without which it is believed that girls could not attain the status of womanhood. Islamic views of female circumcision are ambiguous. The operation was performed long before the rise of Islam, and it is not a practice in many Muslim countries, including Saudi Arabia, Tunisia, Iran, and Turkey. There is

nothing in the Qur'an that sanctions female circumcision, especially its most severe form, infibulation. The Prophet opposed the custom, found among pre-Islamic Arabs, since he considered it harmful to women's sexual well-being. Yet the official position adopted by a majority of Sunni jurists is that female circumcision is sanctioned by the tradition. They concede, however, that the Shari'ah does not regard it as an obligatory requirement.

ARE HUMANS FREE AGENTS OF GOD?

Muslims, like Christians, have raised critical questions about human responsibility in view of God's overpowering will. In the first half of the eighth century, the rudiments of the earliest systematic theology were developed by a group called the Mu'tazilites. Before them, some Muslim thinkers had developed theological arguments, including a doctrine of God and human responsibility. The Mu'tazilites undertook to show that there was nothing repugnant to reason in the Islamic revelation. Their theological system was worked out under

five headings: (1) belief in God's unity, which rejected anything that smacked of anthropomorphism; (2) the justice of God, which denied any ascriptions of injustice to God's judgment of human beings, with the consequence that humans alone were responsible for all their acts and thus punishable for evil actions; (3) the impending judgment, which underscored the importance of daily righteousness and rejected laxity in matters of faith; (4) the middle position of the Muslim sinner, who, because of disobeying God's commandments was neither condemned to hell nor rewarded with paradise; and (5) the duty to command the good and forbid evil to ensure an ethical social order.

The traditionalist Ash'arites, reacting to Mu'tazilite rationalism, limited speculative theology to a defense of the doctrines given in the hadith, which were regarded as more reliable than abstract reason in deriving individual doctrines. The Ash'arites emphasized the absolute will and power of God and denied nature and humankind any decisive role. In their effort to maintain the effectiveness of a God who could and did intervene in human affairs, they maintained that good and evil are what God decrees them to be. Accordingly, good and evil cannot be known from nature but must be discovered in the Qur'an and the tradition. Ash'arite theological views have remained dominant throughout Islamic history, well into modern times, and had a profound effect upon scientific theory and practice among the Sunni.

The attitude of resignation, a by-product of belief in predestination, is summed up in the Sunni creedal confession: "What reaches you could not possibly have missed you; and what misses you could not possibly have reached you" (*Fiqh akbar,* Article 3).

The Shiite Muslims, on the other hand, have developed a rational theology and ethical doctrines resembling those of the Mu'tazilites. Hence, they believe that humans are free agents of God who are responsible for their own actions. Moreover, the justice of God requires that God provide a constant source of guidance through reason and exemplary leaders, known as imams, for human advancement toward perfection. This belief is the source of the emergence of Khomeini-like leadership in Shitte Iran today.

MYSTICAL DIMENSION OF ISLAM

From the early days of the Islamic empire (eighth century) the ascetic reaction to growing worldliness in the Muslim community took the form of mysticism of personality in Islam, whose goal was spiritual and moral perfection of an individual. Sufism, as Islamic mysticism came to be known, aimed to internalize the ritual acts by emphasizing rigorous self-assessment and self-discipline. In its early form Sufism was mainly a form of ascetic piety that involved ridding oneself of any dependence on satisfying one's desire, in order to devote oneself entirely to God. Mystical practices developed by the Sufi masters comprised a moral process to gain the relative personal clarity that comes at moments of retreat and reflection.

From daily moments of reflection the mystic experienced more intense levels of awareness, which could take ecstatic forms, including ecstatic love of God. This aspect of Sufism brought the mystics into direct conflict with the traditionalist Muslims, who emphasized active obedience to God as the highest goal of religious meaning and purpose.

By the eleventh century, the Sufi masters had developed a new form of religious orientation that brought about the acceptance of Sufism by the ordinary people in many places. Near the end of the twelfth century, the Sufi organized several formal brotherhoods or orders (*tariqa*) in which women also participated. Each order taught a pattern of invocation and meditation that used devotional practices to organize a group of novices under a master. Through special control of breath and bodily posture accompanied by invocative words or syllables, they developed more intense concentration.

These brotherhoods, however, degenerated into antisocial groups that caused much damage to the teachings of Islam about societal and familial obligations. Moreover, because of their unquestioning devotion to the Sufi masters, both living and dead, a shrine culture leading to almost saint worship took deep roots among ordinary peoples attracted to this folk Islam. This condition elicited a strong reaction against Sufism in the Muslim world in modern times. Both the traditionalist reformers, like the Wahhabis of Saudi Arabia, and the champions of secularist modernism, like the founder of modern Turkey, Kemal Atatürk (1881–1938), disbanded Sufism as being totally un-Islamic.

Nevertheless, the formal approval of Sufism as a genuine form of Islamic piety by the great scholar Abu Hamid al-Ghazal (1058–1111), who taught Islamic law and theology in Baghdad, has been revived in many countries. There sufism continues to thrive as a bastion of religious tolerance and free-spirited religiosity.

ISLAM TODAY

Islam as a religion, culture, and civilization continues to inspire a billion people worldwide to take up the challenge to go beyond one's self-centered existence to establish a just society that will

Although its interaction with history is not free of tension, and even contradictions, on the whole Islam has developed an enviable system of coexistence among religious communities.

reflect "submission to God's will." As an Abrahamic faith, Islam has accepted the pluralism of human responses to spiritual guidance as a divine mystery. And although its interaction with history is not free of tension, and even contradictions, on the whole Islam has developed an enviable system of coexistence among religious communities. Its vision of a global community working toward the common good of humanity has been overshadowed by political upheavals in the postcolonial Muslim world. Unless the violated justice of the ordinary people is restored, like its other Abrahamic forebears Islam will continue to inspire activist response to social and political injustices in the Muslim world.

Abdulaziz Sachedina is professor of religious studies at the University of Virginia.

Unit 5

Key Points to Consider

❖ How did Spain achieve such brilliance under the Arabs?

❖ How is our view of the Vikings changing according to recent investigations? How did Britain change as a result of the Norman Conquest?

❖ What was life like for women during medieval times? What special problems do we face in trying to learn about medieval women?

❖ Why did the medieval Italian cities institute intramural games?

❖ What were the effects on medieval civilization as a result of the "Black Death"?

❖ Were the Knights Templar seen as "saints" or "sinners" in medieval Europe?

 **Links** **www.dushkin.com/online/**

These sites are annotated on pages 4 and 5.

In the aftermath of barbarian invasions, Western civilization faced several important challenges: to assimilate Roman and Germanic people and cultures, to reconcile Christian and pagan views, and to create new social, political, and economic institutions to fill the vacuum left by the disintegration of the Roman order—in sum, to shape a new unity out of the chaos and diversity of the post-Roman world. The next millennium (c. 500–c. 1500) saw the rise and demise of a distinctive phase of Western experience—medieval civilization.

Medieval culture expressed a uniquely coherent view of life and the world, summarized here by literary scholar C. S. Lewis:

> Characteristically, medieval man was not a dreamer, nor a spiritual adventurer; he was an organizer, a codifier, a man of system.... Three things are typical of him. First, that small minority of his cathedrals in which the design of the architect was actually achieved (usually, of course, it was overtaken in the next wave of architectural fashion long before it was finished).... Secondly, the *Summa* of Thomas Aquinas. And thirdly, the *Divine Comedy* of Dante. In all these alike we see the tranquil, indefatigable, exultant energy of the mass of heterogeneous details into unity. They desire unity and proportion, all the classical virtues, just as keenly as the Greeks did. But they have a more varied collection of things to fit in. And they delight to do it. (*Studies in Medieval and Renaissance Literature,* Cambridge University Press, 1966)

This outlook also expressed itself in a distinctly medieval social ideal. In theory, medieval society provided a well-ordered and satisfying life. The Church looked after people's souls, the nobility maintained civil order, and a devoted peasantry performed the work of the world. Ideally, as historian Crane Brinton explains, "a beautifully ordered nexus of rights and duties bound each man to each, from swineherd to emperor and pope."

Of course, medieval society, like our own, fell short of its ideal. Feudal barons warred among themselves. Often the clergy was ignorant and corrupt. Peasants were not always content and passive. And medieval civilization had other shortcomings. During much of the Middle Ages there was little interest in nature and how it worked. While experimentation and observation were not unknown, science (or "natural philosophy") was subordinate to theology, which generally attracted the best minds of the day. An economy based on agriculture and a society based on inherited status had little use for innovation. Aspects of medieval society are treated in the articles "Scissors or Sword: The Symbolism of a Medieval Haircut," "Women Pilgrims of the Middle Ages," "Britain

1100," and "Girls Growing Up in Later Medieval England." The article on the Knights Templar, "Saints or Sinners? The Knights Templar in Medieval Europe," explores facts of medieval warfare.

All this is not to suggest that the medieval period was static and sterile. Crusaders, pilgrims, and merchants enlarged Europe's view of the world. And there were noteworthy mechanical innovations: the horse collar, which enabled beasts of burden to pull heavier loads; the stirrup, which altered mounted combat; mechanical clocks, which made possible more exact measurement of time; the compass, which brought the age of exploration closer; and the papermaking process, which made feasible the print revolution as Jay Tolson's article, "The Paris Bibles and the Making of a Medieval Information Revolution," describes it. All played key roles in the Reformation and the scientific revolution. "The Amazing Vikings" demonstrates that during the Dark Ages there existed possibilities for enterprise and progress. "The Golden Age of Andalusia under the Muslim Sultans," by Stanley Meisler, recounts the brilliant mulitcultural accomplishments made possible by Muslim rule in medieval Spain, while the article by Malcolm Barber, "How the West Saw Medieval Islam," shows how the Crusades intensified hostilities and misperceptions between Christians and Muslims. In "Monsters and Christian Enemies," Debra Higgs Strickland contends that medieval artists and writers depicted these foreigners as monsters since they had failed to embrace Christianity. Still the military encounter between the two faiths produced cross-cultural influences that contributed to fundamental economic, military, and political changes in the West.

The medieval order broke down in the fourteenth and fifteenth centuries. Plague, wars, and famines produced a demographic catastrophe that severely strained the economic and political systems. Charles Mee's article, "How a Mysterious Disease Laid Low Europe's Masses," explains how the Black Death affected many aspects of medieval life. During this period, social discontent took the form of peasant uprisings and urban revolts. Dynastic and fiscal problems destablized England and France. The Great Schism and the new heresies divided the Church. Emerging capitalism gradually undermined an economy based on landed property. Yet these crises generated the creative forces that would give birth to the Renaissance and the modern era. The nation-state, the urban way of life, the class structure, and other aspects of modern life existed in embryonic form in the Middle Ages. These aspects are treated in "War-Games of Central Italy" by Raymond Role who recounts Italian urban life. And, as historian William McNeill has written, it was in medieval Europe that the West prepared itself for its modern role as "chief disturber and principal upsetter of other people's ways."

The Medieval Period

Scissors or Sword? The Symbolism of a Medieval Haircut

Simon Coates explores the symbolic meanings attached to hair in the early medieval West, and how it served to denote differences in age, sex, ethnicity and status.

WHILST RESIDING in Paris in the sixth century, Queen Clotild (d. 554), the widow of the Merovingian ruler Clovis, became the unwilling subject of the inveterate plotting of her sons, Lothar and Childebert, who were jealous of her guardianship of her grandsons, the children of their brother, Chlodomer. Childebert spread the rumour that he and his brother were to plan the coronation of the young princes and sent a message to Clotild to that effect. When the boys were despatched to their uncles they were seized and separated from their household. Lothar and Childebert then sent their henchman Arcadius to the Queen with a pair of scissors in one hand and a sword in the other. He offered the Queen an ultimatum. Would she wish to see her grandsons live with their hair cut short? or would she prefer to see them killed? Beside herself with grief, Clotild stated that if they were not to succeed to the throne she would rather see them dead than with their hair cut short. Rejecting the scissors, she opted for the sword.

The sequel to this story, told by Gregory of Tours (d. 594), reveals an alternative to death or short-haired dishonour. A third grandson, Chlodovald, was well guarded and escaped his uncles. Seeking to escape the fate of his brothers, he cut his hair short with his own hands and became a priest. Voluntary tonsuring did not carry the ignominy of shearing under duress.

To a twentieth-century audience this story seems strange. Why should a queen choose to have her grandsons killed rather than submitting them to a haircut? In the world of Merovingian Gaul, however, the story had a potent resonance and hair itself was of the utmost importance. The Merovingian kings, who had established themselves in the ruins of Roman Gaul, were known as the *Reges criniti,* the long-haired kings. For them, their long hair symbolised not only their aristocratic status but also their status as kings. It was invested with a sacral quality and believed to contain magical properties. The Byzantine poet and historian Agathias (c.532-c.582) had written:

> It is the rule for Frankish kings never to be shorn; indeed their hair is never cut from childhood on, and hangs down in abundance on their shoulders . . . their subjects have their hair cut all round and are not permitted to grow it further.

The ultimatum offered by Lothar and Childebert thus hit straight to the heart of Merovingian high politics. What they were effectively saying was 'Do you wish to live non-regally or to die?'. Determined to compromise their nephews' rights to rule they utilised the scissors as a potent symbolic weapon. In sixth-century Gaul a haircut meant political coercion and social exclusion. If you removed the long hair of a king, you removed his claims to kingship itself.

The obituary of the long-haired kings was written into the history of the family who supplanted them in 751, the Carolingians. According to Einhard, the biographer of the most famous Carolingian, Charlemagne, the later Merovingians were *rois fainéants,* decadent and do-nothing kings, whose power had been effectively supplanted by the Carolingian dynasty in the form of Mayors of the Palace. The last Merovingian, Childeric III, was king in name and hair only, reduced to travelling around his kingdom in a cart pulled by oxen. The scissors came out again. The Carolingians, with papal backing, cut off Childeric's hair and incarcerated him in a monastery. They also effectively desacralised the significance of hair. Charlemagne's head—and his right to rule—was distinguished not by his hair but by his coronation and anointing at the hand of the pope. Holy oil, not holy hair, made a king.

Furthermore, the Carolingians prided themselves on being descendants of a saint who had not been subjected to the ritual of forcible tonsuring. Gertrude, the daughter of a high-ranking Frankish nobleman, Pippin, was to be married off to the family's advantage. Pippin, however, died before he was able to enforce his will and carry out his plan, leaving Gertrude in the charge of her mother, Itta. Acquiring the support of a holy man, Amandus, mother and daughter decided to found a convent at Nivelles and, 'so that the violators of souls should not drag her daughter by force back into the illicit pleasures of the world', Gertrude's mother 'seized iron shears and cut her

 This article first appeared in *History Today,* May 1999, pp. 7-13. © 1999 by History Today, Ltd. Reprinted by permission.

daughter's hair in the shape of a crown'. Gertrude was the great aunt of the Carolingian Mayor of the Palace, Charles Martel, and became a patron saint of the Carolingian house. The long-haired kings were deposed by a family who cultivated the cult of a tonsured nun. Whereas forcible tonsuring was perceived as shaming, the cutting of hair in accordance with a vow could be regarded as meritorious.

Hair was able to carry such symbolic meanings because it is a body part which is easily subject to change: it can be dyed, shaped, worn loose, bound or be removed. Moreover, since it surrounds the most expressive part of the body, the face, any changes made to it are inherently visible and noticeable. Once rules were prescribed about its meaning, function and treatment, it acquired a particular resonance depending on the way in which it was understood in local communities. These meanings were, of course, highly contextualised. A monk awaiting tonsure would recognise that the presence of a pair of scissors marked the point where he fulfilled his vow to leave behind the secular world and become a servant of God. Unless the monk was unsure of his vocation, this would be unlikely to induce panic. The situation would, however, appear very different to a Merovingian king.

The relationship between long hair and high birth was an ancient one and was present in societies other than Merovingian Gaul. In Ireland, for example, cropped hair denoted a servant or slave. Tacitus had noted the importance of long hair in early Germanic society, commenting that it was the sign of free men. Hair colour, too, bore social significance. In the Irish epic, *Táin bó Cúailnge*, King Conchobar has golden hair which is associated with royalty, while brown and black hair are also attributed to chieftains and heroes. The association of long hair with a warrior class possessed strong Biblical validation in the story of Samson in *Judges* 16:17. Long hair denoted strength and virility. In women, moreover, it represented fertility. Since long hair was part of the social badge of a warrior aristocracy, it was protected by law. In the lawcodes of the Alamans, Frisians, Lombards and Anglo-Saxons, the cutting of hair brought forth penalties. According to the Laws of King Alfred, anyone who cut off a man's beard had to pay a compensation of 20 shillings,

Charles the Bald, who inherited the western portion of Francia after the Treaty of Verdun of 843, and was crowned king of Lotharingia in 869 (as seen here) was apparently nicknamed for his exceptionally full head of hair.

and in Frederick Barbarossa's *Landfried* of 1152, it was forbidden either to seize a man by the beard or to tear any hairs from his head or beard. In the Frankish *Pactus Legis Salicae,* if a *puer crinitus* (long-haired boy) was shorn without the consent of his parents, the heavy fine of forty-five solidi was imposed, while among the Burgundians there were heavy fines for cutting the hair of a freewoman. Beards were perceived as a sign of masculinity, separating men from boys. According to the Anglo-Norman historian, Orderic Vitalis, William the

Conqueror complained that he had to defend Normandy 'whilst still unbearded' referring to the manner in which he was placed in charge of the defence of the duchy when still only a boy.

A particularly ancient function of hair treatment was the manner in which it denoted ethnicity and hence could be used to distinguish different ethnic groups. Tacitus thought that the Suevi were characterised by their distinctive, knotted, hair. Other groups like the Lombards and the Frisians were named after their particular fashion for styling beard or hair. The Byzantines, for example, remarked how the Avars 'wore their hair very long at the back, tied with bands and braided'. Both the great sixth-century Spanish churchman, Isidore of Seville, the author of the *Etymologiae,* a concise encyclopedia of classical culture, and Paul the Deacon, the historian of the Lombards, derived the name Lombard from the German *Langbärte* or long beard. Gregory of Tours recounts how, in 590, Queen Fredegund ordered the army of the Saxons in the Bayeux area to attack a Frankish duke but to disguise themselves as Bretons by cutting their hair in the Breton way and wearing Breton clothing. William of Malmesbury's *Gesta Regum* distinguished Saxons from Normans at the time of the Norman Conquest by reference to the differences between the hair styles of the two ethnic groups. Just before the Norman invasion of England, Harold sent some spies who reported that all the Norman soldiers were priests,

> . . . because they have their entire face, with both lips, shaved, whereas the English left the upper lip uncut, with the hairs ceaselessly flourishing.

William was writing in the twelfth century, but his evidence is confirmed by the Bayeux Tapestry which shows almost all the Norman soldiers clean shaven and the Anglo-Saxon soldiers with long moustaches.

Hair treatment could also be used to denote age categories, as we have already seen with regard to the possession of beards. One of the most distinctive rites of passage in the early medieval West was the ritual cutting of hair to mark the transition from infant to the very young. These ancient ceremonies known as *barbatoria* created a spiritual bond between the cutter and the cut. In the late 730s, the Carolingian Mayor of the Palace, Charles Martel, sent his son Pippin to the Lombard King Liutprand in order that the King might cut the boy's hair and hence become as a father to him. The importance of such fictive kindred is also evident in the story surrounding the ancestry of Miesko, first Christian ruler of Poland, whose father, Semovith, underwent a ritual haircut at the hands of two strangers during a drunken feast where a barrel of beer refilled itself miraculously. The establishment of the strangers as Semovith's

patrons marked the foundation of a new dynasty when Semovith expelled the former duke and appointed himself in his place. As with the emergence of the Carolingians, hair was one issue on which the outcome of dynastic politics could be constructed.

Haircutting could also serve as a marker of sexual difference. On the basis of St Paul's words in *I Corinthians 11:4,* long hair was considered a glory for a woman so long as she kept it covered in public, whilst shorter hair was deemed most appropriate for men. The Romans had valued short hair. All Roman men of power and standing wore their hair short, a sign that it was under control. Fourth-century emperors generated a close-shaven public image. Long hair, hairdressing, and facial hair were

---

The ritual cutting of hair marked the transition from infant to the very young.

---

deemed characteristic of women and barbarians. Aristocrats accused each other of looking like harlots for the way they wore their hair. The emperor Julian the Apostate (r. 361–363) shocked observers less by his attempts to restore the old gods than by his beard. He thus wrote the *Misopogon* or Beard Hater in which he castigated the smooth-shaven Antiochenes who had made fun of his long beard and unkempt hair.

Whereas the period between the fall of the Roman Empire and the emergence of the Carolingian Empire seems to have been dominated by a tolerant, and indeed encouraging, attitude towards facial hair and beards, the Carolingian period and the subsequent post-millennial European world saw the development of a hostility towards long hair and considered it an issue characterised by scandal. In the eighth century, Bede had written that, ' . . . the beard which is a mark of the male sex and of

age, is customarily put as an indication of virtue'. However, on Ash Wednesday 1094, Archbishop Anselm of Canterbury refused to give either ashes or his blessing to men who 'grew their hair like girls'. At Rouen in 1096, a church council decreed 'that no one should grow his hair long but have it cut as a Christian'.

Both William of Malmesbury and Orderic Vitalis associated the long hair of William Rufus's court with moral scandal. Orderic wrote how:

> are crazy and wear little beards, openly proclaiming by such a token that they revel in filthy lusts like stinking goats.

In Carentan in Normandy the Archbishop of Séez rebuked Henry I and his courtiers for their long hair, produced a pair of scissors and cut it on the spot. William of Malmesbury was particularly vituperative about aristocrats with flowing locks. To him long hair was a sign of homosexuality and decadence. It made men effeminate and blurred the differences between the sexes. He told a moral tale about how one knight who gloried in his luxuriant hair dreamt that he was choked by his own locks and subsequently quickly spread the news that haircuts were necessary throughout England. William was so concerned about the decadence represented by long hair that he even blamed it for the Norman Conquest on the grounds that it led men who should have vociferously defended their kingdom to behave no better than women.

Others had more practical reasons for disliking long hair. Bishop Ernulf of Rochester (1114–24) remarked how men with long beards often dipped hairs into liquid when drinking from a cup. The rhetoric of monastic writers thus identified long hair with youth, decadence and the court. It is difficult, however, to draw a hard and fast line between an earlier tolerance of long hair and a gradual distaste for its cultivation. An imperial decree of 390, for example, forbade women to cut off their hair and threatened a bishop who allowed such a woman to enter a church with deposition, while the Council of Agde in 506 said that clerics who allowed their hair to grow long would have it cut by the archdeacon. The sixth-century Irish monk Columbanus, who founded a series of monasteries in Gaul, prescribed penance for deacons who refused to cut their beards.

One area where treatment of hair was particularly seen as denoting differences in sex lay in the field of mourning the dead. The public ritual of mourning involving emotional display and the tearing out of hair was commonly seen as a woman's business. Men, however, were not immune to such activity as is evident in the story of the later Merovingian king, Dagobert III (d.715), who, after a terrifying nocturnal vision, was found the next morning to have cut his long fingernails and then remained in his bedroom ordering his hair to be cut off. According to Tacitus, it was women, however, who engaged in lamentation either by pulling out their hair or letting it down to the extent that they became a common sight at funerals. Reginald of Durham, a twelfth-century writer of saints' lives, describes how after a young man was injured and presumed dead both men and women mourned through tears and wailing but only the women let their hair down in lamentation. The ninth-century author, Agnellus of Ravenna, meanwhile, describes the crowds of women who appeared at funeral ceremonies in the city where he was archbishop. The extravagant behaviour of women at funerals became so great that in the thirteenth century, Italian communes passed restrictive legislation against funerary practices in an attempt to curtail the crowds at funerals and restore social order.

The ecclesiastical counter to the aristocratic cultivation of long hair lay in the monastic tonsure. According to Bede, the tonsure separated the cleric from the layman. It, rather than dress, was the distinguishing badge of those who had entered the clerical profession. Bede's *Ecclesiastical History of the English People* preserves a letter reputed to have been written by Ceolfrid, the abbot of his own monastery, Wearmouth-Jarrow, to Nechtan, the king of the Picts which, in addition to commenting on the teaching of the Roman Church with regard to the calculation of Easter, made some notable remarks about the tonsure. While acknowledging that there were variations in the style of tonsure adopted by clerics, the letter recommended the cultivation of the Petrine tonsure which took the form of a crown in imitation of Christ's crown of thorns, rather than the tonsure associated with Simon Magus which was still worn by some in the Irish Church, and which left a fringe at the front of the head. Early discussions

of the symbolism of the tonsure make no reference to the corona, but Isidore of Seville noted how the crown was symbolic of the authority of the priest, recalling the tiara of the Hebrew priests. Isidore established the symbolic significance of the tonsure by associating it with a ritual of renunciation which viewed it as a pact made with God. According to Isidore, the tonsure of priests was visible on their bodies but had its effect on their souls:

> By this sign, the vices in religion are cut off, and we strip off the crimes of the body like hairs. This renewal fittingly takes place in the mind, but it is shown on the head where the mind is known to reside.

The ceremony of tonsure accomplished a ritual of separation from the community. It stood as a symbol of renunciation, not only because it signified shame and humility, but also because it was a denial of the free status that had been the birthright of most clerics, and was to be followed by a lifestyle that was a negation of the norms of lay society. The act of tonsure made the cleric an outsider. Unlike the forcible tonsuring of deposed Merovingian rulers, however, the cleric accepted this badge of shame voluntarily. But like the coercion of long-haired kings, the cultivation of short hair through the tonsure bore with it political resonance.

Bede was bothered about the Irish sporting the tonsure associated with Simon Magus on the grounds that it separated them from the Roman Church, along with the fact that they calculated Easter in a different manner. The decision taken by the Northumbrian Church at the Synod of Whitby in 664 to follow Roman practice over the calculation of Easter and over the tonsure, was thus a sign of public allegiance to the world of Rome. The Spanish Church had recognised the value of the tonsure in the form of the corona at the fourth council of Toledo in 633 where it was decreed that 'all clerics must shave the whole front part of the hair, leaving only a circular crown on the back'. The idea, however, had clearly spread earlier since Gregory of Tours's uncle Nicetius was reputed to have been born with his hair growing in a circle on top of his head, revealing from birth that he was intended for the episcopate.

Whereas ecclesiastical legislation might prescribe short hair as an essential sign of clerical status, ambiguities about hair treatment remained even in the tighter moral world of the eleventh and twelfth centuries. The custom of clerical shaving was less universal than some writers in the Western Church implied, although reformers in the eleventh century sought to enforce the canonical decrees on this and other matters, as was evident in Pope Gregory VII's order that the shaving of beards was a distinctive mark of the clerical order in society. Many clerics, however, still let their beards grow in times of fast and did not shave when travelling. Canonical rules were thus widely disregarded.

There was no single standard with regard to shaving in religious communities. Whereas the monks at St Augustine's, Canterbury, between 1090 and 1120 are depicted as beardless, those at Mont-St-Michel in the second half of the twelfth century are shown with beards. Hermits, anchorites, recluses and ascetics commonly did not shave and their reputation for unshaven holiness was parodied in the remark made by Bishop Eugenius of Toledo in the seventh century that 'If a beard makes a saint, nothing is more saintly than a goat'. Moreover, despite the denunciation of long hair by writers such as William of Malmesbury, many rulers began actively to cultivate beards. The historian Percy Ernst Schramm noted how the full beard appears in iconographical representations of rulership at the turn of the millennium. Towards the end of their reigns, the rulers of Germany, Otto I and Otto II, had beards. These iconographical sources are, however, at variance with written sources which refer to laymen who cut off their beards to become monks. One such was the ninth-century Carolingian count, Gerald of Aurillac, who shaved his beard to live like a monk. Since he was a layman, however, Gerald was caught between the world of aristocratic mores and the secluded world of clerics:

> He cut his beard as though it were a nuisance, and since his hairs flowed down from the back of his head, he hid the crown on top, which he also covered with a cap.

On October 14th, 680, Wamba, the Visigothic King of Spain, fell unconscious in his palace at Toledo. Julian, the Archbishop of Toledo, was called by the courtiers who feared that the King was near death. He cut Wamba's hair and clothed him in a monastic habit. Emerging from his coma, the king discovered that he had become a monk and could not resume royal office since the law of the Church enshrined in the Council of Chalcedon of 451 decreed that 'those that have become clerics or who have entered a monastery should neither enter the army nor take on secular honours'. Wamba therefore signed documents attesting his acceptance of clerical status and named one of his nobles, Erwig, as his successor.

The forcible tonsure of kings was known in all the pre-Carolingian barbarian kingdoms of Western Europe but, like the issues of tonsuring and clerical beards, it was characterised by ambiguity. Although the hair of secular rulers could be cut off, it could also grow back. The Merovingian ruler Childeric I dealt with his rebellious son, Merovech, by tonsuring him and throwing him into a monastery but Merovech soon escaped and fled to Tours. King Theuderic III was tonsured but grew his hair again and regained power. The Mayor of the Palace, Ebroin, was stripped of his power, tonsured and thrown into a monastery at Luxeuil in Burgundy. He waited for his hair to grow back before gathering an army and attempting to regain control in Francia. Similarly, in Anglo-Saxon England, King Ceolwulf of Northumbria was tonsured and thrown into the monastery at Lindisfarne only to return as king. In 737, however, he was tonsured again at his own request, abdicated as king and entered the monastery voluntarily. Having decided to take the tonsure, he would thus be compelled to keep his hair short. He had no need to grow it since, like Wamba, he was now a monk and no longer a king.

In the early Middle Ages, the language of hair treatment was open to as many interpretations as the treatment of hair itself. What is clear is that hair and its appearance mattered in both secular and clerical society. Men may have lived by the sword but they could metaphorically die by the scissors. Childeric III knew that when the Carolingians bore the scissors his days were numbered. It only took one bad hair day to turn his fear into living panic.

FOR FURTHER READING

J. M. Wallace-Hadrill, *The Long-Haired Kings* (Methuen, 1962); E. James, 'Bede and the Tonsure Question', *Peritia, 3* (1984); R. Bartlett, 'Symbolic Meanings of Hair in the Middle Ages', *TRHS*, Sixth Series 4 (1994), 43–60; Conrad Leyser, 'Longhaired kings and short-haired nuns: Power and gender in Merovingian Gaul', *Medieval World*, (March-April 1992); Giles Constable, 'Introduction: Beards in the Middle Ages', in *Burchard of Bellevaux, Apologia de Barbis*, (ed. R. B. C. Huygen), in *Apologiae duae, Corpus Christianorum Continuatio Mediaevalis*, LXII (Turnhout, 1985); Clare Stancliffe, 'Kings who opted out', in Patrick Wormald, Donald Bullough and Roger Collins (eds), *Ideal and Reality in Frankish and Anglo-Saxon Society: Studies Presented to J. M. Wallace-Hadrill* (OUP, 1983).

Simon Coates is a British Academy Post-doctoral Research Fellow at King's College, University of London, and author of The Early Anglo-Saxon Church c.597–c.900: A Social and Cultural History *(Scolar Press, forthcoming).*

The Amazing Vikings

They earned their brutal reputation—but the Norse were also
craftsmen, explorers and believers in democracy

By Michael D. Lemonick and Andrea Dorfman

RAVAGERS, DESPOILERS, PAGANS, HEA-thens—such epithets pretty well summed up the Vikings for those who lived in the British Isles during medieval times. For hundreds of years after their bloody appearance at the end of the 8th century A.D., these ruthless raiders would periodically sweep in from the sea to kill, plunder and destroy, essentially at will. "From the fury of the Northmen, deliver us, O Lord" was a prayer uttered frequently and fervently at the close of the first millennium. Small wonder that the ancient Anglo-Saxons—and their cultural descendants in England, the U.S. and Canada—think of these seafaring Scandinavians as little more than violent brutes.

But that view is wildly skewed. The Vikings were indeed raiders, but they were also traders whose economic network stretched from today's Iraq all the way to the Canadian Arctic. They were democrats who founded the world's oldest surviving parliament while Britain was still mired in feudalism. They were master metalworkers, fashioning exquisite jewelry from silver, gold and bronze. Above all, they were intrepid explorers whose restless hearts brought them to North America some 500 years before Columbus.

The broad outlines of Viking culture and achievement have been known to experts for decades, but a spate of new scholarship, based largely on archaeological excavations in Europe, Iceland, Greenland and Canada, has begun to fill in the elusive details. And now the rest of us have a chance to share in those discoveries with the opening last week of a wonderfully rich exhibition titled "Vikings: The North Atlantic Saga" at the National Museum of Natural History in Washington.

Timed to commemorate the thousand-year anniversary of Leif Eriksson's arrival in North America, the show examines the Vikings and their Norse descendants from about A.D. 740 to 1450—focusing especially on their westward expansion and on the persistent mysteries of how extensively the Vikings explored North America and why they abandoned their outpost here.

In doing so, the curators have laid to rest a number of popular misconceptions, including one they perpetuate in the show's title. The term Viking (possibly from the Old Norse *vik*, meaning bay) refers properly only to men who went on raids. All Vikings were Norse, but not all Norse were Vikings—and those who were did their viking only part time. Vikings didn't wear horned helmets (a fiction probably created for 19th century opera). And while rape and pillage were part of the agenda, they were a small part of Norse life.

In fact, this mostly blue-eyed, blond or reddish-haired people who originated in what is now Scandinavia were primarily farmers and herdsmen. They grew grains and vegetables during the short summer but depended mostly on livestock—cattle, goats, sheep and pigs. They weren't Christian until the late 10th century, yet they were not irreligious. Like the ancient Greeks and Romans, they worshiped a pantheon of deities, three of whom—Odin, Thor and Freya—we recall every week, as Wednesday, Thursday and Friday were named after them. (Other Norse words that endure in modern English: berserk and starboard.)

Nor were the Norse any less sophisticated than other Europeans. Their oral literature—epic poems known as *Eddas* as well as their sagas—was Homeric in drama and scope. During the evenings and throughout the long, dark winters, the Norse amused themselves with such challenging board games as backgammon and chess (though they didn't invent them). By day the women cooked, cleaned, sewed and ironed, using whalebone plaques as boards and running a heavy stone or glass smoother over the seams of garments.

The men supplemented their farmwork by smelting iron ore and smithing it into tools and cookware; by shaping soapstone into lamps, bowls and pots; by crafting jewelry; and by carving stone tablets with floral motifs, scenes depicting Norse myths and runic inscriptions (usually to commemorate a notable deed or personage).

Most important, though, they made the finest ships of the age. Thanks to several Viking boats disinterred from burial mounds in Norway, archaeologists know beyond a doubt that the wooden craft were "unbelievable—the best in Europe by far," according to William Fitzhugh, director of the National Museum's Arctic Studies Center and the exhibition's chief curator. Sleek and streamlined, powered by both sails and oars, quick and highly maneuverable, the boats could operate equally well in shallow waterways and on the open seas.

With these magnificent craft, the Norse searched far and wide for goods

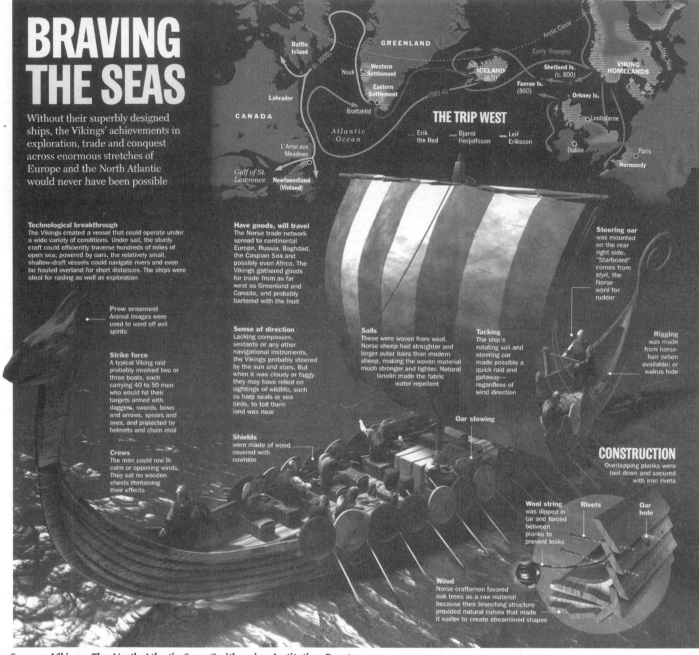

Source: *Vikings: The North Atlantic Sage* (Smithsonian Institution Press)

they couldn't get at home: silk, glass, sword-quality steel, raw silver and silver coins that they could melt down and rework. In return they offered furs, grindstones, Baltic amber, walrus ivory, walrus hides and iron.

At first, the Norse traded locally around the Baltic Sea. But from there, says Fitzhugh, "their network expanded to Europe and Britain, and then up the Russian rivers. They reached Rome, Baghdad, the Caspian Sea, probably Africa too. Buddhist artifacts from northern India have been found in a Swedish Viking grave, as has a charcoal brazier

from the Middle East." The Hagia Sophia basilica in Istanbul has a Viking inscription in its floor. A Mycenaean lion in Venice is covered with runes of the Norse alphabet.

Sometime in the late 8th century, however, the Vikings realized there was a much easier way to acquire luxury goods. The monasteries they dealt with in Britain, Ireland and mainland Europe were not only extremely wealthy but also situated on isolated coastlines and poorly defended—sitting ducks for men with agile ships. With the raid on England's Lindisfarne monastery in 793, the

reign of Viking terror officially began. Says archaeologist Colleen Batey of the Glasgow Museums: "They had a preference for anything that looked pretty," such as bejeweled books or gold, silver and other precious metals that could be recrafted into jewelry for wives and sweethearts. Many monasteries and trading centers were attacked repeatedly, even annually. In some cases the Vikings extorted protection money, known as danegeld, as the price of peace.

The Vikings didn't just pillage and run; sometimes they came to stay. Dublin became a Viking town; so did Lincoln and York, along with much of the surrounding territory in northern and eastern England. In Scotland, Vikings maintained their language and political links to their homeland well into the 15th century. Says Batey: "The northern regions of Scotland, especially, were essentially a Scandinavian colony up until then." Vikings also created the duchy of Normandy, in what later became France, as well as a dynasty that ruled Kiev, in Ukraine.

Given their hugely profitable forays into Europe, it's not entirely clear why the Vikings chose to strike out across the forbidding Atlantic. One reason might have been a growing population; another might have been political turmoil. The search for such exotic trade goods as furs and walrus ivory might have also been a factor. The timing, in any event, was perfect: during the 9th century, when the expansion began, the climate was unusually warm and stable. Pastures were productive, and the pack ice that often clogged the western North Atlantic was at a minimum.

So westward the Vikings went. Their first stop, in about 860, was the Faeroe Islands, northwest of Scotland. Then, about a decade later, the Norse reached Iceland. Experts believe as many as 12,000 Viking immigrants ultimately settled there, taking their farm animals with them. (Inadvertently, they also brought along mice, dung beetles, lice, human fleas and a host of animal parasites, whose remains, trapped in soil, are helping archaeologists form a detailed picture of early medieval climate and Viking life. Bugs, for example, show what sort of livestock the Norse kept.)

Agriculture was tough in Iceland; it was too cold, for instance, to grow barley for that all important beverage beer. "They tried to grow barley all over Iceland, but it wasn't economical," says archaeologist Thomas McGovern of New York City's Hunter College. Nevertheless, the colony held on, and in 930 Iceland's ruling families founded a general assembly, known as the Althing, at which representatives of the entire population met annually to discuss matters of importance and settle legal disputes. The institution is still in operation today, more than a thousand years later.

Viking Vs. Norse

"Viking" refers only to those among the Norse who went out on raiding parties. Plenty of Norse—including all the women—weren't Vikings at all, and others were Vikings only some of the time

In 982 the Althing considered the case of an ill-tempered immigrant named Erik the Red. Erik, the saga says, had arrived in Iceland several years earlier after being expelled from Norway for murder. He settled down on a farm, married a Christian woman named Thjodhild (the Norse were by now starting to convert) and had three sons, Leif, Thorvald and Thorstein, and one daughter, Freydis. It wasn't long, though, before Erik began feuding with a neighbor—something about a cow and some wallboards—and ended up killing again.

The Althing decided to exile him for three years, so Erik sailed west to explore a land he had heard about from sailors who had been blown off course. Making his way around a desolate coast, he came upon magnificent fjords flanked by lush meadows and forests of dwarf willow and birch, with glacier-strewn mountain ranges towering in the distance. This "green land," he decided (in what might have been a clever bit of salesmanship), would be a perfect place to live. In 985 Erik returned triumphantly to Iceland and enlisted a group of followers to help him establish the first Norse outposts on Greenland. Claiming the best plot of land for himself, Erik established his base at Brattahlid, a verdant spot at the neck of a fjord on the island's southwestern tip, across from what is now the modern airport at Narsarsuaq. He carved out a farm and built his wife a tiny church, just 8 ft. wide by 12 ft. long. (According to one legend, she refused to sleep with him until it was completed.)

The remains of this stone-and-turf building were found in 1961. The most spectacular discovery from the Greenland colonies was made in 1990, however, when two Inuit hunters searching for caribou about 55 miles east of Nuuk (the modern capital) noticed several large pieces of wood sticking out of a bluff. Because trees never grew in the area, they reported their discovery to the national museum. The wood turned out to be part of an enormous Norse building, perfectly sealed in permafrost covered by 5 ft. of sand: "definitely one of the best-preserved Norse sites we have," says archaeologist Joel Berglund, vice director

of the Greenland National Museum and Archives in Nuuk.

According to Berglund, a leader of the dig at the "Farm Beneath the Sand" from 1991 through 1996, the site was occupied for nearly 300 years, from the mid-11th century to the end of the 13th century. "It went from small to big and then from big to small again," he explains. "They started with a classic longhouse, which later burned down." The place was abandoned for a while and then rebuilt into what became a "centralized farm," a huge, multifunction building with more than 30 rooms housing perhaps 15 or 20 people, plus sheep, goats, cows and horses.

The likeliest reason for this interspecies togetherness was the harsh climate. Observes Berglund: "The temperature today gets as cold as -50°C [-58°F]." Bones recovered from trash middens in the house indicate that the occupants dined mostly on wild caribou and

Days of the Week

<u>Wednesday</u>
Odin

<u>Thursday</u>
Thor

<u>Friday</u>
Freya

seals, which were plentiful along the coast. (The domesticated animals were apparently raised for their wool and milk, not meat.) Scientists recovered more than 3,000 artifacts in the ruins, including a wooden loom, children's toys and combs. Along with hair, body lice and animal parasites, these items will be invaluable in determining what each room was used for. Researchers also found bones and other remnants from meals, and even a mummified goat. That means, says Berglund, "we'll even be able to tell whether there was enough food and whether the people and animals were healthy."

As Greenland's overlord, Erik the Red took a cut of virtually everyone's profits from the export of furs and ivory. Material success apparently did not keep Erik and his family content, though; they undoubtedly heard of a voyage by a captain named Bjarni Herjolfsson, who had been blown off course while en route to Greenland from Iceland. After drifting for many days, Bjarni spotted a forested land. But instead of investigating this unknown territory, he turned back and reached Greenland.

Intrigued by this tale, Erik's eldest son Leif, sometime between 997 and 1003, decided to sail westward to find

Vikings *and History*

Events in the Viking world (bold) can be seen in parallel with what the rest of the world was doing (italic)

A.D. 793: Viking Age begins with the raid on England's Lindisfarne monastery

800: Charlemagne is crowned Emperor

802: Khmer kingdom is created in Cambodia

841: Vikings found Dublin, in Ireland

845: First Viking assault on Paris

850–900: Maya civilization in Mesoamerica begins to decline

862–82: Viking princes become rulers of Novgorod and Kiev

871: Colonization of Iceland begins

886: Alfred the Great divides England with the Danes under the Danelaw pact

911: Viking chief Rollo founds the duchy of Normandy (now in France)

930: Iceland's parliament, the Althing, is established

969: Fatimids, Muhammad's descendants, sweep across North Africa and make Cairo their capital

982–85: Erik the Red explores Greenland, starts a settlement there

985–86: Icelandic trader Bjarni Herjolfsson sights a lush, forested shore, apparently North America, but opts not to inspect it

c. 1000: Leif Eriksson sets up camp at L'anse aux Meadows, Newfoundland

1000: Iceland adopts Christianity

1042: Accession of Edward the Confessor ends Danish rule in England

1054: Final schism of Roman Catholic Orthodox churches

1066: William the Conqueror, a Norman, defeats England's King Harold at the Battle of Hastings, ending the Viking Age

1077: Completion of the Bayeux tapestry, depicting the Battle of Hastings and showing Viking ships

1095–96: Europe's Christians launch the first Crusades to recapture the Holy Land

1206: Genghis Kahn crowned Emperor of the Mongols, launches wars of conquest

1215: England's King John signs the Magna Carta

1271: Marco Polo sets off for Asia

1337: Beginning of the Hundred Years War between England and France

1347: Plague (Black Death) erupts in Europe

c. 1350: Little Ice Age leads to end of Western Settlement on Greenland

1370: Tamerlane sets out to restore the Mongol empire

1431: Joan of Arc is burned at the stake in Rouen

c. 1450: Last Norse leave Greenland

1492: Christopher Columbus lands in the New World

the new land. First, say the sagas, the crew came to a forbidding land of rocks and glaciers. Then they sailed on to a wooded bay, where they dropped anchor for a while. Eventually they continued south to a place he called Vinland ("wineland," probably for the wild grapes that grew there). Leif and his party made camp for the winter, then sailed home. Members of his family returned in later years, but Leif never did. Erik died shortly after his son returned, and Leif took over the Greenland colony. Though he retained ownership of the Norse base in North America and received a share of the riches that were brought back, he stopped exploring.

This much had long been known from the Icelandic sagas, but until 1960 there was no proof of Leif's American sojourns. In retrospect, it is astonishing that the evidence took so long to be found. That year Norwegian explorer Helge Ingstad and his wife, archaeologist Anne Stine Ingstad, went to Newfoundland to explore a place identified on an Icelandic map from the 1670s as "Promontorium Winlandiae," near the small fishing village of L'Anse aux Meadows, in the province's northern reaches. They were certain that it marked the location of an ancient Norse settlement.

Finding the settlement turned out to be absurdly easy. When the Ingstads asked the locals if there were any odd ruins in the area, they were taken to a place known as "the Indian camp." They immediately recognized the grass-covered ridges as Viking-era ruins like those in Iceland and Greenland.

During the next seven years, the Ingstads and an international team of archaeologists exposed the foundations of eight separate buildings. Sitting on a narrow terrace between two bogs, the buildings had sod walls and peaked sod roofs laid over a (now decayed) wooden

frame; they were evidently meant to be used year-round. The team also unearthed a Celtic-style bronze pin with a ring-shaped head similar to ones the Norse used to fasten their cloaks, a soapstone spindle whorl, a bit of bone needle, a small whetstone for sharpening scissors and needles, lumps of worked iron and iron boat nails. (All these items helped win over detractors, since the artifacts were clearly not native to America.)

Further excavations in the mid-1970s under the auspices of Parks Canada, the site's custodian, made it plain that this was most likely the place where Leif set up camp. Among the artifacts turned up: loom weights, another spindle whorl, a bone needle, jasper fire starters, pollen, seeds, butternuts and, most important, about 2,000 scraps of worked wood that were subsequently radiocarbon dated to between 980 and 1020—just when Leif visited Vinland.

The configuration of the ruined buildings, the paucity of artifacts and garbage compared with those found at other sites, and the absence of a cemetery, stables and holding pens for animals have convinced Birgitta Linderoth Wallace, the site's official archaeologist, that L'Anse aux Meadows wasn't a permanent settlement and was used for perhaps less than 10 years.

Instead, she believes, it served as a base camp for several exploratory expeditions up and down the coast, perhaps as far south as the Gulf of St. Lawrence. "We know this because of the butternuts," she says. "The closest places they grow are east of Quebec near the Gulf of St. Lawrence or in eastern New Brunswick. They are too heavy for birds to carry, and they can't float. And we know the Norse considered them a delicacy."

The National Museum's Fitzhugh notes that the location of the camp was advantageous for various reasons. "L'Anse aux Meadows is rocky and dangerous," he admits. "There are much better places just a few miles away—but there's a good view. They could watch out for danger, and they could bring their boats in and keep an eye on them." What's more, Fitzhugh says, "they would have built where they could easily be found by other people. That's why they chose the tip of a peninsula. All they had to tell people was, 'Cross the Big Water, turn left and keep the land on your right.'" With fair winds, the voyage would have taken about two weeks; a group of men who tried it in the replica Viking ship Snorri (named after the first European born in America) in 1998 were stuck at sea for three months.

Despite all the natural resources, the Norse never secured a foothold in the New World. Within a decade or so after Leif's landing at L'Anse aux Meadows, they were gone. Wallace, for one, believes that there were simply too few people to keep the camp going and that those stationed there got homesick: "You had a very small community that could barely sustain itself. Recent research has shown it had only 500 people, and we know you need that many at a minimum to start a colony in an uninhabited area. They had barely got started in Greenland when they decided to go to North America. It wasn't practical, and I think they missed their family and friends."

Fitzhugh offers another theory. "I think they recognized that they had found wonderful resources but decided they couldn't defend themselves and were unable to risk their families to stay there," he says. "Imagine 30 Norsemen in a boat on the St. Lawrence meeting a band of Iroquois. They would have been totally freaked out."

As for discovering additional Norse outposts in North America, most experts think the chances are very slim. "These areas were heavily occupied by Native Americans," says archaeologist Patricia Sutherland of the Canadian Museum of Civilization in Hull, "so while there may have been some trade, relations would have been hostile. Maybe someone will find an isolated Norse farm on the coast of Labrador or Baffin Island, but not an outpost."

That's not to say Norse artifacts haven't been discovered south of Newfoundland—but aside from a Norse penny, minted between 1065 and 1080 and found in 1957 at an Indian site near Brooklin, Maine, nearly all of them have turned out to be bogus. The Newport (R.I.) Tower, whose supposed Viking origin was central to Longfellow's epic poem *The Skeleton in Armor*, was built by an early Governor of Rhode Island. The Kensington Stone, a rune-covered slab unearthed on a Minnesota farm in

1898 that purportedly describes a voyage to Vinland in 1362, is today widely believed to be a modern forgery. So is Yale's Vinland Map, a seemingly antique chart with the marking "Vinilanda Insula" that surfaced in the 1950s bound into a medieval book.

To the north, though, it's a different story. Digs at dozens of ancient Inuit sites in the eastern Canadian Arctic and western Greenland have turned up a wealth of Norse artifacts, indicating that the Europeans and Arctic natives interacted long after Leif Eriksson and his mates left. Says Sutherland: "The contact was more extensive and more complex than we suspected even a couple of months ago."

The Norse referred to the indigenous peoples they encountered in Greenland and the New World as *skraeling,* a derogatory term meaning wretch or scared weakling, and the sagas make it clear that the Norse considered the natives hostile. But the abundance of Norse items found at Inuit sites—some 80 objects from a single site on Skraeling Island, off the east coast of Ellesmere Island, including a small driftwood carving of a face with European features— suggests that there was a lively trade between the groups (as well as an exchange of Norse goods among the Inuit).

The Vikings held out in their harsh Greenland outposts for several centuries, but by 1450 they were gone. One reason was climate change. Starting about 1350, global temperatures entered a 500-year slump known as the Little Ice Age. Norse hunting techniques and agriculture were inadequate for survival in this long chill, and the Vikings never adapted the Inuit's more effective strategies for the cold.

Another factor was the rapacious overuse of resources. The goats, pigs and sheep brought by the Norse ate or trampled the forests and shrub lands, eventually transforming them into bare ground. Without enough fodder, the farm animals could not survive. The Norse were forced to eat more seal, seabirds and fish—and these too became locally scarce. The depletion of Greenland's meager trees and bushes meant no wood for fuel or for repairing ships.

To make matters worse, demand for the trade goods that Greenlanders exported to Europe plummeted. Not only was African ivory once again available (the supply had been cut off during the Crusades), but the material was falling out of fashion. And Europeans had their own problems: plague, crops failing in the colder conditions and city dwellers rioting in search of food. By the time the last Norse departed Greenland, the colonies had become so marginal that it took several hundred years before some Europeans realized they were gone. The Icelandic colony suffered too, though it managed to hang on.

But the true Vikings—those marauders of monasteries, those fearsome invaders from the north—had long since vanished, except in myth. As Europe's weak feudal fiefs had grown into powerful kingdoms, the Norse raiders had run out of easy victims. In England the victory in 1066 of William the Conqueror—a descendant of Norsemen from Normandy—marked the end of Viking terror.

Indeed, fear of the Vikings had played a pivotal role in reshaping Europe. "They helped develop nations and forced the Europeans to unite and defend themselves," says Fitzhugh. "It was a turning point in European history."

Back in their Scandinavian homeland, the Vikings' descendants also united into kingdoms, ultimately establishing Norway, Sweden and Denmark and pursuing a history no more or less aggressive than that of any other Europeans. The transfer of the Orkney Islands from Danish to Scottish control in 1468, for example, came not as the result of a bloody battle but as part of a royal wedding dowry.

As for the Norse settlements scattered around Britain and Europe, their inhabitants intermarried with the locals and finally disappeared as a distinct people. All that remains of them is their language and genes, spread widely through the Western world. Unlike Columbus, the Vikings may not have established a permanent presence in North America the first time around. But given the millions of Americans who share at least a bit of Viking blood, they are still there— and in considerable force.

The Golden Age of Andalusia Under the Muslim Sultans

From the 8th to the 15th century, Islam ruled in Spain's rich southern region

Stanley Meisler

Stanley Meisler, former Madrid correspondent for the Los Angeles Times, *wrote on the Prado in January and on Berlin's Pergamon Museum in October 1991.*

On January 2 [1992], several thousand festive Spaniards crowded into the downtown streets of Granada to celebrate the 500th anniversary of the surrender of the last Islamic stronghold in Spain to King Ferdinand and Queen Isabella in 1492. That event, as every schoolchild in Spain knows, completed the Reconquest—the final defeat of the Muslims who had occupied much of the Iberian Peninsula for more than 700 years, the final victory of Christianity over Islam in Spain. For the anniversary ceremonies, priests celebrated a mass at the cathedral where Ferdinand and Isabella, known in Spain as the Catholic Monarchs, are buried, and dignitaries led a procession back to the city hall, where Mayor Jesús Quero shouted to a cheering crowd, "Granada! Granada! Granada! In the name of the illustrious Ferdinand of Aragon and Isabella of Castile, long live Spain! Long live the King! Long live Andalusia! Long live Granada!"

A half-mile away, however, in the Albaicín, the old Arabic quarter of narrow streets, mazelike alleys and whitewashed stucco homes that nestles opposite the great hill of the Alhambra, perhaps 50 Spaniards, some of them converts to Islam, gathered. They met by the monastery that now stands on the spot where, according to legend, the submissive and chastened Sultan Boabdil handed the keys of the city to the triumphant Catholic Monarchs.

Now, half a millennium later, the small group of Spaniards marked that surrender with a few moments of silence. Then their leader, Aberraman Medina, lamented, "The conquest of Granada in 1492 was a rehearsal for what would happen later in America—a liquidation of cultures, traditions and beliefs."

This conflict of moods in Granada reflects the excitement and anguish of history in today's Spain. Ever since the death of the dictator Francisco Franco in 1975 and the transformation of Spain into a democracy, Spaniards have felt the need to examine their past and their identity. It is an examination that often brings pain and confusion and controversy, but this does not halt the search.

The self-examination is intensifying in this 500th-anniversary year. The rest of the world knows 1492 as the year that Christopher Columbus discovered America. But Spaniards know it, as well, as the year Ferdinand and Isabella defeated the Arabs in Granada and then expelled the Jews from Spain. They also know that all these cataclysmic events are interrelated. Columbus, in fact, accompanied the Catholic Monarchs to Granada and could not get approval and funds for his voyage until Ferdinand and Isabella diverted their attention from the Arabs to his scheme. And the crusading victory over Islam nourished a Christianity in the Catholic Monarchs so fervent and exclusive that they refused to tolerate Jews in their kingdom.

Spaniards have been aided in their quest for the past by an extraordinary exhibition entitled "Al-Andalus: The Art of Islamic Spain." Earlier this year [1992], it was mounted within the walls of the renowned palaces of the Alhambra, which were built by the sultans of Granada in the dying years of their dynasty. It then moved [in the] summer to the Metropolitan Museum of Art in New York, where it remain[ed] on view until September 27. Displaying 97 pieces of Spanish Islamic art of every variety, from ceramics and carpets to swords and manuscripts, "Al-Andalus" gives Americans one of their first looks at the little-known but splendid Islamic side of Spain.

It is not easy to sort out history and identity in Spain. Too much has been cloaked for centuries by Spaniards trying to hide their antecedents from a society that discriminated against those who could not prove what was called "purity of blood"—a line of descent from old Spanish Christians and not from converted Arabs or Jews. One of Spain's most distinguished journalists José Antonio Martínez Soler, who grew up on the heavily Arab-influenced Almería coast, is now studying Arabic to understand his roots. He has an ironic line about the confusion over the search for self-identity these days. "I like to say," he told me recently, "that all of Spain now believes it is one-half Arabic, one-half Jewish and one-half Spanish."

AN OPULENT STAGE SET FOR THE LAST ACT

Even appearances sometimes get in the way of understanding history. The breathtaking palaces of the Alhambra are not what they seem, for their grand splendor represents defeat, not triumph. "The Alhambra is like a big stage set," says Jerrilynn D. Dodds, an associate professor of architectural history at the City University of New York and a special consultant to the Met. "It was cheaply done but in an opulent way. It was an incredibly defiant gesture. They were defying the Christian onslaught with their own sophisticated culture. But it's also a melancholy monument trying to ward off eventual demise."

The history needs to be sketched briefly, for not much is known outside Spain about the farthest reach of Islam into Europe. In the year 711, a Berber commander led 7,000 Arab and Berber troops from North Africa across the narrow Strait of Gibraltar into a weak and divided Visigothic Christian Spain. Within months, the Muslim invaders captured the Christian center of Toledo in central Spain. Continuing their northern march, they were finally turned back 20 years later in southern France. They then consolidated their hold on Spain, ruled most of it without challenge for three centuries, and then slowly retreated under Christian attack over the centuries until the final defeat in 1492.

The Muslims called Spain *al-Andalus* (a name that survives as "Andalusia," the southern region of Spain). Although the colonists were Arabs from the Middle East, and Berbers and mixed Arab-Berbers from North Africa, Spaniards tended not to make distinctions but usually called them all Moors (*Moros*, in Spanish) or sometimes all Arabs.

In less than two centuries, al-Andalus was transformed from a distant outpost to a center of Islam. Its capital of Córdoba, which grew to a population of one million, soon had few rivals in power and wealth anywhere in the world. As Desmond Stewart wrote in his book *The Alhambra*, by the mid-8th century Córdoba was regarded as the "first true metropolis in the West since the fall of Rome." Exporting lustrous ceramics, intricate textiles, wools, silks, felts, linens, carved ivory and European slaves throughout the Muslim world, the city was challenged as a market only by Constantinople and Baghdad. Its librar-

ies and poets were celebrated. Sultan Abd al-Rahman I and his successors built the Great Mosque of Córdoba, an astounding work of architecture, to symbolize the political and religious power of al-Andalus. In 929, Abd al-Rahman III proclaimed himself a caliph, a successor to the Prophet Muhammad, thus assuming the same status as the rulers of Baghdad and Constantinople.

Within a century, however, the dynasty collapsed, and al-Andalus splintered into a cluster of petty kingdoms. Taking advantage of this weakness, the Spanish Christians in the north reconquered Toledo in 1085. The loss provoked the fearful kings into calling for help from a powerful and puritanical Muslim dynasty in North Africa. Two waves of Islamic zealots, the Almoravids and then the Almohads, ruled al-Andalus for 146 years, but their hold weakened under the pressure of the Christian armies in Spain and North African rivals in Morocco. When the Christians captured the Almohad capital of Seville in 1248, their chroniclers described the conquest as "one of the greatest and noblest that was ever . . . accomplished in the whole world."

Al-Andalus then found itself reduced to a mountainous domain in the southeastern corner of Spain, with 250 miles of coastline near North Africa. A succession of sultans from the Arab-descended Nasrid dynasty ruled this domain from Granada for 254 years. Perhaps because they were the last, perhaps because they built the Alhambra, the Nasrid sultans have been romanticized and celebrated by poets and novelists more than any other Islamic rulers of Spain.

For more than two centuries, the Nasrids staved off the Christians with a series of vassalage treaties continually signed and broken, and with a succession of skirmishes halted by truces. In fact, Boabdil, the last sultan, had received Christian help in his battles with his father and uncle for the throne, and had even sent congratulations to the Catholic Monarchs upon the defeat of his fellow Muslims at Málaga. But when the Christians began to devastate the farmlands that supplied Granada, Boabdil's forces attacked Christian fortresses. Ferdinand and Isabella then vowed to march onward without stopping until they placed a cross upon the towers of the Alhambra.

The Alhambra, which means "red citadel" in Arabic, takes its name from a fort that had been built from the red clay on the hill many years before. Looking for a stronghold in perilous times, the Nasrids had created a royal fortress city on this hill during the 14th century with palaces, enormous walls, formidable gates, military towers, a mosque, sumptuous gardens, and crowded residential and shopping streets for artisans and servants.

The Alhambra never fell in battle. Boabdil, facing certain defeat, negotiated a treaty of surrender with Ferdinand and Isabella, who pledged, falsely as it turned out, to allow their subjects to keep their Islamic faith and customs. According to legend, Boabdil, as he headed south into exile, looked back at Granada and the Alhambra and burst into tears. His mother, whose scheming had helped put Boabdil on the throne, told him with contempt, "You do well to weep like a woman for what you could not defend like a man."

It was a jubilant triumph for Christianity. The politically powerful Cardinal Mendoza of Spain carried the silver cross that Ferdinand had borne throughout the crusade and hoisted it upon the tower of the Alhambra fortress. An eyewitness wrote to the Bishop of León, "It was the most notable and blessed day that there ever was in Spain." In Rome, the bells of St. Peter's rang out as the pope and his cardinals led a solemn procession to celebrate high mass for the victory.

"A MOSLEM PILE IN A CHRISTIAN LAND"

Spain has no finer and more intact monument from the Islamic era than the Alhambra. Victor Hugo called it a "palace that the genies have gilded like a dream and filled with harmony." Washington Irving, who lived there for a few months, did more to popularize the Alhambra throughout the Western world than any other writer in the 19th century. He described it as a Moslem pile in the midst of a Christian land, an Oriental palace amidst the Gothic edifices of the West, an elegant memento of a brave, intelligent, and graceful people who conquered, ruled and passed away. A Spanish poet wrote of a blind beggar in Granada pleading with a woman leaving church, "Give me alms, my lady, for there is no worse affliction in life than to be blind in Granada."

Every year, 1.5 million people, half of them foreigners, visit the Alhambra. Of the six palaces, five of which perched on the escarpment overlooking Granada, two—the Palace of Comares and the Palace of the Lions—remain in almost pristine form. On walls and ceilings, swirls, strange geometric shapes, flowers, leaves, vines, acorns, shells and Arabic calligraphy twist in and out of one another. The patterns are sometimes symmetrical but, because of the calligraphy, often not. Most of the work has been done in stucco—plaster mixed from lime and earth—supplemented by ceramic tiles and carved cedar wood. Except for a few traces, mostly of blues, the once-polychrome stucco has lost its color, but the tiles bring color into every room.

Architecture and decoration are sometimes indistinguishable. Many of the rooms have ceilings fashioned with layers of hanging stucco stalactites; a visitor looking up has an illusion that the ceiling soars forever. Within the Palace of Comares' Hall of the Ambassadors, the sultan's reception room for envoys, every arched window frames a different view of Granada below. The magnificent Court of the Lions, with its famous fountain, is the inner patio of the Palace of the Lions that sultans used for relaxation and pleasure. Here, strolling among various arches and columns, one will see what seem like a dozen different patios.

The calligraphy on the walls of the Alhambra is so intricate that it is sometimes difficult to distinguish the Arabic script from the weaving vines and flowers. The motto of the Nasrid dynasty is repeated scores of times: "There is no conqueror but God." The simple prayers "Blessing" and "Happiness" can be found just as often. Nearby, at the library of the Renaissance palace that Charles V of Spain, the Holy Roman Emperor, built after the Reconquest, Emilia Jiménez is preparing her doctoral dissertation for the University of Granada. It is a study of the Arabic inscriptions of the Alhambra. Jiménez explained to me that several different subjects are treated. "You can find dynastic mottoes, brief prayers, quotations from the Koran, maxims, notes about the construction, instructive information, praises of the sultans, and poetry," she said.

"I AM THE GARDEN, I AWAKE ADORNED IN BEAUTY"

There are, in fact, 30 poems scattered throughout the palace and its grounds, poems often brimming with adulation for the Alhambra itself. "I am the garden, I awake adorned in beauty: Gaze on me well, know what I am like. . . . What a delight for the eyes! The patient man who looks here realizes his spiritual desires," sings 14th-century poet Ibn Zamrak in an inscription in one of the chambers surrounding the Court of the Lions.

It is surprising that so much of the Alhambra has been preserved for more than 600 years. When Washington Irving arrived in 1829, he reported that its palaces had been filled only a few years earlier "with a loose and lawless population—contrabandistas who . . . [carried] on a wide and daring course of smuggling; and thieves and rogues of all sorts. . . . It is difficult to believe that so much has survived the wear and tear of centuries, the shocks of earthquakes, the violence of war, and the quiet, though no less baneful, pilferings of the tasteful traveller." Irving concluded that Granadians could be right when they insisted that the Alhambra was "protected by a magic charm."

Preservation, however, probably owes more to the interest of the Spanish kings. In awe of its beauty, the monarchs designated the Alhambra as their royal residence in Granada. Although few of them actually spent time there, the status ensured funds for maintenance. But by the 18th century this royal interest had slackened. When Napoleon occupied Spain, his troops used the Alhambra as their barracks in Granada. Irving commended the French for repairing and restoring the Alhambra, even though the troops tried to dynamite all its towers before fleeing Granada in 1812. A daring Spanish soldier managed to cut the main fuse leading to the dynamite, but he could not prevent all damage. Partly in response to pleas from Irving, whose book *Legends of the Alhambra* achieved worldwide popularity, the Spanish kings resumed the funding of repairs and upkeep. In 1870, the Alhambra was declared a national monument with its maintenance assured by an annual appropriation from the government.

"As a result of this, we have been restoring the Alhambra all the time for 120 years," says Mateo Revilla Uceda, the 43-year-old former professor of art history who has been director of the Alhambra for the past five years. "But deterioration is not a major problem. There is no contamination at the Alhambra. And the climate is dry." The Alhambra seems to have benefited as well from the choice of material. "The main material of the Alhambra—stucco—is very flexible, but it is also very resistant," says Revilla Uceda. "All the decoration gives the material an illusion of richness."

The idea for the exhibition came out of a chance conversation five years ago between the Metropolitan's assistant director, Mahrukh Tarapor, and Spain's Minister of Culture, Javier Solana. Solana had come to the Met to see an exhibition of the paintings of Francisco de Zurbarán, which Tarapor had organized. After the opening, the minister asked her to take him through her favorite gallery in the museum. The Bombay-born Tarapor, a specialist in Islamic art, led Solana to the small Islamic rooms and told him there was so little space devoted to Islamic Spain because there still had not been enough study of this period. "Do you think the time is right for such study now?" Solana asked. "Would it be appropriate to prepare an exhibition on such art in Spain for 1992? Will you do it? Let's shake on it." Though somewhat surprised by this sudden proposal, Tarapor agreed to explore the idea.

The result is a rare look at the variety of the arts of al-Andalus. Newcomers to Islamic art sometimes feel that it all looks alike. There is an obvious reason for this. Islamic art tends not to strive for blatant novelty but to take familiar models and rework them with only subtle changes. Although it is not true, as many people believe, that the depiction of people and animals is forbidden in the Koran, much of Islamic art uses abstract patterns rather than realistic figures, and this tends to foster a mood of sameness. This seeming uniformity is reinforced as well by the heavy use of the Arabic script in design—a script that is familiar to most Muslims throughout the world. Yet, within this seeming uniformity, there are significant regional and epochal differences, which the Metropolitan exhibit makes clear.

Spain has a special place in Islamic art. The most striking features of the Great Mosque of Córdoba, for example, are the myriad double arches—one horseshoe arch perched on another—throughout its interior. This arrangement had been used before, but never to such startling effect. Spain's ceramic luster-ware (plates and tall Alhambra vases that shone and glittered, often in green and manganese colors), intricate silk textiles, and elaborately carved ivory boxes were widely acclaimed and sought. Many of the artworks of al-Andalus were luxury goods, reflecting the wealth and power of the succession of sultanates in Spain.

The stellar pieces in the exhibition include a 10th-century Cordoban pyxis on loan from the Louvre in Paris. A pyxis is an ivory box fashioned from the natural cylindrical shape of a tusk and probably used to hold gifts of ambergris, musk and camphor—aromatics used as cosmetics and medicines. This one is carved with a host of elaborate scenes, including one showing two horsemen, accompanied by cheetahs and birds, picking dates off a tree.

The exhibition also feature[d] a 15th-century steel sword with a carved ivory hilt that once belonged to Sultan Boabdil, a sword that is usually on display in the Museum of the Army in Madrid. The pieces from the Met's own Islamic collection include a fragment of a 14th-century silk textile with designs that look like the stuccowork of the Alhambra. The Hermitage in St. Petersburg has contributed an enormous, lustrous, 14th-century earthenware vase, four feet high, known as an "Alhambra vase." It has wings like flying buttresses against its neck and Arabic inscriptions calling for "pleasure" and "health" and "blessing." It is believed that the Nasrids placed vases like this throughout the Alhambra for no other function than decoration. With this cachet of royal chic, Alhambra vases were to become some of the most cherished exports from al-Andalus.

A novice to Spain might be surprised that the Spanish Christians allowed so much art to remain from a civilization that had been defeated in a religious crusade. "Christians didn't look down on Islamic art," said Jerrilynn Dodds. "They treated it as the latest fashion. Muslim textiles were so prized that the Christians wrapped relics in them. When Christians expelled the Muslims,

they turned the mosques into Christian churches."

At the Met, the exhibition include[d] a small part of the Alhambra itself—a part that has been missing from Granada for a century. In the 19th century, when governments were lackadaisical about their archaeological treasures, a German banker, Arthur Gwinner Dreiss, bought the Tower of the Ladies in one of the ramparts of the Alhambra. Before leaving Spain he sold the structure back, but he dismantled the wooden ceiling with its intricate geometric patterns and took it with him to Germany. It now belongs to the Museum of Islamic Art in the Berlin suburb of Dahlem, which is loaning the ceiling to the Met. Ironically, the ceiling that visitors to the Alhambra see in the Tower of the Ladies is a reproduction put up years ago.

The fall of Granada in 1492 did not end the story of Islam in Spain. Ferdinand and Isabella promised that the Muslims could continue practicing Islam in peace, but the promise was soon broken. Cardinal Francisco Jiménez de Cisneros ordered a campaign of forced conversion and mass baptism under threat of torture and prison. By 1500 he could report back to the Catholic Monarchs that "there is now no one in the city who is not a Christian, and all the mosques are churches." The converts were known as Moriscos.

But most Moriscos knew little about Christianity and kept to their Muslim ways while going to churches that were once mosques. The Inquisition sent its agents to Granada to punish the new Christians who were backsliding into Islamic heresy. Royal edicts banned Arabic customs: Moriscos couldn't use the Arabic language, especially to name their children. Women had to drop their veils. Even the public Arab baths were closed as dens of sin. In vain, a Morisco leader protested that these baths were used only for cleanliness; men and women were never allowed in at the same time. If sinful women wanted to meet their lovers, he said, "they would manage this more readily by going on social calls, or visiting churches, or going to religious festivities and plays where men and women were mixed up together."

BUYING UP MORISCO LAND AT BARGAIN RATES

In 1568 the desperate Moriscos rose in rebellion in the Alpujarra Mountains between Granada and the Mediterranean Sea. The Spaniards suppressed this uprising with great ferocity and brutality and, to make sure this would never happen again, forced most Moriscos to leave the Granada region and live elsewhere in Spain. Spaniards were invited to pour into Granada and buy up Morisco land at bargain rates. All this, however, did not solve what the Spaniards regarded as their "Morisco problem"—a large population of seemingly unchristian Christians. In 1609, Spain, claiming that this population might somehow become a fifth column for the Islamic Turks threatening Europe, decided to expel all its Moriscos, just as it had expelled all its Jews a little more than a century before. It is estimated that, within five years, 300,000 Moriscos were forced out of Spain. Perhaps 20,000, for one reason or another, managed to elude the expulsion order and remain.

They did not lose all their ways in a rural and provincial Spain that entered the modern age only a few decades ago. "When I grew up on the Almería coast, Martínez Soler told me, "there were women who wore veils and carried jugs of water on their heads. As late as 30 years ago, you could still see women with veils, even in church. Just a few years ago, I was the master of ceremonies at a music festival and was amazed at some of the songs of the people who came down from the Alpujarra Mountains. The words of their religious hymns were Catholic, but the music was Arabic."

Spaniards, in fact, are now proud that they did not wipe out all the traces of Islam. During a visit in 1986 to the unique cathedral that was created centuries ago out of the Great Mosque of Córdoba, King Juan Carlos, the successor to Ferdinand and Isabella in democratic Spain, said, "The light that shines upon us from the cathedral of Córdoba is neither moribund nor tremulous. It is intense, penetrating, illuminating the way. It represents the embrace of all the communities of the world."

How The West Saw Medieval Islam

Worthy opponents or agents of Antichrist? **Malcolm Barber** *on how Western Christendom viewed its Muslim adversaries.*

Since the Christians are not at peace with the Saracens, O Lord', wrote the Mallorcan Ramon Lull, in his *Book of Contemplation on God* in the early 1270s:

> . . . they dare not hold dis-cussions upon the faith with them when they are among them. But were they at peace together, they could dispute with each other peacefully concerning the faith, and then it would be possible for the Christians to direct and enlighten the Saracens in the way of truth, through the grace of the Holy Spirit and the true rea-sons that are signified in the perfection of Thy attributes.

Lull was a prolific writer on the subject of Christian rela-tions with the Muslim world; indeed, he can perhaps be seen as the most outstanding of the many crusade theo-rists who clamoured for at-tention in the late thirteenth and early fourteenth centu-ries. Not only was he the most original writer among them, but he was also the most active, both as author and missionary. It is not surprising to find that such a man did not manage to maintain consistency throughout a long career: in his later life, even he was to regard such peaceful approaches as impractical. Nevertheless, his view en-capsulates a basic truth about Christian-Muslim relations during this period.

Whatever the personal inclinations, ex-periences, or education of individuals, the fundamental fact that Western Chris-tendom and Islam were in the state of permanent war which Urban II had in-

Worlds apart: Christians and pagans point to their respective places of worship in this French illustration to Augustine's *City of God*. Echoes of the East are seen in the pagans' headdresses and the round roofs of their temple, topped significantly with a naked idol.

augurated in 1095 pervaded every Chris-tian perception of Islam throughout the twelfth and thirteenth centuries.

The First Crusade engendered a mass of writing from both participants and other commentators, who explained how Jerusalem had been captured in 1099 and why, in the years that followed, it

had been necessary to establish settle-ments to protect the holy places. The na-ture of Islam and the behaviour of its adherents inevitably formed a central feature of such work and, in these cir-cumstances, it can hardly be expected that it would be objective. Albert of Aachen was one of the most impor-tant of these commentators. He was a member of the Im-perial Collegiate Church in that city and an assiduous collector of stories about the First Crusade and the adven-tures of the early settlers in Palestine and Syria.

One of Albert's stories concerns the fate of a re-nowned French knight, Ger-vase of Bazoches, who had been granted the fief of Galilee by King Baldwin I. In the spring of 1108 Ger-vase and his men were cap-tured by Toghtekin, Atabeg of Damascus, and then of-fered to the king in ex-change for the cities of Acre, Haifa, and Tiberias. Baldwin told him that he was prepared to pay a large sum of money, but that he had no intention of giving up these cities, even 'if you were hold-ing in chains my own blood-brother and my entire family and all the leaders of the Christian people', much less for the life of a single man. Nevertheless, if Toghtekin did kill Gervase, he must ex-pect the Christians to exact retribution. Consequently, Albert continues, Gervase was brought out into the middle of the city of Damascus and after much mockery, shot to death with arrows:

> Soboas, one of the most powerful of the Turks, ordered his head to be cut off, and the skin of his head, with his hair which was white and abundant and had not been cut for a long time, to be pulled off and dried, because it was wonderfully ornamental and so that it might always be borne aloft on the tip of his spear, as a token and memorial of the victory and to stir up the grief of the Christians.

There is no reason to disbelieve Albert's story: there are numerous other examples of similar treatment of prisoners on both sides in the crusader era. This one is not exceptional other than in the rather bizarre way that the Turks chose to mark their victory.

The point is that Islam had to be presented as the enemy. Consequently, Muslim belief had to be disproved or mocked, and Muslim social behaviour distorted and denigrated. If the stories could be enlivened by an appeal to listeners' sexual prurience, then so much the better. All Western perceptions were affected by this context; even when a favourable view of specific Muslims appears it is presented in a manner which shows how the individual concerned overcame the disadvantages of such an alien upbringing, sometimes with the help of innate qualities derived from ancestors in which Latin blood could be discerned.

Albert's description of incidents such as the capture of a large number of noblewomen near Mersivan in Northern Asia Minor during the crusade of 1101, offered a golden opportunity for such fantasies. These women, abandoned by most of their male military protectors—who had apparently fled in panic—were either slaughtered (if unattractive) or carried off to harems in Khorasan where they were kept to satisfy the unbridled sexual appetites of the Turks.

In an earlier story, intended to show the extent of the crisis overcome by the armies of the First Crusade at the battle of Dorylaeum of July 1096, Albert presents the 'delicate and very nobly born' girls in the Christian camp as 'hastening to get themselves dressed up' so that the Turks, 'roused and appeased by love of their beautiful appearance', might spare them once the crusaders had been defeated. Two stereotypes—feminine moral

weakness and Turkish male libido—are neatly combined here, although the story of the defeat at Mersivan does little to strengthen a third, that of the innate chivalry of the Latin knight.

Although there was a common context, it was evident that an understanding of Islam and the Muslim world could take place at different levels. The anonymous author of the *Gesta Francorum*, who took part in the First Crusade, and whose text was extensively used by later writers, is among those nearest to popular belief. Most of his picture of Islam is based upon a series of imaginary conversations of Kerbogha, Atabeg of Mosul, who was defeated by the crusaders outside Antioch in June, 1098. Kerbogha, bombastic and overconfident before the battle, is depicted as writing a letter to what the author calls 'the khalif our pope and the lord sultan our king', in which he tells the Muslims of Khorasan:

> Enjoy yourselves, rejoicing with one accord, and fill your bellies, and let commands and injunctions be sent throughout the whole country that all men shall give themselves up to wantonness and lust, and take their pleasure in getting many sons who shall fight bravely against the Christians and defeat them.

The letter concludes:

> Moreover, I swear to you by Mohammed and by all the names of our gods that I will not appear again before your face until I have conquered, by the strength of my right arm, the royal city of Antioch and all Syria, Rum, Bulgaria and even as far as Apulia, to the glory of the Gods and of you and of all who are sprung from the race of the Turks.

This author's creative fantasies about the motivations and attitudes of the Muslims were not unique among the Normans, who appear to have had a penchant for such tales. In August, 1100, Bohemond of Taranto, who had been consolidating his hold on Antioch, seized in the course of the First Crusade, was captured by Malik-Ghazi, a Danishmend Turk who was emir of Sebastea, and imprisoned in the castle of Niksar in north-eastern Anatolia. He was not released until the spring of 1103, when King Baldwin of Jerusalem coordinated payment of a ransom of 100,000 be-

sants. However, sometime after 1106, Orderic Vitalis, the chronicler of St Evroult in Normandy, apparently using a contact he had among Bohemond's followers, wrote up the episode in the form of a romantic story in which Melaz, the beautiful and intelligent daughter of the emir, is presented as instrumental in obtaining Bohemond's release. No mention is made of any ransom.

According to Orderic, Melaz:

> ...loved the Franks passionately when she heard of their great feats, and was so eager to enjoy their company that often, after distributing liberal bribes to the guards, she would go down into the dungeon and engage in subtle discourse with the captives about the Christian faith and true religion, learning about it by constant discussion interspersed with deep sighs.

When war broke out between Malik-Ghazi and Kilij Arslan, the Seljuk sultan of Rum, she determined to test out the famed chivalry of the Franks by releasing Bohemond and his companions to fight on her father's side. Predictably, Bohemond plays a central role in the resulting defeat of Kilij Arslan. He does not, however, use the battle as an opportunity to escape, remaining loyal to his oath, sworn to Melaz, that he will return to the castle, where he is able to protect her from her father's wrath at what he regards as her treachery. In the key speech, Melaz informs her father that she has become a Christian. 'For the religion of the Christians is holy and honourable, and your religion is full of vanities and polluted with all filth'. Angry as he is, Malik-Ghazi accepts that he has little alternative but to negotiate, and Richard of the Principate, Bohemond's cousin, is sent to Antioch for this purpose. Here the situation is reversed. When Richard proposes an exchange of prisoners, the daughter of Yaghi-Siyan, the former governor of Antioch, is distraught. Asked why, she replies that:

> It was because in future she would not be able to eat the excellent pork that Christians eat. The Turks and many other Saracen peoples detest the flesh of pigs, although they eat with enjoyment the flesh of dogs and wolves, demonstrating in this way that they hold to the law neither of Moses nor of Christ, and are neither Jews nor Christians.

For her part, Melaz is baptised and marries Roger of Salerno, son of Richard of the Principate. Orderic's version of this story seems to be the earliest in the medieval Christian West, although the structure owes much to one of the stories in the *Arabian Nights*. Whatever its origin, thereafter, baptised Muslim princesses, beautiful and noble, and wise enough to see the errors of the society and religion of their birth, become as much part of the popular image of the Muslims as the boastful emir who foolishly relies upon the fickle support of his own false gods.

While such stories have much in common with twelfth-century *chansons de geste* and it may be that the audience was not expected to take them entirely seriously, they are nevertheless consistent with more educated views which present a more systematic picture of the role of Islam as part of the working out of a divine plan. It was inconceivable that God should actually approve of the possession of the holy places by the Muslims: therefore His purpose must be to activate faithful Christians. Fulcher of Chartres, who was initially attached to the armies led by Stephen of Blois and Robert of Normandy on the First Crusade, may have been present at Clermont. His version of the speech of Urban II was that it was the duty and obligation of able-bodied Christians to rescue the holy places from desecration and pollution at the hands of barbaric races in the grip of the pernicious teachings of Mohammed. According to him, the pope had taxed his audience with the disgrace which would befall them 'if a race so despicable, degenerate, and enslaved by demons should thus overcome a people endowed with faith in Almighty God and resplendent in the name of Christ'. God himself would reproach them if they failed to help fellow Christians, now conquered by the 'vile race' of the Turks.

Urban presented the Turks as usurpers of what he called 'our lands', a belief which Fulcher confirmed from his own experience in Jerusalem where, in what he calls the Temple of the Lord (that is the Dome of the Rock on the Temple platform), the Muslims had 'preferred to say the prayers of their faith, although such prayers were wasted because offered to an idol set up in the name of Mohammed'. Once in Christian hands however, the Rock—'which disfigured the Temple of the Lord'—was covered over with marble on which the crusaders placed an altar.

Fulcher's view is not an isolated one. All the chroniclers who participated in the First Crusade maintained that Muslim occupation had resulted in the pollution of the holy places and the persecution of God's faithful.

Once the news of the capture of Jerusalem reached the West, several monastic writers set themselves the task of explaining what had taken place. Two of them—Guibert, abbot of the small house of Nogent, near Laon, and William, a monk at Malmesbury abbey in Wiltshire—had certainly read Fulcher and were influenced by him, but at the same time they were concerned to place the events in a wider historical perspective, which meant some consideration of the nature of Islam itself. Both tried to research the matter to the best of their ability and resources, although neither could transcend the contemporary context of hostility towards Islam.

Guibert's work presented a picture of a religion founded by an epileptic, who was exploited by both the devil and by a renegade Christian hermit. Guided by the hermit, Mohammed produced the Koran, the chief message of which was the encouragement of sexual promiscuity. They persuaded the people that the message had come from Heaven, although in fact it had been brought on the horns of a cow, trained for the purpose. Mohammed's death came about as a result of his epilepsy:

> . . . it happened once, while he was walking about alone, that he was struck by the illness in that place and fell down. While tormented by this suffering, he was found by pigs and so badly torn to pieces that no remains of him were found except his ankles.

William of Malmesbury rejected the popular conception of Muslims as idolaters and, to some extent, succeeded in placing Islam within the context of Jewish and Christian history. In his *Commentary on Lamentations* (written *c* 1136), he says that the Slav peoples "to this day breathe out only pagan superstitions about all matters', but that 'the Saracens and Turks devote themselves to God the Creator, believing Mohammed not to be a God but their prophet'. Moreover, although the Christians, Saracens and Jews have contending opinions about the Son, 'nevertheless all both believe in the heart and confess in the mouth in God the Father, Creator of things'.

However, William's grasp of these points did nothing to mitigate the severity of his condemnation of Muslim usurpation of the holy places. In his *Deeds of the Kings of England,* William's account of the pope's speech emphasises the way Muslims insolently controlled most of the world, including Asia, where 'the shoots of our devotion first sprouted' and which all but two of the apostles 'consecrated' with their deaths. 'There in our time the Christians, if there are any left, suffering starvation from an impoverished agriculture, pay tribute to these abominable people, and with inward sighs, long for the experience of our liberty, since they have lost their own'. Muslim occupation of Africa was damaging to Christian honour, since it had been the home of St Augustine and other distinguished Church Fathers. Even Europe, 'the third part of the world', was under threat, since for 300 years the Muslims had held Spain and the Balearics.

Whatever the level of understanding of individual writers there was no escape from this context of conflict. In this sense there was little change in attitudes until the crises of the late thirteenth century began to encourage men like Ramon Lull to consider alternatives to violence, but even he, fighting against the tide of crusading polemic, was unable to sustain this position for very long. This is not surprising. Contemporaneously with William of Malmesbury, the great Bernard of Clairvaux had lent his support to the view that the Muslims had no right to occupy the holy places of the Christians. Those who failed to understand this deserved their fate. In his treatise *In Praise of the New Knighthood,* he presented the Templars as moved by the example of Christ, who had driven the moneychangers out of the Temple:

> The devoted army, doubtless judging it far more intolerable for the holy places to be polluted by the infidel than infested by merchants, remain in the holy house with horses and arms, driving forth from this place, as from all holy places, the filthy and tyrannical madness of infidelity.

By the thirteenth century, such perceptions of Islam were being placed within an apocalyptic structure, strengthened in the course of the century by the increasing interest in the prophecies of the eccentric Cistercian abbot, Joachim of

Fiore, who had died in 1202. In a striking passage in his crusading bull, *Quia Maior* (April 1213), Pope Innocent III set Islam within the Christian concept of historical time:

> The Christian peoples, in fact, held almost all the Saracen provinces up to the time of Blessed Gregory; but since then a son of perdition has arisen, the false prophet Mohammed, who has seduced many men from the truth by worldly enticements and the pleasures of the flesh. Although his treachery has prevailed up to the present day, we nevertheless put our trust in the Lord who has already given us a sign that good is to come, that the end of this beast is approaching, whose *number,* according to the Revelation of St John, will end in 666 years, of which already nearly 600 have passed.

In the midst of all this belligerence there were no students of the sociology of comparative religion, but there was one man who made a genuine attempt to understand Islam. This was Peter the Venerable, Abbot of Cluny, who, in 1142, in the course of a journey to Spain, commissioned translators to provide him with five important Islamic works, including the Koran. At Nájera he met Robert of Ketton, Hermann of Dalmatia, Peter of Toledo and, said Peter the Venerable, in order that nothing should be omitted or hidden from him, 'a Saracen' whose name was Mohammed. These men appear to have begun work even before Peter had completed his Spanish journey. Among the translations were Ketton's version of the Koran completed in 1143, and Peter of Toledo's rendering of an Arabic work, the *Apologia for Christianity* of al-Kindi, which the abbot said informed him of many things of which he had previously been ignorant.

Armed with these materials, Peter was able to compose both a concise handbook which explained Islamic beliefs as he understood them (*Compendium of all the Heresies of the Saracens*) and a treatise intended to prove the errors of Islam (*Book against the Sect or Heresy of Islam*). He hoped (in the end fruitlessly) that Bernard of Clairvaux would take up the cause of refuting what he regarded as the only heresy to which the faithful had not made proper reply, despite the fact that it had brought almost limitless confusion to the human race. Even Peter the Venerable, however, was prepared to give vigorous support to the crusades when the occasion seemed to demand it, so it does appear that the protestations of peaceful intent with which he prefaces his polemic against the Saracens were intended for a Muslim rather than a Christian audience.

If the major formative influence upon the Western views of Islam in the twelfth and thirteenth centuries was that of confrontation, both physical and intellectual, it did not always follow that the contact which this brought produced an entirely negative conclusion. Admiration of their fighting qualities and indeed chivalry was not unknown among those who actually did battle with the Turks. Here, there is an interesting contrast between William of Malmesbury, who probably never met a Muslim, and the author of the *Gesta Francorum* who experienced the bitter years of the First Crusade.

William professed to believe that Urban II had described the Turks as favouring a manner of warfare based upon swift flight, as a consequence of both lack of courage and thinness of blood. It was apparent to William that:

> ... every race, born in that region, dried out by the excessive heat of the sun, has indeed more discretion but less blood; and thus they retreat from fighting at close quarters, because they know that they do not have enough blood.

Not so the Franks, who as a people originating in the more temperate provinces of the world could afford to be more prodigal of blood. The author of the *Gesta* was under no such illusions, however:

> What man, however experienced or learned, would dare to write of the skill and prowess of the Turks, who thought that they would strike terror into the Franks, as they had done into the Arabs and Saracens, Armenians, Syrians and Greeks, by the menace of their arrows?

For many crusaders, they were certainly preferable to the Greeks. Odo of Deuil, the St Denis chronicler, who blamed the Byzantines for the failure of the Second Crusade, was pleased to draw lessons following a battle with the Turks near Adalia:

> By the blood of these soldiers the Turks' thirst was quenched and the Greeks' treachery was transformed into violence, for the Turks returned to see the survivors and then gave generous aims to the sick and the poor, but the Greeks forced the stronger Franks into their service and beat them by way of payment.

Far fewer Westerners actually lived in a Muslim society, but one who did was the Dominican missionary, Ricoldo da Monte Croce, who was in Baghdad in 1291 when Acre fell to the Mamluks. The very nature of his profession of course made any religious accommodation impossible, for he shared many of the assumptions of his Christian contemporaries, but he is fulsome in his praise of the personal conduct of the Muslims he met and observed in Baghdad, and does not miss the opportunity to point up Christian moral deficiencies in contrast. Neither the author of the *Gesta* at the end of the eleventh century, nor Ricoldo da Monte Croce two centuries later, would have conceded that Muslims could in any way be 'right', but they do show that even in the midst of the crusades observation sometimes modified stereotyping.

FOR FURTHER READING

Matthew Bennett, 'First Crusaders' Images of Muslims: The Influence of Vernacular Poetry?' *Forum for Modern Language Studies,* 22 (1986); Peny Cole, '"O God, the Heathen have come into your inheritance" (Ps. 78.1). The Theme of Religious Pollution in Crusade Documents, 1095–1188," in *Crusaders and Muslims in Twelfth-Century Syria,* ed. M. Shatzmiller (E.J. Brill. 1993); Norman Daniel, *Islam and the West. The Making of an Image* (Edinburgh University Press, 1960); Benjamin Z. Kedar, *Crusade and Mission. European Approaches toward the Muslims* (Princeton University Press, 1984); James Kritzeck, *Peter the Venerable and Islam* (Princeton University Press, 1964); Richard Southern, *Western Views of Islam in the Middle Ages* (Harvard University Press, 1962); Rodney Thomson, *William of Malmesbury* (Boydell and Brewer, 1987).

The quotations from Albert of Aachen's *Historia* are from the draft translation by Susan Edgington. The text will be published in the Oxford Medieval Texts series in 1998.

Malcolm Barber *is Professor of History at the University of Reading and the author of* The New Knighthood *(Cambridge University Press, 1994). He is currently writing a history of the Cathars.*

Monsters and Christian Enemies

Debra Higgs Strickland *examines the extraordinary demonology of medieval Christendom and the way it endowed strangers and enemies with monstrous qualities.*

WESTERN MEDIEVAL CHRISTIANS saw many monsters, both living and imaginary. Although very real to believers, demons and the elusive 'Monstrous Races' did not really exist; but Jews, Muslims, Mongols, and Black Africans—all deemed 'monstrous' by the Christian majority—actually did. But not every monster was necessarily bad; holy persons and even God himself were sometimes represented as 'monsters'. Highlighting what these disparate groups had in common from the Christian viewpoint helps explain what being a 'monster' meant in the later Middle Ages.

The imaginary Monstrous Races may be defined as malformed, malcontented and misbehaving creatures believed to inhabit the periphery of the known world, primarily India, Ethiopia, and the far North. The race of *Panotii,* for example, whose name means 'all ears', were believed to possess ears so large they could sleep in them. The *Cynocephali,* or Dogheads, communicated only by barking. The *Blemmyai* were headless and had their faces on their chests. The *Sciopods,* although one-legged, were very swift and used their single large feet as parasols.

Much of the lore concerning the Monstrous Races was inherited and expanded during the Middle Ages from classical Greek sources, especially Pliny's *Natural History.* We know from medieval sources such as the *Book of Monsters* and the *Marvels of the East* that the Monstrous Races were elusive, either very aggressive or very shy, and often cannibalistic. Their truly unifying feature, however, was their physical abnormality, which may be explained through recourse to various ancient scientific theories, attributable to Hippocrates and Galen, among others. For example, application of climatic theory suggests that the Monstrous Races were physically abnormal owing to the hostile climates they lived in, as harsh environmental conditions were believed to affect physical form in adverse ways. Or, if one follows the implications of classical physiognomical theory, which states that external appearance is a visual manifestation of inner character, the Monstrous Races were malformed owing to their various moral shortcomings.

In fact, it was the 'Christianisation' of physiognomical theory that inspired many interpretations of the Monstrous Races by medieval moralists, who recognised their potential as effective symbolic vehicles. In collections of moralised tales, such as the *Gesta Romanorum* and other *exempla* used in medieval sermons, the particular physical deformity of a given race is interpreted under the assumption that it signified a particular sin or moral shortcoming. For example, the *Panotii* were said to use their huge ears to hear evil, while barking Dogheads were compared to bad preachers. The *Blemmyae,* with their heads on their chests, were compared to gluttons; and Pygmies who fought cranes were said to be 'short' with respect to a good life.

Not all of the Monstrous Races were interpreted as signs of vice; in certain contexts, some were viewed as signs of virtue. Hence, the sheltering foot of the *Sciopod* was the virtue of love, which allows swift gains in the heavenly kingdom. The sharp-shooting *Maritimi* had one each of his four eyes on God, the world, the devil, and the flesh; in order to live rightly, flee the world, resist the devil, and mortify the flesh.

> *Like the Monstrous Races, devils were considered aggressive, murderous and malformed.*

No roster of medieval monsters would be complete without demons, arguably the most well-developed concept of evil and moral bankruptcy ever devised. Images and descriptions of demons reinforced the medieval Christian belief that once Lucifer was kicked out of heaven for his excessive pride, he transmogrified permanently into the dark and hideous Satan and relentlessly sought revenge for his lost status by seducing and destroying human souls with the aid of his numberless minions.

Like the Monstrous Races, devils were considered aggressive, murderous and malformed, but they were not especially elusive. On the contrary: they were always around and eager to snare the souls of good Christians. The thought of encountering an angry, club-wielding *Blemmyae* doubtless inspired fear, but being captured by the devil was a much graver threat, as this might well result in eternal torture and suffering in hell.

Such was the threat posed by demons for St Guthlac, according to Felix's eighth-century *Life of St Guthlac,* as illustrated in the thirteenth-century Guthlac Roll. In an especially harrowing episode, the saint is seized by bestial demons, who torture him and attempt to hurl him into the menacing hellmouth below. The Guthlac Roll artist was clearly inspired by Felix's wonderfully lurid description of demon physiognomy:

> For they were ferocious in appearance, terrible in shape with great heads, long necks, thin faces, yellow complexions, filthy beards, shaggy ears, wild foreheads, fierce eyes, foul mouths, horses' teeth, throats vomiting flames, twisted jaws, thick lips, strident voices, singed hair, fat cheeks, pigeon breasts, scabby thighs, knotty knees, crooked legs, swollen ankles, splay feet, spreading mouths, raucous cries.
>
> For they grew so terrible to hear with their mighty shriekings that they filled almost the whole intervening space between earth and heaven with their discordant bellowings.

In the image, note the contrast between the grotesque devils with the elegant beauty of St Guthlac and St Bartholomew (who is handing his fellow saint a scourge for self-defence). In many artistic and literary contexts, just as distorted physical form signifies moral corruption, beautiful form signifies divine virtue.

So much for imaginary monsters. What of actual living groups also characterised as 'monstrous'? Black Africans, or 'Ethiopians', are one such group. Ethiopians were considered one of the Monstrous Races and are described alongside the *Blemmyai* and *Sciopods* in medieval sources. The Ethiopians are distinguishable in pictorial imagery by what appear to be the naturalistic physiognomical features of dark skin, tightly curled hair, thick lips, and broad noses. A dark blue Ethiopian shooting an arrow at a white Sciopod in

the margins of the thirteenth-century Rutland Psalter gives a good idea of this physical type.

Interestingly, Ethiopians were often idealised as a pious and 'blameless' people in the writings of the ancient Greeks, such as Homer. But in European Christian eyes, Ethiopians were monstrous principally owing to their black skin, which was considered a demonic feature. Black was a colour associated with evil, sin, and the devil, especially in patristic writings. For example, in another vivid Christian application of the physiognomical theory, St Jerome stated that Ethiopians will lose their blackness once they are admitted to the New Jerusalem, meaning that their external appearance will change once they become morally perfect.

On a far less spiritual plane, black African physiognomical features were considered ugly by white European Christians, who often compared black people to apes or demons. For example, Marco Polo, writing near the end of the thirteenth-century, had only this to say of the inhabitants of Zanzibar:

> They are quite black and go entirely naked except that they cover their private parts. Their hair is so curly that it can scarcely be straightened out with the aid of water. They have big mouths and their noses are so flattened and their lips and eyes so big that they are horrible to look at. Anyone who saw them in another country would say they were devils.

Marco's description points up the fact that in addition to physiognomical strangeness, another characteristic of the monstrous outsider is a lack of civilisation, expressed often in pictorial art and narrative descriptions by nudity or scanty dress. Ethiopians, like many of the other Monstrous Races, are often depicted wearing loincloths or less, as a sign of their extreme barbarity.

Another aspect of Ethiopians that condemned them as monstrous was their habitat. During the Middle Ages, Ethiopia was more of an idea than an actual place. It was generally considered a marvellous region whose flora, fauna, and inhabitants were aberrant, strange, and fearful, and was positioned at the edges of the earth on many of the world maps. Ethiopians therefore took on the characteristics of their exotic landscape, especially prior to contact between black Africans and Latin missionaries in

the thirteenth and fourteenth centuries. There were hardly any black Africans living in Europe before the twelfth century, which left Europeans free to formulate the nature of Ethiopians almost entirely in the abstract.

In medieval parlance, the term, 'monster' was also applied specifically to non-Christians, all of whom shared a common monstrous flaw; the failure to embrace the true Christian faith. So even though they possessed an extremely well-developed set of monotheistic beliefs which provided the infrastructure for Christianity itself, the Jews were viewed as idol-worshipping, demonic pagans, principally owing to the Christian conviction that they were responsible for the death of Christ.

The thirteenth-century *Salvin Hours* contains typically monstrous portrayals of Jews in a representation of Christ before Caiaphas, the high priest. The Jews are instantly recognizable from their grotesque physiognomy, featuring dark skin, hooked noses, and evil grimaces. Some also wear pointed caps, which in this type of image have pejorative associations.

A representation of the betrayal and flagellation of Christ in the twelfth-century *Winchester Psalter* emphasises the depravity and physical ugliness of the Jews. In addition, the Black African physiognomy of one of Christ's tormentors indicates that by this time, Ethiopians functioned as general figures of evil, and found their place in works of art alongside Jews as co-representatives of moral depravity.

The conventional Christian line on the Jews—that as the killers of Christ, all Jews are forever damned—fuelled paranoid accusations of ritual murder, blood libel, and plots to overthrow Christendom made against Jews throughout the later Middle Ages, especially in England, France, and Germany. It also provided useful ideological ammunition for those whose hatred of Jews stemmed from economic conflicts. Many ecclesiastics, kings, and Christian merchants were indebted to and dependent upon Jewish moneylenders for funding important political and social projects, from the building of churches and monasteries to the financing of the Crusades. When the borrowers had to default on their loans, they blamed the Jews for their misfortune, and condemned them as 'usurers', claiming that to profit from money-lending was a grave sin. This helps to explain why later medieval images of Jews not only represent them as physically ugly but also sometimes show them clutching money-bags.

Pejorative images of Jews abound not only in illuminated manuscripts but also in public art, including monumental sculpture, wall painting, stained glass, and liturgical objects. It may be assumed, therefore, that nearly everyone saw this imagery, which formed part of a much larger literary, political, and theological propaganda campaign designed to discredit both Jews and Judaism. Anti-Jewish sentiment culminated in the actual physical expulsion of the Jews: from England in 1290; from France in 1306, 1322 and 1394; from Spain in 1492; and from many German principalities and towns during the later Middle Ages. Jews were also expelled from Italy towards the end of this period: by the mid-1500s, there were practically no Jews left in western Europe.

The Jews were not the only threat to Christendom. During the period of the Crusades, other groups were also targets of Christian hatred, mainly the Muslims, who opposed the Crusaders' attempts to regain control of the Holy Land. Muslims are referred to as 'Saracens' in medieval sources. Like the Jews, Saracens were viewed (with equal error) as idol-worshippers, or as heretics. The Prophet Muhammad was declared an agent of Satan, a precursor of Antichrist, or—as Pope Innocent III asserted—Antichrist himself.

The destruction of the Saracens fits conveniently into the larger Christian notion of Holy War, which maintained that knights could redeem their sins and help to bring about the triumph of Christianity by crushing the pagan infidel. Consequently, Saracens are often depicted as pagan devils and monstrous, archenemies of Christendom in works of art and literature, such as the *Song of Roland* and other *chansons de geste*. Like the Ethiopians, Saracens are often described as black, and sometimes they are also repellent giants. They typically demonstrate very loose morals and evoke their pagan gods on the battlefield.

A depiction of Saracens warring against Christian knights from a fourteenth-century copy of the *Romance of Godefroi* again reveals the consistency with which Christian artists portrayed non-Christian enemies with distorted physiognomy and dark skin as a sign of

their rejected status. The Saracens in this image are identifiable by their characteristic headbands. Their shields and trappers feature profile Ethiopian heads and wild boars, which to contemporary viewers were equally evocative of wild savagery.

However, not all Saracens were portrayed as ugly and demonic in the *chansons de geste*. In fact, many Saracens were lauded for their military heroism and even their physical good looks. Tellingly, however, these 'good' Saracens inevitably converted at the end, thereby explaining their virtue and beauty as latently Christian. Conversely, however, the ugly, evil, and unconverted ones were always slain, as a symbol of the ultimate failure of non-Christian religions and perhaps also as anominous warning to their adherents.

An even more terrifying political enemy were the 'Tartars', a pejorative term referring to the combined central Asian peoples, especially the Mongols, who overran much of Asia and eastern Europe during the thirteenth-century. The Tartars were dreaded owing to their shocking ruthlessness in war. Slaughtering Christians and Muslims alike, they ranked among the most thoroughly monstrous of contemporary Christian enemies. In his *Chronica majora*, Matthew Paris gives a vivid, albeit embellished, contemporary account of the Tartar ravages of 1240:

> The Tartar chief, with his dinner guests and other [cannibals], fed upon their carcasses as if they were bread and left nothing but the bones for the vultures. . . .
>
> The old and ugly women were given to the cannibals . . . as their daily allowance of food; those who were beautiful were not eaten, but were suffocated by mobs of ravishers in spite of all their cries and lamentations. Virgins were raped until they died of exhaustion; then their breasts were cut off to be kept as dainties for their chiefs, and their bodies furnished an entertaining banquet for the savages. . . .
>
> [The Tartars] have hard and robust chests, lean and pale faces, rigid and erect shoulders, short and distorted noses; their chins are sharp and prominent, the upper jaw low and deep, the teeth long and few; their eyebrows grow from the hairline to the nose, their eyes are shifty and black, their countenances oblique and fierce, their extremities bony and

nervous, their legs thick but short below the knee. . . .

In this passage and in the accompanying image, the Tartars are maligned in the traditional way, as physiognomically distorted, vicious, cannibalistic savages.

As they moved across eastern Europe during 1240s, the Tartars unleashed such horrors that they became identified with Gog and Magog, the ferocious, monstrous hordes described in the biblical Apocalypse. According to medieval legend, Gog and Magog were locked up by Alexander the Great behind a gate in the Caspian Mountains. But at the end of time, Gog and Magog were expected to burst forth from behind the gate, and under the leadership of Antichrist, unleash a mighty attack on all of Christendom.

Not all monsters represented enemies of the Church; some represented its most sacred membership.

By the thirteenth century, Alexander's Gate functioned as a handy ideological vehicle to enclose not only Gog and Magog, but also contemporary enemies of the Church. In a complex geneaological manoevre, the tradition of the Ten Lost Tribes of Israel was merged with the idea of Gog and Magog, from whom it was said that the Tartars themselves claimed descent. Medieval artists had further expanded the concept of Gog and Magog to incorporate even the Monstrous Races. That Gog and Magog, Jews, Tartars, Ethiopians, and other Monstrous Races were all at various times locked up behind Alexander's Gate points up another important element of the medieval view of monsters: the desire to isolate and to contain them.

Not all monsters represented despised enemies of the Church; some actually represented its most sacred membership. One especially impressive example is an image of the Trinity, prefigured in the Old Testament episode of

Abraham before the three angels, depicted in a thirteenth-century English psalter. If monstrosity signifies moral degeneracy and evil in medieval thought, then what can we make of this image? On the one hand, a three-headed Trinity is a creative means of visualising the doctrine of the simultaneous unity and separate aspects of the Godhead, as well as the idea of Three Persons of equal rank (although the centre head differentiated by the orange halo does suggest a measure of primacy). But in spite of its conventional theological meaning, this type of image was somewhat problematic precisely because the visual result was monstrous—a bit too closely related to portraits of Cerberus, for example.

Besides the Trinity, other revered Christian figures were represented with monstrous features during the later Middle Ages. For example, according to the eastern version of his legend, St Christopher originally was a Doghead. He was known as Reprobus before his conversion to Christianity, and was identified as a Giant of the Race of *Cynocephali.* Dogheaded St Christopher portraits are fairly common in Byzantine art, but in the West there is only one known example. But even without his dog head, St Christopher was never entirely dissociated from the Monstrous Races, in that he was almost always depicted as a Giant, often carrying the Christ child across a river. Giants were a very popular Monstrous Race who are characterised in the Old Testament and in later medieval commentaries as wholly evil. How is it, then, that one of the most popular of medieval saints was identified with two known monsters of such bad repute?

Clearly, a broad definition of medieval monstrosity is required in order to accommodate its application to both the holiest of Christian figures and the worst enemies of the Church. Apropos the enemies, most of the written and pictorial sources examined here reveal that a monster is a metaphor for unacceptability. More specifically, in certain contexts, a monster represented the antithesis of the Christians' view of themselves, which means that descriptions and images of the Monstrous Races, demons, Ethiopians, Jews, Muslims, and Tartars clarified by negative example what it meant to be a good Christian. This was done by attributing to the monsters those traits considered most abhorrent to Christians, such as idolatry, savagery, cannibalism, and rejection of Christ. This theory also has a flip-side, which is the possibility that this type of monster, based as it was on a perversion of good Christian values, was also an expression of what could go wrong with the faith. For example, it is possible that the fear of Christian conversion to Judaism or to Islam helped motivate Christian theologians and artists to portray these groups as monstrous and as rejected by God.

Monstrous portrayals of Christian divinities are quite puzzling given that monstrosity was such a familiar way of characterising non-Christian outcasts. But the fact that the holiest of figures are sometimes rendered as monsters casts doubt on the notion that monstrosity is necessarily a negative state. That is, it is clear that some of the same visual signs used to denote monstrosity in a negative sense can also be used to convey notions of virtue or even divinity. In these cases, the monster must be considered something positive, a visual metaphor for holiness. This theory might explain the portrayals of a Giant or dog-headed St Christopher, or of a three-headed Trinity. In the latter case, monstrosity is also a way of signaling the entirely different substance of God himself. During the later Middle Ages,

other monstrous depictions of holy figures may be observed, such as St John the Baptist 'wildmen' and Ethiopian magi or priests. That monstrous features can be signs of divinity accords very well with the strain of medieval moralisation that interprets the physical abnormalities of the Monstrous Races as signs of virtues rather than vices. In the end, investigating the problem of monstrosity highlights what is perhaps the only consistent feature of symbology in medieval art and literature: its inconsistency, and it also underscores the medieval love of the duality believed to be inherent in any given idea.

FOR FURTHER READING:

R. Mellinkoff, Outcasts: *Signs of Otherness in Northern European Art of the Late Middle Ages* (University of California Press, 1993); J.B. Friedman, *The Monstrous Races in Medieval Art and Thought* (Harvard University Press, 1981); R.M. Wright, *Art and Antichrist in Medieval Europe* (University of Manchester Press, 1995); J. Devisse and M. Mollat, *The Image of the Black in Western Art: From the Early Christian Era to the "Age of Discovery"* (Menil Foundation, 1979); K.R. Stow, *Alienated Minority: The Jews of Medieval Latin Europe* (Harvard University Press, 1992); M.C. Jones, *'The Conventional Saracen of The Songs of Geste'*, Speculum, 17 (1942); J.J. Saunders, *'Matthew Paris and the Mongols'*, in *Essays in Medieval History Presented to Berrie Wilkinson,* ed. T.A. Sandquist and M.R. Powicke (University of Toronto Press, 1969).

Dr Debra Higgs Strickland is Visiting Lecturer in the Department of Fine Art, University of Edinburgh.

Women Pilgrims of the Middle Ages

'There's no discouragement
Shall make him once relent
His first avowed intent
To be a pilgrim.'

Women, however, endured vexations of their own as **Diana Webb** *outlines.*

Do you not realise you are a woman and cannot go just anywhere?' with these words, the holy man Abba Arsenius, somewhere around the beginning of the fifth century, rebuked 'a very rich and God-fearing virgin of senatorial rank' from Rome who had sought him out in his Egyptian solitude. His anxiety was on his own account, not on hers: 'it is through women that the enemy wars against the Saints'. He conjured up a nightmare vision that she would encourage her Roman sisters to 'turn the sea into a thoroughfare with women coming to see me'. Pious women were in this period indeed eagerly engaged in pilgrimages, which often combined visiting the Holy Places with seeking out prominent holy men. Arsenius was not alone in feeling that God-fearing virgins should be discouraged from this inappropriate mobility and encouraged to gratify their ascetic impulses in seclusion. It was a sentiment with a big future.

However popular pilgrimage became in the medieval centuries, and however meritorious it was generally believed to be, it was never officially regarded as indispensable to salvation. This of course made it easier to forbid it to certain Christians, and from its earliest days it was the object of criticism. This tended to focus on two issues which frequently became inextricably intertwined. On the one hand, the idea that

the holy could be found concentrated in particular places was thought to contradict the essentially spiritual nature of Christianity; on the other, gadding about to shrines could easily degenerate into mere tourism or worse, a spiritually aimless wandering affording opportunity for all sorts of immorality away from the eyes of neighbours and superiors.

In principle these criticisms applied to pilgrimage undertaken by men and women alike. What came to be the standard version of the religious life in the West, Benedictine monasticism, enjoined stability on both monks and nuns. St Benedict's well-known denunciation of wandering monks amounted to a rejection of a conception of pilgrimage which had taken root especially among Celtic Christians: the perpetual uprooting of the self from familiar surroundings into penitential wandering, possibly lifelong and not always directed to particular shrines. To judge from the words of an Irish female recluse to St Columbanus, some time around 560, women who sought perfection within this tradition were aware of some limitations:

I, too, as far as I have been able have gone out to war. It is fifteen years since I left my home and sought out this place of pilgrimage . . . and if my fragile sex had not stood in the way, I would have crossed the sea and

sought out a place of more fitting pilgrimage.

Did the words 'fragile sex' denote moral or physical weakness, or both?

It certainly became the orthodox view that stability and seclusion were particularly vital to female religious, and it followed that they should be debarred from pilgrimage as from other excuses to leave the cloister. Not all women were nuns, however. Did the belief that women could not 'go about as they pleased' influence later attitudes to the practice of pilgrimage by laywomen?

It might justly be contended that neither men nor women were often totally free to go as they pleased in the Middle Ages. Few were exempt from the supervisory power of social or ecclesiastical superiors. Monks, like nuns, were bound to seek permission to leave the cloister. The male serf was no less securely tied to the soil than his womenfolk; Richard II's government tried to prevent both male and female serfs from leaving their appointed places 'by colour of pilgrimage'. Noble men and ladies were well-advised to seek licence and safe-conduct from their rulers if they wished to travel abroad. It is against this background that any greater degree of reserve about female freedom of movement has to be assessed, and we need also to ask exactly from what roots it grew. Did wan-

This article first appeared in *History Today,* July 1998, pp. 20-26. © 1998 by History Today, Ltd. Reprinted by permission.

dering women pose a moral and spiritual threat principally to men or to themselves? Was there, perhaps, concern that because they were more vulnerable to physical danger while travelling, they inevitably imposed a burden of responsibility and protection on men? It may of course be difficult to disentangle these lines of thought; and one man's views might be ambivalent.

In 747, St Boniface wrote to Cuthbert, Archbishop of Canterbury, advising him to take steps to prevent 'matrons and veiled women' from making frequent pilgrimages to Rome. 'There are very few towns in Lombardy or Frankland or Gaul' he wrote, 'where there is not a courtesan or a harlot of English stock. It is a scandal and a disgrace to your whole church.' It has been suggested that this letter shows Boniface changing his mind about the desirability of female pilgrimage. Some years earlier he had written to the Abbess Eadburga, refusing to take it upon himself to advise her for or against a pilgrimage to Rome, but quoting with approval the words of 'our sister Wiethburga', who had found peace of mind at the shrine of St Peter. We know from a letter of King Aethelberht II of Kent that Eadburga in fact made her pilgrimage and met Boniface himself at Rome, perhaps in 745 when he attended a council there. Does the letter to Archbishop Cuthbert, only a few years later, indicate sudden misgivings Boniface had not felt earlier? Or was he neither the first nor the last man in recorded history to express generalised doubts about women which he did not feel about individuals who were well known to him?

Boniface identifies two classes of women, *matronae* (married women or, more likely, widows) and nuns, who were by the middle of the eighth century flocking from England to Rome. We can follow the imaginary trails left by these two classes of female pilgrim down through the centuries to a fictional Canterbury in 1370: one trail ends with Chaucer's Prioress, who perhaps really should not have been out of her cloister, and the other with the Wife of Bath, a *matrona* several times over. Her activities may have raised eyebrows, but was her right to go on pilgrimage open to question?

In 791, less than half a century after Boniface's letter to Cuthbert, the Synod of Friuli legislated to safeguard and enforce the enclosure of 'monasteries of maidens living under a rule'. The rele-

vant canon includes a specific prohibition of pilgrimage, and the terms it employs are suggestive:

> At no time whatsoever shall it be permitted to an abbess or any nun to go to Rome and tour other holy places, if Satan should transform himself into an angel of light and suggest it to them as if for the sake of prayer. For no one can be so obtuse or stupid as not to realise how irreligious and blameworthy it is [for them] to have dealings with men because of the necessities of travel. . . .

That women, lay or religious, could not travel without men in their company was a truth universally acknowledged. For female religious this was (or should have been) an insuperable difficulty; for female pilgrims in general it was a problem, as we shall see more fully later.

In theory strict enclosure was required of monks and nuns alike. Four hundred years after the Synod of Friuli, efforts were being made in England to limit the mobility of religious in general. A legatine council held at York in June 1195 by Archbishop Hubert Walter, for example, ruled that monks, regular canons and nuns should not be permitted to leave their houses without just cause and without appropriate escort. Pilgrimage was mentioned among the causes of 'wandering' which were to be forbidden. However, the saving clause 'without specific and reasonable cause' potentially furnished a very elastic loophole, and the additional note that nuns in particular were not to leave the cloister unless accompanied by the abbess or prioress indicated that enclosure was not in fact expected to be total.

Later legislation repeated these prohibitions, tending to focus more narrowly on nuns. Cardinal Ottobuon Fieschi's legatine council of 1268 in London decreed that the abbess and other superiors were only to leave the convent in case of evident necessity, the other nuns never, but again there was the inevitable saving clause, 'unless for just and reasonable cause'. Here, no specific mention was made of pilgrimage and when in 1298 Pope Boniface VIII pronounced on the subject in the ominously entitled Bull *Pericoloso* he focused on secular and legal business as the causes most likely to drag nuns out of the cloister. The English bishops dutifully disseminated this Bull. Archbishop Thomas Corbridge of York, interpreting it as en-

joining 'perpetual enclosure', made a spirited attempt to enforce it on the nuns of his diocese, which evidently met with an equally spirited response. In 1344 Bishop Hamo de Hethe of Rochester complained that the nuns of Malling had been infringing on their enclosure in all sorts of ways, including wandering around the country 'by colour of pilgrimage and visiting your friends', and he exacted an oath of amendment from the abbess and convent.

Some restrictions were clearly widely accepted. Philip VI of France failed to persuade Pope Clement VI to grant the benefits of the 1350 Roman Jubilee Indulgence to 'enclosed nuns' who, among other classes of people, were not able to make the journey. The name of only one nun, the Abbess of Barking, appears among the permissions granted by the English royal government to go to Rome for the Jubilee. It was not just in 1350 that this was exceptional. No other nun appears among the fairly abundant records of royal permissions to go abroad on pilgrimage which survive in the Patent and Close Rolls in the thirteenth and fourteenth centuries. Abbots occur occasionally, while monks sometimes went with or without the permission of their superiors. Domestic pilgrimage, which leaves less mark on the record, was probably less contentious, and it is a fair inference that it was on modest little pilgrimages within the kingdom that nuns like Chaucer's Prioress betook themselves from time to time. Occasionally the popes gave permission for a female recluse—a different category of religious woman—to go on pilgrimage.

What of the Prioress's fellow-pilgrim, the Wife of Bath, and other *matronae?* There was no legislation to stop married women going on pilgrimage, even without their husbands, as long as they had obtained a public statement of their spouse's permission, a requirement laid down by the Council of Westminster in 1195 which in theory applied to married people of both sexes. Two hundred years later, Margery Kempe of Lynn was well aware of the need for her husband's consent to her pilgrimages, but she resisted the demand of the hostile 'doctor' who arraigned her in the chapter-house at York, while she was visiting the shrine of St William, that she should be able to produce a written permission:

> Sir, my husband gave me permission with his own mouth. Why do you pro-

ceed in that way with me more than you do with other pilgrims who are here, and who have no letter any more than I have?'

Occasionally feminine disobedience to husbands in the matter of pilgrimage appears as a motif in a miracle-collection of saint's *Life*. There is an example among the tenth-century miracles of Ste Foy at Conques: a woman in an advanced state of pregnancy had come to the shrine against her husband's will and was suddenly seized by the pains of impending labour. The saint intervened and on consideration of the gift of a ring from the woman's finger arrested the course of nature, so that she could return safely to her husband and give birth in due time. This and other miracle-collections provide abundant evidence that women were constant customers of the saints, petitioning or giving thanks on their own account, sometimes on that of their husbands, above all on that of their children.

Women expected to have access to popular relics. Early in the ninth century mixed crowds flocked to the abbey of Fleury when new relics were brought there. As women could not enter the monastery church, the relics were exhibited at fixed times in a marquee outside. A similar well-publicised instance occurred in the thirteenth century at the Cistercian abbey of Pontigny. Edmund of Abingdon, late Archbishop of Canterbury, was buried there in 1240 and on his canonisation in 1246 flocks of pilgrims had recourse to his tomb, including many Englishwomen of rank. Popes Innocent IV and Alexander IV successively issued special permissions for women to enter the abbey to do reverence to the saint. The chronicler of another Cistercian house, Meaux in Yorkshire, many years later gave a sardonic version of these events. The monks of Pontigny, he said, had favoured the women's devotion and, still more to the point, had been reluctant to forego their offerings. So they had detached the saint's arm and exhibited it separately at the gates of the monastery, 'so that the women were not totally disappointed of their devotion, and they themselves obtained no small profit from their offerings'. God and the saint himself, however, were not best pleased by these proceedings, and refused to work any more miracles.

Another monastic establishment, the cathedral priory of Durham, prevented women from approaching the shrines of St Cuthbert. This exclusion had a different result. Two-thirds of the miracles recorded in the late twelfth century as performed by Godric (d. 1170), the saint of neighbouring Finchale, benefited women, and in at least one instance St Cuthbert himself directed the sufferer to Finchale for her cure. Other saints and shrines catered for a distinctively feminine clientele. In the earlier sixteenth century Sir Thomas More poked gentle fun at housewives who spent more on a pilgrimage to the housekeeper-saint Zita in order to find lost keys than the keys were worth in the first place.

Women, it may be suggested, were essential contributors to the shrine economy; and it seems that their right to participate in pilgrimage, as it became more and more integral to lay religious practice, was taken largely for granted. Restrictions on that participation, particularly on long-distance pilgrimage, may well have been imposed as much by practical as by moralistic considerations. A head-count of pilgrims would undoubtedly show men in a large majority, and there were good reasons why this should be so. Such head-counts of course are not easy to achieve, for lack of sufficiently detailed evidence, but one example can be quoted. The *Opera,* or office of works, of St James in the cathedral of the Tuscan city of Pistoia from about 1360 kept a record of its almsgiving to pilgrims, mostly *en route* to Compostela. Between 1360 and 1460 some 3,000 pilgrims were recorded, most though not all of them by name. (There must have been many more, because there is a gap in the record from 1407–17.) The interesting fact is that only two hundred or so of the named pilgrims were women and the vast majority of them, for some reason, performed their pilgrimages before 1400 rather than after.

Among these few women, however, were some of lowly social rank (a laundress and a cook) and one or two who went both to Compostela and the Holy Land. The popularisation of pilgrimage down the social scale, which potentially opened it up to such women, must also, however, have created many situations in which the man went on pilgrimage and the woman stayed behind to mind the shop. Wives with their husbands, mothers with their sons, and perhaps above all widows, in groups or suitably accompanied according to their rank,

nonetheless, figure prominently among recorded pilgrims of the central and later Middle Ages.

The young Dominican friar, Felix Fabbri of Ulm, gives a vivid picture of the six rich old women who took ship with him at Venice on his first pilgrimage to Jerusalem in 1480. They were 'through old age scarcely able to support their own weight'. Some of the noblemen in the party objected to their presence, but they proved their worth when sickness broke out on the ship between Cyprus and the Holy Land and they, completely unscathed, nursed the rest of the company. Felix compared them favourably with the one woman, the wife of a Flemish pilgrim, who was on the ship he took on his second pilgrimage in 1483: 'restless and inquisitive', she realised all men's worst fears, he complained, 'as she ran hither and thither incessantly about the ship . . . wanting to hear and see everything.'

The spiritual value of pilgrimage, for men or women, might be debatable, though it was widely believed in; its physical hazardousness was beyond dispute. It would have been a rash man who set off to Compostela or the Holy Land, or indeed on any considerable journey, totally unaccompanied. Many all-male parties of pilgrims got together for the sake of safety and company, whether or not they knew one another previously, and women sometimes attached themselves to such groups of men or to family parties. There is an illustrative anecdote in the life of Bona (d. 1207), who lived as a semi-recluse under the supervision of the Augustinian canons of San Martino in Pisa. At an early age she acquired the habit of seeing Christ, his mother, her sisters and St James in visions, and they subsequently accompanied her on her various pilgrimages. She was especially devoted to St James and on her frequent journeys to and from Compostela, she was sometimes escorted by an old man whom she, if no one else, knew to be the saint himself. More normally she travelled in groups of the usual kind, 'with other pilgrims'. On one of these journeys, a male pilgrim got separated from the rest of his party and was promptly set upon by a robber. We are given this illustration of the dangers of solitude only because Bona took it upon herself to intervene, knowing that being wounded and left for dead was the least of the pilgrim's worries; he had two unconfessed mortal sins

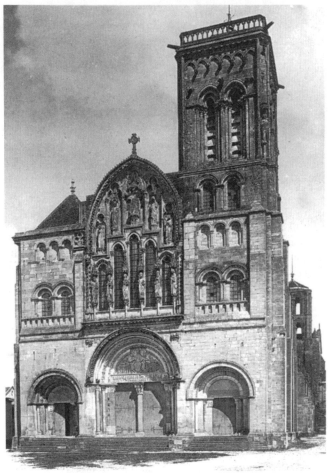

The abbey church of Vezelay, central France, built from the late 12th century, attracted pilgrims in their thousands to its relics of St. Mary Magdalene.

on his conscience which would damn him unless she cured him. (She got him his money back as well, and converted the robber to the religious life: a good day's work.)

On another occasion, Bona went to the superiors who had charge of her and asked for permission to go on pilgrimage to Rome. This was granted, but she was asked with whom she proposed to travel. Merrily she replied, 'Guido, Guida and Pietro', meaning by Guido and Guida Christ himself and the Virgin, her 'guides'. Perhaps aware that there was a lingering reservation in the minds of her superiors, she asked that a servant called Jacopo, 'who had often accompanied her', should go with her to a riverside meadow where she expected to meet her three escorts. Jacopo's evidently burning desire to be allowed to accompany her to Rome himself is let down gently; he is deeply suspicious of

the youth and beauty of Guido-Christ, and needs a great deal of reassurance, to the amusement of all the party, that Bona is not going to be the object of this particular guide's improper attentions.

It is hard to imagine the life of a male pilgrim-saint including such elaborate reference to the provision for his safety *en route*. In the case of women such as Bona, vowed to the religious life, there was, of course, additional reason for anxiety, since their chastity was their indispensable stock in trade. Two centuries later, Margery Kempe of Lynn, who despite the numerous children she had borne in her early sinful life, had to her own satisfaction mastered the difficult art of how to become a virgin, felt a keen anxiety on the same account. Although Christ himself had assured her that he would keep her 'from all wicked men's power', Margery shows recurrent concern about how, and by whom, she

was to be escorted on her various pilgrimages. Abandoned at Venice by the party with which she had gone to the Holy Land, she met Richard the 'broken-backed man' who, it had been foretold, would accompany her. He was nervous of the responsibility, not unreasonably thinking that one man, unarmed, was no great defence for a woman against the hazards of the road. At Assisi, he was only too glad to hand her over to the care of Margaret Florentyne, who had come from Rome for the indulgence of the Portiuncula fittingly accompanied by 'many knights of Rhodes, many gentlewomen and a fine equipage'.

Later in life, having escorted her widowed German daughter-in-law back home, Margery undertook the pilgrimage to Wilsnack on the assurance of the company of a man who promised to see her home to England; but he turned out to be in a perpetual state of nerves, and, she thought, made every effort to be rid of her. Finding herself again abandoned, she made her way to Aachen with a group of rather verminous poor people and saw the relics. Meeting here 'a worthy woman' from London, who was travelling more conventionally as 'a widow with a large retinue', she thought herself assured of company home, but was disappointed. She then joined forces with a solitary poor friar, but that she should travel alone with him seemed improper to an innkeeper's wife, who got her accepted into a passing party of pilgrims. In the next town she tried once again to attach herself to the widow from London and was harshly rebuffed. Back in company with the poor friar, who by all accounts was having almost as bad a time as she was, she suffered horribly from fears of rape, especially at night: 'She dared trust no man; whether she had reason or not, she was always afraid.'

It was a stressful experience, especially given Margery's anxious personality, but by no means an unintelligible one, nor one that would seem altogether unfamiliar to many modern female travellers. The poor friar, who represents millions of nameless innocuous men throughout the ages, had, she acknowledged, 'been most kindly and decently behaved to her during the time that they travelled together'. It would be interesting to have his journal: did it add to the stress of *his* journey—like that of the broken-backed Richard years before, or the querulous man on the road to Wilsnack—that he felt responsible for this woman?

It was not primarily the extra hazards that female travellers faced that Abba Arsenius had in mind when he suggested that the pious Roman virgin could not go just anywhere. His view of the restrictions that women should observe were in later centuries enforced (insofar as they were successfully enforced) only on some women, those who entered the institutionalised religious life. Laywomen who wanted to go on pilgrimage obviously encountered certain problems which flowed from their gender and its perceived frailties. (The pilgrim who in 1370 gave birth to a male child in the hospital of San Jacopo at Pistoia was an extreme case.) The monk-custodians of popular relics might, with some grumbling, have to take steps to safeguard their purity against invading female pilgrims; but the devotion and the offerings of these women were worth having. It is hard to imagine the shrines of the Middle Ages without their female clientele.

FOR FURTHER READING:

Jonathan Sumption, *Pilgrimage: an image of medieval religion* (Faber, 1975); Ronald Finucane, *Miracles and Pilgrims* (Macmillan, 1995); Benedicta Ward, *Miracles and the Medieval Mind* (Wildwood House, 1987); Michael Goodich, *Violence and Miracle in the Fourteenth Century: Private Grief and Public Salvation;* Chicago University Press, 1994); On Margery, *The Book of Margery Kempe,* translated into modern English by B.A. Windeatt (Penguin Classics, 1985); Clarissa Atkinson, *Mystic and Pilgrim: The Book and the World of Margery Kempe* (Cornell University Press, 1983).

Diana Webb is Lecturer in Medieval History at King's College, The University of London, and the author of Patrons and Defenders: The Saints in the Italian City States *(I.B. Tauris, 1996).*

BRITAIN 1100

BRIAN GOLDING *LOOKS AT LIFE UNDER THE NORMAN YOKE DURING THE CONSOLIDATING REIGN OF HENRY I*

ON AUGUST 2ND, 1100, William II Rufus was killed in a hunting accident in the New Forest. His body was immediately taken to Winchester Cathedral for burial. Three days later, his younger brother, Henry (who may possibly have been implicated in Rufus's death), was crowned at Westminster. The New Forest, Winchester, Westminster: all these sites have resonances in Anglo-Norman England. Though Anglo-Saxon kings had been keen huntsmen, the creation of a new landscape whose primary function was hunting rather than agriculture was a Norman innovation which came to be seen by contemporaries and later polemicists alike as the most enduring symbol of alien domination, the 'Norman Yoke'. Winchester had long been the ritual capital of the Wessex dynasty, but Rufus was the last king to be buried there as Winchester inexorably shrank from being the pre-eminent royal power base to merely an important regional and episcopal centre. Its ceremonial function was already being usurped by the new abbey of Westminster as the new centre of the English monarchy. Shortly before his death, Rufus had completed a magnificent new hall in the palace complex adjacent to the abbey, clearly proclaiming the imperial pretensions of the new order. Westminster Hall has remained at the heart of government for 900 years.

Henry I (r. 1100–35) inherited an administrative system of considerable sophistication. The long-established institutions of English government were the most highly developed in western Europe. A grid of hundreds (or their Anglo-Danish equivalents, the wapentakes) and shires overlay almost the entire country, though in the north governmental structures remained fluid. Through their courts justice was administered—and to contemporaries Henry I was the 'lion of justice' and the *rex pacificus*—and taxes were raised. These were both onerous and efficiently collected. Here, too, royal writs were proclaimed conveying the executive will from the centre to the localities. Henry I was almost certainly the last king before Henry VII to die solvent. By expanding the competence of the royal courts, by maximising the profits of royal justice, and by the subtle use of patronage, the political centre of gravity was gradually shifting to the king's benefit. Under Henry royal administration grew both in the localities and at the centre. The Exchequer began to audit the sheriffs' accounts: it and the Treasury can be seen as the first 'government departments' in England. However, in spite of this, royal government and administration, though increasingly systematised and reliant on written records, remained essentially personal, not bureaucratic.

When Henry I succeeded to the throne the Norman Conquest of England was substantially, though not entirely, complete. Early Norman incursions and settlement in Wales had been largely thrust back, to be resumed during Henry's reign, while there had, as yet, been no significant Norman penetration of Scotland. It was only with the accession of David I in 1124 that Normans settled the Lowlands by royal invitation, though there were already some cultural and religious ties fostered by Margaret of Scotland (1046–93), a descendant of the Wessex dynasty; both Anglo-Saxon and Norman exiles had taken refuge there. Neither had Normans yet ventured into the troubled waters of Ireland, though archbishops of Canterbury had begun to interfere in Irish ecclesiastical politics, and Ireland, too, had proved a convenient refuge for some, like the sons of Harold Godwineson, who were

> *The reallocation of land by the Normans was unequalled until the dissolution of the monasteries.*

hostile to the Anglo-Norman regime.

At this point, therefore, the Norman settlement was essentially of England alone. Even here it was drawn-out and long unsure, and the northern shires were only fully colonised during Henry's reign. But this colonisation now encountered no opposition. In the years immediately following 1066, Anglo-Saxon resistance was endemic across the country, especially in the north: this was followed by a major baronial revolt in 1075, which involved not only disaffected Norman magnates, but Anglo-

This article first appeared in *History Today*, April 2000, pp. 10-17. © 2000 by History Today, Ltd. Reprinted by permission.

Saxons and Danes. Thereafter there was little more native hostility, although tensions remained high as antipathies within the ruling dynasty itself dominated political life, and occasionally led to outright war. Familial rivalries between William I and his eldest son, Robert, and then between Robert and his brothers, William II Rufus and Henry I, focused on Robert's claim to rule Normandy. This claim was supported by the king of France, who saw these disputes as a means to maintain control over a principality which, though theoretically subordinate, was by virtue of its inclusion in the Anglo-Norman realm, far more economically and militarily powerful than his own.

Though the Norman settlement was protracted, it was certainly far-reaching. There had been earlier re-distributions of property on a large scale following conquest, for example during the reign of Cnut, but the appropriation of land and its reallocation by the Normans was unequalled until the dissolution of the monasteries. None profited more than the king himself. The royal demesne doubled in extent, ensuring a significant shift in the balance of power between king and aristocracy, such that the Norman kings were never threatened by an over-mighty subject as Edward the Confessor had been by Earl Godwine and his family. Not only were royal revenues greatly enhanced, but more land was available to reward loyal service, thereby further consolidating royal power. The new king had benefited most from the Conquest: beneath him a tightly-knit group of magnates emerged, often related to each other and to the new dynasty by marriage. These men might dominate whole shires, as did William I's half-brother, Robert of Mortain, in Cornwall, or Hugh of Avranches in Cheshire. While many were already well-established in Normandy, others came from nowhere. The origins, for example, of William de Briouze, a major beneficiary of royal patronage in Sussex, whose family was to play a major role in thirteenth-century politics, are extremely obscure.

Not all of these aristocratic families survived more than one generation: the wheel of fortune that had brought them such wealth kept on spinning. 'New' men, such as Robert fitzHaimo and William of Warenne, emerged through the patronage of William Rufus and Henry I; other families, like the Clares, continued to reap further rewards for their enduring loyalty. But many others lost out. The royal family itself was not exempt from fortune's reversal. William I's other half-brother, Odo, bishop of Bayeux and earl of Kent, had lost his lands and liberty in 1082. Odo's brother, Robert of Mortain, temporarily lost his lands in 1088, following his support of Duke Robert of Normandy against Rufus, while William of Mortain, Robert's son, irretrievably fell in 1106 after the battle of Tinchebrai, in which, like his father before him, he fought for Duke Robert. Already in 1102 Robert of Bellême had had all his estates confiscated: a generation earlier Earl Ralph of Hereford had paid the price for his role in the baronial rebellion of 1075.

Most studies of the Norman settlement have traditionally concentrated on this aristocracy but the colonisation ran much deeper. Incomers included not only great lords and their military vassals, prelates and monks, but also *francigenae,* the lesser men and women, and servants such as the gardener recorded at the Bishop of Lincoln's manor of Buckden early in the twelfth century. While most of the incomers were Normans, others came from Brittany, Anjou and elsewhere in France. Some were merchants, who often settled in their own quarter in towns, as, for example, in Southampton or Norwich. They may often have enjoyed a favoured status as merchants, giving them an advantage over native traders, as they certainly did in Hereford. By 1100 the first Jewish settlers since Roman times were established in London. Most came from Rouen, where there was already one of the largest Jewish communities north of the Alps.

The colonisers inhabited a country that, in Reginald Lennard's memorable words, was already old. Unlike the Saxons in England or the Vikings in both England and Normandy, the Normans named few places in England or Wales, and those they did, like Montgomery or Caus, generally reflect an attachment to the home country rather than the establishment of new settlements. Most changes in the landscape were more attributable to economic developments, and in particular to the needs of a rising population, than they were to Norman settlement. The creation of royal forests and other hunting preserves after the Conquest was essentially a legal development which was keenly resented.

Their remnants are among the most enduring elements on the modern landscape—above all the Norman kings' New Forest, recently declared a National Park—where other woodland has been lost over the intervening centuries. Hunting was both enjoyed as sport (albeit a dangerous one: two brothers of Henry I had been killed in hunting accidents), and had a considerable economic function: it is no coincidence that Henry I's reign probably saw the introduction into England of the rabbit, the fallow deer, and the pheasant.

Some new lords were clearly keen to exploit the economic potential of their estates. Ernulf de Hesdin was praised by William of Malmesbury both for his charity to the poor and for his hands-on management of his lands, but Domesday Book reveals many other lords who had increased the value of their lands, sometimes by none too scrupulous means. With a firm grasp on the controls of government and with the support of a considerable clientage, local bosses like Robert d'Oilly, castellan of Oxford, or Picot, sheriff of Cambridgeshire, could tyrannise their regions and appropriate land from monasteries and laity alike.

In most instances increases in agricultural production were the result of a more rigorous exploitation of existing resources, for the Norman Conquest itself introduced no agricultural or technological innovations. The manorialisation of rural society that had quickened in the later Anglo-Saxon period continued as large estates were fragmented into smaller, often more regimented, holdings typified by common fields and nucleated villages. It is not anachronistic to see their lords as country gentry cultivating their lands through the labour of a dependent peasantry, and receiving rents from the freer peasants. For these dependent peasants the Conquest may have had little impact: the few surviving late Anglo-Saxon estate documents suggest that their burdens were not dissimilar from those endured by their thirteenth-century descendants, when the plight of the unfree peasantry has traditionally been supposed to be at its worst. Some certainly benefited. Slaves were a familiar feature of pre-Conquest rural society, and were particularly concentrated in some regions such as the West Midlands. In the post-Conquest generations they gradually disappeared, not because the colonisers had a greater respect for human rights, but because it made better economic sense for lords to exploit a labour force which cultivated its own smallholdings and provided services in return, rather than to maintain slaves at their own expense. Nucleation of settlements may well have accelerated in the post-Conquest world. Certainly, in the north new 'planned' villages can be attributed to the new order.

The north had suffered more than any other region from violent economic and social disruption in the years following 1066. Refugees had swarmed south and the impact of the 'harrying' was still apparent generations afterwards. Whole communities were displaced, and their resettlement in regularly laid-out villages gave both protection and the opportunity for greater control. Yet even in areas less seriously affected by conquest, life was unpredictable and uncertain. Taxation levels were harsh and sometimes punitive: the Anglo-Saxon Chronicle for 1097 records that 'this was a very disastrous year because of excessive taxation'. It continues: 'and on account of the heavy rains which did not leave off throughout the whole year: nearly all the cultivated land in low-lying districts was ruined'. Such catastrophes were not unusual. The following year 'the incoming tide rushed up so strongly and did so much damage that no one remembered anything like it before'. 1102 'was a very disastrous year . . . by reason of numerous taxes and also as a result of murrain and the ruin of the harvest, both of the corn and of the fruit on all the trees. Further (on August 10th) the wind did such great damage here in the land to all the crops that nobody remembered anything like it before.' Such entries remind us that, although overall climatic conditions in Europe had been improving since the tenth century, with the weather becoming warmer and, perhaps, wetter, conditions were always precarious. Even when there were not famines, local shortages could be serious and hard to overcome given the poor communications.

Much of the initiative for the major developments in the landscape and the rural economy, the reclamation of marsh and fen and the clearances of woodland and 'waste', came from the great Benedictine monasteries such as Ely or Glastonbury. Some of this activity was already under way before the Conquest. It was frequently these religious communities, too, that were at the forefront

of urban development as small trading centres developed outside their gates. This had already happened at St Albans and Bury St Edmunds, but it was also apparent at new foundations such as Battle, the monastery established by William I on the site of his victory of 1066. Greater and lesser secular lords also saw the advantage of fostering towns on their estates and, as did Robert fitzHaimo at Burford, offered commercial inducements to merchants willing to

---

The Conquest itself introduced no agricultural or technological innovations.

---

settle in these new communities. Many lords established towns near their castles which not only provided protection and a market for goods but also served—as in the countryside—to dominate the local population. More than twenty years ago J.H. le Patourel drew attention to the colonising trilogy of castle, borough, and monastery. Many lords endeavoured to make the *capita* of their estates focal points of administrative, commercial, and religious activity. Thus, Henry de Ferrers founded a priory beneath his castle at Tutbury, which also overlooked his new town, while in Cornwall, Robert of Mortain built a castle at Launceston and developed a small priory, moving this community from its original site outside Launceston and aggressively transferring its market into his own castle. Older established towns also felt the positive and negative impact of the new order. Many of the castles recorded in Domesday Book were urban structures. The construction of most of these resulted in substantial disruption as houses were demolished and trade dislocated. But at the same time, castles might provide protection and generate commercial demand. There seems little doubt that Rufus's new castle on the Tyne was a powerful catalyst to the growth of the town that took its name from that fortification. Towns, too, might be exorbi-

tantly taxed as Norwich and Oxford certainly were. Both, moreover, had had castles imposed on them, and yet within one or two generations both flourished as commercial, administrative and ecclesiastical centres as never before.

In no way was the coming of a new order more evident in the landscape than in the appearance of castles and churches. According to Domesday Book there were about fifty castles in 1086, but this figure is almost certainly a considerable understatement, and may well refer only to the largest of private fortifications. Few were stone-built. Those that were were either royal and intended to promote an imperial vision, as at the White Tower (London) or Colchester, or belonged to the greatest of the lay magnates like Richard de Lacy at Ludlow, or Count Alan of Brittany at Richmond (Yorkshire). Far more typical were the wooden and earthen fortifications of motte and bailey type, which were intended to dominate and defend their immediate locality. Their densest concentrations were along debated frontiers such as Herefordshire. Often, too, these new castles were in close proximity to new churches. William of Malmesbury famously commented that the Conquest resulted in a dramatic increase in new churches: 'now you may see in every village, town and city churches and monasteries rising in a new style of architecture'. Though some of this rebuilding, particularly of cathedrals and abbey churches, can certainly be attributed to the colonisers' desire to impress their arrival on the land, such an interpretation is too simple. At a local level the dynamic for building was both economic and institutional. Not only did a rising population require more churches, especially in new regions of cultivation where no settlements had previously existed, but the old ecclesiastical organisational structure was fracturing. The parish system that has survived into the present century was essentially a creation of the century-and-a-half following the Conquest. Late Anglo-Saxon lords had already begun to build estate churches, carving them out from the jurisdiction of the old mother or minster-churches, installing priests and enjoying the proceeds of their tenants' tithes. Reforming bishops such as Wulfstan of Worcester or Lanfranc of Canterbury also encouraged the creation of new parishes. Such activity was not confined to England. The early twelfth-century

DOMESDAY BOOK
AT THE TOWER OF LONDON

There is no mention in Domesday of the Tower of London, which this month becomes home to one of the volumes of Great Domesday as part of a new exhibition exploring the castle's role as a repository for state papers.

The value of the survey lies in the vivid snapshot it provides of a country in the throes of traumatic change. William's agents recorded not only who owned the land in 1086, but who had owned it before the Norman Conquest: we get an idea of the wholesale displacement of Anglo-Saxon landowners by Normans, of the King and his most powerful barons, and of institutions like the Church. More than 25,000 slaves are mentioned. The woodland and mills are listed, together with the acreage of pasture and arable land. There are occasional references to other forms of industry, such as stone quarrying (as at Taynton in Oxfordshire, the source of some of the stone for the building of the Tower of London). Most crucially, several of the commissions looked into the possibility of extracting more profit from the manor than had hitherto been taken.

The document could have been even more detailed: what survives today is only a digest of the returns from the survey, much condensed and re-ordered. Some idea of the earlier stages of Domesday can be obtained from two other surviving documents, for the South-West and East Anglia. The latter document was never revised but was entered into the final survey in its long and unedited form. It is now known as Little Domesday, and the main document as Great Domesday. Coverage of parts of the North of England were extremely sketchy—for example, the region between the Ribble and the Mersey—or missed altogether (Durham) because the hold of the Normans over these areas was tenuous. In addition, the greatest cities of Norman England, Winchester and London, were omitted, possibly because it was thought too complicated to describe the ownership of every single property in them.

Besides volumes of both the Great and Little Domesday, the exhibition will contain other important medieval manuscripts connected with the administration of the kingdom, including Hundred Rolls (from the reign of Edward I) and Pipe Rolls (the annual records of the medieval Exchequer). There will also be artefacts connected with the storage and transportation of the documents between the various royal palaces. For sheer eloquence, all of these are overshadowed by the body of a rat discovered inside one of the Pipe Rolls. There can be few more telling indications of the neglect that the manuscripts have occasionally suffered.

While Domesday was historically kept secure in the royal treasury in Winchester and later at the Palace of Westminister, many other administrative documents of England were for centuries kept at the Tower, notably in William the Conqueror's magnificent keep. It is here in the White Tower that the Domesday Book goes on display. What better time than the Millennium Year for these two great icons of the Norman Conquest, a document and a building, to be brought together?

Jeremy Ashbee, Tower of London

communities. The first house of this order was founded in Colchester in c.1100 and Augustinian priories were soon to be the foundation of choice for both Henry I and his court—and for David I, king of Scotland. The Cistercians took a little longer to arrive. Though Cîteaux itself was founded in 1098, the Order's first abbey was not established in England (Waverley) until 1128, Wales (Tintern) in 1131, Scotland (Melrose) in 1136, and Ireland (Mellifont) in 1142. There were also increasingly more opportunities for religious women. Anglo-Saxon nunneries, like their Continental counterparts, had been founded by and for the higher aristocracy, but in the century following the Conquest a number of new communities were established for women of lesser rank, the most interesting experiment being the Gilbertines, who were given their rule around 1148.

Such changes were not, of course, directly attributable to the new political order, and more profound and far-reaching structural changes within the English Church took their inspiration from Rome rather than Normandy. Until the mid-eleventh century papal authority was severely limited: popes were subordinate to the Western Emperors and often dominated by the Roman aristocracy at home, while ecclesiastical power in the regions was held by bishops. However, under the leadership of reforming and centralising popes, notably Gregory VII, the papacy acquired a harder ideological edge and began the extension of its temporal and spiritual authority that was to reach its apogee under Innocent III and Boniface VIII. These supranational ambitions were reflected in Urban II's preaching of the First Crusade in 1095, in the hope that a military expedition under papal leadership would free the Holy Places for Christendom and reassert papal hegemony over the Eastern Church. Several Anglo-Norman magnates had answered the papal call. In 1100, when William Rufus was killed, Duke Robert of Normandy himself was on his way home from Jerusalem. Papal influence was increasingly felt in other ways. Archbishop Lanfranc of Canterbury, though a conscientious reformer, had kept the papacy at arm's length, always managing to avoid attendance at papal synods to which he was repeatedly summoned, and acting in close alliance with William I to create an ecclesiastical polity di-

Prince of Gwynedd, Gruffudd ap Cynan, was praised by his biographer for his extensive church-building, and in Scotland the process seems to have been encouraged by David I. Bishops and abbots too were rebuilding their cathedrals and abbey churches on a much grander scale, sometimes modelling them on examples in the Norman homeland but also borrowing from elsewhere, in particular from the western Empire.

At the same time the Anglo-Norman aristocracy were also active in the founding of new monasteries, and though these were rarely as well-endowed as the Anglo-Saxon communities some, like Shrewsbury or St Werburgh's, Chester, became the dominant abbeys in their regions. By 1100 there were eight Cluniac priories in England, and others soon followed, while some Anglo-Norman lords chose to patronise native communities, such as Gloucester abbey which underwent considerable expansion at this time. Others were patrons of hermits, or even became hermits themselves, and some hermits' settlements soon formed the nucleus of Augustinian

rected from Canterbury—not Rome. His successor, Anselm, however, based his policy on close obedience to the papacy and had since 1097 been in self-imposed exile in protest at the King's refusal to allow him to hold a Church Council or to consult the pope on ecclesiastical matters.

The reign of Henry I has traditionally been seen as a period of assimilation between native English and colonising Normans, an interpretation that is found at least as early as the last quarter of the twelfth century. It was symbolised by the King's own marriage in 1110 to Eadgith, the daughter of Malcolm III Canmore, king of Scots, and Malcolm's English wife, Margaret, daughter of Edward the Atheling. Intermarriage was an effective strategy of conquest. Marriage to a native heiress could be used to legitimate the settlement and validate the appropriation of property. Yet the fact that Eadgith changed her name to a Norman one, Matilda, suggests a certain unease that may be connected to William of Malmesbury's report that Henry and Eadgith were mockingly referred to by the archetypal English names, Godric and Godgifu, suggesting that the Norman Henry had 'gone native' by marrying a woman of English descent. William, like his fellow contemporary historians, Orderic Vitalis and Henry of Huntingdon, was himself the offspring of a mixed marriage. Like Eadgith, Orderic acquired a new, more acceptable Norman name when as a small boy he entered the Norman monastery of St Evroul. Such re-namings were not uncommon: the adoption by natives of more fashionable Norman names for themselves or their children was a strategy for social advancement in a changing world. No wonder the granting of miraculous bi—or even trilingualism is found in several twelfth-century miracle collections. Nor is it surprising to find interpreters recorded in Domesday Book and elsewhere. Such specialists were essential in post-Conquest England: their skills valued by English and Normans alike. As the Normans began their colonisation of Wales, interpreters were

also needed there and might similarly have enjoyed substantial rewards. Intermarriage, too, of course, contributed to bilingualism. Though it was rare during the twelfth century for English men and women to understand Anglo-Norman, unless they belonged to the upper ranks of the Church, the reverse was no longer true. Though Anglo-Norman was the language of the dominant elite, that does not mean that the Norman aristocracy could not understand and speak English:

> *The native adoption of more fashionable Norman names was a strategy for social advancement.*

the clerical aristocracy was often trilingual, while those with interests in Wales could even, like Gerald of Wales in the second half of the century, be quadrilingual.

In the 1130s, a Norman clerk, Gaimar, incorporated a translation of the Anglo-Saxon Chronicle (written, of course, in the vernacular) into his Anglo-Norman verse romance, *Estorie des Engleis* (History of the English), written for Constance, the English wife of a Norman lord. What she or Gaimar or their contemporaries meant by 'Engleis' is not entirely clear. What is certain is that Gaimar and Constance inhabited a world of social, cultural and linguistic fluidity where identities were rapidly shifting.

The Norman aristocracy increasingly identified with their conquered land; their estates on this side of the Channel were, after all, normally worth far more than their ancestral properties. They gave their political loyalties to leaders who were likely to be the most success-

ful protectors of their English lands; their religious loyalties, also, were increasingly focused on monastic foundations in England rather than Normandy, and it was within these English churches that they found burial. Conversely, not all the English had gone down in the wreckage of 1066. Whether specialists like huntsmen or interpreters, high-status moneyers who sometimes established themselves in urban patriciates, local administrators, or churchmen such as Samson, who became abbot of Bury St Edmunds at the end of the twelfth century, some survived and prospered.

The extent to which changes in British society following 1066 were consequent upon the Conquest or merely coincidental remains a lively historiographic issue, but one thing is certain. For the first time (with the brief exception of 1016-35, when Cnut had made England part of his Scandinavian empire) the country was now part, and in many ways the dominant part, of a state divided by water. The English Channel could be both a barrier or a bridge, but the dynamics of government were transformed by the creation of the Anglo-Norman realm. Few political changes in British history have been more significant or enduring. Though Anglo-Norman kings would rule both territories only between 1066 and 1087 and again from 1106 to 1135, the French connection thus forged was to dominate foreign policy throughout the Middle Ages and well beyond.

FURTHER READING

R. Fleming, *Kings and Lords in Conquest England* (CUP, 1991); B. Golding, *Conquest and Colonisation: the Normans in Britain,* 1066–1100 (Macmillan, 1994); J.A. Green, *The Aristocracy of Norman England* (CUP, 1959): A. Williams, *The English and the Norman Conquest* (Boydell and Brewer, 1995).

Brian Golding is Reader in History at the University of Southampton.

The Paris Bibles and the Making of a Medieval Information Revolution

After 13th-century Paris scribes began churning out large numbers of portable Bibles, reading and scholarship changed forever

Jay Tolson

Jay Tolson, editor of The Wilson Quarterly *and author of* Pilgrim in the Ruins: A Life of Walker Percy, *came across the story of the Paris Bibles while doing research for a novel about the son of Abelard and Heloise. "Living in the distant past at least part of the time has its rewards. One was stumbling across the fact that in 13th-century Paris the Bible became pretty much the book it is today—a little fact with wide, and ever-widening, ramifications."*

The year is 1232; the place, the Ile-de-la-Cité, core of medieval Paris, royal seat of Capetain France, and one of Europe's great centers of ecclesiastical, commercial and scholarly life. In a boardinghouse on rue St. Christofe, a street thick with student dwellings, a young canon who has come to Paris to study at the university's faculty of theology sits reading at a rude table in his upstairs room, one of three rented out by his landlady, and tries to ignore the din outside the window. The noise comes mainly from fellow students at a nearby tavern, but to their clamor now are added the harsh declamations of the *crieur,* who from the mud-black street shouts out the provenance and price of his wine while he drums a stick against a large bowl. Our

20-year-old scholar, born less than a league from Nantes, the second son of a minor nobleman, tries again to focus on the Latin text before him, a passage form the Pauline Epistles. In the last light of this early spring day, he squints to read the small script squeezed onto the silky-thin page of his Bible.

Though our canon thinks about it less often now, the fact that he became the first member of his family to own a copy of the Holy Bible was, when he purchased it the year before, the cause of considerable pride (although he does not easily forget his father's anger upon learning the price of his purchase). But as often as our young cleric has thought about his prized possession, we can be altogether certain that he never thinks of it as part of an information revolution.

Yet an information revolution unquestionably took place between the last quarter of the 12th century and the first quarter of the 13th on and around the Ile-de-la-Cité. There, for the first time, the central text of Christendom was produced in great numbers in a single-volume, portable format. And that was only part of the revolution. The Bible also then acquired several distinctive textual and design features that endure to this day, including the standardized ordering of Old Testament and New Testament

books; the division of the individual books into numbered chapters; the octavo-sized, almost sheer vellum page; the extremely small script and a fixed palette of colors (black, blue and red) for the covers and page edges of the books. In short, by 1230 at the latest, the Bible had become very much the book that we know today—in look, in heft, in organization. Manuscript specialist Christopher de Hamel, in his elegant and learned study, A *History of Illuminated Manuscripts* (1986), describes this publishing event as "one of the most phenomenal successes in the history of book production," a claim that is in no way overstated.

Compared to the telephone or the television or the information superhighway, complete with semiconductor chips and fiber-optic wiring, the packaging of a book may seem a minor affair. We should remember, though, that great historical changes have been wrought by the most technically modest innovations. The simple stirrup decisively transformed the art of warfare in medieval Europe, and the invention of the humble plow contributed greatly to the rise of settled communities, the earliest towns. And what other technical innovation has proved more consequential than the book itself? The centuries-long refine-

 From *Civilization* magazine, January/February 1996, pp. 52–57. © 1996 by Jay Tolson. Reprinted by permission of the author.

ment of this remarkable information tool may not have been the prerequisite to reading and writing. After all, evidence of literacy can be found as early as 4000 B.C. But the book, particularly after Johannes Gutenberg's invention of movable type in 1455, did more than any other tool to foster the spread of literacy, as well as to extend and deepen the possible uses of that skill.

The story of the book and its connections with literacy is so momentous that even its smaller chapters hint at the larger importance. Such is the case with what came to be known as the Paris Bibles. With the entire text of the Christian faith accessible to a growing number of readers—because of both its manageable size and its orderly format—Christians could begin to examine the foundations of their faith in a more independent and critical fashion. Though most of these readers were clerics, the example of their style of reading would inspire individuals outside the clergy—would indeed be a step toward the kind of close, analytical reading practiced by the Renaissance humanists and their successors, both inside and outside the academy. (Not coincidentally, the Latin Bible was translated into French for the first time in Paris sometime between 1235 and 1260, when the production of pocket Bibles was at its peak.) Why and how the Paris Bibles acquired their characteristic appearance and format, and the consequences of this development, are all bound up with forces that made this time one of the great transitional moments in human history.

The Rennaissance of the 12th century," as it is often called, was an age of great intellectual activity marked as much by innovation as by rediscovery. Certainly, ancient works and authors were recovered, often by way of Latin translations of the works of Greco-Arabic scholars in Spain. But as historian Norman Cantor explains in his *Civilization of the Middle Ages,* 12th-century thinkers were interested not merely in reclaiming an older tradition but in using the classical heritage "to provide a starting point for new directions and dimensions in all facets of civilized life: religion, law, government, economy, ethics, and education, as well as in art, literature, philosophy, and science."

What gave impetus and direction to this great awakening was, of course, the Christian faith, institutionally upheld and nurtured by the Catholic Church. Whether it was the recovery and extensive study of Roman civil law and the related formation of an administrative-political class, or the gradual transformation of the cathedral schools into the great universities of Oxford, Bologna and Paris, it was the church and churchmen, with the backing of devout worldly rulers, that drove this intense burst of civilizing activity.

This was nothing altogether new, of course. Since Rome's demise in the fifth century, the zealous efforts of churchmen—missionaries, monks, simple parish priests and politically astute bishops—helped to spread northward the learning and many of the institutions of the defunct Roman imperium, even as they gave these Roman legacies a Christian purpose. Monasteries established in the far-flung lands of the Franks, Celts, Angles, Saxons and other pagan peoples functioned as bastions of learning and the civilized arts as well as sites of spiritual withdrawal. By the end of the sixth century, in fact, Celts and Anglo-Saxons had themselves become vigorous bearers of the Christian torch, working as missionaries and scholars on the Continent as well as in the British Isles.

During that long stretch once crudely called the Dark Ages, many monasteries took on the task of teaching the seven liberal arts, the trivium (grammar, rhetoric and dialectic) and the quadrivium (arithmetic, geometry, astronomy and music), to the children of the powerful. Just as important, the monks in these fortresslike institutions copied the manuscript books, or codices, that were central to Christian worship and education—the Sacred Scriptures, the missals, the Psalters and the various writings of the church fathers—and also certain works of classical antiquity and even redactions of local vernacular literature.

The production of manuscripts in the hushed scriptoria of the monasteries was truly a labor of devotion and painstaking craftsmanship. Carefully penned with quills on large sheets of vellum (made from the skin of goats, sheep or calves), the manuscripts were often beautifully illuminated with ornate lettering or pictures or, in most cases, both. Large objects of unwieldy dimensions—up to 20 by 14 inches—these books could also be quite heavy (a comparable three-volume Bible from the 13th century weighed 88 pounds). Though many of the books were used by the monks in their services and their teaching, a fair number were made for—and even commissioned by—emperors, kings and lesser nobles. Some of the more beautiful examples of the monks' handiwork survive, including the Lindisfarne Gospels, the Book of Durrow and, perhaps most famous of all, the Book of Kells.

Given the ongoing production of manuscripts, it is perhaps surprising that, before 1200, the Vulgate (as the Latin Bible translated by St. Jerome in the late fourth and early fifth centuries was called) seldom appeared as a single volume. Christians, in fact, thought of the Bible as a set of scriptures that could be read in any order. A burst of single-volume Bible production did occur in the early ninth century, particularly at St. Martin's Abbey in Tours under the leadership of an English abbot named Alcuin. This flurry of activity accompanied the intellectual stirrings of the early Carolingian period, when monks at certain monasteries attempted not only to weed out impurities that had crept into the Vulgate but also to refine their own style of biblical interpretation, or exegesis. (Their approach, far less systematic and analytical than that of 12th- and 13th-century scholastic theologians, emphasized the inculcation of piety and devotion.) But even at its peak of Bible-related labors, according to David Ganz and other historians, St. Martin's seldom produced more than two large single-volume Bibles a year—no great surprise, really, considering the time and the material required for their making. (For example, the skins of approximately 225 sheep were needed to provide the parchment for just one such Bible.)

The renown of the few single-volume Bibles produced before the 13th century—the Codex Amiatinus, made at Wearmouth-Jarrow in England around 715, as well as the later Alcuinian Bibles—stands as probably the best proof of their rarity. Until the 13th century, the Bible was usually divided into huge "glossed" volumes (with commentary inscribed in small script in the margins of the text), typically 20 in number. The glossed volumes were seldom if ever removed from the monastery refectories where they were kept, and students had little cause to consult them directly. While monks would interpret passages from the Bible for their homilies, and students would memorize selected passages for prayer and worship, the curriculum of the monastery schools focused more on the rudiments of rhetoric and grammar, and to a lesser degree on arithmetic and astronomy, than on the critical study of the Bible.

Why then did the single-volume Bible—the *porto,* as students of Paris dubbed it—become a widespread possession in the early 13th century? The answer lies primarily in the birth of new educational institutions, the first of which began to appear in some of the larger northern European cathedrals and churches in the ninth and 10th centuries. The emergence of these cathedral schools, and of the new approaches to learning they introduced, accompanied the rise of cities and the flowering of urban culture, itself a rich and complex story. Suffice it to say that bishops, wise to the ways of the world, saw such schools as a means of augmenting the prestige and influence of their cathedrals and, by extension, their own temporal sway. The masters at their schools were clerics, but of the secular clergy. ("Cleric" was then a far more flexible and capacious term than it is now, and was not limited to ordained priests.) These masters were also usually itinerant, moving from school to school according to their ability to draw and hold students.

Like the monastery schools, cathedral schools taught the seven liberal arts, but with greater rigor and thoroughness. Besides reshaping the arts into specialized academic disciplines, schoolmen of the 12th century began to take a keener interest in the formerly neglected art of dialectic, the most philosophical of the disciplines, and one that relied heavily on the logical writings of Aristotle.

Related to this intellectual interest was the schools' sponsorship of a new academic discipline, theology, which merged the critical-analytical approaches of philosophy with the study of Sacred Scripture and the works of the church fathers. It was not long before certain masters—above all, Peter Abelard (1079–1142)—became wildly popular for bravado lectures in which they subjected Scripture and doctrine to probing logical analysis. This was considered exhilarating stuff by students hungry for intellectual pyrotechnics, but it was not looked upon kindly by all churchmen. Leaders of the monastic orders such as the Cistercian Bernard of

Clairvaux attacked these agile masters as breeders of impiety, schism and heterodoxy, and a number of the schoolmen were brought before church councils to account for their teachings.

At the university in Paris, every theology student was expected to study and teach the Old and New Testament—and hence, if possible, to have his own copy of the Bible.

But scholastic theology was not to be quashed. Indeed, it became an even more formal discipline when it acquired its own faculty in the newest of Europe's educational establishments, the universities. No one knows exactly when the university emerged in Paris—or for that matter in other European scholastic centers. But sometime around the end of the 12th century or in the early 13th, the masters of the various Parisian cathedral and church schools, particularly those associated with the schools of Notre Dame, began to teach under the aegis of a new corporate entity, the University of Paris, complete with its own charter and chancellors. Here, theology became, along with the arts, law and medicine, a formal faculty in which students could earn the degrees of bachelor, master and doctor. More to the point, every student in the faculty of theology was expected to study and teach the Old and New Testament—and hence, if possible, to have his own copy of the Bible.

Theology candidates were not the only source of demand for individual Bibles. In 1229 the Dominican order, founded by St. Dominic (1170–1221) to combat heresy by teaching the correct doctrines of the faith, opened a school of theology in Paris to train its friars. (It was here, at St. Jacques, that the most agile *magister* of all, Thomas Aquinas,

author of the *Summa Theologiae,* did much of his lecturing and writing.) Two years later, the Franciscans followed suit by establishing their own school in the city. While the emphasis of the two orders was different—Franciscans claimed to put holiness before learning—they were alike in seeing their mission as active engagement with the world rather than ascetic withdrawal. After their schooling, friars from their respective schools went forth to preach and teach the Word, and invariably they had their portable Bibles tucked away in their satchels.

We should not imagine, though, that Paris Bibles, with their characteristic look and format, suddenly appeared around the year 1230. As historian Laura Light has shown in her careful examination of the subject, it was during the first 30 or so years of the 13th century "that a one-volume format was adopted as the usual format for the Vulgate." The early-13th-century precursors of the Paris Bibles tended to be larger and more finely worked than the *portos.* (Many were produced in privately owned workshops, or ateliers, that specialized in costly illuminated manuscripts.) But though these Bibles ranged in size from 10 by 8 inches to 19 by 12 inches, according to Light, they employed the smaller compressed script (developed first by Carolingian scribes) and wide margins that would be used in later Paris Bibles.

That was not the only similarity. The new critical approach to biblical studies that had begun during the previous century—and perhaps, Light speculates, an extensive revision of the Vulgate around the year 1200—accounts for many of the organizational features that were adopted in the single-volume precursors of the Paris Bibles. Until this burst of scholarly criticism, the order of books in most Bibles, such as the famous ninth-century Alcuinian Bibles, followed St. Jerome's arrangement, with some minor adjustments. Beginning in the 12th century, thanks to closer biblical study by scholars such as Hugh of St. Victor (1097–1141), arguments were made, Light explains, for "a grouping of the biblical books which corresponds to their literal meaning." As a result, Bibles of the early 13th century were the first in which "all of the historical books are grouped together to form an unbroken series at the beginning of the Old Testament." Similarly, all books classified as "doctrinal" (e.g., Job, the Psalms) were arranged together. Intended or not, this new ordering came very close to the one urged many centuries before by St. Augustine. Moreover, it was the one that would be employed in the more voluminously produced Paris Bibles—and indeed, with some variations, in most Bibles to this day.

Other features established around the beginning of the 13th century include the incorporation of Jerome's *Interpretation of Hebrew Names,* additions to and changes in his book prologues, and modifications of the capitula lists (the chapter-by-chapter summaries appearing at the beginning of each book). The introduction of chapter divisions within the individual books occurred somewhat earlier than the other innovations, perhaps in the last quarter of the 12th century, and was most likely the work of Stephen Langton (who after his years as the theologian in Paris became archbishop of Canterbury and, more memorably, drafted the Magna Carta). Curiously enough, verse divisions did not appear until much later—in a Greek New Testament issued by a Geneva printer, Robert Etienne, in 1550. But even without verse divisions, the organizational changes made at the turn of the century and incorporated in the *portos* made the Bible a much more userfriendly text. Allowing scholars to examine passages in the context of entire chapters or books, the changes facilitated the new scholarly style of exegesis, one that was far more critical, analytical and comparative than the older, devotionally oriented monastic style.

An important question remains: How was it possible to meet the sudden rise in demand for Bibles? Clearly the limited and painstaking output of the monasteries and the fancier ateliers would not have sufficed. The labor would have been too lengthy and the resulting product far too costly for most students. We know that some of the Dominican and Franciscan institutions made many of their own Bibles, but according to Christopher de Hamel, the Franciscan order in 1260 specifically prohibited its friars from producing Bibles for sale. (Meaning, as de Hamel shrewdly deduced, that many of the friars had been doing just that—no doubt to the neglect of their friarly duties.) But even if some friars continued to moonlight, demand still would have eclipsed supply. Something new was aborning, a new kind of book

business involving a new breed of booksellers.

Scholars who have looked into this business—including the late pioneer of the field, Jean Destrez, and, more recently, Robert Branner and Mary and Richard Rouse—have shown how establishments called *librarii* and *stationarii* came to play a central role in the Paris book trade by the middle of the 13th century. In most respects identical, both establishments, the Rouses note, "were regulated by the university; both were heavily involved in the secondhand trade; both produced new books; and both . . . were roundly damned by the university as frauds, cheats, and thieving rascals."

The new single-volume portable Bibles poured forth in such numbers that they met much of the demand for the next two centuries, until the advent of movable type.

Unlike modern bookstores, the *librarii* and *stationarii* did not carry new books on their shelves. They did stock used manuscripts, but university rules prohibited the booksellers from functioning as anything more than brokers between the original owner and the prospective buyer, or from earning any more than 1.7 percent on any transaction. (Hence the enmity between merchants and the university—and widespread cheating among the former.) The stores did sell new manuscripts, of course, but only upon commission. A prospective buyer who came looking for a copy of the Bible or any other manuscript would pay the bookseller, who would then engage his scribes (in-house or freelance) to execute the commission. Depending on the buyer's taste and purse size, the manuscript, after being copied, might be sent to an atelier for illumination. For a relatively low-cost *porto,* illumination might

be limited to initial letters at the beginning of a book or chapter. In general, the smaller, octavo-sized pages, tightly packed with script, left little room for artistic extravagance.

But why the distinction between the *stationarii* and the *librarii?* According to the Rouses, universities empowered the *stationarii,* and the *stationarii* alone, to engage in a form of book production that scholars call the *pecia* system. In this system, the bookseller held a master copy, or exemplar, of a text whose accuracy was certified and routinely checked by university officials. The exemplar was divided into numbered sections, or *peciae* (gatherings, or quires, of several pages of a text). These *peciae* were used by scribes employed by the store to fulfill the commissions, or alternatively, rented to people who wanted to produce their own manuscripts or fulfill commissions they had received on their own. "The *peciae* were never divided among several scribes at once," the Rouses explain, "but rather each scribe copied each *pecia* in turn." As a result, rather than one copy being made rapidly, many copies were made almost at the same time.

Not all Paris Bibles were produced under the *pecia* system. In fact, in her survey of surviving manuscripts, Laura Light finds relatively few Paris Bibles with the telltale *pecia* numbers in the corner of the pages. But whether they were made by *librarii, stationarii,* fancy ateliers, religious institutions, freelance scribes (often students or other clerics) or by the owners themselves, the new single-volume portable Bibles poured forth in such great numbers that they met not only the immediate demand but much of the demand for the next two centuries, until the advent of movable type. Today, indeed, surviving copies of the 13th-century Paris Bibles far outnumber those of any other species of pre-printing press book. The Library of Congress, for example, holds three.

Portability, accessible format and availability do not in themselves explain why the Paris Bibles constituted a kind of information revolution. The reason lies more directly in the role they played in propelling Europeans toward new ways of understanding the foundations of their faith. These ways reflected, above all, a quite remarkable confidence—shared by Peter Abelard, Thomas Aquinas and many other schoolmen—that reason and learning applied to matters of faith would not only strengthen the individual Christian's convictions but also buttress the authority of the church. It was a confidence not shared by all leaders of the church, but by and large it prevailed.

It did so in part because certain purely pragmatic considerations moved the church hierarchy toward the position of the champions of learning. Well-educated clerics made ideal functionaries in the fledgling royal bureaucracies, and the proximity of clerics to the crowned heads of Europe strengthened bonds between church and state. Moreover, clerics armed with a surer knowledge of the Word—and trained in its proper interpretation—made better foot soldiers in the struggle against heresies that were gaining ground in parts of Europe. Catholic clerics ignorant of their own

Bible would be of little use in opposing the growing Albigensian movement in southern France, a heresy that, in addition to having a dualistic theology, had its own version of the Bible.

The confidence the church placed in reason and learning was no foolish miscalculation. It certainly proved more effective than brutal inquisitorial methods in keeping the faithful within the bounds of orthodoxy. And it gave Western Christianity an intellectual vibrancy that survives to this day.

Nevertheless, the Christian rationalism fostered in this time could exist only in fragile equipoise—the authority of individual reason (enhanced by learning) balanced against the authority of Scripture and tradition. History would soon show how decisively this balance could be upset. However much the critical approach to the central text of the Chris-

tian tradition might have bolstered the position of the church in the short run, it fostered new habits of mind that in the long run weakened the church's authority.

Foremost among these habits were the growing power and confidence of individuals—from the clergy and aristocracy at first, but soon those from other social strata as well—to determine, through reading, reflection and study, their relation to the truth. This development in turn expanded the very scope and meaning of individualism. When the Bible became a text that people could more directly read, study and grapple with, civilized life in the West was set on a course that those who initiated the change most likely would have considered had they lived to see the Reformation, the Enlightenment and the modern world—ironic.

Girls Growing Up in Later Medieval England

*Teenage pregnancy and street gossip—but also lessons in housekeeping and good husbandry. **Jeremy Goldberg** draws on contemporary documents to assess the pluses and minuses of entering adulthood as a woman in the late Middle Ages.*

Jeremy Goldberg is a Lecturer in History at the University of York. He is author of Women, Work, and Life Cycle in a Medieval Economy, *(Clarendon, 1992), and editor of* Woman is a Worthy Wight *(Alan Sutton, 1992).*

Children, our grandparents were told, should be seen and not heard. The historian of the later Middle Ages finds that children, and particularly younger children, are rarely either seen or heard. And if this is not so true of boys, it is rather more true of girls. Most medieval sources are concerned with householders. Householders were exclusively adults and predominantly adult males, who enter administrative, judicial or fiscal records because they tended to carry obligations of service or taxation, or because they were held responsible for their own transgressions or those of their dependants, be they wives, servants or children. We lack the diaries, letters or autobiographical materials that do so much to illuminate the childhoods of at least a literate few from the end of the sixteenth century. Those sources that do exist, be they sermons or advice manuals, tend to be prescriptive rather than simply narrative.

It is in the absence of sources that obviously reflect affective relationships that a particular historiography of medieval childhood has emerged. We are told that children were born into a hostile or at least uncaring world. Numbers of girl babies were disposed of at birth as a burden to their parents. There was little bond between mother and child as many children passed their infancy suckled by a wet-nurse. As an infant the child was constrained in swaddling bands and left unattended and unchanged for many hours on end. Until the child reached her fifth birthday, she was treated with indifference because high rates of infant and child mortality warned parents against investing emotionally in such fragile lives. Parents regularly brutalised their children by beating them. From the age of about seven to nine a girl might be sent into hard service. There she might be ill-treated or sexually abused by masters or other males within the household. By the time she reached her twelfth birthday a girl was of age to be married. This would be a business transaction in which the girl was merely a chattel transferred from the patriarchal authority of her father to that of a husband and

a father-in-law. She would pass from a childhood largely devoid of nurturing, of play, or of what we would recognise as education, to the role of wife and mother whilst still a teenager. Happily, two of the most recent monograph studies of medieval childhood reject some elements of this particular story, but the discussion that follows is predicated against this background.

We may not be overburdened with sources, but we do have some that take us a bit further. They need to be treated with caution, however, as they may dazzle and mislead. Juries' verdicts contained in coroners rolls, for example, concerned as they are with both homicides and accidental deaths can offer unique insight into the lives of even very young children, but only because they have suffered some fatal misfortune. For every baby in its cradle gored by a passing pig or toddler drowned whilst exploring its environment, thousands of others probably survived or failed to survive for more mundane—hence unrecorded—reasons. Similarly, lore of childbirth or childcare would be passed down by experience and word of mouth. Let us begin with a story derived from the consistory court of the Archbishop of York relating to the disputed marriage of one Alice, the daughter and heiress of the former Gervase de Rouclif, and lady of the manor of Rawcliffe (near York). Alice was born c. 1353 in a basement room within her parents' manor house. Her mother, Elena, was attended at the birth by one Elena Taliour, who had been hired to be the baby's wet-nurse, and another older woman whom we may presume to have been the midwife. That same day Alice was carried by her nurse the couple of miles to the parish church of St Olave in York to be baptised.

Some months later Elena was churched (the ceremony of ritual purification) in respect of Alice's birth and her husband held a feast to celebrate the churching. Shortly before Christmas some eleven years later Alice formally exchanged words of matrimony with one John Marrays and immediately after went to live with John's married sister at Kennythorpe near Malton. During the following summer John Marrays visited his child bride and had sex with her on at least one occasion. Shortly after Alice was abducted by armed men and taken into the custody of her uncle, Brian. John Marrays, supported by Alice's mother, who seems to have arranged her daughter's marriage, then brought an action within the York consistory for restitution of conjugal rights. This was challenged by Brian de Rouclif who claimed that Alice had still not reached her twelfth birthday by the time of the abduction and was therefore not lawfully married. Alice thus became the victim of a particularly cruel tug of love between her mother and her uncle in effect for control of her marriage and the property to which she was heiress.

This is only a story, or rather a narrative web composed of many stories, for it is made up from the depositions of some fifty-seven witnesses who appear variously to show that Alice was of age (i.e. twelve or more) and had contracted a valid marriage, or that she was not and had not. We cannot know for sure what really happened. Nor does that matter. Throughout the proceedings of the court Alice was silent. The circumstances of her birth and marriage, even her own words, were narrated at second hand in response to set questions asked of witnesses and set down in an abbreviated Latin translation. But, nevertheless, there is much that we may learn from this episode.

Alice's birth within a basement room is typical of the darkened enclosed womblike space into which Early Modern mothers were known to have given birth. Elena was attended by two women, though rather larger numbers of attendants seem to have been common. Likewise Alice's urgent baptism was normal, as was Elena's subsequent churching, in an era when it was believed that a child unbaptised, and thus uncleansed of original sin, was condemned to eternal damnation. Indeed, in the absence of parish registers only introduced from 1538, our only record of births is from the very rare survival of clerical accounts recording payments for the churching of women. Thus we have from Hornsea in 1482–83 such laconic entries as:

> Item, for the purification of Henry Schomaker's wife, 1½d.
> Item, for the purification of John Major's wife, 1½d.
> Item, for the purification of six different women, 8d.

That baby Alice was provided with a wet-nurse who had been hired in anticipation of her mother giving birth is a reflection of her mother's social standing as a member of the landed gentry and for whom the physicality of feeding and of changing soiled swaddling clothes would have been demeaning. There is elsewhere evidence that some Hull merchants employed wet-nurses, but, unlike parts of Mediterranean Europe, no evidence to suggest that the practice ever extended beyond this social élite. Most mothers probably suckled their own children and for periods of eighteen months to two years, a custom documented in the Rouclif case which would have reduced the mother's fertility, but would also have increased the chances of the infant surviving the first few months of life.

The American social historian, Barbara Hanawalt, is right to argue that infanticide is hardly to be found in the records, but perhaps mistaken to conclude that it was consequently equally rare. Infanticide is by nature a secret crime committed by the desperate and we cannot expect to know about it save in rare cases. Certainly there were seduced or abused teenagers and young adults who saw little alternative. An example from an early sixteenth-century visitation is particularly revealing:

> Alice Ridyng, unmarried, the daughter of John Ridyng of Eton in the diocese of Lincoln appeared in person and confessed that she conceived a boy child by one Thomas Denys, then chaplain to Master Geoffrey Wren, and gave birth to him at her father's home at Eton one Sunday last month and immediately after giving birth, that is within four hours of the birth, killed the child by putting her hand in the baby's mouth and so suffocated him. After she had killed the child she buried it in a dung heap in her father's orchard. At the time of the delivery she had no midwife and nobody was ever told as such that she was pregnant, but some women of Windsor and Eton had suspected and said that she was pregnant, but Alice always denied this saying that something else was wrong with her belly. On the Tuesday after the delivery of the child, however, the women and honest wives of Windsor and Eton took her and inspected her belly and her breasts by which they knew for certain that she had given birth.

Here is telling evidence of the do-gooding, moral supervision that a group of older women felt moved to exercise in this increasingly puritanical era over a girl who had gone astray. Alice could only attempt to minimise her crime by causing her clerical seducer maximum embarrassment:

> Examined further she said by virtue of the oath she had taken on the gospels that she had never been known carnally by anyone other than the said Thomas and that nobody else urged or agreed to the child's death. She also said that the child had been conceived on the feast of the Purification of the Blessed Virgin Mary last at the time of high mass in the house of Master Geoffrey Wren at Spytell where Master Geoffrey was then infirmarer.

Coroners' rolls provide some insight into childhood accidents and hence, somewhat obliquely, aspects of child development and childcare. Barbara Hanawalt's pioneering analysis of these perhaps too readily leaves the impression that young children were often neglected by hard-pressed mothers and that children were regularly burned in cradle fires or drowned in ditches. But these are the records of the unfortunate and the atypical. There is no reason to believe that other demands on a mother's time were necessarily incompatible with childcare, nor that babies and young children were not regularly supervised, if not by the mother then by servants, older siblings or neighbours. The jury's verdict in an accidental death case from Bedfordshire in 1276, for example, records that 'Maud, daughter of Ellis Batte of Sutton was sitting in William's house keeping watch over Emma's child Rose, who was lying in a cradle' at the time that Emma herself became the victim of a work-related accident.

Hanawalt has argued that male toddlers were more adventurous than female toddlers and hence more likely to suffer accidental deaths. It may be, however, that the deaths of boys were more likely to be reported to the coroner and thus become the subject of record than those of their sisters. Most children were, in fact, much more vulnerable to a litany of childhood illnesses. Sex ratio evidence from the 1377 poll tax does not reveal the sort of imbalance in favour of males that was so conspicuous in Tuscany only half a century later, and hence there is little reason to believe that the sort of adverse welfare of girls that may underlie that imbalance operated in English society. Hanawalt's finding, supported by evidence from manor court rolls, that at about the age of seven girls as well as boys began to be engaged in household chores, fetching wood, tending livestock, or picking berries seems much more plausible.

Sadly we know all too little about play. Froissart provides a nostalgic picture of a childhood spent chasing butterflies and playing with mud cakes and we get little glimpses in Flemish marginalia or the paintings of Pieter Breughel, though again small boys tend to be more conspicuous than small girls. Of education we know still less, but mothers probably taught their daughters the Creed, Paternoster (Lord's Prayer), and Ave (Hail Mary) from a comparatively early age, and in some more well-to-do households taught them to read. Some girls, particularly in an urban environment, may have enjoyed some instruction at the local nunnery or even, when a little older, at grammar school.

Another point that Hanawalt has effectively demonstrated is the love and concern that parents were capable of showing towards even very young children. A single example she cites from the Bedfordshire rolls dated 1270 will suffice:

> Emma, daughter of Richard Toky of Southill went to 'Houleden' in Southill to gather wood. Walter Garglof of Stanford came carrying a bow and a small sheaf of arrows. He seized Emma and tried to throw her to the ground and rape her, but she immediately shouted and her father came. Walter shot an arrow at him, striking him on the right side of the forehead and mortally wounding him. He shot him again with an arrow under the right side and so into the stomach. Seman of Southill came and asked why he wanted to kill Richard. Walter immediately shot an arrow at him and struck him in the back so that his life was despaired of. Walter then fled . . .

There is indeed little reason to believe that relations between daughters and parents were other than the usual mixture of affection and infuriation. Parents no doubt backed moral instruction and discipline with physical chastisement, though the frequency with which they were urged not to spare the rod may tell of parents' own reluctance to strike their offspring too readily. That many parents sent their daughters into service once they had reached their teens, and, according to contemporary theory, were deemed capable of rational choice is not evidence of a lack of parental concern any more than is the case of the modern parent who sends their child to school. But in going on to write about servants and service, I do not wish to imply that no daughters remained with their parents into adulthood. In rural areas it was not uncommon for daughters to remain, and this may have been especially true where mothers were widowed. In such instances adolescent daughters may have been an essential part of the familial work-force and essential to the mother's survival in old age. In urban society especially, however, it would appear that very few girls in their teens remained at home, but went instead into service.

Let us consider another story. The words are those of a Venetian who spent time based in London at the very end of the fifteenth century:

> The want of affection in the English, is strongly manifested towards their children, for after having kept them at home until they arrive at the age of seven or nine years at the utmost, they put them out, both males and females, to hard service in the houses of other people, binding them generally for another seven or nine years. And these are called apprentices, and during that time they perform all the most menial offices, and few are born who are exempted from this fate, for everyone, however rich he may be, sends away his children into the houses of others, whilst he, in return, receives those of strangers into his own. And on inquiring their reason for this severity, they answered that they did it in order that their children might learn better manners. [He continues] But I, for my part, believe that they do it because they like to enjoy all their comforts themselves, and that they are better served by strangers than they would be by their own children. . . . If the English sent their children away from home to learn virtue and good manners, and took them back again when their apprenticeship was over, they might, perhaps, be excused. But they never return, for the girls are settled by their patrons, and the boys make the best marriages they can and, assisted by their patrons, not by their fathers, they also open a house and strive diligently by this means to make some fortune for themselves. . . .

How are we to read this text? The Venetian author of the so-called *Italian Relation* reflects the characteristic prejudices of the tourist. Those aspects of the local culture that he finds alien, he castigates in moralistic terms. In Northern Italian society servants were comparatively few in number, almost exclusively female, drawn from a variety of age groups, and exclusively low status. For the fatherless daughter or the poor widow, service was better than walking the streets, but the social gulf between servant and master, and the power the master could exercise, and all too easily abuse, was widely understood. Thus the Venetian writer found the idea of both boys and girls sent into service, and from well-to-do as well as more humble backgrounds, evidence of a lack of parental affection.

Certain important points emerge from the Venetian's narrative that may be corroborated from other sources. First, servanthood was a stage in growing up; it owed more to considerations of age than to status or gender. Second, that just as servants became, to a greater or lesser degree, dependants of their employers, so they became independent of their own parents and natal families. If we add to this the observation that girls might have entered service from as early as their thirteenth year (somewhat later than our shocked Venetian would have it) but would not have married until well into their twenties, and that rather than being tied to a single employer for several years at a time, servants would have moved freely from employer to employer every year or so, then service begins to beg all sorts of questions about the nature of later medieval English society and the experiences of young women.

We may deduce something of the structure of female services from deposition evidence from the York consistory. Numbers of deponents were either currently or formerly servants. Since deponents are often identified by age and marital status, we can know that young women alike can often be found as servants during their teens and earlier twenties, and that they were always unmarried. Depositions also reveal that servants were regularly hired at customary dates, these being Pentecost and Martinmas (November 11th) in the North, Michaelmas (September 29th) in the Midlands, and that most servants stayed with a particular employer only a year or perhaps two years at a time. They further show that servants were sometimes related by blood or marriage to their employers. Testamentary evidence extends this picture by revealing ties of trade or locality that explain how a girl in search of service came to be taken on by a particular master or mistress.

Poll tax evidence from 1377 and 1379, which lists large numbers of servants of sufficient age to pay these taxes on heads, further shows that female servants were particularly in demand in towns, and probably in similar numbers to male servants, but that females were much less in demand than males in the countryside. Probably nearly a third of all women over fourteen in York in 1377 were then employed as servants whereas the equivalent proportion for rural Rutland was less than 8 per cent.

The depositions provide further insights. We glimpse female servants at work, assisting in their employers' shops, running errands, fetching water, washing cloth to be dyed, fetching food and lighted candles, or clearing and washing tables. A celebrated case of 1429 from Norwich tells how, when sent on an errand to a neighbour, the fourteen-year-old Agnes Bethom's curiosity helped bring a heresy charge against that neighbour. Finding the neighbour not at home on entering, Agnes could not resist peeking inside the covered cooking pot simmering on the open fire. Inside she found some bacon cooking, a find she immediately reported back to her mistress for it was the first week of the Lenten fast when the eating of meat was taboo.

Poll tax evidence, supported by testamentary evidence, further suggests that mercantile, textile, and victualling traders were especially likely to employ female servants. In a rural context, women servants were more numerous in pastoral and mixed economies than in arable regions, an observation that accords with evidence from other sources that caring for livestock, dairy work, washing and shearing sheep, making hay, and managing poultry were all seen as primarily 'women's work'. We may also assume that female servants may have assisted with child care, preparing meals, purchasing goods in the market, and generally helping out.

For our Venetian tourist, service was a means by which employers got good help cheaply. In one sense he was correct. In the labour-starved decades following the Black Death of 1348–49, waged labour became very expensive, but since live-in servants were remunerated primarily in terms of board and lodging, they were in particular demand at this time. The shift towards mixed and pastoral farming, another product of demographic contraction, likewise created demand for servants, employed for a year at a time, as against day labour that was better adapted to the more highly seasonalised work pattern of an arable economy. But female servants are found before the plague and continue to be found even when the real cost of hired labour had fallen with renewed demographic growth from the end of the fifteenth century. Such economic factors do little to explain this distinctive feature of late medieval English, and indeed north-western European culture. So why else did parents send their daughters and sons into service, and merchants, artisans, and substantial peasants, not to mention lords and clergy, prefer to employ other peoples' angst-ridden adolescents rather than

their own? 'To learn better manners' was the answer suggested to our Venetian.

This may not be so far off the mark if we understand manners potentially to include how to manage a household, reckon up accounts, keep shop, run a dairy, judge a good cut of meat, or know the price of a dozen tallow candles, in addition to how a young woman should conduct herself in public. It may be that people found it easier to teach such things to strangers than to their own daughters. More importantly not all parents had the knowledge or the means. Though servant girls appear to have been drawn from across the social spectrum so that the rural labourer's daughter was as likely to be found in service in town as the daughter of the merchant, only better off householders had need of the labour that servants could provide or could offer training in the work or running of such households.

Labourers, journeymen and peasant smallholders had neither need for their daughters' labour, nor the means to support a growing teenager. The mobility of servants further ensured that employers had a continual supply of youngsters of the appropriate ages for the tasks required of them. There was little purpose in employing a young woman who was a skilled goldsmith or accomplished needlewoman to run the errands that a girl half her age could just as well manage.

Youngsters themselves probably had little choice as to whether they went into service or stayed at home. Even the aristocracy commonly sent their daughters into service in households of similar, or preferably superior social rank as a sort of finishing school, trusting that they would grow up able to speak French prettily.

But being in service had certain advantages. There were, for example, lots of other young people in the same position. In York in 1377 only one servant in five worked on their own and nearly a third of all servants worked in households with at least three others. The opportunities for making friends with fellow servants or with those from neighbouring households were considerable.

Service provided a degree of security. Many youngsters might have expected to lose one or both parents between their teens and mid-twenties, i.e., precisely at the time they were most likely to have been already economically and emotionally independent of their natal families. It is possible that some of the small proportion of female apprentices found in London records, who unlike servants were bound to their employers for a period of some seven years or more in order to learn a specific craft such as embroidery or working in silk, were in fact orphans, and that apprenticeship was seen as an appropriate way to provide for them.

Employers were obliged to feed and clothe their servants, and, we may surmise, to care for them in illness, counsel them in trouble, and punish them if they went astray. There were, however, clear bounds beyond which an employer might not go with impunity as servants or their parents were quite capable of bringing charges of physical assault or neglect. Similarly, though female servants were periodically seduced or sexually abused by masters or even sons, we should not imagine that such exploitation was the norm. Mistresses, perhaps rather than masters, may have given moral and religious instruction and may sometimes even have encouraged them to read. Certainly a didactic text like *How the Good Wife Taught her Daughter* would have provided suitable instruction for a female servant and good reading practice. Finally, to judge from testamentary evidence, employers' interest in their women servants could sometimes extend beyond a simple money contract and that some provided for their future careers by providing them with cooking utensils, beds and bedding, and very occasionally even houses or shops.

Servants were exclusively single, but many might expect to marry when, or shortly after, they left service. Many young servant women would have conducted courtships, often with fellow servants. We can see this clearly, from disputed marriage cases in the York consistory. These suggest that young women in service enjoyed particular freedom of courtship, but since such women also enjoyed a modest degree of economic autonomy so long as they remained unmarried in service, they were able to exercise considerable choice over whom and when they married. Before the advent of effective forms of artificial contraception, women would, if given the choice, prefer to delay marriage and hence childbirth and childbearing. The wise young woman might engage in serious courtship perhaps only in her early twenties, before eventually marrying by about her mid-twenties.

The wise woman would not have engaged in sexual intercourse as such until she and her partner had agreed to marry; more cautious conduct nevertheless incurring the disapproval of the moral minority by the eve of the Reformation, as a case from a visitation of 1520 demonstrates:

> Agnes Plumrige of Fingerst, the wife of John Plumrige, appeared and confessed that she had been known and made pregnant by her husband before their marriage. The bishop ordered her to go round her neighbours on the feast of the Purification of Mary openly carrying a candle costing four pence.

Having agreed between themselves that they intended marriage, the couple might then be handfast (exchange words of consent while holding hands) before witnesses. Such handfastings of servants were commonly witnessed by employers and friends but not necessarily by parents or other close kin where the young people were no longer living at home. If the words used were in the present tense, e.g. 'I take you John to be my husband and to this I plight you my troth', then in canon law, and probably in the minds of those making the contract, the marriage was immediately binding. Only subsequently might banns be read and the marriage solemnised at the church door, but this seems to have been an elaboration that poorer members of society might, before perhaps the later fifteenth century, choose to forego.

Not all young women were so wise or so lucky. The popular literature of the day is full of clerical seducers, of maidens made pregnant whilst suspecting no guile, of girls abandoned by their fickle lovers. In part, no doubt, this literature served a didactic function, but it also reflects the negative aspect of a society, unlike that of Renaissance Tuscany, that allowed young women below the ranks of the aristocracy and perhaps the peasant and mercantile elites, relative freedom of courtship. Perhaps the greatest danger a young woman could run was to agree to sex before she had any openly witnessed contract of marriage. The deposition of Alice, wife of Adam de Baumburght of York, made in 1381, illustrates the point:

> On Monday night before the feast of the Ascension last she came to a certain high room located inside the dwellinghouse of the said witness where she found, as she says, Robert and Agnes lying alone together in one bed. The witness asked Robert, 'What are you doing here, Robert?' To this Robert replied, 'I'm already here'. The witness said to him, 'Take Agnes by the hand in order to betroth her'. Robert said to the witness, 'I beg you wait until the morning'. The witness said to him in reply, 'By God, no. You'll do it now'. Then Robert took Agnes by the hand and said, 'I will take you as my wife'. The witness said to him, 'You will speak in this manner: I take you Agnes to my wife and to this I plight you my troth', and Robert, thus instructed by the witness, took Agnes by the right hand and contracted with her using the words just recited, viz. 'Here I take you etc.'. Asked how Agnes replied to Robert, she said that Agnes replied to him that she considered herself satisfied. She did not depose further save that she went away and left them alone.

The contract, of course, was subsequently a matter of litigation, hence the record, but Alice's single testimony would have been insufficient proof for canon law required two witnesses to the same event.

Another hazard that the young unmarried woman had to cope with was that of reputation. In a culture that depended so much on the word on the street for information, and where a woman's honour was construed in purely sexual terms, loose talk could cause cruel damage. As the Goodwife warned her daughter, 'A slander raises ill/is evil for to still'. We may cite the example of Isabel Gremmesby from a laconic visitation entry for Grainthorpe in Lincolnshire in 1519:

> Thomas Dam slandered Isabel Gremmesby so that William Pennyngton will not have her for his wife.

Such slander could only be nullified by public denial, as seen for example in a similar entry from Brill in Buckinghamshire of 1494:

> Joan Baron publicly defamed of the sin of fornication done, it is said, with one[. . .] Trussell. She appeared and denied the article and purged herself with Elizabeth Forster, Elina Godynton, Alice Fuller and Alice Pym. A proclamation was made etc. and because no opposer lawfully appeared,

the judge admitted her to her purgation and restored her to her good standing and she was dismissed.

Though not all young women who reached adulthood married, by the time they were of age to marry and have children, we may regard them as having grown up. Elena Couper of Welton near Hull, the heroine of our final story, illustrates this point. She was growing tired of her young man, John Wistow, putting off their marriage, even though she knew that her father disapproved of him strongly. On Sunday before Pentecost, 1491 she confronted him with these words:

John, there are two young men about me in town to have me to wife. And I have loved you these two years. And you know well that you and I are hand-fast between us. And because you shall not vary nor take another better than me, we will be handfast here before these folk that they may bear record thereupon.

John duly obliged, but Elena's mother was less convinced:

You filth and harlot. Why, are you handfast with John Wistow? When your father knows it, he will 'dynge' you and 'myschew' you. [A translation seems superfluous].

Elena took refuge with a friend who only admitted her angry father on condition that he did her no harm. Elena threw herself on her knees, reminded her father that in law she was now married, and said that she asked no inheritance, but only a paternal blessing. This he granted and Elena then sent for her young man, telling him that they could go ahead and set up house together, to which John replied, 'we must tarry, the house is not yet ready'. Such a strong-minded woman surely deserved better. History, however, like real life, does not always have a happy ending.

FOR FURTHER READING:

B. A. Hanawalt, *The Ties that Bound: Peasant Families in Medieval England* (Oxford University Press, 1986); B. A. Hanawalt, *Growing Up in Medieval London* (Oxford University Press, 1993); N. Orme, *From Childhood to Chivalry* (Methuen, 1984); S. Shahar, *Childhood in the Middle-Ages* (Routledge, 1990); P. J. P. Goldberg, *Women, Work, and Life Cycle in a Medieval Economy* (Clarendon, 1992).

War-Games of Central Italy

Modern Italian cities hold annual intramural games dating back to the Middle Ages. **Raymond E. Role** *explores their evolution and the cultural, political and social landscape where these paramilitary sports originated.*

ITALY'S ENERVATING SUMMERS are invigorated by the pageantry of annual sporting events, with Siena's bare-back horse race, *La Corsa del Palio,* being the most famous. Unforgettable as visual experiences, full of the bold patterns and colours of period costumes, these events have roots that reach deep into a less languid medieval past.

Almost a century before the First Crusade (1095–99), Christendom's first counter-assaults against Islam had been launched from Pisa and Genoa, re-opening western Mediterranean sea routes and stimulating a revival of commerce and industry in the Italian peninsula on the foundations of the urban network of ancient Rome. Over the following centuries, their growing economic power enabled Italian cities to develop the most advanced culture in Europe; yet they remained volatile and violent places.

Beginning around the year 1080 in a few cities like Pisa and Lucca, the commune, a republican form of political system, emerged, and by 1143 communes had been established in all major cities from Rome to the Alps. City-dwellers were elevated to citizenship by taking an oath of obedience to the commune, which in effect governed a city-state whose inhabitants spanned all circumstances and means. Italian nobility increasingly participated in the commercial life of the cities, while the urban merchant class steadily increased its wealth, so that many of the distinctions between these two classes diminished. They began to share a common style of life, and became the cities' political class.

As the rural nobility began living in cities during the early twelfth century, they brought their aristocratic mentality with them. Soon city folk of middling rank were emulating the nobles' ostentatious, arrogant and violent behaviours, including the vendetta. With lawlessness endemic among the urban elite, the custom of the vendetta seems to have spread quickly to all levels of society, so no medieval citizen was ever far from a potential street fight.

> *The very fabric of the medieval Italian city was a constant invitation to future violence.*

Men instinctively turned first to their relatives and then to their friends for protection. Kinship ultimately determined status, power and security. By the mid-twelfth century, large kinship groups, or clans, had incorporated themselves into defensive alliances or *consorterie,* while groups of smaller, unrelated families had bound themselves together by solemn oaths into mutual defence associations called 'tower societies'. Consequently, communal governments had constantly to struggle to assert their nascent right to govern and to establish their authority over an unruly populace, while simultaneously striving to unify their citizenry into something more than a quarrelsome tangle of rival factions.

Within the walls of the cities, inhabitants' mutual fear can be seen reflected in their arrangement of housing—a patchwork of neighbourhoods, each the stronghold either of a *consorteria* or of a 'tower society'. The architectural nucleus of such a neighbourhood was its stout stone or brick tower, like those surviving at San Gimignano or Lucca's Torre Guinigi, designed for throwing, shooting or catapulting projectiles at rival fellow-citizens and/or their property nearby. Built tightly around this fortification were the houses of the members of its *consorteria* or its 'tower society', along with their parish church. This whole complex formed a compact urban refuge, whose narrow alleyways could be easily barricaded off and defended when vendettas flared up. The very fabric of the medieval Italian city was a constant invitation to future violence.

Even beyond the city walls, this parochial mentality can be seen in the medieval map of northern and central Italy—a patchwork of city-states, each trying to expand at the expense of the other. The survival of a city as an independent state ultimately rested on its armed forces, which comprised combat

This article first appeared in *History Today,* June 1999, pp. 8-13. © 1999 by History Today, Ltd. Reprinted by permission.

units levied from each of its semi-autonomous neighbourhoods. If the internal divisions from within the city were allowed to reach the battlefield, they could destroy military cohesion and possibly endanger the city itself.

Legislative attempts to curb blood-feuds occurred as early as 1100 when Pisa limited the height of towers and forbade private possession of catapults, mangonels, crossbows and ammunition. City governments, often in concert with the local bishops, demanded oaths of peace *en masse* from their citizens and extracted sums of money from past offenders as surety bonds. Punishments usually took the form of fines, confiscation of property, razing of family palazzi or towers, permanent exile or death—but the clannish nature of the vendetta was so engrained that some legislation, such as the Florentine Ordinances of Justice enacted in 1293, went so far as to punish not only those guilty of violence, but their innocent relatives as well. Some punishments even included a grant of immunity from prosecution to victims' families, in order to allow its members to take revenge with impunity upon the peace-breakers, their close relatives, even their children as yet unborn.

Communal governments also developed a safety-valve to release built-up rancour at a diminished level of violence, and in doing so demonstrated their authority over their disorderly constituents. They coupled major annual religious festivals with a government-sponsored intramural game, or *giocca*, a mock combat pitting contestants from rival neighbourhoods against one another. This offered a non-lethal outlet with, hopefully, a cathartic outcome as a substitute for the vendetta. Such events were preceded by impressive religious-civic processions, formally manifesting the government's jurisdiction. Today, the direct descendants of these paramilitary games come alive each summer.

Almost as old as the communes themselves was the most widespread of all the intramural games, the *Giocca di Mazzascuda;* or the Game of Club and Shield, where fully armoured foot soldiers sought to drive their opponents from the field with blows from wooden maces. Known to have been played at various times in almost every city throughout Tuscany and Umbria, and at Pavia and Gubbio too, this 'sport' was probably played widely elsewhere in Italy as well.

From at least the early thirteenth century, the communal government of Pisa encouraged its citizens to play the *Giocca di Mazzascuda* annually between Christmas and Shrove Tuesday. To underscore governmental control and sponsorship, a field was set up directly in front of Palagio Maggiore, Pisa's seat of government, in the city's main piazza, the Piazza dei Anziani (now Piazza dei Cavalieri di San Stefano). This large circular enclosure, surrounded by a cordon of chains with entrances at two opposing points, was guarded from dawn to dusk by Pisa's police forces to maintain order among combatants and spectators alike. This field of honour was available daily, except Sundays, for privately arranged contests, either single or group combat, a handy place to settle a grudge, even a score, or repay an insult. On January 17th, the feast day of St Anthony Abbot, the government also sponsored a large group combat, similar to a popular knightly tournament called a *melée,* or *battagliaccia.* This civic 'sport' allowed even humble citizens to publicly display their martial skills on foot in the same vainglorious way as the noble citizens displayed their derring-do on horseback. For centuries this annual martial exercise kept its citizen-soldiers in fighting trim, but in 1406 Pisa lost its independence to the Florentines, who swiftly confiscated the Pisans' arms, including their wooden maces for playing the *Giocca di Mazzascuda.*

Undiminished by Florentine rule, however, internecine violence continued at Pisa throughout the fifteenth century, taking on the form of rock-throwing incidents between the then unarmed neighbourhood factions, often staged impromptu on the narrow bridges spanning the Arno. Since little was needed to convert this spontaneous mayhem into a new government-sponsored martial arts tournament, Lorenzo de' Medici, towards the end of the century, encouraged the establishment of the *Giocca del Ponte* to be held on June 17th, the feast day of San Ranieri, patron saint of Pisa. The earliest form of the *Giocca del Ponte* probably consisted of two numerically equal squads of combatants, armed with blunt weapons and protected by shields and armour, contesting the crossing of a bridge. There were no rules, but the first squad to bludgeon its way across to the opponent's side won.

The rules of the *Giocca del Ponte* were made slightly more genteel in the early sixteenth century, by limiting contestants to just six per side, defining the martial techniques permitted and eliminating some of the game's more entertaining 'plays' such as tossing a heavily armoured opponent into the Arno. Gone too were the traditional wooden club and shield, replaced by the *targone,* a long narrow type of wooden shield, a meter long with a semi-circular top 25cm wide, tapering to a blunt point 5cm wide. Fitted with horizontal wooden hand grips top and bottom, the *targone* could be used both defensively, to parry opponents' blows, and offensively, to push and to 'butt end' by gripping its handles or to club by holding its small end. The *Battagliaccia del Giorno di San Antonio* was also reinstated on January 17th, preserving the no-holds-barred style of 'play'—a kind of minor league event where aspiring combatants could hone their skills.

In the late sixteenth century the game was reorganised into just two large opposing teams, called Tramontana and Mezzogiorno, representing the northern and southern sides of the city divided by the Arno, each incorporating the neighbourhood squads. This arrangement forced those in adjacent neighbourhoods—normally the most mutually antagonistic and vendetta-prone groups—to work together as teammates and future comrades-in-arms. Organized in military fashion into six companies of sixty each, with a captain and commanded by a general, these small armies battled against each other for two hours (later reduced to one hour and then to forty-five minutes). These rule changes ushered in a period of increased popularity for the *Giocca del Ponte,* that lasted from 1600 to 1785, when Pietro Leopoldo I, Grand Duke of Tuscany, an enlightened Austrian, banned it, considering it a barbarous anachronism.

After a suspension of over a century and a half, Pisa's city government reinstated the annual *Giocca del Ponte,* in 1947. Its combatants then became contestants in a modernised game, a tense 'push-of-war' with neighborhood squads pushing in opposite directions against a seven-ton carriage, or *carrello,* mounted on a fifty-metre metal track running the length of Ponte di Mezzo. Reborn as Tramontana and Mezzogiorno, each team now composed of six squads of twenty, still representing the same neighbourhoods on opposite sides of the Arno, compete in six consecutive contests. As riotous as the conclusion of any single contest may be, the end of the deciding contest that awards the annual victory to either Tramontana or Mezzogiorno is pandemonium—with unofficial fireworks and the unfurling of homemade banners, while the winners' side of the Arno is brilliantly lit up, leaving the losing side to brood in twilight.

Florence's Calcio *derives from a conditioning exercise for Roman legionaries akin to rugby.*

Medieval Florence had its own version of the *Giocca di Mazzascuda,* but also had long played an indigenous ball game called *Calcio,* a descendant of *Arapasto,* a conditioning exercise for Roman legionaries akin to rugby but more violent. It was not until the early fourteenth century, when Florence's communal government was first able to divide the city into four sub-divisions or *quartieri,* that it also began to sponsor a *Calcio* tournament at Carnevale. Its purpose was to force adjacent neighbourhoods in each *quartiere,* from which Florence also mustered its militia, to work together as teammates, just as at Pisa.

Each quartiere fielded a team of twenty seven players for a three-game, 'sudden death' tournament played on a rectangular field (one hundred metres by forty six), set-up in one of the city's larger piazzas, usually Piazza Santa Croce or Piazza Signoria. The object was to throw a 25cm diameter ball into the opponent's goal, a net 1.2 metres high stretching the full width of the field—one point if successful, but a half-point to the opponent if unsuccessful. The rules were almost nonexistent. Played annually until the late 1700s, this cross between wrestling, boxing, rugby,

basketball and soccer was reinstated with its original rules and staged in its traditional venues in 1930. Known today as *Calcio Storico Fiorentino,* it continues as an annual outlet for (still quite lively) intramural animosities. In 1997, the final match had to be cancelled when disgruntled fans from one *quartiere* violently assaulted a player from a rival *quartiere* as he left his home, in retaliation for his particularly foul play in the semifinal match; and the 1998 final was marred when fans purposely injured an opposing player by throwing fireworks into the field during the pre-game festivities.

If old habits refuse to die at Florence, they are as healthy as ever at Siena, whose very urban structure on its three hills has caused dissension for so long that the city was already referred to in the plural by the ancient Romans—the Sienas. During the Dark Ages, residents descended from the hills into the valley between them to trade with each other in a large, open field, a market site that was to become the heart of the medieval city, Piazza del Campo. Commercial disputes regularly led from quarrels to blows and bloodshed, particularly during the weeks before Lent when scarcity caused high prices. After 1125, a communal government was established in a tripartite manner with each hill becoming a political unit of the city, or *terziere,* with equal representation in the government. Each had its own internal governmental structure.

These initial building blocks of Sienese political life must have been the clan and the 'tower society', which provided Siena's armed forces. A series of devastating wars, along with the Black Death outbreaks in 1348 and thereafter, combined to decrease drastically the numerical strength of *consorteria* and 'tower society' alike, so that by the late 1400s, the survivors had to seek protection from each other by banding together in a new type of association called a *contrada.* A *contrada* was begun by unrelated families living in a neighbourhood as a corporation with a written constitution, laws, membership requirements, dues, officers, a court, a headquarters, a parish church, a patron saint, geographical boundaries, an army, a heraldic symbol, colours, a banner, allies, enemies and vendettas. Originally numbering as many as sixty, depopulation caused some *contrade* to merge until the last geographic revision, in 1729,

reduced them to their present number, seventeen. Today, the Sienese *contrada,* demilitarised yet militant, retains all of its other original elements. It is still a

The Giocca della Pugna *seemed to satisfy the blood-lust of the Sienese, with 1,200 participating in a city-wide contest in 1324.*

mutual aid society and social club. needy members are aided by funds raised from its dues, philanthropic contributions, rental properties, bar and social events such as dances. Each *contrada* sponsors a club for women and another for children, while its headquarters are bar [and] are a focus for male social activity. With both its original structure and social mission preserved, the *contrada* is more modernised than evolved, generating an intense sense of identity and loyalty among those born within its boundaries.

Faced with an already centuries-old culture of intramural violence, Siena's earliest communal governments sought to condone and control what they could not eliminate by also initiating an annual Sienese version of the *Giocca di Mazzascuda* 'played' at the end of Carnevale. Called the *Giocca dell' Elmora,* the Game of the Helmet, it was a citywide group combat, pitting Siena's most populous *terziere* against the other two. For generations, thousands of Sienese, participating under their military banners, wielding wooden weapons (maces, swords and spears) and throwing stones, sought to drive their fellow citizens from Piazza del Campo under the watchful eyes of their elected officials looking on from the windows of Palazzo Pubblico, the seat of government. Sheer numbers, however, made effective control nearly impossible. When even the intervention of the city's police forces still failed to prevent ten fatalities in 1291, sufficient political will was finally generated to ban the 'game' permanently.

Besides the *Giocca dell' Elmora,* its less life-threatening and much older, possibly Etruscan relative, the *Giocca della Pugna,* or the Fist Fight, was a favourite pastime in medieval Siena. Wearing cloth caps with protective cheek-pieces tied together under the chin similar to the sparring headgear of modern boxers, and with their fists wrapped in cloth bindings to protect their knuckles, participants sought to drive their fellow citizens from one of the city's piazzas. Whether arranged in advance or held impromptu between just two neighbourhoods in a nearby piazza, or organized by the communal government between the full *terzieri* in Piazza del Campo, the Giocca della Pugna seemed to satisfy the bloodlust of the Sienese, judging from the participation of 1,200 in a city-wide *pugna,* in 1324. During the Renaissance, bans did little to dull the appetite for the 'game' among the Sienese, who staged a *pugna* just as heartily in 1536 to celebrate the visit of newly crowned Holy Roman Emperor, Charles V, as they did nearly twenty years later to raise their own morale during the siege of the city by his Imperial troops. *La pugna* survived even Napoleon, with the students of Siena University's class of 1816 being the last to enjoy the exhilaration of this 'sport'.

Siena's communal government, like those of other cities in Italy, originally linked their paramilitary games to celebrations of some annual religious festivals, but by the mid-twelfth century it had also coupled as many as six horse races with other religious events. Beginning at some point outside the city walls, these horse races ran a course,

point-to-point or *al lungo,* through Siena's streets to a finishing line at the cathedral, where the winner received as a prize, a bolt of expensive cloth, or *palio.* Later, a single *contrada,* in celebration of the feast day of its patron saint, would periodically stage a *palio,* inviting others to participate. It is uncertain when the *contrade* began to send entrants to the annual city-wide races, but by the last half of the fifteenth century they sponsored all the contestants.

After Siena lost its independence to Florence in 1555, Duke Cosimo I de' Medici, fearing massive public gatherings, reduced the number of races to just one, honouring St Mary, patron saint of Siena, on August 15th, in commemoration of her Assumption. In 1656, a second race was permitted on July 2nd to commemorate the Visitation and the purely local feast day of St Mary of Provenzano—a race run *alla tonda,* three times around Piazza del Campo, allowing viewing of the race start-to-finish for the first time. So exciting was this new form that a third race, also *alla tonda,* was soon added on August 16th. Although the older race, *al lungo,* on August 15th failed to survive the nineteenth century, the other two races, both now called *La Corsa del Palio,* have been run continuously ever since, under the sponsorship of the competing *contrade.* Such longevity is due in part to the incorporation within them of many aspects of Siena's former paramilitary games and races so that, with the partisan enthusiasm for all of them distilled into these two events, *La Corsa del Palio* releases the seemingly eternal fanaticism of the *contrade.*

Lucca's *Tiro dei Balestrieri,* where cross-bow men test their archery skill, Arezzo's *Giostra del Saracino* and Pis-

toia's *Giostra del Orso,* where teams of modern-day knights tilt at the quintain, and Gubbio's *La Corsa dei Ceri,* where teams race up-hill carrying thousand-pound weights, are some of the other sporting events whose origins are entwined in their cities' history. Each is unique yet quintessentially Italian, not so much folkloristic re-enactments as modern expressions of the passions that generated their institution.

FOR FURTHER READING

Violence and Civil Disorder in Italian Cities, 1200–1500, ed. Lauro Martines (University of California Press, 1972); D. and F. W. Kent *Neighbors and Neighborhood in Renaissance Florence: the District of the Red Lion in the Fifteenth Century* (J.J. Augustin Publisher, New York, 1982); Nicholas A. Eckstein *The District of the Green Dragon: Life and Social Change in Renaissance Florence* (Leo S. Olschki Editore, Florence, 1990); E. Cristiani, *Nobilità e Popolo nel commune di Pisa* (Instituto Italiano Per Gli Studi Storici, Naples 1962); L. Artusi, *Il Palagio Parte Guelfa e il Calcio in Costume a Firenze* (Edizioni Scramasax, Florence 1997); W. Heywood *Palio e Ponte* (Hacker Art Books, New York, 1969); A. Dundes & A. Falussi *La Terra in Piazza* (University of California Press, 1975); V. Grassi *Le Contrade di Siena e le loro feste: il Palio attuale* (2 Vol., Periccioli Editore, Siena, 1972).

Raymond E. Role is a practising architect and freelance writer based in Lucca, Italy.

How a Mysterious Disease Laid Low Europe's Masses

In the 1300s, a third of the population died of plague brought by fleas, shocking the medieval world to its foundations.

Charles L. Mee Jr.

In all likelihood, a flea riding on the hid of a black rat entered the Italian port of Messina in 1347, perhaps down a hawser tying a ship up at the dock. The flea had a gut full of the bacillus *Yersinia pestis.* The flea itself was hardly bigger than the letter "o" on this page, but it could carry several hundred thousand bacilli in its intestine.

Scholars today cannot identify with certainty which species of flea (or rat) carried the plague. One candidate among the fleas is *Xenopsylla cheopis,* which looks like a deeply bent, bearded old man with six legs. It is slender and bristly, with almost no neck and no waist, so that it can slip easily through the forest of hair in which it lives. It is outfitted with a daggerlike proboscis for piercing the skin and sucking the blood of its host. And it is cunningly equipped to secrete a substance that prevents coagulation of the host's blood. Although *X. cheopis* can go for weeks without feeding, it will eat every day if it can, taking its blood warm.

One rat on which fleas feed, the black rat *(Rattus rattus),* also known as the house rat, roof rat or ship rat, is active mainly at night. A rat can fall 50 feet and land on its feet with no injury. It can scale a brick wall or climb up the inside of a pipe only an inch and a half in diameter. It can jump a distance of two feet straight up and four horizontally, and squeeze through a hole the size of a quarter. Black rats have been found still swimming days after their ship has sunk at sea.

A rat can gnaw its way through almost anything—paper, wood, bone, mortar, half-inch sheet metal. It gnaws constantly. Indeed, it *must* gnaw constantly. Its incisors grow four to five inches a year: if it were to stop gnawing, its lower incisors would eventually grow—as sometimes happens when a rat loses an opposing tooth—until the incisors push up into the rat's brain, killing it. It prefers grain, if possible, but also eats fish, eggs, fowl and meat—lambs, piglets and the flesh of helpless infants or adults. If nothing else is available, a rat will eat manure and drink urine.

Rats prefer to move no more than a hundred feet from their nests. But in severe drought or famine, rats can begin to move en masse for great distances, bringing with them any infections they happen to have picked up, infections that may be killing them but not killing them more rapidly than they breed.

Rats and mice harbor a number of infections that may cause diseases in human beings. A black rat can even tolerate a moderate amount of the ferocious *Yersinia pestis* bacillus in its system without noticeable ill effects. But bacilli breed even more extravagantly than fleas or rats, often in the millions. When a bacillus finally invades the rat's pulmonary or nervous system, it causes a horrible, often convulsive, death, passing on a lethal dose to the bloodsucking fleas that ride on the rat's hide.

THE ULTIMATE BACILLUS BREEDER

When an afflicted rat dies, its body cools, so that the flea, highly sensitive to changes in temperature, will find another host. The flea can, if need be, survive for weeks at a time without a rat host. It can take refuge anywhere, even in an abandoned rat's nest or a bale of cloth. A dying rat may liberate scores of rat fleas. More than that, a flea's intestine happens to provide ideal breeding conditions for the bacillus, which will eventually multiply so prodigiously as finally to block the gut of the flea entirely. Unable to feed or digest blood, the flea desperately seeks another host. But now, as it sucks blood, it spits some

From *Smithsonian* magazine, February 1990, pp. 67–74, 76, 78. © 1990 by Charles L. Mee, Jr. Reprinted by permission of the author.

out at the same time. Each time the flea stops sucking for a moment, it is capable of pumping thousands of virulent bacilli back into its host. Thus bacilli are passed from rat to flea to rat, contained, ordinarily, within a closed community.

For millions of years, there has been a reservoir of *Yersinia pestis* living as a permanently settled parasite—passed back and forth among fleas and rodents in warm, moist nests—in the wild rodent colonies of China, India, the southern part of the Soviet Union and the western United States. Probably there will always be such reservoirs—ready to be stirred up by sudden climatic change or ecological disaster. Even last year, four authentic cases of bubonic plague were confirmed in New Mexico and Arizona. Limited outbreaks and some fatalities have occurred in the United States for years, in fact, but the disease doesn't spread, partly for reasons we don't understand, partly because patients can now be treated with antibiotics.

And at least from biblical times on, there have been sporadic allusions to plagues, as well as carefully recorded outbreaks. The emperor Justinian's Constantinople, for instance, capital of the Roman empire in the East, was ravaged by plague in 541 and 542, felling perhaps 40 percent of the city's population. But none of the biblical or Roman plagues seemed so emblematic of horror and devastation as the Black Death that struck Europe in 1347. Rumors of fearful pestilence in China and throughout the East had reached Europe by 1346. "India was depopulated," reported one chronicler, "Tartary, Mesopotamia, Syria, Armenia, were covered with dead bodies; the Kurds fled in vain to the mountains. In Caramania and Caesarea none were left alive."

Untold millions would die in China and the rest of the East before the plague subsided again. By September of 1345, the *Yersinia pestis* bacillus, probably carried by rats, reached the Crimea, on the northern coast of the Black sea, where Italian merchants had a good number of trading colonies.

From the shores of the Black Sea, the bacillus seems to have entered a number of Italian ports. The most famous account has to do with a ship that docked in the Sicilian port of Messina in 1347. According to an Italian chronicler named Gabriele de Mussis, Christian merchants from Genoa and local Muslim residents in the town of Caffa on the Black Sea got into an argument; a serious fight en-

sued between the merchants and a local army led by a Tartar lord. In the course of an attack on the Christians, the Tartars were stricken by plague. From sheer spitefulness, their leader loaded his catapults with dead bodies and hurled them at the Christian enemy, in hopes of spreading disease among them. Infected with the plague, the Genoese sailed back to Italy, docking first at Messina.

Although de Mussis, who never traveled to the Crimea, may be a less-than-reliable source, his underlying assumption seems sound. The plague did spread along established trade routes. (Most likely, though, the pestilence in Caffa resulted from an infected population of local rats, not from the corpses lobbed over the besieged city's walls.)

In any case, given enough dying rats and enough engorged and frantic fleas, it will not be long before the fleas, in their search for new hosts, leap to a human being. When a rat flea senses the presence of an alternate host, it can jump very quickly and as much as 150 times its length. The average for such jumps is about six inches horizontally and four inches straight up in the air. Once on human skin, the flea will not travel far before it begins to feed.

The first symptoms of bubonic plague often appear within several days: headache and a general feeling of weakness, followed by aches and chills in the upper leg and groin, a white coating on the tongue, rapid pulse, slurred speech, confusion, fatigue, apathy and a staggering gait. A blackish pustule usually will form at the point of the fleabite. By the third day, the lymph nodes begin to swell. Because the bite is commonly in the leg, it is the lymph nodes of the groin that swell, which is how the disease got its name. The Greek word for "groin" is *boubon*—thus, bubonic plague. The swelling will be tender, perhaps as large as an egg. The heart begins to flutter rapidly as it tries to pump blood through swollen, suffocating tissues. Subcutaneous hemorrhaging occurs, causing purplish blotches on the skin. The victim's nervous system begins to collapse, causing dreadful pain and bizarre neurological disorders, form which the "Dance of Death" rituals that accompanied the plague may have taken their inspiration. By the fourth or fifth day, wild anxiety and terror overtake the sufferer—and then a sense of resignation, as the skin blackens and the rictus of death settles on the body.

In 1347, when the plague struck in Messina, townspeople realized that it must have come from the sick and dying crews of the ships at their dock. They turned on the sailors and drove them back out to sea—eventually to spread the plague in other ports. Messina panicked. People ran out into the fields and vineyards and neighboring villages, taking the rat fleas with them.

When the citizens of Messina, already ill or just becoming ill, reached the city of Catania, 55 miles to the south, they were at first taken in and given beds in the hospital. But as the plague began to infect Catania, the townspeople there cordoned off their town and refused—too late—to admit any outsiders. The sick, turning black, stumbling and delirious, were objects more of disgust than pity; everything about them gave off a terrible stench, it was said, their "sweat, excrement, spittle, breath, so foetid as to be overpowering; urine turbid, thick, black or red. . . ."

Wherever the plague appeared, the suddenness of death was terrifying. Today, even with hand-me-down memories of the great influenza epidemic of 1918 (SMITHSONIAN, January 1989) and the advent of AIDS, it is hard to grasp the strain that the plague put on the physical and spiritual fabric of society. People went to bed perfectly healthy and were found dead in the morning. Priests and doctors who came to minister to the sick, so the wild stories ran, would contract the plague with a single touch and die sooner than the person they had come to help. In his preface to *The Decameron,* a collection of stories told while the plague was raging, Boccaccio reports that he saw two pigs rooting around in the clothes of a man who had just died, and after a few minutes of snuffling, the pigs began to run wildly around and around, then fell dead.

"Tedious were it to recount," Boccaccio thereafter laments, "brother was forsaken by brother, nephew by uncle, brother by sister and, oftentimes, husband by wife; nay what is more and scarcely to be believed, fathers and mothers were found to abandon their own children, untended, unvisited, to their fate, as if they had been strangers. . . ."

In Florence, everyone grew so frightened of the bodies stacked up in the streets that some men, called *becchini,* put themselves out for hire to fetch and carry the dead to mass graves. Having in this way stepped over the boundary into the land of the dead, and no doubt feeling doomed themselves, the *becchini* became an abandoned, brutal lot. Many roamed the streets, forcing their way into private homes and threatening to carry people away if they were not paid off in money or sexual favors.

VISITING MEN WITH PESTILENCE

Some people, shut up in their houses with the doors barred, would scratch a sign of the cross on the front door, sometimes with the inscription "Lord have mercy on us." In one place, two lovers were supposed to have bathed in urine every morning for protection. People hovered over latrines, breathing in the stench. Others swallowed pus from the boils of plague victims. In Avignon, Pope Clement was said to have sat for weeks between two roaring fires.

The plague spread from Sicily all up and down the Atlantic coast, and from the port cities of Venice, Genoa and Pisa as well as Marseilles, London and Bristol. A multitude of men and women, as Boccaccio writes, "negligent of all but themselves . . . migrated to the country, as if God, in visiting men with this pestilence in requital of their iniquities, would not pursue them with His wrath wherever they might be. . . ."

Some who were not yet ill but felt doomed indulged in debauchery. Others, seeking protection in lives of moderation, banded together in communities to live a separate and secluded life, walking abroad with flowers to their noses "to ward off the stench and, perhaps, the evil airs that afflicted them."

It was from a time of plague, some scholars speculate, that the nursery rhyme "Ring Around the Rosy" derives: the rose-colored "ring" being an early sign that a blotch was about to appear on the skin; "a pocket full of posies" being a device to ward off stench and (it was hoped) the attendant infection; "ashes, ashes" being a reference to "ashes to ashes, dust to dust" or perhaps to the sneezing "a-choo, a-choo" that afflicted those in whom the infection had invaded the lungs—ending, inevitably, in "all fall down."

In Pistoia, the city council enacted nine pages of regulations to keep the plague out—no Pistoian was allowed to leave town to visit any place where the plague was raging; if a citizen did visit

a plague-infested area he was not allowed back in the city; no linen or woolen goods were allowed to be imported; no corpses could be brought home from outside the city; attendance at funerals was strictly limited to immediate family. None of these regulations helped.

In Siena, dogs dragged bodies from the shallow graves and left them half-devoured in the streets. Merchants closed their shops. The wool industry was shut down. Clergymen ceased administering last rites. On June 2, 1348, all the civil courts were recessed by the city council. Because so many of the laborers had died, construction of the nave for a great cathedral came to a halt. Work was never resumed: only the smaller cathedral we know today was completed.

In Venice, it was said that 600 were dying every day. In Florence, perhaps half the population died. By the time the plague swept through, as much as one-third of Italy's population had succumbed.

In Milan, when the plague struck, all the occupants of any victim's house, whether sick or well, were walled up inside together and left to die. Such draconian measures seemed to have been partially successful—mortality rates were lower in Milan than in other cities.

Medieval medicine was at a loss to explain all this, or to do anything about it. Although clinical observation did play some role in medical education, an extensive reliance on ancient and inadequate texts prevailed. Surgeons usually had a good deal of clinical experience but were considered mainly to be skilled craftsmen, not men of real learning, and their experience was not much incorporated into the body of medical knowledge. In 1300, Pope Boniface VIII had published a bull specifically inveighing against the mutilation of corpses. It was designed to cut down on the sale of miscellaneous bones as holy relics, but one of the effects was to discourage dissection.

Physicians, priests and others had theories about the cause of the plague. Earthquakes that released poisonous fumes, for instance. Severe changes in the Earth's temperature creating southerly winds that brought the plague. The notion that the plague was somehow the result of a corruption of the air was widely believed. It was this idea that led people to avoid foul odors by holding flowers to their noses or to try to drive out the infectious foul odors by inhaling the alternate foul odors of a latrine. Some thought that the plague came from

the raining down of frogs, toads and reptiles. Some physicians believed one could catch the plague from "lust with old women."

Both the pope and the king of France sent urgent requests for help to the medical faculty at the University of Paris, then one of the most distinguished medical groups in the Western world. The faculty responded that the plague was the result of a conjunction of the planets Saturn, Mars and Jupiter at 1 P.M. on March 20, 1345, an event that caused the corruption of the surrounding atmosphere.

Most Christians believed the cause of the plague was God's wrath at sinful Man.

Ultimately, of course, most Christians believed the cause of the plague was God's wrath at sinful Man. And in those terms, to be sure, the best preventives were prayer, the wearing of crosses and participation in other religious activities. In Orvieto, the town fathers added 50 new religious observances to the municipal calendar. Even so, within five months of the appearance of the plague, Orvieto lost every second person in the town.

There was also some agreement about preventive measures one might take to avoid the wrath of God. Flight was best: away from lowlands, marshy areas, stagnant waters, southern exposures and coastal areas, toward high, dry, cool, mountainous places. It was thought wise to stay indoors all day, to stay cool and to cover any windows that admitted bright sunlight. In addition to keeping flowers nearby, one might burn such aromatic woods as juniper and ash.

The retreat to the mountains, where the density of the rat population was not as great as in urban areas, and where the weather was inimical to rats and fleas, was probably a good idea—as well as perhaps proof, of a kind, of the value of empirical observation. But any useful notion was always mixed in with such wild ideas that it got lost in a flurry of desperate (and often contrary) stratagems. One should avoid bathing because that opened the pores to attack from the corrupt atmosphere, but one should wash face and feet, and sprinkle them with rose water and vinegar. In the morning, one might eat a couple of figs with rue and filberts. One expert advised eating ten-year-old treacle mixed with several dozen items, including chopped-up snake. Rhubarb was recommended, too, along with onions, leeks and garlic. The best spices were myrrh, saffron and pepper, to be taken late in the day. Meat should be roasted, not boiled. Eggs should not be eaten hard-boiled. A certain Gentile di Foligno commended lettuce; the faculty of medicine at the University of Paris advised against it. Desserts were forbidden. One should not sleep during the day. One should sleep first on the right side, then on the left. Exercise was to be avoided because it introduced more air into the body; if one needed to move, one ought to move slowly.

By the fall of 1348, the plague began to abate. But then, just as hopes were rising that it had passed, the plague broke out again in the spring and summer of 1349 in different parts of Europe. This recurrence seemed to prove that the warm weather, and people bathing in warm weather, caused the pores of the skin to open and admit the corrupted air. In other respects, however, the plague remained inexplicable. Why did some people get it and recover, while other seemed not to have got it at all—or at least showed none of its symptoms—yet died suddenly anyway? Some people died in four or five days, others died at once. Some seemed to have contracted the plague from a friend or relative who had it, others had never been near a sick person. The sheer unpredictability of it was terrifying.

In fact, though no one would know for several centuries, there were three different forms of the plague, which ran three different courses. The first was simple bubonic plague, transmitted from rat to person by the bite of the rat flea. The second and likely most common form was pneumonic, which occurred when the bacillus invaded the lungs. After a two- or three-day incubation period, anyone with pneumonic plague would have a severe, bloody cough; the sputum cast into the air would contain *Yersinia pestis*. Transmitted through the air from person to person, pneumonic plague was fatal in 95 to 100 percent of all cases.

The third form of the plague was septocemic, and its precise etiology is not entirely understood even yet. In essence, however, it appears that in cases of septocemic plague the bacillus entered the bloodstream, perhaps at the moment of the fleabite. A rash formed and death occurred within a day, or even within hours, before any swellings appeared. Septocemic plague always turned out to be fatal.

Some people did imagine that the disease might be coming from some animal, and they killed dogs and cats—though never rats. But fleas were so much a part of everyday life that no one seems to have given them a second thought. Upright citizens also killed gravediggers, strangers from other countries, gypsies, drunks, beggars, cripples, lepers and Jews. The first persecution of the Jews seems to have taken place in the South of France in the spring of 1348. That September, at Chillon on Lake Geneva, a group of Jews were accused of poisoning the wells. They were tortured and they confessed, and their confessions were sent to neighboring towns. In Basel all the Jews were locked inside wooden buildings and burned alive. In November, Jews were burned in Solothurn, Zofingen and Stuttgart. Through the winter and into early spring they were burned in Landsberg, Burren, Memmingen, Lindau, Freiburg, Ulm, Speyer, Gotha, Eisenach, Dresden, Worms, Baden and Erfurt. Sixteen thousand were murdered in Strasbourg. In other cities Jews were walled up inside their houses to starve to death. That the Jews were also dying of the plague was not taken as proof that they were not causing it.

On the highways and byways, meanwhile, congregations of flagellants wandered about, whipping themselves twice a day and once during the night for weeks at a time. As they went on their way they attracted hordes of followers and helped spread the plague even farther abroad.

The recurrence of the plague after people thought the worst was over may have been the most devastating development of all. In short, Europe was swept not only by a bacillus but also by a widespread psychic breakdown—by abject terror, panic, rage, vengefulness, cringing remorse, selfishness, hysteria, and above all, by an overwhelming sense of utter powerlessness in the face of an inescapable horror.

After a decade's respite, just as Europeans began to recover their feeling of well-being, the plague struck again in 1361, and again in 1369, and at least once in each decade down to the end of the century. Why the plague faded away is still a mystery that, in the short run, apparently had little to do with improvements in medicine or cleanliness and more to do with some adjustment of equilibrium among the population of rats and fleas. In any case, as agents for Pope Clement estimated in 1351, perhaps 24 million people had died in the first onslaught of the plague; perhaps as many as another 20 million died by the end of the century—in all, it is estimated, one-third of the total population of Europe.

Very rarely does a single event change history itself. Yet an event of the magnitude of the Black Death could not fail to have an enormous impact.

Very rarely does a single event change history by itself. Yet an event of the magnitude of the Black Death could not fail to have had an enormous impact. Ironically, some of the changes brought by the plague were for the good. Not surprisingly, medicine changed—since medicine had so signally failed to be of any help in the hour of greatest need for it. First of all, a great many doctors died—and some simply ran away. "It has pleased God," wrote one Venetian-born physician, "by this terrible mortality to leave our native place so destitute of upright and capable doctors that it may be said not one has been left." By 1349, at the University of Padua there were vacancies in every single chair of medicine and surgery. All this, of course, created room for new people with new ideas. Ordinary people began wanting to get their hands on medical guides and to take command of their own health. And gradually more medical texts began to appear in the vernacular instead of in Latin.

AN OLD ORDER WAS BESIEGED

Because of the death of so many people, the relationship between agricultural supply and demand changed radically, too. Agricultural prices dropped precipitously, endangering the fortunes and power of the aristocracy, whose wealth and dominance were based on land. At the same time, because of the deaths of so many people, wages rose dramatically, giving laborers some chance of improving their own conditions of employment. Increasing numbers of people had more money to buy what could be called luxury goods, which affected the nature of business and trade, and even of private well-being. As old relationships, usages and laws broke down, expanding secular concerns and intensifying the struggle between faith and reason, there was a rise in religious, social and political unrest. Religious reformer John Wycliffe, in England, and John Huss, in Bohemia, were among many leaders of sects that challenged church behavior and church doctrine all over Europe. Such complaints eventually led to the Protestant Reformation, and the assertion that Man stood in direct relation to God, without need to benefit from intercession by layers of clergy.

Indeed, the entire structure of feudal society, which had been under stress for many years, was undermined by the plague. The three orders of feudalism—clergy, nobility and peasantry—had been challenged for more than a century by the rise of the urban bourgeoisie, and by the enormous, slow changes in productivity and in the cultivation of arable land. But the plague, ravaging the weakened feudal system from so many diverse and unpredictable quarters, tore it apart.

By far the greatest change in Western civilization that the plague helped hasten was a change of mind. Once the immediate traumas of death, terror and flight had passed through a stricken town, the common lingering emotion was that of fear of God. The subsequent surge of religious fervor in art was in many ways nightmarish. Though medieval religion had dealt with death and dying, and naturally with sin and retribution, it was only after the Black Death that painters so wholeheartedly gave themselves over to pictures brimming with rotting corpses, corpses being consumed by snakes and toads, swooping birds of prey appearing with terrible suddenness, cripples gazing on the figure of death with longing for deliverance, open graves filled with blackened, worm-eaten bodies, devils slashing the faces and bodies of the damned.

Well before the plague struck Europe, the role of the Catholic Church in Western Europe had been changing. The Papacy had grown more secular in its concerns, vying with princes for wealth and power even while attempts at reform were increasing. "God gave us the Papacy," Pope Leo X declared. "Let us enjoy it." The church had suffered a series of damaging losses in the late 1200s—culminating in 1309 when the Papacy moved from Rome to Avignon. But then, the Black Death dealt the church a further blow, for along with renewed fear and the need for new religious zeal came the opposite feeling, that the church itself had failed. Historical changes rarely occur suddenly. The first indications of change from a powerful catalyst usually seem to be mere curiosities, exceptions or aberrations from the prevailing worldview. Only after a time, after the exceptions have accumulated and seem to cohere, do they take on the nature of a historical movement. And only when the exceptions have come to dominate, do they begin to seem typical of the civilization as a whole (and the vestiges of the old civilization to seem like curiosities). This, in any case, is how the great change of mind occurred that defines the modern Western world. While the Black Death alone did not cause these changes, the upheaval it brought about did help set the stage for the new world of Renaissance Europe and the Reformation.

As the Black Death waned in Europe, the power of religion waned with it, leaving behind a population that was gradually but certainly turning its attention to the physical realm in which it lived, to materialism and worldliness, to the terrible power of the world itself, and to the wonder of how it works.

Saints Or Sinners?
The Knights Templar in Medieval Europe

During the trials that destroyed one of 14th-century Europe's most celebrated crusading military orders, witnesses claimed all manner of abuses had been going on for years. But how true were these claims? And what did contemporaries think about them and the other military orders—such as the Knights Hospitaller and Teutonic Knights? **Helen Nicholson** *investigates.*

Helen Nicholson lectures in history at the University of Wales College of Cardiff. She is currently working on a translation of the Itinerarium Peregrinorum et Gesta Regis Ricardi, *a chronicle of the Third Crusade.*

In October 1307, by order of Philip IV of France, all the Knights Templar within the French domains were arrested. In November, Pope Clement V sent out orders for the arrest of the Templars throughout Europe. The brothers were accused of a variety of crimes, which were said to be long-established in the order. There were, it was claimed, serious abuses in the admission ceremony, where the brothers denied their faith in Christ. The order encouraged homosexual activity between brothers. The brothers worshipped idols. Chapter meetings were held in secret. The brothers did not believe in the mass or other sacraments of the church and did not carry these out properly, defrauding patrons of the order who had given money for masses to be said for their families' souls.

What was more, it was alleged that the Templars did not make charitable gifts or give hospitality as a religious order should. The order encouraged broth-ers to acquire property fraudulently, and to win profit for the order by any means possible.

During the trial of the Templars witnesses claimed that the order's abuses had been notorious for many years and under interrogation, including torture, many brothers confessed to at least some of these crimes. In March 1312, Pope Clement dissolved the Order of the Temple, giving its property to the Order of the Hospital, and assigning the surviving brothers to other religious orders. Despite this, the question of the order's guilt has never been settled. Just what were the accusations made against the Templars before 1300, and were these related to the trial? What did contemporaries think about the other military orders, such as the Knights Hospitaller and the Teutonic Knights?

The Order of the Temple was a military order, a type of religious order. It had been founded in the early twelfth century, in the wake of the Catholic conquest of the Holy Land, to protect pilgrims travelling to the holy places against bandits. This role soon grew to protecting Christian territory in Spain as well as the Holy Land. The order gained its name because the King of Jerusalem had given the brothers his palace in the al-Aqsa mosque, which the Christians called 'the Temple of Solomon', to be their headquarters. In Europe the members' lifestyle was much like that of ordinary monks. The order's rule laid down a strict regime on clothing, diet, charitable giving and other living arrangements. In theory only men could join the order, but in practice some women were also admitted.

The Order of the Temple was the first military order, but others soon followed. The Order of the Hospital of St John of Jerusalem had been founded as a hospice for pilgrims in the eleventh century, but by the 1130s the Hospital was employing mercenaries to protect pilgrims from bandits, and was soon involved in the defence of the frontiers of the Kingdom of Jerusalem alongside the Order of the Temple. These brothers became known as the Hospitallers.

The Hospital of St Mary of the Teutons was set up at the siege of Acre during the Third Crusade (1189–92) to care for German pilgrims and was then re-launched in 1198 as a military order. The brothers were known as the Teutonic Knights. These were the most famous of the international military orders,

 This article first appeared in *History Today*, December 1994, pp. 30–36. © 1994 by History Today, Ltd. Reprinted by permission.

but the concept was so popular that others were founded wherever Christians confronted non-Christians: in Spain, where the Muslim frontier was slowly retreating, and in the Baltic and Prussia where pagan tribes threatened Christian settlements and converts. From the 1230s onwards the Teutonic order became prominent in the Baltic area.

The concept of the military order was a natural development from the concept of the crusade. Rather than taking up weapons for a short period to defend Christ's people, the members of a military order did so for life. In return, they expected to receive pardon for their sins and immediate entry into heaven if they died in action against the enemies of their faith.

In western Europe, far from the battlefield, some of the clergy were doubtful whether a military order could be a valid religious order. Around 1150, the Abbot of Cluny wrote to Pope Eugenius III that he and many of his monks regarded the brothers of the Temple as only knights, not monks, and believed that fighting the Muslims overseas was less important than suppressing bandits at home. Letters written to encourage the early Templars also hint at this sort of opposition. But the bulk of the surviving evidence is warmly in praise of the Templars, and clergy and knightly classes alike welcomed the new order with generous donations. In fact the Hospital of St John seems to have attracted more donations as it became more of a military order. By 1200 the military orders had become part of the religious establishment and criticism of the concept ceased.

However, other criticism arose which tended to fluctuate with events. During a crusade, while crusaders wrote home with accounts of the military orders' courage and self-sacrifice, criticism was overlooked. Between crusades, as Europeans received news of territorial losses to the Muslims, they forgot the military orders' heroism and concluded that these defeats were God's punishment for sin. For surely God would not allow godly men to suffer such setbacks.

Political views also shaped criticism, especially during the period 1229–50, while pope and emperor were at loggerheads. The Temple, and to a lesser degree the Hospital, supported the pope, while the Teutonic order supported the emperor. So observers sympathetic to the emperor's policies in the Holy Land, such as Matthew Paris, chronicler of St

Albans abbey, criticised the Templars and Hospitallers. Yet there was praise from those who opposed the emperor in the Holy Land, such as Philip of Novara and the Powerful Ibelin family of Cyprus who were Philip's lords.

Chroniclers tended to be critical, for they wished to draw a moral from contemporary events for the edification of future generations. In other forms of literature, romance, epic or farce, the Templars, Hospitallers and Teutonic Knights appeared as brave knights of Christ combating the Muslim menace, or as helpers of lovers, or as good monks. It is interesting that although monks and parish priests came under heavy criticism for their immorality in the 'fables' or farces, the military orders were not criticised. Obviously they were not regarded as womanisers.

Between the Second and Third Crusades of 1148–49 and 1189, the generous donations of money and privileges to the Templars and Hospitallers became a major cause of resentment. This was hardly surprising. All religious orders aroused complaints about their privileges, and the Templars and Hospitallers never attracted such severe criticism as the Cistercians and friars.

But the Templars and the Hospitallers caused particular annoyance because their houses were so widely scattered. Their legal privileges were especially resented. In 1236 Pope Gregory IX wrote to the Templars and hospitallers in western France ordering them not to abuse the privileges granted to them by the papal see. The brothers had been summoning their legal opponents to courts in far-off places which they had no hope or reaching by the specified day, so that they were then fined for failing to appear. The brothers had also been taking annual payments for clergy and laity in return for allowing them to share their legal privileges.

Forty years later, when Edward I's commissioners were conducting the Hundred Roll inquiries to establish where royal rights had been usurped in each locality, there were similar protests. Some people who had no proper connection with the Templars and Hospitallers were claiming their privileges, in Warwickshire and Derbyshire there were complaints that the orders' privileges 'impede and subvert all common justice and excessively oppress the people', while the burghers of Totnes and Grimsby had been summoned to courts

in the four corners of England by the Hospitallers and Templars respectively.

Despite their extensive possessions, the Templars and Hospitallers were always claiming to be poverty-stricken. They sent out alms-collectors on a regular basis, to collect money from lay-people and clergy for their work in the Holy Land. Matthew Paris was probably expressing a widely-felt discontent when he wrote around 1245:

> The Templars and Hospitallers . . . receive so much income form the whole of Christendom, and, only for defending the Holy Land, swallow down such great revenues as if they sink them into the gulf of the abyss . . .

Whatever did they do with all their wealth? Some Europeans concluded that they must be using their resources very inefficiently.

The orders were not only wealthy and privileged, they were proud and treacherous. Pride, the first of the seven deadly sins, was already the military orders' most infamous vice by the 1160s. As the years passed it became a stock complaint against the Templars and Hospitallers, as if it was 'their' sin. Pride made the orders jealous of each other and of other Christians, so that they fought each other instead of fighting the Saracens. The Templars and Hospitallers' quarrels became notorious, although in fact the orders went to great lengths to ensure peaceful relations. The troubadour, Daspol, writing in around 1270, neatly summed up the problem: because the Templars and Hospitallers had become proud and greedy and did evil instead of good, they were unable or unwilling to defend the Holy Land against the Saracens.

In 1289 a Flemish satirist, Jacquemart Giélée, depicted the Templars' and Hospitallers' bitter quarrels in his satire, *Renart le Nouvel,* the new Renart, based on the old theme of the unscrupulous fox. A Hospitaller is shown denigrating the Templars in order to win Renart for his order. After the final loss of Acre in 1291, Pope Nicholas IV suggested that the military order's quarrels had been a contributory factor in the defeat, and many chroniclers and churchmen agreed.

The charge that the Order of the Temple encouraged the brothers to acquire property fraudulently and to win profit by all possible means clearly reflects these complaints against the Templars and Hospitallers. For at least 150 years contemporaries had accused the military orders of lying and cheating because of their greed for wealth. In 1312 the same old criticisms against the Hospitallers arose again at the Council of Vienne, as the pope planned to bestow on them the former property of the Templars.

Interestingly, no critic before 1300 accused the Templars of immorality. In the mid-thirteenth century an English poet, writing in Anglo-Norman French, surveyed the whole of society and accused most of the clergy of womanising, even dropping hints about the Hospitallers. But he exempted the Templars, who were too busy making money to have time for sex:

> The Templars are most doughty men and they certainly know how to look after themselves, but they love pennies too much; when prices are high they sell their wheat instead of giving it to their dependants. Nor do the lords of the Hospital, have any desire for buying women's services, if they have their palfreys and horses, I don't say it for any evil . . .

A more explicit charge of immorality against the Hospitallers appeared in March 1238, when a French crusade was preparing to depart for the Holy Land. Pope Gregory IX wrote a letter of rebuke to the Hospitallers in Acre. He had heard that the brothers kept harlots in their villages, had been cheating the dying into bequeathing their property to them and (among other crimes) that several of the brothers were guilty of heresy. As for the Templars, he only complained that they were not keeping the roads safe for pilgrims!

Although the Templars were not accused of immorality, they were linked with traditional romantic love. A late thirteenth-century French verse romance, *Sone de Nausay,* depicts the Master of the Temple in Ireland as the go-between in a love affair, while a French Arthurian romance of the same period, *Claris et Laris,* depicts the Templars as friends to lovers. But this was a wholly sympathetic view, and saw the Templars as servants of lovers rather than as lovers themselves. None of the military orders were accused of sodomy, although such accusations were occasionally made against ordinary monks.

There were many other complaints against the military orders before 1300. Perhaps the most significant were the divided opinions over their record of fighting the Muslims (and other non-Christians). Many complained that they were not sufficiently enthusiastic about defending Christendom and winning back lost territory, while others complained that they were too eager to fight those who could be won to Christ by peaceful means.

Some contemporaries alleged that the military orders were unwilling to fight the Muslims because they were secretly in alliance with them. The military orders certainly did make alliances with Muslim rulers on various occasions, but these alliances were intended to promote the Christian cause, not to hinder it.

The chroniclers also alleged that the Muslims exploited the brothers' greed. There was a legend in circulation which recounted how the Christians had failed to capture a Muslim fortress because some of the Christian leaders had been bribed by Muslim gold to raise the siege. This gold subsequently turned out to be copper. This story appeared in various forms and with various parties in the role of dupe from the mid-twelfth century onwards. By the early thirteenth century the Templars had become the dupes, and by the mid-thirteenth century the Hospitallers had joined them. The fortress also changed identity several times! In fact this is a very old story, and versions of it appear in Gregory of Tours' *History of the Franks,* written in the sixth century, and in the collection of ancient Welsh legends known as the *Mabinogion.*

Many accusations that the military orders were unwilling to attack the Muslims arose from a misunderstanding of the true situation in the Holy Land. The Templars were criticised for refusing to help the Third Crusade besiege Jerusalem in 1191–92, but the brothers believed that the city could not be held after the crusaders had returned home, and that the security of the holy places were better served by attacking Egypt. In 1250, during the crusade of Louis IX of France, Count Robert of Artois decided to lead the vanguard of the crusading army to attack the Muslims in Mansourah. The Templars and Hospitallers advised against this, whereupon the count accused them of laziness and trying to impede the Christian cause and advanced. Anxious not to be accused of cowardice, the military orders accompanied him and, as they had predicted, the Christian army was cut to pieces. This was a terrible defeat, but something of a propaganda coup for the military orders, who had fearlessly died for Christ against hopeless odds.

Other critics felt that the military orders were *too* eager to fight. Thirteenth-century literature depicted the ideal knight as one who only fought when necessary. The military orders' self-sacrifice for Christ seemed rash and irrational. Some of the clergy believed that the orders' love of violence and domination impeded or prevented conversions. This accusation was made against the Templars in the 1180s by Walter Map, Archdeacon of Oxford, and against the Teutonic order by some unknown critics and around 1266–68 by Roger Bacon, an English Franciscan friar imprisoned in Paris for his unorthodox views.

The unknown critics may have been the Polish princes who opposed the expansion of the Teutonic order's power in Prussia. In 1258, letters were sent to Pope Alexander IV from the order's friends in Poland and Prussia, defending them against various accusations. Apparently the brothers had been accused of forbidding the preaching of Christianity to the pagan Prussians, preventing the establishment of churches, destroying old churches, impeding the sacraments and enslaving new converts. Roger Bacon's criticisms echoed these: the Teutonic order wanted to subjugate the Prussians and reduce them to slavery, and refused to stop attacking them in order to allow peaceful preaching. He added that the order had deceived the Roman Church for many years as to its true motives in Prussia.

The peak of criticism of the military orders came around 1250. After this they faded from the chronicles and critical writings. Many critics of the church omitted them. Others showed little actual knowledge of them. Although there was a vast number of newsletters coming from the Holy Land, so the chroniclers could hardly have been short of information on events, they seem to have chosen to ignore this. News was almost invariably bad, and chroniclers probably believed that the loss of the Holy Land was only a matter of time. There were many crises closer to home to occupy their pens.

As a result, after 1250, the image of the military orders expressed in the chronicles and other writing shows a relative improvement. Day-to-day relations between the military orders and their neighbours and the authorities were usually peaceful. Bishops' registers, royal administrative records and the records of the nobility where these survive, show that although there were disputes generally the military orders were obedient subjects and reliable servants. As Walter Map had remarked, whatever the Templars did in the Holy Land, in England they lived peacefully enough.

Despite the sorry state of the Latin Christian settlement in the Holy Land, after 1250 the military orders were still well regarded in Europe. Donations to the orders had fallen in most areas, but all religious orders were suffering in this respect. Some commentators, while agreeing that even the Templars had declined in spirituality along with all other religious orders, depicted them as having previously been among the most spiritual of the religious orders. This was a far cry from their original foundation, when some had doubted that the order could have a spiritual dimension at all!

So, how far were the Templars' accusers of 1307 justified in their case against the order? Contemporaries would certainly have agreed with the charge that they lied and cheated in order to satisfy their greed. Yet there is no hint before 1300 that the Templars did not carry out the sacraments; although the Teutonic order were accused of impeding the sacraments in Prussia. It was true that the proceedings of the order's chapter meetings were kept secret, but this was the custom among military orders.

The accusation that the order did not practice charity and hospitality may have sprung from the rivalry between the Temple and the Hospital. The Hospitallers were always at pains to emphasise their dual hospitable-military role, in contrast to the solely military role of the Templars. A few contemporaries were struck by the difference: a German pilgrim, John of Würzburg, remarked dismissively in around 1170 that the Temple's charitable giving was not a tenth of the Hospital's. Of course, the Order of the Temple did practise charity, as it was obliged to do under its religious rule, but most contemporaries seemed to have regarded the defence of pilgrims as charity in itself.

There is no indication before 1300 of public scandal over the order abusing admission procedures, or of heresy, idolatry or homosexuality within the order. Only the Hospital was accused of heresy. Interestingly, the Teutonic Knights' rivals in Livonia were accusing them of pagan practices and witchcraft by 1306. This suggests that such charges were politically motivated, rather than based on fact.

The accusations of denial of Christ, sodomy and idolatry had been standard accusations against heretics for centuries, most recently against the Waldensians and the Cathars. Therefore, to accuse a rival of such crimes was to accuse them of heresy. Orthodox Christian belief was believed to be essential for the health of society and to ensure God's favour. Heresy was seen as a disease which must be eradicated before it overcame the whole Christian body. Powerful political rivals could use the charge of heresy with devastating effect against their opponents: it had been deployed by Pope Innocent IV against the emperor Frederick II during the 1240s, and from 1303 by Philip IV's government against Pope Boniface VIII, who had infuriated Philip by asserting the supremacy of the church over secular rulers. Boniface was accused of heresy, sodomy, witchcraft and magic. Later Guichard, Bishop of Troyes, and Louis of Nevers, son of the Count of Flanders, were accused of similar crimes after incurring Philip's enmity.

Certainly any wealthy, privileged religious order with close ties to the papacy, such as the Cistercians, Friars, Hospitallers or Templars, was likely to incur a monarch's enmity. Yet the Templars were no more disliked than other military orders, and less criticised than some other religious orders. They had a long history of faithful service to the French crown. So why were they singled out for attack?

The Templars had a special position in the defence of the Holy Land. According to Jacquemart Giélée, the brothers claimed to be sole 'Defenders of the Holy Church'. They were depicted as principal defenders of the Holy Land by the Parisian poet Rutebuef in 1277. Templars were mentioned in chronicles and literature in general more than other military orders. They were invariably listed first whenever anyone thought about military orders. They had been the first military order, and were one of the richest and most far-flung. Yet this particular prominence also left them particularly vulnerable when they failed in their duty.

When the city of Acre finally fell to the Muslims in May 1291, several reports of the disaster depicted the Templars as chiefly responsible for the defence of the city. The chronicler of Erfut, writing in the summer of 1291, depicted the Templars dying like true knights of Christ, fighting to the last. Thaddeo of Naples, a priest, praised the courage of the brothers of the military orders who died, and portrayed the death of the master of the Temple, William of Beaujeu, as the decisive blow which led to the loss of the Holy Land. For after Acre fell, the remaining Latin Christian possessions in the East surrendered to the Muslims.

But the order's prominence could also be its undoing. The most popular account of the defeat, which was reproduced in many chronicles, dismissed the Templars as totally ineffective and only concerned to save their treasure. The true hero of the tragedy was now Brother Matthew of Claremont, marshal of the Hospital, who was 'a faithful warrior, knight of Christ', and died a martyr's death. Ricoldo of Monte Cruce, a Dominican Friar who was on a preaching mission in the Middle East when he heard of the disaster, compared William of Beaujeu to the notorious King Ahab, husband of Queen Jezebel and the worst king of Israel in the Old Testament. Certainly he was an excellent soldier, but God rejected him because of his sins. The loss of Acre was not mentioned among the charges brought against the Templars in 1307, but it was understood that the brothers' alleged abuses were responsible for the disaster.

From the evidence, the famous, shocking charges brought against the Templars in 1307 were unknown before 1300. The order was certainly guilty of fraud and unscrupulous greed, but so too were other religious orders. The brothers' real crime was their failure to protect the Holy Land after claiming to be solely responsible for its defence.

FOR FURTHER READING:

M. Barber, 'Propaganda in the Middle Ages: the charges against the Templars', *Nottingham Medieval Studies,* 17 (1973); M. Barber, *The Trial of the Templars* (Cambridge University Press, 1978); M. Barber, *The New Knighthood: a History of the Order of the Temple* (Cambridge University Press, 1993); H. Nicholson, *Templars, Hospitallers and Teutonic Knights: Images of the military orders, 1128–1291* (Leicester University Press, 1993); J. Upton-Ward, (trans.) *The Rule of the Templars: the French text of the Rule of the Order of Knights Templar* (Boydell Press, 1992).

Unit 6

Unit Selections

35. **Marsilio Ficino, Renaissance Man,** Valery Rees
36. **Machiavelli,** Vincent Cronin
37. **Women of the Renaissance,** J. H. Plumb
38. **Columbus—Hero or Villain?** Felipe Fernández-Armesto
39. **Sir Francis Drake Is Still Capable of Kicking Up a Fuss,** Simon Winchester
40. **Luther: Giant of His Time and Ours,** *Time*
41. **Explaining John Calvin,** William J. Bouwsma
42. **She-Devils, Harlots and Harridans in Northern Renaissance Prints,** Julia Nurse

Key Points to Consider

❖ How did politics change at the beginning of the modern era? What part did the ideas of Machiavelli play in the shift from medieval to modern politics?

❖ Did Renaissance humanism influence the place of women in European life? Why were some women depicted as She-Devils, Harlots, and Harridans?

❖ Compare the lives of Sir Francis Drake and Columbus.

❖ What are the ideas of Martin Luther and John Calvin?

 **Links**   **www.dushkin.com/online/**

These sites are annotated on pages 4 and 5.

The departure from medieval patterns of life was first evident in Renaissance Italy. There the growth of capital and the development of distinctly urban economic and social organizations promoted a new culture. This culture, which spread to other parts of Europe, was dominated by townsmen whose tastes, abilities, and interests differed markedly from those of the medieval clergy and feudal nobility.

The emerging culture was limited to a minority—generally those who were wealthy. But even in an increasingly materialistic culture it was not enough just to be wealthy. It was necessary to patronize the arts, literature, and learning, and to demonstrate skill in some profession. The ideal Renaissance man, as Robert Lopez observes (in *The Three Ages of the Italian Renaissance,* University of Virginia Press, 1970) "came from a good old family, improved upon his status through his own efforts, and justified his status by his own intellectual accomplishments."

The new ideal owed much to the classical tradition. Renaissance man, wishing to break out of the other-worldly spirituality of the Middle Ages, turned back to the secular naturalism of the ancient world. Indeed, the Renaissance was, among other things, a heroic age of scholarship that restored classical learning to a place of honor. It was classical humanism in particular that became the vogue. The article "Marsilio Ficino, Renaissance Man" exemplifies these ideas. And in the new spirit of individualism, humanism was transformed. The classical version, "man is the measure of all things," became, in poet and scholar Leon Alberti's version, "A man can do all things, if he will." No one better illustrates Alberti's maxim than Leonardo da Vinci.

Civic humanism was another Renaissance modification of the classical heritage. It involved a new philosophy of political engagement, a reinterpretation of political history from the vantage point of contemporary politics, and a recognition that men would not simply imitate the ancients but rival them. Of course, humans being what we are, Renaissance humanism had its darker side. And the Renaissance ideal did not fully extend to women, as J. H. Plumb's essay, "Women of the Renaissance," explains.

Renaissance art and architecture reflected the new society and its attitudes. Successful businessmen were as likely as saints to be the subjects of the portraits. Equestrian statues of warriors and statesmen glorified current heros while evoking memories of ancient Rome. Renaissance painters rediscovered nature, which generally had been ignored by medieval artists, often depicting it as an earthly paradise—the appropriate setting for humanity in its new image. And in contrast to the great medieval cathedrals, which glorified God, Renaissance structures focused on humanity.

Some of these developments in art and architecture indicate changes in the role of Christianity and the influence of the Church, which

no longer determined the goals of Western civilization as they had during the medieval period. Increasingly, civil authorities and their symbols competed with churchmen and their icons, while Machiavelli (treated in the article by Vincent Cronin) and other writers provided a secular rationale for a new political order. Nonetheless, most Europeans, including many humanists, retained a deep and abiding religious faith.

The Reformation, with its theological disputes and wars of religion, is a powerful reminder that secular concerns had not entirely replaced religious ones, especially in northern Europe. The great issues that divided Protestant and Catholic—the balance between individual piety and the Church's authority, the true means of salvation, and so on—were essentially medieval in character. Indeed, in their perceptions of humanity, their preoccupation with salvation and damnation, and their attacks upon the church's conduct of its affairs, Martin Luther, John Calvin, Ulrich Zwingli, and other Protestant leaders echoed the views of medieval reformers. Luther's lasting influence is examined in "Luther: Giant of His Time and Ours." As for Calvinism, see William Bouwsma's essay, "Explaining John Calvin," in which the author attempts to correct modern misperceptions of the Swiss reformer.

Taken together, then, the Renaissance and Reformation constituted a new compound of traditional elements—classical and medieval, secular and religious—along with elements of modernity. The era was a time of transition, or as Lynn White describes it, "This was a time of torrential flux, of fearful doubt, making the transition from the relative certainties of the Middle Ages to the new certainties of the eighteenth and nineteenth centuries." Such "fearful doubts" were expressed in the witch hunts of the period and the depiction of women as seen in Julia Nurse's, "She-Devils, Harlots and Harridans in Northern Renaissance Prints."

Other troubling facts of the era surfaced when Western civilization reached across the Atlantic. Many of these concerns were revived during the Columbus quincentenary. These matters are addressed in "Columbus—Hero or Villain?" and in Simon Winchester's article, "Sir Francis Drake Is Still Capable of Kicking Up a Fuss," which shows us another man of action and his impact on the fortunes of England and the world.

Marsilio Ficino, Renaissance Man

Valery Rees looks at the Florentine scholar Marsilio Ficino and finds a man whose work still speaks to us today.

IN OCTOBER [1999] it will be 500 years since Marsilio Ficino died in Florence. Although we risk becoming sated with centenaries, some events and individuals stand out as deserving of celebration: Marsilio Ficino is one of these.

If his name is not as well known as those of his illustrious followers, it is not surprising, as we shall see from his career. Nor would this state of affairs have entirely displeased him, for he was a modest man.

Marsilio Ficino was the son of Cosimo de' Medici's physician. Born in 1433, he received his early training in medicine, on the reasonable assumption that he would follow his father's career. However an early interest in philosophy (especially in Lucretius and Plato) soon brought him to Cosimo's attention. Around 1456 Cosimo redirected him to learning more Greek so that he could pursue these studies with greater effect. Cosimo was actively looking for a suitable candidate to translate the texts that were being brought to Florence by his own trading agents as well as by Greek scholars fleeing the fall of Constantinople. Ficino's progress in Greek clearly pleased Cosimo. Early fruits of it were translations of Orphic and Homeric hymns. Then Cosimo gave him two extraordinary gifts: the first, in 1462, was a manuscript of the works of Plato, the only known complete codex of Plato's works. This was almost certainly the very copy which the Greek emperor had brought to the Council of Florence in 1438 and which had been so much admired by the Italian participants there. The second gift, the follow-ing year, was of a villa and land in Careggi, close to Cosimo's own favourite country seat. This facilitated the work of translation, and participation in those meetings of like-minded scholars, poets and statesmen that formed the Platonic Academy of Florence. In fact, Ficino became the leader of that circle, and from his correspondence, which he himself collected and published in twelve volumes in his lifetime, we can see that the circle of his influence was wide indeed.

Ficino started work on the Platonic dialogues at once, but soon Cosimo asked him to lay that aside and concentrate on a text called the *Poimandres* ('Shepherd of Men'), which one of his agents had just acquired in Macedonia. Its contents, written in Greek, were curious: it consisted of writings attributed to Hermes Trismegistus (thrice greatest Hermes) who was thought to be a contemporary of Moses, and was related to or even identified with the divine being Thoth (Tehuti). Tehuti figures in Egyptian representations of the weighing of the heart, ie. the judgement of the soul at death. He had human form but the head of an ibis, recognisable by its long beak. He shared the qualities of the Greek Hermes, as a messenger between divine and human realms, and was the embodiment of eloquence, reason and the discursive mind. To the Egyptians he was the inventor of language and writing, master of knowledge, with power to guide souls at the time of death.

The importance of finding this Hermetic work cannot be overestimated. One Hermetic text, the *Asclepius*, had been known since Classical times, though often attributed to its reputed Latin translator Apuleius rather than Hermes. Whereas the *Asclepius* clearly deals in mysteries and magic, the *Poimandres* (now generally known as the *Corpus Hermeticum*) is full of powerful poetry highly reminiscent of the biblical books of Genesis and Job and other Hebrew/Aramaic sources. Thus the *Poimandres,* then thought to date from the time of Moses, appeared to provide the much desired missing link between the philosophy of Graeco-Roman antiquity and the revealed wisdom of holy scripture. Moses had been brought up as an Egyptian, and, according to the tradition endorsed by St Augustine, both Plato and Pythagoras had studied in Egypt. Hence the divergent strands of Greek philosophy and Christian apologetics now seemed to share a common source.

In the seventeenth century the Hermetic writings were subjected to intensive critical scrutiny, and their Egyptian origins rejected, in favour of a late Hellenistic date, reflecting a syncretic philosophy that contained elements of the Greek and Hebrew traditions. Yet more recent scholarship tends once more to emphasise the indigenous Egyptian elements within the Hermetic Corpus. But none of this later critical scholarship detracts from the fact that Ficino's generation genuinely believed the Hermetic texts to represent an early link in the chain of transmission of a very ancient and unified tradition of wisdom, which he called the *prisca theologia,* a theology that underlay but predated the coming of Christ. Indeed the subtitle of the *Poimandres* is 'On the Power and Wisdom of God.'

If theology was so old, and included pre-Christian sources within it, no longer need Classical philosophy be regarded as the enemy of religion, as had often been the case. Plato and Pythagoras became respectable, and a *pia philosophia* could be traced back beyond them all the way to Zoroaster, the Sixth century B.C. founder of the Parsee religion, and to the Chaldaean civilisation who were believed to be the most ancient sources. The early Church Fathers, especially Origen and Clement of Alexandria, could be seen as the direct heirs of this tradition.

The *Poimandres* translation was finished in 1463, and printed in 1471. It immediately became a very popular and influential work. The Platonic dialogues took longer to appear, coming into print only in 1484, though versions of them were being circulated and discussed in manuscript form much earlier. Indeed, the intervening years were extremely fruitful.

When Cosimo died in 1464, Ficino was able to continue his work under the patronage of Cosimo's son, Piero de' Medici, who also appointed him as tutor to his own sons Lorenzo and Giuliano. This period saw the publication of his translations of two Platonic works, Alcinous on *Plato's Doctrine* and the Platonic *Definitions* of Speusippus. Ten of the dialogues were also ready before Cosimo died as well as Ficino's major commentaries on Plato's *Philebus* (published 1464), on ethics and the highest Good, and on the *Symposium* (published 1469). This period also marks the beginnings of Ficino's public career, with lectures on the Philebus commentary in the Church of Santa Maria degli Angeli in Florence. 'Since philosophy' he said on this occasion, 'is defined by all men as love of wisdom . . . and wisdom is the contemplation of the divine, then certainly the purpose of philosophy is knowledge of the divine.' This quest was to remain the constant imperative throughout his life and work, a rule to live by as well as a system of thought. According to Plato, 'the minds of those practising philosophy, having recovered their wings through wisdom and justice . . . fly back to the heavenly kingdom.' The study and practice of philosophy is thus the ascent of the mind from the lower regions to the highest, and from darkness to light. Its origin is an impulse of the divine mind; its middle steps are the faculties and the disciplines

which we have described; and its end is the possession of the highest good. Finally, its fruit is the right government of men.

The *Symposium* commentary, known as *De Amore,* is arguably an original work rather than a commentary, so far does it carry Plato's themes into new territory. It became one of the best known and best loved works of interpretation, serving as inspiration for generations of writers on the theme of love, sometimes filtered through its early emulators, Pietro Bembo, Leone Ebreo and Castiglione, then translated into Italian in 1544, and French in 1545 and 1578, and thus making its mark directly or indirectly on English and French literature, in the verses of Sidney, Chapman, Spenser and Shakespeare, of Ronsard and Scève.

Between 1469 and 1473 the work of translation proceeded apace. Yet it appears that these were difficult times for Ficino personally. He speaks of 'a certain bitterness of spirit' and often refers to the influence of Saturn, dominant at his birth, as favouring discipline and contemplation but incurring melancholy also. It was perhaps a time of deep anxi-

According to Plato, the practice of philosophy is the ascent of the mind from darkness to light.

ety: working so closely with Plato and the later Platonists brought up many questions of a metaphysical and philosophical nature that Ficino needed to resolve to his own satisfaction, quite apart from the requirement to avoid heresy. By 1473, it seems his concerns were reasonably resolved, and he took ordination as a priest. By 1474, he was sufficiently sure of his ground to complete his own major work, the *Platonic Theology,* though he continued to revise it up to its publication in 1482. It is a master work of exposition of the arguments

for the immortality of the soul, aiming at a proper synthesis of Platonic philosophy and Christian theology. His title was not new: Proclus had written on a similar theme in the fifth century. Ficino studied in detail his extant works, as well as those of all the other major writers in the Platonic tradition, both Latin and Greek, Christian and anti-Christian.

Also in 1474, prompted by his recovery from a serious illness, Ficino published a smaller work on similar themes, known as the *Christian Religion,* and in 1476, a treatise dealing with Paul's rapture into the third heaven, pursuing the idea of a positive interaction between divine inspiration and providence and human imagination and will. His primary concern in all these works was to clarify the underlying concordance between the Christian/Aristotelian outlook of his own education and the apparently contradictory ideas that he found in Plato and the later Platonists. Chief among these was the concept of the immortality of the individual human soul. Aristotle had denied this, and traditional scholastic theology was inconsistent with it. Strange though it may seem to us, the concept of an immortal individual soul did not become an article of Christian dogma until 1512. Other crucial questions included the nature of the will, whether it is free or not; the role of love and beauty in drawing mankind naturally towards the divine; whether only Christians could be so drawn, through Christ's redemption, or whether all peoples share in divine Grace. Similarly, is human love the first step along that path of attraction to the divine, or is it a falling away from spiritual development? These were questions whose changing answers mark a real turning point in European culture. They reverberated through the art and literature of the period, and they became burning issues that rent communities apart during the Reformation. Yet with one slight exception, Ficino managed to present and represent these issues, expanding, expounding and elaborating on their themes without incurring the wrath or censure of the Church.

That wrath could be expressed in many ways: following the failure of the Pazzi conspiracy against the Medici family, Florence was put under interdict by the Pope, and was then attacked in a bitter war. By 1478, largely as a result of the war, there was an outbreak of plague in the city. Ficino's response was to publish a very different work, a practical guide to the treatment of plague. This was written in Tuscan to be immediately accessible and of use to his fellow citizens at a time of great need. It was subsequently translated into Latin by Hieronymus Ricci in 1516 and published alongside Galen's work on fevers, as a standard medical work. It is easy to forget that all Ficino's works of profound contemplation and leisurely presentation were written against a backdrop of intense social and political disturbances.

During the following years, Ficino continued to revise his Plato translations, and to write summaries and commentaries. The complete Plato dialogues were published in 1484, making a reliable version of Plato available to a much wider reading public. They were enormously influential, and a second edition was printed in 1496. Meanwhile a series of later works in the Platonic-Pythagorean tradition followed in 1488, including *Synesius on Dreams; Iamblichus on the Egyptian Mysteries; Psellus on Daemons; Priscan on the Soul; Porphyry and Proclus on Sacrifice and Magic;* the *Mystical Theology and Divine Names of Dionysius;* and in 1492, the long awaited *Enneads of Plotinus.* Finally, in 1495 he allowed the printing and publication of his *Letters* that he had been collecting and circulating in manuscript form for many years. So successful was this publication that three further editions, or reprintings, followed within two years. At the time of his death in 1499, Ficino was still working on a commentary to St Paul's *Epistles to the Romans.*

Ficino returned again and again to favourite themes, presenting them in order to convince and persuade others. He wrote on light and the sun, on dreams, on resurrection and rebirth; he became interested in astronomy and mathematics, together with their sister arts of astrological influences and natural magic. This was where he narrowly avoided censure, for in the third of his three books *On Life,* magic and astrology play a prominent part, and he had to defend himself from criticism. Interestingly enough, this third book had started out as an attempt to understand and explain a mystifying passage in Plotinus. Ficino was never one to shirk from following the full implications of what he was studying, however unfashionable or disturbing. Nor did he neglect to put what

The concept of an immortal soul did not become an article of Christian dogma until 1512.

he learned into practice, living a Platonic life and putting all his wisdom and experience at the disposal of others, through teaching, through letters, through sermons but perhaps above all through his own personal example.

He described his life's work to Giovanni Niccolini, Archbishop of Amalfi, at Rome in a letter written shortly before the publication of his Plato translations:

> Being initially guided by the authority of Saint Augustine and then being strengthened in resolve by the testimony of many holy Christians, I therefore considered that, since I needed to apply myself to philosophy, it would be well worth doing so mainly in an academy. But wishing the Platonic teaching to shine out further still, since it is related to the divine law of both Moses and Christ as the moon is to the sun, I translated all the books of Plato from Greek into Latin. In addition, so that no one's eyes would be blinded by seeing this new light, I wrote a book by way of exposition, divided into eighteen parts [The Platonic Theology]. Here the Platonic mysteries are set forth as clearly as possible, so that we may follow Plato's mind rather than his words and so that, removing the poetic veils, we may reveal the Platonic teaching, which is in complete accord with divine law. I believe, and with good reason, that this has been decreed by divine providence, so that all those subtle minds who find it difficult to yield to the sole authority of divine law may at least yield in the end to the reasoning of Plato, which gives its full support to religion.

Through Ficino the writings of the ancients not only became available, but became a powerful enlivening force. He is known to posterity principally for these translations. But he was not the

first to explore this literature, nor the first to translate, emulate and adapt what was found to meet the needs of the day. Among the most brilliant of his predecessors, Leonardo Bruni had translated some of Plato's dialogues and had thereby reshaped Florentine political thinking along Republican lines; Valla had developed critical linguistics; Leon Battista Alberti had translated Vitruvius, the key to new ideas of harmony and proportion in art and architecture. Ficino's task was more comprehensive, for he sought not just to borrow, imitate or adapt but to effect a real synthesis between classical philosophy and Christianity. This is what made it ultimately more influential. He would not himself have claimed to be providing anything new, yet his interpretations gave strength and impetus to new ways of looking at the world.

This comes through clearly in his *Letters.* Their hallmarks are clarity, eloquence, honesty and integrity. They show a man engaged in a life-long quest for real and substantial happiness, not just for himself but for all who care to partake of it. He is deeply pious but his piety has been forged in the fires of profound, persistent questioning. As a friend, he is a source of wise counsel, though he often wraps it up in playful terms. One interesting example of this is his correspondence with Callimachus in the mid 1480s, a series of witty exchanges, but underneath the banter is a serious intent. Callimachus had had to flee from Rome when the Roman Academy was disbanded for trying to plot against the Pope. The Florentine Academy was also subject to suspicion by association, yet Ficino's correspondence with Callimachus during his lengthy exile is warm and friendly. In his first letter, a response to Callimachus's challenge over the existence of daemons, Ficino shows how Callimachus is nonetheless beneficiary of the gifts of such daemons. When Callimachus complained of fiery spirits, that had caused his house to burn down, Ficino turns serious: picking up his cue from an Orphic poem Callimachus had sent him earlier, he reminds him that fire will bring the ultimate destruction of the whole creation. 'Besides,' he says, 'you were looking for light in your books and your books were turned into light for you.' Then on a more serious note, 'What can we divine from this for you, my friend? You will in the end shine more in death than in life,' for it is the soul that shines, and its light is eternal.

The themes covered in Ficino's letters are of universal, not just historical interest. They include love, pain, coping with adversity; how to study, how to balance the various demands on one's life; they discuss unity and individuality, beauty, medicine and astrology. They expound Plato, they refer to Hermes and the Neoplatonists, to Augustine and the Church Fathers, they contain passing Biblical commentary, always related to the particular problem that concerns his correspondent at the time. The forms of expression are varied to suit the circumstance, ranging from simple exposition to the imaginative creativity of fables or the famous letter of 1479 to Ferrante, king of Naples, where the spirit of Ferrante's father Alfonso is invoked to deliver a strong moral and spiritual message to his son directly from the realm of the angels. Always of prime concern to Ficino is the life of the soul. Its twin needs, for love and reason (or wisdom and justice, as quoted above, or faith and judgement, devotion and discrimination) form a recurrent motif in his work. When these twin needs are met, the soul recovers its two wings to fly back to its true home.

There are letters to political leaders and princes, to churchmen and scholars, both in Italy and elsewhere: his contacts stretched to England (Colet), the French court (de Gannay), humanists in Germany (Prenninger) and the Low Countries (Paul of Middleburgh) and with Hungary he enjoyed a very fruitful period of collaboration with Matthias Corvinus via Francesco Bandini and Nicholas Bathory. In Italy his correspondents include Lorenzo de' Medici; Ferrante, King of Naples; Federico da Montefeltro, Duke of Urbino; Pope Six-

Always of prime concern to Ficino was the life of the soul. Its twin needs, love and reason, form a recurrent motif in his work.

tus IV; Giovanni Cavalcanti the poet; Ermolao Barbaro; Bernardo Bembo; Pier Leone of Spoleto, Marco Barbo, and other scholars and churchmen too numerous to be listed.

The latest volume of these *Letters* in English translation, published in June 1999, deals principally with concerns in Italy in the years 1481–83. It contains the letter to Niccolini quoted above, as well as letters on the war, on daemons, on medicine, the Graces, astrology, and a fascinating series of Apologi or Fables. It also adds to our picture of Ficino as a person.

Ficino's writings were studied closely for many years as a principal means of access to the great philosophers of ancient Greece and Egypt. Through his translations and commentaries, his teaching and his letters, the wisdom of these texts came vividly to life and helped the shape the thinking of his time. Naturally, his own concerns coloured his interpretation of the past, and this Ficinian Christian Platonism began to have a far-reaching influence.

Through the Medicis, Ficini's ideas blossomed in Florentine art and literature and travelled, via Venice, to Hungary, Germany and France. By the end of the sixteenth century we can find in Shakespeare's plays perfect resonances of Ficini's ideas, though no outward evidence of direct transmission can easily be demonstrated.

As long as Classical influence reigned, Ficini's work continued to inform and inspire. Artists as diverse as Michelangelo and the metaphysical poets bear the stamp of his approach. Although Plato scholarship has now moved on, and for most purposes we have no need to rely on Ficino to decipher the Greeks today, the questions that he tried to answer are still relevant today, and will always remain so. He speaks of the soul, nature, and human behaviour with intelligence, wisdom and compassion. There is still much for us to learn from the writings of this remarkable man.

FOR FURTHER READING

The Letters of Marsilio Ficino (Shepheard-Walwyn, six vols. 1975-1999); A. Goodman & A. MacKay, *The Impact of Humanism on Western Europe* (Longman,1990); M.J.B. Allen, *Plato's Third Eye* (Variorium, 1995); and *Synoptic Art* (Olschki, 1998); C.V. Kaske and J.R. Clarke, *Three Books on Life,* (Binghampton, N.Y. 1998); D. Van Oyen, C. Salaman & William Wharton, *The Way of Hermes,* (Duckworth, 1999.)

Valery Rees has been translating Ficino's letters for many years. She organised the conference 'Marsilio Ficino: His Sources, His Circle, His Legacy' in London in June.

Machiavelli

Would you buy a used car from this man?

Vincent Cronin

Machiavelli—the most hated man who ever lived: charged, down the centuries, with being the sole poisonous source of political monkey business, of the mocking manipulation of men, of malfeasance, misanthropy, mendacity, murder, and massacre; the evil genius of tyrants and dictators, worse than Judas, for no salvation resulted from *his* betrayal; guilty of the sin against the Holy Ghost, knowing Christianity to be true, but resisting the truth; not a man at all, but Antichrist in apish flesh, the Devil incarnate, Old Nick, with the whiff of sulphur on his breath and a tail hidden under his scarlet Florentine gown.

Machiavelli is the one Italian of the Renaissance we all think we know, partly because his name has passed into our language as a synonym for unscrupulous schemer. But Niccolò Machiavelli of Florence was a more complex and fascinating figure than his namesake of the English dictionary, and unless we ourselves wish to earn the epithet Machiavellian, it is only fair to look at the historical Machiavelli in the context of his age.

He was born in 1469 of an impoverished noble family whose coat of arms featured four keys. Niccolò's father was a retired lawyer who owned two small farms and an inn, his mother a churchgoer who wrote hymns to the Blessed Virgin. Niccolò was one of four children; the younger son, Totto, became a priest, and the idea of a confessional occupied by a Father Machiavelli is one that has caused Niccolò's enemies some wry laughter.

Niccolò attended the Studio, Florence's university, where he studied the prestigious newly-discovered authors of Greece and Rome. Like all his generation, he idolized the Athenians and the Romans of the Republic, and was to make them his models in life. This was one important influence. The other was the fact that Florence was then enjoying, under the Medici, a period of peace. For centuries the city had been torn by war and faction; but now all was serene, and the Florentines were producing their greatest achievements in philosophy, poetry, history, and the fine arts.

This point is important, for too often we imagine the Italian Renaissance as a period of thug-like *condottieri* and cruel despots forever locked in war. We must not be deceived by the artists. Uccello and Michelangelo painted bloody battles, but they were battles that had taken place many years before. If we are to understand Machiavelli, we must picture his youth as a happy period of civilization and peace: for the first time in centuries swords rusted, muscles grew flabby, fortress walls became overgrown with ivy.

In 1494, when Machiavelli was twenty-five, this happiness was shattered. King Charles VIII of France invaded Italy to seize the kingdom of Naples; Florence lay on his route. In the Middle Ages the Florentines had fought bravely against aggressors, but now, grown slack and effete, they were afraid of Charles's veterans and his forty cannon. Instead of manning their walls, they and their leading citizen, Pietro de' Medici, meekly allowed the French king to march in; they even paid him gold not to harm their country.

This debacle led to internal wars, to economic decline, in which Niccolò's father went bankrupt, to much heart-searching, and to a puritanical revolution. Savonarola the Dominican came to rule from the pulpit. Thundering that the French invasion was punishment for a pagan way of life, he burned classical books and nude pictures and urged a regeneration of Florence through fasting and prayer. The French just laughed at Savonarola; he lost the confidence of his fellow citizens and was burned at the stake in 1498.

In that same year, Machiavelli became an employee of the Florentine Republic, which he was to serve ably as diplomat and administrator. Machiavelli scorned Savonarola's idea of political regeneration through Christianity; instead, he persuaded the Florentines to form a citizen militia, as was done in Republican Rome. In 1512 Florence's big test came. Spain had succeeded France as Italy's oppressor, and now, at the instigation of the Medici, who had been exiled from Florence in 1494 and wished to return, a Spanish army of five thousand marched against Tuscany. Four thousand of Machiavelli's militia were defending the strong Florentine town of Prato. The Spaniards, ill-fed and unpaid, launched a halfhearted attack. The Florentines, instead of resisting, took to their heels. Prato was sacked, and a few days later Florence surrendered without a fight. The Medici returned, the Republic came to an end, Machiavelli lost his job and was tortured and exiled to his farm. For the second time in eighteen years he had witnessed a defeat that was both traumatic and humiliating.

In the following year an out-of-work Machiavelli began to write his great book *The Prince*. It is an attempt to answer the question implicit in Florence's two terrible defeats: what had gone wrong? Machiavelli's answer is this: for all their classical buildings and pictures, for all the Ciceronian Latin and readings from Plato, the Florentines had never really revived the essence of classical life—that military vigor and patriotism unto death that distinguished the Greeks and Romans. What then is the remedy? Italy must be regenerated—not by Savonarola's brand of puritanism, but by a soldier-prince. This prince must subordinate every aim to military efficiency. He must personally command a citizen army and keep it disciplined by a reputation for cruelty.

But even this, Machiavelli fears, will not be enough to keep at bay the strong new nation-states, France and Spain. So, in a crescendo of patriotism, Machiavelli urges his prince to disregard the accepted rules of politics, to hit below the belt. Let him lie, if need be, let him violate treaties: "Men must be either pampered or crushed, because they can get revenge for small injuries but not for fatal ones"; "A prudent ruler cannot, and should not, honor his word when it places him at a disadvantage and when the reasons for which he made his promise no longer exist"; "If a prince wants to maintain his rule he must learn how not to be virtuous."

Machiavelli develops his concept of a soldier-prince with a couple of portraits. The first, that of the emperor Alexander Severus, is an example of how a prince should not behave. Alexander Severus, who reigned in the third century, was a man of such goodness it is said that during his fourteen years of power he never put anyone to death without a trial. Nevertheless, as he was thought effeminate, and a man who let himself be ruled by his mother, he came to be scorned, and the army conspired against him and killed him. Machiavelli scorns him also: "Whenever that class of men on which you believe your continued rule depends is corrupt, whether it be the populace, or soldiers, or nobles, you have to satisfy it by adopting the same disposition; and then *good deeds are your enemies."*

Machiavelli's second portrait is of Cesare Borgia, son of Pope Alexander VI, who carved out a dukedom for himself and then brought it to heel by appointing a tough governor, Ramiro. Later, says Machiavelli, Cesare discovered that "the recent harshness had aroused some hatred against him, and wishing to purge the minds of the people and win them over . . . he had this official (Ramiro) cut in two pieces one morning and exposed on the public square . . . This ferocious spectacle left the people at once *content and horrified."*

The words I have italicized show Machiavelli's peculiar cast of mind. He grows excited when goodness comes to a sticky end and when a dastardly deed is perpetrated under a cloak of justice. He seems to enjoy shocking traditional morality, and there can be little doubt that he is subconsciously revenging himself on the Establishment responsible for those two profound military defeats.

Machiavelli wrote *The Prince* for Giuliano de' Medici. He hoped that by applying the lessons in his book, Giuliano would become tough enough to unite Italy and drive out the foreigner. But Giuliano, the youngest son of Lorenzo the Magnificent, was a tubercular young man with gentle blue eyes and long sensitive fingers, the friend of poets and himself a sonneteer. He was so soft that his brother Pope Leo had to relieve him of his post as ruler of Florence after less than a year. Preparations for war against France taxed his feeble constitution; at the age of thirty-seven he fell ill and died. Machiavelli's notion of turning Giuliano into a second Cesare Borgia was about as fantastic as trying to turn John Keats into a James Bond.

This fantastic element has been overlooked in most accounts of Machiavelli, but it seems to me important. Consider the *Life of Castruccio Castracani,* which Machiavelli wrote seven years after *The Prince.* It purports to be a straight biography of a famous fourteenth-century ruler of Lucca, but in fact only the outline of the book is historically true. Finding the real Castruccio insufficiently tough to embody his ideals, Machiavelli introduces wholly fictitious episodes borrowed from Diodorus Siculus's life of a tyrant who really was unscrupulous: Agathocles. As captain of the Syracusans, Agathocles had collected a great army, then summoned the heads of the Council of Six Hundred under the pretext of asking their advice, and put them all to death.

Machiavelli in his book has Castruccio perform a similar stratagem. Just as in *The Prince* the second-rate Cesare Borgia passes through the crucible of Machiavelli's imagination to emerge as a modern Julius Caesar, so here a mildly villainous lord is dressed up as the perfect amoral autocrat. In both books Machiavelli is so concerned to preach his doctrine of salvation through a strong soldier-prince that he leaves Italy as it really was for a world of fantasy.

Machiavelli had a second purpose in dedicating *The Prince* to Giuliano de' Medici (and when Giuliano died, to his almost equally effete nephew Lorenzo). He wished to regain favor with the Medici, notably with Pope Leo. This also was a fantastic plan. Machiavelli had plotted hand over fist against the Medici for no less that fourteen years and was known to be a staunch republican, opposed to one-family rule in Florence. Pope Leo, moreover, was a gentle man who loved Raphael's smooth paintings and singing to the lute; he would not be interested in a book counseling cruelty and terror.

How could a man like Machiavelli, who spent his early life in the down-to-earth world of Italian politics, have yielded to such unrealistic, such fantastic hopes? The answer, I think, lies in the fact that he was also an imaginative artist—a playwright obsessed with extreme dramatic situations. Indeed, Machiavelli was best known in Florence as the author of *Mandragola*. In that brilliant comedy, a bold and tricky adventurer, aided by the profligacy of a parasite, and the avarice of a friar, achieves the triumph of making a gulled husband bring his own unwitting but too yielding wife to shame. It is an error to regard Machiavelli as primarily a political theorist, taking a cool look at facts. *The Prince* is, in one sense, the plot of a fantastic play for turning the tables on the French and Spaniards.

What, too, of Machiavelli's doctrine that it is sometimes wise for a prince to break his word and to violate treaties? It is usually said that this teaching originated with Machiavelli. If so, it would be very surprising, for the vast majority of so-called original inventions during the Italian Renaissance are now known to have been borrowed from classical texts. The Florentines valued wisdom as Edwardian English gentlemen valued port—the older the better.

In 1504 Machiavelli wrote a play, which has been lost, called *Masks*. It was in imitation of Aristophanes' [The] *Clouds,* the subject of which is the Sophists, those men who claimed to teach "virtue" in a special sense, namely, efficiency in the conduct of life. The Sophists emphasized material success and the ability to argue from any point of view, irrespective of its truth. At worst, they encouraged a cynical disbelief in all moral restraints on the pursuit of selfish, personal ambition.

Florentines during their golden age had paid little attention to the Sophists, preferring Plato, who accorded so well with Christianity and an aesthetic approach to life; but after the collapse in 1494 it would have been natural for a man like Machiavelli to dig out other, harder-headed philosophers.

The source for his doctrine of political unscrupulousness may well have been the Sophists as presented in Aristophanes' play. The following sentence from one of Machiavelli's letters in 1521 is close to many lines in *The Clouds:* "For that small matter of lies," writes Machiavelli, "I am a doctor and hold my degrees. Life has taught me to confound false and true, till no man knows either." In *The Prince* this personal confession becomes a general rule: "One must know how to color one's actions and to be a great liar and deceiver."

How was it that an undisputably civilized man like Machiavelli could advise a ruler to be cruel and deceitful and to strike terror? The answer lies in the last chapter of *The Prince,* entitled "Exhortation to liberate Italy from the barbarians." Often neglected, it is, in fact, the most deeply felt chapter of all and gives meaning to the rest. "See how Italy," Machiavelli writes, "beseeches God to send someone to save her from those barbarous cruelties and outrages"—he means the outrages perpetrated by foreign troops in Italy, a land, he goes on, that is "leaderless, lawless, crushed, despoiled, torn, overrun; she has had to endure every kind of desolation."

Machiavelli is a patriot writing in mental torment. He seldom mentions the deity, but in this chapter the name God occurs six times on one page, as an endorsement for this new kind of ruler. Machiavelli really believes that his deceitful prince will be as much an instrument of God as Moses was, and this for two reasons. First, Italy is an occupied country, and her survival is at stake; and just as moral theologians argued that theft becomes legitimate when committed by a starving man, so Machiavelli implies that deceit, cruelty, and so on become legitimate when they are the only means to national survival.

Secondly, Machiavelli had seen honest means tried and fail. Savonarola had hoped to silence cannon by singing hymns; Machiavelli himself had sent conscripts against the Spaniards. But the Italians had been then—and still were—bantams pitted against heavyweights. They could not win according to the rules, only with kidney punches. And since they had to win or cease to be themselves—that is, a civilized people as compared with foreign "barbarians"—Machiavelli argues that it is not only right but the will of God that they should use immoral means.

We must remember that *The Prince* is an extreme book that grew out of an extreme situation and that its maxims must be seen against the charred, smoking ruins of devastated Italy. The nearest modern parallel is occupied France. In the early 1940's cultivated men like Camus joined the Resistance, committing themselves to blowing up German posts by night and to other sinister techniques of *maquis* warfare. Like Machiavelli, they saw these as the only way to free their beloved country.

But the most original and neglected aspect of Machiavelli is his method. Before Machiavelli's time, historians had been the slaves of chronology. They started with the Creation, or the founding of their city, and worked forward, year by year, decade by decade, chronicling plague, war, and civil strife. Sometimes they detected a pattern, but even when they succeeded in doing so, the pattern was *sui generis,* not applicable elsewhere. Machiavelli was the first modern historian to pool historical facts from a variety of authors, not necessarily of the same period, and to use these facts to draw general conclusions or to answer pertinent questions.

He applies this method notably in his *Discourses on Livy,* and among the questions he answers are these: "What causes commonly give rise to wars between different powers?" "What kind of reputation or gossip or opinion causes the populace to begin to favor a particular citizen?" "Whether the safeguarding of liberty can be more safely entrusted to the populace or to the upper class; and which has the stronger reason for creating disturbances, the 'have-nots' or the 'haves'?"

Machiavelli does not wholly break free from a cyclical reading of history—the term Renaissance is itself a statement of the conviction that the golden age of Greece and Rome had returned. Nor did he break free from a belief in Fortune—what we would now call force of circumstance—and he calculated that men were at the mercy of Fortune five times out of ten. Nevertheless, he does mark an enormous advance over previous historical thinkers, since he discovered the method whereby man can learn from his past.

Having invented this method, Machiavelli proceeded to apply it imperfectly. He virtually ignored the Middle Ages, probably because medieval chronicles were deficient in those dramatic human twists, reversals, and paradoxes that were what really interested him. This neglect of the Middle Ages marred his study of how to deal with foreign invaders. Over a period of a thousand years Italy had constantly suffered invasion from the north; the lessons implicit in these instances would have helped Machiavelli to resolve his main problem much better than the more remote happenings he chose to draw from Livy. For example, at the Battle of Legnano, near Milan, in 1176, a league of north Italian cities won a crushing victory over Frederick Barbarossa's crack German knights. The Italians didn't employ duplicity or dramatic acts of terrorism, just courage and a united command.

So much for Machiavelli's teaching and discoveries. It remains to consider his influence. In his own lifetime he was considered a failure. Certainly, no soldier-prince arose to liberate Italy. After his death, however, it was otherwise. In 1552 the Vatican placed Machiavelli's works on the Index of Prohibited Books, because they teach men "to appear good for their own advantage in this world—a doctrine worse than heresy." Despite this ban, Machiavelli's books were widely read and his political teaching became influential. It would probably have confirmed him in his pessimistic view of human nature had he known that most statesmen and thinkers would seize on the elements of repression and guile in his teachings to the exclusion of the civic sense and patriotism he equally taught.

In France several kings studied Machiavelli as a means of increasing their absolutism, though it cannot be said that he did them much good. Henry III and Henry IV were murdered, and in each case on their blood-soaked person was found a well-thumbed copy of *The Prince.* Louis XIII was following Machiavelli when he caused his most powerful subject, the Italian-born adventurer

Concini, to be treacherously killed. Richelieu affirmed that France could not be governed without the right of arbitrary arrest and exile, and that in case of danger to the state it may be well that a hundred innocent men should perish. This was *raison d'état,* an exaggerated version of certain elements in *The Prince,* to which Machiavelli might well not have subscribed.

In England Machiavelli had little direct influence. England had never been defeated as Florence had been, and Englishmen could not understand the kind of desperate situation that demanded unscrupulous political methods. The political diseases Machiavelli had first studied scientifically were in England called after his name, rather as a physical disease—say Parkinson's—is called not after the man who is suffering from it but after the doctor who discovers it. Machiavelli thus became saddled with a lot of things he had never advocated, including atheism and any treacherous way of killing, generally by poison. Hence Flamineo in Webster's *White Devil:*

> O the rare tricks of a Machivillian!
> Hee doth not come like a grosse plodding slave
> And buffet you to death: no, my quaint knave—
> Hee tickles you to death; makes you die laughing,
> As if you had swallow'd a pound of saffron.

The eighteenth century, with its strong belief in man's good nature and reason, tended to scoff at Machiavelli. Hume wrote: "There is scarcely any maxim in *The Prince* which subsequent experience has not entirely refuted. The errors of this politician proceed, in a great measure, from his having lived in too early an age of the world to be a good judge of political truth." With Hume's judgment Frederick the Great of Prussia would, in early life, have agreed. As a young man Frederick wrote an *Anti-Machiavel,* in which he stated that a ruler is the first servant of his people. He rejected the idea of breaking treaties, "for one has only to make one deception of this kind, and one loses the confidence of every ruler." But Frederick did follow Machiavelli's advice to rule personally, to act as his own commander in the field, and to despise flatterers.

Later, Frederick began to wonder whether honesty really was the best policy. "One sees oneself continually in danger of being betrayed by one's allies, forsaken by one's friends, brought low by envy and jealousy; and ultimately one finds oneself obliged to choose between the terrible alternative of sacrificing one's people or one's word of honor." In old age, Frederick became a confirmed Machiavellian, writing in 1775: "Rulers must always be guided by the interests of the state. They are slaves of their resources, the interest of the state is their law, and this law may not be infringed."

During the nineteenth century Germany and Italy both sought to achieve national unity, with the result that writers now began to play up Machiavelli's other side, his call for regeneration. Young Hegel hails the author of *The Prince* for having "grasped with a cool circumspection the necessary idea that Italy should be saved by being combined into one state." He and Fichte go a stage further than Machiavelli: they assert that the conflict between the individual and the state no longer exists, since they consider liberty and law identical. The necessity of evil in political action becomes a superior ethics that has no connection with the morals of an individual. The state swallows up evil.

In Italy Machiavelli's ideal of a regenerated national state was not perverted in this way and proved an important influence on the *risorgimento.* In 1859 the provisional government of Tuscany, on the eve of national independence, published a decree stating that a complete edition of Machiavelli's works would be printed at government expense. It had taken more than three hundred years for "a man to arise to redeem Italy," and in the event the man turned out to be two men, Cavour and Garibaldi. Both, incidentally, were quite unlike the Prince: Cavour, peering through steel-rimmed spectacles, was a moderate statesman of the center, and Garibaldi a blunt, humane, rather quixotic soldier.

Bismarck was a close student of Machiavelli, but Marx and Engels did not pay much attention to him, and the Florentine's books have never exerted great influence in Russia. In contemporary history Machiavelli's main impact has been on Benito Mussolini. In 1924 Mussolini wrote a thesis on *The Prince,* which he described as the statesman's essential vade mecum. The Fascist leader deliberately set himself to implement Petrarch's call quoted on the last page of *The Prince:*

> *Che l'antico valore*
> Nell' italici cor non è ancor morto.

> Let Italians, as they did of old,
> Prove that their courage has not grown cold.

After a course of muscle building, Mussolini sent the Italian army into Ethiopia to found a new Roman Empire. He joined Hitler's war in 1940, only to find that he had failed to impart to modern Italians the martial qualities of Caesar's legions. The final irony occurred in 1944, when the Nazis were obliged to occupy northern Italy as the only means of stopping an Allied walkover, and Italy again experienced the trauma of 1494 and 1512. Mussolini's failures discredit, at least for our generation, Machiavelli's theory that it is possible for one man to effect a heart transplant on a whole people.

What is Machiavelli's significance today? His policy of political duplicity has been found wanting in the past and is probably no longer practicable in an age of democracy and television. His policy of nationalism is also beginning to date as we move into an era of ideological blocs. His insistence on the need for military preparedness has proved of more durable value and is likely to remain one of the West's key beliefs. His technique for solving political problems through a study of the past is practiced to some extent by every self-respecting foreign minister of our time.

Was Machiavelli, finally, an evil man? He made an ethic of patriotism. In normal times that is a poisonous equation, but defensible, I believe, in the context of sixteenth-century Italy. Machiavelli wrote on the edge of an abyss: he could hear the thud of enemy boots, had seen pillage, profanation, and rape by foreign troops. Imaginative as he was, he could sense horrors ahead: the ending of political liberty and of freedom of the press, which put the lights out in Italy for 250 years. He taught that it is civilized man's first duty to save civilization—at all costs. Doubtless he was mistaken. But it is not, I think, the mistake of an evil man.

Women of the Renaissance

J. H. Plumb

François Villon, the vagabond poet of France, wondered, as he drifted through the gutters and attics of fifteenth-century Paris, where were the famous women of the days long past? Where Héloïse, for whom Abelard had endured such degradation? Where Thaïs, Alis, Haremburgis, where the Queen Blanche with her siren's voice, where were these fabled, love-haunted, noblewomen, of more than human beauty? Gone, he thought, gone forever. Even the rough Viking bards sang of their heroic women, of Aud the Deep-minded, who "hurt most whom she loved best." The lives of these fateful, tragic women, medieval heroines of love and sorrow became themes of epic and romance that were told in the courts of princes; yet even as Villon bewailed their loss, men were growing tired of them.

The age of heroes was dying. The unrequited love of Dante for Beatrice, the lyrical attachment of Petrarch for Laura, and, in a different mood, the agreeable pleasantries of Boccaccio, had domesticated love, making it more intimate. The dawn of a carefree, less fate-ridden attitude to woman was gentle, undramatic, and slow beginning way back with the wandering troubadours and the scholars who moved from castle to farm, from monastery to university, singing their lighthearted lyrics to earn their keep:

Down the broad way do I go,
Young and unregretting,
Wrap me in my vices up,
Virtue all forgetting,
Greedier for all delight
Than heaven to enter in:
Since the soul in me is dead,
Better save the skin.
Sit you down amid the fire,
Will the fire not burn you?
Come to Pavia, will you
Just as chaste return you?
Pavia, where Beauty draws
Youth with finger-tips,
Youth entangled in her eyes,
Ravished with her lips.

So sang the nameless Archpoet, young, consumptive, in love, as he wandered down to Salerno to read medicine. The time was the twelfth century—three hundred years before the haunting love poems of Lorenzo de' Medici were written. Yet the sentiments of both men were a part of the same process, part of the lifting tide of Southern Europe's prosperity, of its growing population, of the sophistication that wealth and leisure brought, for in leisure lies dalliance. The wandering scholars were few; their mistresses, chatelaines or girls of the town. Yet they were the naive harbingers of a world that was to reach its fullness in Italy in the fifteenth century.

It was the new prosperity that influenced the lives of women most profoundly. It brought them fresh opportunities for adornment; it increased their dowries and their value. It emancipated many from the drudgery of the household and from the relentless, time-consuming demands of children. Women entered more fully into the daily lives and pursuits of men. And, of course, the new delights of the Renaissance world—painting, music, literature—had their feminine expression. Much of the artistic world was concerned with the pursuit of love in all its guises. Women were a part of art.

Except for the very lowest ranks of society, women were inextricably entangled in the concept of prosperity, and their virtue was a marketable commodity. They were secluded from birth to marriage, taught by women and priests, kept constantly under the closest supervision in the home or in the convent. Marriage came early: twelve was not an uncommon age, thirteen usual, fifteen was getting late, and an unmarried girl of sixteen or seventeen was a catastrophe. Women conveyed property and could often secure a lift in the social scale for their families. Even more important was the use of women to seal alliances between families, whether princely, noble, or mercantile. The great

Venetian merchants interlocked their adventures overseas with judicious marriages at home. The redoubtable Vittoria Colonna was betrothed at the age of four to the Marquis of Pescara to satisfy her family's political ambition. Lucrezia Borgia's early life was a grim enough reminder of the dynastic value of women. Her fiancés were sent packing, her husbands murdered or declared impotent, so that Alexandere VI could use her again and again in the furtherance of his policies.

In less exalted ranks of society women were still traded. It took Michelangelo years of horse trading to buy a young Ridolfi wife for his nephew and so push his family up a rank in Florentine society. Marriages so arranged were symbolic of power and social status as well as wealth, and their celebration, in consequence, demanded the utmost pomp and splendor that the contracting parties could afford. Important Venetian marriages were famed for an extravagance that not even the Council of Ten could curb.

The festivities began with an official proclamation in the Doge's Palace. The contracting parties and their supporters paraded the canals *en fete*. Gondoliers and servants were dressed in sumptuous livery; the facades of the palaces were adorned with rare Oriental carpets and tapestries; there were bonfires, fireworks, balls, masques, banquets, and everywhere and at all times—even the most intimate serenades by gorgeously dressed musicians. Of course, such profusion acted like a magnet for poets, dramatists, rhetoricians, painters, and artists of every variety. For a few ducats a wandering humanist would pour out a few thousand words, full of recondite references to gods and heroes; poets churned out epithalamiums before they could be asked; and painters immortalized the bride, her groom, or even, as Botticelli did, the wedding breakfast. And they were eager for more mundane tasks, not for one moment despising an offer to decorate the elaborate *cassoni* in which the bride took her clothes and linen to her new household. Indeed, the competitive spirit of both brides and painters in *cassoni* became so fierce that they ceased to be objects of utility and were transformed into extravagant works of art, becoming the heirlooms of future generations.

The artistic accompaniment of marriage became the height of fashion. When the Duke and Duchess of Urbino returned to their capital after their wedding, they were met on a hilltop outside their city by all the women and children of rank, exquisitely and expensively dressed, bearing olive branches in their hands. As the Duke and Duchess reached them, mounted choristers accompanied by nymphs à *la Grecque* burst into song—a special cantata that had been composed for the newlyweds. The Goddess of Mirth appeared in person with her court, and to make everyone realize that jollity and horseplay were never out of place at a wedding, hares were loosed in the crowd. This drove the dogs insane with excitement, to everyone's delight. No matter how solemn the occasion, marriage always involved coarse farce, usually at the climax of the wedding festivities, when the bride and the groom were publicly bedded. Although there was no romantic nonsense about Italian weddings—certainly few marriages for love—everyone knew that the right, true end of the contract was the bed. The dowager Duchess of Urbino, something of a blue-stocking and a Platonist and a woman of acknowledged refinement, burst into her niece's bedroom on the morning after her marriage and shouted, "Isn't it a fine thing to sleep with the men?"

Marriage for the women of the Renaissance gave many their first taste of opulence, leisure, and freedom. They were very young; the atmosphere of their world was as reckless as it was ostentatious; and furthermore, they had not chosen their husbands, who frequently were a generation older than they. Their men, who often were soldiers or courtiers living close to the razor-edge of life, fully enjoyed intrigue, so the young wife became a quarry to be hunted. As she was often neglected, the chase could be brief. Even Castiglione, who was very fond of his wife, treated her somewhat casually. He saw her rarely and made up for his absence with affectionate, bantering letters. Of course, she was a generation younger than he and therefore

hardly a companion. Such a situation was not unusual: a girl of thirteen might excite her mature husband, but she was unlikely to entertain him for long. She fulfilled her tasks by bearing a few children and running a trouble-free household, and neither matter was too onerous for the rich. Nurses took over the children as soon as they were born; a regiment of servants relieved wives of their traditionally housewifely duties. So the leisure that had previously been the lot of only a few women of very high birth became a commonplace of existence for a multitude of women.

The presence of these leisured women in society helped to transform it. It created the opportunity for personality to flourish, for women to indulge the whims of their temperaments—free from the constraining circumstances of childbirth, nursery, and kitchen. There were men enough to adorn their vacant hours. Italy was alive with priests, many of them urbane, cultured, and idle, whose habit acted as a passport, hinting a security for husbands that their actions all too frequently belied. Nevertheless, they were the natural courtiers of lonely wives, and they swarmed in the literary salons of such distinguished women as Elisabetta Gonzaga at Urbino, the Queen of Cyprus at Asolo, or Vittoria Colonna at Rome.

Soldiers as well as priests needed the sweetness of feminine compassion to soften their tough and dangerous lives. Fortunately, military campaigns in Renaissance Italy were short and usually confined to the summer months, and so the horseplay, the practical jokes, and the feats of arms that were as essential to the courtly life as literary conversations or dramatic performances were provided by the knights.

In addition to soldiers and priests, there were the husbands' pages, all in need of the finer points of amorous education. For a princess, further adornment of the salon was provided by an ambassador—often, true enough, a mere Italian, but at times French or Spanish, which gave an exotic touch that a woman of fashion could exploit to her rivals' disadvantage. Naturally, these courts became highly competitive: to have Pietro Bembo sitting at one's feet, reading his mellifluous but tedious essays on the beauties of Platonic love, was sure to enrage the hearts of other women. In fact, the popularity of Bembo illustrates admirably the style of sophis-

ticated love that the extravagant and princely women of Italy demanded.

Pietro Bembo was a Venetian nobleman, the cultivated son of a rich and sophisticated father who had educated him in the height of humanist fashion at the University of Ferrara, where he acquired extreme agility in bandying about the high-flown concepts of that strange mixture of Platonism and Christianity that was the hallmark of the exquisite. Petrarch, of course, was Bembo's mentor, and like Petrarch he lived his life, as far as the pressures of nature would allow him, in literary terms. He fell verbosely and unhappily in love with a Venetian girl; his ardent longings and intolerable frustrations were committed elegantly to paper and circulated to his admiring friends.

This experience provided him with enough material for a long epistolary exchange with Ercole Strozzi, who was as addicted as Bembo to girls in literary dress. Enraptured by the elegance of his sentiments, Strozzi invited Bembo to his villa near Ferrara, doubtless to flaunt his latest capture, Lucrezia Borgia, as well as to indulge his insatiable literary appetite. However, the biter was quickly bitten, for Bembo was just Lucrezia's cup of tea. A mature woman of twenty-two, thoroughly versed in the language as well as the experience of love, she was already bored with her husband, Alfonso d'Este, and tired of Strozzi. Soon she and Bembo were exchanging charming Spanish love lyrics and far larger homilies on aesthetics. After a visit by Lucrezia to Bembo, sick with fever, the pace quickened. Enormous letters followed thick and fast. Bembo ransacked literature to do homage to Lucrezia; they were Aeneas and Dido, Tristan and Iseult, Lancelot and Guinevere—not, however, lover and mistress.

For a time they lived near each other in the country while Ferrara was plague-ridden. Proximity and the furor of literary passion began to kindle fires in Bembo that were not entirely Platonic, and, after all, Lucrezia was a Borgia. Her tolerant but watchful husband, however, had no intention of being cuckolded by an aesthete, and he rattled his sword. Bembo did not relish reliving the tragedy of Abelard; he might love Lucrezia to distraction, but he cherished himself as only an artist can, so he thought it discreet to return to Venice (he had excuse enough, as his brother was desperately sick). There he consoled himself by polishing his dialogue, *Gli Asolani,* which already enjoyed a high reputation among those to whom it had been circulated in manuscript. Resolving to give his love for Lucrezia its final, immortal form, he decided to publish it with a long dedication to her. To present her with his divine thoughts on love was a greater gift by far, of course, than his person. Doubtless both Lucrezia and her husband agreed; whether they read further than the dedication is more doubtful.

Bembo had written these highfalutin letters—informal, mannered, obscure, and so loaded with spiritual effusions on love, beauty, God, and women that they are almost unreadable—during a visit to that tragic and noblewoman Caterina Cornaro, Queen of Cyprus. The daughter of a Venetian aristocrat, she had been married as a girl to Giacomo II of Cyprus for reasons of state and declared with infinite pomp "daughter of the republic." Bereaved of both husband and son within three years, she had defied revolution and civil war and maintained her government for fourteen years until, to ease its political necessities, Venice had forced her abdication and set her up in a musical-comedy court at Asolo. There she consoled herself with the world of the spirit, about which Bembo was better informed than most, and he was drawn to her like a moth to a flame. Her court was elegant, fashionable, and intensely literary. *Gli Asolani,* published by Aldus in 1505, made Bembo the archpriest of love as the *Courtier* was to make Castiglione the archpriest of manners. Indeed, Bembo figures in the *Courtier,* and Castiglione adopted his literary techniques. These two subtle and scented bores were destined to turn up together, and nowhere was more likely than the court of Elisabetta Gonzaga at Urbino, for her insatiable appetite for discussion was equal to their eloquence; her stamina matched their verbosity; and night after night the dawn overtook their relentless arguments about the spiritual nature of love. Neither, of course, was so stupid as to think that even the high-minded Caterina or Elisabetta could live by words alone, and Bembo, at least, always interlarded the more ethereal descriptions of Platonic love with a warm eulogy of passion in its more prosaic and energetic aspects. Indeed, he was not above appearing (not entirely modestly disguised) as an ambassador of Venus, in order to declaim in favor of

natural love. After six years of this excessively cultured refinement at Urbino, Bembo became papal secretary to Leo X in Rome. Appropriately, at Rome the word became flesh, and Bembo settled into the comfortable arms of a girl called Morosina, who promptly provided him with three children. It is not surprising, therefore, that Bembo's interests became more mundane, turning from Platonic philosophy to the history of Venice. After the death of his mistress, the life of the spirit once more claimed him, and he entered the College of Cardinals in 1538. More than any other man of his time, he set the pattern of elegant courtship, so that the flattery of the mind, combined with poetic effusions on the supremacy of the spirit, became a well-trodden path for the courtier. It possessed the supreme advantage of passionate courtship without the necessity of proof—a happy situation, indeed, when the object was both a blue stocking and a queen.

Yet it would be wrong to think that the gilded lives of Renaissance princesses were merely elegant, sophisticated, and luxurious or that flirtation took place only in the most refined language. Few could concentrate their thoughts year in, year out, on the nobility of love like Vittoria Colonna. She, who inspired some of Michelangelo's most passionate poetry, even into old age, could and did live in an intense world of spiritual passion, in which the lusts of the flesh were exorcised by an ecstatic contemplation of the beauties of religion. She managed to retain her charm, avoid the pitfalls of hypocrisy, and secure without effort the devotion of Castiglione and Bembo as well as Michelangelo. Even the old rogue Aretino attempted to secure her patronage, but naturally she remained aloof. In her the Platonic ideals of love and beauty mingled with the Christian virtues to the exclusion of all else. Amazingly, no one found her a bore. However, few women could live like Vittoria: they sighed as they read Bembo, became enrapt as they listened to Castiglione, but from time to time they enjoyed a quiet reading of Boccaccio and, better still, Bandello.

Matteo Bandello had been received as a Dominican and spent many years of his live at the Convento delle Grazie, at Milan, which seems to have been a more exciting place for a short-story teller than might be imagined. He acted for a time as ambassador for the Ben-

tivoglio and so came in contact with that remarkable woman Isabello d'Este Gonzaga, whose court at Mantua was as outstanding for its wit, elegance, and genius as any in Italy. There Bandello picked up a mistress, which put him in no mind to hurry back to his brother monks. At Mantua, too, he laid the foundations of his reputation for being one of the best raconteurs of scandal in all Italy, Aretino not excepted. How true Bandello's stories are is still a matter of fierce warfare among scholars, but this they agree on: they did not seem incredible to those who read them. That being so, they give a hair-raising picture of what was going on at courts, in monasteries, in nunneries, in merchant houses, in the palaces and the parsonages of Italy. The prime pursuit, in the vast majority of Bandello's stories, is the conquest of women, and to achieve success, any trick, any falsehood, any force, is justifiable. His heroes' attitude toward success in sex was like Machiavelli's toward politics—the end justified any means. The aim of all men was to ravish other men's wives and daughters and preserve their own women or revenge them if they failed to do so. Vendettas involving the most bloodcurdling punishments were a corollary to his major theme. In consequence, Bandello's stories, cast in a moral guise, nevertheless read like the chronicles of a pornographer. Here are the themes of a few that were thought to be proper entertainment for the lighter moments of court life or for quiet reading by a bored wife: the marriage of a man to a woman who was already his sister and to his daughter; the adultery of two ladies at court and the death of their paramours, which is a vivid record of sexual pleasure and horrifying punishment; the servant who was decapitated for sleeping with his mistress; the death through excessive sexual indulgence of Charles of Navarre; Gian Maria Visconti's burial of a live priest; the autocastration of Fra Filippo—and so one might go on and on, for Bandello wrote hundreds of short stories, and they were largely variations of a single theme. The women of the Renaissance loved them, and few storytellers were as popular as Bandello (such abilities did not go unmarked, and he finished his career as Bishop of Agen). Nor was Bandello exceptional: there were scores of writers like him. Malicious, distorted, exaggerated as these tales were, they were based on the realities of Italian life.

Undoubtedly the increased leisure of men and women released their energies for a more riotous indulgence of their sexual appetites.

However daring the Italian males of the Renaissance were, the prudence of wives and the vigilance of husbands prevailed more often than not. The Emilia Pias, Elisabetta Gonzagas, Isabello d'Estes, Lucrezia Borgias, Costanza Amarettas, and Vittoria Colonnas were rare—particularly for cardinals and bishops ravenous for Platonic love. So in Rome, in Florence, in Venice, and in Milan there developed a class of grand courtesans, more akin to geisha girls than to prostitutes, to the extent that the *cortesane famose* of Venice despised the *cortesane de la minor sorte* and complained of their number, habits, and prices to the Senate (they felt they brought disrepute on an honorable profession). Grand as these Venetian girls were, they could not compete with the great courtesans of Rome, who not only lived in small palaces with retinues of maids and liveried servants but also practiced the literary graces and argued as learnedly as a Duchess of Urbino about the ideals of Platonic love.

Italy during the Renaissance was a country at war, plagued for decades with armies. A well-versed condottiere might battle with skill even in the wordy encounters of Platonic passion, but the majority wanted a quicker and cheaper victory. For months on end the captains of war had nothing to do and money to spend; they needed a metropolis of pleasure and vice. Venice, with its quick eye for a profit, provided it and plucked them clean. There, women were to be had for as little as one *scudo*, well within the means even of a musketeer. And it was natural that after Leo X's purge, the majority of the fallen from Rome should flow to Venice. That city, with its regattas, *feste*, and carnivals, with its gondolas built for seclusion and sin, became a harlot's paradise. The trade in women became more profitable and extensive than it had been since the days of Imperial Rome. The Renaissance recaptured the past in more exotic fields than literature or the arts.

Life, however, for the noblewomen of the Renaissance was not always cakes and ale; it could be harsh and furious: the male world of war, assassination, and the pursuit of power frequently broke in upon their gentle world of love and dalliance. Indeed, Caterina Sforza, the woman whom all Italy saluted as its *prima donna,* won her fame through her dour courage and savage temper. Castiglione tells the story of the time she invited a boorish condottiere to dinner and asked him first to dance and then to hear some music—both of which he declined on the grounds that they were not his business. "What is your business, then?" his hostess asked. "Fighting," the warrior replied. "Then," said the virago of Forlì, "since you are not at war and not needed to fight, it would be wise for you to have yourself well greased and put away in a cupboard with all your arms until you are wanted, so that you will not get more rusty than you are." Caterina was more a figure of a saga than a woman of the Renaissance. Three of her husbands were assassinated. At one time she defied the French, at another Ceasare Borgia, who caught her and sent her like a captive lioness to the dungeons of Sant' Angelo. She told her frantic sons that she was habituated to grief and had no fear of it, and as they ought to have expected, she escaped. Yet tough and resourceful as she was, Caterina could be a fool in love—much more than the Duchess of Urbino or Vittoria Colonna. Time and time again her political troubles were due to her inability to check her strong appetite, which fixed itself too readily on the more monstrous of the Renaissance adventurers. So eventful a life induced credulity, and like the rest of her family, Caterina believed in the magical side of nature, dabbled in alchemy and mysteries, and was constantly experimenting with magnets that would produce family harmony or universal salves or celestial water or any other improbable elixir that the wandering hucksters wished on her. At any age, at any time, Catarina would have been a remarkable woman, but the Renaissance allowed her wild temperament to riot.

Certainly the women of the Renaissance were portents. Elisabetta Gonzaga and Isabello d'Este are the founding sisters of the great literary salons that were to dominate the fashionable society of Western Europe for centuries. But the courts of Italy were few, the families that were rich enough to indulge the tastes and pleasures of sophisticated women never numerous. The lot of most women was harsh; they toiled in the home at their looms or in the fields alongside their men. They bred early and died young, untouched by the growing civility about them, save in their piety. In the churches where they sought ease for their sorrows, the Mother of God shone with a new radiance, a deeper compassion, and seemed in her person to immortalize their lost beauty. Even the majority of middle-class women knew little of luxury or literary elegance. Their lives were dedicated to their husbands and their children; their ambitions were limited to the provision of a proper social and domestic background for their husbands; and they were encouraged to exercise prudence, to indulge in piety, and to eschew vanities. Yet their lives possessed a civility, a modest elegance, that was in strong contrast to the harsher experiences and more laborious days of medieval women. Their new wealth permitted a greater, even if still modest, personal luxury. They could dress themselves more finely, acquire more jewels, provide a richer variety of food for their guests, entertain more lavishly, give more generously to charity. Although circumscribed, their lives were freer, their opportunities greater. It might still be unusual for a woman to be learned or to practice the arts, but it was neither rare nor exotic. And because they had more time, they were able to create a more active social life and to spread civility. After the Renaissance, the drawing room became an integral part of civilized living; indeed, the Renaissance education of a gentleman assumed that much of his life would be spent amusing women and moving them with words. As in so many aspects of life in Renaissance Italy, aristocratic attitudes of the High Middle Ages were adopted by the middle classes. Courtesy and civility spread downward, and the arts of chivalry became genteel.

Columbus—Hero or Villain?

Felipe Fernández-Armesto *weighs up the case for and against the man of the hour and finds a Columbus for all seasons.*

Felipe Fernández-Armesto is a member of The Faculty of Modern History of Oxford University.

This year, his statue in Barcelona exchanged symbolic rings with the Statue of Liberty in New York; meanwhile, the descendants of slaves and peons will burn his effigy. In a dream-painting by Salvador Dali, Columbus takes a great step for mankind, toga-clad and cross-bearing—while a sail in the middle distance drips with blood. The Columbus of tradition shares a single canvas with the Columbus of fashion, the culture-hero of the western world with the bogey who exploited his fellowman and despoiled his environment. Both versions are false and, if historians had their way, the quincentennial celebrations ought to stimulate enough educational work and research to destroy them. Instead, the polemical atmosphere seems to be reinforcing *à parti pris* positions.

It is commonly said that the traditional Columbus myth—which awards him personal credit for anything good that ever came out of America since 1492—originated in the War of Independence, when the founding fathers, in search of an American hero, pitched on the Genoese weaver as the improbable progenitor of all-American virtues. Joel Barlow's poem, *The Vision of Columbus,* appeared in 1787. Columbus remained a model for nineteenth-century Americans, engaged in a project for taming their own wilderness. Washington Irving's perniciously influential *History of the Life and Voyages of Christopher Columbus* of 1828—which spread a lot of nonsense including the ever-popular folly that Columbus was derided for claiming that the world was round—appealed unashamedly to Americans' self-image as promoters of civilisation.

Yet aspects of the myth are much older—traceable to Columbus' own times and, to a large extent, to his own efforts. He was a loquacious and indefatigable self-publicist, who bored adversaries into submission and acquired a proverbial reputation for using more paper than Ptolemy. The image he projected was that of a providential agent, the divinely-elected 'messenger of a new heaven', chosen to bear the light of the gospel to unevangelised recesses of the earth—the parts which other explorers could not reach. His plan for an Atlantic crossing 'God revealed to me by His manifest hand'. Playing on his christian name, he called himself 'Christo ferens' and compiled a book of what he said were biblical prophecies of his own discoveries. Enough contemporaries were convinced by his gigantic self-esteem for him to become literally a legend in his own lifetime. To a leading astrological guru at the court of Spain, he was 'like a new apostle'. To a humanist from Italy who taught the would-be Renaissance men of Castile, he was 'the sort of whom the ancients made gods'.

The image of Columbus-as-victim of the Spanish courts is explained by his relishing his own misfortunes as good copy and good theatre.

From his last years, his reputation dipped: writers were obliged to belittle him in the service of monarchs who were locked in legal conflict with Columbus' family over the level of reward he had earned. Yet his own self-perception was passed on to posterity by influential early books. Bartolomé de Las Casas—Columbus' editor and historian—professed a major role for himself in the apostolate of the New World and heartily endorsed Columbus' self-evaluation as an agent of God's purpose. Almost as important was the *Historie dell'Ammiraglio,* which claimed to be a work of filial piety and therefore presented Columbus as an unblemished hero, with an imputed pedigree to match his noble soul.

Claims to having access to a divine hot-line are by their nature unverifiable. Demonstrably false was the second element in Columbus' self-made myth: his image of tenacity in adversity—a sort of *Mein Kampf* version of his life, in which he waged a long, lone and unremitting struggle against the ignorance and derision of contemporaries. This theme has echoed through the historical tradition. That 'they all laughed at Christopher Columbus' has been confirmed by modern doggerel. Vast books have been wasted in an attempt to explain his mythical perseverance by ascribing to him 'secret' foreknowledge of the existence of America. Yet almost all the evidence which underlies it comes straight out of Columbus' own propaganda, according to which he was isolated, ignored, victimised and persecuted, usually for the numinous span of 'seven' years; then, after fulfilling his destiny, to the great profit of his detractors he was returned to a wilderness of contumely and neglect, unrewarded by the standard of his deserts, in a renewed trial of faith.

The images of Columbus-as-hero and Columbus-as-villain have a long historical and literary tradition.

These passages of autobiography cannot be confirmed by the facts. The documented length of his quest for patronage was less than five years. Throughout that time he built up a powerful lobby of moral supporters at the Castilian court and financial backers in the business community of Seville. His own protestations of loneliness are usually qualified by an admission that he was unsupported 'save for' one or two individuals. When added together, these form an impressive cohort, which includes at least two archbishops, one

court astrologer, two royal confessors, one royal treasurer and the queen herself. In his second supposed period of persecution, he was an honoured figure, loaded with titles, received at court, consulted by the crown and—despite his woebegone protestations of poverty—amply moneyed.

The explanation of the image of Columbus-as-victim must be sought in his character, not in his career. He was what would now be called a whinger, who relished his own misfortunes as good copy and good theatre. When he appeared at court in chains, or in a friar's habit, he was playing the role of victim for all it was worth. His written lamentations—which cover many folios of memoranda, supplications and personal letters—are thick with allusions to Jeremiah and Job. The notions of patience under suffering and of persecution for righteousness' sake fitted the hagiographical model on which much of his self-promotional writing was based: a flash of divine enlightenment; a life transformed; consecration to a cause; unwavering fidelity in adversity.

The most successful promotional literature is believed by its own propagators. To judge from his consistency, Columbus believed in his own image of himself. It is not surprising that most readers of his works, from Las Casas onwards, have been equally convinced. Columbus seems to have been predisposed to self-persuasion by saturation in the right literary models: saints, proph-

ets and heroes of romance. Despite his astonishing record of achievement, and his impressive accumulation of earthly rewards, he had an implacable temperament which could never be satisfied, and an unremitting ambition which could never be assuaged. Such men always think themselves hard done by. His extraordinary powers of persuasion—his communicator's skills which won backing for an impossible project in his lifetime—have continued to win followers of his legend ever since his death.

Like Columbus-the-hero, Columbus-the-villain is also an old character in a long literary tradition. Most of the denunciations of him written in his day have not survived but we can judge their tenor from surviving scraps. The usual complaints against servants of the Castilian crown in the period are made: he acted arbitrarily in the administration of justice; he exceeded his powers in enforcing his authority; he usurped royal rights by denying appeal to condemned rebels; he alienated crown property without authorisation; he deprived privileged colonists of offices or perquisites; he favoured his own family or friends; he lined his pockets at public expense. In the course of what seems to have been a general campaign against Genoese employees of the crown in the late 1490s, he was 'blamed as a foreigner' and accused of 'plotting to give the island of Hispaniola to the Genoese'.

Other allegations attacked his competence rather than his good faith, generally with justice. It was true, for instance, that he had selected an unhealthy and inconvenient site for the settlement of Hispaniola; that he had disastrously misjudged the natives' intentions in supposing them to be peaceful; and that his proceedings had so far alienated so many colonists that by the time of his removal in 1500 it was a missionary's opinion that the colony would never be at peace if he were allowed back. All these complaints reflect the priorities of Spaniards and the interests of the colonists and of the crown. There were, however, some charges against Columbus which anticipated the objections of modern detractors, who scrutinise his record from the natives' point of view, or who look at it from the perspective of fashionably ecological priorities.

First, there was the issue of Columbus' activities as a slaver. Coming from a Genoese background, Columbus never understood Spanish scruples about slavery, which had been characterised as an unnatural estate in the most influential medieval Spanish law-code, and which the monarchs distrusted as a form of intermediate lordship that reserved subjects from royal jurisdiction. Castilian practice was, perhaps, the most fastidious in Christendom. The propriety of slavery was acknowledged in the cases of captives of just war and offenders against natural law; but such cases were reviewed with rigour and in the royal courts, at least, decision-making tended to be biased in favour of the alleged slaves.

Shortly before the discovery of the New World, large numbers of Canary Islanders, enslaved by a conquistador on the pretext that they were 'rebels against their natural lord' had been pronounced free by a judicial inquiry commissioned by the crown, and liberated, in cases contested by their 'owners', in a series of trials. This does not seem, however, to have altered Columbus to the risks of slap-happy slaving.

Although the ferocious Caribs of the Lesser Antilles were generally deemed to be lawful victims of enslavement (since the cannibalism imputed to them seemed an obvious offence against natural law) Columbus' trade was chiefly in Arawaks, who, by his own account, were rendered exempt by their amenability to evangelisation. By denying that the Arawaks were idolatrous, Columbus exonerated them of the one possible charge which might, in the terms of the time, be considered an 'unnatural' of-

fence. Even when the monarchs reproved him and freed the Arawaks he sold, Columbus was astonishingly slow on the uptake. In a colony where the yield of other profitable products was disappointing, he traded slaves to allay the colony's grievous problems of supply. 'And although at present they die on shipment,' he continued, 'this will not always be the case, for the Negroes and Canary Islanders reacted in the same way at first'. In one respect, contemporary criticisms of the traffic differed from those made today. The friars and bureaucrats who denounced Columbus for it did so not because it was immoral, but because it was unlawful.

Slavery was only one among many ills which Columbus was said to have inflicted on the natives. The current myth incriminates him with 'genocide'. In the opinion of one *soi-disant* Native American spokesman, 'he makes Hitler look like a juvenile delinquent'. This sort of hype is doubly unhelpful: demonstrably false, it makes the horrors of the holocaust seem precedented and gives comfort to Nazi apologists by making 'genocide' an unshocking commonplace. Though he was often callous and usually incompetent in formulating indigenist policy, the destruction of the natives was as far removed from Columbus' thoughts as from his interests. The Indians, he acknowledged, were 'the wealth of this land'. Their conservation was an inescapable part of any rational policy for their exploitation. Without them the colony would have no labour resources. At a deeper level of Columbus' personal concerns, they were the great glory of his discovery: their evangelisation justified it and demonstrated its place in God's plans for the world, even if the material yield was disappointing to his patrons and backers. And Columbus had enough sense to realise that a large and contented native population was, as the monarchs said, their 'chief desire' for his colony. 'The principal thing which you must do,' he wrote to his first deputy,

> is to take much care of the Indians, that no ill nor harm may be done them, nor anything taken from them against their will, but rather that they be honoured and feel secure and so should have no cause to rebel.

Though no contemporary was so foolish as to accuse Columbus of wil-

fully exterminating Indians, it was widely realised that his injunctions were often honoured in the breach and that his own administrative regulations sometimes caused the natives harm. The missionaries almost unanimously regarded him as an obstacle to their work, though the only specific crime against the natives to survive among their memoranda—that 'he took their women and all their property'—is otherwise undocumented. The imposition of forced labour and of unrealistic levels of tribute were disastrous policies, which diverted manpower from food-growing and intensified the 'culture-shock' under which indigenous society reeled and tottered, though Columbus claimed they were expedients to which he was driven by economic necessity.

Some contemporaries also condemned the sanguinary excesses of his and his brother's punitive campaigns in the interior of Hispaniola in 1495–96. It should be said in Columbus' defence, however, that he claimed to see his own part as an almost bloodless pacification and that the 50,000 deaths ascribed to these campaigns in the earliest surviving account were caused, according to the same source, chiefly by the Indians' scorched-earth strategy. The outcome was horrible enough, but Columbus' treatment of the Indians inflicted catastrophe on them rather by mistakes than by crimes. In general, he was reluctant to chastise them—refusing, for instance, to take punitive measures over the massacre of the first garrison of Hispaniola; and he tried to take seriously the monarchs' rather impractical command to 'win them by love'.

It would be absurd to look for environmental sensitivity of a late twentieth-century kind in Columbus' earliest critics. Yet the accusation of over-exploitation of the New World environment, which is at the heart of the current, ecologically-conscious anti-Columbus mood, was also made before the fifteenth century was quite over. According to the first missionaries, members of Columbus' family were 'robbing and destroying the land' in their greed for gold. Though he declined to accept personal responsibility, Columbus detected a similar problem when he denounced his fellow-colonists' exploitative attitude: unmarried men, with no stake in the success of the colony and no intention of permanent residence, should be excluded, he thought. They merely mulcted the island for what they could get before rushing home to Castile.

The danger of deforestation from the demand for dyestuffs, building materials and fuel was quickly recognised. The diversion of labour from agriculture to gold-panning aroused friars' moral indignation. The usefulness of many products of the indigenous agronomy was praised by Columbus and documented by the earliest students of the pharmacopoeia and florilegium of the New World. The assumption that there was an ecological 'balance' to be disturbed at hazard was, of course, impossible. On the contrary, everyone who arrived from the Old World assumed that the natural resources had to be supplemented with imported products to provide a balanced diet, a civilised environment and resources for trade. The modifications made by Columbus and his successors were intended, from their point of view, to improve, not to destroy. They introduced sources of protein—like livestock; comforts of home—like wheat and grapes; and potential exports—like sugar, whether these changes were really disastrous is hard to judge dispassionately. The loss of population in the early colonial period was probably due to other causes. In the long run, colonial Hispaniola proved able to maintain a large population and a spectacular material culture.

Since it was first broached in Columbus' day, the debate about the morality of the colonisation of the New World has had three intense periods: in the sixteenth century, when the issues of the justice of the Spanish presence and the iniquity of maltreatment of the natives were raised by religious critics and foreign opportunists; in the late eighteenth century, when Rousseau and Dr Johnson agreed in preferring the uncorrupted wilderness which was thought to have preceded colonisation; and in our own day. Until recently, Columbus managed largely to avoid implication in the sins of his successors. Las Casas revered him, and pitied, rather than censured, the imperfections of his attitude to the natives. Eighteenth-century sentimentalists regretted the colonial experience as a whole, generally without blaming Columbus for it. This was fair enough. Columbus' own model of colonial society seems to have derived from Genoese precedents: the trading factory, merchant quarter and family firm. The idea of a 'total' colony, with a population and environment revolutionised by the impact and image of the metropolis, seems to have been imposed on him by his Castilian masters. In making him personally responsible for everything which followed—*post hunc ergo propter hunc*—his modern critics have followed a convention inaugurated by admirers, who credited Columbus with much that [h]as nothing to do with him—including, most absurdly of all—the culture of the present United States. Columbus never touched what was to become US territory except in Puerto Rico and the Virgin Islands. The values which define the 'American ideal'—personal liberty, individualism, freedom of conscience, equality of opportunity and representative democracy—would have meant nothing to him.

Columbus deserves the credit or blame only for what he actually did: which was to discover a route that permanently linked the shores of the Atlantic and to contribute—more signally, perhaps, than any other individual—to the long process by which once sundered peoples of the world were brought together in a single network of communications, which exposed them to the perils and benefits of mutual contagion and exchange. Whether or not one regards this as meritorious achievement, there was a genuine touch of heroism in it—both in the scale of its effects and in the boldness which inspired it. There had been many attempts to cross the Atlantic in central latitudes, but all—as far as we know—failed because the explorers clung to the zone of westerly winds in an attempt to secure a passage home. Columbus was the first to succeed precisely because he had the courage to sail with the wind at his back.

Historians, it is often said, have no business making moral judgements at all. The philosophy of the nursery-school assembly, in which role-models and culprits are paraded for praise or reproof seems nowadays to belong to a hopelessly antiquated sort of history, for which the reality of the past mattered less than the lessons for the present and the future. A great part of the historian's art is now held to consist in what the examiners call 'empathy'—the ability to see the past with the eyes, and to reconstruct the feelings, of those who took part in it. If value judgements are made at all, they ought at least to be controlled by certain essential disciplines. First, they must be consistent with the facts: it is unhelpful to accuse of 'genocide', for instance, a colonial administrator who was anxious for the preservation of the native labour force. Secondly, they should be made in the context of the value-system of the society scrutinised, at the time concerned. It would be impertinent to expect Columbus to regard slavery as immoral, or to uphold the equality of all peoples. Conquistadors and colonists are as entitled to be judged from the perspective of moral relativism as are the cannibals and human-sacrificers of the indigenous past. Thirdly, moral judgements should be expressed in language tempered by respect for the proper meanings of words. Loose talk of 'genocide' twists a spiral to verbal hype. Useful distinctions are obliterated; our awareness of the real cases, when they occur, is dulled.

Columbus was a man of extraordinary vision with a defiant attitude to what was possible; he could not anticipate the consequences of his discovery.

Finally, when we presume to judge someone from a long time ago, we should take into account the practical constraints under which they had to operate, and the limited mental horizons by which they were enclosed. Columbus was in some ways a man of extraordinary vision with a defiant attitude to the art of the possible. Yet he could not anticipate the consequences of his discovery or of the colonial enterprise confided to him. Five hundred years further on, with all our advantages of hindsight, we can only boast a handful of 'successful' colonial experiments—in the United States, Siberia, Australia and New Zealand—in all of which the indigenous populations have been exterminated or swamped. The Spanish empire founded by Columbus was strictly unprecedented and, in crucial respects, has never been paralleled. The problems of regulating such vast dominions, with so many inhabitants, so far away, and with so few resources, were unforeseeable and proved unmanageable. Never had so many people been conquered by culture-shock or their immune-systems invaded by irresistible disease. Never before had such a challenging environment been so suddenly transformed in an alien image. In these circumstances, it would be unreasonable to expect Columbus' creation to work well. Like Dr Johnson's dog, it deserves some applause for having performed at all.

So which was Columbus: hero or villain? The answer is that he *was* neither but has *become* both. The real Columbus was a mixture of virtues and vices like the rest of us, not conspicuously good or just, but generally well-intentioned, who grappled creditably with intractable problems. Heroism and villainy are not,

however, objective qualities. They exist only in the eye of the beholder.

In images of Columbus, they are now firmly impressed on the retinas of the upholders of rival legends and will never be expunged. Myths are versions of the past which people believe in for irrational motives—usually because they feel good or find their prejudices confirmed. To liberal or ecologically conscious intellectuals, for instance, who treasure their feelings of superiority over their predecessors, moral indignation with Columbus is too precious to discard. Kinship with a culture-hero is too profound a part of many Americans' sense of identity to be easily excised.

Thus Columbus-the-hero and Columbus-the-villain live on, mutually sustained by the passion which continuing

controversy imparts to their supporters. No argument can dispel them, however convincing; no evidence, however compelling. They have eclipsed the real Columbus and, judged by their effects, have outstripped him in importance. For one of the sad lessons historians learn is that history is influenced less by the facts as they happen than by the falsehoods men believe.

FOR FURTHER READING:

J. H. Elliott, *The Old World and the New* (Cambridge University Press, 1970); A. W. Crosby, *Columbian Exchange: Biological and Cultural Consequences of 1492* (Greenwood, 1972); J. Larner 'The Certainty of Columbus', *History*, lxxiii (1987); F. Fernández-Armesto, *Columbus* (Oxford University Press, 1991).

Sir Francis Drake is still capable of kicking up a fuss

Westward the corsair of England's empire made his way, plundering Spain for queen and country; now modern moralists are nibbling at his fame

Simon Winchester

Simon Winchester is a frequent contributor to SMITHSONIAN. *His latest book is entitled* The River at the Center of the World *(Henry Holt, 1996).*

Perched in front of me as I write is a small and elegantly made tablet of milk chocolate, brought from England by a kindly relation who paid the rather alarming sum of £10 sterling for a box of it. She had discovered it in the tourist souvenir stall that has just been built (to widespread shudders) inside the now publicly accessible quarters of Buckingham Palace.

It is sold as a commemoration of one of England's greatest heroes. "Sir Francis Drake, 1540–96," declares the wrapper. "Famous Circumnavigator and Admiral."

The text notes that Drake was knighted by Queen Elizabeth I in 1581, won fame by contributing to the defeat of the Spanish Armada in 1588 and lives on "as the hero of many popular legends." He was certainly part of the imprint of pride stamped on all miniature Britons of my generation, who learned stories about Drake almost with our mother's milk.

They were stories that began in a period when tiny newly Protestant England faced Catholic Spain, then a globe-girdling imperial power. That period ended with Spain defeated, her power waning, Protestantism no longer under threat, and the long slow rise of the Brit-

ish Empire about to begin. Francis Drake, the stories taught us, was the man who more than any other helped set the change in motion. Boys of my age could rattle off the most famous lines from Sir Henry Newbolt's poem "Drake's Drum," rollicking lines that were supposedly called down by the departed Drake from the company of angels: "If the Dons sight Devon, I'll quit the port of Heaven / And drum them up the Channel as we drummed them long ago."

That all went well with other sagas of my youth—the D-Day invasion and the climbing of Mount Everest and the coronation of the young Queen Elizabeth II, the playing in those postwar days of Sir Edward Elgar's thumping "Land of Hope and Glory." In the early Fifties I even journeyed down to Plymouth with my uncle and walked through empty streets to the green expanse of Plymouth Hoe where Drake's statue stands.

Plymouth Hoe is the site of a famous Drake story, a moment on a July evening in 1588 when the Spanish Armada had just been spotted off England. The first in the chain of signal bonfire beacons to alert southern England against invasion had been lit. The little captain general (he was probably under 5 feet 5 inches) was playing at bowls on Plymouth Hoe as breathless aides told him about the almost solid wall of Spanish vessels, ready for attack. Would Sir Francis put

to sea immediately? No, Drake is supposed to have said: "There is plenty of time to finish the game and beat the Spaniards, too."

The man was born 450 years ago on a tenant farm in a broad valley near Tavistock, a lush corner of far western England hard by the great granite dome of Dartmoor. Recent research suggests that his father, Edmund, a fiery part-time Protestant preacher, was exiled to Kent for stealing horses. There the young Drake grew up and learned seamanship, living in a hulk on the River Medway. In the Drake story, historic context is crucial. When Drake was born, in about 1543, the Protestant Reformation was still shaky; all Protestant Europe feared Catholics and especially Catholic Spain. In England, the Reformation had barely begun. Henry VIII's recent divorce had brought a tidal wave of events including England's break with the Church of Rome and the creation of the Church of England.

During Drake's career the slaughter of thousands of Protestants, on and after the St. Bartholomew's Day Massacre of 1572, occurred throughout France; and Philip II of Spain (SMITHSONIAN, December 1987) dispatched an army to suppress a Protestant revolt in the Low Countries. In England, after Henry died, his Catholic daughter, Mary, briefly ruled. Married to King Philip, she had a number of Protestant leaders burned at the stake, whence her nickname "Bloody Mary." After her half-sister Elizabeth became queen in 1558, Catholics in England were officially despised, their influence personified by fear and loathing of Spain and Philip II. He was savagely caricatured as a monster of cruelty, of papist power in general, the essence of Spain's seemingly unassailable "Evil Empire."

By comparison, England was of little consequence in global terms. It was only in Elizabeth's reign that the situation began to change. Always careful not to offend Philip too much, the queen nevertheless built up England's maritime strength, as relations with Spain evolved from uneasy alliance to strained peace to something like cold war and, finally, in 1588, to war itself.

Even while Spain and England were still officially at peace, Drake began helping this process along by raiding Spain's holdings in the Caribbean. His motivations involved an anti-Catholic religious zeal, patriotism and the possibility of huge profit for himself—and eventually for the queen's treasury—in gold and jewels originally stolen by Spain from the Aztecs and Incas.

His first attempts, after he shipped out at age 23 aboard a slaving vessel owned by his cousin John Hawkins, were by all accounts fumbling. (He was uncomfortable, it now seems, with taking part in slaving commerce, anyway.) But by the summer of 1573, ranging far from home in his own ships with a trusted band of west country seamen, he had captured "the Treasure-house of the World," the tiny port of Nombre de Dios, on the north coast of what is now Panama. As became his custom, he enlisted the help of *cimarrones,* African slaves who had escaped from the Spaniards, and marched through the jungle with them to intercept Spanish mule trains bringing sacks of treasure across the isthmus for transshipment to Spain. *"Qué gente?"* a perplexed Spanish sentry challenged as Drake's Devonians and black allies poured down on the caravan from the bushes. "Englishmen," replied Drake, coldly.

Many of the 73 men who had sailed with him the year before—two of his brothers among them—were left dead.

But his ships headed home loaded with gold coins, ingots, raw and uncut diamonds and emeralds from Chile and Peru, as well as engraved scimitars, guns and charts, and Spanish secrets. When the tiny fleet entered Plymouth Sound one Sunday in August 1573, people burst out of church in mid-sermon to greet him.

Within weeks England had a new hero. Now Drake could buy land and houses and, for the first time, deal as an equal with men way above his social station. He was just turning 30, already famous for pluck and vigor, and ready to become a byword in the Virgin Queen's memorable reign. That year Elizabeth was 40; already 15 years on the throne, the monarch was willing to back Drake's exploits at sea in secret and profit hugely from his prizes. Much of the gold from his Caribbean raids enabled her to build up her own army and, most crucially, expand England's lately reorganized navy. It made good sense, she and her courtiers thought, to use this brash newcomer to let the world know that, at sea, England was Spain's rival—and more. Thus was launched Drake's celebrated circumnavigation of the globe.

Years earlier, Ferdinand Magellan sailed from Portugal to the Philippines only to be killed there (SMITHSONIAN, April 1991), though one of his ships completed the circumnavigation of the globe. But no one since then had made the trip and no English ship had sailed the Pacific. When Drake set out from Plymouth on November 15, 1577, with four tiny vessels and 164 men, he was undertaking a stupendous venture.

The publicly stated purpose of the voyage was clear. With private backing from rich nobles, the queen and her favorite, the earl of Leicester, Drake was officially bound on a voyage of trade and exploration. There was even some talk of finding the mysterious Strait of Anian, as the elusive Northwest Passage was then known.

Drake's unofficial agenda was very different. Queen Elizabeth and King Philip were not yet officially at war, but Drake was to capture Spanish ships carrying the wealth of Peru and Mexico up to the west coast of South America to the Isthmus of Panama.

His four ships were puny by any standard—puny in relation to more than 30,000 miles of unknown ocean ahead of them, puny when compared with Spanish galleons that tended to displace hundreds of tons, often carrying heavy guns under mountains of sail. Drake's largest ship, the *Pelican,* measured 70 feet from stem to stern; she had just 18 small cannon. For security purposes Drake told the men they would be gone only a short while. But he had loaded his great cabin with books on navigation, as well as his Protestant Bible and John Foxe's history of Protestant martyrs, and carried musicians to boost morale. He held prayer sessions morning and evening. Dreadful weather set in quickly. Early on, too, he began having trouble with a gentleman member of the expedition named Thomas Doughty.

From the bulge of Africa they crossed to Brazil, and worked their way down to the Río de la Plata, hunting seals for meat, and taking on fresh fruit to ward off scurvy, from which—to Drake's credit—his crewmen almost never suffered. By June 1578, they were off Patagonia and headed for a hellish, labyrinthine passage known as the Strait of Magellan. It was there, before that challenge, that Drake brought disciplinary matters to a head. Drake was a defiantly common man and a seaman who on occasion hauled on the lines with the crew, and he expected gentlemen to do the same. Doughty was an arrogant, well-connected aristocrat and a representative of the expedition's noble financial backers. From the outset he treated his captain like a social upstart. In Port St. Julian, Drake ordered Doughty to stand trial for planning mutiny. He was charged with challenging Drake's authority and fomenting trouble by urging that the expedition reach the Pacific by sailing around the tip of Africa. Several times he had disobeyed Drake's orders to the fleet.

A jury of his shipmates found the man guilty. Though Drake was on shaky legal ground, because he seems not to have carried an official commission from Queen Elizabeth, he ordered Doughty beheaded.

The night before, both men were shriven of their sins, and Doughty and Drake had dinner together. But once the ax had fallen next morning, Drake had the prize held up by its hair. "Lo," he said, "this is the end of traitors." He was troubled by the execution, however. And he swiftly renamed his ship. The *Pelican* was rechristened the *Golden Hind,* now one of the most famous vessels in history. Drake's latter-day detractors, largely overlooking the crucial danger of a divided command at sea under such circumstances, make much of the execution and even the name change. The new name, they point out, had immediate political and fiscal advantages: it was chosen to curry favor with Sir Christopher Hatton, one of the rich backers in England (and a close friend of Doughty's), who sported a hind on his coat of arms.

ONLY THE *GOLDEN HIND* WAS LEFT

Drake's three remaining ships made swift passage through the strait, 363 nautical miles in 16 days. Then a terrific storm fell upon them, pounding and battering for 52 days. The fleet lost contact. The *Golden Hind* was driven miles south and had to fight its way back. When the storm blew itself out, only the *Golden Hind* was left. One ship had turned over, and the other turned back, eventually limping home to England where Drake was duly reported drowned and his ship lost. Sometime after the storm, Drake put ashore on Horn Island, at the extreme tip of the continent, in search of new antiscorbutic fruits. Fifty years later the Dutch claimed the first sighting of the Horn, but a few contemporary charts show that it was Drake who first discovered the fearsome cape.

Free of the Horn, he swept north off Chile and Peru, taking ship after ship from astounded and outraged Spaniards. This, at last, was what he had come for: to plunder the papists in the name of the Protestant Queen! The process reached a nautical and remunerative climax with the capture of *Nuestra Señora de la Concepción,* a galleon loaded with silver, gold and diamonds worth £125,000 in Tudor money, billions today.

Eventually he sailed north past what is now California, to reach a latitude possibly as far north as Vancouver. Finding no sign of the Northwest Passage, he turned south to find a safe place to haul his bar-

nacle-heavy and leaking vessel and careen it for caulking and repair. On June 17, 1579, he made landfall. Exactly where has been hotly disputed, but commonsense odds are that it was just north of San Francisco, in an estuary known today as Drake's Estero, at the western end of Marin County's seemingly endless Sir Francis Drake Boulevard.

For five weeks his exhausted men rested, replenished supplies, worked on the ship and built a small settlement. They also mingled enough with peaceable locals to introduce genes that led to blue-eyed Miwok Indians being spotted in the forests as late as the 18th century. Drake left a brass plate (with a sixpenny piece hammered into it for authenticity) formally annexing the land—New Albion, he called it—in England's name. The debate over the exact site of New Albion has been peppered by forgery, fracas and false claims, including the "discovery" in 1937 of a phony brass plate. But there is little hope of settling it beyond all question. Queen Elizabeth acquired Drake's personal log upon his return, keeping it secret to avoid trouble with Spain, and it has not been seen since.

The *Golden Hind* took 68 days to cross 7,000 miles of Pacific, touching first at Palau in Micronesia and then at Mindanao in what Spain had just named the Philippines—after archenemy Philip II. Near the Celebes, Drake's extraordinary feat of navigation in chartless waters almost ended tragically when the *Golden Hind* grounded on an isolated reef surrounded by deep water. They could not get off, and most of the crew had prepared for a slow death when, the following day, a wind shift and a high tide floated the *Hind,* and she proved miraculously without serious hull damage.

"IS OUR QUEEN ALIVE?" HE SAID

Ten thousand mostly unrecorded miles— from Java round what was not yet called the Cape of Good Hope, up the slave coast of West Africa, past Spain and Ushant—still separated them from home. But we know Drake's first words when, on September 26, 1580, the *Golden Hind*

at last encountered English fishermen off the Scilly Isles. "Is our queen alive?" he called.

Another monarch might perhaps have felt obliged to punish his depredations among Spanish shipping, word of which had long since reached Europe, stirring Philip's demands for restitution. Elizabeth did do some diplomatic maneuvering, worried that too much public approval would further anger the Spanish monarch, but she was royally pleased with Drake.

His booty—worth a quarter of a million Elizabethan pounds, less the 10 percent she secretly granted him—was soon surrendered to the Crown. All over again, Drake became a national hero and now a court favorite as well. It was then that the queen had Drake knighted, musing mischievously as he knelt before her that instead of having him dubbed "Sir Francis" she could quite as easily have had his head lopped off with the sword, a course that King Philip had specifically urged upon her. Drake bought himself a big country estate, Buckland Abbey, and became a member of Parliament and mayor of Plymouth. Still, he found time for a few more raids on Spanish holdings in the New World. Returning from one of them he destroyed a Spanish fort in St. Augustine, and moving up the coast, he picked up desperate English colonists from Roanoke Island to ferry them home.

Philip II did not take action against heretical England because he was deep into a campaign to recover the breakaway Protestant provinces of Holland—for Spain, the tactical equivalent of America's Vietnam War. But by 1586, the long-threatened conflict between Philip and Elizabeth seemed inevitable, and a pair of exploits soon secured Drake's reputation as a naval hero twice over.

The first, in 1587, was an astonishing raid on the Spanish shipping assembled in the Bay of Cádiz as part of Spain's preparation for an attack on England. In command of a small fleet, Drake had been prowling along the Iberian coast, trying to ferret out Spain's plans for war, when he learned of the fleet's whereabouts. The Spanish ships were at anchor in a confined harbor, backed by shore batteries and attended by maneuverable armed galleys. Nobody except Drake, who believed in tactical surprise, would have had the audacity to attack them. When he did, it seemed a breathtaking gamble—and turned out to be a masterly display of cool courage and world-class seamanship. His fleet sailed straight in on a following breeze, right past the guns onshore, and sank or drove off the galleys. Then the English spent hours dashing in and out among the Spanish ships, eventually setting fire to many of them.

In all, 39 Spanish ships were sunk or put permanently out of commission, delaying Philip's war preparations. All Europe was stirred by the exploit. "Singeing the King of Spain's beard," Drake called it, and everyone followed suit. To this day in England, schoolchildren know it as such. To this day, partly because of it, Britons vacationing on Andalusian beaches sometimes find Spaniards less welcoming than they hoped.

On the way home from Cádiz, Drake's flotilla captured the *San Felipe,* the king of Spain's personal treasure ship, bound home with a cargo of pepper, calico, cinnamon, cloves, ebony, silk, saltpeter, china, indigo, nutmeg, gold and silver, not to mention 22 brass cannon, scores of iron cannon and 659 passengers who could be richly ransomed. The loss of the *San Felipe* was a second terrible humiliation for the proud Spanish. On Philip's orders, the duke of Medina Sidonia, a noble soldier who knew little about sea warfare, completed the assembly of a huge, brandnew and terrifying navy—*la Felicissima Armada*—set to sail northward. Its declared aim was to pick up thousands of Spanish troops in Dunkirk, there as a result of the war in the Low Countries, and ferry them across the English Channel. Once landed, they would have Protestant England and arrogant Elizabeth at their mercy. It was July 1588. Under command of the fleet admiral, Lord Howard of Effingham, British ships, though outsized and outnumbered, were ready, and it was at this point that Drake made his remark about finishing that game of bowls.

Or did he? Probably not. The remark was first quoted in 1736, a century and

a half later. Besides, on the particular afternoon in question, there was not a thing that Drake could have done about the Armada; his part of the combined British fleet was locked up in Plymouth Harbor by a wind blowing out of the south.

In the nine-day running sea fight that followed, the heavier Spanish ships never succeeded in coming into close quarters with the faster, better gunned English, and the English inflicted little damage on the Armada. They did herd it along eastward, and when it finally anchored at a point where Spanish troops might have been taken aboard, English fire ships forced the Spanish to cut their anchor lines. Then a steady wind from the west blew the Armada eastward, beyond hope of return or of carrying troops anywhere.

Through all this, Drake, in *Revenge,* commanded a quarter of the English fleet and did characteristically bold service. Because he was already so famous, he perhaps has been given more credit than was his due. But nowadays, Drake debunkers tend to accentuate the negative and, with regard to the Armada, concentrate on the *Rosario* incident, the one thing that Drake did that stirred angry criticism from a few contemporaries. On the first night after the Armada had been engaged, Drake, under orders from Lord Howard, was leading the fleet eastward along the English Channel, keeping track of Medina Sidonia's ships. He was supposed to mount a light on the *Revenge's* sternpost so the rest of the English ships could follow him through the darkness. But he veered off secretly (later saying he had seen some sails) and then found, and took the surrender of, a badly crippled Armada treasure ship, the *Rosario.* The English fleet was left to its own devices during a windy Channel night. Drake, it was claimed, had more pressing matters on his mind: namely greed.

England and the queen were delighted to receive the bulk of the *Rosario's* treasure, however. It was used to help pay the cost of the Netherlands' soldiers still busily fighting against Spanish invaders, and to pay for the building of nearly a dozen warships. That may be why, at the time, Drake's

only serious accuser was Sir Martin Frobisher (SMITHSONIAN, January 1993), who was angry because he did not share in the spoils. Drake's behavior, Frobisher told the High Lords of Admiralty, endangered England's cause, and it was prompted by the greatest flaw in Drake's character—his avarice.

A number of historians, professional and amateur, have since held that Drake's impetuousness and desire for riches did on this and other occasions overcome him. But after a close study of the papers of the day, a recent biographer, John Sugden, thinks otherwise. Brought out in 1990, Sugden's was the first serious biography of Drake since Sir Julian Corbett's famous hagiography from the 1890s, and it comes to Drake's support, not only in this incident, but in other character-questioning controversies that have resulted from recent revisionism.

For instance, was Drake heavily involved in John Hawkins' slave trade? No, says Sugden. In fact, he freed all the Spanish-held slaves he took. Had he been too Machiavellian in the renaming of the *Pelican* after Doughty's execution? Again, no. In Sugden's view, Drake simply had to flatter his wealthy patrons, as was customary in Elizabethan times.

Still, the present age would radically alter the old view of Drake. His patriotism and his religious zeal as a Protestant do not stir a responsive chord in a secular world; his exhortations sometimes sound like bombast to a modern ear. By today's standards, revisionists like to say, Drake was little more than a licensed pirate and a sometime slave trader, a man responsible for shedding much blood, the leader of ventures that were sometimes fiascoes morally, tactically and even financially. Sugden points out that the Elizabethan navy, as well as exploration at the time, was regularly paid for by investors hoping for gain. Drake began as a corsair, but he came to command large forces of men and ships in Elizabeth's name and was privy to the highest councils of his country. But Drake's muscular nationalism has been long out of favor, and we now tend to see the outward course of empire as at best a tawdry enterprise.

When I went down to Plymouth to look at Drake's huge bronze statue for the first time in 40 years, I met a Spaniard, and once we had fallen into conversation, I told him I had just been to see Drake's great manor house, Buckland Abbey, which stood nearby. I thought that four centuries might have softened the Spanish view of their onetime scourge, but I was wrong. "Ah . . . *el Draque*." He almost spat the words out. "The dragon." And he stirred sugar into his coffee in a menacing way. "This house you speak of," he went on. "It was built with stolen money. Our money. It is still not forgiven."

It is now 400 years since the little captain general died off Puerto Bello, Panama, suffering from dysentery, then known as the "bludie flux." Despite arguments over his reputation, a group recently came forward with plans to find his coffin and bring his body home.

Memories of Drake do rather run to blood, guns and treasure. Yet there is in Devon a small and charming and very innocent memorial. It was created during the calm years after the circumnavigation, when Drake was mayor of Plymouth. During his tenure he became concerned—obsessed, even—with the problem of how the citizens of the fast-growing seaport might get their fresh water.

He designed and built a tiny canal—six feet wide, three feet deep and nearly 20 miles long. It still exists. Known as Drake's Leat, it snakes its way, mossy and green and now water-filled only after heavy rains, between one of the Dartmoor tors and the leafy suburbs of a great naval port. He completed it under budget and well inside the planned schedule. Residents of Plymouth who complain about water costs or water quality sometimes write letters to the local paper suggesting that old Drake's Leat be reopened.

The palace chocolate that offers the most admiring assessment of his life is still before me. Whether it eventually melts away or becomes a victim to my own sweet tooth, the man whom it memorializes has a reputation that may well change and change again. All one can say with certainty is that Sir Francis Drake occupies a pivotal place in British history—and even in world history—that assuredly will not vanish, even after yet another four centuries have gone by.

Luther: Giant of His Time and Ours

Half a millennium after his birth, the first Protestant is still a towering force

It was a back-room deal, little different from many others struck at the time, but it triggered an upheaval that altered irrevocably the history of the Western world. Albrecht of Brandenburg, a German nobleman who had previously acquired a dispensation from the Vatican to become a priest while underage and to head two dioceses at the same time, wanted yet another favor from the Pope: the powerful archbishop's chair in Mainz. Pope Leo X, a profligate spender who needed money to build St. Peter's Basilica, granted the appointment—for 24,000 gold pieces, roughly equal to the annual imperial revenues in Germany. It was worth it. Besides being a rich source of income, the Mainz post brought Albrecht a vote for the next Holy Roman Emperor, which could be sold to the highest bidder.

In return, Albrecht agreed to initiate the sale of indulgences in Mainz. Granted for good works, indulgences were papally controlled dispensations drawn from an eternal "treasury of merits" built up by Christ and the saints; the church taught that they would help pay the debt of "temporal punishment" due in purgatory for sins committed by either the penitent or any deceased person. The Pope received half the proceeds of the Mainz indulgence sale, while the other half went to repay the bankers who had lent the new archbishop gold.

Enter Martin Luther, a 33-year-old priest and professor at Wittenberg University. Disgusted not only with the traffic in indulgences but with its doctrinal underpinnings, he forcefully protested to Albrecht—never expecting that his action would provoke a sweeping uprising against a corrupt church. Luther's challenge culminated in the Protestant Reformation and the rending of Western Christendom, and made him a towering figure in European history. In this 500th anniversary year of his birth (Nov. 10, 1483), the rebel of Wittenberg remains the subject of persistent study. It is said that more books have been written about him than anyone else in history, save his own master, Jesus Christ. The renaissance in Luther scholarship surrounding this year's anniversary serves as a reminder that his impact on modern life is profound, even for those who know little about the doctrinal feuds that brought him unsought fame. From the distance of half a millennium, the man who, as Historian Hans Hillerbrand of Southern Methodist University in Dallas says, brought Christianity from lofty theological dogma to a clearer and more personal belief is still able to stimulate more heated debate than all but a handful of historical figures.

Indeed, as the reformer who fractured Christianity, Luther has latterly become a key to reuniting it. With the approval of the Vatican, and with Americans taking the lead, Roman Catholic theologians are working with Lutherans and other Protestants to sift through the 16th century disputes and see whether the Protestant-Catholic split can some day be overcome. In a remarkable turnabout, Catholic scholars today express growing appreciation of Luther as a "father in the faith" and are willing to play down his excesses. According to a growing consensus, the great division need never have happened at all.

Beyond his importance as a religious leader, Luther had a profound effect on Western culture. He is, paradoxically, the last medieval man and the first modern one, a political conservative and a spiritual revolutionary. His impact is most marked, of course, in Germany, where he laid the cultural foundations for what later became a united German nation.

When Luther attacked the indulgence business in 1517, he was not only the most popular teacher at Wittenberg but also vicar provincial in charge of eleven houses of the Hermits of St. Augustine. He was brilliant, tireless and a judicious administrator, though given to bouts of spiritual depression. To make his point on indulgences, Luther dashed off 95 theses condemning the system ("They preach human folly who pretend that as soon as money in the coffer rings, a soul from purgatory springs") and sent them to Archbishop Albrecht and a number of theologians.*

The response was harsh: the Pope eventually rejected Luther's protest and demanded capitulation. It was then that Luther began asking questions about other aspects of the church, including the papacy itself. In 1520 he charged in an open letter to the Pope, "The Roman Church, once the holiest of all, has become the most licentious den of thieves, the most shameless of brothels, the kingdom of sin, death and hell." Leo called Luther "the wild boar which has invaded the Lord's vineyard."

The following year Luther was summoned to recant his writings before the Diet of Worms, a council of princes convened by the young Holy Roman Emperor Charles V. In his closing defense, Luther proclaimed defiantly: "Unless I

---

*Despite colorful legend, it is not certain he ever nailed them to the door of the Castle Church.

 From *Time*, October 31, 1983, pp. 100–103. © 1983 by Time Inc. Magazine Company. Reprinted by permission.

am convinced by testimony from Holy Scriptures and clear proofs based on reason—because, since it is notorious that they have erred and contradicted themselves, I cannot believe either the Pope or the council alone—I am bound by conscience and the Word of God. Therefore I can and will recant nothing, because to act against one's conscience is neither safe nor salutary. So help me God." (Experts today think that he did not actually speak the famous words, "Here I stand. I can do no other.")

This was hardly the cry of a skeptic, but it was ample grounds for the Emperor to put Luther under sentence of death as a heretic. Instead of being executed, Luther lived for another 25 years, became a major author and composer of hymns, father of a bustling household and a secular figure who opposed rebellion—in all, a commanding force in European affairs. In the years beyond, the abiding split in Western Christendom developed, including a large component of specifically "Lutheran" churches that today have 69 million adherents in 85 nations.

The enormous presence of the Wittenberg rebel, the sheer force of his personality, still broods over all Christendom, not just Lutheranism. Although Luther declared that the Roman Pontiffs were the "Antichrist," today's Pope, in an anniversary tip of the zucchetto, mildly speaks of Luther as "the reformer." Ecumenical-minded Catholic theologians have come to rank Luther in importance with Augustine and Aquinas. "No one who came after Luther could match him," says Father Peter Manns, a Catholic theologian in Mainz. "On the question of truth, Luther is a lifesaver for Christians." While Western Protestants still express embarrassment over Luther's anti-Jewish rantings or his skepticism about political clergy, Communist East Germany has turned him into a secular saint because of his influence on German culture. Party Boss Erich Honecker, head of the regime's *Lutherjahr* committee, is willing to downplay Luther's antirevolutionary ideas, using the giant figure to bolster national pride.

Said West German President Karl Carstens, as he opened one of the hundreds of events commemorating Luther this year: "Luther has become a symbol of the unity of all Germany. We are all Luther's heirs."

After five centuries, scholars still have difficulty coming to terms with the contradictions of a tempestuous man. He was often inexcusably vicious in his writings (he wrote, for instance, that one princely foe was a "faint-hearted wretch and fearful sissy" who should "do nothing but stand like a eunuch, that is, a harem guard, in a fool's cap with a fly swatter"). Yet he was kindly in person and so generous to the needy that his wife despaired of balancing the household budget. When the plague struck Wittenberg and others fled, he stayed behind to minister to the dying. He was a powerful spiritual author, yet his words on other occasions were so scatological that no Lutheran periodical would print them today. His writing was hardly systematic, and his output runs to more than 100 volumes. On the average, Luther wrote a major tract or treatise every two weeks throughout his life.

The scope of Luther's work has made him the subject of endless reinterpretation. The Enlightenment treated him as the father of free thought, conveniently omitting his belief in a sovereign God who inspired an authoritative Bible. During the era of Otto von Bismarck a century ago, Luther was fashioned into a nationalistic symbol; 70 years later, Nazi propagandists claimed him as one of their own by citing his anti-Jewish polemics.

All scholars agree on Luther's importance for German culture, surpassing even that of Shakespeare on the English-speaking world. Luther's masterpiece was his translation of the New Testament from Greek into German, largely completed in ten weeks while he was in hiding after the Worms confrontation, and of the Old Testament, published in 1534 with the assistance of Hebrew experts. The Luther Bible sold massively in his lifetime and remains today the authorized German Protestant version. Before Luther's Bible was published, there was no standard German, just a profusion of dialects. "It was Luther," said Johann Gottfried von Herder, one of Goethe's mentors, "who has awakened and let loose the giant: the German language."

Only a generation ago, Catholics were trained to consider Luther the arch-heretic. Now no less than the Vatican's specialist on Lutheranism, Monsignor Aloys Klein, says that "Martin Luther's action was beneficial to the Catholic Church." Like many other Catholics, Klein thinks that if Luther were living today there would be no split. Klein's colleague in the Vatican's Secretariat for Promoting Christian Unity, Father Pierre Duprey, suggests that with the Second Vatican Council (1962–65) Luther "got the council he asked for, but 450 years too late." Vatican II accepted his contention, that in a sense, all believers are priests; while the council left the Roman church's hierarchy intact, it enhanced the role of the laity. More important, the council moved the Bible to the center of Catholic life, urged continual reform and instituted worship in local languages rather than Latin.

One of the key elements in the Reformation was the question of "justification," the role of faith in relation to good works in justifying a sinner in the eyes of God. Actually, Catholicism had never officially taught that salvation could be attained only through pious works, but the popular perception held otherwise. Luther recognized, as University of Chicago Historian Martin Marty explains, that everything "in the system of Catholic teaching seemed aimed toward appeasing God. Luther was led to the idea of God not as an angry judge but as a forgiving father. It is a position that gives the individual a great sense of freedom and security." In effect, says U.S. Historian Roland Bainton, Luther destroyed the implication that men could "bargain with God."

Father George Tavard, a French Catholic expert on Protestantism who teaches in Ohio and has this month published *Justification: An Ecumenical Study* (Paulist; $7.95), notes that "today many Catholic scholars think Luther was right and the 16th century Catholic polemicists did not understand what he meant. Both Lutherans and Catholics agree that good works by Christian believers are the result of their faith and the working of divine grace in them, not their personal contributions to their own salvation. Christ is the only Savior. One does not save oneself." An international Lutheran-Catholic commission, exploring the basis for possible reunion, made a joint statement along these lines in 1980. Last month a parallel panel in the U.S. issued a significant 21,000-word paper on justification that affirms much of Luther's thinking, though with some careful hedging from the Catholic theologians.

There is doubt, of course, about the degree to which Protestants and Catholics can, in the end, overcome their differences. Catholics may now be permitted to sing Luther's *A Mighty For-*

tress Is Our God or worship in their native languages, but a wide gulf clearly remains on issues like the status of Protestant ministers and, most crucially, papal authority.

During the futile Protestant-Catholic reunion negotiations in 1530 at the Diet of Augsburg, the issue of priestly celibacy was as big an obstacle as the faith *vs.* good works controversy. Luther had married a nun, to the disgust of his Catholic contemporaries. From the start, the marriage of clergy was a sharply defined difference between Protestantism and Catholicism, and it remains a key barrier today. By discarding the concept of the moral superiority of celibacy, Luther established sexuality as a gift from God. In general, he was a lover of the simple pleasures, and would have had little patience with the later Puritans. He spoke offhandedly about sex, enjoyed good-natured joshing, beer drinking and food ("If our Lord is permitted to create nice large pike and good Rhine wine, presumably I may be allowed to eat and drink"). For his time, he also had an elevated opinion of women. He cherished his wife and enjoyed fatherhood, siring six children and rearing eleven orphaned nieces and nephews as well.

But if Luther's views on the Catholic Church have come to be accepted even by many Catholics, his anti-Semitic views remain a problem for even his most devoted supporters. Says New York City Rabbi Marc Tanenbaum: "The anniversary will be marred by the haunting specter of Luther's devil theory of the Jews."

Luther assailed the Jews on doctrinal grounds, just as he excoriated "papists" and Turkish "infidels." But his work titled *On the Jews and Their Lies* (1543) went so far as to advocate that their synagogues, schools and homes should be destroyed and their prayer books and Talmudic volumes taken away. Jews were to be relieved of their savings and put to work as agricultural laborers or expelled outright.

Fortunately, the Protestant princes ignored such savage recommendations, and the Lutheran Church quickly forgot about them. But the words were there to be gleefully picked up by the Nazis, who removed them from the fold of religious polemics and used them to but-

tress their 20th century racism. For a good Lutheran, of course, the Bible is the sole authority, not Luther's writings, and the thoroughly Lutheran Scandinavia vigorously opposed Hitler's racist madness. In the anniversary year, all sectors of Lutheranism have apologized for their founder's views.

Whatever the impact of Luther's anti-Jewish tracts, there is no doubt that his political philosophy, which tended to make church people submit to state authority, was crucial in weakening opposition by German Lutherans to the Nazis. Probably no aspect of Luther's teaching is the subject of more agonizing Protestant scrutiny in West Germany today.

Luther sought to declericalize society and to free people from economic burdens imposed by the church. But he was soon forced, if reluctantly, to deliver considerable control of the new Protestant church into the hands of secular rulers who alone could ensure the survival of the Reformation. Luther spoke of "two kingdoms," the spiritual and the secular, and his writings provided strong theological support for authoritarian government and Christian docility.

The Lutheran wing of the Reformation was democratic, but only in terms of the church itself, teaching that a plowman did God's work as much as a priest, encouraging lay leadership and seeking to educate one and all. But it was Calvin, not Luther, who created a theology for the democratic state. A related aspect of Luther's politics, controversial then and now, was his opposition to the bloody Peasants' War of 1525. The insurgents thought they were applying Luther's ideas, but he urged rulers to crush the revolt: "Let whoever can, stab, strike, kill." Support of the rulers was vital for the Reformation, but Luther loathed violent rebellion and anarchy in any case.

Today Luther's law-and-order approach is at odds with the revolutionary romanticism and liberation theology that are popular in some theology schools. In contrast with modern European Protestantism's social gospel, Munich Historian Thomas Nipperdey says, Luther "would not accept modern attempts to build a utopia and would argue, on the contrary, that we as mortal sinners are incapable of developing a paradise on earth."

Meanwhile, the internal state of the Lutheran Church raises other questions about the lasting power of Luther's vision. Lutheranism in the U.S., with 8.5 million adherents, is stable and healthy. The church is also growing in Third World strongholds like racially torn Namibia, where black Lutherans predominate. But in Lutheranism's historic heartland, the two Germanys and Scandinavia, there are deep problems. In East Germany, Lutherans are under pressure from the Communist regime. In West Germany, the Evangelical Church in Germany (E.K.D.), a church federation that includes some non-Lutherans, is wealthy (annual income: $3 billion), but membership is shrinking and attendance at Sunday services is feeble indeed. Only 6% of West Germans—or, for that matter, Scandinavians—worship regularly.

What seems to be lacking in the old European churches is the passion for God and his truth that so characterizes Luther. He retains the potential to shake people out of religious complacency. Given Christianity's need, on all sides, for a good jolt, eminent Historian Heiko Oberman muses, "I wonder if the time of Luther isn't ahead of us."

The boldest assertion about Luther for modern believers is made by Protestants who claim that the reformer did nothing less than enable Christianity to survive. In the Middle Ages, too many Popes and bishops were little more than corrupt, luxury-loving politicians, neglecting the teaching of the love of God and using the fear of God to enhance their power and wealth. George Lindbeck, the Lutheran co-chairman of the international Lutheran-Catholic commission, believers that without Luther "religion would have been much less important during the next 400 to 500 years. And since medieval religion was falling apart, secularization would have marched on, unimpeded."

A provocative thesis, and a debatable one. But with secularization still marching on, almost unimpeded, Protestants and Catholics have much to reflect upon as they scan the five centuries after Luther and the shared future of their still divided churches.

—By Richard N. Ostling. Reported by Roland Flamini and Wanda Menke-Glückert/Bonn, with other bureaus.

Explaining John Calvin

John Calvin (1509–64) has been credited, or blamed, for much that defines the modern Western world: capitalism and the work ethic, individualism and utilitarianism, modern science, and, at least among some devout Christians, a lingering suspicion of earthly pleasures. During [a] recent American presidential campaign, the two candidates appealed to "values" that recall the teachings of the 16th-century churchman, indicating that what William Pitt once said of England—"We have a Calvinist creed"—still may hold partly true for the United States. But the legend of the joyless tyrant of Geneva obscures both the real man, a humanist as much as a religious reformer, and the subtlety of his thought. Here his biographer discusses both.

William J. Bouwsma

William J. Bouwsma, 65, is Sather Professor of History at the University of California, Berkeley. Born in Ann Arbor, Michigan, he received an A.B. (1943), an M.A. (1947), and a Ph.D. (1950) from Harvard. He is the author of, among other books, Venice and the Defense of Republican Liberty *(1968) and* John Calvin: A Sixteenth-Century Portrait *(1988).*

Our image of John Calvin is largely the creation of austere Protestant churchmen who lived during the 17th century, the century following that of the great reformer's life. The image is most accurately evoked by the huge icon of Calvin, familiar to many a tourist, that stands behind the University of Geneva. There looms Calvin, twice as large as life, stylized beyond recognition, stony, rigid, immobile, and—except for his slightly abstracted disapproval of whatever we might imagine him to be contemplating—impassive.

Happily, the historical record provides good evidence for a Calvin very different from the figure invoked by his 17th-century followers. This Calvin is very much a man of the 16th century, a time of religious strife and social upheaval. His life

and work reflect the ambiguities, contradictions, and agonies of that troubled time. Sixteenth-century thinkers, especially in Northern Europe, were still grappling with the rich but incoherent legacy of the Renaissance, and their characteristic intellectual constructions were less successful in reconciling its contradictory impulses than in balancing among them. This is why it has proved so difficult to pigeon-hole such figures as Erasmus and Machiavelli or Montaigne and Shakespeare, and why they continue to stimulate reflection. Calvin, who can be quoted on both sides of most questions, belongs in this great company.

Born in 1509 in Noyon, Calvin was brought up to be a devout French Catholic. Indeed, his father, a lay administrator in the service of the local bishop, sent him to the University of Paris in 1523 to study for the priesthood. Later he decided that young John should be a lawyer. Accordingly, from 1528 to 1533, Calvin studied law. During these years he was also exposed to the evangelical humanism of Erasmus and Jacques Lefèvre d'Étaples that nourished the radical student movement of the time. The students called for salvation by grace rather than by good works and ceremonies—a position fully compatible with

Catholic orthodoxy—as the foundation for a general reform of church and society on the model of antiquity.

To accomplish this end, the radical students advocated a return to the Bible, studied in its original languages. Calvin himself studied Greek and Hebrew as well as Latin, the "three languages" of ancient Christian discourse. His growing interest in the classics led, moreover, to his first publication, a moralizing commentary on Seneca's essay on clemency.

Late in 1533, the French government of Francis I became less tolerant of the Paris student radicals, whom it saw as a threat to the peace. After helping to prepare a statement of the theological implications of the movement in a public address delivered by Nicolas Cop, rector of the University, Calvin found it prudent to leave Paris. Eventually he made his way to Basel, a Protestant town tolerant of religious variety.

Up to this point, there it little evidence of Calvin's "conversion" to Protestantism. Before Basel, of course, he had been fully aware of the challenge Martin Luther posed to the Catholic Church. The 95 Theses that the German reformer posted in Wittenberg in 1517 attacked what Luther believed were corruptions of true Christianity and, by im-

From *The Wilson Quarterly*, New Year's 1989 edition, pp. 68–75. © 1989 by William J. Bouwsma. Reprinted by permission of the author.

plication, the authors of those errors, the Renaissance popes. Luther, above all, rejected the idea of salvation through indulgences or the sacrament of penance. Excommunicated by Pope Leo X, he encouraged the formation of non-Roman churches.

In Basel, Calvin found himself drawing closer to Luther. Probably in part to clarify his own beliefs, he began to write, first a preface to his cousin Pierre Olivétan's French translation of the Bible, and then what became the first edition of the *Institutes,* his masterwork, which in its successive revisions became the single most important statement of Protestant belief. Although he did not substantially change his views thereafter, he elaborated them in later editions, published in both Latin and French, in which he also replied to his critics; the final versions appeared in 1559 and 1560.

The 1536 *Institutes* had brought him some renown among Protestant leaders, among them Guillaume Farel. A French Reformer struggling to plant Protestantism in Geneva, Farel persuaded Calvin to settle there in late 1536. The Reformation was in trouble in Geneva. Indeed, the limited enthusiasm of Geneva for Protestantism—and for religious and moral reform—continued almost until Calvin's death. The resistance was all the more serious because the town council in Geneva, as in other Protestant towns in Switzerland and southern Germany, exercised ultimate control over the church and the ministers.

The main issue was the right of excommunication, which the ministers regarded as essential to their authority but which the town council refused to concede. The uncompromising attitudes of Calvin and Farel finally resulted in their expulsion from Geneva in May of 1538.

Calvin found refuge for the next three years in Protestant Strasbourg, where he was pastor of a church for French-speaking refugees. Here he married Idelette de Bure, a widow in his congregation. Theirs proved to be an extremely warm relationship, although none of their children survived infancy.

During his Strasbourg years, Calvin learned much about church administration from Martin Bucer, chief pastor there. Attending European religious conferences, he soon became a major figure in the international Protestant movement.

Meanwhile, without strong leadership, the Protestant revolution in Geneva foundered. In September of 1541, Calvin was invited back, and there he remained until his death in 1564. He was now in a stronger position. In November the town council enacted his *Ecclesiastical Ordinances,* which provided for the religious education of the townspeople, especially children, and instituted his conception of church order. It established four groups of church officers and a "consistory" of pastors and elders to bring every aspect of Genevan life under the precepts of God's law.

The activities of the consistory gave substance to the legend of Geneva as a joyless theocracy, intolerant of looseness or pleasure. Under Calvin's leadership, it undertook a range of disciplinary actions covering everything from the abolition of Catholic "superstition" to the enforcement of sexual morality, the regulation of taverns, and measures against dancing, gambling, and swearing. These "Calvinist" measures were resented by many townsfolk, as was the arrival of increasing numbers of French Protestant refugees.

The resulting tensions, as well as the persecution of Calvin's followers in France, help to explain the trial and burning of one of Calvin's leading opponents, Michael Servetus. Calvin felt the need to show that his zeal for orthodoxy was no less than that of his foes. The confrontation between Calvin and his enemies in Geneva was finally resolved in May of 1555, when Calvin's opponents overreached themselves and the tide turned in his favor. His position in Geneva was henceforth reasonably secure.

But Calvin was no less occupied. He had to watch the European scene and keep his Protestant allies united. At the same time, Calvin never stopped promoting his kind of Protestantism. He welcomed the religious refugees who poured into Geneva, especially during the 1550s, from France, but also from England and Scotland, from Italy, Germany, and the Netherlands, and even from Eastern Europe. He trained many of them as ministers, sent them back to their homelands, and then supported them with letters of encouragement and advice. Geneva thus became the center of an international movement and a model for churches elsewhere. John Knox, the Calvinist leader of Scotland, described Geneva as "the most perfect school of Christ that ever was on the Earth since the days of the Apostles." So while Lutheranism was confined to parts of Germany and Scandinavia, Calvinism spread into Britain, the English-speaking colonies of North America, and many parts of Europe.

Academic efforts to explain the appeal of Calvinism in terms of social class have had only limited success. In France, his theology was attractive mainly to a minority among the nobility and the urban upper classes, but in Germany it found adherents among both townsmen and princes. In England and the Netherlands, it made converts in every social group, Calvinism's appeal lay in its ability to explain disorders of the age afflicting all classes and in the remedies and comfort it provided, as much by its activism as by its doctrine. Both depended on the personality, preoccupations, and talents of Calvin himself.

Unlike Martin Luther, Calvin was a reticent man. He rarely expressed himself in the first person singular. This reticence has contributed to his reputation as cold and unapproachable. Those who knew him, however, noted his talent for friendship as well as his hot temper. The intensity of his grief on the death of his wife in 1549 revealed a large capacity for feeling, as did his empathetic reading of many passages in Scripture.

In fact, the impersonality of Calvin's teachings concealed an anxiety, unusually intense even in an anxious age. He saw anxiety everywhere, in himself, in the narratives of the Bible, and in his contemporaries. This feeling found expression in two of his favorite images for spiritual discomfort: the abyss and the labyrinth. The abyss represented all the nameless terrors of disorientation and the absence of familiar boundaries. The labyrinth expressed the anxiety of entrapment: in religious terms, the inability of human beings alienated from God to escape from the imprisonment of self-concern.

One side of Calvin sought to relieve his terror of the abyss with cultural constructions and patterns of control that might help him recover his sense of direction. This side of Calvin was attracted to classical philosophy, which nevertheless conjured up for him fears of entrapment in a labyrinth. Escape from this, however, exposed him to terrible uncertainties and, once again, to the horrors of the abyss. Calvin's ideas thus tended to oscillate between those of freedom and order. His problem was to strike a balance between the two.

He did so primarily with the resources of Renaissance humanism, applying its philological approach to recover a biblical understanding of Christianity. But humanism was not only, or even fundamentally, a scholarly movement. Its scholarship was instrumental to the recovery of the communicative skills of classical rhetoric. Humanists such as Lorenzo Valla and Erasmus held that an effective rhetoric would appeal to a deeper level of the personality than would a mere rational demonstration. By moving the heart, Christian rhetoric would stimulate human beings to the active reform of both themselves and the world.

Theological system-building, Calvin believed, was futile and inappropriate. He faulted the medieval Scholastic theologians for relying more on human reason than on the Bible, which spoke uniquely to the heart. The teachings of Thomas Aquinas, and like-minded theologians, appealed only to the intellect, and so were lifeless and irrelevant to a world in desperate need.

As a humanist, Calvin was a *biblical* theologian, prepared to follow Scripture even when it surpassed the limits of human understanding. And its message, for him, could not be presented as a set of timeless abstractions; it had to be adapted to the understanding of contemporaries according to the rhetorical principle of decorum—i.e. suitability to time, place, and audience.

Calvin shared with earlier humanists an essentially biblical conception of the human personality, not as a hierarchy of faculties ruled by reason but as a mysterious unity. This concept made the feelings and will even more important aspects of the personality than the intellect, and it also gave the body new dignity.

Indeed, Calvin largely rejected the traditional belief in hierarchy as the general principle of all order. For it he substituted the practical (rather than the metaphysical) principle of *utility*. This position found expression in his preference, among the possible forms of government, for republics. It also undermined, for him, the traditional subordination of women to men. Calvin's Geneva accordingly insisted on a single standard of sexual morality—a radical departure from custom.

Calvin's utilitarianism was also reflected in deep reservations about the capacity of human beings to attain anything but practical knowledge. The notion that they can know anything absolutely, as God knows it, so to speak, seemed to him deeply presumptuous. This helps to explain his reliance on the Bible: Human beings have access to the saving truths of religion only insofar as God has revealed them in Scripture. But revealed truth, for Calvin, was not revealed to satisfy human curiosity; it too was limited to meeting the most urgent and practical needs, above all for individual salvation. This practicality also reflects a basic conviction of Renaissance thinkers: the superiority of an active life to one of contemplation. Calvin's conviction that every occupation in society is a "calling" on the part of God himself sanctified this conception.

But Calvin was not only a Renaissance humanist. The culture of 16th-century Europe was peculiarly eclectic. Like other thinkers of his time, Calvin had inherited a set of quite contrary tendencies that he uneasily combined with his humanism. Thus, even as he emphasized the heart, Calvin continued to conceive of the human personality as a hierarchy of faculties ruled by reason; from time to time he tried uneasily, with little success, to reconcile the two conceptions. This is why he sometimes emphasized the importance of rational control over the passions—an emphasis that has been reassuring to conservatives.

Calvin's theology has often been seen as little more than a systematization of the more creative insights of Luther. He followed Luther, indeed, on many points: on original sin, on Scripture, on the absolute dependence of human beings on divine grace, and on justification by faith alone. Other differences between Calvin and Luther are largely matters of emphasis. His understanding of predestination, contrary to a general impression, was virtually identical to Luther's; it was not of central importance to his theology. He believed that it meant that the salvation of believers by a loving God was absolutely certain.

In major respects, however, Calvin departed from Luther. In some ways he was more radical, but most of his differences suggest that he was closer to Catholicism than Luther, as in his insistence on the importance of the historical church. He was also more traditional in his belief in the authority of clergy over laity, perhaps as a result of his difficulties with the Geneva town council. Even more significant, especially for Calvinism as a historical force, was Calvin's attitude toward the everyday world.

Luther had regarded this world and its institutions as incorrigible, and was prepared to leave them to the devil. But for Calvin this world, created by God, still belonged to Him; it remained potentially His kingdom; and every Christian was obliged to devote his life to make it so in reality by reforming and bringing it under God's law.

Calvin's thought was less a theology to be comprehended by the mind than a set of principles for the Christian life: in short, spirituality. He was more concerned with the experience and application of Christianity than with mere reflection about it. His true successors were Calvinist pastors rather than Calvinist theologians. Significantly, in addition to devoting much of his energy to the training of other pastors, Calvin was himself a pastor. He preached regularly: some 4,000 sermons in the 13 years after his return to Geneva.

Calvin's spirituality begins with the conviction that we do not so much "know" God as "experience" him indirectly, through his mighty acts and works in the world, as we experience but can hardly be said to know thunder, one of Calvin's favorite metaphors for religious experience. Calvin also believed that human beings can understand something of what God is like in the love of a father for his children, but also—surprisingly in one often identified with patriarchy—in the love of a mother. He denounced those who represented God as dreadful; God for him is "mild, kind, gentle, and compassionate."

Nevertheless, in spite of this attention to God's love for mankind, Calvin gave particular emphasis to God's power because it was this that finally made his love effective in the work of redemption from sin. God, for Calvin, represented supremely all the ways in which human beings experience power: as energy, as warmth, as vitality, and, so, as life itself.

Sin, by contrast, is manifested precisely in the negation of every kind of power and ultimately of the life force given by God. Sin *deadens* and, above all, deadens the feelings. Saving grace, then, must be conceived as the transfusion of God's power—his warmth, passion, strength, vitality—to human beings. It was also essential to Calvin's spirituality, and a reflection of his realism, that this "transfusion" be not instantaneous but gradual.

Calvin's traditional metaphor for the good Christian life implied activity:

"Our life is like a journey," he asserted, but "it is not God's will that we should march along casually as we please, but he sets the goal before us, and also directs us on the right way to it." This way is also a struggle.

Complex as his ideas were, it is easy to see how the later history of Calvinism has often been obscured by scholars' failure to distinguish among (1) Calvinism as the beliefs of Calvin himself, (2) the beliefs of his followers, who, though striving to be faithful to Calvin, modified his teachings to meet their own needs, and (3) more loosely, the beliefs of the Reformed tradition of Protestant Christianity, in which Calvinism proper was only one, albeit the most prominent, strand.

The Reformed churches in the 16th century were referred to in the plural to indicate, along with what they had in common, their individual autonomy and variety. They consisted originally of a group of non-Lutheran Protestant churches based in towns in Switzerland and southern Germany. These churches were jealous of their autonomy; and Geneva was not alone among them in having distinguished theological leadership. Ulrich Zwingli and Heinrich Bullinger in Zurich and Martin Bucer in Strasbourg also had a European influence that combined with that of Calvin, especially in England, to shape what came to be called "Calvinism."

Long after Calvin's death in 1564, the churchmen in Geneva continued to venerate him and aimed at being faithful to his teaching under his successors, first among them Theodore de Bèze. But during what can be appropriately described as a Protestant "Counter Reformation," the later Calvinism of Geneva, abandoning Calvin's more humanistic tendencies and drawing more on other, sterner aspects of his thought, was increasingly intellectualized. Indeed, it grew to resemble the medieval Scholasticism that Calvin had abhorred.

Predestination now began to assume an importance that had not been attributed to it before. Whereas Calvin had been led by personal faith to an awed belief in predestination as a benign manifestation of divine providence, predestination now became a threatening doctrine: God's decree determined in advance an individual's salvation or damanation. What good, one might wonder, were one's own best efforts if God had already ruled? In 1619 these tendencies reached a climax at the Synod of Dort in the Netherlands, which spelled out various corollaries of predestination, as Calvin had never done, and made the doctrine central to Calvinism.

Calvinist theologians, meanwhile, apparently finding Calvin's loose rhetorical style of expression unsatisfactory, began deliberately to write like Scholastic theologians, in Latin, and even appealed to medieval Scholastic authorities. The major Calvinist theological statement of the 17th century was the *Institutio Theologiae Elencticae* (3 vols., Geneva, 1688) of François Turretin, chief pastor of Geneva. Although the title of this work recalled Calvin's masterpiece, it was published in Latin, its dialectical structure followed the model of the great *Summas* of Thomas Aquinas, and it suggested at least as much confidence as Thomas in the value of human reason. The lasting effect of this shift is suggested by the fact that "Turretin," in Latin, was the basic theology textbook at the Princeton Seminary in New Jersey, the most distinguished intellectual center of American Calvinism until the middle of the 19th century.

Historians have continued to debate whether these developments were essentially faithful to Calvin or deviations from him. In some sense they were both. Later Calvinist theologians, as they abandoned Calvin's more humanistic tendencies and emphasized his more austere and dogmatic side, found precedents for these changes in the contrary aspects of his thought. They were untrue to Calvin, of course, in rejecting his typically Renaissance concern with balancing contrary impulses. One must remember, however, that these changes in Calvinism occurred during a period of singular disorder in Europe, caused by, among other things, a century of religious warfare. As a result, there was a widespread longing for certainty, security, and peace.

One or another aspect of Calvin's influence has persisted not only in the Reformed churches of France, Germany, Scotland, the Netherlands, and Hungary but also in the Church of England, where he was long as highly regarded as he was by Puritans who had separated from the Anglican establishment. The latter organized their own churches, Presbyterian or Congregational, and brought Calvinism to North America 300 years ago.

Even today these churches, along with the originally German Evangelical and Reformed Church, remember Calvin—that is, the strict Calvin of Geneva—as their founding father. Eventually Calvinist theology was also widely accepted by major groups of American Baptists; and even Unitarianism, which broke away from the Calvinist churches of New England during the 18th century, reflected the more rational impulses in Calvin's theology. More recently, Protestant interest in the social implications of the Gospel and Protestant Neo-Orthodoxy, as represented by Karl Barth and Reinhold Niebuhr, reflect the continuing influence of John Calvin.

Calvin's larger influence over the development of modern Western civilization has been variously assessed. The controversial "Weber thesis" attributed the rise of modern capitalism largely to habits encouraged by Puritanism, but Max Weber (1864–1920) avoided implicating Calvin himself. Much the same can be said about efforts to link Calvinism to the rise of early modern science; Puritans were prominent in the scientific movement of 17th-century England, but Calvin himself was indifferent to the science of his own day.

A somewhat better case can be made for Calvin's influence on political theory. His own political instincts were highly conservative, and he preached the submission of private persons to all legitimate authority. But, like Italian humanists of the 15th and 16th centuries, he personally preferred a republic to a monarchy; and in confronting the problem posed by rulers who actively opposed the spread of the Gospel, he advanced a theory of resistance, kept alive by his followers, according to which lesser magistrates might legitimately rebel against kings. And, unlike most of his contemporaries, Calvin included among the proper responsibilities of states not only the maintenance of public order but also a positive concern for the general welfare of society. Calvinism has a place, therefore, in the evolution of liberal political thought. His most durable influence, nevertheless, has been religious. From Calvin's time to the present, Calvinism has meant a peculiar seriousness about Christianity and its ethical implications.

She-Devils, Harlots and Harridans in Northern Renaissance Prints

The social, sexual and demonic power of women
was an important theme in the popular print of Germany and the Low Countries
in the 16th century, as **Julie Nurse** shows.

They beat men, stole their money, killed them even, and they could fly—a veritable feat for any ordinary woman. The Renaissance woman was, indeed, a she-devil or so we are led to believe from prints by German and Netherlandish artists of the fifteenth and sixteenth centuries currently on show at the British Museum, in an exhibition *The 'Power of Women' and the Northern Renaissance Print.*

The 'Power of Women', or '*Weibermacht*' as the theme was known in Germany, was a popular subject for artists and writers during the Renaissance period. It was not an early form of feminism, as the term might suggest, but a concept that emerged out of the complex religious and social turmoil that was provoked by the European Reformation of the sixteenth century. The idea achieved popularity largely through the format of the print, a medium that rose in status to rival painting as a respected art form during the Renaissance period. To meet the growing demand for images that disseminated the changing ideas of the Protestant Reformation, entrepreneurial publishers developed the print production process into a commercial enterprise. This was particularly so in the North European regions of Germany and the Netherlands. Furthermore, the iconoclastic clampdown on religious, didactic forms of art throughout

Europe meant that painters were forced to seek other avenues for work.

Although it is not clear who first coined the term *Weibermacht,* it is evident that the theme gained currency, while the 'print series' helped to popularise the topic. In 1511, the Flemish artist Lucas van Leyden (c.1494–1533) was the first printmaker to produce such a series on a commercial basis. The success of this series is reflected in the apparent trend for 'Power of Women' sequences thereafter: Lucas van Leyden produced a second smaller version in 1516 and many other printmakers, like Phillip Galle ('Women's Tricks in the Old Testament'), followed suit throughout the sixteenth century. The theme applied not only to biblical women. Mythological and secular scenarios were also seized upon by printmakers as marketable subjects for their prints.

The cultural climate of Northern Europe was ripe for the production of images reflecting the deep-seated prejudices that embodied the *Weibermacht* idea. A liberal atmosphere prevailed in cities like Leyden, Strasbourg and, in particular, Nuremberg—the city that produced Albrecht Dürer and many other innovative printmakers. Artists were allowed a freedom unmatched elsewhere. Compared to the elitism of more traditional forms of art, the print medium offered a portable format that

was not only accessible to wider audiences, but gave the freedom to illustrate everyday anxieties and fears.

The 'Southern' Renaissance region of Italy presented a marked contrast. Here, artists were conditioned, controlled even, by the intellectual tastes of their wealthy patrons—the demand, in short, for images that enhanced Italy's great classical tradition. To Northern European artists, this was a borrowed legacy and an archaic one from which they were able to distance themselves. Of course, Italian artists also produced powerful images of the women of mythology and the Bible, but the emphasis was different. The images were at once lush and bathed in the natural warmth of the Mediterranean imagination as opposed to the quirky, bizarre and often coldly grotesque interpretations that flourished in Northern Europe.

Although the *Weibermacht* idea was more suited to the print album of the specialist or the domestic decor of the ordinary citizen than to the public sphere, it was deemed fashionable enough to be considered for major art commissions. Albrecht Dürer was initially commissioned to decorate the great hall of Nuremberg's Town Hall with scenes on the theme of *Weibermacht* in 1520–21. But this plan was rejected in favour of loftier sentiments that celebrated justice and political order.

Other forms of the minor decorative arts—misericords, maiolica, trinkets and metal-work—drew freely on the theme. Crucially, however, the initial or original designs came from the printmakers.

The basis for the *Weibermacht* theme was the age-old idea of role-reversal, or the 'battle of the sexes'. The theme re-emerged in deeply misogynistic literature of the fourteenth and fifteenth centuries as a means of explaining the evils of society at large. Plague, war, crop failures and a population explosion had left much of Europe in turmoil by the end of the medieval period. Fears and threats to the status quo had to be resolved. Scapegoats were sought—and women were a convenient 'weak' target. Men became increasingly alienated from the sphere of women, not only through fear of succumbing to their powers of seduction, deviousness and sorcery, but also for economic reasons. War had left a surplus of available single women by the beginning of the sixteenth century, many of whom were forced to work, beg or prostitute themselves. The status quo within marriage was threatened as role-reversal became an inevitable consequence of this sexual imbalance. Warnings were issued like this example of 1527:

Best be unbound to woman
Rich the man without a wife.

Many secular prints were produced to demonstrate the perceived consequences of marriage. Distorted fears became dangerously entangled with the drive for moral improvement and, in reaction, writers and artists enforced an ideal vision of female chastity, austerity and obedience as a sharp contrast to the disobedient and uncontrollable ways of the 'bad' woman.

The late-fifteenth-century 'satirical' prints of the German engraver Israel van Meckenham seem to have been directly influenced by such medieval thoughts and traditions. Echoing the tone adopted in the Old Testament, reprehension of men and women appears to be the predominant theme in his integral suite of profane scenes, so called *'Alltagsleben'* ('Everyday Life') of 1495, a novel and moralistic interpretation of love and marriage. Prior to this date, print series were almost inevitably religious and didactic in nature. Affection and romanticism are nowhere to be seen among Meckenham's couple, but boredom, stu-

pidity and anger are apparent. The henpecked husband was a popular topic in literature of the fourteenth and fifteenth centuries and helped to reinforce men's fear of women's wiles.

Perhaps the most vehemently satirical in Meckenham's *Alltagsleben* series is 'The Angry Wife': a woman stands on the foot of her husband whose wrist she grabs as she battles with him for his breeches that lie on the floor. She raises her distaff, traditional symbol of domesticity, in preparation to strike him. Her rage is accentuated by the demon of anger hovering above the pair. Domestic disputes of this kind were popular with printmakers as allegorical examples of the topsy-turvey world that they lived in. In Martin Treu's version of this print, the woman wears the man's breeches, thereby emphasizing her role as dominatrix.

In an anonymous print produced at this time in the Netherlands, a horde of gargoyles in skirts descend on two helpless men, one of whom helps a woman to put on some breeches—a traditional symbol of power along with the keys she holds in her pocket. A banner is held up victoriously with the inscription 'upper hand'—the meaning is quite clear: women are dominating to the extreme in this case. The fact that the inscriptions within the image are not only in Dutch but also Latin and French suggests that this print was not intended for the ordinary uneducated public but for a more learned audience.

The medieval preaching tradition illustrating biblical texts with scenes from daily life continued to influence artists and writers of the sixteenth century. In Rotterdam, Erasmus pulled no punches: he adopted the moralistic tone of the Old Testament to warn fellow men of women, in particular wives, ' . . . a sex so unalterably simple, that for any of them [men] to thrust forward, and reach at the name of wife, is but to make themselves the more remarkable fools. . . .' (*In Praise of Folly*, 1511). Similarly, the German poet Hans Sachs wrote a number of popular verses based on marital discordance with a misogynistic bent, in particular, the carnival play *The Angry Wife* of 1533, in which he warns men:

Go ahead and act like a man!
Otherwise she'll end up riding you
And before long she'll
Deprive you of your pants, your purse and your sword,

Which will make us all ashamed of you
Do not give her too much rein,
But rather take an oak cudgel
And beat her soundly between the ears!

The proverbial act of 'riding' a man was interpreted by printmakers, not only in secular contexts, but also in mythological ones. It was, in fact, fifteenth-century anonymous Florentine artists who first interpreted the idea of 'women on top' from spurious medieval tales. The plight of the Greek philosopher, Aristotle, who was fooled by the courtesan, Phyllis, was one of many fictitious stories about duped intelligent men that emerged at this time in the absence of solid information about them. It was said that Aristotle warned Alexander to control his passion for Phyllis because women had undone many heroes of antiquity. In revenge, Phyllis sought to kindle Aristotle's desire for her. Once he was smitten, she demanded to ride astride him as proof of his passion. When Alexander witnessed the unlikely scene of the subservient philosopher on all fours being whipped by the courtesan, he learned never to become infatuated with a woman again. Although this and other similar tales had gone out of fashion in Italy by the sixteenth century, they remained popular in Germany where the iconography of the 'ridden' man became more satirical. The so-called Master of the House-book, a prolific German engraver active between about 1470 and 1500, was perhaps the first artist to depict the scene of Aristotle being 'ridden' by Phyllis in a derogatory manner. Copies and imitations of his prints were transmitted to artists and patrons beyond his own circle which led to a new burst of interest in the theme. One of the most spirited interpretations of the story was that of the printmaker known as Matthaus Zaisinger (or MZ), who is believed to have worked in Nuremberg around 1500.

The Roman poet, Virgil, was mocked in a similar manner for allegedly falling for the emperor's daughter, another fictitious tale that tarnished his reputation during the sixteenth century. Alarmed at the prospect of Virgil's passion, the emperor's daughter sought to make a fool of the poet. She promised to raise him to her room via a pulley and basket but, instead, left him hanging half way in view of the mocking public below. Although this was a popular subject in other media, Lucas van Leyden was one of the few printmakers to include this sequence in his 'Power of Women' woodcut series of 1511. Virgil's predicament is given prominence to emphasise the ultimate gullibility of man, however intelligent he may be, at the hands of woman. Other tales reproduced in Leyden's woodcut series were taken from the Old Testament and further demonstrated the cunning of biblical women: Eve, Delilah, Jezebel, Salome and Jael all duped men either for sexual, patriotic or simply cunning reasons.

As the first woman to seduce man, Eve was an obvious inspiration for the *Weibermacht* theme. Though she featured in many other forms of art, it was through the print that she became lustful, notably in Hans Baldung's woodcut of 1511. The carnal implications of this tale are reinforced by the presence of the rabbits in the bottom left-hand corner, a reminder of one of the seven deadly sins—lust. In the second of the two Genesis versions of the story of Adam and Eve, the Old Testament implied that Eve was unequal to Adam, having been created from the rib of man, while the later New Testament interpretation is that men and women were equal from the beginning. Medieval and Renaissance society preferred the former tale, which reinforced the belief that women's inferiority was justified. Adam's fall from grace was viewed as a direct result of Eve's actions.

Delilah's betrayal of Samson was as popular as Eve's disobedience in *Weibermacht* illustrations. Samson, normally a figure of Herculean strength, revealed the secret of his strength—his long hair—to his love, Delilah. The scene in which Delilah cuts off the hair of a sleeping Samson must have provided great amusement for Renaissance society, judging by the popularity of the story with artists. Lucas van Leyden produced the scene several times. His engraved version of 1508 was a particularly graphic one in which Samson's shield lies discarded in the foreground, a potent symbol of his defenceless state.

The 'power' of biblical women was not just evil, as Judith and Jael both demonstrated. On the contrary, their stories were based on patriotism and, as such, they were often paired together in images, as in Philip Galle's prints from his series devoted to 'Women's Tricks in the Old Testament'. Judith and her patriotic deed of beheading the enemy

Holofernes was a classic example of female omnipotence. Her courage, piety and determined action made her a standard example of fortitude and prudence for many other Renaissance artists. Michelangelo, for one, included her in his designs for the Sistine Chapel fresco in Rome. According to the Book of Judges, Judith played on her beauty to attract the enemy Holofernes who subsequently invited her into his tent for a feast. After his commanders had withdrawn, Judith plied Holofernes with wine and beheaded him, placing his head in a bag.

Renaissance prints of biblical and mythological heroes and heroines were made to be collected and looked at as objects and models of human behaviour. However, since Judith did not conform with contemporary notions of how women were to behave, images of her at this time tend to be ambiguous; beneath her 'womanliness' lies a sense of threat. While some artists depicted her as a patriotic and physically strong figure others played on her sexual attraction. Alternatively, some printmakers preferred simply to accentuate the violence of her actions, as in the case of Philip Galle's version.

The tale of Jael's murder of the Canaanite warrior and enemy, Sisera, had patriotic parallels with Judith's story. Jael hammers a tent peg into Sisera's temple: a particularly violent action that inspired sixteenth-century printmakers throughout Northern Europe. Although Leyden set a precedent by producing the image in his early woodcut series, the scenario was treated with increasing vigour as the sixteenth century progressed. Philip Galle's later engraving draws attention to the hammer in Jael's hand, emphasising the villainous act which she is about to perform.

Man's folly was as much to blame for women's deceptive behaviour according to sixteenth-century society. This ultimate weakness was highlighted in classical, mythological tales too. Hercules and Omphale were a particularly appealing pair in this respect: normally a figure of great strength and accentuated masculinity, Hercules was punished for killing the brother of Iole—the passion of his life—by becoming a servant to Queen Omphale of Lydia. He was forced to surrender his hero's lion-skin cloak and club, dress in women's garb and perform the spinning work of women. Such role-reversal fitted in with

contemporary Northern Renaissance artistic trends. Among the various artists who produced images of this scenario was Bartholomous Spranger. The engraved version of Spranger's painting by Aegidius Sadeler (late sixteenth century), portrays Omphale as both dominant and alluring as she smirks at the audience from beneath the lion skin, almost as if she is amused by Hercules' fate.

Although not strictly part of the 'Power of Women' series, the witch, as a symbol of the demonic side of woman, remained the most realistic threat to mankind. The social and moral upheaval of the Reformation had effectively weakened the foundations of the Christian faith, a situation which gave rise to increased fear of the occult. It was believed that Satan and his followers—human witches—were gaining control of the spiritual world. In an attempt to control the increase in medieval sorcery the *Malleus Maleficarum* (The Witches Hammer), a manual on witchcraft, was written by two Dominicans in Strasbourg in 1487 to raise awareness of the practice and legitimise the need to suppress it. The witch-hunt that soon took Europe by storm was based on an idea that fed deeply on in-built prejudices and fears about the power of female sexuality and capacity for evil. The idea of the act of carnal intercourse with the devil led men to believe that women were more prone to seduction by Satan and, thereby, to witchcraft. Since chasteness was upheld as an essential quality for women, those who appeared to subvert this ideal were condemned. For printmakers, witches and lewd women represented a contrasting image to that of the pious virgin.

Hans Baldung brought the domain of the occult to the fore in his numerous prints on the subject, particularly so in 'The Witches' Sabbath' of 1510 in which a group of witches are engaged in sinister and perverse activities associated with the devil. The Sabbath was believed to be a secret night meeting that witches conducted with Satan. This assembly was central to the idea of the uncontrollable sexual appetite of women and justified the need for the witch-hunt. Baldung, a well-respected figure in Strasbourg, was one of the first printmakers to introduce colour to prints and was no doubt considered as an important innovator in the eyes of print collectors. From this elevated position, he was able to disseminate and popularise his obsession with the evil aspect of women.

Similarly preoccupied with the evils of society, was the printmaker Daniel Hopfer. His violent image portraying three old hags beating a devil reinforces the associations that women were believed to have had with the devil. Yet, witches had the power to invoke both good and bad deeds. It has been suggested that this print may have been an allegory for war and peace although, more specifically, the idea of a woman beating the devil into submission was also equated with that of the wife beating the husband into subservience. Such allegories would have been understood only by learned audiences able to decipher them.

Women did not have to be witches to perform devilish deeds, however. Ordinary 'bad' women were seen to encourage man's indulgent ways too, as Jacob Matham illustrated in his series of four prints entitled Drunkenness in which a woman induces a man to become inebriated in order to dupe him. Indeed male over-indulgence was as much a concern as female cunning. Young women were often depicted with lascivious or debauched men to accentuate the stupidity of such behaviour. This is demonstrated in Urs Graf's image where a woman allows an old fool to grope her as a means of stealing his money which she promptly hands over to her real lover. As a mercenary and wife-beater in real life Graf's images are perhaps best seen as a crude satirical view of convenient relationships between men and women.

Man's folly was the basis for many other secular interpretations of *Weibermacht,* none more so than in Erhard Schön's prints. As a citizen of the free-thinking city of Nuremberg Schön, a devout supporter of Lutheran reformation, was at liberty to depict the corruption that he saw around him. His illustrated broadsheets offered scathing attacks which were aimed not only at the Catholic clergy, but also at the folly of mankind in general. Even without the text, it is clear that 'The Snare of the Fowler' concerns the entrapment of foolish men by women.

The 'Power of Women' theme continued to be popular with Northern Renaissance artists up to the seventeenth century. In particular, the printed image offered a convenient means of disseminating popular ideas of this sort to wider audiences than was possible in other forms of art. The subject provided entertainment not only to aristocratic collectors, but to the population at large via peddlers roaming the countryside. However, as the tension of the Reformation eased, satirical images began to lose their bite and gradually the idea of the fallen state of the world on which *Weibermacht* was based, sank to the level of an amusing game in the popular art of the printed broadsheet. Despite this, the moralising tradition that was promoted by writers and artists like Hans Sachs and Erhard Schon, continued to surface in the arts of Northern Europe. So too, did the universal theme of role reversal and classic tales like Samson and Delilah. Yet there was an essential difference in the way women were interpreted. Perhaps because of the gradual move away from the superstitious and irrational beliefs of the medieval period towards a commercially ordered and humanistic society, women ceased to be viewed as such an evil threat to mankind.

FOR FURTHER READING:

Lene Dresen-Coenders (ed). *'Saints and She-Devils': Images of Women in the 15th and 16th Centuries* (Rubicon Press, 1985); D. Schoenhern *Eve and Ava: Women in Renaissance and Baroque prints,* (National Gallery of Art, Washington, 1992); C.Zika, *Fears of Flying: Representations of Witchcraft and Sexuality in early 16th century Germany,* Australian Journal of Art VII, (Melbourne, 1989); P. Parshall and D. Landau, *The Renaissance Print 1470–1550,* (Yale University Press, 1994); Giulia Bartrum *German Renaissance Prints 1490–1550* (British Museum Press, 1995).

Julia Nurse *is Curatorial Assistant in the Department of Prints and Drawings at the British Museum.*

Test Your Knowledge Form

We encourage you to photocopy and use this page as a tool to assess how the articles in **Annual Editions** expand on the information in your textbook. By reflecting on the articles you will gain enhanced text information. You can also access this useful form on a product's book support Web site at **http://www.dushkin.com/ online/.**

NAME: _____ DATE: _____

TITLE AND NUMBER OF ARTICLE: _____

BRIEFLY STATE THE MAIN IDEA OF THIS ARTICLE: _____

LIST THREE IMPORTANT FACTS THAT THE AUTHOR USES TO SUPPORT THE MAIN IDEA:

WHAT INFORMATION OR IDEAS DISCUSSED IN THIS ARTICLE ARE ALSO DISCUSSED IN YOUR TEXTBOOK OR OTHER READINGS THAT YOU HAVE DONE? LIST THE TEXTBOOK CHAPTERS AND PAGE NUMBERS:

LIST ANY EXAMPLES OF BIAS OR FAULTY REASONING THAT YOU FOUND IN THE ARTICLE:

LIST ANY NEW TERMS/CONCEPTS THAT WERE DISCUSSED IN THE ARTICLE, AND WRITE A SHORT DEFINITION:

ANNUAL EDITIONS revisions depend on two major opinion sources: one is our Advisory Board, listed in the front of this volume, which works with us in scanning the thousands of articles published in the public press each year; the other is you—the person actually using the book. Please help us and the users of the next edition by completing the prepaid article rating form on this page and returning it to us. Thank you for your help!

ANNUAL EDITIONS: World Civilization, Volume I, Eleventh Edition

ARTICLE RATING FORM

Here is an opportunity for you to have direct input into the next revision of this volume. We would like you to rate each of the 42 articles listed below, using the following scale:

1. Excellent: should definitely be retained
2. Above average: should probably be retained
3. Below average: should probably be deleted
4. Poor: should definitely be deleted

Your ratings will play a vital part in the next revision. So please mail this prepaid form to us just as soon as you complete it. Thanks for your help!

RATING

ARTICLE

1. Hatshepsut: The Female Pharaoh
2. Correspondence in Clay
3. The Cradle of Cash
4. Shards of Speech
5. The Coming of the Sea Peoples
6. Grisly Assyrian Record of Torture and Death
7. Winning at Olympia
8. The Athenian Democracy and Its Slaves
9. Re-Running Marathon
10. Love and Death in Ancient Greece
11. Cleopatra: What Kind of a Woman Was She, Anyway?
12. In the Year 1, Augustus Let the Good Times Roll
13. Chariot Racing in the Ancient World
14. Friends, Romans, or Countrymen? Barbarians in the Empire
15. Jews and Christians in a Roman World
16. The Other Jesus
17. Women and the Bible
18. Ecstasy in Late Imperial Rome
19. Who the Devil Is the Devil?
20. The Survival of the Eastern Roman Empire
21. Byzantium: The Emperor's New Clothes?
22. What Is Islam?
23. Scissors or Sword? The Symbolism of a Medieval Haircut

RATING

ARTICLE

24. The Amazing Vikings
25. The Golden Age of Andalusia under the Muslim Sultans
26. How the West Saw Medieval Islam
27. Monsters and Christian Enemies
28. Women Pilgrims of the Middle Ages
29. Britain 1100
30. The Paris Bibles and the Making of a Medieval Information Revolution
31. Girls Growing Up in Later Medieval England
32. War-Games of Central Italy
33. How a Mysterious Disease Laid Low Europe's Masses
34. Saints or Sinners? The Knights Templar in Medieval Europe
35. Marsilio Ficino, Renaissance Man
36. Machiavelli
37. Women of the Renaissance
38. Columbus—Hero or Villain?
39. Sir Francis Drake Is Still Capable of Kicking Up a Fuss
40. Luther: Giant of His Time and Ours
41. Explaining John Calvin
42. She-Devils, Harlots and Harridans in Northern Renaissance Prints

(Continued on next page)

We Want Your Advice

**ANNUAL EDITIONS: WESTERN CIVILIZATION, Volume 1,
Eleventh Edition**

ABOUT YOU

Name   Date

Are you a teacher? ☐ A student? ☐
Your school's name

Department

Address   City   State   Zip

School telephone #

YOUR COMMENTS ARE IMPORTANT TO US !

Please fill in the following information:
For which course did you use this book?

Did you use a text with this *ANNUAL EDITION*? ☐ yes ☐ no
What was the title of the text?

What are your general reactions to the *Annual Editions* concept?

Have you read any particular articles recently that you think should be included in the next edition?

Are there any articles you feel should be replaced in the next edition? Why?

Are there any World Wide Web sites you feel should be included in the next edition? Please annotate.

May we contact you for editorial input? ☐ yes ☐ no
May we quote your comments? ☐ yes ☐ no